Fodor's

FLORENCE, TUSCANY & UMBRIA

9th Edition

Fodor's Travel Publications   New York, Toronto, London, Sydney, Auckland
www.fodors.com

Be a Fodor's Correspondent

Your opinion matters. It matters to us. It matters to your fellow Fodor's travelers, too. And we'd like to hear it. In fact, we need to hear it.

When you share your experiences and opinions, you become an active member of the Fodor's community. That means we'll not only use your feedback to make our books better, but we'll publish your names and comments whenever possible. Throughout our guides, look for "Word of Mouth," excerpts of your unvarnished feedback.

Here's how you can help improve Fodor's for all of us.

Tell us when we're right. We rely on local writers to give you an insider's perspective. But our writers and staff editors—who are the best in the business—depend on you. Your positive feedback is a vote to renew our recommendations for the next edition.

Tell us when we're wrong. We're proud that we update most of our guides every year. But we're not perfect. Things change. Hotels cut services. Museums change hours. Charming cafés lose charm. If our writer didn't quite capture the essence of a place, tell us how you'd do it differently. If any of our descriptions are inaccurate or inadequate, we'll incorporate your changes in the next edition and will correct factual errors at fodors.com immediately.

Tell us what to include. You probably have had fantastic travel experiences that aren't yet in Fodor's. Why not share them with a community of like-minded travelers? Maybe you chanced upon a beach or bistro or B&B that you don't want to keep to yourself. Tell us why we should include it. And share your discoveries and experiences with everyone directly at fodors.com. Your input may lead us to add a new listing or highlight a place we cover with a "Highly Recommended" star or with our highest rating, "Fodor's Choice."

Give us your opinion instantly at our feedback center at www.fodors.com/feedback. You may also e-mail editors@fodors.com with the subject line "Florence, Tuscany & Umbria Editor." Or send your nominations, comments, and complaints by mail to Florence, Tuscany & Umbria Editor, Fodor's, 1745 Broadway, New York, NY 10019.

You and travelers like you are the heart of the Fodor's community. Make our community richer by sharing your experiences. Be a Fodor's correspondent.

Buon viaggio! (Or simply: Happy traveling!)

Tim Jarrell, Publisher

FODOR'S FLORENCE, TUSCANY & UMBRIA
Editor: Matthew Lombardi

Editorial Production: Astrid deRidder
Editorial Contributors: Peter Blackman, Linda Cabasin, Shannon Kelly, Ann Reavis, Patricia Rucidlo, Mark Sullivan, Jonathan Willcocks
Maps & Illustrations: Henry Colomb and Mark Stroud, Moon Street Cartography, David Lindroth, Inc.; William Wu; Bob Blake and Rebecca Baer, *map editors*
Design: Fabrizio LaRocca, *creative director*; Guido Caroti, Siobhan O'Hare, *art directors*; Tina Malaney, Chie Ushio, Ann McBride, *designers*; Melanie Marin, *senior picture editor;* Moon Sun Kim, *cover designer*
Cover Photo: Ponte Vecchio, Florence: SIME s.a.s/eStock Photo
Production/Manufacturing: Angela L. McLean & Matthew Struble

COPYRIGHT

9th Edition

ISBN 978-1-4000-0754-7

ISSN 1533-1628

SPECIAL SALES

This book is available at special discounts for bulk purchases for sales promotions or premiums. Special editions, including personalized covers, excerpts of existing books, and corporate imprints, can be created in large quantities for special needs. For more information, write to Special Markets/Premium Sales, 1745 Broadway, MD 6-2, New York, New York 10019, or e-mail specialmarkets@randomhouse.com.

AN IMPORTANT TIP & AN INVITATION

Although all prices, opening times, and other details in this book are based on information supplied to us at press time, changes occur all the time in the travel world, and Fodor's cannot accept responsibility for facts that become outdated or for inadvertent errors or omissions. So **always confirm information when it matters,** especially if you're making a detour to visit a specific place. Your experiences—positive and negative— matter to us. If we have missed or misstated something, **please write to us.** We follow up on all suggestions. Contact the Florence, Tuscany & Umbria editor at editors@fodors.com or c/o Fodor's at 1745 Broadway, New York, NY 10019.

PRINTED IN SINGAPORE
10 9 8 7 6 5 4 3 2 1

CONTENTS

FLORENCE, TUSCANY & UMBRIA IN FOCUS

CONTENTS

ABOUT THIS BOOK

Our Ratings

Sometimes you find terrific travel experiences and sometimes they just find you. But usually the burden is on you to select the right combination of experiences. That's where our ratings come in.

As travelers we've all discovered a place so wonderful that its worthiness is obvious. And sometimes that place is so experiential that superlatives don't do it justice: you just have to be there to know. These sights, properties, and experiences get our highest rating, **Fodor's Choice**, indicated by orange stars throughout this book.

Black stars highlight sights and properties we deem **Highly Recommended**, places that our writers, editors, and readers praise again and again for consistency and excellence.

By default, there's another category: any place we include in this book is by definition worth your time, unless we say otherwise. And we will.

Disagree with any of our choices? Care to nominate a place or suggest that we rate one more highly? Visit our feedback center at www.fodors.com/feedback.

Budget Well

Hotel and restaurant price categories from ¢ to $$$$ are defined in the opening pages of each chapter. For attractions, we always give standard adult admission fees; reductions are usually available for children, students, and senior citizens. Want to pay with plastic? **AE, D, DC, MC, V** following restaurant and hotel listings indicate if American Express, Discover, Diners Club, MasterCard, and Visa are accepted.

Restaurants

Unless we state otherwise, restaurants are open for lunch and dinner daily. We mention dress only when there's a specific requirement and reservations only when they're essential or not accepted—it's always best to book ahead.

Hotels

Hotels have private bath, phone, TV, and air-conditioning. We indicate whether they operate on the European Plan (a.k.a. EP, meaning without meals), Breakfast Plan (BP, with a full breakfast), Modified American Plan (MAP, with breakfast and dinner), or American Plan (AP, including all meals). We always list facilities but not whether you'll be charged an extra fee to use them, so when pricing accommodations, find out what's included.

Many Listings

★	Fodor's Choice
★	Highly recommended
⊠	Physical address
✛	Directions
⌂	Mailing address
☎	Telephone
🖷	Fax
⊕	On the Web
✎	E-mail
▨	Admission fee
☉	Open/closed times
Ⓜ	Metro stations
▭	Credit cards

Hotels & Restaurants

▣	Hotel
↳	Number of rooms
⚲	Facilities
⭑◯⭑	Meal plans
✕	Restaurant
⌫	Reservations
⤡	Smoking
BYOB	BYOB
✕▣	Hotel with restaurant that warrants a visit

Outdoors

⛳	Golf
⛺	Camping

Other

☾	Family-friendly
⇨	See also
⊠	Branch address
☞	Take note

Experience Florence, Tuscany & Umbria

1

WHAT'S NEW

A Streetcar Named Discontent

Perugia's minimetrò got off to a smooth start in January 2008, connecting a large parking lot near the soccer stadium with the old center of Umbria's capital, and enhancing an already extensive system of public escalators built to reduce traffic congestion. In Florence, though, attempts to come to grips with traffic are plagued by bureaucratic, physical, and ecological problems.

Work began in 2005 on a projected three-line tram system designed to crisscross central Florence. Traveling almost entirely aboveground, the first line will connect the central Santa Maria Novella train station with Scandicci, a suburb to the southwest of Florence.

Work proceeds extremely slowly. Traffic is disrupted where the tramline crosses busy streets, and trees have been cut down by the hundreds to make way for the project—both circumstances that have not pleased the average Florentine. In fact, the second line, planned to pass very close to both the Baptistery and the Duomo, in the very heart of town, has caused such an uproar that a growingly popular movement, Salviamo Firenze—Fermiamo il Tram! (Save Florence—Stop the Tram!), threatens to entirely halt the second section of the project. In 2008 a confusingly worded referendum, requiring citizens to vote either "no" if they are in favor of the tram or "yes" to stop everything, may determine whether visitors to Florence, during the next five years or more, will be greeted by extensive roadwork in the city center.

Other Transportation News

In early 2008 money was finally allocated to a huge enterprise involving the Alta Velocità (High Speed) train system between Milan and Naples, passing through Florence.

During the years to come (the unlikely date of 2010 has been given for completion), the central Santa Maria Novella train station will take on secondary importance, and the previously peripheral Campo di Marte station, with high-speed tracks taking trains through a tunnel beneath Florence, will take on the primary role. Campo di Marte (to be given a new design by London-based architects Norman Foster & Partners) will become the main hub of the Florentine rail network, and then be linked, perhaps by tram, to the center of town.

David on the Move?

It's obvious that none of Italy's medieval town centers was originally designed for automobile traffic. This, coupled with the huge influx of tourists (as many as 11 million annually), make Florence's relatively small historic center highly congested, especially during the peak tourist seasons.

In 2008, with an idea for tackling at least one cause of the problem, a top cultural official daringly suggested moving one of the city's top tourist attractions, Michelangelo's *David,* away from the center of town. But with most Florentines shaking their heads in disbelief and the mayor indicating that such a move cannot take place at any time "in the near future," it seems unlikely that visitors will have to look for the *David* anywhere other than in the Accademia Gallery, its present home, for quite some time.

BEATING THE EURO

Below are suggestions for ways to save money on your trip, courtesy of the Travel Talk Forums at Fodors.com.

Transportation

"I take regional trains instead of the Eurostar trains. For example, Florence to Rome on Eurostar is 32.50 euro; the regional train is 15.80 euro. That's half the price; so what if it takes 15 minutes longer...big deal." —JoanneH

"In Florence, the no. 7 bus will take you from the Santa Maria Novella train station up to Fiesole for 1 euro. After visiting the town and the Etruscan ruins, you can watch the sun set over the city from the terrace of the Bar Blu for the price of a glass of wine." —ira

"We used Siena as a base and visited several Hill Towns including San Gimignano by local bus. The schedules were convenient and the fares were very cheap." —basingstoke2

Food & Drink

"In Volterra, buy a bottle of wine, some cheese and crackers and enjoy a relaxing picnic in the lovely park that is adjacent to Fortezza Medicea, which still serves as a prison after hundreds of years. Afterward, meander through Volterra until you reach an overlook where you can see the well-preserved remains of Volterra's Roman theater and baths." —maitaitom

"When we rented a house in Umbria, we were just up the hill from a wine co-op. You could buy a jug (or two!) and then get it filled with wine for really very little. The wine was very drinkable, especially when you were sitting in a grove of olive trees admiring the sun setting behind the hills." —txtree

"Buy snacks and bottled water in bulk at a neighborhood supermarket at the beginning of your stay and keep them cool in your apartment or hotel fridge. Grab a bottle each when leaving in the AM and that way avoid buying expensive water or snacks near tourist attractions, where prices are much higher. Save your euros for espresso or gelato." —cruisinred

Sights

"The small cities can be less expensive but still fabulous. We were just in Assisi—all the sites were free, a delicious dinner for two with wine was 22 euros, and our hotel was reasonable at 65 euros per night." —rosetravels

"Visiting the beautiful Abbazia di Sant'Antimo outside Montalcino is free. This abbey is set in a lovely valley, surrounded by cypress and olive trees. We visited on a Sunday morning, mass was going on, and it was an unbelievably beautiful experience." —dina4

Lodging

"Everyone talks about going in the off season and mentions November or March. But in Florence at least, July is a shoulder season. I got a hotel room for half to a third the cost of the same room during the high season." —isabel

"We try to book apartments whenever we can in Florence and Rome and in Tuscany we rent farm houses or something similar. Especially if you are traveling with more than 2 persons these are usually much more reasonable." —caroltis

WHAT'S WHERE

The following numbers refer to chapters.

2 **Florence.** In the 15th century Florence was at the center of the artistic revolution that would come to be known as the Renaissance. Today, the Renaissance remains the main reason people visit here—the abundance of art treasures is mind-boggling.

3 **Northwest Tuscany.** West of Florence the main attractions are **Pisa,** home of the Leaning Tower, and **Lucca,** a town with a charming historic center. Farther north and west are snowcapped peaks, thermal waters, and miles of Mediterranean coast, including, across the regional border in Liguria, the **Cinque Terre**—five fishing villages that have become a major destination.

4 **Central Tuscany.** The hills spreading south from Florence to Siena make up **Chianti,** a region of sublime wine and fabulous views. **Siena** was once Florence's main rival, and it remains one of Italy's most appealing medieval towns. To its northwest, **San Gimignano** is famous for its 15th-century towers. Farther west still is **Volterra,** a town dating back to the Etruscans.

5 **Eastern Tuscany.** **Arezzo,** Tuscany's third largest city (after Florence and Pisa), has a car-free historic center and a basilica containing fabulous frescoes. **Cortona,** perched on a steep hill with sweeping views, exemplifies an alluringly old-fashioned way of life.

6 **Southern Tuscany.** In the **Val d'Orca** the towns of **Montalcino** and **Montepulciano** are surrounded by some of Italy's finest vineyards, and **Pienza** is a unique example of Renaissance urban planning. Farther south is the **Maremma,** Tuscany's cattle-ranching country. Off the coast, the rocky island of **Elba** is a popular resort destination.

7 **Northern Umbria.** Like Tuscany, Umbria has beautiful rolling hills topped by attractive old towns. **Perugia** is Umbria's largest city, but it's far from overwhelming, and it has a well-preserved medieval core. In **Assisi,** birthplace of Saint Francis, the grand basilica draws millions of pilgrims annually. To the east in the Marches region, **Urbino** is famed for its splendid Renaissance palace.

8 **Southern Umbria.** **Spoleto** is a quiet, elegant hill town, but each summer it brims with activity during the Festival dei Due Mondi. To its east, mountainous **Valnerina** may be Umbria's most beautiful region. The town of **Orvieto** sits atop a tufa plateau; its magnificent Duomo can be seen for miles around.

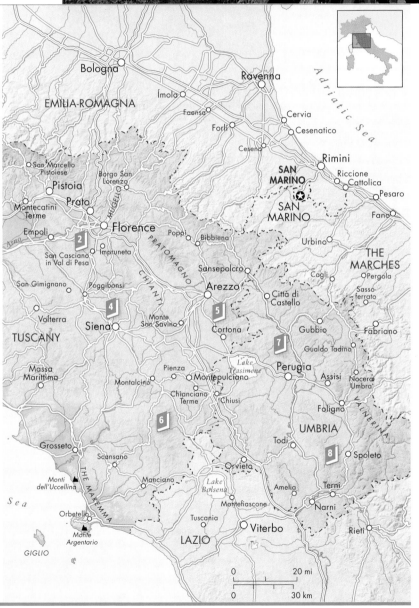

Map Labels

EMILIA-ROMAGNA

Bologna
Ímola
Faenza
Forlì
Cesena
Cervia
Cesenatico
Ravenna

Adriatic Sea

Rimini
Riccione
Cattolica
Pesaro
Fano

SAN MARINO
SAN MARINO

San Marcello
Pistoiese
Borgo San
Lorenzo
Pistoia
Prato
Montecatini
Terme
Empoli
Florence
Poppi
Bibbiena
Urbino
THE MARCHES

San Casciano
in Val di Pesa
Impruneta
Sansepolcro
Cagli
Pergola
Sasso-
ferrato

San Gimignano
Poggibonsi
Arezzo
Città di
Castello
Gubbio
Fabriano

Volterra
Monte
San Savino
Cortona
Gualdo Tadino

TUSCANY
Siena
Lake Trasimeno
Perugia
Assisi
Nocera
Umbra

Massa
Marittima
Pienza
Montepulciano
Montalcino
Chianciano
Terme
Chiusi
Foligno

VALNERINA

Grosseto
UMBRIA
Todi
Spoleto

Scansano
Orvieta
Amelia
Terni

Monti
dell'Uccellina
Lake Bolsena
Manciano
Montefiascone
Narni
Rieti

Sea
Orbetello
Tuscania
Viterbo

Monte
Argentario
LAZIO

GIGLIO

Arno
PRATOMAGNO
MUGELLO
CHIANTI
THE MAREMMA

2 4 5 6 7 8

0 _____ 20 mi
0 _____ 30 km

FLORENCE, TUSCANY & UMBRIA PLANNER

Getting Here

Most flights to Tuscany originating in the United States stop either in Rome, London, Paris, or Frankfurt, and then connect to Florence's small **Aeroporto A. Vespucci** (commonly called **Peretola**), or to Pisa's **Aeroporto Galileo Galilei**. The only exception at this writing is Delta's New York/JFK flight going directly into Pisa.

There are several other alternatives for getting into the region. If you want to start your trip in Umbria, it works to fly into Rome's Aeroporto Leonardo da Vinci (commonly called Fiumicino); from Rome it's an hour by train or an hour and a half by car to reach the lovely town of Orvieto. You can also fly to Milan and pick up a connecting Alitalia flight to Pisa, Florence, or Perugia. Finally, from May through September (as of this writing), the carrier Eurofly has nonstop flights between New York and Bologna, which is an hour by train or an hour and a half by car from Florence.

What to Pack

In summer, stick with light clothing, as things can get steamy in June, July and August, but throw in a sweater in case of cool evenings, especially if you're headed for the mountains and/or islands. Sunglasses, a hat, and sunblock are essential. Brief summer afternoon thunderstorms are common in inland cities, so an umbrella will come in handy. In winter, bring a coat, gloves, hats, scarves, and boots. In winter, weather is generally milder than in the northern and central United States, but central heating may not be up to your standards, and interiors can be cold and damp; take wools or flannel rather than sheer fabrics. Bring sturdy shoes for winter and comfortable walking shoes in any season.

As a rule, Italians dress exceptionally well. They do not usually wear shorts. Men aren't required to wear ties or jackets anywhere, except in some of the grander hotel dining rooms and top-level restaurants, but are expected to look reasonably sharp—and they do. Formal wear is the exception rather than the rule at the opera nowadays, though people in expensive seats usually do get dressed up.

A certain modesty of dress (no bare shoulders or knees) is expected in churches, and strictly enforced in many.

For sightseeing, **pack a pair of binoculars**; they will help you get a good look at painted ceilings and domes. If you stay in budget hotels, **take your own soap.** Many such hotels do not provide it or give guests only one tiny bar per room. Washcloths, also, are rarely provided even in three- and four-star hotels.

Restaurants: The Basics

A meal in Tuscany and Umbria (and elsewhere in Italy) has traditionally consisted of five courses, and every menu you encounter will still be organized along this five-course plan:

First up is the antipasto (appetizer), often consisting of cured meats or marinated vegetables. Next to appear is the primo, usually pasta or soup, and after that the secondo, a meat or fish course with, perhaps, a contorno (vegetable dish) on the side. A simple dolce (dessert) rounds out the meal.

This, you've probably noticed, is a lot of food. Italians have noticed as well—a full, five-course meal is an indulgence usually reserved for special occasions. Instead, restaurant meals are a mix-and-match affair: you might order a primo and a secondo, or an antipasto and a primo, or a secondo and a contorno.

The crucial rule of restaurant dining is that you should order at least two courses. It's a common mistake for tourists to order only a secondo, thinking they're getting a "main course" complete with side dishes. What they wind up with is one lonely piece of meat.

Hotels: The Basics

Hotels in these regions are usually well maintained (especially if they've earned our recommendation in this book), but in some respects they won't match what you find at comparably priced U.S. lodgings. Keep the following points in mind as you set your expectations, and you're likely to have a good experience:

■ First and foremost, rooms are usually smaller, particularly in cities. If you're truly cramped, ask for another room, but don't expect things to be spacious.

■ A "double bed" is usually two singles pushed together.

■ In the bathroom, tubs are not a given—request one if it's essential. In budget places, showers sometimes use a drain in the middle of the bathroom floor. And washcloths are a rarity.

■ Most hotels have satellite TV, but there are fewer channels than in the United States, and only one or two will be in English.

■ Wall-to-wall carpet is uncommon. Terra-cotta floors are the norm.

How's the Weather?

Throughout Tuscany and Umbria, the best times to visit are spring and fall. Days are warm, nights are cool, and though there are still tourists, the crowds are smaller. In the countryside the scenery is gorgeous, with abundant greenery and flowers in spring, and burnished leaves in autumn.

July and August are the most popular times to visit. Note, though, that the heat is often oppressive and mosquitoes are prevalent. Try to start your days early and visit major sights first to beat the crowds and the midday sun. For relief from the heat, head to the mountains of the Garfagnana, where hiking is spectacular, or hit the beach at resort towns such as Forte dei Marmi and Viareggio, along the Maremma coast, or on the island of Elba.

November through March, you might wonder who invented the term "sunny Italy." The panoramas are still beautiful, even with overcast skies, frequent rain, and occasional snow. In winter Florence benefits from shorter museum lines and less competition for restaurant tables. Outside the cities, though, many hotels and restaurants close for the season.

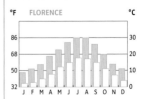

FLORENCE, TUSCANY & UMBRIA TODAY

The People

"And what greater fortune, if in Italy there were more Tuscans and fewer Italians," writes Curzio Malaparte (Prato, 1898–Rome, 1957) in his celebrated novel *Maledetti Toscani* (*Those Cursed Tuscans*). He's being provocative and arrogant, qualities of which his fellow Tuscans, especially the Florentines, are often accused.

The Florentines, for their own part, acknowledge all this with evident pride, even using the term *toscanaccio* (nasty Tuscan) to describe themselves. Many attempts have been made to identify Italy's regional differences. In the "you are what you eat" category is Marcella Hazan's description (in the introduction to *The Classic Italian Cookbook*) of the "careful and calculating" Florentine, "a man who knows the measure of all things," whose "cooking is an austerely composed play upon essential and unadorned themes." There are historical reasons and age-old disputes underlying it all. The Sienese, called "genteel" by Malaparte, are the first to say, "it's an ill-wind that blows from the direction of Arezzo!" *Meglio un morto in casa, che un Pisano all'uscio* (Better a death in the house, than a Pisan at the door), states a Florentine proverb.

In recent years, accelerated by Italy's entry into the European Union, another phenomenon has made itself apparent, in the rapid growth of the immigrant populations in both Tuscany and Umbria. Florence alone has 35,000 legally registered foreign residents—and the number is rising. They're predominantly Albanians, Chinese, Peruvians, Filipinos, and Romanians. Continuing to arrive, these different groups are having a profound impact on the economy and cultural makeup of the city. How well these new Tuscans and Umbrians adapt, and how well their hosts receive them, remains to be seen.

Culture & Tradition

In the 1950s, when Italy's largely agrarian population began to move to the city, large numbers of farmhouses in Tuscany and Umbria were abandoned. The essentially feudal system of land usage, called *mezzadria* (sharecropping), also disappeared, taking with it a long and very rich tradition of *contadino* (peasant) culture. The abandoned farmhouses were restored as summer homes or permanent residences for the numerous English, Germans, and Americans who began to buy here. The contadini, on the other hand, were largely forced into the drab state-funded housing projects found on the outskirts of old towns in both regions.

In the 1970s and '80s a sort of "folk revival" began, with interest developing in the festivals, food, popular theater, songs, and local religious events that were once a vital part of local tradition. Today the calendar overflows with resurrected sagre (festivals or fairs) that derive from contadino practice. You'll find them all through Tuscany and Umbria, in towns large and small, January through December, with names like Sagra del Cinghiale (Wild Boar Festival), Sagra della Castagna (Chestnut Festival), Festa del Fungo (Mushroom Festival). There's the Befanate (celebrating Italy's witch-like Santa equivalent) in Grosseto during Epiphany, the Teatro Povero (a folk theater production) in Monticchiello in July, and, throughout the Maremma on the night of April 30 they perform the Canta il Maggio (Songs for Spring). They're fun, and there's often delicious traditionally

prepared food to be had. You can check with the local or regional tourist information offices for the dates and times of any *sagre* that happen to coincide with your visit.

Politics

Astonishingly frequent storms may rock Italy's national political boat, but the situation in Tuscany and Umbria, at the local and regional levels, is comparatively even-keeled. Along with the Marches and the Emilia-Romagna regions, Tuscany and Umbria form the so-called red quadrilateral of central Italy, each with strong left-wing political inclinations that date to World War II.

To cite but a few local leaders, the mayors of Perugia, Pisa, Siena, and Florence all wet their political feet either as members of the former Partito Comunista Italiano (PCI) or, as is the case with the younger Leonardo Domenici, mayor of Florence, with the post-communist Partito Democratico della Sinistra (the PDS, formed in 1991 to replace the PCI). All are now aligned with the center-left Partito Democratico (PD), formed in 2007. The names of Italy's political parties change with a frequency that boggles the minds of Italians and foreigners alike, but one thing remains certain: Tuscans and Umbrians will always side with the left.

Some think that this has brought stability; others, stagnation. As a woman from Perugia recently wrote on the blog of a national right-wing magazine, "We all know that Locchi is the mayor [of Perugia], that Boccali [of the same party] will be his successor, I can even hazard a guess at the name of the mayor after that. For thirty years I know who'll be governing Perugia—and they know it too."

The Economy

With Italy's boom years of the 1960s long since over, the more recent adoption of the euro (which seemed to double the price of many commodities overnight), and the relative stability of the average wage, many Tuscans and Umbrians are finding it difficult, as the catch-phrase has it, "to make it to the end of the month." Some blame the euro, some the politicians, others the employers, or the "system" as a whole. Whatever the cause, it must also be admitted that Italy has been forced to undergo great change in the last 40 years. An essentially agrarian economy in the '50s, Italy was heavily industrialized in the '60s, with rapid urbanization and depopulation of the countryside being the direct results.

Today, with large Italian industrial companies struggling to compete in a global market (here everyone blames the politicians), the new trend is to encourage small and mid-size business ventures that emphasize the concept "Made in Italy." With tourism and the general service industries comfortably accounting for two-thirds of their economies, Tuscany and Umbria have also tried to support the production of what are essentially traditional local goods: leather and shoes in Florence; textiles and clothing in Prato and Perugia; jewelry in Arezzo; paper products in northern Umbria and the valleys between Florence and Pisa; furniture in both regions. Not to mention that Gucci, Ferragamo, and Pucci are all internationally recognized Florentine labels and that the fashion designers Dolce & Gabbana now have a clothing factory in the Val d'Arno, just south of Florence.

TOP FLORENCE, TUSCANY & UMBRIA ATTRACTIONS

Galleria degli Uffizi, Florence

(A) Florence has many museums, but the Uffizi is king. Walking its halls is like stepping into an art-history textbook, except here you're looking at the genuine article—masterpieces by Leonardo, Michelangelo, Raphael, Botticelli, Caravaggio, and dozens of other luminaries. When planning your visit, make a point to reserve a ticket in advance. (⇨ Chapter 2.)

Duomo, Florence

(B) The Cathedral of Santa Maria del Fiore, commonly known as the Duomo, is Florence's most distinctive landmark, sitting at the very heart of the city and towering over the neighboring rooftops. Its massive dome is one of the world's great engineering masterpieces. For an up-close look, you can climb the 463 steps to the top—then gaze out at the city beneath you. (⇨ Chapter 2.)

Leaning Tower, Pisa

(C) This tower may be too famous for its own good (it's one of Italy's most popular tourist attractions), but there's something undeniably appealing about its perilous tilt, and climbing to the top is a kick. The square on which it sits, known as the Campo dei Miracoli, has a majestic beauty that no quantity of tourists can diminish. (⇨ Chapter 3.)

Piazza del Campo, Siena

(D) The sloping, fan-shaped square in the heart of Siena is one of the best places in Italy to engage in the distinctly Italian activity of hanging out and people-watching. The flanking Palazzo Vecchio and Torre del Mangia are first-rate sights. (⇨ Chapter 4.)

San Gimignano, Central Tuscany

(E) This classic Tuscan hill town has been dubbed a "medieval Manhattan" because of its numerous towers, built by

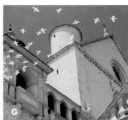

noble families of the time, each striving to outdo its neighbors. The streets fill with tour groups during the day, but if you stick around till sunset the crowds diminish and you see the town at its most beautiful. (⇨ Chapter 4.)

Abbazia di Sant'Antimo, Southern Tuscany

In a peaceful valley, surrounded by gently rolling hills, olive trees, and thick oak woods, Sant'Antimo is one of Italy's most beautifully situated abbeys—and a great "off the beaten path" destination. Stick around for mass and you'll hear the halls resound with Gregorian chants. (⇨ Chapter 6.)

Palazzo Ducale, Urbino, the Marches

(F) East of Umbria in the Marches region, Urbino is a college town in the Italian style—meaning its small but prestigious university dates to the 15th century. The highlight here is the Palazzo Ducale, a palace that exemplifies the Renaissance ideals of grace and harmony. (⇨ Chapter 7.)

Basilica di San Francesco, Assisi

(G) The basilica, built to honor Saint Francis, consists of two great churches—one Romanesque, fittingly solemn with its low ceilings and guttering candles; the other Gothic, with soaring arches and stained-glass windows (the first in Italy). They're both filled with some of Europe's finest frescoes. (⇨ Chapter 7.)

Duomo, Orvieto

(H) The facade of Orvieto's monumental Duomo contains a bas-relief masterpiece depicting the stories of the Creation and the Last Judgment (with the horrors of hell shown in striking detail). Inside, there's more glorious gore in the right transept, frescoed with Luca Signorelli's *Stories of the Antichrist and the Last Judgment*. (⇨ Chapter 8.)

TOP EXPERIENCES

The View from Florence's Piazzale Michelangelo

One of the best ways to introduce yourself to Florence is by walking up to this square on the hill south of the Arno. From here you can take in the whole city, and much of the surrounding countryside, in one spectacular vista. To extend the experience, linger at one of the outdoor cafés, and for the finest view of all, time your visit to correspond with sunset.

Strolling the Ramparts of Lucca

Lucca, 80 km (50 mi) west of Florence, isn't situated on a hilltop in the way commonly associated with Tuscan towns, and it doesn't have quite the abundance of art treasures that you find in Siena or Pisa (to say nothing of Florence). Yet for many visitors, Lucca is a favorite Tuscan destination, and the source of its appeal has everything to do with its ramparts. These hulking barricades have surrounded the city center since the 17th century; built as a source of security, they now are an elevated, oval park, complete with walkways, picnic areas, grass, and trees. The citizens of Lucca spend much of their spare time here, strolling, biking, and lounging, oblivious to the novelty of their situation but clearly happy with it.

Taking the Waters at a Tuscan Spa

Tuscany is dotted throughout with small *terme* (thermal baths), where hot water flows from natural springs deep beneath the earth's surface. It's been believed for millennia that these waters have the power to cure whatever ails you; although their medicinal power may be questionable, that doesn't keep a dip from being an extremely pleasant way to spend an afternoon. In northwest Tuscany you can take the waters at Montecatini Terme (made famous as a setting for Fellini's 8½ and seemingly little changed since then) or Bagni di Lucca (which had its heyday in the era of the 19th-century Romantic poets). To the south, Saturnia is the biggest draw, along with the more humble Chianiano Terme and Bagno Vignoni.

Discovering the Cinque Terre

A short trip west across the Tuscan border, along the Ligurian coast, are five tiny, remote fishing villages known collectively as the Cinque Terre. Tourism here was once limited to backpackers, but the beauty of the landscape—with steep, vine-covered hills pushing smack-dab against an azure sea—and the charm of the villages have turned the area into one of Italy's top destinations. The number-one activity is hiking the trails that run between the villages—the views are once-in-a-lifetime gorgeous—but if hiking isn't your thing, you can still have fun lounging about in cafés, admiring the water, and perhaps sticking a toe in it.

Wine-tasting in Chianti

The gorgeous hills of the Chianti region, between Florence and Siena, produce exceptional wines, and they never taste better than when sampled on their home turf. Many Chianti vineyards are visitor-friendly, but the logistics of a visit are different from what you may have experienced in other wine regions. If you just drop in, you're likely to get a tasting, but for a tour you usually need to make an appointment several days ahead of time. The upside is that your tour may end up being a half day of full immersion—including extended conversation with the winemakers and even a meal.

Passeggiata along Corso Vanucci, Perugia

The *passeggiata*—the evening stroll—is a ritual practiced in towns throughout Italy. One of its most pleasant manifestations is along Perugia's Corso Vanucci, a wide, pedestrians-only boulevard through the heart of the city, lined with elegant palaces—and many bars where you can stop for a pre-dinner aperitivo and watch the world go by.

Sampling Umbrian Truffles

The truffle (*tartufo* in Italian) is a peculiar delicacy—a gnarly clump of fungus that grows wild in the forest a few inches underground, is hunted down by specially trained truffle-sniffing dogs (or sometimes pigs), and can sell for a small fortune. The payoff is a powerful, perfumy flavor that makes gourmets swoon. Umbria is Italy's richest truffle-hunting ground, and in many of the region's restaurants you'll encounter truffle-infused dishes or be offered a shaving of truffle over your pasta. Indulge yourself at least once—it's an experience you won't forget.

Hiking in the footsteps of Saint Francis

Umbria, which bills itself as "Italy's Green Heart," is fantastic hiking country. Among the many options are two with a Franciscan twist: from the town of Cannara, 16 km (10 mi) south of Assisi, an easy half-hour walk leads to the fields of Pian d'Arca, where Saint Francis delivered his sermon to the birds. For slightly more demanding walks, you can follow the saint's path from Assisi to the Ermeo delle Carceri (Hermitage of Prisons), where Francis and his followers went to "imprison" themselves in prayer, and from here continue along the trails that crisscross Monte Subasio.

Spoleto's Festival dei Due Mondi

For two weeks in late June–early July, the Umbrian town of Spoleto is entirely given over to the Festival dei Due Mondi (Festival of the Two Worlds), one of Europe's great performing-arts events. Classical music, opera, dance, and theater fill every conceivable venue with performances that mix old with new and tradition with innovation. In many cases it's the opportunity to see world-renowned talent in one-of-a-kind, intimate settings. Attending the festival takes planning months in advance—most events sell out, and hotel rooms are at a premium—but for a dedicated arts lover, it's an effort that's richly rewarded.

Il Dolce Far Niente

"The sweetness of doing nothing" has long been an art form in Italy. This is a country in which life's pleasures are warmly celebrated, not guiltily indulged. Of course, doing "nothing" doesn't really mean nothing. It means doing things differently. It means lingering over a glass of wine for the better part of an evening just to watch the sun slowly set. It means savoring a slow and flirtatious evening passeggiata along the main street of a little town, a procession with no destination other than the town and its streets. And it means making a commitment—however temporary—to thinking, feeling, and believing that there is nowhere that you have to be next, that there is no other time than the magical present.

QUINTESSENTIAL FLORENCE, TUSCANY & UMBRIA

Il Caffè (Coffee)

The Italian day begins and ends with coffee, and more cups of coffee punctuate the time in between. To live like the Italians do, drink as they drink, standing at the counter or sitting at an outdoor table of the corner bar. (In Italy, a "bar" is a coffee bar.) A primer: *caffè* means coffee, and Italian standard issue is what Americans call espresso—short, strong, and usually taken very sweet. *Cappuccino* is a foamy half-and-half of espresso and steamed milk; cocoa powder *(cacao)* on top is acceptable, cinnamon is not. If you're thinking of having a cappuccino for dessert, think again—Italians drink only caffè or caffè *macchiato* (with a spot of steamed milk) after lunchtime. Confused? Homesick? Order caffè *americano* for a reasonable facsimile of good-old filtered joe.

Il Calcio (Soccer)

Imagine the most rabid American football fans—the ones who paint their faces on game day and sleep in pajamas emblazoned with the logo of their favorite team. Throw in a dose of melodrama along the lines of a tear-jerking soap opera. Ratchet up the intensity by a factor of 10, and you'll start to get a sense of how Italians feel about their national game, soccer—known in the mother tongue as *calcio*. On Sunday afternoons throughout the long September-to-May season, stadiums are packed throughout Italy. Those who don't get to games in person tend to congregate around television sets in restaurants and bars, rooting for the home team with a passion that feels like a last vestige of the days when the country was a series of warring medieval city-states. How calcio mania affects your stay in Italy depends on how eager you are to get involved. At the very least,

If you want to get a sense of contemporary Italian culture and indulge in some of its pleasures, start by familiarizing yourself with the rituals of daily life. These are a few highlights—things you can take part in with relative ease.

you may notice an eerie Sunday-afternoon silence on the city streets, or erratic restaurant service around the same time, accompanied by cheers and groans from a neighboring room. If you want a memorable, truly Italian experience, attend a game yourself. Availability of tickets may depend on the current fortunes of the team in the town where you're staying, but they often can be acquired with help from your hotel concierge.

Il Gelato (Ice Cream)

During warmer months, *gelato*—the Italian equivalent of ice cream—is a national obsession. It's considered a snack rather than a dessert, bought at stands and shops in piazzas and on street corners, and consumed on foot, usually at a leisurely stroll *(see* La Passeggiata, *following)*. Gelato is softer, less creamy, and more intensely flavored than its American counterpart. It comes in simple flavors that capture the essence of the main ingredient. (You won't find Chunky Monkey or Cookies 'n' Cream.) At most gelaterias choices include pistachio, *nocciola* (hazelnut), caffè, and numerous fruit varieties. Quality varies; the surest sign that you've hit on a good spot is a line at the counter.

La Passeggiata (Strolling)

A favorite Italian pastime is the *passeggiata* (literally, the promenade). In the late afternoon and early evening, especially on weekends, couples, families, and packs of teenagers stroll the main streets and piazzas of Italy's towns. It's a ritual of exchanged news and gossip, window-shopping, flirting, and gelato-eating that adds up to a uniquely Italian experience. To join in, simply hit the streets for a bit of wandering. You may feel more like an observer than a participant, until you realize that observing is what la passeggiata is all about.

IF YOU LIKE...

Renaissance Art

Travel veterans will tell you that the seemingly countless masterpieces of Italian art can cause first-time visitors—eyes glazed over from a heavy downpour of images, dates, and names—to lean, Pisa-like, on their companions for support. After a surfeit of Botticellis and Raphaels, even the miracle of the High Renaissance may begin to pall. The secret is to act like a tortoise, not a hare, and take your sweet time.

Instead of trotting after brisk tour guides, allow the splendors of the age to unfold slowly. Don't stop at the museums; get out and explore the chapels, palaces, and town squares for which Italy's marvelous art was conceived centuries ago and where much of it remains. Take in Michelangelo's *David* in Florence's Accademia, but then meander down the nearby 15th-century street where the sculptor was born.

Those caveats aside, here are the places to go when you're ready for an art feast:

Galleria degli Uffizi, Florence. Allow the better part of a day to explore the world's greatest collection of Italian Renaissance art.

Basilica di San Francesco, Arezzo, Eastern Tuscany. Piero della Francesa's *Legend of the True Cross* merits a pilgrimage to this Tuscan town.

Galleria Nazionale dell Umbria, Perugia. At one of Italy's finest small museums, the art is the star, but the first-class presentation adds to the appeal.

Palazzo Ducale, Urbino, the Marches. Head off the beaten path to visit a palace that perfectly displays the values of the Renaissance.

Monumental Churches

Few images are more identifiable with Italy than the country's great churches, stunning works of architecture that often took one or even two centuries to build.

The name duomo (derived from the Latin for "house," domus, and the root of the English "dome") is used to refer to the principal church of a town or city.

Generally speaking, the bigger the city, the more splendid its duomo. Still, some impressive churches inhabit some unlikely places—in the Umbrian hill towns of Assisi and Orvieto, for example.

Duomo, Florence. Brunelleschi's beautiful dome, the most recognizable in Italy, is an unequaled feat of 15th-century engineering.

Santa Croce, Florence. The resting place of Michelangelo, Galileo, and Machiavelli also contains the most important art of any church in Florence.

Cripta, Siena, Central Tuscany. Siena's Duomo is large and lush with art, but the vivid frescoes in its crypt merit special mention.

Basilica di San Francesco, Assisi. The fresco cycle here illustrating the life of Saint Francis is counted among the masterpieces of the Renaissance; the massive double basilica is a striking contrast of darkness and light.

Duomo, Orvieto, Southern Umbria. Few cathedrals can claim masterpieces inside and out, but here you'll find Italy's most perfect Gothic facade matched with Luca Signorelli's phenomenal frescoes in the Cappella di San Brizio.

Traditional Cooking

Italian cuisine all comes back to *la cucina di casa* (home cooking). From *ribollita* (bread soup) to a simply grilled whole fish from along the Ligurian coastline, the finest plates are often the simplest. The emphasis is on exceptionally good *materie prime* (primary ingredients) handled with skill and with respect for the foods themselves and for the traditional methods of preparing them.

Within Tuscany and Umbria, towns and regions have their own time-tested specialties that are a source of local pride, and even sophisticated restaurants often maintain an orthodox focus on generations-old recipes. Chefs revere the most humble ingredients, devoting the same attention to day-old bread that they do to costly truffles. Here are a few places where the simplest food will take your breath away:

Antico Noe, Florence. If Florence had diners, this unpretentious restaurant would be the best diner in town. What's on the menu depends on what's best that day at the market.

Buca di Sant'Antonio, Lucca, Northwest Tuscany. Simple, traditional Tuscan cuisine is created here with exceptional grace.

Osteria del Coro, Siena, Central Tuscany. Chef Stefano Azzi is a champion of traditional Sienese fare, but that doesn't keep him from turning out fabulous pizzas as well.

La Pallotta, Assisi, Northern Umbria. It's a family affair at this homey trattoria, which is a true gem among Assisi's hit-or-miss dining options.

Shopping

"Made in Italy" is synonymous with style, quality, and craftsmanship, whether it refers to high fashion or Maserati automobiles.

The best buys include leather goods of all kinds (from gloves to bags to jackets); silk goods; knitwear; ceramics; and, of course, the country's world-famous food products, from artisanal pasta sauces to world-class wine to extra-virgin olive oil.

Every region has its specialties. Florence is known for straw goods, gold jewelry, leather, and paper products (including beautiful handmade notebooks); Assisi for embroidery; and much of Umbria for ceramics.

And almost every town in Tuscany and Umbria has its own candidate for Italy's best olive oil.

And in Florence, as well as the other midsize cities, Italy's famous fashion names are never hard to find.

Via Tornabuoni, Florence. Whether you're looking to splurge or just browsing, Florence's most chic shopping street is the place to find Italian high style.

Via Tiberina Nord, Deruta, Northern Umbria. Deruta is the top spot for Umbrian ceramics; along this road you'll find one factory after another selling first-class wares.

Enoteca Italia, Siena, Central Tuscany. Italy's only state-sponsored wineshop is like a library of wine (with a vast collection).

IF YOU LIKE...

Hiking

After you've gotten an eyeful of the gorgeous landscapes of Tuscany and Umbria, it's only natural that you'll want to get out into them. Both regions are crisscrossed with countless hiking paths; you won't have a problem finding one suited to your fitness level. Tourist information offices in most towns can give you directions for walks lasting from an hour to a full day.

Cinque Terre, Liguria. They're not undiscovered, as they once were—you'll hear English spoken everywhere—but these five villages clinging to the cliffs of the Riviera di Levante, along the coast just west of Tuscany, are still spectacular, and they're all connected by invigorating hiking trails with memorable views of the towns, the rocks, and the Ligurian Sea.

Badia a Coltibuono, Gaiole in Chianti, Central Tuscany. It's more a walk than a hike, but the paths at this 2,000-acre estate take you through oak, fir, and chestnut woods and past two small lakes; it's Chianti at its most idyllic.

The Paths of St. Francis, Umbria. Outside Assisi, an easy half-hour walk takes you from the town of Cannara to Pian d'Arca, site of Saint Francis's sermon to the birds. It takes a bit more effort to make the walk from Assisi to the Eremo delle Carceri; from here you can head up to the summit of Monte Subasio, where you have views for miles in every direction.

Festivals

Celebrations can be serious business in Italy. From avant-garde musical performances to ribald street fairs, tremendous effort is expended to see that things are done right, with the pride of the community resting on the success of the event. The result is usually a fabulous time for those who attend.

Carnevale, Viareggio, Northwest Tuscany. For the two weeks leading up to Lent, this coastal town does its own fanciful version of Mardi Gras.

Palio, Siena, Central Tuscany. Twice a year, on July 2 and August 16, Siena goes medieval with this bareback horse race around its main square.

Festa dei Ceri, Gubbio, Northern Umbria. Mid-May marks Gubbio's Festival of the Candles, highlighted by townsmen racing up a hill carrying three huge pillars—just as they've been doing every year since 1160.

Festival dei Due Mondi, Spoleto, Southern Umbria. Star performers from around the world flock to this Umbrian hill town every summer for two weeks to do their thing in piazzas and intimate theaters.

FAQS

How likely am I to find English-speaking locals? English is widely spoken, especially in the cities. Odds are if the person you want to speak to doesn't know English, there will be someone within earshot who can translate. Nonetheless, if you pick up a few common phrases in Italian, your effort will be appreciated.

Are Italian drivers as crazy as I've heard? Yes—at least some of them are. Americans tend to be well schooled in defensive-driving techniques, but many Italians are not. When you hit the road, don't be surprised to encounter tailgating and high-risk passing. Your best response is to take the same safety-first approach you use at home; on the road is one place where you don't want to be mistaken for a local. On the up side, Italy's roads are very well maintained. Note that wearing a seat belt and having your lights on at all times are required by law.

Is it okay to drink cappuccino after 11 am? For most Italians, a frothy cappuccino is a morning thing: drinking milk later in the day is thought to be bad for the stomach. So, if you order a cappuccino in the afternoon or evening, you'll give yourself away as a tourist, and you may encounter a hint of condescension from the barista. But unless you're trying to pass as a local, there's no reason not to order whatever suits your fancy.

What's the best thing to do with the kids? One tried-and-true way of keeping kids entertained while giving then some exercise is to have them climb a tower. There are plenty of medieval towers to choose from, including the Campanile in Florence, the Torre del Mangia in Siena, the Torre Grossa in San Gimignano, and the Torre Guigini in Lucca, just for starters.

Note that the Leaning Tower in Pisa doesn't permit climbers under the age of eight.

Is the Cinque Terre a viable day trip from Florence? Technically it's doable, but we don't recommend it. You'll spend about five hours on the train round-trip, or something close to that if you go by car. And if it's summer and you want to hike the trails (which most people do), you're better off getting started early in the morning so you can beat the heat. The Cinque Terre is a beautiful, one-of-a-kind destination, and it deserves an overnight—but if you're set on a day trip, you're better off starting from Pisa or Lucca.

What's crime like in Florence and the other cities of Tuscany and Umbria? By and large, the cities of the region are remarkably crime -ree. The exceptions, unfortunately, are the tourist-focused crimes of purse snatching and pickpocketing. It would be an overstatement to say these crimes are rampant, but they do happen on a regular basis, particularly around train stations and major tourist attractions. They're commonly perpetrated by groups of street kids and by well-dressed professionals cruising for easy targets. A little common sense goes a long way toward keeping you safe: if children approach you, don't be reluctant to shoo them away firmly; don't keep your wallet in your back pocket; carry a purse with a shoulder strap, and wear it across your chest, so it can't be separated from you with a simple tug.

A GREAT ITINERARY

Day 1: Florence

If you're coming in on an international flight, you'll probably settle in Florence in time for an afternoon stroll or siesta (depending on your jet-lag strategy) before dinner.

Logistics: On your flight in, read through the restaurant listings in this guide and begin anticipating the first dinner of your trip. Look for a place near your hotel, and when you arrive, reserve a table (or have your concierge do it for you). Making a meal the focus of your first day is a great way to ease into Italian life.

Day 2: Florence

Begin your morning at the **Uffizi Gallery** (reserve your ticket in advance). The extensive collection will occupy much of your morning. Next, take in the neighboring **Piazza della Signoria**, Florence's most impressive square, then head a few blocks north to the **Duomo.** There, check out Ghiberti's famous bronze doors on the **Battistero,** and work up an appetite by climbing the 463 steps to the cupola of Brunelleschi's splendid cathedral dome, atop which you'll experience a memorable vista. Spend the afternoon relaxing, shopping, and wandering Florence's medieval streets; or, if you're up for a more involved journey, head out to **Fiesole** to experience the ancient amphitheater and beautiful views of the Tuscan countryside.

Day 3: Florence

Keep the energy level up for your second full day in Florence, sticking with art and architecture for the morning, trying to see most of the following: Michelangelo's *David* at the **Galleria dell'Accademia,** the **Palazzo Pitti** and **Boboli Gardens,** the **Medici Chapels,** and the churches of **Santa Maria**

Novella and **Santa Croce.** If it's a clear day, spend the afternoon on a trip up to the **Piazzale Michelangelo,** high on a hill above Florence, for sweeping views of the idyllic Florentine countryside. Given all the walking you've been doing, tonight would be a good night to recharge by trying the famed *bistecca alla fiorentina* (a grilled T-bone steak with olive oil).

Logistics: You can get up to the Piazzale Michelangelo by taxi or by taking Bus 7 from Santa Maria Novella. Otherwise, do your best to get around on foot; Florence is a brilliant city for walking.

Day 4: San Gimignano

Now that you've been appropriately introduced to the bewildering splendor of Renaissance Italy, it's time for a change of pace—and time for a rental car, which will enable you to see the back roads of Tuscany and Umbria. After breakfast, pick up your car, stop back at your hotel for your luggage, and head on out. On a good day the lazy drive from Florence to **San Gimignano,** past vineyards and typical Tuscan landscapes, is truly spectacular. The first thing that will hit you when you arrive at the hill town of San Gimignano will be the towers everywhere. The medieval skyscrapers of Italy, they also once occupied the role now played by Ferraris or Hummers: they were public displays of wealth. After finding your way to a hotel in the old town, set out on foot and check out the city's turrets and alleyways, doing your best to get away from the trinket shops, and later enjoying a leisurely dinner with the light but delicious local white wine, Vernaccia di San Gimignano.

Logistics: Some hotels might be able to coordinate with some rental-car agencies so that your car can be brought to your

hotel for you. Once you navigate your way out of Florence (no easy task), San Gimignano is only 57 km (35 mi) to the southwest, so it's an easy drive; you could even take a detour on the SS222 (Strada Chiantigiana), stop at one of the Chianti wine towns, and visit a winery along the way.

Day 5: Siena

In the morning, set out for nearby **Siena,** which is known worldwide for its Palio, a festival that culminates in an elaborate horse-race competition among the 17 *contrade* (medieval neighborhoods) of the city. Because of the enormous influx of tourists, especially in summer, Siena isn't everyone's cup of tea, but it's still one of Tuscany's most impressive sights; however many tourists you have to bump elbows with, it's hard not to be blown away by the city's precious medieval streets and memorable fan-shape **Piazza del Campo.** Not to be missed while in town are the spectacular **Duomo,** the **Battistero,** and the **Spedale di Santa Maria della Scala,** an old hospital and hostel that now contains an underground archaeological museum.

Logistics: It's a short and pretty drive from San Gimignano to Siena, but once there, parking can be a challenge. Look for the *stadio* (soccer stadium), where there's a parking lot that often has space.

Day 6: Arezzo/Cortona

Get an early start, because there's a lot to see today. From Siena you'll first head to **Arezzo,** home to the **Basilica di San Francesco,** which contains important frescoes by Piero della Francesca. Check out the **Piazza Grande** along with its beautiful Romanesque church of **Pieve di Santa Maria.** Try to do all of this before lunch, after which you'll head straight to **Cortona.** If Arezzo didn't capture your imagination, Cortona, which dates to the 5th century BC, will. Olive trees and vineyards give way to a medieval hill town with views over ridiculously idyllic Tuscan countryside and Lake Trasimeno. Cortona is a town for walking and relaxing, not sightseeing, so enjoy yourself, wandering through the **Piazza della Repubblica** and **Piazza Signorelli,** perhaps doing a bit of shopping.

Logistics: Siena to Arezzo is 63 km (39 mi) on the E78. From Arezzo to Cortona, it's just 30 km (18 mi)—take S71.

Day 7: Assisi

Today you'll cross over into Umbria, a region just as beautiful as Tuscany but still less trodden. Yet another impossibly beautiful hill town, **Assisi,** is the home of

A GREAT
ITINERARY

Saint Francis and host to the many religious pilgrims that come to celebrate his legacy. Going here is the most treasured memory of many a traveler's visit to Italy. Upon arriving and checking into your lodging, head straight for the **Basilica di San Francesco**, which displays the coffin of Saint Francis and dozens of unbelievable frescoes. From here take Via San Francesco to **Piazza del Commune** and see the **Tempio di Minerva** before a break for lunch. After lunch, see **San Rufino**, the town cathedral, and then go back through the piazza to Corso Mazzini and see **Santa Chiara**. If you're a true Franciscan, you could instead devote the afternoon to heading out 16 km (10 mi) to **Cannara**, where Saint Francis delivered his sermon to the birds.

Logistics: From Cortona take the S71 to the A1 autostrada toward Perugia. After about 40 km (24 mi), take the Assisi exit (E45), and it's another 14 km (8 mi) to Assisi.

Day 8: Spoleto

This morning will take you from a small Umbrian hill town to a slightly bigger one: **Spoleto**, a walled city that's home to a world-renowned arts festival each summer. But Spoleto needs no festival to be celebrated. Its **Duomo** is wonderful. Its fortress, **La Rocca**, is impressive. And the **Ponte delle Torri**, a 14th-century bridge that separates Spoleto from Monteluco, is a marvelous sight, traversing a gorge 260 feet below and built upon the foundations of a Roman aqueduct. See all these during the day, stopping for a light lunch of a *panino* (sandwich) or salad, saving your appetite for a serious last dinner in Italy: Umbrian cuisine is excellent everywhere, but Spoleto is a memorable culinary destination. Do your best to sample black

AN ITINERARY TIP

Because of spotty train service to Tuscan hill towns, this itinerary is extremely difficult to complete without a car. Driving is easy and relaxing in the region, whose roads can be winding but are generally wide, well kept, well marked, and not too crowded. If you absolutely don't want to drive, buses are the best way to go, but you'll often have to change buses in hubs like Florence, and it would be best to cut out some of the smaller Tuscan hill towns and spend extra time in Siena and Spoleto.

truffles, a proud product of the region; they're delicious on pasta or meat.

Logistics: One school of thought would be to time your visit to Spoleto's world-renowned arts festival that runs from mid-June through mid-July. Another would be to do anything you can to avoid it. It all depends on your taste for big festivals and big crowds. The trip from Assisi to Spoleto is a pretty 47-km (29-mi) drive (S75 to the S3) that should take you less than an hour.

Day 9: Spoleto/Departure

It's a fair distance from Spoleto to the Florence airport, your point of departure. Depending on your comfort level with Italian driving, allow at least 2½ hours to reach Florence's airport.

Logistics: An alternative possibility would be to try to get a flight out of Perugia's tiny airport, which is a lot closer to Spoleto than Florence. It offers connections to Milan and Rome (Ciampino)—but not many. Otherwise, just get an early start and drive to Florence along the A1 autostrada.

WHO'S WHO IN RENAISSANCE ART

Michelangelo. Leonardo da Vinci. Raphael. This heady triumvirate of the Italian Renaissance is synonymous with artistic genius. Yet they are only three of the remarkable cast of characters whose work defines the Renaissance, that extraordinary flourishing of art and culture in Italy, especially in Florence, as the Middle Ages drew to a close. The artists were visionaries, who redefined painting, sculpture, architecture, and even what it means to be an artist.

THE PIONEER. In the mid-14th century, a few artists began to move away the flat, two-dimensional painting of the Middle Ages. **Giotto**, who painted seemingly three-dimensional figures who show emotion, had a major impact on the artists of the next century.

THE GROUNDBREAKERS. The generations of **Brunelleschi** and **Botticelli** took center stage in the 15th century. **Ghiberti, Masaccio, Donatello, Uccello, Fra Angelico**, and **Filippo Lippi** were other major players. Part of the Renaissance (or "re-birth") was a renewed interest in classical sources—the texts, monuments, and sculpture of Ancient Greece and Rome. Perspective and the illusion of three-dimensional space in painting was another discovery of this era, known as the Early Renaissance. Suddenly the art appearing on the walls looked real, or more realistic than it used to.

Roman ruins were not the only thing to inspire these artists. There was an incredible exchange of ideas going on. In Santa Maria del Carmine, Filippo Lippi was inspired by the work of Masaccio, who in turn was a friend of Brunelleschi. Young artists also learned from the masters via the apprentice system. Ghiberti's workshop (*bottega* in Italian) included, at one time or another, Donatello, Masaccio, and Uccello. Botticelli was apprenticed to Filippo Lippi.

THE BIG THREE. The mathematical rationality and precision of 15th-century art gave way to what is known as the High Renaissance. **Leonardo, Michelangelo**, and **Raphael** were much more concerned with portraying the body in all its glory and with achieving harmony and grandeur in their work. Oil paint, used infrequently up until this time, became more widely employed: as a result, Leonardo's colors are deeper, more sensual, more alive. For one brief period, all three were in Florence at the same time. Michelangelo and Leonardo surely knew one another, as they were simultaneously working on frescoes (never completed) inside Palazzo Vecchio.

When Michelangelo left Florence for Rome in 1508, he began the slow drain of artistic exodus from Florence, which never really recovered her previous glory.

A RENAISSANCE TIMELINE

IN THE WORLD

▼ Black Death in Europe kills one third of the population, 1347-50.

▼ Joan of Arc burned at the stake, 1431.

IN FLORENCE

▼ Founding of the Medici bank, 1397.

▼ Medici family made official papal bankers.

▼ 1434, Cosimo il Vecchio becomes de facto ruler of Florence. The Medici family will dominate the city until 1494.

▼ Dante, a native of Florence, writes *The Divine Comedy*, 1302-21.

1300

1400

IN ART

EARLY RENAISSANCE

▼▼ Masaccio and Masolino fresco Santa Maria del Carmine, 1424-28.

GIOTTO (ca. 1267-1337)

BRUNELLESCHI (1377-1446)

▼▼ Giotto frescoes in Santa Croce, 1320-25.

LORENZO GHIBERTI (ca. 1381-1455)

DONATELLO (ca. 1386-1466)

PAOLO UCCELLO (1397-1475)

FRA ANGELICO (ca. 1400-1455)

▼ 1334, 67-year-old Giotto is appointed chief architect of Santa Maria del Fiore, Florence's Duomo (below). He begins to work on the Campanile, which will be completed in 1359, after his death.

MASACCIO (1401-1428)

FILIPPO LIPPI (ca. 1406-1469)

▼ Donatello sculpts his bronze *David*, ca. 1440.

▼▼ Fra Angelico frescoes friars' cells in San Marco, ca. 1438-45.

▼ Uccello's *Sir John Hawkwood*, ca. 1436.

▼ Ghiberti wins the competition for the Baptistery doors (above) in Florence, 1401.

▼ Brunelleschi wins the competition for the Duomo's cupola (right), 1418.

▼ Gutenberg Bible is printed, 1455.

▼ Columbus discovers America, 1492.

▼ Martin Luther posts his 95 theses on the door at Wittenberg, kicking off the Protestant Reformation, 1517.

▼ Constantinople falls to the Turks, 1453.

▼ Machiavelli's *Prince* appears, 1513.

▼ Copernicus proves that the earth is not the center of the universe, 1530-43.

Lorenzo "il Magnifico" (right), the Medici patron of the arts, rules in Florence, 1449-92.

▼ Two Medici popes Leo X (1513-21) and Clement VII (1523-34) in Rome.

▼ Catherine de'Medici becomes Queen of France, 1547.

1450 **1500** **1550**

HIGH RENAISSANCE MANNERISM

▼ Fra Filippo Lippi's *Madonna and Child*, ca. 1452.

▼ 1508, Raphael begins work on the chambers in the Vatican, Rome.

▼ Giorgio Vasari publishes his first edition of *Lives of the Artists*, 1550.

▼ 1504, Michelangelo's *David* is put on display in Piazza della Signoria, where it remains until 1873.

▼ Botticelli paints the *Birth of Venus*, ca. 1482.

▼ Michelangelo begins to fresco the Sistine Chapel ceiling, 1508.

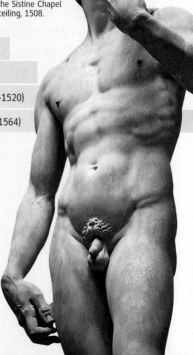

BOTTICELLI (ca. 1444-1510)

LEONARDO DA VINCI (1452-1519)

RAPHAEL (1483-1520)

MICHELANGELO (1475-1564)

▼▼ Leonardo paints *The Last Supper* in Milan, 1495-98.

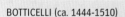

Giotto's *Nativity*   Donatello's *St. John the Baptist*   Ghiberti's *Gates of Paradise*

GIOTTO (CA. 1267-1337)
Painter/architect from a small town north of Florence.
He unequivocally set Italian painting on the course that led to the triumphs of the Renaissance masters. Unlike the rather flat, two-dimensional forms found in then prevailing Byzantine art, Giotto's figures have a fresh, life-like quality. The people in his paintings have bulk, and they show emotion, which you can see on their faces and in their gestures. This was something new in the late Middle Ages. Without Giotto, there wouldn't have been a Raphael.
In Florence: **Santa Croce; Uffizi; Campanile; Santa Maria Novella**
Elsewhere in Italy: **Scrovegni Chapel, Padua; Vatican Museums, Rome**

FILIPPO BRUNELLESCHI (1377-1446)
Architect/engineer from Florence.
If Brunelleschi had beaten Ghiberti in the Baptistery doors competition in Florence, the city's Duomo most likely would not have the striking appearance and authority that it has today. After his loss, he sulked off to Rome, where he studied the ancient Roman structures first-hand. Brunelleschi figured out how to vault the Duomo's dome, a structure unprecedented in its colossal size and great height. His Ospedale degli Innocenti employs classical elements in the creation of a stunning, new architectural statement; it is the first truly Renaissance structure.
In Florence: **Duomo; Ospedale degli Innocenti; San Lorenzo; Santo Spirito; Baptistery Doors Competition Entry, Bargello; Santa Croce**

LORENZO GHIBERTI (CA. 1381-1455)
Sculptor from Florence.
Ghiberti won a competition—besting his chief rival, Brunelleschi—to cast the gilded bronze North Doors of the Baptistery in Florence. These doors, and the East Doors that he subsequently executed, took up the next 50 years of his life. He created intricately worked figures that are more true-to-life than any since antiquity, and he was one of the first Renaissance sculptors to work in bronze. Ghiberti taught the next generation of artists; Donatello, Uccello, and Masaccio all passed through his studio.
In Florence: **Door Copies, Baptistery; Original Doors, Museo dell'Opera del Duomo; Baptistry Door Competition Entry, Bargello; Orsanmichele**

DONATELLO (CA. 1386-1466)
Sculptor from Florence.
Donatello was an innovator who, like his good friend Brunelleschi, spent most of his long life in Florence. Consumed with the science of optics, he used light and shadow to create the effects of nearness and distance. He made an essentially flat slab look like a three- dimensional scene. His bronze *David* is probably the first free-standing male nude since antiquity. Not only technically brilliant, his work is also emotionally resonant; few sculptors are as expressive.
In Florence: ***David*, Bargello; *St. Mark*, Orsanmichele; Palazzo Vecchio; Museo dell'Opera del Duomo; San Lorenzo; Santa Croce**
Elsewhere in Italy: **Padua; Prato; Venice**

Fra Angelico's *The Deposition*   Masaccio's *Trinity*   Filippo Lippi's *Madonna and Child*

PAOLO UCCELLO (1397-1475)
Painter from Florence.
Renaissance chronicler Vasari once observed that had Uccello not been so obsessed with the mathematical problems posed by perspective, he would have been a very good painter. The struggle to master single-point perspective and to render motion in two dimensions is nowhere more apparent than in his battle scenes. His first major commission in Florence was the gargantuan fresco of the English mercenary Sir John Hawkwood (the Italians called him Giovanni Acuto) in Florence's Duomo.
In Florence: **Sir John Hawkwood, Duomo; *Battle of San Romano*, Uffizi; Santa Maria Novella**
Elsewhere in Italy: **Urbino**

FRA ANGELICO (CA. 1400-1455)
Painter from a small town north of Florence.
A Dominican friar, who eventually made his way to the convent of San Marco, Fra Angelico and his assistants painted frescoes for aid in prayer and meditation. He was known for his piety; Vasari wrote that Fra Angelico could never paint a crucifix without a tear running down his face. Perhaps no other painter so successfully translated the mysteries of faith and the sacred into painting. And yet his figures emote, his command of perspective is superb, and his use of color startles even today.
In Florence: **Museo di San Marco; Uffizi**
Elsewhere in Italy: **Vatican Museums, Rome; Fiesole; Cortona; Perugia; Orvieto**

MASACCIO (1401-1428)
Painter from San Giovanni Valdarno, southeast of Florence.
Masaccio and Masolino, a frequent collaborator, worked most famously together at Santa Maria del Carmine. Their frescoes of the life of St. Peter use light to mold figures in the painting by imitating the way light falls on figures in real life. Masaccio also pioneered the use of single-point perspective, masterfully rendered in his *Trinity*. His friend Brunelleschi probably introduced him to the technique, yet another step forward in rendering things the way the eye sees them. Masaccio died young and under mysterious circumstances.
In Florence: **Santa Maria del Carmine; *Trinity*, Santa Maria Novella**

FILIPPO LIPPI (CA. 1406-1469)
Painter from Prato.
At a young age, Filippo Lippi entered the friary of Santa Maria del Carmine, where he was highly influenced by Masaccio and Masolino's frescoes. His religious vows appear to have made less of an impact; his affair with a young nun produced a son, Filippino (Little Philip, who later apprenticed with Botticelli), and a daughter. His religious paintings often have a playful, humorous note; some of his angels are downright impish and look directly out at the viewer. Lippi links the earlier painters of the 15th century with those who follow; Botticelli apprenticed with him.
In Florence: **Uffizi; Palazzo Medici Riccardi; San Lorenzo; Palazzo Pitti**
Elsewhere in Italy: **Prato**

| Botticelli's *Primavera* | Leonardo's *Portrait of a Young Woman* | Raphael's *Madonna on the Meadow* |

BOTTICELLI (CA. 1444-1510)
Painter from Florence.
Botticelli's work is characterized by stunning, elongated blondes, cherubic angels (something he undoubtedly learned from his time with Filippo Lippi), and tender Christs. Though he did many religious paintings, he also painted monumental, nonreligious panels—his *Birth of Venus* and *Primavera* being the two most famous of these. A brief sojourn took him to Rome, where he and a number of other artists frescoed the Sistine Chapel walls.
In Florence: **Birth of Venus, Primavera, Uffizi; Palazzo Pitti**
Elsewhere in Italy: **Vatican Museums, Rome**

LEONARDO DA VINCI (1452-1519)
Painter/sculptor/engineer from Anchiano, a small town outside Vinci.
Leonardo never lingered long in any place; his restless nature and his international reputation led to commissions throughout Italy, and took him to Milan, Vigevano, Pavia, Rome, and, ultimately, France. Though he is most famous for his mysterious *Mona Lisa* (at the Louvre in Paris), he painted other penetrating, psychological portraits in addition to his scientific experiments: his design for a flying machine (never built) predates Kitty Hawk by nearly 500 years. The greatest collection of Leonardo's work in Italy can be seen on one wall in the Uffizi.
In Florence: **Adoration of the Magi, Uffizi**
Elsewhere in Italy: **Last Supper, Santa Maria delle Grazie, Milan**

RAPHAEL (1483-1520)
Painter/architect from Urbino.
Raphael spent only four highly productive years of his short life in Florence, where he turned out made-to-order panel paintings of the Madonna and Child for a hungry public; he also executed a number of portraits of Florentine aristocrats. Perhaps no other artist had such a fine command of line and color, and could render it, seemingly effortlessly, in paint. His painting acquired new authority after he came up against Michelangelo toiling away on the Sistine ceiling. Raphael worked nearly next door in the Vatican, where his figures take on an epic, Michelangelesque scale.
In Florence: **Uffizi; Palazzo Pitti**
Elsewhere in Italy: **Vatican Museums, Rome**

MICHELANGELO (1475-1564)
Painter/sculptor/architect from Caprese.
Although Florentine and proud of it (he famously signed his St. Peter's *Pietà* to avoid confusion about where he was from), he spent most of his 90 years outside his native city. He painted and sculpted the male body on an epic scale and glorified it while doing so. Though he complained throughout the proceedings that he was really a sculptor, Michelangelo's Sistine Chapel ceiling is arguably the greatest fresco cycle ever painted (and the massive figures owe no small debt to Giotto).
In Florence: **David, Galleria dell'Accademia; Uffizi; Casa Buonarroti; Bargello**
Elsewhere in Italy: **St. Peter's Basilica, Vatican Museums, and Piazza del Campidoglio in Rome**

Florence

WORD OF MOUTH

"Michelangelo, Dante, Galileo. Gelato, red wine, amazing food. Some of the most wonderful art and architecture. Firenze is a magical city (and where my fiancé and I got engaged). It is an absolute gem."

–Kristin

WELCOME TO FLORENCE

TOP REASONS TO GO

★ **Galleria degli Uffizi:** Italian Renaissance art doesn't get much better than this vast collection bequeathed to the city by the last Medici, Anna Maria Luisa.

★ **The dome of the Duomo:** Brunelleschi's work of engineering genius is the city's undisputed centerpiece.

★ **Michelangelo's *David*:** One look and you'll know why this is the Western world's most famous sculpture.

★ **The view from Piazzale Michelangelo:** From this perch the city is laid out before you. The colors at sunset heighten the experience.

★ **Piazza Santa Croce:** After you've had your fill of Renaissance masterpieces, hang out here and watch the world go by.

1 **The Duomo to the Ponte Vecchio.** You're in the heart of Florence here. Among the numerous highlights are the city's greatest museum **(the Uffizi)** and its most impressive square **(Piazza della Signoria).**

2 **San Lorenzo to the Accademia.** The blocks from the church of **San Lorenzo** to the **Accademia** museum bear the imprints of the Medici and of Michelangelo, culminating in his masterful *David*. Just to the north, the former convent of **San Marco** is an oasis decorated with ethereal frescoes.

3 **Santa Maria Novella to the Arno.** This part of town includes the train station, 15th-century palaces, and the city's most chic shopping street, **Via Tornabuoni**.

4 **Santa Croce.** The district centers around its namesake basilica, which is filled with the tombs of Renaissance luminaries. The area is also known for its leather shops, some of which have been in operation since the 16th century.

5 **The Oltrarno.** Across the Arno you encounter the massive Palazzo Pitti and the narrow streets of the **Santo Spirito** district, which is filled with artisans' workshops and antique stores. A climb to **Piazzale Michelangelo** gives you a spectacular view of the city.

Piazza del Duomo

Santa Croce Church

2

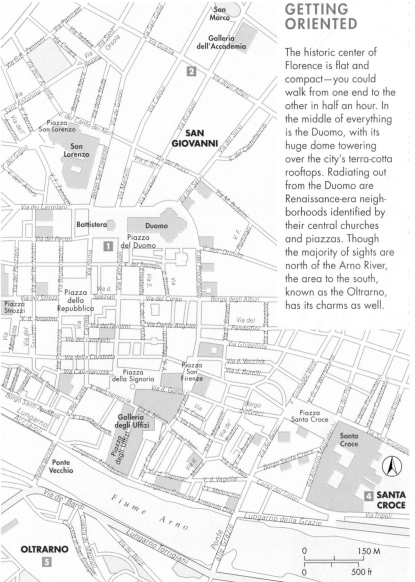

GETTING ORIENTED

The historic center of Florence is flat and compact—you could walk from one end to the other in half an hour. In the middle of everything is the Duomo, with its huge dome towering over the city's terra-cotta rooftops. Radiating out from the Duomo are Renaissance-era neighborhoods identified by their central churches and piazzas. Though the majority of sights are north of the Arno River, the area to the south, known as the Oltrarno, has its charms as well.

San Marco

Galleria dell'Accademia

SAN GIOVANNI

San Lorenzo

Piazza San Lorenzo

Battistero

Duomo

Piazza del Duomo

Piazza della Repubblica

Piazza Strozzi

Piazza San Firenze

Piazza della Signoria

Galleria degli Uffizi

Piazza degli Uffizi

Ponte Vecchio

Piazza Santa Croce

Santa Croce

4 SANTA CROCE

OLTRARNO
5

F i u m e   A r n o

| 0 | | 150 M |
| 0 | | 500 ft |

FLORENCE PLANNER

Avoiding an Art Hangover

Even for the most dedicated art enthusiast, trying to take in Florence's abundance of masterpieces can turn into a headache—there's just too much to see. Especially if you don't count yourself as an art lover, remember to pace yourself. Allow time to wander and follow your whims, and ignore any pangs of guilt if you'd rather relax in a café and watch the world go by than trudge on sore feet through another breathtaking palace or church.

Florence isn't a city that can be "done." It's a place you can return to again and again, confident there will always be more treasures to discover.

Making the Most of Your Time

With some planning, you can see Florence's most famous sights in a couple of days. Start off at the city's most awe-inspiring work of architecture, the **Duomo,** climbing to the top of the dome if you have the stamina. On the same piazza, check out Ghiberti's bronze doors at the **Battistero.** (They're actually high-quality copies; the Museo dell'Opera del Duomo has the originals.) Set aside the afternoon for the **Galleria degli Uffizi,** making sure to reserve tickets in advance.

On Day Two, visit Michelangelo's *David* in the **Galleria dell'Accademia**—reserve tickets here, too. Linger in the **Piazza della Signoria,** Florence's central square, where a copy of *David* stands in the spot the original occupied for centuries, then head east a couple of blocks to **Santa Croce,** the city's most artistically rich church. Double back and walk across Florence's landmark bridge, the **Ponte Vecchio.**

Do all that, and you'll have seen some great art, but you've just scratched the surface. If you have more time, put the **Bargello,** the **Museo di San Marco,** and the **Cappelle Medicee** at the top of your list. When you're ready for an art break, stroll through the **Boboli Gardens** or explore Florence's lively shopping scene, from the food stalls of the **Mercato Centrale** to the chic boutiques of the **Via Tornabuoni.**

Piazza della Signoria

Tourist Offices

The Florence tourist office, known as the APT (☎055/290832 ⊕ *www.comune.firenze.it*), has branches next to the Palazzo Medici-Riccardi, in the main train station, and around the corner from the Basilica di Santa Croce. The offices are generally open from 9 in the morning until 7 in the evening. The multilingual staff will give you directions (but usually not free maps) and the latest on happenings in the city. It's particularly worth a stop if you're interested in finding out about performing-arts events. The APT Web site is in Italian only.

Titian's *Venus of Urbino*

Florentine Hours

Florence's sights keep tricky hours. Some are closed on Wednesday, some on Monday, some on every other Monday. Quite a few shut their doors each day (or on most days) by 2 in the afternoon. Things get even more confusing on weekends. Make it a general rule to check the hours closely for any place you're planning to visit; if it's somewhere you have your heart set on seeing, it's worthwhile to call to confirm.

Here's a selection of major sights that might not be open when you'd expect—consult the sight listings within this chapter for the full details. And be aware that, as always, hours can and do change.

■ The **Uffizi** and the **Accademia** are both closed Monday. All but a few of the galleries at Palazzo Pitti are closed Monday as well.

■ The **Duomo** closes at 3:30 on Thursday (as opposed to 5:30 on other weekdays, 4:45 on weekends). The dome of the Duomo is closed on Sunday.

■ The **Battistero** is open from noon until 7, Monday through Saturday, and on Sunday from 8:30 to 2.

■ The **Bargello** closes at 1:50 PM, and is closed entirely on alternating Sundays and Mondays.

■ The **Cappelle Medicee** are closed on alternating Sundays and Mondays.

■ **Museo di San Marco** closes at 1:50 on weekdays but stays open until 7 on weekends—except for alternating Sundays and Mondays, when it's closed entirely.

■ **Palazzo Medici-Riccardi** is closed Wednesday.

With Reservations

At most times of day you'll see a line of people snaking around the Uffizi. They're waiting to buy tickets, and you don't want to be one of them. Instead, call ahead for a reservation (055/294883; reservationists speak English). You'll be given a reservation number and a time of admission—the further in advance you call, the more time slots you'll have to choose from. Go to the museum's reservation door at the appointed hour, give the clerk your number, pick up your ticket, and go inside. You'll pay €3 for this privilege, but it's money well spent. At this writing, an on-line reservation option has also been launched at ⊕*www.polomuseale.firenze. it; the booking process at this point is awkward, but it's likely to improve.*

Use the same reservation service to book tickets for the Galleria dell'Accademia, where lines rival those of the Uffizi. (Reservations can also be made for the Palazzo Pitti, the Bargello, and several other sights, but they aren't needed.) An alternative strategy is to check with your hotel—many will handle reservations.

Top Passeggiata

Via dei Calzaiuoli, between Piazza del Duomo and Piazza della Signoria, is where Florence comes out for its evening stroll.

GETTING HERE & AROUND

Getting Here by Car

Florence is connected to the north and south of Italy by the Autostrada del Sole (A1). It takes about one hour and a half of driving on scenic roads to get to Bologna (although heavy truck traffic over the Apennines often makes for slower going), about three hours to Rome, and 3 to 3½ hours to Milan. The Tyrrhenian Coast is an hour west on the A11.

Getting Here by Bus

Long-distance buses provide inexpensive if somewhat claustrophobic service between Florence and other cities in Italy and Europe. **Lazzi Eurolines** (⊠ *Via Mercadante 2, Santa Maria Novella* ☎ *055/363041* ⊕ *www.lazzi.it*) and **SITA** (⊠ *Via Santa Caterina da Siena 17/r, Santa Maria Novella* ☎ *055/214721* ⊕ *www.sita-online.it*)are the major lines; they have neatly divided up their routes, so there's little overlap.

Getting Here by Air

Florence's small **Aeroporto A. Vespucci** (✛ *10 km [6 mi] northwest of Florence* ☎ *055/373498* ⊕ *www.aeroporto.firenze.it*) commonly called **Peretola**, is located just outside of town and receives flights from Milan, Rome, London, and Paris. To get into the city center from the airport by car, take the autostrada A11. Tickets for the local bus service into Florence are sold at the airport's second-floor bar—Bus 62 runs once an hour directly to the train station at Santa Maria Novella. The airport's bus shelter is beyond the parking lot.

Pisa's **Aeroporto Galileo Galilei** (✛ *12 km [7 mi] south of Pisa and 80 km [50 mi] west of Florence* ☎ *050/849300* ⊕ *www.pisa-airport.com*) is the closest landing point with significant international service, including (at this writing) a few direct flights from the United States each week on Delta. It's a straight shot down SS67 to Florence. A train service connects Pisa's airport station with Santa Maria Novella, roughly a 1½-hour trip. Trains start running about 7 AM from the airport, 6 AM from Florence, and continue service every hour until about 7 PM from the airport, 4 PM from Florence.

For flight information, call the airport or **Florence Air Terminal** (⊠ *Stazione Centrale di Santa Maria Novella* ☎ *055/216073*)—which, despite the misleading name, is simply an office at the Santa Maria Novella train station, around the corner from train tracks 1 and 2.

Getting Here by Train

Florence is on the principal Italian train route between most European capitals and Rome, and within Italy it is served frequently from Milan, Venice, and Rome by Intercity (IC) and nonstop Eurostar trains. **Stazione Centrale di Santa Maria Novella** (☎ *892021* ⊕ *www.trenitalia.com*) is the main station and is in the center of town. Avoid trains that stop only at the Campo di Marte or Rifredi stations, which are not convenient to the city center.

Neptune Fountain, Piazza della Signoria

Getting Around by Bus

Florence's flat, compact city center is made for walking, but when your feet get weary, you can use the efficient bus system, which includes small electric buses making the rounds in the center. Buses also climb to Piazzale Michelangelo and San Miniato south of the Arno.

Maps and timetables for local bus service are available for a small fee at the ATAF (Azienda Trasporti Area Fiorentina) booth next to the train station, or for free at visitor information offices. Tickets must be bought in advance from tobacco shops, newsstands, automatic ticket machines near main stops, or ATAF booths. The ticket must be canceled in the small validation machine immediately upon boarding.

You have several ticket options, all valid for one or more rides on all lines. A €1.20 ticket is good for one hour from the time it is first canceled. A multiple ticket—four tickets, each valid for 70 minutes—costs €4.50. A 24-hour tourist ticket costs €5. Two-, three-, and seven-day passes are also available.

Getting Around by Taxi

Taxis usually wait at stands throughout the city (in front of the train station and in Piazza della Repubblica, for example), or you can call for one (☎ 055/4390 or 055/4798). The meter starts at €2.30, with a €3.60 minimum and extra charges at night, on Sunday, and for radio dispatch.

Getting Around by Bike & Moped

Brave souls (cycling in Florence is difficult at best) may rent bicycles at easy-to-spot locations at Fortezza da Basso, the Stazione Centrale di Santa Maria Novella, and Piazza Pitti. Otherwise try **Alinari** (✉ *Via Guelfa 85/r, San Marco* ☎ *055/280500* ⊕ *www. alinarirental.com*). You'll be up against hordes of tourists and those pesky *motorini* (mopeds). (For a safer ride, try Le Cascine, a former Medici hunting ground turned into a large public park with paved pathways.) The historic center can be circumnavigated via bike paths lining the *viali*, the ring road surrounding the area. If you want to go native and rent a noisy Vespa (Italian for "wasp") or other make of motorcycle or *motorino*, you may do so at **Maxirent** (✉ *Borgo Ognissanti 155/r, Santa Maria Novella* ☎ *055/265420*) or **Massimo** (✉ *Via Campo d'Arrigo 16/r* ☎ *055/573689*). However unfashionable, helmets must be rented at either place, and are mandatory.

Getting Around by Car

An automobile in Florence is a major liability. If your itinerary includes parts of Italy where you'll want a car (such as Tuscany), pick the vehicle up on your way out of town.

EATING & DRINKING WELL IN FLORENCE

Food in Florence is not about sauces, foams, or fusion. Simply prepared meats, grilled or roasted, are the stars, and pair well with seasonal vegetables like artichokes, porcini, and cannellini beans. Bistecca's big here, but there's plenty more that tastes great on the grill, too.

Traditionalists (and many Florentines are) go for their gustatory pleasures in trattorie and osterie, places where décor is unimportant, place mats are mere paper, and service is often perfunctory. Culinary innovation comes slowly in this town, though some cutting-edge restaurants have been appearing, usually with young chefs who've traveled and worked outside Italy. Some of these places lack charm (many have an international, you-could-be-anywhere feel), but their menus offer exciting, updated versions of Tuscan standards

By American standards, Florentines eat late: 1:30 or 2 is typical for lunch, and 9 for dinner. Consuming a primo, secondo, and dolce is largely a thing of the past, and no one looks askance if you don't order the whole nine yards. For lunch, many Florentines simply grab a panino and a glass of wine at a bar. Those opting for a simple trattoria lunch often order a plate of pasta and dessert.

STALE AND STELLAR

Florence lacks signature pasta and rice dishes, perhaps because the town's content to have raised frugality with bread to culinary craft. Stale bread is the basis for three classic Florentine primi: pappa al pomodoro, ribollita, and panzanella. "Pappa" is made with either fresh or canned tomatoes and that stale bread. Ribollita is a vegetable soup fortified with cavolo nero (sometimes called Tuscan kale elsewhere), cannellini beans, and thickened with bread. Panzanella, a summertime dish, is reconstituted Tuscan bread combined with tomatoes, cucumber, and basil. They all are greatly enhanced with a generous application of fragrant Tuscan olive oil.

2

A CLASSIC ANTIPASTO:
CROSTINI DI FEGATINI

This beloved dish consists of a chicken liver spread, served warm or at room temperature, on toasted, garlic-rubbed bread. It can be served smooth, like a pâté, or in a rougher spread. It's made by sautéeing chicken livers with finely diced carrot and onion, enlivened with the addition of wine, broth, or Marsala reductions, and mashed anchovies and capers.

A CLASSIC SECONDO:
BISTECCA FIORENTINA

The town's culinary pride and joy is a thick slab of beef, resembling a T-bone steak, from large white oxen called Chianina. The meat's slapped on the grill and served rare, sometimes with a pinch of salt. It's always seared on both sides, and just barely cooked inside (experts say five minutes per side, and then fifteen minutes with the bone sitting perpendicularly on the grill). To ask for it more well done is to incur disdain; some restaurants simply won't serve it any other way than rare.

A CLASSIC CONTORNO:
CANNELLINI BEANS

Simply boiled, they provide the perfect accompaniment to a bistecca. The small white beans are best when they go straight from the garden into the pot.

They should be annointed with a generous outpouring of Tuscan olive oil; the combination is oddly felicitous, and it goes a long way toward explaining why Tuscans are referred to as *mangiafagioli* (bean eaters) by other Italians..

A CLASSIC DOLCE:
BISCOTTI DI PRATO

These are sometimes the only dessert on offer, and are more or less an afterthought to the glories that have proceeded them. "Biscotti" means twice-cooked (or, in this case, twice baked) hard almond cookies which soften considerably when dipped languidly into *vin santo* ("holy wine"), a sweet dessert wine, or into a simple *caffè*.

A CLASSIC WINE: CHIANTI CLASSICO

This blend from the region just south of Florence relies mainly on the local, hardy sangiovese grape; it's aged for at least one year before hitting the market. (*Riserve*—reserves—are aged at least an additional six months.) Chianti is usually the libation of choice for Florentines, and it pairs magnificently with grilled foods and seasonal vegetables. Traditionalists opt for the younger, fruitier (and usually less expensive) versions often served in straw flasks. You can sample *Chianti classico* all over town, and buy it in local *salumerie*, *enoteche*, and supermarkets.

Updated
by Patricia
Rucidlo

FLORENCE, THE CITY OF THE LILY, gave birth to the Renaissance and changed the way we see the world. For centuries it has captured the imagination of travelers, who have come seeking rooms with views and phenomenal art. Florence's is a subtle beauty—its staid, unprepossessing palaces built in local stone are not showy. They take on a certain magnificence when day breaks and when the sun sets; their muted colors glow in this light. A walk along the Arno offers views that don't quit and haven't much changed in 700 years; navigating Piazza della Signoria, almost always packed with tourists and locals alike, requires patience. There's a reason why everyone seems to be here, however. It's the heart of the city, and home to the Uffizi—arguably the world's finest repository of Renaissance art.

Florence was "discovered" in the 1700s by upper-class northerners making the grand tour. It became a mecca for travelers, particularly the Romantics, who were inspired by the elegance of its palazzi and its artistic wealth. Today millions of modern visitors follow in their footsteps. When the sun sets over the Arno and, as Mark Twain described it, "overwhelms Florence with tides of color that make all the sharp lines dim and faint and turn the solid city to a city of dreams," it's hard not to fall under the city's spell.

THE DUOMO TO THE PONTE VECCHIO

The heart of Florence, stretching from the Piazza del Duomo south to the Arno, is as dense with artistic treasures as anyplace in the world. The churches, medieval towers, Renaissance palaces, and world-class museums and galleries contain some of the most outstanding aesthetic achievements of Western history.

Much of the *centro storico* (historic center) is closed to automobile traffic, but you still must dodge mopeds, cyclists, and masses of fellow tourists as you walk the narrow streets, especially in the area bounded by the Duomo, Piazza della Signoria, Galleria degli Uffizi, and Ponte Vecchio.

THE MAIN ATTRACTIONS

8 Bargello. During the Renaissance, this building was headquarters for the ★ chief of police. It also was used as a prison, and the exterior served as a "most wanted" billboard: effigies of notorious criminals and Medici enemies were painted on its walls. Today it houses the **Museo Nazionale,** home to what is probably the finest collection of Renaissance sculpture in Italy. The concentration of masterworks by Michelangelo (1475–1564), Donatello (circa 1386–1466), and Benvenuto Cellini (1500–71) is remarkable; the works are distributed among an eclectic collection of arms, ceramics, and miniature bronzes, among other things. For Renaissance art lovers, the Bargello is to sculpture what the Uffizi is to painting.

In 1401 Filippo Brunelleschi (1377–1446) and Lorenzo Ghiberti (circa 1378–1455) competed to earn the most prestigious commission of the day: the decoration of the north doors of the Baptistery in Piazza

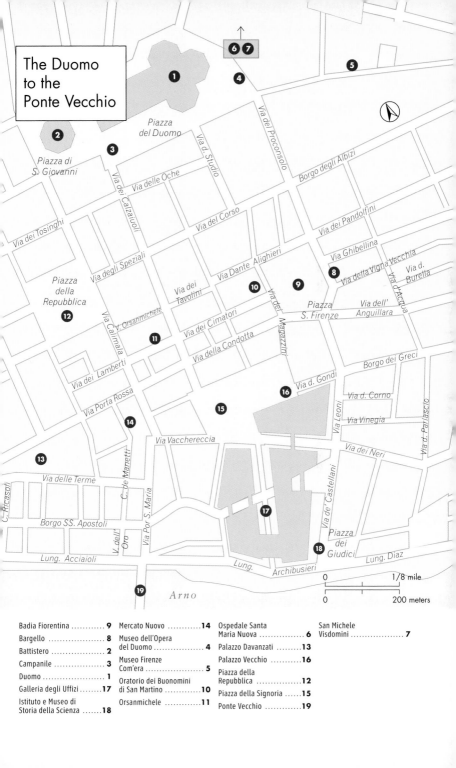

The Duomo
to the
Ponte Vecchio

Piazza del Duomo

Piazza di S. Giovanni

Via del Proconsolo

Borgo degli Albizi

Via d. Studio

Via delle Oche

Via del Corso

Via dei Calzaiuoli

Via dei Pandolfini

Via dei Tosinghi

Via degli Speziali

Via Ghibellina

Via della Vigna Vecchia

Via d. Burella

Via Dante Alighieri

Piazza della Repubblica

Via dei Tavolini

Via d. Magazzini

Piazza S. Firenze

Via dell' Anguillara

Via d'Acqua

v. Orsanmichele

Via dei Cimatori

Via Calimala

Via della Condotta

Borgo dei Greci

Via dei Lamberti

Via d. Gondi

Via d. Corno

Via d. Parlascio

Via Porta Rossa

Via Leoni

Via Vinegia

Via Vacchereccia

Via dei Neri

Via delle Terme

C. Arcasoli

C. de Manetti

Via de' Castellani

Piazza dei Giudici

Borgo SS. Apostoli

Via Por S. Maria

V. dell' Oro

Lung. Acciaioli

Lung. Diaz

Lung. Archibusieri

Arno

0   1/8 mile

0   200 meters

FLORENCE THROUGH THE AGES

Guelph vs. Ghibelline. Though Florence can lay claim to a modest importance in the ancient world, it didn't come into its own until the Middle Ages. In the early 1200s the city, like most of the rest of Italy, was rent by civic unrest. Two factions, the Guelphs and the Ghibellines, competed for power. The Guelphs supported the papacy, and the Ghibellines supported the Holy Roman Empire. Bloody battles—most notably one at Montaperti in 1260—tore Florence and other Italian cities apart. By the end of the 13th century the Guelphs ruled securely and the Ghibellines had been vanquished. This didn't end civic strife, however: the Guelphs split into the Whites and the Blacks for reasons still debated by historians. Dante, author of The Divine Comedy, was banished from Florence in 1301 because he was a White.

The Guilded Age. Local merchants had organized themselves into guilds by 1250. In that year they proclaimed themselves the "*primo popolo*" (literally, "first people"), making a landmark attempt at elective, republican rule. Though the episode lasted only 10 years, it constituted a breakthrough in Western history. Such a daring stance by the merchant class was a by-product of Florence's emergence as an economic powerhouse. Florentines were papal bankers; they instituted the system of international letters of credit; and the gold florin became the international standard of currency. With this economic strength came a building boom. Palaces and basilicas were erected, enlarged, or restructured. Sculptors such as Donatello and Ghiberti decorated them; painters such as Giotto and Botticelli frescoed their walls.

Mighty Medici. Though ostensibly a republic, Florence was blessed (or cursed) with one very powerful family, the Medici, who came to prominence in the 1430s and were the de facto rulers of Florence for several hundred years. It was under patriarch Cosimo il Vecchio (1389–1464) that the Medici's position in Florence was securely established. Florence's golden age occurred during the reign of his grandson Lorenzo de' Medici (1449–92). Lorenzo was not only an astute politician but also a highly educated man and a great patron of the arts. Called "Il Magnifico" (the Magnificent), he gathered around him poets, artists, philosophers, architects, and musicians.

Lorenzo's son, Piero (1471–1503), proved inept at handling the city's affairs. He was run out of town in 1494, and Florence briefly enjoyed its status as a republic while dominated by the Dominican friar Girolamo Savonarola (1452–98). After a decade of internal unrest, the republic fell and the Medici were recalled to power, but Florence never regained its former prestige. By the 1530s most of the major artistic talent had left the city—Michelangelo, for one, had settled in Rome. The now-ineffectual Medici, eventually attaining the title of grand dukes, remained nominally in power until the line died out in 1737, after which time Florence passed from the Austrians to the French and back again until the unification of Italy (1865–70), when it briefly became the capital under King Vittorio Emanuele II.

del Duomo. For the contest, each designed a bronze bas-relief panel depicting the sacrifice of Isaac; the panels are displayed together in the room devoted to the sculpture of Donatello, on the upper floor. The judges chose Ghiberti for the commission; see if you agree with their choice. ⊠ *Via del Proconsolo 4, Bargello* ☎*055/294883* ⊕*www.polo-museale.firenze.it* ☐*€4* ⊙*Daily 8:15–1:50; closed 2nd and 4th Mon. of month and 1st, 3rd, and 5th Sun. of month.*

> **WORD OF MOUTH**
>
> "I think the Bargello might be the most underrated museum in Florence, if not Italy." –Jess

❷ **Battistero** *(Baptistery)*. The octagonal Baptistery is one of the supreme monuments of the Italian Romanesque style and one of Florence's oldest structures. Local legend has it that it was once a Roman temple dedicated to Mars; modern excavations, however, suggest that its foundations date from the 4th to 5th and the 8th to 9th centuries AD, well after the collapse of the Roman Empire. The round Romanesque arches on the exterior probably date from the 11th century. The interior dome mosaics from the beginning of the 14th century are justly renowned, but—glittering beauties though they are—they could never outshine the building's famed bronze Renaissance doors decorated with panels crafted by Lorenzo Ghiberti. The doors—or at least copies of them—on which Ghiberti worked most of his adult life (1403–52) are on the north and east sides of the Baptistery, and the Gothic panels on the south door were designed by Andrea Pisano (circa 1290–1348) in 1330. The original Ghiberti doors were removed to protect them from the effects of pollution and acid rain and have been beautifully restored; they are now on display in the Museo dell'Opera del Duomo.

Ghiberti's north doors depict scenes from the life of Christ; his later east doors (dating from 1425–52), facing the Duomo facade, render scenes from the Old Testament. Both merit close examination, for they are very different in style and illustrate the artistic changes that marked the beginning of the Renaissance. Look at the far right panel of the middle row on the earlier (1403–24) north doors (*Jesus Calming the Waters*). Ghiberti here captured the chaos of a storm at sea with great skill and economy, but the artistic conventions he used are basically pre-Renaissance: Jesus is the most important figure, so he is the largest; the disciples are next in size, being next in importance; the ship on which they founder looks like a mere toy.

The exquisitely rendered panels on the east doors are larger, more expansive, more sweeping—and more convincing. The middle panel on the left-hand door tells the story of Jacob and Esau, and the various episodes of the story—the selling of the birthright, Isaac ordering Esau to go hunting, the blessing of Jacob, and so forth—have been merged into a single beautifully realized street scene. Ghiberti's use of perspective suggests depth: the background architecture looks far more credible than on the north-door panels, the figures in the foreground are grouped realistically, and the naturalism and grace of the poses (look at Esau's left leg and the dog next to him) have nothing to do with the sacred message being conveyed. Although the religious content remains, the figures and their place in the natural world are given new prominence and are portrayed with a realism not seen in art since the fall of the Roman Empire nearly a thousand years before.

As a footnote to Ghiberti's panels, one small detail of the east doors is worth a special look. To the lower left of the Jacob and Esau panel, Ghiberti placed a tiny self-portrait bust. From either side, the portrait is extremely appealing—Ghiberti looks like everyone's favorite uncle—but the bust is carefully placed so that you can make direct eye contact with the tiny head from a single spot. When that contact is made, the impression of intelligent life—of *modern* intelligent life—is astonishing. It's no wonder that these doors received one of the most famous compliments in the history of art from an artist known to be notoriously stingy with praise: Michelangelo declared them so beautiful that they could serve as the Gates of Paradise. ⊠ *Piazza del Duomo* ☎ *055/2302885* ⊕ *www.operaduomo.firenze.it* ☑ *€3* ⊙ *Mon.–Sat. noon–7, Sun. 8:30–2; 1st Sat. of month 8:30–2.*

⑰ **Galleria degli Uffizi.** The venerable Uffizi Gallery occupies the top floor
Fodor'sChoice of the U-shaped **Palazzo degli Uffizi** fronting on the Arno, designed
★ by Giorgio Vasari (1511–74) in 1560 to hold the *uffizi* (administrative offices) of the Medici grand duke Cosimo I (1519–74). Later, the Medici installed their art collections here, creating what was Europe's first modern museum, open to the public (at first only by request) since 1591. Hard-core museum aficionados can pick up a complete guide to the collections at bookshops and newsstands.

Among the highlights are Paolo Uccello's *Battle of San Romano,* its brutal chaos of lances one of the finest visual metaphors for warfare ever captured in paint; the *Madonna and Child with Two Angels,* by Fra Filippo Lippi (1406–69), in which the impudent eye contact established by the angel would have been unthinkable prior to the Renaissance; the *Birth of Venus* and *Primavera* by Sandro Botticelli (1445–1510), the goddess of the former seeming to float on air and the fairy-tale charm of the latter exhibiting the painter's idiosyncratic genius at its zenith; the portraits of the Renaissance duke Federico da Montefeltro and his wife, Battista Sforza, by Piero della Francesca (circa 1420–92); the *Madonna of the Goldfinch* by Raphael (1483–1520), which, though darkened by time, captures an aching tenderness between mother and child; Michelangelo's *Doni Tondo*; a *Self-Portrait as an Old Man* by Rembrandt (1606–69); the *Venus of Urbino* by Titian (circa 1488/90–1576); and the splendid *Bacchus* by Caravaggio (circa 1571/72–1610). In the last two works, the approaches to myth and sexuality are diametrically opposed, to put it mildly. Six additional exhibition rooms opened in 2004, convoluting the way you exit the museum. Many of the more than 400 works now displayed would have been better left in storage, though a couple of Caravaggios at the very end of your hike out are well worth a look.

Late in the afternoon is the least crowded time to visit. For a €3 fee, advance tickets can be reserved by phone or, once in Florence, at the

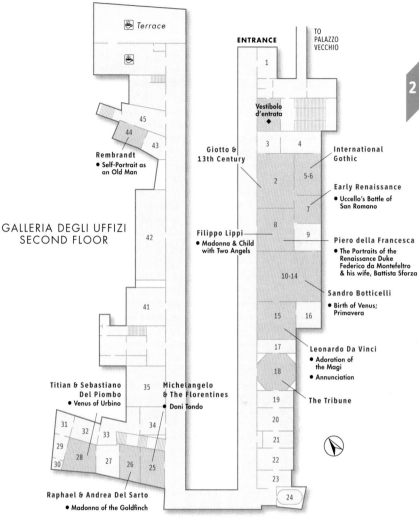

Terrace

ENTRANCE

TO PALAZZO VECCHIO

1

Vestibolo d'entrata ◆

45

44

43

Rembrandt
● Self-Portrait as an Old Man

3   4

Giotto & 13th Century

International Gothic

2

5-6

Early Renaissance
● Uccello's Battle of San Romano

7

8

9

Filippo Lippi
● Madonna & Child with Two Angels

Piero della Francesca
● The Portraits of the Renaissance Duke Federico da Montefeltro & his wife, Battista Sforza

10-14

Sandro Botticelli
● Birth of Venus; Primavera

15   16

GALLERIA DEGLI UFFIZI SECOND FLOOR

42

41

17

Leonardo Da Vinci
● Adoration of the Magi
● Annunciation

18

19

The Tribune

20

Titian & Sebastiano Del Piombo
● Venus of Urbino

35

Michelangelo & The Florentines
● Doni Tondo

31   32   33   34

29

30   28   27   26   25

21

22

23

24

Raphael & Andrea Del Sarto
● Madonna of the Goldfinch

2

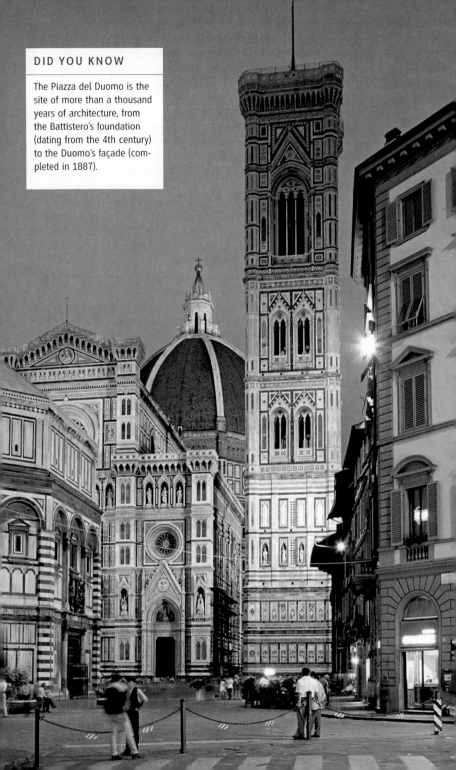

Uffizi reservation booth at least one day in advance of your visit. At this writing, an online reservation option has also been launched at ⊕*www. polomuseale.firenze.it;* the booking process at this point is awkward, but it's likely to improve. If you book by phone, remember to keep the confirmation number and take it with you to the door at the museum marked "Reservations." Usually you're ushered in almost immediately. Come with cash, because credit cards are not accepted (though you can use a credit card when booking online.) When there's a special exhibit on, which is often, the base ticket price goes up to €10. ⊠*Piazzale degli Uffizi 6, Piazza della Signoria* ☎*055/23885 advance tickets* ⊠*Consorzio ITA, Piazza Pitti 1, 50121* ☎*055/294883* ⊕*www.uffizi.firenze. it; reservations www.polomuseale.firenze.it* ▤*€6.50, reservation fee €3* ☉*Tues.–Sun. 8:15–6:50.*

⓯ Piazza della Signoria. This is by far the most striking square in Florence.
★ It was here, in 1497, that the famous "bonfire of the vanities" took place, when the fanatical friar Savonarola induced his followers to hurl their worldly goods into the flames; it was also here, a year later, that he was hanged as a heretic and, ironically, burned. A bronze plaque in the piazza pavement marks the exact spot of his execution.

The statues in the square and in the 14th-century **Loggia dei Lanzi** on the south side vary in quality. Cellini's famous bronze *Perseus* holding the severed head of Medusa is certainly the most important sculpture in the loggia. Other works here include *The Rape of the Sabine* and *Hercules and the Centaur,* both late-16th-century works by Giambologna (1529–1608), and in the back, a row of sober matrons dating from Roman times.

In the square, the Neptune Fountain, created between 1550 and 1575, takes something of a booby prize. It was created by Bartolomeo Ammannati, who considered it a failure himself. The Florentines call it Il Biancone, which may be translated as "the big white man" or "the big white lump." Giambologna's equestrian statue, to the left of the fountain, pays tribute to Grand Duke Cosimo I. Occupying the steps of the Palazzo Vecchio are a copy of Donatello's proud heraldic lion of Florence, the *Marzocco* (the original is now in the Bargello); a copy of Donatello's *Judith and Holofernes* (the original is in the Palazzo Vecchio); a copy of Michelangelo's *David* (the original is in the Galleria dell'Accademia); and Baccio Bandinelli's *Hercules* (1534). The Marzocco, the Judith, and the David were symbols of Florentine civic pride—the latter two subjects had stood up to their oppressors. They provided apt metaphors for the republic-loving Florentines, who often chafed at Medici hegemony.

⓳ Ponte Vecchio *(Old Bridge).* This charmingly simple bridge is to Florence
★ what the Tower Bridge is to London. It was built in 1345 to replace an earlier bridge that was swept away by flood, and its shops housed first butchers, then grocers, blacksmiths, and other merchants. But in 1593 the Medici grand duke Ferdinand I (1549–1609), whose private corridor linking the Medici palace (Palazzo Pitti) with the Medici offices (the Uffizi) crossed the bridge atop the shops, decided that all this plebeian

commerce under his feet was unseemly. So he threw out the butchers and blacksmiths and installed 41 goldsmiths and eight jewelers. The bridge has been devoted solely to these two trades ever since.

The **Corridoio Vasariano** (⌗ *Piazzale degli Uffizi 6, Piazza della Signoria* ☎ *055/23885 or 055/294883*), the private Medici corridor, was built by Vasari in 1565. Though the ostensible reason for its construction was one of security, it was more likely designed so that the Medici family wouldn't have to walk amid the commoners. The corridor is notoriously fickle with its operating hours; at this writing it was temporarily closed, but it can often be visited by prior special arrangement. Call for the most up-to-date details. Take a moment to study the Ponte Santa Trinita, the next bridge downriver, from either the bridge or the corridor. It was designed by Bartolomeo Ammannati in 1567 (possibly from sketches by Michelangelo), blown up by the retreating Germans during World War II, and painstakingly reconstructed after the war. The view from the Ponte Santa Trinita is beautiful, which might explain why so many young lovers seem to hang out there.

ALSO WORTH SEEING

❾ Badia Fiorentina. Originally endowed by Willa, Marquess of Tuscany, in 978, this ancient church is an interesting mélange of 13th-century, Renaissance, baroque, and 18th-century architectural refurbishing. Its graceful bell tower, best seen from the interior courtyard, is beautiful for its unusual construction—a hexagonal tower built on a quadrangular base. The interior of the church (open Monday afternoon only) was halfheartedly remodeled in the baroque style during the 17th century. Three tombs by Mino da Fiesole (circa 1430–84) line the walls, including the *monumento funebre di Conte Ugo* (tomb sculpture of Count Ugo), widely regarded as Mino's masterpiece. Executed in 1469–81, it shows Mino at his most lyrical: the faces seem to be lit from within—no small feat in marble. The best-known work of art here is the delicate *Vision of St. Bernard,* by Filippino Lippi (circa 1457–1504), on the left as you enter. The painting—one of Filippino's finest—is in superb condition; note the Virgin Mary's hands, perhaps the most beautifully rendered in the city. On the right side of the church, above the **cappella di San Mauro,** is a monumental organ dating from 1558. Constructed by Onofrio Zeffirini da Cortona (1510–86), it's largely intact but is missing its 16th-century keyboard. ⌗ *Via Dante Alighieri 1, Bargello* ☎ *055/264402* ⌗ *Free* ⊙ *Mon. 3–6.*

❸ Campanile. The Gothic bell tower designed by Giotto (circa 1266–1337) is a soaring structure of multicolor marble originally decorated with reliefs that are now in the Museo dell'Opera del Duomo. A climb of 414 steps rewards you with a close-up of Brunelleschi's cupola on the Duomo next door and a sweeping view of the city. ⌗ *Piazza del Duomo* ☎ *055/2302885* ⊕ *www.operaduomo.firenze.it* ⌗ *€6* ⊙ *Daily 8:30–7:30.*

⓲ Istituto e Museo di Storia della Scienza *(Museum of the History of Science).* Although it tends to be obscured by the glamour of the neighboring Uffizi, this science museum has much to commend it: Galileo's own instruments, antique armillary spheres—some of them real works of art—and other reminders that the Renaissance made not only artistic but also scientific history. Note that the museum was closed for renovations in 2008 and will likely remain closed into 2009. ⊠ *Piazza dei Giudici 1, Piazza della Signoria* ☏ *055/265311* ⊕ *www.imss.fi.it* ✏ *€7.50* ⊙ *Mon., Wed., Fri., and Sat. 9:30–5, Thurs. 9:30–1; last Thurs. of June and Aug. 8 am–11 pm, 1st Thurs. of July and Sept. 8 am–11 pm.*

> ### WORD OF MOUTH
>
> "I strongly recommend making reservations for both the Accademia and the Uffizi. We saved ourselves a ton of time. We walked right into the Accademia and right past the line of unreserved people." –Ivy

NEED A BREAK? Calling itself a "zupperia," La Canova di GustaVino (⊠ *Via della Condotta 29/r, Piazza della Signoria* ☏ *055/2399806*) keeps several hearty, restorative soups on hand. Solid fare includes mixed cheese plates (both French and Italian), as well as *tomino con prosciutto* (mild cow's cheese, topped with thin slices of prosciutto) run under the broiler.

⓮ Mercato Nuovo *(New Market).* The open-air loggia, built in 1551, teems with souvenir stands, but the real attraction is a copy of Pietro Tacca's bronze *Porcellino* (which translates as "little pig" despite the fact the animal is, in fact, a wild boar). The *Porcellino* is Florence's equivalent of the Trevi Fountain: put a coin in his mouth, and if it falls through the grate below (according to one interpretation), it means you'll return to Florence someday. The statue dates from around 1612, but the original version, in Palazzo Pitti, is an ancient Greek work. ⊠ *Corner of Via Por Santa Maria and Via Porta Rossa, Piazza della Repubblica* ⊙ *Market: Tues.–Sat. 8–7, Mon. 1–7.*

Museo dei Ragazzi. Florence's "Children's Museum" may be the best-kept public-access secret in Florence. A series of interactive tours includes "Encounters with History," during which participants meet and talk with Giorgio Vasari or Galileo Galilei and explore secret passageways. Events occur at three separate venues (Palazzo Vecchio, Museo Stibbert, and the Istituto e Museo di Storia della Scienza). Tours are in English and absolutely must be booked in advance. ⊠ *Piazza della Signoria 1* ☏ *055/2768224* ⊕ *www.museoragazzi.it* ✏ *€6* ⊙ *By reservation only.*

❹ Museo dell'Opera del Duomo *(Cathedral Museum).* Ghiberti's original Baptistery door panels and the *cantorie* (choir loft) reliefs by Donatello and Luca della Robbia (1400–82) keep company with Donatello's *Mary Magdalene* and Michelangelo's *Pietà* (not to be confused with his more famous *Pietà* in St. Peter's in Rome). Renaissance sculpture is in part defined by its revolutionary realism, but in its palpable suffering Donatello's *Magdalene* goes beyond realism. Michelangelo's heart-wrenching *Pietà* was unfinished at his death; the female figure supporting the body of Christ on the left was added by Tiberio

Continued on page 61

THE DUOMO
FLORENCE'S BIGGEST MASTERPIECE

For all its monumental art and architecture, Florence has one undisputed centerpiece: the Cathedral of Santa Maria del Fiore, better known as the Duomo. Its cupola dominates the skyline, presiding over the city's rooftops like a red hen over her brood. Little wonder that when Florentines feel homesick, they say they have *"nostalgia del cupolone."*

The Duomo's construction began in 1296, following the design of Arnolfo da Cambio, Florence's greatest architect of the time. By modern standards, construction was slow and haphazard—it continued through the 14th and into the 15th century, with some dozen architects having a hand in the project.

In 1366 Neri di Fioravanti created a model for the hugely ambitious cupola: it was to be the largest dome in the world, surpassing Rome's Pantheon. But when the time finally came to build the dome in 1418, no one was sure how—or even if—it could be done. Florence was faced with a 143-ft hole in the roof of its cathedral, and one of the greatest challenges in the history of architecture.

Fortunately, local genius Filippo Brunelleschi was just the man for the job. Brunelleschi won the 1418 competition to design the dome, and for the next 18 years he oversaw its construction. The enormity of his achievement can hardly be overstated. Working on such a large scale (the dome weighs 37,000 tons and uses 4 million bricks) required him to invent hoists and cranes that were engineering marvels. A "dome within a dome" design and a novel herringbone bricklaying pattern were just two of the innovations used to establish structural integrity. Perhaps most remarkably, he executed the construction without a supporting wooden framework, which had previously been thought indispensable.

Brunelleschi designed the lantern atop the dome, but he died soon after its first stone was laid in 1446; it wouldn't be completed until 1461. Another 400 years passed before the Duomo received its façade, a 19th-century neo-Gothic creation.

DUOMO TIMELINE

1296 Work begins, following design by Arnolfo di Cambio.

1302 Arnolfo dies; work continues, with sporadic interruptions.

1331 Management of construction taken over by the Wool Merchants guild.

1334 Giotto appointed project overseer, designs campanile.

1337 Giotto dies; Andrea Pisano takes leadership role.

1348 The Black Plague; all work ceases.

1366 Vaulting on nave completed; Neri di Fioravanti makes model for dome.

1417 Drum for dome completed.

1418 Competition is held to design dome.

1420 Brunelleschi begins work on the dome.

1436 Dome completed.

1446 Construction of lantern begins; Brunelleschi dies.

1461 Michelozzo completes lantern.

1469 Gilt copper ball and cross added by Verrocchio.

1588 Original façade is torn down by Medici court.

1871 Emilio de Fabris wins competition to design new façade.

1887 Façade completed.

WHAT TO LOOK FOR INSIDE THE DUOMO

The interior of the Duomo is a fine example of Florentine Gothic with a beautiful marble floor, but the space feels strangely barren—a result of its great size and the fact that some of the best art has been moved to the nearby **Museo dell'Opera del Duomo**.

Notable among the works that remain are two towering equestrian frescoes of famous soldiers: *Niccolò da Tolentino* (1456), by Andrea del Castagno, and *Sir John Hawkwood* (1436), by Paolo Uccello. There's also fine terra-cotta work by Luca della Robbia. Ghiberti,

Brunelleschi's great rival, is responsible for much of the stained glass, as well as a reliquary urn with gorgeous reliefs. A vast fresco of the Last Judgment, painted by Vasari and Zuccari, covers the dome's interior. Brunelleschi had wanted mosaics to go there; it's a shame he didn't get his wish.

In the crypt beneath the cathedral, you can explore excavations of a Roman wall and an 11th-century cemetery; entry is near the first pier on the right. On the way down you pass Brunelleschi's modest tomb.

1. Entrance; stained glass by Ghiberti
2. Fresco of Niccolò da Tolentino by Andrea del Castagno
3. Fresco of John Hawkwood by Paolo Uccello
4. *Dante and the Divine Comedy* by Domenico di Michelino
5. Lunette: *Ascension* by Luca della Robbia
6. Above altar: two angels by Luca della Robbia. Below the altar: reliquary of St. Zenobius by Ghiberti.
7. Lunette: *Resurrection* by Luca della Robbia
8. Entrance to dome
9. Bust of Brunelleschi by Buggiano
10. Stairs to crypt
11. Campanile

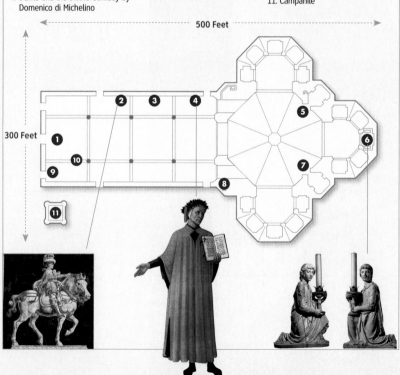

MAKING THE CLIMB

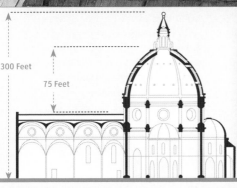

Climbing the 463 steps to the top of the dome is not for the faint of heart—or for the claustrophobic—but those who do it will be awarded a smashing view of Florence ❶. Keep in mind that the way up is also the way down, which means that while you're huffing and puffing in the ascent, people very close to you in a narrow staircase are making their way down ❷.

300 Feet

75 Feet

DUOMO GOOD TO KNOW

• Even first thing in the morning during high season (May through September), a line is likely to have formed to climb the dome. Expect an hour wait.

• For an alternative to the dome, consider climbing the less trafficked campanile, which gives you a view from on high of the dome itself.

• Dress code essentials: covered shoulders, no short shorts, and hats off upon entering.

✉ Piazza del Duomo

☎ 055/2302885

⊕ www.operaduomo.firenze.it

🎫 Free, crypt €3, cupola €6

🕐 Crypt: Mon.–Wed., Fri., Sun. 10–5; Thurs. 10–4:30; Sat. 10–5:45; first Sat. of month 10–3:30. Cupola: Weekdays 8:30–7, Sat. 8:30–5:40, 1st Sat. of month 8:30–4. Duomo: Mon.–Wed. and Fri. 10–5, Thurs. 10–4:30, Sat., 10–4:45, Sun 1:30–4:45, 1st Sat. of month 10–3:30.

BRUNELLESCHI vs. GHIBERTI
The Rivalry of Two Renaissance Geniuses

In Renaissance Florence, painters, sculptors, and architects competed for major commissions, with the winner earning the right to undertake a project that might occupy him (and keep him paid) for a decade or more. Stakes were high, and the resulting rivalries fierce—none more so than that between Filippo Brunelleschi and Lorenzo Ghiberti.

The two first clashed in 1401, for the commission to create the bronze doors of the Baptistery. When Ghiberti won, Brunelleschi took it hard, fleeing to Rome, where he would remain for 15 years. Their rematch came in 1418, over the design of the Duomo's cupola, with Brunelleschi triumphant. For the remainder of their lives, the two would miss no opportunity to belittle each other's work.

FILIPPO BRUNELLESCHI (1377–1446)

MASTERPIECE: The dome of Santa Maria del Fiore.

BEST FRIENDS: Donatello, whom he stayed with in Rome after losing the Baptistery doors competition; the Medici family, who rescued him from bankruptcy.

SIGNATURE TRAITS: Paranoid, secretive, bad tempered, practical joker, inept businessman.

SAVVIEST POLITICAL MOVE: Feigned sickness and left for Rome after his dome plans were publicly criticized by Ghiberti, who was second-in-command. The project proved too much for Ghiberti to manage on his own, and Brunelleschi returned triumphant.

MOST EMBARRASSING MOMENT: In 1434 he was imprisoned for two weeks for failure to pay a small guild fee. The humiliation might have been orchestrated by Ghiberti.

OTHER CAREER: Shipbuilder. He built a huge vessel, *Il Badalone*, to transport marble for the dome up the Arno. It sank on its first voyage.

INSPIRED: The dome of St. Peter's in Rome.

LORENZO GHIBERTI (1378–1455)

MASTERPIECE: *The Gates of Paradise,* the ten-paneled east doors of the Baptistery.

BEST FRIEND: Giovanni da Prato, an underling who wrote diatribes attacking the dome's design and Brunelleschi's character.

SIGNATURE TRAITS: Instigator, egoist, know-it-all, shrewd businessman.

SAVVIEST POLITICAL MOVE: During the Baptistery doors competition, he had an open studio and welcomed opinions on his work, while Brunelleschi labored behind closed doors.

OTHER CAREER: Collector of classical artifacts, historian.

INSPIRED: *The Gates of Hell* by Auguste Rodin.

The Gates of Paradise detail

Calcagni (1532–65), and never has the difference between competence and genius been manifested so clearly. ⊠ *Piazza del Duomo 9* ☏ *055/2302885* ⊕ *www.operaduomo.firenze.it* 🎫 €6 ⊙ *Mon.–Sat. 9–7:30, Sun. 9–1:40.*

WORD OF MOUTH

"The Duomo was a truly amazing cathedral. We visited it twice, once to attend mass (in English, which we appreciated), and once to look at its architecture and art and to climb up to the top. Although the climb is definitely a bit tiring, it was well worth it—the view from the top was incredible." –Gina

5 **Museo Firenze Com'era.** The name of this museum translates as "Florence as it was"; it has prints, paintings, and other exhibits designed to show how Florence looked once upon a time. A diorama renders Roman Florence, of which very little remains today. The rest of the museum is dedicated to Florence during and after the Renaissance. Pre-19th-century prints and paintings show the unfinished facades of the Duomo and Santa Croce. Also note the sweeping size of various *piazze* and the wide streets—clearly, wishful thinking on the part of the artists. ⊠ *Via dell'Oriuolo 24* ☏ *055/2616545* 🎫 €2.70 ⊙ *Mon.–Wed. 9–2, Sat. 9–7.*

10 **Oratorio dei Buonomini di San Martino.** Founded in 1441 by Antoninus, Bishop of Florence, to offer alms to the *poveri vergognosi* (the ashamed poor), this one-room oratory is decorated with 15th-century frescoes by the school of Ghirlandaio that vividly depict the confraternity's activities. More than 500 years later, the Compagnia dei Buonomini, or Confraternity of the Good Men, continues to perform charitable works, linking Renaissance notions of charity to the 21st century. ⊠ *Piazza San Martino, Bargello* ☏ *No phone* 🎫 *Free* ⊙ *Mon.–Thurs. and Sat. 10–noon and 3–5, Fri. 10–noon.*

11 **Orsanmichele.** This multipurpose structure, which is closed indefinitely for restoration at this writing, began as an 8th-century oratory and then in 1290 was turned into an open-air loggia for selling grain. Destroyed by fire in 1304, it was rebuilt as a loggia-market. Between 1367 and 1380 the arcades were closed and two stories were added above; finally, at century's end it was turned into a church. Inside is a beautifully detailed 14th-century Gothic tabernacle by Andrea Orcagna (1308–68). The exterior niches contain sculptures dating from the early 1400s to the early 1600s by Donatello and Verrocchio (1435–88), among others, that were paid for by the guilds. Although it is a copy, Verrocchio's *Doubting Thomas* (circa 1470) is particularly deserving of attention. Here you see Christ, like the building's other figures, entirely framed within the niche, and St. Thomas standing on its bottom ledge, with his right foot outside the niche frame. This one detail, the positioning of a single foot, brings the whole composition to life. Most of the sculptures have since been replaced by copies; however, it's possible to see nearly all of them at the **Museo di Orsanmichele** (also closed at this writing for restoration). ⊠ *Via dei Calzaiuoli, Piazza della Repubblica* ☏ *055/284944* 🎫 *Free* ⊙ *Closed for restoration.*

⑥ Ospedale Santa Maria Nuova. Folco Portinari, the father of Dante's Beatrice, founded this sprawling complex in 1288. It was originally a hostel for visiting pilgrims and travelers. During the Black Death of 1348, it served as a hospice for those afflicted. At another point it served as an office where money could be exchanged and deposited and letters could be received; Michelangelo did his banking here. It had been lavishly decorated by the top Florentine artists of the day, but most of the works, such as the frescoes by Domenico Veneziano and Piero della Francesca, have disappeared or been moved to the Uffizi for safekeeping. Today it functions as a hospital in the modern sense of the word, but you can visit the single-nave church of **Sant'Egidio,** in the middle of the complex, where the frescoes would have stood. Imagine, too, Hugo van der Goes's (1435–82) magnificent *Portinari Altarpiece,* which once crowned the high altar; it's now in the Uffizi. Commissioned by Tommaso Portinari, a descendent of Folco, it arrived from Brugge in 1489 and created quite a stir. Bernardo Rossellino's immense marble tabernacle (1450), still in the church, is worth a look. ⊠ *Via Sant'Egidio and Piazza di Santa Maria Nuova, San Lorenzo.*

⑬ Palazzo Davanzati. The prestigious Davanzati family owned this 14th-century palace in one of Florence's swankiest medieval neighborhoods. It reopened in May 2005 after a lengthy, 10-year restoration. The place is a delight, as you can wander through the surprisingly light-filled courtyard, and climb the steep stairs to the *piano nobile,* where the family did most of its living. The beautiful *Sala dei Pappagalli* (Parrot Room) is adorned with trompe-l'oeil tapestries and gaily painted birds. Though some claim that these date from the 14th century, many art historians are much less sure. ⊠ *Piazza Davanzati 13, Piazza della Repubblica* ☎ *055/2388610* ✆ *Free* ☾ *Daily 8:15–1:50. Closed 1st, 3rd, and 5th Sun. of month; closed 2nd and 4th Mon. of month.*

⑯ Palazzo Vecchio *(Old Palace).* Florence's forbidding, fortresslike city hall was begun in 1299, presumably designed by Arnolfo di Cambio, and its massive bulk and towering campanile dominate Piazza della Signoria. It was built as a meeting place for the heads of the seven major guilds governing the city at the time; over the centuries it has served lesser purposes, but today it is once again City Hall. The interior courtyard is a good deal less severe, having been remodeled by Michelozzo (1396–1472) in 1453; a copy of Verrocchio's bronze *puttino* (cherub), topping the central fountain, softens the space.

The main attraction is on the second floor: two adjoining rooms that supply one of the most startling contrasts in Florence. The first is the vast **Sala dei Cinquecento** (Room of the Five Hundred), named for the 500-member Great Council, the people's assembly established after the death of Lorenzo the Magnificent, that met here. The sala was decorated by Giorgio Vasari, around 1563–65, with huge—almost grotesquely huge—frescoes celebrating Florentine history; depictions of battles with nearby cities predominate. Continuing the martial theme, the sala also contains Michelangelo's *Victory,* intended for the never-completed tomb of Pope Julius II (1443–1513), plus other sculptures of decidedly lesser quality.

The second room is the little **Studiolo,** to the right of the sala's entrance. It was the study of Cosimo I's son, the melancholy Francesco I (1541–87). It was designed by Vasari and decorated by Vasari and Bronzino (1503–72), and is intimate, civilized, and filled with complex, questioning, allegorical art. ⊠ *Piazza della Signoria* ☎ *055/2768465* 🎟 *€6* 🕓 *Mon.–Wed. and Fri.–Sun. 9–7, Thurs. 9–2.*

⓬ **Piazza della Repubblica.** The square marks the site of the ancient forum that was the core of the original Roman settlement. The street plan around the piazza still reflects the carefully plotted Roman military encampment. The Mercato Vecchio (Old Market), which had been here since the Middle Ages, was demolished and the current piazza was constructed between 1885 and 1895 as a neoclassical showpiece. The piazza is lined with outdoor cafés, affording an excellent opportunity for people-watching.

❼ **San Michele Visdomini.** Aficionados of the 16th-century mannerists should stop in this church, which has a *Sacra Conversazione* by Jacopo Pontormo (1494–1556). The early work, said by Vasari to have been executed on paper, is in dire need of a cleaning. Its palette is somewhat bereft of the lively colors typically associated with Pontormo. ⊠ *Via dei Servi at Via Bufalini, Duomo* ☎ *No phone* 🎟 *Free* 🕓 *Daily 7–noon and 3–6.*

SAN LORENZO TO THE ACCADEMIA

A sculptor, painter, architect, and even a poet, Florentine native son Michelangelo was a consummate genius, and some of his finest creations remain in his hometown. The Biblioteca Medicea Laurenziana is perhaps his most fanciful work of architecture. A key to understanding Michelangelo's genius can be found in the magnificent Cappelle Medicee, where both his sculptural and architectural prowess can be clearly seen. Planned frescoes were never completed, sadly, for they would have shown in one space the artistic triple threat that he certainly was. The towering yet graceful *David*, his most famous work, resides in the Galleria dell'Accademia.

After visiting San Lorenzo, resist the temptation to explore the market that surrounds the church. You can always come back later, after the churches and museums have closed; the market is open until 7 PM. Note that the Museo di San Marco closes at 1:50 on weekdays.

THE MAIN ATTRACTIONS

❸ ★ **Cappelle Medicee** *(Medici Chapels).* This magnificent complex includes the **Cappella dei Principi,** the Medici chapel and mausoleum that was begun in 1605 and kept marble workers busy for several hundred years, and the **Sagrestia Nuova** (New Sacristy), designed by Michelangelo and so called to distinguish it from Brunelleschi's Sagrestia Vecchia (Old Sacristy) in San Lorenzo.

Michelangelo received the commission for the New Sacristy in 1520 from Cardinal Giulio de' Medici (1478–1534), who later became Pope

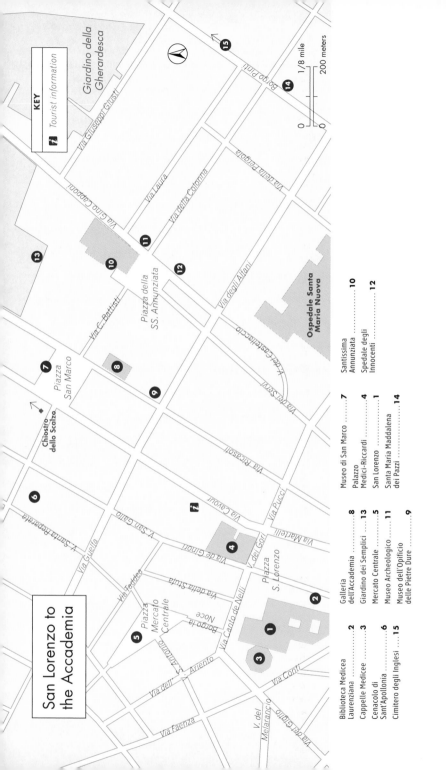

San Lorenzo to the Accademia

KEY

i Tourist Information

Giardino della Gherardesca

Giardino dei Semplici **13**

Ospedale Santa Maria Nuova

Chiostro dello Scalzo

Piazza San Marco

Piazza della SS. Annunziata

Piazza S. Lorenzo

Piazza Mercato Centrale

1/8 mile

200 meters

Clement VII and who wanted a new burial chapel for his cousins Giuliano (1478–1534) and Lorenzo (1492–1519). The result was a tour de force of architecture and sculpture. Architecturally, Michelangelo was as original and inventive here as ever, but it is, quite properly, the powerful sculptural compositions of the sidewall tombs that dominate the room. The scheme is allegorical: on the tomb on the right are figures representing Day and Night, and on the tomb to the left are figures representing Dawn and Dusk; above them are idealized sculptures of the two men, usually interpreted to represent the active life and the contemplative life. But the allegorical meanings are secondary; what is most important is the intense presence of the sculptural figures and the force with which they hit the viewer. ⊠*Piazza di Madonna degli Aldobrandini, San Lorenzo* ☎*055/294883 reservations* 🎫*€6* ⊙*Daily 8:15–4:50. Closed 1st, 3rd, and 5th Mon. and 2nd and 4th Sun. of month.*

❽ Galleria dell'Accademia *(Accademia Gallery).* The collection of Florentine paintings, dating from the 13th to the 18th centuries, is largely unremarkable, but the sculptures by Michelangelo are worth the price of admission. The unfinished *Slaves,* fighting their way out of their marble prisons, were meant for the tomb of Michelangelo's overly demanding patron Pope Julius II (1443–1513). But the focal point is the original *David,* moved here from Piazza della Signoria in 1873. *David* was commissioned in 1501 by the Opera del Duomo (Cathedral Works Committee), which gave the 26-year-old sculptor a leftover block of marble that had been ruined by another artist. Michelangelo's success with the block was so dramatic that the city showered him with honors, and the Opera del Duomo voted to build him a house and a studio in which to live and work.

Today *David* is beset not by Goliath but by tourists, and seeing the statue at all—much less really studying it—can be a trial. Save yourself a long and tiresome wait in line by reserving tickets in advance. A Plexiglas barrier surrounds it, following a 1991 attack upon the sculpture by a hammer-wielding artist who, luckily, inflicted only a few minor nicks on the toes. A 2004 restoration in honor of his 500th birthday has, at the very least, cleaned up the sculpture. The statue is not quite what it seems. It is so poised and graceful and alert—so miraculously alive—that it is often considered the definitive embodiment of the ideals of the High Renaissance in sculpture. But its true place in the history of art is a bit more complicated.

As Michelangelo well knew, the Renaissance painting and sculpture that preceded his work were deeply concerned with ideal form. Perfection of proportion was the ever-sought Holy Grail; during the Renaissance, ideal proportion was equated with ideal beauty, and ideal beauty was equated with spiritual perfection. But *David,* despite its supremely calm and dignified pose, departs from these ideals. Michelangelo didn't give the statue perfect proportions. The head is slightly too large for the body, the arms are too large for the torso, and the hands are dramatically large for the arms. The work was originally commissioned to adorn the exterior of the Duomo and was intended to be seen from a distance and on high. Michelangelo knew exactly what he was doing, calculating that the perspective of the viewer would be such that, in order for the statue to appear proportioned, the upper body, head, and arms would have to be bigger as they are farther away from the viewer's line of vision. But he also did it to express and embody, as powerfully as possible in a single

figure, an entire biblical story. David's hands *are* big, but so was Goliath, and these are the hands that slew him. ⊠ *Via Ricasoli 60, San Marco* ☎*055/294883 reservations, 055/2388609 gallery* ⌨*€6.50, reservation fee €3* ⊙*Tues.–Sun. 8:15–6:50.*

❼ **Museo di San Marco.** A former Dominican convent adjacent to the church of San Marco now houses this museum, which contains many stunning works by Fra Angelico (circa 1400–55), the Dominican friar famous for his piety as well as for his painting. When the friars' cells were restructured between 1439 and 1444, he decorated many of them with frescoes meant to spur religious contemplation. His unostentatious and direct paintings exalt the simple beauties of the contemplative life. Fra Angelico's works are everywhere, from the friars' cells to the superb panel paintings on view in the museum. Don't miss the famous *Annunciation,* on the upper floor, and the works in the gallery off the cloister as you enter. Here you can see his beautiful *Last Judgment*; as usual, the tortures of the damned are far more inventive and interesting than the pleasures of the redeemed. ⊠*Piazza San Marco 1* ☎*055/2388608* ⌨*€4* ⊙ *Weekdays 8:15–1:50, weekends 8:15–6:50. Closed 1st, 3rd, and 5th Sun., and 2nd and 4th Mon. of month.*

❶ **San Lorenzo.** Filippo Brunelleschi designed this basilica, as well as that of Santo Spirito in the Oltrarno, in the early 15th century. He never lived to see either finished. The two interiors are similar in design and effect, and proclaim with ringing clarity the beginning of the Renaissance in architecture. San Lorenzo, however, has a grid of dark, inlaid marble lines on the floor, which considerably heightens the dramatic effect. The grid makes the rigorous geometry of the interior immediately visible and is an illuminating lesson on the laws of perspective. If you stand in the middle of the nave at the church entrance, on the line that stretches to the high altar, every element in the church—the grid, the nave columns, the side aisles, the coffered nave ceiling— seems to march inexorably toward a hypothetical vanishing point beyond the high altar, exactly as in a single-point-perspective painting. Brunelleschi's **Sagrestia Vecchia** (Old Sacristy) has stucco decorations by Donatello; it's at the end of the left transept. ⊠*Piazza San Lorenzo* ☎*055/2645144* ⌨*€2.50* ⊙*Mon.–Sat. 10–5; Mar.–Oct., Sun. 1:30–5. Closed Sun. Nov.–Feb.*

ALSO WORTH SEEING

❷ **Biblioteca Medicea Laurenziana** *(Laurentian Library)*. Michelangelo the architect was every bit as original as Michelangelo the sculptor. Unlike Brunelleschi (the architect of the Spedale degli Innocenti), however, he

CLOSE UP

Florence's Trial by Fire

One of the most striking figures of Renaissance Florence was Girolamo Savonarola, a Dominican friar who, for a moment, captured the conscience of the city. In 1491 he became prior of the convent of San Marco, where he adopted a life of austerity and delivered sermons condemning Florence's excesses and the immorality of his fellow clergy. Following the death of Lorenzo de' Medici, Savonarola was instrumental in the formation of the republic of Florence, ruled by a representative council with Christ enthroned as monarch. In one of his most memorable acts, he urged Florentines to toss worldly possessions—from frilly dresses to Botticelli paintings—onto a "bonfire of the vanities" in Piazza della Signoria. Savonarola's antagonism toward church hierarchy led to his undoing: he was excommunicated in 1497, and the following year was hanged and burned on charges of heresy. Today, at the Museo di San Marco, you can visit Savonarola's cell and see his arresting portrait.

2

wasn't obsessed with proportion and perfect geometry. He was interested in experimentation and invention and in the expression of a personal vision at times highly idiosyncratic.

It was never more idiosyncratic than in the Laurentian Library, begun in 1524 and finished in 1568, and its famous **vestibolo**. This strangely shaped anteroom has had scholars scratching their heads for centuries. In a space more than two stories high, why did Michelangelo limit his use of columns and pilasters to the upper two-thirds of the wall? Why didn't he rest them on strong pedestals instead of on huge, decorative curlicue scrolls, which rob them of all visual support? Why did he recess them into the wall, which makes them look weaker still? The architectural elements here do not stand firm and strong and tall, as inside San Lorenzo, next door; instead, they seem to be pressed into the wall as if into putty, giving the room a soft, rubbery look that is one of the strangest effects ever achieved by classical architecture. It's almost as if Michelangelo intentionally flouted the conventions of the High Renaissance to see what kind of bizarre, mannered effect might result. His innovations were tremendously influential and produced a period of architectural experimentation. As his contemporary Giorgio Vasari put it, "Artisans have been infinitely and perpetually indebted to him because he broke the bonds and chains of a way of working that had become habitual by common usage."

The anteroom's staircase (best viewed straight-on), which emerges from the library with the visual force of an unstoppable lava flow, has been exempted from the criticism, however. In its highly sculptural conception and execution, it is quite simply one of the most original and fluid staircases in the world. ⊠*Piazza San Lorenzo 9, entrance to the left of San Lorenzo* ☎*055/210760* ⊕*www.bml.firenze.sbn.it* ✉*Special exhibitions €5*, museum €3 ⊙*Sun. –Fri. 9–1.*

❻ Cenacolo di Sant'Apollonia. The frescoes of the refectory of a former Benedictine nunnery were painted in sinewy style by Andrea del Castagno, a follower of Masaccio (1401–28). The *Last Supper* is a powerful version of this typical refectory theme. From the entrance, walk around the corner to Via San Gallo 25 and take a peek at the lovely 15th-century cloister that belonged to the same monastery but is now part of the University of Florence. ⊠ *Via XXVII Aprile 1, San Marco* ☎*055/2388607* ⊘ *Daily 8:15–1:50. Closed 1st and 3rd Sun. of month.*

⓯ Cimitero degli Inglesi. Familiarly known by its English-language name, the English Cemetery, this is the final resting place for some 1,400 souls. It was designed in 1828 by Carlo Reishammer and originally intended for the Swiss community in Florence. Just outside Florence's 14th-century walls (no longer visible), the cemetery grew to accommodate other foreigners living here, and thus earned another of its names, the Protestant Cemetery. Perhaps its most famous resident is Elizabeth Barrett Browning (1809–61), who spent the last 15 years of her life in the city. Other expats, including Arthur Clough, Walter Savage Landor, Frances Trollope (mother of Anthony), and the American preacher Theodore Parker are buried in this cemetery, which is also referred to as the "Island of the Dead." (Swiss painter Arnold Böcklin [1827–1901] used the cemetery as inspiration for his haunting painting of that name.) ⊠ *Piazzale Donatello 38, Santa Croce* ☎*055/582608* 🎫 *Free; suggested €3 per person for large groups* ⊘ *Nov.–Mar., Mon. 9–noon, Tues.–Fri. 2–5; Apr.–Sept., Mon. 9–noon, Tues.–Fri. 3–6.*

⓭ Giardino dei Semplici. Created by Cosimo I in 1550, this delightful garden was designed by favorite Medici architect Niccolò Tribolo. Many of the plants here have been grown since the 16th century. Springtime, especially May, is a particularly beautiful time to visit, as multitudes of azaleas create a riot of color. ⊠ *Via Pier Micheli 3, San Marco* ☎*055/2757402* ⊕*www.unifi.it* 🎫*€4* ⊘ *Thurs.–Tues. 9–1.*

❺ Mercato Centrale. Some of the food at this huge, two-story market hall is remarkably exotic. The ground floor contains meat and cheese stalls, as well as some very good bars that have *panini* (sandwiches), and the second floor teems with vegetable stands. ⊠*Piazza del Mercato Centrale, San Lorenzo* ☎*No phone* ⊘*Mon.–Sat. 7–2.*

⓫ Museo Archeologico *(Archaeological Museum).* Of the Etruscan, Egyptian, and Greco-Roman antiquities here, the Etruscan collection is particularly notable—one of the largest in Italy. The famous bronze *Chimera* was discovered (without the tail, a reconstruction) in the 16th century. ⊠ *Via della Colonna 38, Santissima Annunziata* ☎*055/23575* ⊕*www.comune.firenze.it/soggetti/sat/didattica/museo.html* 🎫*€4* ⊘ *Mon. 2–7, Tues. and Thurs. 8:30–7, Wed. and Fri.–Sun. 8:30–2.*

❾ Museo dell'Opificio delle Pietre Dure. Adjacent to this fascinating small museum is an *opificio*, or workshop, that Ferdinand I established in 1588 to train craftsmen in the art of working with precious and semi-precious stones and marble (*pietre dure* means "hard stones"). Four hundred–plus years later, the workshop is renowned as a center for the restoration of mosaics and inlays in semiprecious stones. The museum is highly informative and includes some magnificent antique examples of this highly specialized and beautiful craft. ✉ *Via degli Alfani 78, San Marco* ☎055/26511 ✉€2 ⊘*Mon.–Wed. and Fri. and Sat. 8:15–2, Thurs. 8:15–7.*

❹ **Palazzo Medici-Riccardi.** The main attraction of this palace, begun in 1444 by Michelozzo for Cosimo de' Medici, is the interior chapel, the so-called **Cappella dei Magi** on the upper floor. Painted on its walls is Benozzo Gozzoli's famous *Procession of the Magi,* finished in 1460 and celebrating both the birth of Christ and the greatness of the Medici family. Gozzoli wasn't a revolutionary painter, and today is considered by some not quite first-rate because of his technique, which was old-fashioned even for his day. Gozzoli's gift, however, was for entrancing the eye, not challenging the mind, and on those terms his success here is beyond question. The paintings are full of activity yet somehow frozen in time in a way that fails utterly as realism but succeeds triumphantly as soon as the demand for realism is set aside. Entering the chapel is like walking into the middle of a magnificently illustrated children's storybook, and this beauty makes it one of the most enjoyable rooms in the city. ✉ *Via Cavour 1, San Lorenzo* ☎055/2760340 ✉€5 ⊘*Thurs.–Tues. 9–7.*

⑭ **Santa Maria Maddalena dei Pazzi.** One of Florence's hidden treasures, a cool and composed *Crucifixion* by Perugino (circa 1445/50–1523), is in the chapter house of the monastery below this church. Here you can see the Virgin Mary and St. John the Evangelist with Mary Magdalene and Sts. Benedict and Bernard of Clairvaux posed against a simple but haunting landscape. The figure of Christ crucified occupies the center of this brilliantly hued fresco. Perugino's colors radiate—note the juxtaposition of the yellow-green cuff against the orange tones of the Magdalene's robe. ✉*Borgo Pinti 58, Santa Croce* ☎055/2478420 ✉*Suggested €1* ⊘*Mon.–Sat. 9–noon, 5–5:20, and 6–7; Sun. 9–noon and 5–6:20.*

⑩ **Santissima Annunziata.** Dating from the mid-13th century, this church was restructured in 1447 by Michelozzo, who gave it an uncommon (and lovely) entrance cloister with frescoes by Andrea del Sarto (1486–1530), Pontormo (1494–1556), and Rosso Fiorentino (1494–1540). The interior is a rarity for Florence: an overwhelming example of the baroque. But it's not really a fair example, because it's merely 17th-century baroque decoration applied willy-nilly to an earlier structure—exactly the sort of violent remodeling exercise that has given the baroque a bad name. The **Cappella dell'Annunziata,** immediately inside the entrance to the left, illustrates the point. The lower half, with its stately Corinthian columns and carved frieze bearing the Medici arms, was commissioned by Piero de' Medici in 1447; the upper half, with its erupting curves and impish sculpted cherubs, was added 200 years later. Each is effective in its own way, but together they serve only to prove that dignity is rarely comfortable wearing a party hat. Fifteenth-century-fresco enthusiasts should also note the very fine *Holy Trinity with St. Jerome* in the second chapel on the left. Done by Andrea del Castagno (circa 1421–57), it shows a wiry and emaciated St. Jerome

with Paula and Eustochium, two of his closest followers. ✉*Piazza di Santissima Annunziata* ☎*055/266186* ⊙*Daily 7–12:30 and 4–6:30.*

⑫ Spedale degli Innocenti. Built by Brunelleschi in 1419 to serve as an orphanage, it takes the historical prize as the very first Renaissance building. Brunelleschi designed its portico with his usual rigor, building it out of the two shapes he considered mathematically (and therefore philosophically and aesthetically) perfect: the square and the circle. Below the level of the arches, the portico encloses a row of perfect cubes; above the level of the arches, the portico encloses a row of intersecting hemispheres. The entire geometric scheme is articulated with Corinthian columns, capitals, and arches borrowed directly from antiquity. At the time he designed the portico, Brunelleschi was also designing the interior of San Lorenzo, using the same basic ideas. But because the portico was finished before San Lorenzo, the Spedale degli Innocenti can claim the honor of ushering in Renaissance architecture. The 10 ceramic medallions depicting swaddled infants that decorate the portico are by Andrea della Robbia (1435–1525/28), done in about 1487.

Within the Spedale degli Innocenti is a small museum, or **Pinacoteca** (⌨€4 ⊙*Thurs.–Tues. 8:30–2*). Most of the objects are minor works by major artists, but well worth a look is Domenico Ghirlandaio's (1449–94) *Adorazione dei Magi* (*Adoration of the Magi*), executed in 1488. His use of color, and his eye for flora and fauna, shows that art from north of the Alps made a great impression on him. ✉*Piazza di Santissima Annunziata 12* ☎*055/20371* ⌨€4 ⊙*Mon.–Sat. 8:30–7, Sun. 8:30–2.*

OFF THE BEATEN PATH

Chiostro dello Scalzo. Often overlooked, this small, peaceful 16th-century cloister was frescoed in grisaille by Andrea del Sarto (1486–1530) and Franciabigio, with scenes from the life of St. John the Baptist, Florence's patron saint. ✉ *Via Cavour 69, San Marco* ☎*055/2388604* ⊙*Mon., Thurs., and Sat. 8:30–1:50.*

SANTA MARIA NOVELLA TO THE ARNO

Piazza Santa Maria Novella, near the train station, suffers a degree of squalor, especially at night. Nevertheless, the streets in and around the piazza have their share of architectural treasures, including some of Florence's most tasteful palaces. Between Santa Maria Novella and the Arno is Via Tornabuoni, Florence's finest shopping street.

THE MAIN ATTRACTIONS

❷ Santa Maria Novella. The facade of this church looks distinctly clumsy by later Renaissance standards, and with good reason: it is an architectural hybrid. The lower half was completed mostly in the 14th century; its pointed-arch niches and decorative marble patterns reflect the Gothic style of the day. About 100 years later (around 1456), architect Leon Battista Alberti was called in to complete the job. The marble decoration of his upper story clearly defers to the already existing work below, but the architectural motifs he added evince an entirely different style. The central doorway, the four ground-floor half-columns with Corinthian capitals, the triangular pediment atop the second story, the inscribed frieze immediately below the pediment—these are borrowings from antiquity, and they reflect the new Renaissance style in architecture, born some 35 years earlier at the Spedale degli Innocenti. Alberti's most important addition, however, the S-curve scrolls that surmount the decorative circles on either side of the upper story, had no precedent whatever in antiquity. The problem was to soften the abrupt transition between wide ground floor and narrow upper story. Alberti's solution turned out to be definitive. Once you start to look for them, you will find scrolls such as these (or sculptural variations of them) on churches all over Italy, and every one of them derives from Alberti's example here.

The architecture of the interior is, like that of the Duomo, a dignified but somber example of Florentine Gothic. Exploration is essential, however, because the church's store of art treasures is remarkable. Highlights include the 14th-century stained-glass rose window depicting the *Coronation of the Virgin* (above the central entrance); the Cappella Filippo Strozzi (to the right of the altar), containing late-15th-century frescoes and stained glass by Filippino Lippi; the *cappella maggiore* (the area around the high altar), displaying frescoes by Ghirlandaio; and the Cappella Gondi (to the left of the altar), containing Filippo Brunelleschi's famous wood crucifix, carved around 1410 and said to have so stunned the great Donatello when he first saw it that he dropped a basket of eggs.

Of special interest for its great historical importance and beauty is Masaccio's *Trinity,* on the left-hand wall, almost halfway down the nave. Painted around 1426–27 (at the same time he was working on his frescoes in Santa Maria del Carmine), it unequivocally announced the arrival of the Renaissance. The realism of the figure of Christ was revolutionary in itself, but what was probably even more startling to contemporary Florentines was the barrel vault in the background. The mathematical rules for employing perspective in painting had just been discovered (probably by Brunelleschi), and this was one of the first works of art to employ them with utterly convincing success.

In the cloisters of the **Museo di Santa Maria Novella** (⊠ *Piazza Santa Maria Novella 19* ☎ *055/282187* ✆ *€2.70* 🕙 *Mon.–Thurs. and Sat. 9–5, Sun. 9–2*), to the left of Santa Maria Novella, is a faded fresco cycle by Paolo Uccello depicting tales from Genesis, with a dramatic vision of the Deluge. Earlier and better-preserved frescoes painted in 1348–55 by Andrea da Firenze are in the chapter house, or the **Cappellone degli Spagnoli** (Spanish Chapel), off the cloister. ☎ *055/210113* ✆ *€2.50 for both museum and chapel* 🕙 *Mon.–Thurs. and Sat. 9–5, Sun. 9–2.*

❾ Santa Trinita. Started in the 11th century by Vallambrosian monks and originally Romanesque in style, the church underwent a Gothic remodeling during the 14th century. (Remains of the Romanesque construction are visible on the interior front wall.) Its major works are the fresco cycle and altarpiece in the Cappella Sassetti, the second to the high altar's right, painted by Ghirlandaio from around 1480 to 1485.

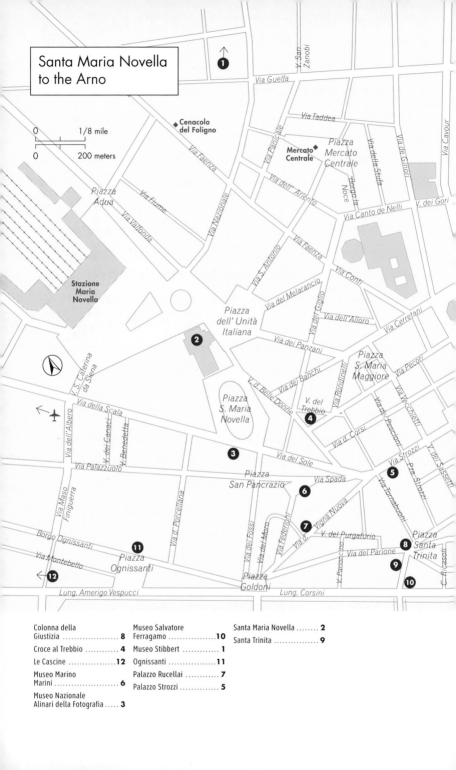

Santa Maria Novella to the Arno

Meet the Medici

The Medici were the dominant family of Renaissance Florence, wielding political power and financing some of the world's greatest art. You'll see their names at every turn around the city. These are some of the clan's more notable members:

Cosimo il Vecchio (1389–1464), incredibly wealthy banker to the popes, was the first in the family line to act as de facto ruler of Florence. He was a great patron of the arts and architecture; he was the moving force behind the family palace and the Dominican complex of San Marco.

Lorenzo il Magnifico (1449–92), grandson of Cosimo il Vecchio, presided over a Florence largely at peace with her neighbors. A collector of cameos, a writer of sonnets, and lover of ancient texts, he was the preeminent Renaissance man.

Leo X (1475–1521), also known as Giovanni de' Medici, became the first Medici pope, helping extend the family power base to include Rome and the Papal States. His reign was characterized by a host of problems, the biggest one being a former friar named Martin Luther.

Catherine de' Medici (1519–89) was married by her cousin Pope Clement VII to Henry of Valois, who later became Henry II of France. Wife of one king and mother of three, she was the first Medici to marry into European royalty. Lorenzo il Magnifico, her great-grandfather, would have been thrilled.

Cosimo I (1537–74), the first grand duke of Tuscany, should not be confused with his ancestor Cosimo il Vecchio.

His work here possesses such graceful decorative appeal as well as a proud depiction of his native city (most of the cityscapes show 15th-century Florence in all her glory). The wall frescoes illustrate scenes from the life of St. Francis, and the altarpiece, depicting the *Adoration of the Shepherds*, veritably glows. ⊠ *Piazza Santa Trinita, Santa Maria Novella* ☎ *055/216912* ✆ *Mon.–Sat. 8–noon and 4–6.*

ALSO WORTH SEEING

8 **Colonna della Giustizia.** In the center of **Piazza Santa Trinita** is this column from Rome's Terme di Caracalla, given to the Medici grand duke Cosimo I by Pope Pius IV in 1560. Typical of Medici self-assurance, the name translates as the Column of Justice. The column was raised here by Cosimo in 1565 to mark the spot where he heard the news that Florentine ducal forces had prevailed over a ragtag army composed of Florentine republican exiles and their French allies at the 1554 battle of Marciano near Prato; the victory made his power in Florence all but absolute. ⊠ *Piazza Santa Trinita, Santa Maria Novella.*

4 **Croce al Trebbio.** In 1338 the Dominican friars (the Dominican church of Santa Maria Novella is down the street) erected this little granite column near Piazza Santa Maria Novella to commemorate a famous local victory: it was here in 1244 that they defeated their avowed enemies, the Patarene heretics, in a bloody street brawl. ⊠ *Via del Trebbio, Santa Maria Novella.*

⑫ Le Cascine. In the 16th century this vast park belonged to the Medici, who allegedly used it for hunting, one of their favorite pastimes. It was opened to the public in the 19th century. The park runs for nearly 3 km (2 mi) along the Arno and has roughly 291 acres. It's ideal for strolling on sunny days, and there are paths for jogging, allées perfect for biking, grassy fields for picnicking, and lots of space for rollerblading (as well as a place to rent skates). At the northern tip of the park is the **piazzaletto dell'Indiano,** an oddly moving monument dedicated to Rajaram Cuttraputti, Marajah of Kolepoor, who died in Florence in 1870. The park hosts sports enthusiasts, a weekly open-air market, and discotheques. But be warned: at night there's a booming sex-for-sale trade. ⊠ *Main entrance: Piazza Vittorio Veneto, Viale Fratelli Roselli (at the Ponte della Vittoria).*

❻ Museo Marino Marini. A 21-foot-tall bronze horse and rider, one of the major works by artist Marini (1901–80), dominates the space of the main gallery here. The museum itself is an eruption of contemporary space in a deconsecrated 9th-century church, designed with a series of open stairways, walkways, and balconies that allow you to peer at Marini's work from all angles. In addition to his Etruscanesque sculpture, the museum houses Marini's paintings, drawings, and engravings. ⊠ *Piazza San Pancrazio, Santa Maria Novella* ☎ *055/219432* ✏ *€4* ⊙ *Wed.–Mon. 10–5. Closed Tues. and all of Aug.*

❸ Museo Nazionale Alinari della Fotografia. Housed in part of what was once an ancient hospice across the piazza from the church of Santa Maria Novella, this museum hosts temporary photography exhibitions in its two largest rooms. The rest of the ground floor and the long narrow hall upstairs hold part of the museum's vast permanent collection devoted to the history of photography. There are many old cameras of all sizes dating as far back as 1820, and special niches dedicated to specific camera models. ⊠ *Piazza Santa Maria Novella 14/a* ☎ *055/216310* ⊕ *www.alinarifondazione.it* ✏ *€9* ⊙ *Thurs., Fri., and Sun.–Tues. 9:30–7:30, Sat. 9:30* AM–11:30 PM.

❿ Museo Salvatore Ferragamo. If there's such a thing as a temple for footwear, this is it. The shoes in this dramatically displayed collection were designed by Salvatore Ferragamo (1898–1960) beginning in the early 20th century. Born in southern Italy, the late master jump-started his career in Hollywood by creating shoes for the likes of Mary Pickford and Rudolph Valentino. He then returned to Florence and set up shop in the basement of the 13th-century Palazzo Spini Ferroni. The collection includes about 16,000 shoes, and those on exhibition are frequently rotated. ⊠ *Via dei Tornabuoni 2, Santa Maria Novella* ☎ *055/3360846* ✏ *€5* ⊙ *Mon. and Wed.–Sun. 10–6.*

❶ Museo Stibbert. Federico Stibbert (1838–1906), born in Florence to an Italian mother and an English father, liked to collect things. Over a lifetime of doing so, he amassed some 50,000 objects. This museum, which was also his home, displays many of them. He had a fascination with medieval armor and also collected costumes, particularly Uzbek costumes, which are exhibited in a room called the Moresque Hall.

These are mingled with an extensive collection of swords, guns, and other devices whose sole function was to kill people. The paintings, most of which date from the 15th century, are largely second-rate. The house itself is an interesting amalgam of neo-Gothic, Renaissance, and English eccentric. To get here, take Bus 4 from the station at Santa Maria Novella, get off at the stop marked FABBRONI 4, and follow signs to the museum. ✉ *Via Federico Stibbert 26* ☎055/475520 ✆€6 ⊙*Mon.–Wed. 10–2, Fri.–Sun. 10–6. Tours every half hr.*

⓫ Ognissanti. The Umiliati owned this architectural hodgepodge of a church before the Franciscans took it over in the mid-16th century. (They were ousted in 2001, and replaced by the Benedictines, who moved out in 2003.) Beyond the fanciful baroque facade by Matteo Nigetti (1560–1649) are a couple of wonderful 15th-century gems. On the right in the nave is *Madonna della Misericordia* by Ghirlandaio; a little farther down is Botticelli's *St. Augustine in His Study.* A companion piece, directly across the way, is Ghirlandaio's *St. Jerome.* Pass through the rather dreadfully frescoed cloister to check out Ghirlandaio's superb *Last Supper*—which proves definitively that Leonardo da Vinci was not the only Tuscan painter who could do them well. ✉*Piazza Ognissanti, Santa Maria Novella* ☎055/2398700 ✆*Free* ⊙*Church: daily 7–noon and 3–6; Last Supper: Mon., Tues., and Sat. 9–noon.*

❼ Palazzo Rucellai. Architect Leon Battista Alberti (1404–72) designed perhaps the very first private residence inspired by antique models—which goes a step further than the Palazzo Strozzi. A comparison between the two is illuminating. Evident on the facade of the Palazzo Rucellai, dating between 1455 and 1470, is the ordered arrangement of windows and rusticated stonework seen on the Palazzo Strozzi, but Alberti's facade is far less forbidding. Alberti devoted a far larger proportion of his wall space to windows, which lighten the facade's appearance, and filled in the remainder with rigorously ordered classical elements borrowed from antiquity. The result, though still severe, is less fortresslike, and Alberti strove for this effect purposely (he is on record as saying that only tyrants need fortresses). Ironically, the Palazzo Rucellai was built some 30 years *before* the Palazzo Strozzi. Alberti's civilizing ideas here, it turned out, had little influence on the Florentine palazzi that followed. To Renaissance Florentines, power—in architecture, as in life—was equally as impressive as beauty. While you are admiring the facade (the palazzo isn't open to the public), turn around and look at the Loggia dei Rucellai across the street. Built in 1463–66, it was the private "terrace" of the Rucellai family, in-laws to the Medici. Its soaring heights and grand arches are a firm testament to the family's status and wealth. ✉ *Via della Vigna Nuova, Santa Maria Novella.*

❺ Palazzo Strozzi. The Strozzi family built this imposing palazzo in an attempt to outshine the nearby Palazzo Medici. Based on a model by Giuliano da Sangallo (circa 1452–1516) dating from around 1489 and executed between 1489 and 1504 under il Cronaca (1457–1508) and Benedetto da Maiaino (1442–97), it was inspired by Michelozzo's earlier Palazzo Medici-Riccardi. The palazzo's exterior is simple, severe, and massive: it's a testament to the wealth of a patrician, 15th-century Florentine family. The interior courtyard, entered from the rear of the palazzo, is another matter altogether. It is here that the classical vocabulary—columns, capitals, pilasters, arches, and cornices—is given uninhibited and powerful expression. Blockbuster art shows frequently occur here. ⊠ *Via Tornabuoni, Piazza della Repubblica* ☎ *055/2776461* ⊕ *www.palazzostrozzi.org and www.contromodafirenze.it* ✆ *Free, except during exhibitions* ⊙ *Daily 10–7.*

OFF THE BEATEN PATH

Cenacolo del Foligno. This delightful *Last Supper*, executed sometime in the 1470s, has been variously attributed to Perugino or to one of his followers. Its placement, at the end of a long room—the former refectory for a group of nuns—is simply breathtaking; because the white walls are otherwise unadorned, the fresco packs quite a visual punch. In the middle of the lunette in the upper center, Christ appears in the Garden of Gethsemane with the sleeping apostles. The delicate brush strokes of the leaves in the trees are exquisite. Judas, as is typical of so many representations of the Last Supper, is shown seated at the other side of the table quite apart from the other 11 apostles. Note how the artist has carefully labeled each apostle except for Judas. The tondi surrounding the fresco show portraits of prominent Franciscans such as St. Anthony of Padua, Francis of Assisi, St. Bernardino of Siena, and St. Louis of Toulouse. ⊠ *Via Faenza 42, Santa Maria Novella* ☎ *055/286982* ✆ *Free* ⊙ *Mon., Tues., and Sat. 9–noon.*

SANTA CROCE

The Santa Croce quarter, on the southeast fringe of the historic center, was built up in the Middle Ages outside the second set of medieval city walls. The centerpiece of the neighborhood was the basilica of Santa Croce, which could hold great numbers of worshippers; the vast piazza could accommodate any overflow and also served as a fairground and, allegedly since the middle of the 16th century, as a playing field for no-holds-barred soccer games. A center of leatherworking since the Middle Ages, the neighborhood is still packed with leatherworkers and leather shops.

THE MAIN ATTRACTIONS

❷ Piazza Santa Croce. Originally outside the city's 12th-century walls, this piazza grew with the Franciscans, who used the large square for public preaching. During the Renaissance it was used for *giostre* (jousts), including one sponsored by Lorenzo de' Medici. "Bonfires of the vanities" occurred here, as well as soccer matches in the 16th century. Lined with many palazzi dating from the 15th century, it remains one of Florence's loveliest piazze and is a great place to people-watch.

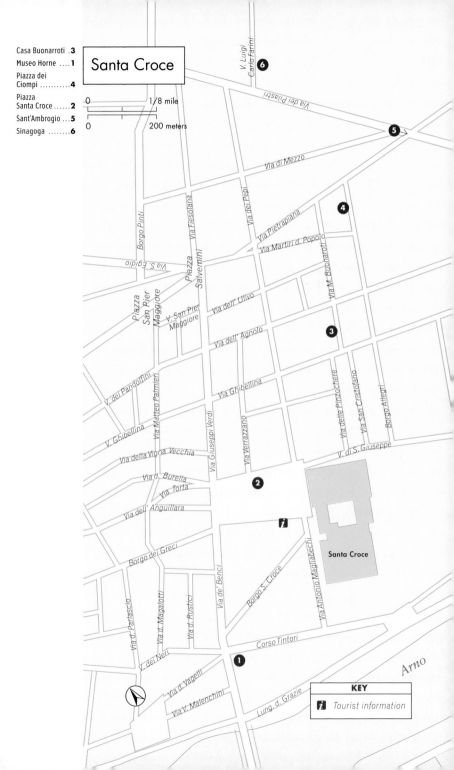

Santa Croce

0   1/8 mile

0   200 meters

V. Luigi Carlo Farini

Via dei Piastri

Borgo Pinti

Via S. Egidio

Via Fiesolana

Piazza Salvemini

Via di Mezzo

Via dei Pepi

Via Pietrapiana

Via Martiri d. Popolo

Via M. Buonarroti

Piazza San Pier Maggiore

V. San Pier Maggiore

Via dell' Ulivo

Via dell' Agnolo

V. dei Pandolfini

V. Ghibellina

Via Matteo Palmieri

Via Ghibellina

Via delle Pinzochere

Via San Cristofano

Borgo Allegri

Via della Vigna Vecchia

Via Giuseppi Verdi

Via Verrazzano

V. di S. Giuseppe

Via d. Buretta

Via Torta

Via dell' Anguillara

Borgo dei Greci

Via de' Benci

Borgo S. Croce

Via Antonio Magliabechi

Santa Croce

V. di Parlascio

Via d. Magalotti

Via d. Rustici

V. dei Neri

Corso Tintori

Arno

Via d. Vagelli

Via V. Malenchini

Lung. d. Grazie

6 **Sinagoga.** Jews were well settled in Florence by 1396, when the first money-lending operations became officially sanctioned. Medici patronage helped Jewish banking houses to flourish, but by 1570 Jews were required to live within the large "ghetto," near today's Piazza della Repubblica, by decree of Cosimo I, who had cut a deal with Pope Pius V (1504–72): in exchange for ghettoizing the Jews, he would receive the title Grand Duke of Tuscany.

Construction of the modern Moorish-style synagogue began in 1874 as a bequest of David Levi, who wished to endow a synagogue "worthy of the city." Falcini, Micheli, and Treves designed the building on a domed Greek cross plan with galleries in the transept and a roofline bearing three distinctive copper cupolas visible from all over Florence. The exterior has alternating bands of tan travertine and pink granite, reflecting an Islamic style repeated in Giovanni Panti's ornate interior. Of particular interest are the cast-iron gates by Pasquale Franci, the eternal light by Francesco Morini, and the Murano glass mosaics by Giacomo dal Medico. The gilded doors of the Moorish ark, which fronts the pulpit and is flanked by extravagant candelabra, are decorated with symbols of the ancient Temple of Jerusalem and bear bayonet marks from vandals. The synagogue was used as a garage by the Nazis, who failed to inflict much damage in spite of an attempt to blow up the place with dynamite. Only the columns on the left side were destroyed, and even then, the Women's Balcony above did not collapse. Note the Star of David in black and yellow marble inlaid in the floor. The original capitals can be seen in the garden.

Some of the oldest and most beautiful Jewish ritual artifacts in all of Europe are displayed upstairs in the small **Museo Ebraico.** Exhibits document the Florentine Jewish community and the building of the synagogue. The donated objects all belonged to local families and date from as early as the late 16th century. Take special note of the exquisite needlework and silver pieces. A small but well-stocked gift shop is downstairs. ⊠ *Via Farini 4, Santa Croce* ☎ *055/2346654* ✉ *Synagogue and museum €5* ⊘ *Apr., May, Sept., and Oct., Sun.–Thurs. 10–5, Fri. 10–2; June–Aug., Sun.–Thurs. 10–6, Fri. 10–2; Nov.–Mar., Sun.–Thurs. 10–3, Fri. 10–2. English guided tours: 10:10, 11, noon, 1, 2 (no tour at 2 on Fri.).*

NEED A BREAK? The only kosher–vegetarian restaurant in Tuscany is Ruth's (⊠ *Via Farini 2/a, Santa Croce* ☎ *055/2480888*), adjacent to Florence's synagogue. On the menu: inexpensive vegetarian and Mediterranean dishes and a large selection of kosher wines. It's closed for Friday dinner and Saturday lunch.

ALSO WORTH SEEING

3 **Casa Buonarroti.** If you are really enjoying walking in the footsteps of the great genius, you may want to complete the picture by visiting the Buonarroti family home, even though Michelangelo never actually lived there. It was given to his nephew, and it was the nephew's son, also called Michelangelo, who turned it into a gallery dedicated to his great-uncle. The artist's descendents filled it with art treasures, some by Michelangelo himself—a marble bas-relief; the *Madonna of the Steps,*

Continued on page 84

SANTA CROCE

The Duomo may catch your eye first, but to discover Florence's most impressive tombs and finest church art, cross town to this Gothic masterpiece.

Construction of Santa Croce was initiated in 1294 by Florence's Franciscan friars, who were aiming to outdo Santa Maria Novella, the church of their Dominican rivals. In the centuries that followed, Santa Croce would fulfill this goal in ways the Franciscans never could have imagined: it became the resting place of Italian geniuses—a sort of Florentine Westminister Abbey—and the site of revolutionary frescoes that helped change the course of Western art.

Clockwise from left: Sacristy inside Santa Croce; Detail from Michelangelo tomb; Exterior of Sante Croce; Dante Alighieri monument.

WHAT TO LOOK FOR INSIDE SANTA CROCE

THE ART WITHIN SANTA CROCE is the most impressive of any church in Florence. Historically, the most significant works are the Giotto frescoes. Time hasn't been kind to them; over the centuries, they've been whitewashed, plastered over, and clumsily restored. But you can still sense the realism and drama of Giotto's work—it may look primitive, but in the 14th century it sparked a revolution. Before Giotto, the role of painting was to symbolize the attributes of God; after him, it was to imitate life.

Giotto fresco, Capella Bardi

Donatello's Crucifixion

ENTRANCE

❶ ❷

BASILICA

❸ ❹ ❺ ❻ ❼ ❽ ❾ ❿ ⓫

CLOISTER 1

⓬ Pazzi Chapel

Sacristy

Museum ⓭

CLOISTER 2

Cimabue's Triumphal Cross

Donatello's Annunciation

6 Donatello's Annunciation (c. 1435) exquisitely renders the surprise of the Virgin as Gabriel announces that the Lord is with her.

9 Donatello's Crucifixion (1425) annoyed his friend Brunelleschi, who complained that it made Christ look like a peasant. Its location is in the Cappella Bardi di Vernio, the chapel at the end of the left transept.

10 Giotto's Cappella Bardi frescoes (1320–30), in the first chapel to the right of the main altar, show scenes from the life of St. Francis.

11 Giotto's Cappella Peruzzi frescoes (1320–30), in the second chapel to the right of the main altar, depict scenes from the lives of John the Evangelist and Baptist.

12 Brunelleschi's Cappella Pazzi (begun 1429) shows the master architect in an intimate light; Brunelleschi did not live to see it completed.

13 Cimabue's Triumphal Cross (1287–88), in the attached Museo dell'Opera di Santa Croce, heartbreakingly shows what damage the flood of 1966 did to some very important pieces of art.

TOMBS & MONUMENTS OF GREAT MEN

1 Galileo Galilei (1564–1642). Galileo's tomb wasn't given prominence until 100 years after his death, as his evidence that the earth was not the center of the universe was highly displeasing to the Church.

2 Lorenzo Ghiberti (1378–1455). The tomb slab of sculptor Lorenzo Ghiberti, who created the Baptistery doors, is on the floor near Galileo's tomb.

3 Michelangelo (1475–1564; tomb shown above). The great master supposedly picked this spot so he'd see Brunelleschi's dome on Judgment Day.

4 Dante Alighieri (1265–1321). A memorial to Dante was built in 1829 to honor the poet, who was banished from Florence and buried in Ravenna.

5 Niccolò Machiavelli (1469–1527). The Renaissance political theoretician, whose brutally pragmatic philosophy so influenced the Medici, has the quote *Tanto nomini nullum par elogium* ("For so great a name, no praise is adequate") on his tomb, built in 1787.

7 Leonardo Bruni (1370–1444). Bernardo Rossellino's *Tomb of Leonardo Bruni* (1444–45), one of Santa Croce's finest works, depicts the humanist chancellor of Florence, the first *uomo illustre* (illustrious man) to be buried in the church.

8 Gioacchino Rossini (1792–1868). The great Italian composer wrote more than 30 operas; his most famous was *Il barbiere di Siviglia* (The Barber of Seville).

Santa Croce Basics

Like the Duomo, Santa Croce is Gothic in design, and in all likelihood the two churches had the same initial architect, Arnolfo di Cambio. In the typical fashion of the Middle Ages, construction continued for decades—the church was finally consecrated by Pope Eugene IV in 1442. And, also like the Duomo, Santa Croce's neo-Gothic façade is a 19th-century addition.

✉ Piazza Santa Croce 16
☎ 055/2466105
🎫 €5 Basilica and museum (combined ticket)
🕐 Mon.–Sat. 9:30–5:30, Sun. 1–5:30.

carved when Michelangelo was only a teenager; and his wooden model for the facade of San Lorenzo—and some by other artists that pay homage to him. ⊠ *Via Ghibellina 70, Santa Croce* ☏*055/241752* ⊕*www. casabuonarroti.it* ⊠*€6.50* ⊙*Fri.–Wed. 9:30–2.*

❶ **Museo Horne.** Englishman Herbert P. Horne (1864–1916), architect, art historian, and collector, spent much of his life in his 15th-century palazzo surrounded by carefully culled paintings, sculptures, and other decorative arts mostly from the 14th to 16th centuries. His home has since been turned into a museum, and although most of the collection is decidedly B-list, it's worth a visit to see how a gentleman lived in the 19th century. Many of the furnishings, such as the 15th-century *lettuccio* (divan), are exemplary. ⊠ *Via dei Benci 6, Santa Croce* ☏*055/244661* ⊠*€5* ⊙*Mon.–Sat. 9–1.*

❹ **Piazza dei Ciompi.** Now the site of a daily flea market, this piazza was a working-class neighborhood of primarily wool- and silk-trade workers in the 14th century. The disenfranchised wool workers, forbidden entry to the Arte della Lana (the Wool Guild, whose members included those who traded in wool), briefly seized control of the government. It was a short-lived exercise in rule by the nonrepresented and was eventually overpowered by the ruling upper class. The loggia, executed in 1567, is by Giorgio Vasari.

❺ **Sant'Ambrogio.** Named for the Bishop of Milan, this 10th-century church once belonged to an order of Benedictine nuns. Just this side of austere, the church is one of the oldest in Florence. Though its facade is 19th-century, inside are 15th-century panel paintings and a lovely but rather damaged 1486 fresco by Cosimo Roselli, in the chapel to the left of the high altar. The tabernacle of the Blessed Sacrament was carved by Mino da Fiesole, who, like Verrocchio, il Cronaca, and Francesco Granacci (1469/77–1543), is buried here. ⊠*Piazza Sant'Ambrogio, Santa Croce* ☏*No phone* ⊠*Free* ⊙*Daily 8–noon and 3–6.*

OFF THE BEATEN PATH

American Military Cemetery. About 8 km (5 mi) south of Florence on the road to Siena is one of two American cemeteries in Italy (the other is in Nettuno). It contains 4,402 bodies of Americans who died in Italy during World War II. Spread across a gently rolling hill, the simple crosses and Stars of David bearing only name, date of death, and state seem to stretch endlessly. At the top of the hill is a place for reflection and large mosaic maps depicting the Allied assault in 1943. The two fronts—called the Gothic Line and the Gustav Line—are vividly rendered. So, too, is the list containing 1,409 names of those missing in action. ⊹ *From Florence, take Via Cassia south to Località Scopeti* ☏*055/2020020* ⊠*Free* ⊙*Daily 9–5.*

Museo del Cenacolo. This way-off-the-beaten-path museum (the name translates as the Museum of the Last Supper) has a stunning fresco by Andrea del Sarto. Begun sometime around 1511 and finished 1526–27, the fresco depicts the moment when Christ announced that one of his apostles would betray him. Andrea has rendered the scene in subtle yet still brilliant colors. Also on display are a couple of lesser-known works by Pontormo and copies of other 16th-century works. (Down the street is the church of San Salvi, founded by John Gualbert and begun in 1048. Though it suffered damage during the siege of 1529–30, the interior has a modest but lovely *Madonna and Child* by Lorenzo di Bicci as well as a 16th-century wood cross on the altar.) To get here, take Bus 6 from Piazza San Marco and get off at the Lungo L'Affrico stop—it's the first stop after crossing the railroad tracks. ⊠ *Via San Salvi 16* ☎*055/2388603* ⌚*Free* ☉*Tues.–Sun. 8:15–1:50.*

THE OLTRARNO

A walk through the Oltrarno (literally "the other side of the Arno") takes in two very different aspects of Florence: the splendor of the Medici, manifest in the riches of the mammoth Palazzo Pitti and the gracious Giardino di Boboli; and the charm of the Oltrarno, a slightly gentrified but still fiercely proud working-class neighborhood with artisans' and antiques shops.

Farther east across the Arno, a series of ramps and stairs climbs to Piazzale Michelangelo, where the city lies before you in all its glory (skip this trip if it's a hazy day). More stairs (behind La Loggia restaurant) lead to the church of San Miniato al Monte. You can avoid the long walk by taking Bus 12 or 13 at the west end of Ponte alle Grazie and getting off at Piazzale Michelangelo; you still have to climb the monumental stairs to and from San Miniato, but you can then take the bus from Piazzale Michelangelo back to the center of town. If you decide to take a bus, remember to buy your ticket before you board.

THE MAIN ATTRACTIONS

❻ Giardino di Boboli *(Boboli Gardens).* The main entrance to these landscaped gardens is from the right wing of ⇨ **Palazzo Pitti.** The gardens began to take shape in 1549, when the Pitti family sold the palazzo to Eleanor of Toledo, wife of the Medici grand duke Cosimo I. The initial landscaping plans were laid out by Niccolò Tribolo (1500–50). After his death, work was continued by Vasari, Ammannati, Giambologna, Bernardo Buontalenti (circa 1536–1608), and Giulio (1571–1635) and Alfonso Parigi (1606–56), among others. Italian landscaping is less formal than French but still full of sweeping drama. A copy of the famous *Morgante,* Cosimo I's favorite dwarf astride a particularly unhappy tortoise, is near the exit. Sculpted by Valerio Cioli (circa 1529–99), the work seems to illustrate the perils of culinary overindulgence. A visit here can be disappointing because the gardens are somewhat under-planted and under-cared for, but it's still a great walk with some fabulous views. ⊠*Enter through Palazzo Pitti* ☎*055/294883* ⊕*www. polomuseale.firenze.it* ⌚ *€6, combined ticket with Galleria del Costume and Giardino Bardini* ☉*Jan., Feb., Nov., and Dec., daily 8:15–4:30; Mar., daily 8:15–5:30; Apr., May, Sept., and Oct., daily 8:15–6:30; June–Aug., daily 8:15–7:30. Closed 1st and last Mon. of month.*

❽ Piazzale Michelangelo. From this lookout you have a marvelous view of Florence and the hills around it, rivaling the vista from the Forte di Belvedere. It has a copy of Michelangelo's *David* and outdoor cafés

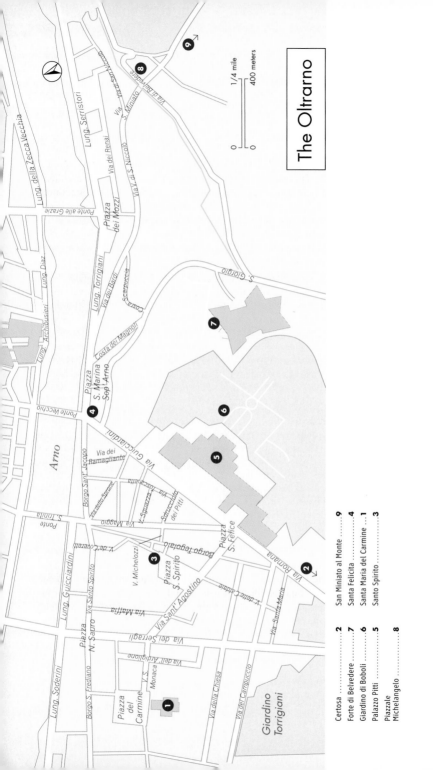

The Oltrarno

0   1/4 mile
0   400 meters

packed with tourists during the day and with Florentines in the evening. In May the **Giardino dell'Iris** (Iris Garden) off the piazza is abloom with more than 2,500 varieties of the flower. The **Giardino delle Rose** (Rose Garden) on the terraces below the piazza is also in full bloom in May and June.

5 **Palazzo Pitti.** This enormous palace is one of Florence's largest architectural set pieces. The original palazzo, built for the Pitti family around 1460, comprised only the main entrance and the three windows on either side. In 1549 the property was sold to the Medici, and Bartolomeo Ammannati was called in to make substantial additions. Although he apparently operated on the principle that more is better, he succeeded only in producing proof that more is just that: more.

Today the palace houses several museums: The **Museo degli Argenti** displays a vast collection of Medici household treasures. The **Galleria del Costume** showcases fashions from the past 300 years. The **Galleria d'Arte Moderna** holds a collection of 19th- and 20th-century paintings, mostly Tuscan. Most famous of the Pitti galleries is the **Galleria Palatina,** which contains a broad collection of paintings from the 15th to 17th centuries. The rooms of the Galleria Palatina remain much as the Medici left them. Their floor-to-ceiling paintings are considered by some to be Italy's most egregious exercise in conspicuous consumption, aesthetic overkill, and trumpery. Still, the collection possesses high points, including a number of portraits by Titian and an unparalleled collection of paintings by Raphael, notably the double portraits of Angelo Doni and his wife, the sullen Maddalena Strozzi. The price of admission to the Galleria Palatina also allows you to explore the former **Appartamenti Reali** containing furnishings from a remodeling done in the 19th century. ✉ *Piazza Pitti* ☎ *055/210323* ✉ *Galleria Palatina and Galleria d'Arte Moderna, combined ticket €8.50; Galleria del Costume, Giardino Bardini, Giardino di Boboli, Museo degli Argenti, and Museo Porcelleane, combined ticket €6* ⊙ *Tues.–Sun. 8:15–6:50.*

9 **San Miniato al Monte.** This church, like the Baptistery, is a fine example of Romanesque architecture and is one of the oldest churches in Florence, dating from the 11th century. A 12th-century mosaic topped by a gilt bronze eagle, emblem of San Miniato's sponsors, the Calimala (cloth merchants' guild) crowns the lovely green-and-white marble facade. Inside are a 13th-century inlaid-marble floor and apse mosaic. Artist Spinello Aretino (1350–1410) covered the walls of the **Sagrestia** with frescoes depicting scenes from the life of St. Benedict. The nearby **Cappella del Cardinale del Portogallo** (Chapel of the Portuguese Cardinal) is one of the richest 15th-century Renaissance works in Florence. It contains the tomb of a young Portuguese cardinal, Prince James of Lusitania, who died in Florence in 1459. Its glorious ceiling is by Luca della Robbia, and the sculpted tomb by Antonio Rossellino

(1427–79). ✉ *Viale Galileo Galilei, Piazzale Michelangelo, Lungarno Sud* ☎*055/2342731* ⊘*Apr.–Oct., daily 8–7; Nov.–Mar., Mon.–Sat. 8–1 and 2:30–6, Sun. 3–5.*

❶ **Santa Maria del Carmine.** The Cappella **Brancacci**, at the end of the right transept of this church, houses a masterpiece of Renaissance painting: a fresco cycle that changed the course of Western art. Fire almost destroyed the church in the 18th century; miraculously, the Brancacci Chapel survived almost intact. The cycle is the work of three artists: Masaccio and Masolino (1383–circa 1447), who began it around 1424, and Filippino Lippi, who finished it some 50 years later after a long interruption during which the sponsoring Brancacci family was exiled. It was Masaccio's work that opened a new frontier for painting, as he was among the first artists to employ single-point perspective; tragically, he died in 1428 at the age of 27, so he didn't live to experience the revolution his innovations caused.

Masaccio collaborated with Masolino on several of the frescoes, but he alone painted the *Tribute Money,* on the upper-left wall; *St. Peter Baptizing,* on the upper altar wall; the *Distribution of Goods,* on the lower altar wall; and the *Expulsion of Adam and Eve,* on the chapel's upper-left entrance pier. If you look closely at the last painting and compare it with some of the chapel's other works, you should see a pronounced difference. The figures of Adam and Eve possess a startling presence primarily thanks to the dramatic way in which their bodies seem to reflect light. Masaccio here shaded his figures consistently, so as to suggest a single, strong source of light within the world of the painting but outside its frame. In so doing, he succeeded in imitating with paint the real-world effect of light on mass, and he thereby imparted to his figures a sculptural reality unprecedented in his day.

These matters have to do with technique, but with the *Expulsion of Adam and Eve* his skill went beyond mere technical innovation. In the faces of Adam and Eve, you see more than finely modeled figures; you see terrible shame and suffering depicted with a humanity rarely achieved in art. Reservations to see the chapel are mandatory, but can be booked on the same day. Your time inside is limited to 15 minutes—a frustration that's only partly mitigated by the 40-minute DVD about the history of the chapel you can watch either before or after your visit. ✉*Piazza del Carmine, Santo Spirito* ☎*055/2768224 reservations* 🎫*€4* ⊘*Mon. and Wed.–Sat. 10–5, Sun. 1–5.*

❸ **Santo Spirito.** The plain, unfinished facade gives nothing away, but the interior, although it appears chilly compared with later churches, is one of the most important examples of Renaissance architecture in Italy. Unfortunately, it's closed to the public except during Mass (Mon.–Sat. 9, Sun. 9, 10:30, and 6). You're welcome to attend the service, but if you go, be prepared to sit through the whole thing.

The interior is one of a pair designed in Florence by Filippo Brunelleschi in the early 15th century (the other is San Lorenzo). It was here that Brunelleschi supplied definitive solutions to the two major problems of interior Renaissance church design: how to build a cross-shaped interior using classical architectural elements borrowed from antiquity and how to reflect in that interior the order and regularity that Renaissance scientists (among them Brunelleschi himself) were at the time discovering in the natural world around them.

Brunelleschi's solution to the first problem was brilliantly simple: turn a Greek temple inside out. While ancient Greek temples were walled buildings surrounded by classical colonnades, Brunelleschi's churches were classical arcades surrounded by walled buildings. This brilliant architectural idea overthrew the previous era's religious taboo against pagan architecture once and for all, triumphantly claiming that architecture for Christian use.

Brunelleschi's solution to the second problem—making the entire interior orderly and regular—was mathematically precise: he designed the ground plan of the church so that all its parts were proportionally related. The transepts and nave have exactly the same width; the side aisles are precisely half as wide as the nave; the little chapels off the side aisles are exactly half as deep as the side aisles; the chancel and transepts are exactly one-eighth the depth of the nave; and so on, with dizzying exactitude. For Brunelleschi, such a design technique was a matter of passionate conviction. Like most theoreticians of his day, he believed that mathematical regularity and aesthetic beauty were flip sides of the same coin, that one was not possible without the other. In the **Santo Spirito refectory** (⊠ *Piazza Santo Spirito 29* ☎ *055/287043*), adjacent to the church, you can see Andrea Orcagna's painting of the Crucifixion. ⊠ *Piazza Santo Spirito* ☎ *055/210030* 🎨 *Church free, refectory €2.20* ☉ *Church: open only during Mass. Refectory: Apr.–Sept., Tues.–Sat. 9–2; Oct.–Mar., Tues.–Sat. 9–1:30.*

ALSO WORTH SEEING

② **Certosa.** The incredible Carthusian complex was largely funded in 1342 by the wealthy Florentine banker Niccolò Acciaolo, whose guilt at having amassed so much money must have been at least temporarily assuaged with the creation of such a structure to honor God. In the grand cloister are stunning frescoes of *Christ's Passion* by Pontormo. Though much of the paint is missing, their power is still unmistakable. Also of great interest are the monks' cells; apparently the monks could spend most of their lives tending their own private gardens without dealing with any other monks. To get here, you must either take Bus 37 and get off at the stop marked CERTOSA, or you need to have a car. Tours, which are mandatory, are given only in Italian, but even if you can't understand what's being said, you can still take in the sights. ⊹ *From Florence, take Viale Petrarca to Via Senese and follow it for about 10 mins; the Certosa is on the right* ☎ *055/2049226* 🎨 *Suggested €3 to €4* ☉ *Tues.–Sun. 9–11:30 and 3–4:15.*

7 **Forte di Belvedere** (*Fort Belvedere*). Built in 1590 to help defend the city against siege, this former first-rate fortification is now a first-rate exhibition venue. Farther up the hill is Piazzale Michelangelo, but as the natives know, the best views of Florence are right here. To the north, all the city's monuments are spread out in a breathtaking panorama. To the south, the nearby hills furnish a complementary rural view, in its way equally memorable. The fortress is adjacent to the top of the Giardino di Boboli. ⊠*Porta San Giorgio, San Niccolò* 🎫*Varies with exhibit.*

4 **Santa Felicita.** This late-baroque church (its facade was remodeled between 1736 and 1739) contains the mannerist Jacopo Pontormo's *Deposition,* the centerpiece of the Cappella Capponi (executed 1525–28) and a masterpiece of 16th-century Florentine art. The remote figures, which transcend the realm of Renaissance classical form, are portrayed in tangled shapes and intense pastel colors (well preserved because of the low lights in the church), in a space and depth that defy reality. Note, too, the exquisitely frescoed *Annunciation,* also by Pontormo, at a right angle to the *Deposition.* The granite column in the piazza was erected in 1381 and marks a Christian cemetery. ⊠*Piazza Santa Felicita, Via Guicciardini, Palazzo Pitti* ⊙*Mon.–Sat. 9–noon and 3–6, Sun. 9–1.*

NEED A BREAK? Cabiria (⊠*Piazza Santo Spirito 4/r* 📞*055/215732*), across the piazza from the church of Santo Spirito, draws funky locals and visitors in search of a cappuccino, a quenching ade, or an expertly mixed drink. When it's warm, sit outside on the terrace.

WHERE TO EAT

Florence's popularity with tourists means that, unfortunately, there's a higher percentage of mediocre restaurants here than you'll find in most Italian towns. Some restaurant owners cut corners and let standards slip, knowing that a customer today is unlikely to return tomorrow, regardless of the quality of the meal. So, if you're looking to eat well, it pays to do some research, starting with the recommendations here—we promise there's not a tourist trap in the bunch.

Dining hours start at around 1 for lunch and 8 for dinner. Many of Florence's restaurants are small, so reservations are a must. You can sample such specialties as creamy *fegatini* (a chicken-liver spread) and *ribollita* (minestrone thickened with bread and beans and swirled with extra-virgin olive oil) in a bustling, convivial trattoria, where you share long wooden tables set with paper place mats, or in an upscale *ristorante* with linen tablecloths and napkins.

Those with a sense of culinary adventure should not miss the tripe sandwich, served from stands throughout town. This Florentine favorite comes with a fragrant *salsa verde* (green sauce) or a piquant red hot sauce—or both. Follow the Florentines' lead and take a break at an *enoteca* (wine bar) during the day and discover some excellent Chianti and Super Tuscans from small producers who rarely export.

BEST BETS, FLORENCE DINING

With hundreds of restaurants to choose from, how will you decide where to eat? Fodor's writers and editors have selected their favorite restaurants by price, cuisine, and experience in the Best Bets lists below. In the first column, Fodor's Choice properties represent the "best of the best."

FODOR'S CHOICE

Cibrèo, $$$$, Santa Croce

L'Ora d'Aria, $$$$, Santa Croce

Taverna del Bronzino, $$$, San Lorenzo & Beyond

Osteria de'Benci, $$–$$$, Santa Croce

Best by Price

BEST ¢

All'Antico Vinaio, Santa Croce

da Nerbone, San Lorenzo & Beyond

da Rocco, Santa Croce

La Mescita, San Lorenzo & Beyond

BEST $

Cibrèo Trattoria, Santa Croce

La Casalinga, Oltrarno

Mario, San Lorenzo & Beyond

Osteria Antica Mescita San Niccolo, Oltrarno

BEST $$

Baldovino, Santa Croce

Frescobaldi Wine Bar, Centro Storico

La Mucca sul Tetto, Santa Croce

Quattro Leoni, Oltrarno

BEST $$$

Beccofino, Oltrarno

Il Latini, Centro Storico

La Giostra, Centro Storico

Osteria de'Benci, Centro Storico

BEST $$$$

Cibrèo, Centro Storico

L'Ora d'Aria, Centro Storico

Simon Boccanegra, Centro Storico

Taverna del Bronzino, San Lorenzo & Beyond

Best Experiences

FOR KIDS

Baldovino, $$, Santa Croce

Danny Rock, ¢, Santa Croce

I Latini, $$$, Centro Storico

ROMANTIC

Enoteca Pinchiorri, $$$$, Santa Croce

L'Ora d'Aria, $$$, Santa Croce

Targa, $$$, Beyond City Center

BISTECCA FIORENTINA (TUSCAN STEAK)

l Latini, $$$, Centro Storico

La Giostra, $$$, Santa Croce

Osteria de'Benci, $$$, Santa Croce

OUTDOOR DINING

Fuori Porta, ¢, Oltrarno

Osteria de'Benci, $$$, Santa Croce

Quattro Leoni, $$, Oltrarno

WINE BARS

Casa del Vino, $, San Lorenzo & Beyond

Fuori Porta, ¢, Oltrarno

Le Volpi e l'Uva, $, Oltrarno

ALTA CUCINA (SOPHISTICATED CUISINE)

Enoteca Pinchiorri, $$$, Santa Croce

L'Ora d'Aria , $$$, Santa Croce

Taverna del Bronzino, $$–$$$, Santa Croce

CASALINGA (HOME COOKING)

La Casalinga, $, Oltrarno

Le Mosacce, ¢–$, Santa Croce

Mario, $, San Lorenzo & Beyond

LUNCH SPOTS

Antico Noe, $$–$$$, Santa Croce

Cantinetta Antinori, $$$, Santa Maria Novella to the Arno

Benvenuto, $, Santa Croce

Frescobaldi Wine Bar, $$, Centro Storico

WINE LIST

Cantinetta Antinori, $$$, Santa Maria Novella to the Arno

Enoteca Pinchiorri, $, Santa Croce

Taverna del Bronzino, $, San Lorenzo & Beyond

WHAT IT COSTS IN EUROS				
¢	$	$$	$$$	$$$$
AT DINNER	under €15	€15–€25	€25–€35	€35–€45	over €45

Prices are for a first course *(primo)*, second course *(secondo)*, and dessert *(dolce)*.

THE DUOMO TO THE PONTE VECCHIO

$–$$ ✕ **Frescobaldi Wine Bar.** This swanky establishment serves both lunch and dinner. The food is typically Tuscan with some flights of fancy, including *acciughe marinate* (marinated anchovies) and *affettati misti* (a selection of sliced, cured meats). There's a separate wine bar within the restaurant called Frescobaldino. ⊠ *Via de' Magazzini 2–4/r, Piazza della Signoria* ☎ *055/284724* ⊟ *MC, V* ☺ *Closed Sun. No lunch Mon.*

$ ✕ **Birreria Centrale.** The feel here is more Munich beer hall than Florentine trattoria; indeed, although the menu lists plenty of Italian dishes, it also emphasizes sausages and sauerkraut. The *würstel rossi con crauti, speck, e patate alla tedesca* (a large and quite plump hotdog with sauerkraut, cured beef, potatoes, and pickles), for instance, comes with a dollop of spicy mustard. Heavy wooden tables are set closely together, and copies of 19th-century paintings adorn the intensely yellow walls, along with two frescoed Michelangelesque nudes that cavort over a brick arch. There's outside seating in warm weather—a great place to enjoy a beer. ⊠ *Piazza Cimatori 1/r, Duomo* ☎ *055/211915* ⊟ *AE, MC, V* ☺ *Closed Sun.*

¢–$ ✕ **Le Mosacce.** Come to this tiny, cramped, and boisterous place for a quick bite to eat. The menu, written in three languages, includes hearty, stick-to-the-ribs Florentine food such as *ribollita*. Seating is communal, and fellow diners share the big, straw-covered flask of wine. Service is prompt and efficient; two nimble cooks with impeccable timing staff the small kitchen. ⊠ *Via del Proconsolo 55/r, Duomo* ☎ *055/294361* ⌦ *Reservations not accepted* ⊟ *AE, DC, MC, V* ☺ *Closed weekends.*

SAN LORENZO & BEYOND

$$$–$$$$ ✕ **Taverna del Bronzino.** Want to have a sophisticated meal in a 16th-century Renaissance artist's studio? The former studio of Santi di Tito, a student of Bronzino's, has a simple, formal decor, with white tablecloths and place settings. The classic, dramatically presented Tuscan food is superb, and the solid, afforable wine list rounds out the menu. The service is outstanding. Reservations are advised, especially for eating at the wine cellar's only table. ⊠ *Via delle Ruote 25/r, San Marco* ☎ *055/495220* ⊟ *AE, DC, MC, V* ☺ *Closed Sun. and 3 wks in Aug.*

Fodor's Choice ★

$$–$$$ ✕ **Le Fonticine.** Owner Silvano Bruci is from Tuscany and his wife, Gianna, is from Emilia-Romagna, and their fine-dining oasis near the train station combines the best of two Italian cuisines. Start with the mixed-vegetable antipasto plate and then move on to any of their housemade pastas. The feathery light tortelloni *nostro modo* ("our way") stuffed with fresh ricotta and served with a tomato and cream sauce should not be missed. The restaurant's interior, filled with the Brucis'

2

painting collection, provides a cheery space for this soul-satisfying food. ⊠ *Via Nazionale 79/r, San Lorenzo* ☎055/282106 ⊟*AE, DC, MC, V* ⊙*Closed Sun., Mon., Nov. 24–Jan. 5, and Jul. 25–Aug. 25.*

$ ✕**Mario.** Florentines flock to this narrow family-run trattoria near San ★ Lorenzo to feast on Tuscan favorites served at simple tables under a wooden ceiling dating from 1536. A distinct cafeteria feel and genuine Florentine hospitality prevail: you'll be seated wherever there's room, which often means with strangers. Yes, there's a bit of extra oil in most dishes, which imparts calories as well as taste, but aren't you on vacation in Italy? Worth the splurge is *riso al ragù* (rice with ground beef and tomatoes). ⊠ *Via Rosina 2/r, corner of Piazza del Mercato Centrale, San Lorenzo* ☎055/218550 ⌫*Reservations not accepted* ⊟*No credit cards* ⊙*Closed Sun. and Aug. No dinner.*

¢ ✕**da Nerbone.** The place has been around since 1872, and it's easy to see why: this tiny stall in the middle of the covered Mercato Centrale has been serving up Florentine food to Florentines who like their tripe. Tasty primi and secondi are available every day, but cognoscenti come for the *panino con il lampredotto* (a type of tripe sandwich). Less adventurous sorts might want to sample the panino con il bollito (a boiled beef sandwich). Ask that the bread be "bagnato" (dipped, briefly, in the tripe cooking liquid), and have both the *salsa verde* (green sauce) and *salsa piccante* (a spicy, cayenne-laced sauce) slathered on top. ⊠ *Mercato San Lorenzo* ☎055/219949 ⊟*No credit cards* ⊙*Closed Sun. No dinner.*

¢ ✕**La Mescita.** Come early (or late) to grab a seat at this tiny spot frequented by Florentine university students and businesspeople. You can get a sandwich to go, or sit and enjoy the day's *primi* (such as a terrific *lasagne*) and follow it with their *polpettona* (meat loaf) and tomato sauce. Though seats are cramped and the wine is no great shakes, the service is friendly and the food hits the spot. Groups of 15 or more can reserve in the evenings for special meals. ⊠ *Via degli Alfani 70/r* ☎*No phone* ⊟*No credit cards* ⊙*Closed Sun. No dinner.*

SANTA MARIA NOVELLA TO THE ARNO

$$$ ✕**Cantinetta Antinori.** After a rough morning of shopping on Via Tornabuoni, stop for lunch in this 15th-century palazzo in the company of Florentine ladies (and men) who lunch and come to see and be seen. The panache of the food matches its clientele: expect treats such as *tramezzino con pane di campagna al tartufo* (country pâté with truffles served on bread) and the *insalata di gamberoni e gamberetti con carciofi freschi* (crayfish and prawn salad with shaved raw artichokes). ⊠*Piazza Antinori 3, Santa Maria Novella* ☎055/292234 ⊟*AE, DC, MC, V* ⊙*Closed weekends, 20 days in Aug., and Dec. 25–Jan. 6.*

$$$ ✕**Il Latini.** It may be the noisiest, most crowded trattoria in Florence, but it's also one of the most fun. The genial host, Torello ("little bull") Latini, presides over his four big dining rooms, and somehow it feels as if you're dining in his home. Ample portions of *ribollita* prepare the palate for the hearty meat dishes that follow. Both Florentines and tourists alike tuck into the *agnello fritto* (fried lamb) with aplomb.

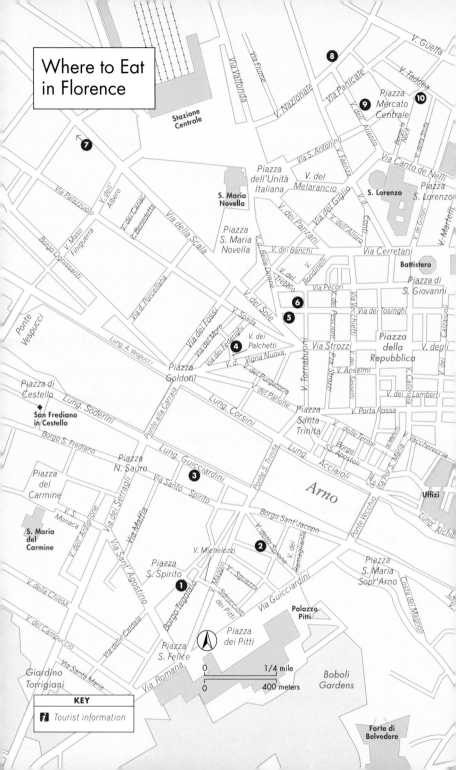

2

Though reservations are advised, there's always a wait anyway. ⊠ *Via dei Palchetti 6/r, Santa Maria Novella* ☎055/210916 ▤*AE, DC, MC, V* ⊘*Closed Mon. and 15 days at Christmas.*

$–$$ ✕**Osteria delle Belle Donne.** Down the street from the church of Santa Maria Novella, this gaily decorated spot, festooned with ropes of garlic and other vegetables, has an ever-changing menu and stellar service led by the irrepressible Giacinto. The kitchen has Tuscan standards, but shakes up the menu with alternatives such as *sedani con bacon, verza, e uova* (thick noodles sauced with bacon, cabbage, and egg). If you want to eat alfresco, request a table outside when booking. ⊠ *Via delle Belle Donne 16/r, Santa Maria Novella* ☎055/2382609 ▤*AE, DC, MC, V.*

SANTA CROCE

$$$$ ✕**Cibrèo.** The food at this upscale trattoria is fantastic, from the creamy
Fodor'sChoice crostini *di fegatini* (a savory chicken-liver spread) to the melt-in-your-
★ mouth desserts. Many Florentines hail this as the city's best restaurant, and Fodor's readers tend to agree—though some take issue with the prices and complain of long waits for a table (even with a reservation). If you thought you'd never try tripe—let alone like it—this is the place to lay any doubts to rest: the *trippa in insalata* (cold tripe salad) with parsley and garlic is an epiphany. The food is traditionally Tuscan, impeccably served by a staff that's multilingual—which is a good thing, because there are no written menus. Around the corner is Cibreino, Cibrèo's budget version, with a shorter menu and a no-reservations policy. ⊠ *Via A. del Verrocchio 8/r, Santa Croce* ☎055/2341100 ⚱*Reservations essential* ▤*AE, DC, MC, V* ⊘*Closed Sun. and Mon. and July 25–Sept. 5.*

$$$$ ✕**Enoteca Pinchiorri.** A sumptuous Renaissance palace with high, frescoed ceilings and bouquets in silver vases provides the backdrop for this restaurant, one of the most expensive in Italy. Some consider it one of the best, and others consider it a non-Italian rip-off, as the kitchen is presided over by a Frenchwoman with sophisticated, yet internationalist, leanings. Prices are high and portions are small; the vast holdings of the wine cellar, as well as stellar service, dull the pain, however, when the bill is presented. Interesting pasta combinations such as the *ignudi*—ricotta-and-spinach dumplings with a lobster-and-coxcomb fricassee—are always on the menu. ⊠ *Via Ghibellina 87, Santa Croce* ☎055/242777 ⚱*Reservations essential* ▤*AE, MC, V* ⊘*Closed Sun., Mon., and Aug. No lunch Tues. or Wed.*

$$$$ ✕**Ora d'Aria.** The name means "Hour of Air" and refers to the time of
Fodor'sChoice day when prisoners were let outside for fresh air—alluding to the fact
★ that this gem is across the street from what was once the old prison. In the kitchen, gifted young chef Marco Stabile turns out exquisite Tuscan classics as well as more fanciful dishes, which are as beautiful as they are delicious; intrepid diners will be vastly rewarded for ordering the tortellini *farciti con piccione* (stuffed with pigeon) if it's on the day's menu. Two tasting menus give Stabile even greater opportunity to shine, and the carefully culled wine list has something to please every palate. Do not miss his tiramisu espresso—something halfway between

a dessert and a coffee. ⊠ *Via Ghibellina 3/c, near Santa Croce* ☏ *055/2001699* ⊟ *AE, DC, MC, V* ⊗ *Closed Sun. No lunch*.

$$$$ ✕ **Simon Boccanegra.** Florentine food cognoscenti flock to this place named for a condottiere (mercenary) hero in a Verdi opera. Under high ceilings, candles on every table cast a rosy glow; the fine wine list and superb service make a meal here a true pleasure. The chef has a deft hand with fish dishes, as well as an inventiveness when it comes to reinterpreting such classics as risotto with chicken liver—he adds leek and saffron to give it a lift. Remember to save room for dessert. A less-expensive, less-formal wine bar serving a basic Tuscan menu is also on the premises. ⊠ *Via Ghibellina 124/r, Santa Croce* ☏ *055/2001098* ✍ *Reservations essential* ⊟ *AE, DC, MC, V* ⊗ *Closed Sun. No lunch*.

$$$ ✕ **La Giostra.** This clubby spot, whose name means "carousel" in Ital-
★ ian, is owned and run by Prince Dimitri Kunz d'Asburgo Lorena, and his way with mushrooms is as remarkable as his charm. The unusually good pastas may require explanation from Soldano, one of the prince's good-looking twin sons. In perfect English he'll describe a favorite dish, *taglierini con tartufo bianco*, a decadently rich pasta with white truffles. Leave room for dessert: this might be the only show in town with a sublime tiramisu *and* a wonderfully gooey Sacher torte. ⊠ *Borgo Pinti 12/r, Santa Croce* ☏ *055/241341* ⊟ *AE, DC, MC, V.*

$$–$$$ ✕ **Antico Noe.** If Florence had diners (it doesn't), this would be the best diner in town. The short menu at the one-room eatery relies heavily on seasonal ingredients picked up daily at the market. The menu comes alive particularly during truffle and artichoke season (don't miss the grilled artichokes if they're on the menu). Locals rave about the tagliatelle *ai porcini* (with mushrooms); the fried eggs liberally laced with truffle might be the greatest truffle bargain in town. Ask for the menu in Italian, as the English version is much more limited. The short wine list has some great bargains. ⊠ *Volta di San Piero 6/r, Santa Croce* ☏ *055/2340838* ⊟ *AE, DC, MC, V* ⊗ *Closed Sun. and 2 wks in Aug.*

$$–$$$ ✕ **Osteria de'Benci.** A few minutes from Santa Croce, this charming oste-
Fodor'sChoice ria serves some of the most eclectic food in Florence. Try the spaghetti
★ *degli eretici* (in tomato sauce with fresh herbs). The grilled meats are justifiably famous; the *carbonata* is a succulent piece of grilled beef served rare. When it's warm, you can dine outside with a view of the 13th-century tower belonging to the prestigious Alberti family. Right next door is Osteria de'Benci Caffè (¢–$), serving selections from the menu from 8 AM to midnight. ⊠ *Via de' Benci 11–13/r, Santa Croce* ☏ *055/2344923* ⊟ *AE, DC, MC, V* ⊗ *Closed Sun. and 2 wks in Aug.*

$$ ✕ **Baldovino.** David and Catherine Gardner, expat Scots, have created this lively, brightly colored restaurant down the street from the church of Santa Croce. From its humble beginnings as a pizzeria, it has evolved into something more. It's a happy thing that pizza is still on the menu, but now it shares billing with sophisticated primi and secondi. The menu changes monthly and has such treats as *filetto di manzo alla Bernaise* (filet mignon with light béarnaise sauce). Baldovino also serves pasta dishes and grilled meat until the wee hours. ⊠ *Via San Giuseppe 22/r, Santa Croce* ☏ *055/241773* ⊟ *MC, V.*

$$ ✕**La Mucca sul Tetto.** The strangely named "Cow on the Roof" has an equally odd, but pleasing, interior: anthracite-sponged walls adorned with Moorish-style stencil work are topped by 15th-century vaulting. The menu, which changes every few weeks, features Tuscan seasonal classics, as well as some unusual, tasty variations. Start with their light-as-a-feather *coccoli* (fried, coin-size discs of dough) served with *stracchino* (a soft, mild cheese) and prosciutto on the side. Meat lovers should not miss the fried lamb chops, whose batter is laden with pistachios. The bilingual staff is happy to guide you through the well-culled wine list, which caters to all budgets and all tastes. ⊠ *Via Ghibellina 134/r, near Santa Croce* ☎ *055/2344810* ▭ *AE, DC, MC, V* ⊘ *No lunch. Closed Sun.*

$–$$ ✕**Cantinetta il Francescano.** Plain wooden tables, muted indigo-gray walls, and fresh flowers provide the backdrop for simple Tuscan food served by a gracious and caring staff. Have a quick lunch here (it's just down the street from Santa Croce), or linger over a candlelit dinner. Start with one of the tasty antipasti, such as the *mozzarella di buffala con pomordori* (buffalo mozzarella with tomato sauce), and follow with one of the hearty pastas; or opt for the *tagliata*, which is done two ways. The standard version has sliced, rare beef topped with arugula and Parmesan; the succulent *tagliata di pollo* is flattened and grilled chicken topped with arugula. Reservations are advised. ⊠ *Largo Bargellini 16, Santa Croce* ☎ *055/241605* ▭ *MC, V* ⊘ *Closed Tues.*

$–$$ ✕**Koime.** If you're looking for a break from the ubiquitous ribollita, stop in at this eatery, which may be the only Japanese restaurant in the world to be housed in a 15th-century Renaissance palazzo. High, vaulted arches frame the Kaiten sushi conveyor belt. It's Japanese food, cafeteria style: selections, priced according to the color of the plate, make their way around a bar, where diners pick whatever they find appealing. Those seeking a more substantial meal head to the second floor, where Japanese barbecue is prepared at your table. The minimalist basement provides a subtle but dramatic backdrop for a well-prepared cocktail. ⊠ *Via de' Benci 41/r, Santa Croce* ☎ *055/2008009* ▭ *AE, DC, MC, V*

$–$$ ✕**La Maremma.** Brightly colored walls and white table linens add some zest to this simple trattoria. It excels at Tuscan classics as well as other dishes from around Italy. Nicely apportioned *primi* (the version here of the Roman *spaghetti alla carbonara* is terrific) prime the taste buds for what follows: the *pollo al aceto* (chicken with balsamic vinegar) is luscious; ham and cheese aficionados shouldn't miss the *salsiccia grigliata con pecorino fresco* (grilled sausage topped with a mild, melted sheep's-milk cheese). Service is courteous and prompt; the wine list is affordable and well thought out. ⊠ *Via Verdi 16/r, Santa Croce* ☎ *055/244615* ▭ *AE, MC, V* ⊘ *Closed Wed.*

$ ✕**Benvenuto.** At this Florentine institution, beloved for decades by locals and Anglophone Renaissance scholars alike, the service is ebullient, the menu long (with often unwittingly humorous English typographical errors), and the food simple, Tuscan, and tasty. The list of primi and secondi is extensive, and there are daily specials as well. Don't miss the *scaloppine all Benvenuto* (veal cutlets with porcini). ⊠ *Via della*

CLOSE UP

What Tripe!

While in Florence, those with a sense of culinary adventure should seek out a tripe sandwich, which is just about as revered by local gourmands as the bistecca alla fiorentina. In this case, however, the treasure comes on the cheap—sandwiches are sold from small stands found in the city center, topped with a fragrant green sauce or a piquant red hot sauce, or both. *Bagnato* means that the hard, crusty roll is first dipped in the tripe's cooking liquid; it's advisable to say *"sì"* when asked if that's how you like it. Sandwiches are usually taken with a glass of red wine poured from the tripe seller's *fiasco* (flask). If you find the tripe to your liking, you might also enjoy *lampredotto*, another, some say better, cut of stomach. For an exalted,

high-end tripe treat, try Fabio Picchi's cold tripe salad, served gratis as an *amuse-bouche* at the restaurant Cibrèo. It could make a convert of even the staunchest "I'd never try *that*" kind of eater.

Tripe carts are lunchtime favorites of Florentine working men—it's uncommon, but not unheard of, to see a woman at a tripe stand. Aficionados will argue which sandwich purveyor is best; here are three that frequently get mentioned: **La Trippaia** (⊠ *Via dell'Ariento, Santa Maria Novella* ☎ *No phone* ⊘ *Closed Sun.*). **Il Trippaio** (⊠ *Via de' Macci at Borgo La Croce, Santa Croce* ☎ *No phone* ⊘ *Closed Sun.*). **Nerbone** (⊠ *Inside the Mercato Centrale, Santa Maria Novella* ☎ *No phone* ⊘ *Closed Sun.*).

Mosca 16/r, at Via de' Neri, Santa Croce ☎ *055/214833* ⊟ *AE, DC, MC, V* ⊘ *Closed Sun.*

$ ✕**Cibrèo Trattoria.** This intimate little trattoria, known to locals as Cibreino, shares its kitchen with the famed Florentine culinary institution that also share's its name. They share the same menu, too, though Cibreino's is much shorter. Start with *il gelatina di pomodoro* (tomato gelatin) liberally laced with basil, garlic, and a pinch of hot pepper, and then sample the justifiably renowned *passato in zucca gialla* (pureed yellow-pepper soup) before moving on to any of the succulent second courses. Save room for dessert, as the pastry chef has a dangerous hand with chocolate tarts. To avoid sometimes agonizingly long waits, come early (7 PM) or late (after 9:30). ⊠ *Via dei Macci 118, Santa Croce* ☎ *055/2341100* ✍ *Reservations not accepted* ⊟ *No credit cards* ⊘ *Closed Sun. and Mon. and July 25–Sept. 5.*

$ ✕**Pallottino.** With its tile floor, photograph-filled walls, and wooden ⟳ tables, Pallottino is the quintessential Tuscan trattoria, with hearty, heartwarming classics such as *pappa al pomodoro* (bread and tomato soup) and *peposa alla toscana* (beef stew laced with black pepper). The menu changes frequently to reflect what's seasonal; the staff is friendly, as are the diners who often share a table and, eventually, conversation. They also do pizza here, as well as great lunch specials. ⊠ *Via Isola delle Stinche 1/r, Santa Croce* ☎ *055/289573* ⊟ *AE, DC, MC, V* ⊘ *Closed Mon. and 2–3 wks in Aug.*

¢–$ ✕**Del Fagioli.** Florentine business types seeking comfort food, Tuscan style, crowd this small place at lunchtime. There's hardly anything on the menu that isn't Tuscan, from the tasty *crostini* starting the meal to the *cantuccini* (local dialect for "biscotti") that finish it. Their ribollita is particularly good. A hearty *salsa verde* (green sauce) accompanies the terrific *bollito misto* (mixed boiled meats)—a particularly soothing dish when it's cold outside. Tuscany dominates the wine list, too. ⊠*Corso Tintori 47/r, Santa Croce* ☎*055/244285* ▭*No credit cards* ☾*Closed weekends.*

¢ ✕**All'Antico Vinaio.** Florentines like to grab a quick bite to eat at this narrow little sandwich shop near the Uffizi. A handful of stools offer a place to perch while devouring one of their very fine sandwiches; most folks, however, simply grab a sandwich, pour themselves a glass of inexpensive wine in a paper cup (more serious wines can be poured into glasses), and mingle on the pedestrians-only street in front. If *porchetta* (a very rich, deliciously fatty roasted pork) is on offer, don't miss it. They also offer first-rate primi, which change daily. ⊠*Via de' Neri 65, Santa Croce* ☎*No phone* ▭*No credit cards* ☾*Closed Sun.*

¢ ✕**Danny Rock.** There's a bit of everything at this restaurant, which is
Ↄ always hopping with Italians eager to eat well-made cheeseburgers and fries or one of the many tasty crepes (served both sweet and savory). You can also find a basic plate of spaghetti as well as a respectable pizza here. Interior decor isn't high on the list: you dine at a green metal table with matching chairs. The young-at-heart feel might explain why the main dining room has a big screen showing *Looney Tunes.* ⊠*Via Pandolfini 13/r, Santa Croce* ☎*055/2340307* ▭*AE, DC, MC, V.*

¢ ✕**da Rocco.** At one of Florence's biggest markets you can grab lunch to go, or you could cram yourself into one of the booths and pour from the straw-cloaked flask (wine here is *da consumo*, which means they charge you for how much you drink). Food is abundant, Tuscan, and fast; locals pack in. The menu changes daily, and the prices are great. ⊠*In Mercato Sant'Ambrogio, Piazza Ghiberti, Santa Croce* ☎*No phone* ⌕*Reservations not accepted* ▭*No credit cards* ☾*Closed Sun. No dinner.*

THE OLTRARNO

$$$ ✕**Beccofino.** Forget that the noise level here often reaches the pitch of the Tower of Babel, and ignore the generic urban decor. Come here for the food: chef Robbie Pepin, who's worked with such heavy hitters as Gordon Ramsey and Alain Ducasse, has breathed life into this very cool place. His cooking, while wholly Italian, has a crisp simplicity reminiscent of Japanese food. He can do just about everything, but shines with fish and shellfish. He takes the Florentine classic gnudi and tops it with prawns, calamari, and fresh tomatoes; it creates a beautiful blend in your mouth. The menu changes frequently, the wine list is divine, and service is exceptional. ⊠ *Piazza Scarlatti 1/r, Lungarno South* ☎ *055/2790076* ⌕ *Reservations essential* ▭ *MC, V* ☾*No lunch.*

$$ ✕**Quattro Leoni.** The eclectic staff at this trattoria in a small piazza is an appropriate match for the diverse menu. In winter you can eat in one of two rooms with high ceilings, and in summer you can sit outside and admire the scenery. Traditional Tuscan favorites, such as *taglierini con porcini* (long, thin, flat pasta with porcini mushrooms), are on the menu, but so, too, are less typical dishes such as the earthy cabbage

salad with avocado, pine nuts, and drops of *olio di tartufo* (truffle oil). Reservations are a good idea. ⊠ *Piazza della Passera, Via dei Vellutini 1/r, Palazzo Pitti* ☎055/218562 ⊟*AE, DC, MC, V* ⊗*No lunch Wed.*

$ ✕**La Casalinga.** *Casalinga* means "housewife," and this place has the nostalgic charm of a 1950s kitchen with Tuscan comfort food to match. If you eat *ribollita* anywhere in Florence, eat it here—it couldn't be more authentic. Mediocre paintings clutter the semipaneled walls, tables are set close together, and the place is usually jammed. The menu is long, portions are plentiful, and service is prompt and friendly. Save room for dessert: the lemon sorbet perfectly caps off the meal. ⊠*Via Michelozzi 9/r, Santo Spirito* ☎055/218624 ⊟*AE, DC, MC, V* ⊗*Closed Sun., 1 wk at Christmas, and 3 wks in Aug.*

$ ✕**Osteria Antica Mescita San Niccolò.** It's always crowded, always good, and always cheap. The osteria is next to the church of San Niccolò, and if you sit in the lower part you'll find yourself in what was once a chapel dating from the 11th century. The subtle but dramatic background is a nice complement to the food, which is simple Tuscan at its best. The *pollo con limone* is tasty pieces of chicken in a lemon-scented broth. In winter try the *spezzatino di cinghiale con aromi* (wild boar stew with herbs). Reservations are advised. ⊠*Via San Niccolò 60/r, San Niccolò* ☎055/2342836 ⊟*AE, MC, V* ⊗*Closed Sun. and Aug.*

¢ ✕**Fuori Porta.** One of the oldest and best wine bars in Florence, this place serves cured meats and cheeses, as well as daily specials such as the sublime spaghetti *al curry. Crostini* and *crostoni*—grilled breads topped with a mélange of cheeses and meats—are the house specialty; the *verdure sott'olio* (vegetables with oil) are divine. All this can be enjoyed at rustic wooden tables, and outdoors when weather allows. One shortcoming is the staff; the members of which are sometimes disinclined to explain the absolutely wonderful wine list. ⊠*Via Monte alle Croci 10/r, San Niccolò* ☎055/2342483 ⊟*AE, MC, V.*

BEYOND THE CITY CENTER

$$$ ✕**Targa.** It looks and feels like California on the Arno at this sleek, airy restaurant a short ride from the city center. Owner-chef Gabriele Tarchiani has spent time in the United States, which shows in the plants that fill the interior as well as the creative touches on the frequently changing menu. Somewhat unusual combinations such as the *fusilli al ragù di anatra e finferli* (fusilli with a minced duck and wild mushroom sauce) provide the perfect prelude for the exquisitely prepared *secondi* that follow. Leave room for dessert—they're culinary masterpieces. No wonder Florentines come here to celebrate special occasions. ⊠*Lungarno Colombo 7, east of city center* ☎055/677377 ⌦*Reservations essential* ⊟*AE, DC, MC, V* ⊗*Closed Sun.*

$$$ ✕**Zibibbo.** Benedetta Vitali, formerly of Florence's famed Cibrèo, has a restaurant of her very own. It's a welcome addition to the sometimes claustrophobic Florentine dining scene—particularly as you have to drive a few minutes out of town to get here. Off a quiet piazza, it has two intimate rooms with rustic, maroon-painted wood floors and a sloped ceiling. The *tagliatelle al sugo d'anatra* (wide pasta ribbons with duck sauce) are aromatic and flavorful, and *crocchette di fave con*

salsa di yogurt (fava bean croquettes with a lively yogurt sauce) are innovative and tasty. ✉ *Via di Terzollina 3/r, northwest of city center* ☎ *055/433383* ⊟ *AE, DC, MC, V* ⊙ *Closed Sun.*

$ ✕ **l'Giuggiolo.** They call themselves an osteria-pizzeria, and certainly many Florentines flock here to indulge in the sinfully rich, thin-crust pizzas turned out by a skilled *pizzaiuolo* (pizza-maker). However, the real thrills come from the fantastic osteria part of the menu. Start with the *bavarese di pomodoro fresco su salsa al basilico* (a chilled tomato concoction spiked with garlic and sauced with basil), sample one of the divine pastas, and then move on to any of the meats, like the *millefoglie di manza con pomodori secchi e parmigiano* (thinly sliced rare roast beef with sun-dried tomatoes and Parmesan). ✉ *Viale Righi 3, northeast of city center* ☎ *055/606240* ✍ *Reservations essential* ⊟ *AE, DC, MC, V.*

CAFÉS

Cafés in Italy serve not only coffee concoctions and pastries but also sweets, drinks, and panini, and some have hot pasta and lunch dishes. They are usually open from early in the morning to late at night and are often closed Sunday.

Caffè Giacosa (✉ *Via della Spada 10/r, Santa Maria Novella* ☎ *055/2776328* ⊕ *www.caffegiacosa.it*) opens early in the morning for coffee, serves tasty light lunches, and makes excellent cocktails in the evening.

Caffè Sant'Ambrogio (✉ *Piazza Sant'Ambrogio 7–8/r, Santa Croce* ☎ *055/2477277*) has outdoor summer seating with a view of an 11th-century church (Sant'Ambrogio) directly across the street.

At night **Capocaccia** (✉ *Lungarno Corsini 12/14r, Lungarno Sud* ☎ *055/210751*) is often a chaotic scene (especially on hot summer nights), but in the daytime it's significantly calmer. Light lunches and a good list of panini are on the menu, and you can nosh at an outdoor table with a view of the Arno. If you're craving Sunday brunch, Capocaccia has that, too.

Gran Caffè (✉ *Piazza San Marco 11/r* ☎ *055/215833*) is down the street from the Accademia, so it's a perfect stop for a marvelous panino or sweet while raving about the majesty of Michelangelo's *David*. Do be aware that sitting at a table is more expensive at most cafes, and this place is particularly notorious in trying to get you to sit down.

⟳ Around the corner from the church of Santa Maria Novella, **i 5 Tavoli** (✉ *Via del Sole 26/r, Santa Maria Novella* ☎ *055/294438*) has only five tables (as its name implies), many fine sandwiches, hot pasta specials, and a very good (and inexpensive) cheeseburger.

i Visacci (✉ *Borgo Albizi 80/r, Santa Croce* ☎ *No phone*), which has great panini and a fine selection of beers on tap (in addition to the ubiquitous wine), is a good place for a light lunch or an aperitivo.

Nannini (⊠ *Borgo San Lorenzo 7/r, San Lorenzo* ☎ *055/212680*) has light lunches and excellent coffee.

Down the street from the church of Santissima Annunziata is **Oliandolo** (⊠ *Via Ricasoli 38–40/r, Santissima Annunziata* ☎ *055/211296*), with an enticing list of panini.

Classy **Procacci** (⊠ *Via Tornabuoni 64/r, Santa Maria Novella* ☎ *055/211656*) is a Florentine institution dating to 1885; try one of the panini tartufati and swish it down with a glass of Prosecco. It's closed Sunday.

Perhaps the best spot for people-watching is **Rivoire** (⊠ *Via Vacchereccia 4/r, Piazza della Signoria* ☎ *055/214412*). Stellar service, light snacks, and terrific aperitivi are the norm. Think twice, however, before ordering more substantial fare; it falls flat.

Rose's (⊠ *Via del Parione 26/r, Santa Maria Novella* ☎ *055/287090*) draws businesspeople at lunch and people with multiple body piercings at night. The Italian lunch menu switches to sushi in the evening.

WINE BARS

Wine bars are found all over Florence, and most of them have light fare as well as lengthy wine lists—perfect places for lunch or dinner. Many are closed on Sunday.

In the heart of the centro storico is **Cantinetta dei Verrazzano** (⊠ *Via dei Tavolini 18/20/r, Piazza della Signoria* ☎ *055/268590*), where serious wines may be had as well as tasty baked treats in the morning and light lunches.

Casa del Vino (⊠ *Via dell'Ariento 16/r, San Lorenzo* ☎ *055/215609*) makes creative *panini,* such as *sgrombri e carciofini sott'olio* (mackerel and marinated baby artichokes), and has an ever-changing list of significant wines by the glass. They also have a well-stocked collection of bottles to go, at more than fair prices.

It's hard to believe that **Coquinarius** (⊠ *Via delle Oche 15/r, Duomo* ☎ *055/2302153*) is as close to the Duomo as it is; the place is serene, sophisticated, and perfect for resting one's soul.

A hop, skip, and a jump from Orsanmichele in the centro storico is **I Fratellini** (⊠ *Via dei Cimatori 38/r, Piazza della Signoria* ☎ *055/2396096*), in existence since 1875. It sells wines by the glass and has a lengthy list of panini, including pecorino with sun-dried tomatoes and spicy wild-boar salami with goat cheese. There are no seats, so perch on the curb and make like a local.

Le Volpi e l'Uva (⊠ *Piazza de' Rossi 1, Palazzo Pitti* ☎ *055/2398132*), off Piazza Santa Trinita, is an oenophile's dream: the waiters pour significant wines by the glass and serve equally impressive cheeses and little sandwiches to go with them.

Olio & Convivium (⊠ *Via Santo Spirito 4, Santo Spirito* ☏*055/2658198*) has a great selection of cheeses and cured meats, wines by the glass, food products to take home (like powdered porcini mushrooms), and daily specials.

At **Pitti Gola** (⊠*Piazza Pitti 16, Palazzo Pitti* ☏*055/212704*), you can order tasty tidbits to accompany your choices from the extensive and impressive wine list. The outdoor seats have a view of Palazzo Pitti.

Semidivino (⊠*Via San Gallo 22/r, San Marco* ☏*055/4620016*) has indoor and outdoor seating, a great list of wines by the glass, light fare at both lunch and dinner, and a charming staff.

FOREIGN FOODS

Eating ethnic in Florence is a hit-or-miss affair. Although numerous Asian restaurants have sprung up since the 1990s, most are nothing to write home about. Still, if you need a break from Italian, some relief is available.

Amon (⊠*Via Palazzuolo 26/28r, Santa Maria Novella* ☏ *No phone*) is a standing-only spot that serves Egyptian and other Middle Eastern fare at rock-bottom prices.

Buddakan (⊠*Largo Bargellini 2, Santa Maria Novella* ☏*055/2346123*) is a pan-Asian experience, offering Thai, Korean, and Chinese dishes. It's popular with young Florentines looking for tasty non-Italian food in a somewhat swank setting.

Dionisio (⊠*Via San Gallo 16/r, San Lorenzo* ☏*055/217882*) draws a mostly student crowd (as it's in the midst of university buildings) enjoying tasty kebabs.

Il Mandarino (⊠*Via Condotta 17/r, Piazza della Signoria* ☏*055/2396130*) has excellent hot-and-sour soup and more-than-passable dumplings. Enjoy them with white linen tablecloths and a bottle of Verdicchio.

If you're craving döner kebab (thin, grilled slices of beef, lamb, or chicken), look no further than **Mavi** (⊠*Via de' Benci 15/r, Santa Croce* ☏*055/2466760*). Portions are copious, and the hot sauce is darn hot.

Tijuana (⊠*Via Ghibellina 156–158/r, Santa Croce* ☏*055/2341330*) is open only at night; it's frequented by young Florentines craving enchiladas and fajitas.

Döner kebabs at **Turkaz** (⊠*Via de'Servi 65/r, Santissima Annunziata* ☏*055/2399959*) have a killer hot sauce; you can order hot rice and meat dishes to eat in or take out. It's generally agreed by aficionados that this is the best kebab in town.

GELATO & PASTRY SHOPS

The convenient **Caffè delle Carrozze** (⊠*Piazza del Pescee 3–5/r, Piazza della Signoria* ☎*055/2396810*) is around the corner from the Uffizi; their gelato (the Italian version of ice cream) is, according to many, the best in the historic center.

The *pasticceria* (bakery) **Dolci e Dolcezze** (⊠*Piazza C. Beccaria 8/r, Sant'Ambrogio* ☎*055/2345458*), on colorful Borgo La Croce, has the prettiest and tastiest cakes, sweets, and tarts in town. It's closed Monday.

Gelaterie Carabe (⊠*Via Ricasoli 60/r, San Marco* ☎*055/289476*) specializes in things Sicilian (including cannoli). Its *granità* (granular flavored ices), made only in the summer, are tart and flavorful—perfect thirst-quenchers.

Florentines with serious sweet tooths come to **I Dolci di Patrizio Corsi** (⊠*Borgo Albizi 15/r, Santa Croce* ☎*055/2480367*), which has a bewildering selection of chocolate- and cream-filled sweets. It's closed on Sunday afternoon.

Grom (⊠*Via del Campanile, Duomo* ☎*055/216158*)is a stone's throw from the Duomo and might be the best gelateria in town. Flavors change frequently according to the season, so expect a fragrant gelato di canella (cinnamon ice cream) in the winter, and lively fresh fruit flavors in the summer.

Vestri (⊠*Borgo Albizi 11/r, Santa Croce* ☎*055/2340374*) is devoted to chocolate in all its guises. The small but sublime selection of chocolate-based gelati includes one with hot peppers.

Most people consider **Vivoli** (⊠*Via Isola delle Stinche 7/r, Santa Croce* ☎*055/292334*) the best gelateria in town, though the cioccolata con caffè is overrated.

PIZZERIAS

Pizzas in Florence can't compete with their counterparts in Rome or Naples, but you can sample a few good approximations.

Baldovino (⊠*Via San Giuseppe 22/r, Santa Croce* ☎*055/241773*) makes pizzas to delight the kids and more sophisticated stuff to satisfy parents.

In the Oltrarno, try **Borgo Antico** (⊠*Piazza Santo Spirito 6/r, Santo Spirito* ☎*055/210437*), which serves pizza and other trattoria fare.

The *pizzaiuoli* (pizza-makers) successfully merge Roman (thin) crust with Neapolitan (thick) crust at **Le Campane** (⊠ *Borgo La Croce 85–87/r, Santa Croce* ☎*055/2341101*).

The **Pizzeria Caffè Italiano** (⊠*Via Isole delle Stinche 11/r, Santa Croce* ☎*055/289368*), a small pizzeria, is favored by locals. Come early to grab one of the few tables, and don't mind the fact that service here is intentionally rushed: turning tables is paramount.

Pugi (⊠ *Piazza San Marco 9/b, San Marco* ☎ *055/280981*), handily across the street from San Marco, sells the popular *pizza a taglio* (pizza by the slice); their *focaccie* and other breads are equally good. It's a great place to grab a quick lunch or snack.

ROSTICCERIE & TAVOLE CALDE

Rosticcerie and *tavole calde* are good alternatives to the more-formal trattorie, osterie, and ristoranti dining options. You can assemble an entire meal at a rosticcerie, which has antipasti, pastas, roasted chicken and other meats, vegetable side dishes, and desserts; sometimes seating is also available. Tavole calde (literally, "hot tables") are sometimes synonymous with rosticcerie, but while a rosticceria almost always has whole roast chickens, that's not always the case with a tavola calda. Both are significantly less expensive than full sit-down service—another part of their appeal.

At **Alfio e Beppe** (⊠ *Via Cavour 118–120/r, San Marco* ☎ *055/214108*), you can watch chickens roast over high flames as you decide which of the other delightful things you're going to eat with it.

The daily specials at **Da Rocco** (⊠ *Piazza Ghiberti, Santa Croce* ☎ *No phone*), in the Mercato Sant'Ambrogio, can include *polpettine alla pizzaiuolo* (veal meatballs in tangy tomato-oregano sauce). Portions are generous. In summer, try the *panzanella*, a salad made with bread crumbs, tomatoes, and basil and doused with extra virgin olive oil.

Near the Uffizi is **Giuliano Centro** (⊠ *Via de' Neri 74/r, Piazza della Signoria* ☎ *055/2382723*), with a mouth-watering assortment of food including crisp *pollo fritto* (fried chicken). If you want to mingle with locals, grab a sandwich and an inexpensive glass of wine at their enoteca directly across the street.

La Ghiotta (⊠ *Via Pietrapiana 7/r, Santa Croce* ☎ *055/241237*) sells whole and half chickens, grilled or roasted, among other things. The baked fennel is also a treat.

Near Santa Maria Novella is **La Spada** (⊠ *Via del Moro 66/r, Santa Maria Novella* ☎ *055/218757*). Walk in and inhale the fragrant aromas of meats cooked in the wood-burning oven. La Spada also has a complete line of takeout.

SALUMERIE

Salumerie, specialty food shops strong on fine fresh ingredients such as meats and cheeses, are great for picking up a picnic lunch or assembling dinner.

Antico Salumificio Anzuini-Massi (⊠ *Via de' Neri 84/r, Santa Croce* ☎ *055/294901*) shrink-wraps their own pork products, making it a snap to take home some *salame di cinghiale* (wild boar salami).

The cheese collection at **Baroni** (⊠*Mercato Central, enter at Via Signa, San Lorenzo* ☎*055/289576*) may be the most comprehensive in Florence.

Conti (⊠*Mercato Centrale, enter at Via Signa, San Lorenzo* ☎*055/2398501*), closed Sunday, sells top-quality wines, olive oils, and dried fruits; they'll shrink-wrap the highest-quality dried porcini for traveling.

'ino (⊠*Via dei Georgofili 3/r–7/r* ☎*055/219208*) sells artisanal products such as olive oil, cheeses from all over Italy, top-notch chocolates, and boutique wines. It's right behind the Uffizi, making it a perfect place to grab a tasty sandwich and glass of wine before forging on to the next museum.

Looking for some cheddar cheese to pile in your panino? **Pegna** (⊠*Via dello Studio 8, Duomo* ☎*055/282701*) has been selling both Italian and non-Italian food since 1860. It's closed Saturday afternoon in July and August, Wednesday afternoon September through June, and Sunday year-round.

Perini (⊠*Mercato Centrale, enter at Via dell'Aretino, San Lorenzo* ☎*055/2398306*), closed Sunday, sells prosciutto, mixed meats, sauces for pasta, and a wide assortment of antipasti. They're generous with their free samples.

WHERE TO STAY

Florence is equipped with hotels for all budgets; for instance, you can find both budget and luxury hotels in the *centro storico* (historic center) and along the Arno. Florence has so many famous landmarks that it's not hard to find lodging with a panoramic vista. The equivalent of the genteel *pensioni* of yesteryear still exist, though they are now officially classified as hotels. Generally small and intimate, they often have a quaint appeal that usually doesn't preclude modern plumbing.

WHAT IT COSTS IN EUROS				
	¢	$	$$	$$$	$$$$
FOR TWO PEOPLE	under €80	€80–€140	€140–€210	€210–€290	over €290

Prices are for a standard double room in high season, including tax and service.

Florence's importance not only as a tourist city but as a convention center and the site of the Pitti fashion collections guarantees a variety of accommodations. The high demand also means that, except in winter, reservations are a must. If you find yourself in Florence with no reservations, go to **Consorzio ITA** (⊠*Stazione Centrale, Santa Maria Novella* ☎*055/282893*). You must go there in person to make a booking.

THE DUOMO TO THE ARNO

$$$$ ⚑**Hotel degli Orafi.** A key scene in *A Room with a View* was shot in this pensione, which is today a luxury hotel adorned with chintz and marble. Many rooms have luscious views of the Arno, and a few have their own terraces. Breakfast is served in opulent surroundings—check out the crystal chandelier and the frescoed ceiling. The affable English-speaking staff members go out of their way to be helpful. **Pros:** Stellar Arno views. **Cons:** Extra charge for Internet use. ✉*Lungarno Archibusieri 4, Piazza della Signoria, 50121* ☎*055/26622* 🖷*055/2662111* ⊕*www.hoteldegliorafi.it* ⟿*42 rooms* ⚿*In-room: safe, refrigerator. In-hotel: concierge, laundry service, public Internet, parking (fee)* ⊟*AE, DC, MC, V* ⓘⓄⓘ*BP.*

$$$$ ⚑**Hotel Helvetia and Bristol.** Painstaking care has gone into making this
★ hotel one of the prettiest and most intimate in town. It has the extra plus of being in the center of the centro storico, making it a luxurious base from which to explore the city. From the cozy yet sophisticated lobby with its stone columns to the guest rooms decorated with prints, you might feel as if you're a guest in a sophisticated manor house. The restaurant serves sumptuous fare in a romantic setting. Pros: Central location, superb staff. Cons: Rooms facing the street get some noise. ✉*Via dei Pescioni 2, Piazza della Repubblica, 50123* ☎*055/26651* 🖷*055/288353* ⊕*www.hbf.royaldemeure.com* ⟿*54 rooms, 13 suites* ⚿*In-room: safe, refrigerator, VCR, Wi-Fi. In-hotel: restaurant, room service, bar, concierge, laundry service, parking (fee), some pets allowed* ⊟*AE, DC, MC, V* ⓘⓄⓘ*EP.*

$$$$ ⚑**Hotel Savoy.** From the outside, it looks very much like the turn-of-the-19th-century building that it is. Inside, sleek minimalism and up-to-the-minute amenities prevail. Sitting rooms have a funky edge, their cream-color walls dotted with contemporary prints. Muted colors dress the rooms, which have streamlined furniture and soaring ceilings; many have views of the Duomo's cupola or the Piazza della Repubblica. The deep marble tubs might be reason enough to stay here—but you'll also appreciate the efficient and courteous staff. **Pros:** Location, trendy clientele (if that's your thing). **Cons:** Smallish rooms, trendy clientele (if that's not your thing). ✉*Piazza della Repubblica 7, 50123* ☎*055/27351* 🖷*055/2735888* ⊕*www.roccofortehotels.com* ⟿*88 rooms, 12 suites* ⚿*In-room: safe, refrigerator, VCR, dial-up, Wi-Fi. In-hotel: restaurant, room service, bar, concierge, children's programs (ages infant–12), laundry service, parking (fee)* ⊟*AE, DC, MC, V* ⓘⓄⓘ*EP.*

$$$ ⚑**Hotel Benivieni.** The tranquil, former 15th-century palace is one block away from the Duomo. Rooms are spacious, with high ceilings, hardwood floors, and sweeping draperies. A winter garden provides a wonderful place to while away some time. The affable Caldana family, wholly fluent in English, ably staffs the front desk. **Pros:** Location. **Cons:** Smallish bathrooms; some Fodor's readers detect street noise, despite triple-glazed windows. ✉*Via delle Oche 5, Duomo, 50122* ☎*055/2382133* 🖷*055/2398248* ⊕*www.hotelbenivieni.it* ⟿*15 rooms* ⚿*In-room: safe, Wi-Fi (some). In-hotel: laundry service, parking (fee), some pets allowed, no-smoking rooms* ⊟*AE, DC, MC, V* ⓘⓄⓘ*BP.*

2

\$\$–\$\$\$ ⬛ **Hermitage.** A stone's throw from the Ponte Vecchio, this is a fine little hotel with an enviable location. All rooms are decorated with lively wallpaper; some have views of Palazzo Vecchio and others of the Arno. The rooftop terrace, where you can have breakfast or an aperitivo, is decked with flowers. The lobby suggests a friend's living room—its warm yellow walls are welcoming. Double glazing and air-conditioning help keep street noise at bay. **Pros:** Views; friendly, English-speaking staff. **Cons:** Short flight of stairs to reach elevator. ✉ *Vicolo Marzio 1, Piazza della Signoria, 50122* ☎ *055/287216* 🖨 *055/212208* 🌐 *www.hermitagehotel.com* 🛏 *27 rooms, 1 suite* ⚴ *In-room: safe. In-hotel: laundry service, public Wi-Fi, parking (fee), some pets allowed* ⊟ *MC, V* ⦿*BP.*

\$\$–\$\$\$
Fodor'sChoice
★ ⬛ **In Piazza della Signoria.** Proprietors Alessandro and Sonia Pini want you to use their house—in this case, part of a 15th-century palazzo—as if it were your own. Such warm sentiments extend to the cozy feeling created in the rooms, all of which are uniquely decorated and lovingly furnished; some have damask curtains, others fanciful frescoes in the bathroom. Pros: Marvelous staff, tasty breakfast with a view of Piazza della Signoria. Cons: Short flight of stairs to reach elevator. ✉ *Via dei Magazzini 2, near Piazza della Signoria 50122* ☎ *055/2399546* 🌐 *www.inpiazzadellasignoria.com* 🛏 *10 rooms, 3 apartments* ⚴ *In-room: safe, kitchen (some), refrigerator (some), Wi-Fi. In hotel: laundry service, public Internet, parking (fee)* ⊟ *AE, DC, MC, V* ⦿*BP.*

\$\$–\$\$\$ ⬛ **Palazzo Niccolini al Duomo.** This 16th-century family palace has been lovingly restored by Ginevra and Filippo Niccolini di Camugliano—the building has been in Filippo's family for more than 100 years. The sumptuous rooms have high ceilings, spacious marble-floored bathrooms (a rarity in restored Renaissance palazzi); some are decorated with sweeping frescoes. A few rooms have views of the Duomo (just down the street); others retain their original Empire furnishings. The Blue Suite accommodates up to four, and comes with its own kitchenette. **Pros:** Steps away from the Duomo. **Cons:** Street noise sometimes a problem. ✉ *Via dei Servi 2, 50122* ☎ *055/282412* 🖨 *055/290979* 🌐 *www.niccolinidomepalace.com* 🛏 *5 rooms, 5 suites* ⚴ *In-room: safe, refrigerator, Wi-Fi. In-hotel: public Internet, Wi-Fi, parking (fee)* ⊟ *AE, DC, MC, V.*

\$ ⬛ **Albergo Firenze.** A block from the Duomo, this hotel is on one of the oldest piazzas in Florence. Though the reception area and hallways have all the charm of a college dormitory, the similarity ends upon entering the spotlessly clean rooms. A good number of triple and quadruple rooms make this a good choice for families. **Pros:** For the location, a great bargain. **Cons:** No-frills public areas. ✉ *Piazza Donati 4, Duomo, 50122* ☎ *055/214203* 🖨 *055/212370* 🌐 *www.hotelfirenze-fi.it* 🛏 *58 rooms* ⚴ *In-hotel: Public Internet (fee), parking (fee)* ⊟ *MC, V* ⦿*BP.*

\$ ⬛ **Cristina.** A friendly and enthusiastic staff runs this tiny hotel one block from the Uffizi and the Bargello. It's a couple of flights up to reach the place, but the price and location make it a bargain. Rooms are large and clean, and have desks and comfortable beds. A few rooms can accommodate up to four. **Pros:** Great deal for families. **Cons:**

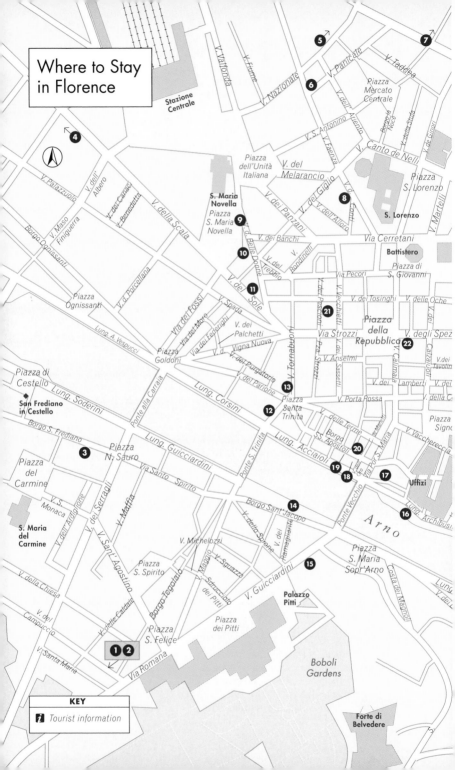

2

Steep flight of stairs, some rooms share bath. ⊠ *Via della Condotta 4, Duomo, 50122* 🖭🖭*055/214484* 🕾*9 rooms, 4 with bath* 🖐*In-room: no a/c, no phone, no TV. In-hotel: no elevator, parking (fee), some pets allowed* ▤*AE, DC, MC, V* 🍽*EP.*

$ 🖻**Sani Tourist House.** Hosts Elizabeth and Remi have taken their former no-frills accommodation and spruced it up a bit, adding such amenities as air-conditioning and the occasional private bath to make a stay here more pleasant. Some rooms have a tremendous view of Orsanmichele or the Casa di Dante. There's no reception area or desk service, but if you're looking for a place to lay your head at a bargain rate, this is a good option. **Pros:** Good deals for single travelers, even lower rates off-season. **Cons:** No reception, shared bath. ⊠*Piazza dei Giuochi 1, Duomo, 50123* 🕾*347/8642573* 🖥*055/2654386* 🌐*www.sanibnb. it* 🕾*6 rooms with shared bath* 🖐*In-room: safe, refrigerator. In-hotel: parking (fee)* ▤*AE, MC, V* 🍽*EP.*

SAN LORENZO & BEYOND

$$–$$$ 🖻**Il Guelfo Bianco.** The 15th-century building has all modern conveniences, but its Renaissance charm still shines. Rooms have high ceilings (some are coffered) and windows are triple-glazed. Contemporary prints and paintings on the walls contrast nicely with classic furnishings. Larger-than-usual single rooms have French-style beds and are a good choice for those traveling alone. Breakfast can be enjoyed in a small outdoor garden when weather permits. Though the hotel is in the centro storico, it still feels somewhat off the beaten path. **Pros:** Stellar multilingual staff. **Cons:** Rooms facing the street can be a little noisy. ⊠ *Via Cavour 29, San Marco, 50129* 🕾*055/288330* 🖥*055/295203* 🌐*www.ilguelfobianco.it* 🕾*40 rooms* 🖐*In-room: safe, refrigerator. In-hotel: concierge, laundry service, public Internet, parking (fee), some pets allowed* ▤*AE, DC, MC, V* 🍽*BP.*

$$–$$$ 🖻**Loggiato dei Serviti.** The Loggiato is tucked away on one of the city's loveliest squares; a mirror image of the architect's famous Spedale degli Innocenti across the way. Occupying a 16th-century former convent, the building was once an inn for traveling priests. Vaulted ceilings, tasteful furnishings (some antique), canopy beds, and rich fabrics make this spare Renaissance building with modern comforts a find. An annex named The Dependance has five rooms of comparable quality. **Pros:** Prime location; helpful, English-speaking staff. **Cons:** Some furnishings show wear; some noise in rooms facing piazza ⊠*Piazza Santissima Annunziata 3, 50122* 🕾*055/289592* 🖥*055/289595* 🌐*www. loggiatodeiservitihotel.it* 🕾*43 rooms* 🖐*In-room: safe, refrigerator, Wi-Fi (some). In-hotel: bar, laundry service, parking (fee), some pets allowed* ▤*AE, DC, MC, V* 🍽*BP.*

$$ 🖻**Bellettini.** You're in good hands at this small hotel run by Gina Naldini and Claudio, her husband. The top floor has two rooms with a view, and all the good-sized guest rooms have Venetian or Tuscan provincial furnishings; bathrooms are bright and modern. Public rooms are simple but comfortable. A handful of triples and quadruples are available. An ample buffet breakfast includes tasty homemade cakes. **Pros:** Excellent

staff. **Cons:** Two rooms have shared bath (but at significantly lower rates). ⊠ *Via dei Conti 7, Santa Maria Novella, 50123* 🕾*055/213561* 🖷*055/283551* ⊕*www.hotelbellettini.com* ⟿*28 rooms, 26 with private bath* ⌂*In-room: safe, refrigerator, ethernet. In-hotel: bar, parking (fee), some pets allowed* ▤*AE, DC, MC, V* ¶◎¶*BP.*

$$ 🏨**Hotel Casci.** In this refurbished 14th-century palace, the home of Giacchino Rossini in 1851–55, the friendly Lombardi family runs a hotel with spotless rooms. Guest rooms are functional, and many of them open out onto various terraces (a view doesn't necessarily follow, however). It's on a very busy thoroughfare, but triple-glazed windows allow for a sound night's sleep. Many rooms easily accommodate an extra bed or two, and there are a number of triples and quads available. **Pros:** Helpful staff, good option for families. **Cons:** Bit of a college-dorm atmosphere; small elevator ⊠ *Via Cavour 13, San Marco, 50129* 🕾*055/211686* 🖷*055/2396461* ⊕*www.hotelcasci.com* ⟿*25 rooms* ⌂*In-room: safe, refrigerator, Wi-Fi. In-hotel: laundry service, public Internet, parking (fee), some pets allowed* ▤*AE, DC, MC, V* ¶◎¶*BP.*

$$ 🏨**Hotel delle Arti.** If Florence had town houses, this would be one: the entrance to the public room downstairs feels as if you're in someone's living room. Pale, pastel walls, polished hardwood floors, and muted fabrics give rooms a simple, elegant look. Breakfast is taken on the top floor, and a small terrace provides city views. The highly capable staff is completely fluent in English. **Pros:** Down the street from the Duomo. **Cons:** Staff goes home at 11. ⊠ *Via dei Servi 38/a, Santissima Annunziata, 50122* 🕾*055/2645307* 🖷*055/290140* ⊕*www.hoteldellearti.it* ⟿*9 rooms* ⌂*In-room: refrigerator. In-hotel: laundry service, some pets allowed (fee)* ▤*AE, DC, MC, V* ¶◎¶*BP.*

$-$$ 🏨 **Firenze.** Each room in the intimate *residenza* is painted a different pastel color—peach, rose, powder-blue. Simple furnishings and double-glazed windows ensure a peaceful night's sleep. You might ask for one of the rooms that has a small private terrace; if you contemplate a longer stay, one of their well-located apartments might suit. Coffee, tea, and fresh fruit, available all day in the sitting room, are on the house. **Pros:** Ample DVD library, honor bar with Antinori wines. **Cons:** Staff goes home at 8, no credit cards accepted. ⊠ *Via San Gallo 72, San Marco, 50129* 🕾*055/4627296* 🖷*055/4634450* ⊕*www.anticadimorafirenze.it* ⟿*6 rooms* ⌂*In-room: safe, refrigerator, dial-up, Wi-Fi* ▤*No credit cards* ¶◎¶*BP.*

$ 🏨**Residenza Johanna I.** Savvy travelers and those on a budget should
★ look no farther, as this *residenza* is a tremendous value for quality and location. Though it's very much in the centro storico, the place is rather homey. You're given a large set of keys to let yourself into the building after 7 PM, when the staff goes home. Simple rooms have high ceilings and pale pastel floral prints. Morning tea and coffee (but no breakfast) are served in your room. **Pros:** Great value. **Cons:** Staff goes home at 7, no credit cards. ⊠ *Via Bonifacio Lupi 14, San Marco, 50129* 🕾*055/481896* 🖷*055/482721* ⊕*www.johanna.it* ⟿*11 rooms* ⌂*In-room: no a/c, no phone, no TV. In-hotel: parking (fee)* ▤*No credit cards* ¶◎¶*EP.*

SANTA MARIA NOVELLA TO THE ARNO

$$$$ ⬚ **Gallery Hotel Art.** High design resides at this art showcase near the Ponte Vecchio. The coolly understated public rooms have a revolving collection of photographs by artists like Helmut Newton adorning the walls; the reception area is subtly but dramatically lit. Rooms are sleek and uncluttered and dressed mostly in neutrals. Luxe touches, such as leather headboards and kimono robes, abound. Both the bar and restaurant attract sophisticated, fashionable locals; brunch happens on the weekends. **Pros:** Cookies in the room, comfortable beds. **Cons:** Sometimes elevator is slow. ✉ *Vicolo dell'Oro 5, Santa Maria Novella, 50123* ☎ *055/27263* 📠 *055/268557* ⊕ *www.lungarnohotels. com* ➽ *65 rooms, 9 suites* ♣*In-room: safe, refrigerator, dial-up, Wi-Fi. In-hotel: restaurant, room service, bar, concierge, laundry service, parking (fee)* ▤ *AE, DC, MC, V* ⏸*BP.*

$$$$ ⬚ **JK Place.** Ori Kafri, the manager of this boutique hotel, refers to it
Fodor's Choice   as a house, and indeed it is a sumptuously appointed home away from
  ★   home. A library serves as the reception room; buffet breakfast is laid out on a gleaming chestnut table in an interior atrium. Soothing earth tones prevail in the rooms, some of which have chandeliers, others canopied beds. A secluded rooftop terrace makes a perfect setting for an aperitivo, as do the ground-floor sitting rooms with large, pillow-piled couches. The place is favored by young fashionistas, their entourages, and other beautiful people. **Pros:** Intimate feel, stellar staff. **Cons:** Breakfast at a shared table. ✉ *Piazza Santa Maria Novella 7, 50123* ☎ *055/2645181* 📠 *055/2658387* ⊕ *www.jkplace.com* ➽ *14 doubles, 6 suites* ♣*In-room: safe, refrigerator, VCR, dial-up, Wi-Fi. In-hotel: bar, concierge, laundry service, parking (fee), some pets allowed* ▤ *AE, DC, MC, V* ⏸*BP.*

$$$ ⬚ **Antica Torre di Via Tornabuoni.** If you're looking for a room with a view, stop here, where just about every one has a window that frames the awe-inspiring Duomo or the Arno (some even have small terraces). When it's warm, you can sit on the rooftop terrace with a glass of wine and enjoy a 360-degree panorama. The tastefully furnished rooms, with their high ceilings and sweeping draperies, create a fine backdrop for historic Florence. This is the perfect place if you desire luxe privacy; since it's a residenza (a residence property), the staff goes home at 7 PM. Charming host Jacopo d'Albasio strives to ensure that all his guests are not only happy, but yearn to come back. **Pros:** Views and terraces. **Cons:** No staff after 7, seemingly ongoing remodeling. ✉ *Via Tornabuoni 1, Santa Maria Novella, 50122* ☎ *055/2658161* 📠 *055/218841* ⊕ *www.tornabuoni1.com* ➽ *11 rooms, 1 suite* ♣*In-room: safe, refrigerator, dial-up, Wi-Fi. In-hotel: bar, parking (fee), some pets allowed* ▤ *AE, DC, MC, V* ⏸*EP.*

$$$ ⬚ **Beacci Tornabuoni.** Florentine pensioni don't get any classier than this.
  ★   It has old-fashioned style and enough modern comfort to keep you happy, and it's in a 14th-century palazzo. The sitting room has a large fireplace, the terrace has a tremendous view of some major Florentine monuments, and the wallpapered rooms are inviting. On Monday, Wednesday, and Friday nights from May through October, the dining room opens, serving Tuscan specialties. **Pros:** Multilingual staff, flower-

filled terrace. **Cons:** Fodor's readers advise to request rooms away from reception area, which can be noisy. ⊠ *Via Tornabuoni 3, Santa Maria Novella, 50123* ☎ *055/212645* 🖷 *055/283594* ⊕ *www.tornabuoni-hotels.com* ⤺ *28 rooms* ⚒ *In-room: refrigerator. In-hotel: restaurant, bar, laundry service, public Internet, parking (fee), some pets allowed* ▭ *AE, DC, MC, V* ⦿ *BP.*

$$ 📷 **Torre Guelfa.** If you want a taste of medieval Florence, try this hotel hidden within a former 13th-century tower. The Torre Guelfa once protected the wealthy Acciaiuoli family; now it's one of the best small hotels in the center of Florence. Each guest room is different, some with canopied beds, some with balconies. Those on a budget might consider one of the six less expensive rooms on the second floor, which are comparable to the rest of the rooms but have no TV. **Pros:** Wonderful staff, some family-friendly triple rooms. **Cons:** Stairs to elevator. ⊠ *Borgo Santi Apostoli 8, Santa Maria Novella, 50123* ☎ *055/2396338* 🖷 *055/2398577* ⊕ *www.hoteltorreguelfa.com* ⤺ *24 rooms, 2 suites* ⚒ *In-room: safe (some), no TV (some). In-hotel: laundry service, public Wi-Fi, parking (fee), some pets allowed* ▭ *AE, MC, V* ⦿ *BP.*

$$ 📷 **Le Vigne.** The small, family-run hotel looks out over one of Florence's most beautiful and central squares. Despite soaring high ceilings, the feeling is comfortable and homey, with rooms furnished in 19th-century Florentine style. Nice touches include complimentary afternoon tea and homemade breakfast jams and cakes. There's also a children's play area. ⊠ *Piazza Santa Maria Novella 24, 50123* ☎ *055/294449* 🖷 *055/2302263* ⊕ *www.florence.ala.it/le_vigne* ⤺ *25 rooms* ⚒ *In-room: safe. In-hotel: bar, laundry service, parking (fee), some pets allowed* ▭ *AE, DC, MC, V* ⦿ *BP.*

$$ 📷 **Villa Azalee.** The 19th-century villa deftly recalls its previous incarnation as a private residence. It's been in the hands of the Brizzi family for more than 100 years, and they understandably take pride in the prettiness of the place. Quilted, floral-print slipcovers dress the furniture; throw rugs pepper the floors. Many rooms have views of the hotel's garden, and some have private terraces. The hotel is five minutes on foot from the train station and steps from the Fortezza da Basso (site of the Pitti fashion shows). **Pros:** Proximity to train station, two garden apartments are wheelchair accessible. **Cons:** Feels a bit out of the way, despite being in city center. ⊠ *Viale Fratelli Rosselli 44, Santa Maria Novella, 50123* ☎ *055/214242* 🖷 *055/268264* ⊕ *www.villa-azalee.it* ⤺ *25 rooms* ⚒ *In-hotel: bar, bicycles, laundry service, public Internet, parking (fee), some pets allowed* ▭ *AE, DC, MC, V* ⦿ *BP.*

$–$$ 📷 **Alessandra.** The location, a block from the Ponte Vecchio, and the clean, ample rooms make this a good choice. The building, known as the Palazzo Roselli del Turco, was designed in 1507 by Baccio d'Agnolo, a contemporary of Michelangelo. Though little remains of the original design save for the high wood ceilings, there's still an aura of grandeur. Friendly hosts Anna and Andrea Gennarini speak fluent English. **Pros:** Several rooms have views of the Arno, the spacious suite is a bargain. **Cons:** Stairs to elevator, some rooms share bath. ⊠ *Borgo Santi Apostoli 17, Santa Maria Novella, 50123* ☎ *055/283438* 🖷 *055/210619* ⊕ *www.hotelalessandra.com* ⤺ *26 rooms, 19 with bath; 1 suite; 1* *apartment* &In-room: safe, refrigerator, dial-up, Wi-Fi. In-hotel: laundry service, parking (fee) ⊟AE, MC, V ⊗Closed Dec. 10–26 ⚏BP.

$ **Pensione Ferretti.** Minutes away from Piazza Santa Maria Novella, this pensione has views onto the tiny piazza containing the Croce al Trebbio, as well as easy access to the historic center. English-speaking owner Roberto Banti and his wife, Sandra, do just about anything to make you feel at home (including providing 24-hour, free Internet access). There's no a/c, but ceiling fans make warmer months more bearable. Though it's housed in a 16th-century palazzo, accommodations are no-frills. **Pros:** Reasonable rates, accommodating owners. **Cons:** One Fodor's reader observes: "more like a hostel than a hotel." ⊠ *Via delle Belle Donne 17, Santa Maria Novella, 50123* ☎*055/2381328* ⧠*055/219288* ⊕ *www.hotelferretti.com* ⤳*16 rooms, 6 with bath; 1 apartment* &In-room: no a/c, no TV. In-hotel: no elevator, public Internet, parking (fee), some pets allowed ⊟AE, DC, MC, V ⚏BP.

¢–$ **Nuova Italia.** The genial English-speaking Viti family runs this hotel near the train station and within walking distance of the sights. Its rooms are clean and simply furnished. Air-conditioning and triple-glazed windows ensure restful nights. Some rooms can accommodate extra beds. **Pros:** Reasonable rates. **Cons:** No elevator. ⊠ *Via Faenza 26, Santa Maria Novella, 50123* ☎*055/268430* ⧠*055/210941* ⊕*www. hotelnuovaitalia.it* ⤳*20 rooms* &In-room: Wi-Fi (some). In-hotel: no elevator, laundry service, public Wi-Fi, parking (fee), some pets allowed ⊟AE, MC, V ⊗Closed Dec. 8–Dec. 26 ⚏BP.

THE OLTRARNO & BEYOND

$$$$ **Lungarno.** Many rooms and suites here have private terraces that jut out right over the Arno, granting stunning views of the Palazzo Vecchio and the Lungarno. Four suites in a 13th-century tower preserve details like exposed stone walls and old archways and look over a little square with a medieval tower covered in jasmine. The very chic interiors approximate breezily elegant homes, with lots of crisp white fabrics with blue trim. A wall of windows and a sea of white couches make the lobby bar one of the most relaxing places in the city to stop for a drink. Inquire about the Lungarno Suites, across the river; they include kitchens, making them attractive if you're planning a longer stay. **Pros:** Upscale without being stuffy. **Cons:** Rooms without Arno views feel less special. ⊠*Borgo San Jacopo 14, Lungarno Sud, 50125* ☎*055/27261* ⧠*055/268437* ⊕*www.lungarnohotels.com* ⤳*60 rooms, 13 suites* &In-room: dial-up, Wi-Fi. In-hotel: restaurant, bar, concierge, laundry service, parking (fee) ⊟AE, DC, MC, V ⚏BP.

$$$$ **Palazzo Magnani Feroni.** The perfect place to play the part of a Florentine aristocrat is here at this 16th-century palazzo, which despite its massive halls and sweeping staircase could almost feel like home. Suites include large sitting rooms and bedrooms, all decorated with luxurious fabrics, chandeliers, and Renaissance-inspired furniture. The rooftop terrace, complete with bar, has citywide views that startle. Though it's only a five-minute walk from the Ponte Vecchio, the street is surprisingly quiet. **Pros:** 24-hour room service. **Cons:** A few steps up to the elevator. ⊠ *Borgo San Frediano 5, Santo Spirito, 50124* ☎ *055/2399544* 🖷 *055/2608908* ⊕ *www.palazzomagnani.feroni* ⇄ *11 suites* &In-room: safe, refrigerator, dial-up, Wi-Fi. In-hotel: room service, bar, laundry service, parking (fee)* ⊟ *AE, DC, MC, V* ¶⚏*BP.*

$$$$ 🏨 **Villa La Vedetta.** A private-villa–turned–luxury hotel perches on the hills of the Arno's south bank, providing phenomenal views. Cool black, gray, and red tones complement Baccarat chandeliers and 19th-century consoles in public rooms. Carefully coordinated color schemes prevail in both the sleeping areas and the bathrooms. The stellar staff is fluent in English and is virtually equal in number to the guests. The Onice Restaurant has an inventive Italian menu with a fine wine list and tip-top wait staff. **Pros:** Luxe experience removed from the city center. **Cons:** It's a taxi ride to the sights. ⊠ *Viale Michelangelo 78, 50125* ☎ *055/681631* 🖷 *055/6582544* ⊕ *www.villalavedettahotel.com* ⇄ *10 rooms, 8 suites* &In-room: safe, refrigerator, Wi-Fi. In-hotel: restaurant, room service, bars, pool, laundry service, parking (no fee), some pets allowed, no-smoking rooms* ⊟ *AE, DC, MC, V.*

$$ 🏨 **Albergo La Scaletta.** For a tremendous view of the Boboli Garden's, look no farther than this exquisite pensione near the Ponte Vecchio and Palazzo Pitti. Simply furnished yet rather large rooms and a sunny breakfast room make this place cozy. In warm weather two flower-bedecked terraces are open; one has a stunning 360-degree view of Florence, and provides a perfect spot to sip a glass of wine. If you give advance notice, hotel staff will arrange for a light dinner to be served there, too. **Pros:** The terrace. **Cons:** Small elevator, many steps ⊠ *Via Guicciardini 13, Palazzo Pitti, 50125* ☎ *055/283028* 🖷 *055/289562* ⊕ *www.lascaletta.com* ⇄ *13 rooms* &In-hotel: parking (fee), some pets allowed* ⊟ *MC, V* ¶⚏*BP.*

$$ 🏨 **Annalena.** The story goes that Annalena, a 15th-century maiden, married a Medici; another man, smitten with her and angry at her refusal to capitulate, murdered her husband and her young son. The devastated widow then turned her private home into a convent. Is it true? Well, it certainly is romantic, as is the former convent, now pensione, that bears her name. With its high ceilings and spacious rooms, it's a perfect place to unwind. Some rooms overlook a private garden, and one has a private terrace; there are also a handful of triples and quads available. **Pros:** The triples and quads are great for families. **Cons:** A hefty flight of stairs to get to reception. ⊠ *Via Romana 34, Santo Spirito/San Frediano, 50125* ☎ *055/222402* 🖷 *055/222403* ⊕ *www.hotelannalena. it* ⇄ *20 rooms* &In-room: refrigerator. In-hotel: no elevator, laundry service, parking (fee), some pets allowed* ⊟ *AE, MC, V* ¶⚏*BP.*

$$ 🏨 **Hotel Silla.** The entrance to this slightly off-the-beaten-path hotel is through a 15th-century courtyard lined with potted plants and sculpture-filled niches. The hotel, formerly a palazzo dating from the 15th century, is up a flight of stairs and has two floors. Rooms are simply furnished and walls are papered; some have views of Via de' Renai and the Arno, while others overlook a less-traveled road. Breakfast may be taken in a room that preserves an Empire feel (including two chandeliers from the early 19th century); when it's warm, a large, sunny terrace is the perfect place to read or to write that postcard.

Pros: A Fodor's reader raves, "It's in the middle of everything except the crowds." **Cons:** Some readers complain of street noise and too-small rooms. ⊠ *Via de' Renai 5, San Niccolò, 50125* ☎*055/2342888* ☏*055/2341437* ⊕*www.hotelsilla.it* ➦*35 rooms* ⚿*In-room: safe, refrigerator, Wi-Fi In-hotel: bar, concierge, laundry service, parking (fee), some pets allowed* ⊟*AE, DC, MC, V* ¶⊚|*BP.*

SANTA CROCE

$$$$ ⛆**Hotel Regency.** The noise and crowds of Florence seem far from this stylish hotel in a residential district near the Sinagoga, though you're not more than 10 minutes from the Accademia and Michelangelo's *David.* Across the street is Piazza d'Azeglio, a small public park that somehow evokes 19th-century middle Europe. Rooms dressed in richly colored fabrics and antique-style furniture remain faithful to the hotel's 19th-century origins as a private mansion. The restaurant here is equally sophisticated. **Pros:** Faces one of the few green parks in the center of Florence. **Cons:** A small flight of stairs takes you to reception. ⊠*Piazza d'Azeglio 3, Santa Croce, 50121* ☎*055/245247* ☏*055/2346735* ⊕*www.regency-hotel.com* ➦*30 rooms, 4 suites* ⚿*In-room: safe, refrigerator, Wi-Fi. In-hotel: restaurant, room service, bar, concierge, laundry service, parking (fee), some pets allowed, no-smoking rooms,* ⊟*AE, DC, MC, V* ¶⊚|*BP.*

$$$$ ⛆**Monna Lisa.** Housed in a 15th-century palazzo, with parts of the
★ building dating from the 13th century, this hotel retains some of its original wood-coffered ceilings from the 1500s, as well as its original marble staircase. Though some rooms are small, they are tasteful, and each is done in different floral wallpaper. The public rooms retain a 19th-century aura, and the intimate bar, with its red velveteen wallpaper, is a good place to unwind. **Pros:** Annex is wheelchair accessible. **Cons:** Rooms in annex are much less charming than those in palazzo. ⊠*Borgo Pinti 27, Santa Croce, 50121* ☎*055/2479751* ☏*055/2479755* ⊕*www.monnalisa.it* ➦*45 rooms* ⚿*In-room: safe, refrigerator. In-hotel: bar, concierge, laundry service, parking (fee), some pets allowed* ⊟*AE, DC, MC, V* ¶⊚|*BP.*

$$$–$$$$ ⛆**J&J.** On a quiet street within walking distance of the sights sits this unusual hotel, a converted 16th-century convent. The large, suite-like rooms are ideal for honeymooners, families, and small groups of friends; some are on two levels, and many are arranged around a central courtyard. Pale travertine tiles used to refit some bathrooms provide a pleasing, ultramodern contrast to more traditional furnishings. Smaller rooms are more intimate, and some open onto a little shared courtyard. The gracious owners enjoy chatting in the light and airy lounge; breakfast is served in a glassed-in Renaissance loggia or in the central courtyard. **Pros:** Large rooms. **Cons:** One flight of steep stairs to get to rooms. ⊠*Via di Mezzo 20, Santa Croce, 50121* ☎*055/26312* ☏*055/240282* ⊕*www.cavalierehotels.com* ➦*19 rooms, 7 suites* ⚿*In-room: dial-up. In-hotel: bar, no elevator, laundry service, public Wi-Fi, parking (fee)* ⊟*AE, DC, MC, V* ¶⊚|*BP.*

$$-$$$ ⛄**Hotel Villa Liana.** With this hotel, it's possible to experience palazzo life without breaking the bank. Steps from the *viali* (the outer limit defining the centro storico) but still very much within the bounds of the historic center, the Liana, originally a 19th-century villa, retains the feel of another era. The lobby has high ceilings and large windows; a sweeping staircase leads to the breakfast room, which has a period fresco on its ceiling. A small bar offers the makings of an aperitivo; sip it in the gazebo in the garden. **Pros:** Good for kids—playground around the corner. **Cons:** Rooms facing street are noisy. ⌂ *Via V. Alfieri 18, Santa Croce, 50121* ☎*055/245303 or 055/245304* 🖨*055/2344596* ⊕*www.hotelliana.com* 🔑*24 rooms* ⌂*In-room: safe, refrigerator, dial-up. In-hotel: bar, laundry service, public Internet, parking (fee), some pets allowed* ▤*AE, DC, MC, V* ⦿*BP.*

$$-$$$ ⛄**Morandi alla Crocetta.** You're made to feel like privileged friends of
★   the family at this charming and distinguished residence near Piazza Santissima Annunziata. The former convent is close to the sights but very quiet, and it's furnished comfortably in the classic style of a gracious Florentine home. One room retains original 17th-century fresco fragments, and two others have small private terraces. The Morandi is not only an exceptional hotel but also a good value. It's very small, so book well in advance. **Pros:** Interesting, offbeat location; terrific staff. **Cons:** Extra charge for breakfast, two flights of stairs to reach reception and rooms. ⌂ *Via Laura 50, Santissima Annunziata, 50121* ☎*055/2344747* 🖨*055/2480954* ⊕*www.hotelmorandi.it* 🔑*10 rooms* ⌂*In-room: safe, refrigerator, dial-up, Wi-Fi. In-hotel: no elevator, concierge, laundry service, parking (fee), some pets allowed, minibar* ▤*AE, DC, MC, V* ⦿*EP.*

¢   ⛄**Albergo Losanna.** Most major sights are within walking distance of this tiny pensione steps away from the *viali*, the edge of the city center. Though dated and a little worn around the edges, the property is impeccably clean and the rooms have high ceilings; the mother and son who run the place are enthusiastic and cordial. Try to get a room facing away from the street; though there aren't any views, you won't hear as much street noise. **Pros:** Bargain price. **Cons:** On a noisy street. ⌂ *Via V. Alfieri 9, Santa Croce, 50121* ☎*055/245840* ⊕*www.albergolosanna.com* 🔑*8 rooms, 3 with bath* ⌂*In-room: no a/c (some), no TV. In-hotel: parking (fee)* ▤*AE, MC, V* ⦿*BP.*

¢   ⛄**Istituto Oblate dell'Assunzione.** Twelve nuns run this convent, which is minutes from the Duomo. Rooms are spotlessly clean and simple; some of them have views of the cupola, and others look out onto a carefully tended garden where you are welcome to relax. Several rooms have three and four beds, making them well suited for families. Curfew is at 11:30 PM. You can join Mass every morning at 7:30. For an additional three euros, you can get a simple continental breakfast, and the nuns provide half or full pension for groups of 10 or more. None of the nuns speaks English, and they don't have a Web presence, so unless you speak Italian, the best way to book is by fax. **Pros:** Bargain price. **Cons:** Curfew, no credit cards. ⌂ *Borgo Pinti 15, Santa Croce, 50121* ☎*055/2480582* 🖨*055/2346291* 🔑*28 rooms, 22 with bath*

⚿In-room: no a/c (some), no phone, no TV. In-hotel: parking (fee) ⊟No credit cards ⏏EP.

OUTSIDE THE CITY

$$$$ ⬚**Villa La Massa.** You approach the tall and imposing villa, 15 minutes out of town, via a gravel drive lined with flowers. The public rooms are outfitted in Renaissance style, with a color scheme of deep green, gold, and crimson. Guest rooms have high ceilings, some with frescoes; plush carpeting; and deep bathtubs. A pool and beautiful views of the Arno are bonuses. The restaurant is superb and serves Tuscan classics as well as less typical fare; a pianist quietly plays old standards while you eat. A shuttle bus runs every hour to and from the center of Florence. **Pros:** Pleasing mix of city and country life. **Cons:** Even with shuttle, a car is a necessity; rooms are grander, but more expensive, in the main villa than in the two other buildings, the Vecchio Mullino and Villino. ⊠*Via della Massa 24, Candeli 50012* ☎*055/62611* ⎙*055/633102* ⊕*www. villalamassa.com* ⇆*19 rooms, 18 suites* ⚿*In-room: safe, refrigerator, dial-up. In-hotel: restaurant, bar, pool, concierge, laundry service, public Internet, parking (fee), some pets allowed* ⊟*AE, DC, MC, V* ⊗*Closed Dec.–Mar.* ⏏*BP.*

$$–$$$$ ⬚**Relais Villa l'Olmo.** Alberto and Claudia Giannotti have turned a former 16th-century country villa into an elegantly comfortable agriturismo 20 minutes south from the center of Florence. If you're looking for a country experience but crave easy access to the city, this place outside the small town of Impruneta does the trick. Many of the apartments look out over a gently terraced field of olive trees. (The estate produces top-notch olive oil, as well as some respectable wine.) The cheerful apartments are suitable for couples; some are adjoining. Unlike many agriturismi, there's no minimum stay during high season here. **Pros:** Good for families and groups. **Cons:** You need a car. ⊠*Via Impruneta 19, Impruneta 50023* ☎*055/2311311* ⎙*055/2311313* ⊕*www.relaisfarmholiday.it* ⇆*8 apartments, 2 cottages, 1 farmhouse* ⚿*In-room: safe, kitchen, refrigerator. In-hotel: pools, bicycles, laundry facilities, laundry service, parking (no fee), some pets allowed, public Internet, no elevator* ⊟*AE, DC, MC, V* ⏏🍽 🚲🐾.

$$$ ⬚**Torre di Bellosguardo.** *Bellosguardo* means "beautiful view"; given the view of Florence you get here, the name is fitting. The hotel, perched atop a hill minutes from the *viale*, is reached via a narrow road dotted with olive trees. Dante's friend Guido Calvacanti supposedly chose this serene spot for his country villa, but little remains from the early 14th century. The reception area, a former ballroom, has soaring ceilings with frescoes by Francavilla (1553–1615). Guest rooms, all with high ceilings, are simple and have heavy wooden furniture. **Pros:** Great for escaping heat of the city in summer. **Cons:** A car is a necessity. ⊠*Via Roti Michelozzi 2, 50124* ☎*055/2298145* ⎙*055/229008* ⊕*www.torrebellosguardo.com* ⇆*9 rooms, 7 suites* ⚿*In-room: no a/c (some), refrigerator, no TV, dial-up. In-hotel: bar, pool, concierge, laundry service, parking (no fee), some pets allowed* ⊟*AE, MC, V.*

$$–$$$ ⌂**Villa Poggio San Felice.** Livia Puccinelli Sannini, the descendant of a
★   famed 19th-century Florentine hotelier, and her husband have turned
her family's former country villa (documented in the 15th century)
into a serene hotel outside the city limits. It retains the intimate feel of
a single-family home with only five high-ceilinged rooms; some have
divine views of Brunelleschi's cupola down below, and others have
working fireplaces. Simple landscaped gardens are peaceful. Though a
daily shuttle service runs to the center of town. **Pros:** Affordable villa
experience, pool is a great advantage in summer. **Cons:** You need a car.
⊠ *Via San Matteo in Arcetri 24, 50125* ☎*055/220016* 🖷*055/2335388*
⊕*www.villapoggiosanfelice.com* ⇆*4 rooms, 1 suite* ♿*In-hotel: pool,
no elevator, laundry service, public Internet, parking (no fee), some pets
allowed* ⊟*AE, MC, V* ☾*Closed Jan. 10–Feb. 28* ⦿*BP.*

NIGHTLIFE & THE ARTS

THE ARTS

Florence has a lively classical music scene. The internationally famous,
annual Maggio Musicale lights up the musical calendar in early summer.
Fans of rock, pop, and hip-hop might be somewhat surprised by the lack
of live acts that make it to town (for such offerings, travel to Rome or
Milan is often a necessity). What it lacks in contemporary music, however, is more than made up for with its many theatrical offerings.

FESTIVALS & SPECIAL EVENTS

Teatro Saschall (⊠*Lungarno Aldo Moro 3* ☎*055/6503068*), a large
exhibition space, is the venue for many events throughout the year,
including a large Christmas bazaar run by the Red Cross and rock
concerts. Around St. Patrick's Day (March 17), Teatro Saschall hosts
the weeklong **Irlanda in Festa** *(Ireland Festival)*, with "seminars" on Irish
beer as well as lots of Irish music.

On **Holy Thursday** at the Duomo, a centuries-old ritual is reenacted
with members of the Compagnia della Misericordia, a lay association
that during the Renaissance comforted those condemned to death and
provided dowries for poor girls as well as other services for its members. (Today the confraternity runs an efficient ambulance service.)
A solemn procession of priests and confraternity members wends its
way into the Duomo, and then the priests wash the feet of the confraternity members.

On Easter Sunday, Florentines and foreigners alike flock to the Piazza
del Duomo to watch the **Scoppio del Carro** *(Explosion of the Cart)*: a
monstrosity of a carriage, pulled by two huge oxen decorated for the
occasion, makes its way through the city center and ends up in the
piazza. Through an elaborate wiring system, an object representing
a "dove" is sent from inside the church to the Baptistery across the
way. The dove sets off an explosion of fireworks that come streaming
from the carriage. You have to see it to believe it. If you don't like

crowds, don't worry: video replays figure prominently on the nightly newscasts afterward.

On June 24 Florence grinds to a halt to celebrate the **Festa di San Giovanni** *(Feast of St. John the Baptist)* in honor of its patron saint. Many shops and bars close, and at night a fireworks display along the Arno attracts thousands.

FILM

The daily Florentine newspaper *La Nazione* (⊕*www.lanazione.it*) has movie listings. Note that most American films are dubbed into Italian rather than subtitled. **Festival dei Popoli** (⊠*Borgo Pinti 82/r, Santa Croce* ☎*055/244778* ⊕*www.festivaldeipopoli.org*) is a weeklong documentary film festival that usually happens in November or December with screenings at various venues around town.

The **Odeon** (⊠*Piazza Strozzi, Piazza della Repubblica* ☎*055/214068* ⊕*www.cinehall.it*) shows first-run English-language films on Monday, Tuesday, and Thursday at its magnificent art-deco theater. The **British Institute of Florence** (⊠*Palazzo Lanfredini, Lungarno Guicciardini 9, Lungarno Sud* ☎*055/26778270* ⊕*www.britishinstitute. it*) runs several English-language film series; they have a bent toward classic movies.

MUSIC

The **Accademia Bartolomeo Cristofori** (⊠*Via di Camaldoli 7/r, Santo Spirito/San Frediano* ☎*055/221646* ⊕*www.accademiacristofori.it*), also known as the Amici del Fortepiano (Friends of the Fortepiano), sponsors fortepiano concerts throughout the year. **Amici della Musica** (⊕*www.amicimusica.fi.it*) organizes concerts at the **Teatro della Pergola** (Box office ⊠*Via Alamanni 39, Santissima Annunziata* ☎*055/210804* ⊕*www.pergola.firenze.it*).

The **Maggio Musicale Fiorentino** (⊠*Via Alamanni 39* ☎*055/210804*), a series of internationally acclaimed concerts and recitals, is held in the **Teatro Comunale** (⊠*Corso Italia 16, Lungarno North* ☎*055/211158* ⊕*www.maggiofiorentino.com*). Within Italy, you can purchase tickets from late April through July directly at the box office or by phone at ☎*800/112211*. You can also buy them online. Other events—opera, ballet, and additional concerts—occur regularly throughout the year at different venues in town.

The **Orchestra da Camera Fiorentina** (⊠*Via E. Poggi 6, Piazza della Signoria* ☎*055/783374*) performs various concerts of classical music throughout the year at Orsanmichele, the grain market–turned–church.

The concert season of the **Orchestra della Toscana** (⊠*Via Ghibellina 101, Santa Croce* ☎*055/2340710*) runs from November to June. You can hear organ music in the baroque church of **Santa Margherita in Maria de' Ricci** (⊠*Via il Corso, Piazza della Signoria* ☎*055/215044*). Free concerts begin every night at 9:15, except Monday.

Visiting rock stars, trendy bands from Germany, and some American groups play at **Tenax** (⊠*Via Pratese 46* ⊕*www.tenax.org*).

THEATER

Theater lovers might want to try an evening at **Teatro della Pergola** (✉ *Via della Pergola 12/r, Santissima Annunziata* ☎*055/2264353* ⊕*www.pergola.firenze.it*). The season runs from mid-October to mid-April. If the idea of hearing a play in Italian is too forbidding, visit the lovely theater. Built in 1656 by Ferdinando Tacca, and once the private theater of the grand dukes, it was opened to the public in 1755. The theater has undergone several metamorphoses; its present incarnation dates to 1828, and the atrium was constructed nine years later.

NIGHTLIFE

Florentines are rather proud of their nightlife options. Most bars now have some sort of happy hour, which usually lasts for many hours and often has snacks that can substitute for a light dinner. (Check, though, that the buffet is free or comes with the price of a drink.) Clubs typically don't open until very late in the evening and don't get crowded until 1 or 2 in the morning. Though the cover charges can be steep, finding free passes around town is fairly easy.

BARS

Capocaccia (✉*Lungarno Corsini 12/14r, Lungarno Sud* ☎*055/210751*) makes great Bloody Marys, and it's the place to be at cocktail time. At night young Florentines crowd the doors and spill out into the street. **Colle Bereto** (✉*Piazza Strozzi 4–6/r, Piazza della Repubblica* ☎*055/283156*) draws in young Florentines and savvy tourists who like well-made cocktails and the huge spread that accompanies them. One of the hottest spots in town is the bar at the Gallery Art Hotel, **Fusion Bar** (✉*Vicolo dell'Oro 5, Santa Maria Novella* ☎*055/27263*). For a swanky experience, lubricated with trademark Bellinis and the best martinis in Florence, head to **Harry's Bar** (✉*Lungarno Vespucci 22/r, Lungarno North* ☎*055/2396700*). The oh-so-cool vibe at **La Dolce Vita** (✉*Piazza del Carmine 6/r, Santo Spirito* ☎*055/284595* ⊕*www.dolcevitaflorence.com*) attracts Florentines and the occasional visiting American movie star. **Negroni** (✉*Via de' Renai 17/r, San Niccolò* ☎*055/243647* ⊕*www.negronibar.com*) teems with well-dressed young Florentines at happy hour. **Rex** (✉*Via Fiesolana 23–25/r, Santa Croce* ☎*055/2480331*) attracts a trendy, artsy clientele. **Zoe** (✉*Via de' Renai1 3/r, San Niccolò* ☎*055/243111*) calls itself a "caffetteria," and while coffee may indeed be served, elegant youngish Florentines flock here for the fine cocktails. Here's people-watching at its very best, done while listening to the latest CDs imported from England. **Zona 15** (✉*Via del Castellaccia 53–55/r [Piazza Brunelleschi], Duomo* ☎*055/211678*) is coolly chic with its pale interior, blond woodwork, and metallic surfaces. Lunch, dinner, cocktails, and live music draw Florentine cognoscenti and others.

NIGHTCLUBS

BeBop (✉*Via dei Servi 76/r, Santissima Annunziata* ☎*No phone*) has loud, live music, Beatles nights, and teems with American kids enjoying their junior year abroad programs. **Central Park** (✉*Via Fosso*

Macinante 2 ☎*055/353505*) is a great spot for those who want to put on their dancing shoes for some house and hip-hop music. **Jazz Club** (✉ *Via Nuova de' Caccini 3, corner of Borgo Pinti, Santa Croce* ☎*055/2479700*) puts on live music in a small basement. When last call's come and gone, go where the bartenders unwind after their shift: **Loch Ness** (✉ *Via de' Benci 19/r, Santa Croce* ☎*No phone*) keeps the drinks flowing until 5 AM.

Maracaná (✉ *Via Faenza 4, Santa Maria Novella* ☎.*055/210298*) is a restaurant and pizzeria featuring Brazilian specialties; at 11 PM it transforms itself into a cabaret floor show, and then into a disco until 4 AM. Book a table if you want to eat. **Meccanò** (✉ *Le Cascine, Viale degli Olmi 1* ☎.*055/331371*) is a multimedia experience in a high-tech disco with a late-night restaurant. People sip cocktails against a backdrop of exotic flowers, leopard-print chairs and chintz, and red walls and floors on the two crowded floors at **Montecarla** (✉ *Via de' Bardi 2, San Niccolò* ☎*055/2340259*). **Space Electronic** (✉ *Via Palazzuolo 37, Santa Maria Novella* ☎*055/293082*) has two floors, with karaoke downstairs and an enormous disco upstairs. **Yab** (✉ *Via Sassetti 5/r, Piazza della Repubblica* ☎*055/215160*) celebrated its 25th anniversary in 2004; it never seems to go out of style, though it increasingly becomes the haunt of Florentine high schoolers and university students intent on dancing and doing vodka shots.

SHOPPING

Window-shopping in Florence is like visiting an enormous contemporary-art gallery. Many of today's greatest Italian artists are fashion designers, and most keep shops in Florence. Discerning shoppers may find bargains in the street markets. ⚠**Do not buy any knockoff goods from any of the hawkers plying their fake Prada (or any other high-end designer) on the streets.** It's illegal, and fines are astronomical if the police happen to catch you. (You pay the fine, not the vendor.)

Shops are generally open 9 to 1 and 3:30 to 7:30 and are closed Sunday and Monday mornings most of the year. Summer (June to September) hours are usually 9 to 1 and 4 to 8, and some shops close Saturday afternoon instead of Monday morning. When looking for addresses, you'll see two color-coded numbering systems on each street. The red numbers are commercial addresses and are indicated, for example, as 31/r. The blue or black numbers are residential addresses. Most shops take major credit cards and ship purchases, but because of possible delays it's wise to take your purchases with you.

MARKETS

Le Cascine's open-air market is held every Tuesday morning. Food, bargain clothing, and gadgets are sold. The **Mercato Centrale** (✉ *Piazza del Mercato Centrale, San Lorenzo*) is a huge indoor food market with a staggering selection of things edible. The clothing and leather-goods stalls of the **Mercato di San Lorenzo** in the streets next to the church of

The bounty at Florence's Mercato Centrale.

San Lorenzo have bargains for shoppers on a budget. It's possible to strike gold at the **Mercato di Sant'Ambrogio** (⊠*Piazza Ghiberti, off Via dei Macci, Santa Croce*), where clothing stalls abut the fruit and vegetables. Every Thursday morning from September through June, the covered loggia in Piazza della Repubblica hosts a **Mercato dei Fiori** (*flower market* ⊠*Piazza della Repubblica*); it's awash in a lively riot of plants and flowers. If you're looking for cheery, inexpensive trinkets to take home, you might want to stop and roam through the stalls under the loggia of the **Mercato del Porcellino** (⊠ *Via Por Santa Maria at Via Porta Rossa, Piazza della Repubblica*). You can find bargains at the **Piazza dei Ciompi flea market** (⊠*Sant'Ambrogio, Santa Croce*) Monday through Saturday and on the last Sunday of the month. The second Sunday of every month brings the **Spirito flea market.** On the third Sunday of the month, vendors at the Fierucola organic fest sell such delectables as honeys, jams, spice mixes, and fresh vegetables.

SHOPPING DISTRICTS

Florence's most fashionable shops are concentrated in the center of town. The fanciest designer shops are mainly on **Via Tornabuoni** and **Via della Vigna Nuova.** The city's largest concentrations of antiques shops are on **Borgo Ognissanti** and the Oltrarno's **Via Maggio.** The **Ponte Vecchio** houses reputable but very expensive jewelry shops, as it has since the 16th century. The area near **Santa Croce** is the heart of the leather merchants' district.

SPECIALTY STORES

ANTIQUES

Galleria Luigi Bellini (✉ *Lungarno Soderini 5, Lungarno Sud* ☎ *055/214031*) claims to be Italy's oldest antiques dealer, which may be true, since Father Mario Bellini was responsible for instituting Florence's international antiques biennial. **Giovanni Pratesi** (✉ *Via Maggio 13, Santo Spirito* ☎ *055/2396568*) specializes in Italian antiques; in this case, it's furniture, with some fine paintings, sculpture, and decorative objects turning up from time to time. Vying with Galleria Luigi Bellini as one of Florence's oldest antiques dealers, **Guido Bartolozzi** (✉ *Via Maggio 18/r, Santo Spirito* ☎ *055/215602*) deals predominately in period Florentine pieces. At **Paolo Paoletti** (✉ *Via Maggio 30/r, Palazzo Pitti* ☎ *055/214728*), look for Florentine antiques with an emphasis on Medici-era objects from the 15th and 16th centuries.

BOOKS & PAPER

Alberto Cozzi (✉ *Via del Parione 35/r, Santa Maria Novella* ☎ *055/294968*) keeps an extensive line of Florentine papers and paper products. The artisans in the shop rebind and restore books and works on paper. **Alice's Masks Art Studio** (✉ *Via Faenza 72/r, Santa Maria Novella* ☎ *055/287370*) preserves the centuries-old technique of papier-mâché masks. On hand are masks typical of 18th-century Venice, as well as some more whimsical ones: a mask of Vincent van Gogh is painted with brushstrokes reminiscent of his own inimitable style. One of Florence's oldest paper-goods stores, **Giulio Giannini e Figlio** (✉ *Piazza Pitti 37/r* ☎ *055/212621*) is *the* place to buy the marbleized stock, which comes in many shapes and sizes, from flat sheets to boxes and even pencils. Photograph albums, frames, diaries, and other objects

★ dressed in handmade paper can be purchased at **Il Torchio** (✉ *Via dei Bardi 17, San Niccolò* ☎ *055/2342862*). The stuff is high-quality, and the prices lower than usual. **La Tartaruga** (✉ *Borgo Albizzi 60/r, Santa Croce* ☎ *055/2340845*) sells brightly colored, recycled paper in lots of guises (such as calendars and stationery), as well as toys for children. **Libreria d'Arte Galleria Uffizi** (✉ *Piazzale degli Uffizi 6, near Palazzo Vecchio* ☎ *055/284508*) carries monographs on famous artists, some of whose work can be found in the Uffizi; it also carries scholarly works in both Italian and English.

Long one of Florence's best art-book shops, **Libreria Salimbeni** (✉ *Via Matteo Palmieri 14–16/r, Santa Croce* ☎ *055/2340905*) has an outstanding selection. **Pineider** (✉ *Piazza della Signoria 13/r, Piazza della Signoria* ☎ *055/284655*) has shops throughout the world, but the business began in Florence and still does all its printing here. Stationery and business cards are the mainstay, but the stores also sell fine leather desk accessories as well as a less stuffy, more lighthearted line of products.

CLOTHING

The usual fashion suspects—Prada, Gucci, Versace, to name but a few—all have shops in Florence.

The sleek, classic boutique **Giorgio Armani** (✉ *Via Tornabuoni 48/r, Santa Maria Novella* ☎ *055/219041*) is a centerpiece of the dazzling high-

FODOR'S FIRST PERSON

First Person Name
First Person Occupation

Since 1970, Valentino Adami, a native of southern Tuscany who has lived all over the world, and his wife, Antonella Chini, a Florentine, have been owners of the ceramics shop Sbigoli Terrecotte. The operation is a family affair: Antonella studied in Faenza, the ceramics center in Emilia-Romagna, and daughter Lorenza holds two certificates in ceramics. Most days, they can be found in the back of the shop, painting vases. Valentino and daughter Chiara run the front of the store, two plain rooms bursting with colorful objects—vases, espresso cups, plates, and patio tables.

Valentino explains what makes Italian ceramics distinctive: "First of all, it's the type of clay we use. The clay we find here is softer. We fire it at a lower temperature [950 degrees Centigrade]. You get better color if you fire it at a lower temperature."

The use of color is crucial. "The color of the sun, of the sea—it gives us confidence with color. Our colors are similar to what the Renaissance masters used, only we don't use lead. Like those Renaissance masters, we used to fire with wood. It would take three or four days. Now we use an electric kiln."

According to Valentino, works from major ceramics-making areas within Italy can be distinguished both by color and type of design. "The further you go south, you'll find that the colors are stronger. Deruta [in Umbria] makes one kind of ceramics, and Montelupo [near Florence] another. The main difference in ceramics from Faenza is that they use faces and produce lots of hunting scenes. In Florence, it's more geometric. Our portraits are rougher compared to Faenza."

end shops clustered in this part of town. **Bernardo** (⊠ *Via Porta Rossa 87/r, Piazza della Repubblica* ☎*055/283333*) specializes in men's trousers, cashmere sweaters, and shirts with details like mother-of-pearl buttons. **Cabó** (⊠ *Via Porta Rossa 77–79/r, Piazza della Repubblica* ☎*055/215774*) carries that sinuous Missoni knitwear. Trendy **Diesel** (⊠ *Via dei Lamberti 13/r, Piazza della Signoria* ☎*055/2399963*) started in Vicenza; its gear is on the "must-have" list of many self-respecting Italian teens. The outlandish designs of native son **Roberto Cavalli** (⊠ *Via Tornabuoni 83/r, Santa Maria Novella* ☎*055/2396226*) appeal to Hollywood celebrities and to those who want a little bit of rock star in their wardrobe. **Emporio Armani** (⊠*Piazza Strozzi 16/r, Santa Maria Novella* ☎*055/284315*), sister store of the Giorgio Armani boutique, has slightly more affordable, funky, nightclub- and office-friendly garb. **Prada** (⊠ *Via Tornabuoni 67/r, Santa Maria Novella* ☎*055/267471*), known to mix schoolmarmish sensibility with sexy cuts and funky fabrics, appeals to an exclusive clientele. The aristocratic Marchese di Barsento, **Emilio Pucci** (⊠ *Via Tornabuoni 20–22/r, Santa Maria Novella* ☎*055/2658082*), became an international name in the late 1950s when the stretch ski clothes he designed for himself caught on with the dolce vita crowd—his pseudopsychedelic prints and "palazzo pajamas" became all the rage. You can take home a custom-

2

made suit or dress from **Giorgio Vannini** (✉ *Borgo Santi Apostoli 43/r, Santa Maria Novella* ☎*055/293037*), who has a showroom for his prêt-à-porter designs. The signature couture collection of **Gianni Versace** (✉*Via Tornabuoni 13–15/r, Santa Maria Novella* ☎*055/2396167*) revolutionized the catwalk with rubber dresses and purple leather pants; sister Donatella continues the line of high-priced, over-the-top couture for rock stars and movie celebs. **Versus** (✉*Via Vigna Nuova 36–38/r, Santa Maria Novella* ☎*055/217619*) is the more playful—and more affordable—Versace line.

The intrepid shopper might want to check out some other, lesser-known shops. Young Florentines have a soft spot in their hearts for the clingy, one-of-a-kind frocks designed by Angela Baldi at her tiny shop, **Babele** (✉*Borgo Pinti 34/r, Santa Croce* ☎*055/244729*). **Blunauta** (✉*Via del Proconsolo 69/r, Duomo* ☎*055/212460*) sells casual, well-made clothes for men and women. At **L'essentiel** (✉ *Via del Corso 10/r, Piazza della Signoria* ☎*055/294713*) Lara Caldieron has spun her club-going years into fashion that also works well on the street and in the office. **Geraldine Tayar** (✉*Sdrucciolo de' Pitti 6/r, Palazzo Pitti* ☎*055/290405*) makes clothing and accessories of her own design in eclectic fabric combinations. **Il Guardaroba/Stock House** (✉*Via Verdi, Santa Croce* ☎*055/2340271*) is where savvy Florentines shop for one-off designer clothes at affordable prices. If you're looking for something hot to wear to the clubs, check out **Liu-Jo** (✉*Via Calimala 14/r, Piazza della Repubblica* ☎*055/216164*). The surreal window displays at **Luisa Via Roma** (✉*Via Roma 19–21/r, Duomo* ☎*055/217826*) hint at the trendy yet tasteful clothing inside this fascinating, *alta moda* (high-style) boutique, which stocks the world's top designers as well as Luisa's own line. **Lo Stock di Max** (✉*Via Pietrapiana 15/r*☎*055/241084*) sells last year's Max Mara stuff at a fraction of the original price.

Maçel (✉ *Via Guicciardini 128/r, Palazzo Pitti* ☎*055/287355*) has collections by lesser-known Italian designers, many of whom use the same factories as the A-list. Florentine designer **Patrizia Pepe** (✉*Piazza San Giovanni 12/r, Duomo* ☎*055/2645056*) has body-conscious clothes perfect for all ages, especially for women with a tiny streak of rebelliousness. Members of the junior set desiring to look well clad, Florentine style, should consider stopping at **Piccolo Slam** (✉ *Via dei Lamberti 13/r, Piazza della Signoria* ☎*055/214504*). **Principe** (✉ *Via del Sole 2, Santa Maria Novella* ☎*055/292764*) is a Florentine institution with casual clothes for men, women, and children at far-from-casual prices. It also has a great housewares department. For cutting-edge fashion, the fun and funky window displays at **Spazio A** (✉*Via Porta Rossa 109–115/r, Piazza della Repubblica* ☎*055/212995*) merit a stop. The shop carries such well-known designers as Alberta Ferretti and Narciso Rodriguez, as well as lesser-known Italian, English, and French designers.

GIFTS & HOUSEWARES

Aromatherapy has been elevated to an art form at **Antica Officina del Farmacista Dr. Vranjes** (✉*Borgo La Croce 44/r, Santa Croce* ☎*055/241748* ✉ *Via San Gallo 63/r* ☎*055/494537*). Dr. Vranjes makes scents for the body and for the house. For housewares, nothing beats **Bartolini** (✉ *Via dei*

Servi 30/r, Santissima Annunziata
☎*055/211895*) for well-designed
practical items. **Brandimarte** (✉ *Via
L. Bartolini 18/r, Santo Spirito/San
Frediano* ☎*055/2286242*), a silver-
smith workshop, can be toured by
prior arrangement; it makes everything from salt and pepper shakers
to gigantic serving trays, for sale in

the attached showroom. **Coltellerie Berti** (✉ *Via Cavour 144/r, San Marco*
☎*055/2741449*) boasts that they have a "long history of iron, of fire,
and knowing hands." They've been making knives since 1895, and
decades of experience have gone into crafting these exquisite objects
which are light in the hand and razor-sharp.

La Bottega dell'Olio (✉ *Piazza del Limbo 2/r, Santa Maria Novella*
☎*055/2670468*) sells olive oil in all its permutations. The shop, which
is tucked into a small piazza, has a great collection of fine olive oils, as
well as bath products made from olive oil. **La Scagliola** (✉ *Piazza Pitti
14/r, Palazzo Pitti* ☎*055/211523*) practices the 17th-century art of
scagliola, a less-expensive alternative to pietre dure; it's a composite
that imitates marble, used here to form handsome tabletops, boxes, and
picture frames. **Lorenzo Villoresi** (✉ *ia de'Bardi 14, Lungarno South* ☎
055/2341187) makes one-of-a-kind fragrances, which he develops after
meeting with you. Such personalized attention does not come cheap.

Mandragora Art Store (✉ *Piazza del Duomo 50/r, Duomo* ☎*055/292559*)
is one of the first attempts in Florence to cash in on the museum-store
craze. Florence has been famous for its straw products for centuries, and
Martini (✉ *Via S. Veridiana 6/r, Santa Croce* ☎*055/2480612*) has been
producing fine baskets, trays, and other household goods since 1921.

The essence of a Florentine holiday is captured in the sachets of the
Officina Profumo Farmaceutica di Santa Maria Novella (✉ *Via della Scala
16, Santa Maria Novella* ☎*055/216276*), an art-nouveau emporium
of herbal cosmetics and soaps that are made following centuries-old
recipes created by friars. **Pitti Mosaici** (✉ *Piazza dei Pitti 23/r, Palazzo
Pitti* ☎*055/282127*) continues the pietre dure tradition that was all the
rage of 16th-century Florence. Stones are worked into exquisite tables,
pictures, and jewelry. **Rampini Ceramiche** (✉ *Borgo Ognissanti 32/34,
Lungarno North* ☎*055/219720*) sells exquisitely crafted, and expensive, ceramics. **Sbigoli Terrecotte** (✉ *Via Sant'Egidio 4/r, Santa Croce*
☎*055/2479713*) carries traditional Tuscan terra-cotta and ceramic
vases, pots, and cups and saucers. What to get that gal (or guy) who
has everything? Drop into the **Shabby Shop** (✉ *Via del Parione 12/r,
Santa Maria Novella* ☎*055/294826*), which specializes in antique silver—mostly English, dating from George I to George III (1698–1811),
and jewelry from the 1950s. For the record: there's nothing shabby
about this shop.

JEWELRY

Angela Caputi (⊠*Borgo Santi Apostoli 44/46*☎*055/292993*) wows Florentine cognoscenti with her highly creative, often outsized plastic jewelry. A small, but equally creative, collection of women's clothing made of fine fabrics is also on offer. **Carlo Piccini** (⊠*Ponte Vecchio 31/r, Piazza della Signoria* ☎*055/292030*) has been around for several generations, selling antique jewelry as well as making pieces to order; you can also get old jewelry reset here. **Cassetti** (⊠*Ponte Vecchio 54/r, Piazza della Signoria* ☎*055/2396028*) combines precious and semiprecious stones and metals in contemporary settings. **Gatto Bianco** (⊠*Borgo Santi Apostoli 12/r, Santa Maria Novella* ☎*055/282989*) has breathtakingly beautiful jewelry worked in semiprecious and precious stones; the feel is completely contemporary. **Gherardi** (⊠*Ponte Vecchio 5/r, Piazza della Signoria* ☎*055/211809*), Florence's king of coral, has the city's largest selection of finely crafted pieces, as well as cultured pearls, jade, and turquoise. **Oro Due** (⊠*Via Lambertesca 12/r, Piazza della Signoria* ☎*055/292143*) sells gold jewelry the old-fashioned way: beauteous objects are priced according to the level of craftsmanship and the price of gold bullion that day. The two women who run **Oreria** (⊠*Borgo Pinti 87/a, Santa Croce* ☎*055/244708*) create divine designs using silver and semiprecious stones. Send suitors to purchase significant gifts here. **Studio Ballerino** (⊠*Borgo Allegri 25/r, Santa Croce* ☎*055/2344658*) has one-of-a-kind pieces crafted in semiprecious stone, gold, and silver. One of Florence's oldest jewelers, **Tiffany** (⊠*Via Tornabuoni 25/r, Santa Maria Novella* ☎*055/215506*) has supplied Italian (and other) royalty with finely crafted gems for centuries. Its selection of antique-looking classics has been updated with a selection of contemporary silver.

LINENS & FABRICS

Antico Setificio Fiorentina (⊠*Via L. Bartolini 4, Santo Spirito/San Frediano* ☎*055/213861*) has been providing damasks and other fine fabrics for royalty and those who aspire to it since 1786. Visits by appointment are preferred. **Blue Home** (⊠*Borgo Santi Apostoli 58/r, Santa Maria Novella* ☎*055/2658262*) sells sumptuous fabrics which can be rendered into sofas, rugs, and other home furnishings to create divinely inspired interiors. Antique and contemporary rugs are also on hand. **Loretta Caponi** (⊠*Piazza Antinori 4/r, Santa Maria Novella* ☎*055/213668*) is synonymous with Florentine embroidery, and the luxury lace, linens, and lingerie have earned the eponymous signora worldwide renown. Luxurious silks, beaded fabrics, lace, wool, and tweeds can be purchased at **Valli** (⊠ *Via Strozzi 4/r, Piazza della Repubblica* ☎*055/282485*). It carries fabrics created by Armani, Valentino, and other high-end designers.

OUTLETS

At **Barberino Designer Outlet** (⊠ *Via Meucci snc,* ☎*055/842161*) you'll find Prada, Pollini, Missoni, and Bruno Magli, among others. To get here, take the A1 to the Barberino di Mugello exit, and follow signs to the mall.

One-stop bargain shopping awaits at **The Mall** (⊠ *Via Europa 8* ☎*055/8657775*), where the stores sell goods by such names as Bottega Veneta, Giorgio Armani, Loro Piana, Sergio Rossi, and Yves St. Laurent. Cognoscenti drive 45 minutes or take the train to Montevarchi, and then taxi out of town to the **Prada Outlet** (⊠ *Levanella Spacceo, Estrada Statale 69, Montevarchi* ☎*055/91911*).

SHOES & LEATHER ACCESSORIES

Florentine women with a sense of whimsical style adore the purses at **Bracciolini** (⊠ *Via delle Vigna Nuova 30/r*). If you're a fan of frogs, you'll adore the frog baguette bag with matching frog wallet.

The colorful, foot-friendly shoes at **Camper** (⊠ *Via Por Santa Maria 47/r, Piazza della Signoria* ☎*055/2670342*) are made in Spain, but they cost less here than they do in the United States. The ultimate fine leathers are crafted into classic shapes at **Casadei** (⊠ *Via Tornabuoni 33/r, Santa Maria Novella* ☎*055/287240*), winding up as women's shoes and bags. The classy **Ferragamo** (⊠ *Via Tornabuoni 2/r, Santa Maria Novella* ☎*055/292123*), in a 13th-century Renaissance palazzo, displays designer clothing and accessories, but elegant footwear still underlies the Ferragamo success. **Pollini** (⊠ *Via Calimala 12/r, Piazza della Repubblica* ☎*055/214738*) has beautifully crafted shoes and leather accessories for those willing to pay that little bit extra.

Beltrami (⊠ *Via della Vigna Nuova 70/r, Santa Maria Novella* ☎*055/287779*), which sells shoes and some apparel, has long been synonymous with style; classic looks are beautifully updated. **Cellerini** (⊠ *Via del Sole 37/r, Santa Maria Novella* ☎*055/282533*) is an institution in a city where it seems that just about everybody wears an expensive leather jacket. **Coccinelle** (⊠ *Via Por Santa Maria 49/r, Piazza della Signoria* ☎*055/2398782*) sells leather accessories in bold colors and funky designs. **Furla** (⊠ *Via Calzaiuoli 47/r, Piazza della Repubblica* ☎*055/2382883*) makes beautiful leather bags and wallets in up-to-the-minute designs. **Giotti** (⊠ *Piazza Ognissanti 3–4/r, Lungarno North* ☎*055/294265*) has a full line of leather goods, including clothing. Florentine perennial **Gucci** (⊠ *Via Tornabuoni 73/r, Santa Maria Novella* ☎*055/264011*) puts its famous initials on just about everything it sells. Beware, however, of shop assistants with severe attitude problems. **Il Bisonte** (⊠ *Via del Parione 31/r, off Via della Vigna Nuova, Santa Maria Novella* ☎*055/215722*) is known for its natural-looking leather goods, all stamped with the store's bison symbol. **Madova** (⊠ *Via Guicciardini 1/r, Palazzo Pitti* ☎*055/2396526*) has high-quality leather gloves in a rainbow of colors and a choice of linings (silk, cashmere, and unlined). **Paolo Carandini** (⊠ *Via de' Macci 73/r, Santa Croce* ☎*055/245397*) works exclusively in leather, producing exquisite objects such as picture frames, jewelry boxes, and desk accessories.

Shoe styles at **Romano** (⊠ *Via Speziali 10/r, Piazza della Repubblica* ☎*055/216535*) span the staid to the offbeat at appealing prices. A consortium of leatherworkers plies its trade at **Scuola del Cuoio** (⊠ *Piazza Santa Croce 16* ☎*055/244533* ⊕*www.leatherschool.com*), in the former dormitory of the convent of Santa Croce; high-quality, fairly priced jackets, belts, and purses are sold here.

SIDE TRIPS FROM FLORENCE

FIESOLE

GETTING HERE

The easiest way to get to Fiesole from Florence is by public bus: Take the number 7, marked "Fiesole," which you can pick up at Santa Maria Novella station or Piazza San Marco. If you decide to drive (the bus is so much easier), go to Piazza Liberta and cross the Ponte Rosso heading in the direction of the SS65/SR65. Turn right on to Via Salviati and continue on to Via Roccettini. Make a left turn to Via Vecchia Fiesolana, which will take you directly in the center of town.

VISITOR INFORMATION

Fiesole tourism office (⊠ *Via Portigiani 3, 50014* ☏*055/598720* ⊕*www. comune.fiesole.fi.it*).

EXPLORING

A half-day excursion to Fiesole, in the hills 8 km (5 mi) above Florence, gives you a pleasant respite from museums and a wonderful view of the city. From here the view of the Duomo gives you a new appreciation for what the Renaissance accomplished. Fiesole began life as an ancient Etruscan and later Roman village that held some power until it succumbed to barbarian invasions. Eventually it gave up its independence in exchange for Florence's protection. The medieval cathedral, ancient Roman amphitheater, and lovely old villas behind garden walls are clustered on a series of hilltops. A walk around Fiesole can take from one to two or three hours, depending on how far you stroll from the main piazza.

The trip from Florence by car or bus takes 20–30 minutes. Take Bus 7 from the Stazione Centrale di Santa Maria Novella, Piazza San Marco, or the Duomo. (You can also get on and off the bus at San Domenico.) A word of caution: pickpockets have been known to frequent this bus, so keep an eye out for reaching hands. There are several possible routes for the two-hour walk from central Florence to Fiesole. One route begins in a residential area of Florence called Salviatino (Via Barbacane, near Piazza Edison, on the Bus 7 route), and after a short time, offers peeks over garden walls of beautiful villas, as well as the view over your shoulder at the panorama of Florence in the valley.

The **Duomo** reveals a stark medieval interior. In the raised presbytery, the **Cappella Salutati** was frescoed by 15th-century artist Cosimo Rosselli, but it was his contemporary, sculptor Mino da Fiesole (1430–84), who put the town on the artistic map. The Madonna on the altarpiece and the tomb of Bishop Salutati are fine examples of the artist's work. ⊠*Piazza Mino da Fiesole* ☏*055/59400* ☉*Nov.–Mar., daily 7:30–noon and 2–5; Apr.–Oct., daily 7:30–noon and 3–6.*

The beautifully preserved 2,000-seat **Anfiteatro Romano** *(Roman Amphi-theater)*, near the Duomo, dates from the 1st century BC and is still used for summer concerts. To the right of the amphitheater are the remains of the **Terme Romani** (Roman Baths), where you can see the gymnasium, hot and cold baths, and rectangular chamber where the water was heated. A beautifully designed **Museo Archeologico**, an intricate series of levels connected by elevators, is built amid the ruins and contains objects dating from as early as 2000 BC. The nearby **Museo Bandini** is filled with the private collection of Canon Angelo Maria Bandini (1726–1803); he fancied 13th- to 15th-century Florentine paintings, terra-cotta pieces, and wood sculpture, which he later bequeathed to the Diocese of Fiesole. ⊠ *Via Portigiani 1* ☎ *055/59477* ☜ *€10, includes access to the archaeological park and museums.* ☉ *Apr.–Sept., daily 9:30–7; Oct.–Mar., Wed.–Mon. 10–4:30.*

The hilltop church of **San Francesco** has a good view of Florence and the plain below from its terrace and benches. Halfway up the hill you'll see sloping steps to the right; they lead to a lovely wooded park with trails that loop out and back to the church.

If you really want to stretch your legs, walk 4 km (2½ mi) toward the center of Florence along Via Vecchia Fiesolana, a narrow lane in use since Etruscan times, to the church of **San Domenico.** Sheltered in the church is the *Madonna and Child with Saints* by Fra Angelico, who was a Dominican friar here. ⊠ *Piazza San Domenico, off Via Giuseppe Mantellini* ☎ *055/59230* ☜ *Free* ☉ *Daily 9–noon.*

From the church of San Domenico it's a five-minute walk northwest to the **Badia Fiesolana,** which was the original cathedral of Fiesole. Dating to the 11th century, it was first the home of Camaldolese monks. Thanks to Cosimo il Vecchio, the complex was substantially restructured. The facade, never completed due to the death of Cosimo, contains elements of its original Romanesque decoration. The attached convent once housed Cosimo's valued manuscripts. Its mid-15th-century cloister is well worth a look. ⊠ *Via della Badia dei Roccettini 11* ☎ *055/59155* ☉ *Weekdays 9–6, Sat. 9:30–12:30.*

WHERE TO STAY & EAT

$$–$$$ ✕ **Le Cave di Maiano.** If you're looking to get out of town, hop in your car (or take a taxi) to this simple trattoria in the hills just outside Florence. Italians flock here for the *buon rapporto fra qualità e prezzo* (the good rapport between quality and price). Tuscan staples are on hand, as is a fine plate of spaghetti with truffled asparagus. They grill well here, so consider something from the grill to follow. By all means leave room for dessert. Though the food is typical, they do it exceedingly well: the *zuppa cotta* should not be missed. ⊠ *Via Cave di Maiano 16* ☎ *055/59133* ▭ *AE, DC, MC, V.*

$ ✕ **San Domenico.** Three-quarters of the way up the hill to Fiesole, this rather industrial-looking spot has tasty *pizze* as well as pastas. If you're hiking in the nearby hills, or going to see the Fra Angelico at the church of San Domenico, this is a perfect place to break for lunch. Outdoor seating in the summer looks directly onto a somewhat busy two-lane road. ✉*Piazza San Domenico* ☎*055/59182* ▭*AE, DC, MC, V* ⊘*Closed Mon.*

$$$$ 🏨**Villa San Michele.** The cypress-lined driveway provides an elegant preamble to this incredibly gorgeous (and very expensive) hotel nestled in the hills of Fiesole. The 16th-century building was originally a Franciscan convent designed by Santi di Tito. Not a single false note is struck in the reception area (formerly the chapel), the dining rooms (a covered cloister and former refectory), or the tasteful antiques and art that decorate the rooms. The open-air loggia, where lunch and dinner are served, provides one of the most stunning views of Florence—a good thing, too, as the food is overpriced and bland. **Pros:** Exceptional convent conversion. **Cons:** Money must be no object. ✉*Via Doccia 4, 50014* ☎*055/59451* 🖷*055/5678250* ⊕*www.villasanmichele.com* ⤳*21 rooms, 24 suites* ♿*In-room: safe, refrigerator, VCR, dial-up, Wi-Fi. In-hotel: restaurant, room service, bar, pool, gym, bicycles, concierge, laundry service, public Internet, parking (no fee), some pets allowed* ▭*AE, DC, MC, V* ⊘*Closed Dec.–Easter.*

$$$ 🏨**Villa Aurora.** The attractive hotel on the main piazza takes advantage of its hilltop spot, with beautiful views in many of the rooms, some of which are on two levels with beamed ceilings and balconies. The building, constructed as a theater in 1860, was transformed into a hotel in the late 19th century. It's fit for queens, and quite a few of them—Queen Victoria and Margherita di Savoia among others—have stayed here. **Pros:** Some rooms have pretty views, air quality better than in Florence. **Cons:** A little worn at the edges. ✉*Piazza Mino da Fiesole 39, 50014* ☎*055/59363* 🖷*055/59587* ⊕*www.villaaurora.net* ⤳*23 rooms, 2 suites* ♿*In-hotel: restaurant, bar, public Internet, some pets allowed* ▭*AE, DC, MC, V* 🍽*BP.*

NIGHTLIFE & THE ARTS

From June through August, **Estate Fiesolana** (✉*Teatro Romano* ☎*055/598720* ⊕*www.comune.fiesole.fi.it*) is a festival of theater, music, dance, and film that takes place in Fiesole's churches and in the Roman amphitheater—demonstrating that the ancient Romans knew a thing or two about acoustics.

SETTIGNANO

When Florence is overcrowded and hot—that is, for most of the summer—this village, a 20-minute car or bus trip east of Florence, is particularly appealing. It was the birthplace of many artists, including the sculptors Desiderio di Settignano (circa 1428–64), Antonio (1427–79) and Bernardo (1409–64) Rossellino, and Bartolomeo Ammannati (1511–92). Michelangelo's wet nurse was the wife of a stonecutter in Settignano, and to her he attributed his later calling in life. Alas, though these artists' works no longer adorn their native town, Settignano is worth a visit simply to breathe its fresh air, walk its tiny streets, and sit in its small **piazza** with an aperitivo.

Gardens Around Florence

Like any well-heeled Florentine, you, too, can get away from Florence's hustle and bustle by heading for the hills. Take a break from city sightseeing to enjoy the gardens and villas. Villa di Castello and Villa La Petraia, both northwest of Florence's historic center, can be explored in one trip. The Italian garden at Villa Gamberaia is an 8-km (5-mi) jaunt east of the center near Settignano. Plan for a full-day excursion, picnic lunch included, if visiting all three gardens. Though Villa Demidoff, originally a Medici country house, is in somewhat dilapidated shape, it's worth a trip to see Giambologna's *Appenino*. For a prime taste of Medici living, venture farther afield to the family's Villa Medicea in Poggio a Caiano, south of Prato (⇨ *Chapter 3, Northwest Tuscany*).

VILLA DI CASTELLO

A fortified residence in the Middle Ages, Villa di Castello was rebuilt in the 15th century by the Medici. The palace isn't open to the public; the gardens, however, are the main attraction.

Though the original garden design has been altered somewhat over the centuries, the allegorical theme of animals, devised by Tribolo in 1537 to the delight of the Medici, is still evident. The artificial cave, Grotta degli Animali (Animal Grotto), displays sculpted animals by Giambologna and his assistants. An Ammannati sculpture, a figure of an old man representing the Appenines, is at the center of a pond on the terrace overlooking the garden. Two bronze sculptures by Ammannati, centerpieces of fountains studding the garden, can now be seen indoors in Villa La Petraia. Allow about 45 minutes to visit the garden; you can easily visit Villa La Petraia from

here, making for a four-hour trip in total.

To get to Villa di Castello by car, head northwest from Florence on Via Reginaldo Giuliani (also known as Via Sestese) to Castello, about 6 km (4 mi) northwest of the city center in the direction of Sesto Fiorentino; follow signs to Villa di Castello. Or take Bus 28 from the city center and tell the driver you want to get off at Villa di Castello; from the stop, walk north about ½ km (¼ mi) up the tree-lined allée from the main road. ⊠ *Via di Castello 47, Castello* ☎ *055/454791* ☞ *Free* ☉ *Garden: Nov.–Feb., daily 8:15–2; Mar.–Oct., daily 9–7. Closed 2nd and 3rd Mon. of month; palace closed to public.*

VILLA LA PETRAIA

The splendidly planted gardens of Villa La Petraia sit high above the Arno with a sweeping view of Florence. The villa was built around a medieval tower and reconstructed after it was purchased by the Medici sometime after 1530. Virtually the only trace of the Medici having lived here are the 17th-century courtyard frescoes.

The garden and the vast park behind the palace suggest a splendid contrast between formal and natural landscapes. Allow 60 to 90 minutes to explore the park and gardens, plus 30 minutes for the guided tour of the so-called museum, the villa interior. This property is best visited after the Villa di Castello.

To get here by car, follow directions to Villa di Castello, but take the right off Via Reginaldo Giuliani, following the sign for Villa La Petraia. You can walk from Villa di Castello to Villa La Petraia in about 15 minutes;

turn left beyond the gate of Villa di Castello and continue straight along Via di Castello and the imposing Villa Corsini; take Via della Petraia uphill to the entrance. ⌗ *Via della Petraia 40, Località Castello* ☎ *055/451208* 🎟 *Free* 🕐 *Oct.–Mar., garden: daily 8:15–4:30, villa tours: daily at 9:15, 10, 10:45, 11:30, 12:10, 1:30, 2:20, 3, and 3:40; Apr., May, and Sept., garden: daily 9–5, villa tours: daily at 9:15, 10, 10:45, 11:30, 12:10, 1:30, 2:20, 3, 3:40, and 4:45; June–Aug., garden: daily 9–7, villa tours: daily at 9:15, 10, 10:45, 11:30, 12:10, 1:30, 2:20, 3, 3:40, 4:45, 5:35, and 6:35. Closed 2nd and 3rd Mon. of month.*

VILLA GAMBERAIA

Villa Gamberaia, near the village of Settignano on the eastern outskirts of Florence, was the rather modest 15th-century country home of Matteo di Domenico Gamberelli, the father of noted Renaissance sculptors Bernardo, Antonio, and Matteo Rossellino. In the early 1600s the villa eventually passed into the hands of the wealthy Capponi family. They spared no expense in rebuilding it and, more importantly, creating its garden, one of the finest near Florence. Studded with statues and fountains, the garden suffered damage during World War II but has been restored according to the original 17th-century design. This excursion takes about 1½ hours, allowing 45 minutes to visit the garden. Parts of the villa are open by appointment.

To get here by car, head east on Via Aretina, an extension of Via Gioberti, which is picked up at Piazza Beccaria; follow the sign to the turnoff to the north to Villa Gamberaia, about 8 km (5 mi) from the center. To go by bus, take Bus 10 to Settignano. From

Settignano's main Piazza Tommaseo, walk east on Via di San Romano; the second lane on the right is Via del Rossellino, which leads southeast to the entrance of Villa Gamberaia. The walk from the piazza takes about 10 minutes. ⌗ *Via del Rossellino 72, near Settignano* ☎ *055/697205* 🎟 *€10* 🕐 *Garden: daily 9–6.*

VILLA DEMIDOFF

Francesco I de' Medici commissioned the multitalented Bernardo Buontalenti in 1568 to build a villa and a grandiose park to accompany it. The park, particularly the colossal and whimsical sculpture of the *Fontana dell'Appenino* (*Fountain of the Appenines*), executed by Giambologna in 1579–89, is worth the price of admission alone. Besides providing a nice excursion from Florence, the villa is an excellent picnic spot.

To get here by car, head north from Florence on the SR65 toward Pratolino and follow signs to the villa. Or take Bus 25 from Piazza San Marco and get off at Pratolino. ⌗ *Località Pratolino, Vaglia* ☎ *055/409427* 🎟 *Free* 🕐 *May–Sept., Thurs.–Sun. 10–7:30.*

To get to the village, take Bus 10 from Florence, from the station at Santa Maria Novella or at Piazza San Marco, all the way to the end of the line, the *capolinea*. It will put you in the middle of Settignano's piazzetta.

A 20-minute walk through scenic countryside from the piazza leads to the **Oratorio della Vannella** (⊠*Località Corbignano*). The exterior, dating from 1719–21, is unremarkable, but the fresco of the *Madonna and Child Enthroned* (circa 1470), attributed to a young Sandro Botticelli (1445–1510), is housed here. It's in sad shape but is said to work miracles. To get here, take Via Desiderio di Settignano, walk around the very modern cemetery, turn left, and then follow the narrow path lined with olive trees. The oratory is open for 6 PM Mass the last Sunday of each month; otherwise, you can call the tourist information office in Florence (☎055/2340444) to open the doors.

WHERE TO STAY & EAT

$$ ✕**Osvaldo.** If you're making the trip to Settignano, this is a great dining option (get off Bus 10 at the stop called Ponte a Mensola). The small, unassuming family-run trattoria is situated along a street and a tiny stream; if you sit outside (there are no views, alas), you might hear the trickle of the stream. The food is terrific, and though it is described as *cucina casalinga* (home cooking), only the portions are home-style. Service is prompt and courteous. Count yourself lucky if the menu includes *fritti di fiori di zucca* (fried zucchini flowers)—probably the lightest fried food you'll find anywhere. ⊠*Via G. D'Annunzio 51/r* ☎*055/603972* ▤*AE, DC, MC, V* ☺*Closed Wed. No lunch Tues.*

$-$$ ✕**Trattoria Casalinga da Graziella.** Though it's a very simple, bare-bones trattoria, the *cucina casalinga* is tasty and inexpensive, and the service is courteous. Generously portioned primi stick to the ribs—the *tortelloni alla mugellana* (potato-stuffed ravioli with a tomato meat sauce) is perfectly executed. The roast piglet, cooked Sardinian style, must be reserved one night in advance. ⊠*Via Cave di Maiano 20* ☎*055/599963* ▤*MC, V* ☺*Closed Tues.*

$ ⌂**Fattoria di Maiano.** In the foothills between Florence and Fiesole are these lovely apartments, which sleep 4 to 11 people and rent by the week. Many apartments are in a former convent, and some are scattered around the farm; all have wood floors, simple and sturdy furniture, and very modern kitchens, and most have splendid views onto olive groves (olive oil is produced by the Fattoria owners). **Pros:** Great way to have a country experience with the city nearby. **Cons:** Requires a week stay ⊠*Via Benedetto da Maiano 11, 50016* ☎*055/599600* 🖷*055/599640* ⊕*www.fattoriadimaiano.com* ⌨*8 apartments* ⌂*In-room: no a/c (some), kitchen. In-hotel: restaurant, some pets allowed* ▤*DC, MC, V* ⍩*EP.*

Pisa, Lucca & Northwest Tuscany

WORD OF MOUTH

"For history and charm the small walled city of Lucca is, I think, absolutely magical. The food in Lucca also eclipses most all of Tuscany too!"

—hanabilly

WELCOME TO NORTHWEST TUSCANY

TOP REASONS TO GO

★ **Leaning Tower of Pisa:** It may be touristy, but now that you can once again climb to the top, it's touristy fun.

★ **Olive-oil tasting in and around Lucca:** Italian olive oil is justifiably world famous, and cognoscenti insist that the best is found here.

★ **Cappella Maggiore, Duomo, Prato:** Filippo Lippi's solemn frescoes depicting scenes from the lives of John the Baptist and Saint Stephen have gotten a big boost from a 2006 restoration.

★ **Bagni di Lucca:** This sleepy little town attracted the English Romantics, among others, who were drawn to its salubrious waters and air.

★ **Tomb of Ilaria del Carretto, Duomo, Lucca:** Check out this moving sculpture by Jacopo della Quercia commemorating a young woman who died in childbirth.

Old city, Pisa

1 **Towns west of Florence.** At industrial centers from the Middle Ages such as **Prato** and **Pistoia** you can relax far from Florence's throngs and savor fine food and some art gems. Fragrant white truffles adorn many a restaurant menu in **San Miniato.**

2 **Pisa.** Thanks to an engineering mistake, the name Pisa is recognized the world over. The Leaning Tower, the baptistery, and the cathedral make an impressive threesome on the **Piazza del Duomo.**

3 **Lucca.** This laid-back yet elegant town is surrounded by tree-bedecked 16th-century ramparts that are now a delightful promenade.

4 **The Garfagnana.** Sports enthusiasts and nature addicts flock to **Abetone** to ski in winter and refresh themselves with cool, mountain air in summer.

5 **The Northwest Coast.** Experience Italian beach culture at **Forte dei Marmi,** a crowded and expensive place to see and be seen. Farther west, it's a worthwhile side trip out of Tuscany to visit the coastal villages of the **Cinque Terre.**

Lucca

TUSCANY

UMBRIA

EMILIA-
ROMAGNA

3

Abetone
12
4
12
San
Marcello
64
Bagni
di Lucca
66
Pistoia
Pescia
Montecatini
A11
Vinci
Mt
Albano
Mt
Pisano
Fucecchio
Arno River
San
Miniato
Empoli
Castelfiorentino
Pontedera
67
429
Certaldo
Volterra
68
68
1
Piombino
Golfo
Di Follónica

65
A1
Borgo
San Lorenzo
EMILIA-
ROMAGNA
67
325
65
Prato
67
Florence
1
Mantelupo
Impruneta
A1
CHIANTI
2
222
Greve
Poggibonsi

0   10 mi
0   10 km

GETTING
ORIENTED

The landscape west of
Florence is flat and generally unremarkable, but
when you reach the coast
there are beautiful sandy
beaches on the Tyrrhe-
nian Sea—and the almost
surreal charm of Pisa's
Piazza del Duomo, with
the Leaning Tower as the
star attraction. Heading
north, lush hills and olive
trees dot the countryside
around Lucca, and the
elevation climbs as you
enter the Garfagnana
and its Alpi Apuane—
the Tuscan Alps.

Montecatini

NORTHWEST TUSCANY PLANNER

On the Waterfront

You may not think of Tuscany as a beach destination, but its long coastline is popular with Italian vacationers. From June through August the resort towns of Viarregio, Forte dei Marmi, and Marina di Massa are packed with beachgoers. Bagni (bathhouses) open, and the sands fill with colorful umbrellas and beach chairs; you can rent your own for about €20 a day. During the rest of year, the beaches are sparsely populated. You can walk for miles along the sand, watching the waves lap against the shore and breathing in the fresh sea breeze.

Crossing the Tuscan border into the region of Liguria brings you to the Cinque Terre, one of Italy's most distinctive seaside locales. Here the main attractions are five isolated fishing villages and the beautiful hiking trails that run between them.

Cinque Terre

Making the Most of Your Time

The majority of first-time visitors to Tuscany start out by exploring Florence and then are lured south by the Chianti district and Siena. Heading west instead is an appealing alternative. **Pisa** is the main attraction, and it certainly isn't short on tourists. If that's all you want (or have time) to see here, you're probably best off doing it as a day trip from Florence. If you want to stick around for a while, consider making **Lucca** your base. It's a tremendously appealing town, with fine food and an easygoing atmosphere.

From Lucca you can discover the rest of the area on day trips. The **Garfagnana** has gorgeous mountain peaks and excellent hiking opportunities (as well as skiing in winter). You can follow a day in the mountains with a day along the coast, at the resort towns along the Ligurian Sea and the **Cinque Terre.**

Finding a Place to Stay

Excluding the beach resort towns, lodging is generally a better deal here than in much of the rest of Tuscany; some real bargains can be found in off-the-beaten-path towns. Consider staying at an *agriturismo*, a farm or vineyard with guest accommodations, which can range from rustic to stately. Many area hotel restaurants serve excellent food, and meal plans are usually available as supplements to your room rate. In summer, when Florence is hot and crowded, it's not a bad plan to base yourself in one of the surrounding towns and use the train to make day trips into the city.

DINING & LODGING PRICE CATEGORIES (IN EUROS)

	¢	$	$$	$$$	$$$$
RESTAU-RANTS	under €15	€15–€25	€25–€35	€35–€45	over €45
HOTELS	under €70	€70–€110	€110–€160	€160–€220	over €220

Restaurant prices are for a first course (*primo*), second course (*secondo*), and dessert (*dolce*). Hotel prices are for two people in a standard double room in high season, including tax and service.

GETTING AROUND

By Car

The best way to explore the region is by car—and part of the fun is stopping to take in the scenery. In the northern part of the region, towns are spread out and driving the winding mountain roads adds to your travel time.

The A1 superstrada connects Florence to Prato; for Pistoia, Montecatini, and Lucca, follow signs for Firenze Nord, which connects to the A11. For Empoli, Pisa, and hill towns west, take the Fi-Pi-Li and sometimes indicated on signage as S.G.C. from Scandicci, just outside Florence. (Note that the Fi-Pi-Li is notorious for its frequent delays due to accidents and construction.) The A12 will take you from near Pisa along the Versilian Coast to La Spezia, entryway to the Cinque Terre. The Cinque Terre itself is impractical for car travel because of the narrow roads and lack of parking (although better access and parking are available at the northern and southern towns of Monterosso al Mare and Riomaggiore); from La Spezia you can take the train, which is the main means of access to the area.

By Train

Two main train lines run from Florence's Santa Maria Novella station into northwest Tuscany—one traveling through Prato, Pistoia, Montecatini, and Lucca; the other through Empoli and Pisa. The two lines meet up on the coast with a line that runs through Livorno, Viareggio, and La Spezia.

Trains are a viable option if you're going to any of these cities. For the rest of northwest Tuscany, train connections are extremely limited or nonexistent. To get to the Cinque Terre, you can take a train to La Spezia and then pick up a local train to any of the five towns.

By Bus

Many of the cities in the region do have bus stations, but service is often sporadic or complicated; it's easier to take the train to Pisa, Prato, Pistoia, Lucca, Montecatini Terme, Livorno, and Empoli, where service is regular and trains run frequently. Pescia is an easy bus ride from the train station at Montecatini Terme; you can purchase bus tickets at the station or at the news vendor. San Miniato and environs are best reached by car, as service is limited.

It's possible to take a bus from Pistoia or Florence to get to Abetone. A car is necessary to see Carrara and the rest of the Versilian Coast, because bus service is sporadic. For the Cinque Terre, the Lazzi bus service will get you to La Spezia, and then you can take the train to Riomaggiore.

There are three primary bus lines. **Copit** (☎ *055/214637 in Florence* ⊕ *www.copitspa. it*). **Lazzi** (☎ *055/363041 in Florence* ⊕ *www.lazzi.it*) **SITA** (☎ *800/373760* ⊕ *www.sita-on-line.it*)

Updated
by Patricia
Rucidlo

LUCCA AND PISA ARE THE MOST-VISITED CITIES of northwest Tuscany, and with good reason: Lucca has a charming historic center set within its 16th century walls, and Pisa is home to what may be the most famous tower in the world. Both cities are due west of Florence; the landscape along the way isn't Tuscany's finest—it's flat, interspersed with factories—but it has several smaller cities with low-key appeal: good restaurants, a few noteworthy sights, and a taste of Italian life away from the main tourism centers.

Farther north, the setting gets more impressive. Craggy, often snow-capped mountains rise above sparsely populated valleys, with narrow roads winding up and down the heights. This is the Garfagnana, Tuscany's most mountainous territory, cut through by the majestic Alpi Apuane (Apuane Alps). The steep terrain rolls down into pine-forested hills and eventually meets the wide, sandy beaches of the Ligurian Sea. Along this stretch, known as the Versilian Coast, are the resort towns of Viareggio and Forte dei Marmi, both of which pack in Italian and other European beachgoers in the summer. Farther west, a hop over the border from Tuscany into Liguria brings you to the Cinque Terre—five tiny, cliff-hugging seaside villages that have become one of Italy's most popular destinations.

ALONG THE ARNO FROM FLORENCE TO PISA

Off the beaten path in Empoli, San Miniato, and the neighboring hill towns are fine examples of art—especially in Empoli and Carmignano—and stirring views. The terrific restaurants in this area are often less expensive than in the larger surrounding cities, and this is also a good place to find local handmade products—ceramics in Montelupo, glass and leather in the Empoli–Vinci area.

MONTELUPO

30 km (19 mi) southwest of Florence, 6 km (4 mi) east of Empoli.

GETTING HERE
Train service does run from Florence's Santa Maria Novella to Montelupo, but it's sporadic. It's an easy drive on the Fi-Pi-Li highway.

VISITOR INFORMATION
Montelupo tourism office (✉ *Via XX settembre 34* ☎ *0571/518993* ⊕ *www.museomontelupo.it*).

EXPLORING
This small town, which straddles the Arno, and the surrounding villages have been producing ceramics for centuries. A ceramics museum proudly displays the work of the past, but the finest tribute to the tradition is the fact that top-quality ceramics are still handmade in the region. Montelupo's *centro storico* (historic center) is filled with shops selling the finished product.

The **Museo Archeologico e della Ceramica** *(Museum of Archaeology and Ceramics)* has some 3,000 pieces of majolica, a glazed pottery made in this region since the early 14th century. The museum includes a good section on archaeology and prehistoric finds, clear explanations of the technology and history of making ceramics from the earliest days to the present, and a beautifully mounted and arranged collection of local work dating from the early

14th to the late 18th centuries. There's also an interesting display of the coats of arms of important Renaissance families such as the Medici and Strozzi. ✉ *Via Bartolomeo Sinibaldi 45* ☎ *0571/51087* 💶 *€3.50, combination ticket €8 (includes Museo Leonardiano in Vinci and Collegiata di Sant'Andrea in Empoli)* ⏱ *Tues.–Sun. 10–6.*

FESTIVAL

Every June, Montelupo is host to the weeklong **Festa della Ceramica** (☎ *0571/518993*) , a ceramics festival that includes exhibitions of local and international art, demonstrations of techniques new and ancient, street theater and music—and, of course, sales of ceramics from around the world. Additional information about the ceramics festival is available from the Montelupo Fiorentino tourist office.

SHOPPING

Many of the pieces for sale at Montelupo's ceramics shops follow traditional styles, but some artists bring modern inspiration to their wheels. Not all of the stores will ship for you, although many will wrap the objects for you to carry home.

Bartoloni: La Ceramica Tradizionale di Montelupo (✉ *Corso Garibaldi 34* ☎ *0571/51242* ⏱ *Daily 10:30–1 and 4:30–8*), down the road from the Museo Archeologico e della Ceramica, produces objects in a range of styles.

Ceramica ND Dolfi (✉ *Via Toscoromagnola 1, Località Antinoro* ☎ *0571/51264* ⏱ *Daily 9–8*) has been in the family for three generations. It's a ceramics-making compound located 3 km (2 mi) from Montelupo on the road heading east toward Florence, where you'll find a sun-drenched *spazio aziendale* (selling floor), a factory workshop, the family residence, and a yard where terra-cotta planters are displayed. The ceramics, all priced reasonably given the high-quality handcrafted work, include large vases, plates suitable for hanging, and brightly colored serving pieces for the table.

Le Ceramiche del Borgo (✉ *Via XX Settembre 30* ☎ *0571/518856* ⏱ *Daily 9–1 and 4–8*) sells the work of Eugenio Taccini, which includes bowls, platters, tiles, and plates. The large shop is next to a bridge in Montelupo's historical center; the store's proprietor (and artist's daughter), Lea Taccini, speaks good English.

Many serious ceramics lovers think **Maioliche Dolfi Otello** (✉ *Via Toscoro-magnola Nord 20/b, Località Camaioni* ☎*0571/910105* ⊕*www.otellodolfi.it* ⊗ *Weekdays 8–noon and 1:30–6:30*) produces the region's finest work. The shop, in the same building as the factory, is a couple of miles outside Montelupo, down the SS67 highway in the direction of Florence. In addition to fine platters, vases, and pitchers, the shop produces devotional ceramics by hand in the style of the della Robbia. You can often watch the artisans at work.

EMPOLI

33 km (21 mi) west of Florence, 50 km (31 mi) east of Pisa.

GETTING HERE

Empoli is an easy 20-minute train ride from Florence's Santa Maria Novella station. If you're driving, take the Fi-Pi-Li armed with patience. The road is regularly under construction, and there are often delays due to accidents. Lazzi provides bus service from Florence to Empoli.

VISITOR INFORMATION

Empoli tourism office (✉ *Piazza Farinata degli Uberti 3* ☎*0571/757729* 🖷*0571/757740*).

EXPLORING

Empoli, roughly halfway between Florence and Pisa, is a small town with a long history. References to the city first appear in documents from the 800s. By the late 12th century it was under the control of Florence. It was here in 1260, after the Battle of Montaperti, that Farinata degli Uberti, leader of the Ghibellines, decided not to burn Florence to the ground. Dante immortalized this decision in Canto X of his *Inferno*.

Now Empoli is a sleepy little town a quick train ride from Florence. If you're traveling in summer, when Florence is at its hottest and most crowded, you might consider staying here and hopping on the train for day trips into the city. But don't overlook the sights of Empoli itself—they're worth seeing.

★ The **Collegiata di Sant'Andrea** is a jewel of a museum, filled with terracotta sculptures from the della Robbia school, including one by Andrea della Robbia. There's also a magnificent 15th-century fresco pietà by Masolino (circa 1383–1440), as well as a small work by Fra Filippo Lippi (1406–69) and a wonderful tabernacle attributed to Francesco Botticini (circa 1446–97) and Antonio Rossellino (1427–79). ✉*Just off Piazza Farinata degli Uberti* ☎*0571/76284* 🖷*€3, combination ticket €8 (includes Museo Leonardiano in Vinci and Museo Archeologico e della Ceramica in Montelupo)* ⊗*Thurs.–Mon. 10–12 and 4–7.*

NEED A BREAK?
Vinegar (✉ *Piazza della Vittoria 36–37* ☎*0571/74630*) a bar near the train station, sells all sorts of *panini* (sandwiches) as well as coffee and *aperitivi* (cocktails). It's a great spot to grab a sandwich before hopping the bus to Vinci.

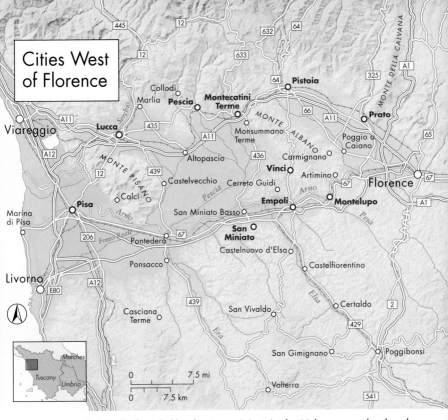

Cities West
of Florence

445
12
632
64
12
633
64 ● **Pistoia**
325 A1

MONTE DELLA CALVANA

Collodi
Marlia **Pescia** **Montecatini**
Terme
64
66
A11

MONTE ALBANO

Prato
Poggio a
Caiano
65

Viareggio
A11 **Lucca** 435
A11
Monsummano
Terme
436 Carmignano

Vinci Artimino
67 **Florence** 67
A1

A12
12 439
Castelvecchio
Cerreto Guidi
Arno

Calci
Pescia
Empoli **Montelupo**
Pesa

MONTE PISANO

Pisa
Arno
San Miniato Basso
Marina
di Pisa
206 Fosso Reale Pontedera 67 **San**
Miniato
Castelnuovo d'Elsa

Ponsacco
Castelfiorentino

Livorno
E80 A12

Casciana
Terme 439
San Vivaldo
Certaldo 2
429

San Gimignano
Poggibonsi

Marches
Tuscany Umbria

0   7.5 mi

0   7.5 km

San Gimignano

Volterra
541

Elsa
Era

Originally founded by the Augustinians in the 11th century, the church of **Santo Stefano** can be visited only by requesting a tour in the Collegiata di Sant'Andrea. It's worth the walk around the corner and down the street to see the *sinopie* (preparatory drawings) by Masolino depicting scenes from the *Legend of the True Cross*. He left without actually frescoing them; it may be that the Augustinian friars were late in making payment. ⌧ *Via de' Neri* ☎*0571/76284* 🖅*Free with admission to the Collegiata* ☉*Thurs.–Mon. 10–12 and 4–7.*

A short but not very scenic walk from the center of town brings you to the little church of **San Michele in Pontorme**, chiefly notable for the gorgeous *St. John the Baptist* and *St. Michael the Archangel*, two works dating from about 1519 by native son Jacopo Carrucci (1494–1556), better known as Pontormo. ⌧*Piazza San Michele* ☎*No phone* 🖅*Free* ☉*Ring bell for sacristan; no set hours, but most consistently open in morning.*

OFF THE
BEATEN
PATH

Villa Medicea. On the night of July 15, 1576, Isabella de' Medici, daughter of the all-powerful Cosimo I, grand duke of Tuscany, was murdered by her husband in the Villa Medicea in the town of Cerreto Guidi for "reasons of honor"—that is, she was suspected of adultery. These days, although the villa's formal garden is in somewhat imperfect condition, the vast halls and chambers within remain majestic. Copies of portraits of various Medici, including Isabella, cover the walls. The villa sits atop the highest point in Cerreto Guidi, encircled by two narrow streets where the daily business of the town goes on. As you stand on the wide, flat front lawn, high above the streets of the town, with the villa behind you and terraced hillsides of olive groves and vineyards stretching into the distance, you can imagine what it was like to be a Medici. To see the villa, ring the bell for the custodian. ⊠ ✛ *8 km (5 mi) west of Empoli, Cerreto Guidi* ☎*0571/55707* ✆*Free* ⊙*Daily 8:30–6:30. Closed 2nd and 3rd Mon. of each month.*

WHERE TO STAY & EAT

$$–$$$ ✕ **Il Galeone.** This relaxed and friendly place is known for its fish, but the meat dishes are just as good. Pale-pink walls and pink tablecloths play off the gray-and-white tile floors. Give the *moscardini con fagioli e rucola* (baby squid gently cooked with cannellini beans, diced tomatoes, and olive oil, served on a bed of arugula) a try; the *spiedini di seppioline e gamberoni* (kebabs of squid with shrimp) are terrific, too. Pizza is also served here. ⊠*Via Curtatone e Montanara 67* ☎*0571/72826* ⊟*AE, DC, MC, V* ⊙*Closed Sun. and Aug.*

$ 🏨 **Hotel Il Sole.** Across the street from the railway station, Il Sole has been in the hands of the Sabatini family since 1905. Each of the 12 rooms is its own eclectic interpretation of the Victorian style. If you are on a budget, this is a good alternative to staying in Florence, which is about a half-hour train ride away. **Pros:** Proximity to train station. **Cons:** It's a little worn at the edges. ⊠*Piazza Don Minzoni 18, 50053* ☎*0571/73779* 🖷*0571/79871* ⇆*12 rooms, 9 with bath* ♿*In-room: no a/c (some). In-hotel: some pets allowed* ⊟*AE, DC, MC, V* 🍴*BP.*

SHOPPING

Women of all shapes and sizes can find something stylish at the high-quality **Modyva outlet** (☎*0571/9501* ⊕*www.modyva.it* ⊙*Mon.–Sat. 9–1 and 3:30–7. Closed Aug.*). It's outside Empoli, hidden away near Modyva's factory with no sign outside. All four of the Modyva fashion house's lines are sold here at reduced prices, with those for irregulars (meticulously marked) lowered further. To get to the outlet, take either of the Empoli Ovest exits from the Fi-Pi-Li autostrada and turn left at the bottom of the ramp; at the traffic light go straight across the road and into the Terrafino industrial park. Modyva's *spazio aziendale* (selling space) is in the first building on your left.

VINCI

10 km (6 mi) north of Empoli, 45 km (28 mi) west of Florence.

GETTING HERE

To get to Vinci via public transportation, take the train to Empoli, and from here catch a Lazzi bus to Vinci.

VISITOR INFORMATION

Vinci tourism office (⊠*Via delle Torre 11* ☎🖷*0571/568012*).

Going Local at Festivals

A great way to get a feel for the region and its people is to attend a local *sagra* (festival). During the summer there's one taking place nearly every weekend in some small town or village, usually with a food theme, such as a *sagra dei funghi* (mushroom festival) or *sagra della zuppa* (soup festival). Held at night, the events dish out plenty to eat and drink, and there's usually dancing, sometimes with live music. Old-school ballroom moves are the norm; you're likely to see couples fox-trotting or doing the tango.

These are village affairs, with few people speaking English. There are no numbers to call for information. The festivals are advertised only by handwritten signs on the side of the road. Attending a sagra is a unique opportunity to experience small-town Italian culture.

EXPLORING

The small hill town from which Leonardo da Vinci derived his name is a short drive or bus ride north of Empoli. At the church of Santa Croce, near the town square, you can see the baptismal font in which Leonardo was baptized. But if you want to see the house where he was born, you'll have to travel to Anchiano, 3 km (2 mi) north of Vinci. Though somewhat of a tourist trap, it's worth a trip to Vinci for the views alone.

The modestly sized **Museo Ideale Leonardo da Vinci** houses an idiosyncratic hodgepodge of items related to the great Renaissance master, including mechanical objects and copies of his sketches, including one of this region. ⊠ *Via Montalbano 2* 📷*0571/56296* 💶*€5* 🕐*Daily 10–6.*

Museo Leonardiano, atop the castle belonging to the Guidi family in the historical center of Vinci, has replicas of many of Leonardo's machines and gadgets. The stunning country views most likely influenced the artist, as some of his painted backgrounds suggest the hills of Vinci. ⊠ *Via della Torre 2* 📷*0571/56055* 💶*€6, €8 combination ticket (includes Collegiata di Sant'Andrea in Empoli and Museo Archeologico e della Ceramica in Montelupo)* 🕐*Daily 9:30–7.*

OFF THE
BEATEN
PATH

Casa Natale di Leonardo. No one knows the precise location of Leonardo da Vinci's birthplace, but this typical 15th-century Tuscan house is in the general vicinity and probably shares much in common with the house where he was born. It's in Anchiano, 3 km (2 mi) from Vinci, and can be reached easily on foot or by car. It has a primitive interior—it hasn't been gussied up for tourists. Note the printed inventory of Leonardo's library. His tastes in literature were wide-ranging, from the ancients to contemporary (15th-century) authors. ⊠ *Località Anchiano* 📷*0571/56519* 💶*Free* 🕐*Mar.–Oct., daily 9:30–7; Nov.–Feb., daily 9:30–6.*

WHERE TO STAY

$ 🖼 **Il Fondaccio.** The Falzari family oversees this moderately priced agriturismo overlooking the hills near Vinci. Five apartments are available for groups of two to six people for one-week stays; one apartment is wheelchair accessible. If you're traveling with children, il Fondaccio is a perfect spot from which to tour the sights (Pisa, Lucca, San Gimignano, and beaches are all nearby); the pool provides a fine option for nonsightseeing days. **Pros:** Central location, good for kids. **Cons:** One-week stay required. ⊠ *Via del Fondaccio 19, 50059* ☎ *0571/559511* 📠 *0571/959703* ⊕ *www.fondaccio.it* ↝ *5 apartments* △ *In-room: no a/c, kitchen, no TV. In-hotel: pool, bicycles* ⊟ *No credit cards* ⊙ *Closed Nov.–Mar.* ⼣ *EP.*

SAN MINIATO

20 km (12 mi) southwest of Vinci, 43 km (27 mi) west of Florence.

GETTING HERE

The easiest way to get to San Miniato is by car via the Fi-Pi-Li. The San Miniato train station is far from the centro storico.

VISITOR INFORMATION

San Miniato tourism office (⊠ *Piazza del Popolo 3* ☎ *0571/418739*).

EXPLORING

San Miniato has a history dating to Etruscan and Roman times; today it's a tiny, pristine hill town of narrow, cobbled streets lined with austere 13th- to 17th-century facades, some covering buildings that are centuries older. The Holy Roman Empire had very strong ties here—the local castle was built in 962 under the aegis of Otto I (912–973). Eventually the town, with its Ghibelline (pro-imperial) sympathies, passed into the hands of the Florentines. San Miniato's artistic treasures are limited by Tuscan standards, but the town's prettiness makes a visit worthwhile. In the first three weekends in November, an annual truffle festival adds to San Miniato's allure.

In 1211 Saint Francis founded the **Convento di San Francesco** *(Convent and Church of St. Francis)*, which contains two cloisters and an ornate wooden choir. For a dose of monastic living, you can stay overnight (€36 for a double room). ⊠ *Piazza San Francesco* ☎ *0571/43051* ⼖ *Free* ⊙ *Daily 9–noon and 3–7 (or ring bell).*

The **Convento e Chiesa di Santi Jacopo e Filippo** *(Convent and Church of Sts. Jacob and Philip)* is also known as the church of San Domenico, which refers to the fact that the Dominicans took over the church in the 14th century. Most of the interior suffers from too much baroque, but there is a lovely sculpted tomb by Bernardo Rossellino for

Giovanni Chellini, a doctor who died in 1461. ⊠*Piazza del Popolo* ☎*0571/418739* ⊠*Free* ⊗*Daily 8:30–noon.*

Bar Cantini (⊠*Via Conti 1* ☎*0571/43030*) is a social hub for San Miniatans; its panini are wonderful, in part because the bread is baked on-site. There are also pizza by the slice, tasty *granita* (flavored ice), and homemade ice cream.

The only thing remarkable about San Miniato's **Duomo**, set in a pretty piazza, is its 13th-century facade, which has been restored. The interior is largely uninteresting, though there's a poignant plaque commemorating the 55 citizens who were killed in this church in July 1944 by German occupying forces. (The Taviani brothers' 1982 movie, *The Night of San Lorenzo*, was about these events.) ⊠*Piazza del Castello* ☎*No phone* ⊠*Free* ⊗*Daily 8–12:30 and 3–6:30.*

Although the **Museo Diocesano** is small, the modest collection incorporates a number of subtle and pleasant local works of art. Note the rather odd Crucifixion by Fra Filippo Lippi, Verrocchio's (1435–88) *Il Redentore*, and the small but exquisite *Education of the Virgin* by Tiepolo (1696–1770). ⊠*Piazza del Castello* ☎*0571/406700* ⊠*€3, combination ticket €5 (includes entry to 8 museums)* ⊗*Tues.–Sun. 10–7.*

The **Torre di Federico II**, dating from the time of Frederick II (1194–1250), was destroyed during World War II. A point of civic pride for San Miniatans and visible for miles, the tower was rebuilt and reopened in 1958. The hapless, ill-fated Pier della Vigna, chancellor and minister to Frederick II, leaped to his death from the tower, earning a mention in Dante's *Inferno*. The hill on which the tower stands—a surprisingly large oval of green grass—is one of the loveliest places in the area to have a picnic, enjoy the 360-degree view, and perhaps join local children in a pickup game of *calcio* (soccer). ⊠*Piazza la Torre* ☎*0571/42745* ⊠*€2.50* ⊗*Tues.–Sun. 10–6.*

WHERE TO STAY & EAT

$$ ✕**Il Convio.** A short drive down a steep, serpentine road from San Miniato brings you to a rustic country *ristorante* with sponged walls, stenciled decorations, and checkered tablecloths. The main courses are mostly Tuscan classics, such as *bistecca fiorentina* (a generous cut of grilled steak). White truffle, the local specialty, is showcased—you can get it with pasta, *crespelle* (thin pancakes filled with ricotta), tripe, eggs, beef fillet, and even pumpkin. There's a good selection of reasonably priced local wines, and service is courteous. ⊠*Via San Maiano 2* ☎*0571/408114* ⊟*AE, DC, MC, V* ⊗*Closed Wed.*

¢ ⌂**Convento di San Francesco.** For a complete change of pace, you can stay in this 13th-century convent in the company of five Franciscan friars. Rooms are simple but quiet. You are given keys, so there's no curfew. You can partake in some spiritual activities or skip them altogether. All rooms have baths, four rooms accommodate three people, and one room has four beds. The city center is a 10-minute walk from the monastery. **Pros:** Price, tranquillity. **Cons:** Conditions are rather spartan, most of staff speaks only Italian. ⊠*Piazza San Francesco,*

56020 ☎*0571/43051* 🖷*0571/43398* 🛏*30 rooms* �*In-room: no a/c, no phone, no TV. In-hotel: no elevator, no kids under 12* ▤*No credit cards* ⑩*EP.*

PISA

If you can get beyond the kitsch of the stalls hawking cheap souvenirs around the Leaning Tower, you'll find that Pisa has much to offer. Its treasures aren't as abundant as those of Florence, to which it is inevitably compared, but the cathedral-baptistery-tower complex of Piazza del Duomo, known collectively as the Campo dei Miracoli (Field of Miracles), is among the most dramatic settings in Italy.

Pisa may have been inhabited as early as the Bronze Age. It was certainly populated by the Etruscans and, in turn, became part of the Roman Empire. In the early Middle Ages it flourished as an economic powerhouse—along with Amalfi, Genoa, and Venice, it was one of the four maritime republics. The city's economic and political power ebbed in the early 15th century as it fell under Florence's domination, though it enjoyed a brief resurgence under Cosimo I in the mid-16th century. Pisa sustained heavy damage during World War II, but the Duomo and Tower were spared, along with some other grand Romanesque structures.

GETTING HERE
Pisa is an easy hour's train ride from Florence. By car it's a straight shot on the Fi-Pi-Li autostrada. The Pisa–Lucca train runs frequently and takes about 30 minutes.

VISITOR INFORMATION
Pisa tourism office (✉*Piazza Vittorio Emanuele II* ☎*050/42291*).

EXPLORING PISA

Pisa, like many Italian cities, is best explored on foot, and most of what you'll want to see is within walking distance. The views along the Arno River are particularly grand and shouldn't be missed—there's a feeling of spaciousness that isn't found on the Arno in Florence.

As you set out, note that there are various combination-ticket options for sights on the Piazza del Duomo.

MAIN ATTRACTIONS
❷ **Battistero.** This lovely Gothic baptistery, which stands across from the Duomo's facade, is best known for the pulpit carved by Nicola Pisano (circa 1220–84; father of Giovanni Pisano) in 1260. Ask one of the ticket takers if he'll sing for you inside; the acoustics are remarkable. ✉*Piazza del Duomo* ☎*050/3872210* ⊕*www.opapisa.it* 🎟*€5, discounts available if bought in combination with tickets for other monuments* ☉*Mar. 1–13, daily 9–6; Mar. 14–20, daily 9–7; Mar. 21–Sept., daily 8–8; Oct., daily 9–7; Nov.–Feb., daily 10–5.*

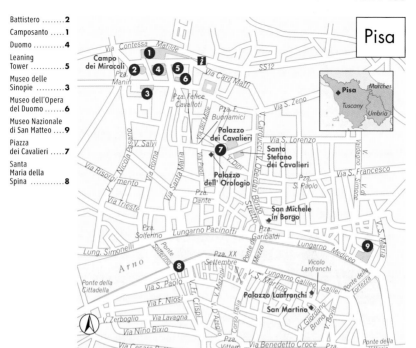

❹ Duomo. Pisa's cathedral brilliantly utilizes the horizontal marble stripe motif (borrowed from Moorish architecture) that became common to Tuscan cathedrals. It is famous for the Romanesque panels on the transept door facing the tower that depict scenes from the life of Christ. The beautifully carved 14th-century pulpit is by Giovanni Pisano (son of Nicola). ⊠*Piazza del Duomo* ☎*050/3872210* ⊕*www.opapisa.it* 🎟*€2, discounts available if bought in combination with tickets for other monuments* ☉*Mar. 1–13, daily 9–6; Mar. 14–20, daily 10–7; Mar. 21–Sept., daily 10–8; Oct., daily 10–7; Nov.–Feb. daily 10–1 and 2–5.*

❺ Leaning Tower *(Torre Pendente)*. Legend holds that Galileo conducted an experiment on the nature of gravity by dropping metal balls from the top of the 187-foot-high Leaning Tower of Pisa. Historians, however, say this legend has no basis in fact—which isn't quite to say that it's false. Work on this tower, built as a campanile (bell tower) for the Duomo, started in 1173: the lopsided settling began when construction reached the third story. The tower's architects attempted to compensate through such methods as making the remaining floors slightly taller on the leaning side, but the extra weight only made the problem worse. The settling continued, and by the late 20th century it had accelerated to such a point that many feared the tower would simply topple over, despite all efforts to prop it up. The structure has since been firmly anchored

FodorśChoice
★

to the earth. The final phase to restore the tower to its original tilt of 300 years ago was launched in early 2000 and finished two years later. The last phase removed some 100 tons of earth from beneath the foundation. Reservations, which are essential, can be made online or by calling the Museo dell'Opera del Duomo; it's also possible to arrive at the ticket office and book for the same day. Note that children under eight years of age are not allowed to climb. ⊠ *Piazza del Duomo* ☎ *050/3872210* ⊕ *www.opapisa.it* ☑ *€17* ⊗ *Mar. 21–Sept., daily 8:30–8:30; Oct., daily 9–7; Nov.–Feb., daily10–5; Mar. 1–Mar. 13, daily 9–6; Mar. 14–Mar. 20, daily 9–7.*

> ### WORD OF MOUTH
>
> "At Pisa we discovered a peaceful haven with relatively few tourists compared with Florence, and a magnificent lawn you could actually walk and sit on. I lay down in the lovely grass and slept in the sun until I was awakened by the cool shadow of the Leaning Tower. It was magic and peaceful and beautiful." –Jo

ALSO WORTH SEEING

❶ Camposanto. According to legend, the cemetery—a walled structure on the western side of the Campo dei Miracoli—is filled with earth that returning Crusaders brought back from the Holy Land. Contained within are numerous frescoes, notably *The Drunkenness of Noah*, by Renaissance artist Benozzo Gozzoli (1422–97), presently under restoration; and the disturbing *Triumph of Death* (14th century; artist uncertain), whose subject matter shows what was on people's minds in a century that saw the ravages of the Black Death. ⊠ *Piazza del Duomo* ☎ *050/3872210* ⊕ *www.opapisa.it* ☑ *€5, discounts available if bought in combination with tickets for other monuments* ⊗ *Mar. 1–13, daily 9–6; Mar. 14–20, daily 9–7; Mar. 21–Sept., daily 8–8; Oct., daily 10–7; Nov.–Feb., daily 10–5.*

❸ Museo delle Sinopie. The well-arranged museum on the south side of the Piazza del Duomo holds the *sinopie* (preparatory drawings) for the Camposanto frescoes. ⊠ *Piazza del Duomo* ☎ *050/3872210* ⊕ *www.opapisa.it* ☑ *€5, discounts available if bought in combination with tickets for other monuments* ⊗ *Mar. 1–13, daily 9–6; Mar. 14–20, daily 9–7; Mar. 21–Sept., daily 8–8; Oct., daily 10–7; Nov.–Feb., daily 10–5.*

❻ Museo dell'Opera del Duomo. At the southeast corner of the sprawling Campo dei Miracoli, this museum holds a wealth of medieval sculptures and the ancient Roman sarcophagi that inspired Nicola Pisano's figures. ⊠ *Piazza del Duomo* ☎ *050/3872210* ⊕ *www.opapisa.it* ☑ *€5, discounts available if bought in combination with tickets for other monuments* ⊗ *Mar. 1–13, daily 9–6; Mar. 14–20, daily 9–7; Mar. 21–Sept., daily 8–8; Oct., daily 10–7; Nov.–Feb., daily 10–5.*

❾ Museo Nazionale di San Matteo. On the north bank of the Arno, this museum contains some incisive examples of local Romanesque and Gothic art. ⊠ *Lungarno Mediceo* ☎ *050/541865* ☑ *€5* ⊗ *Tues.–Sat. 9–7, holidays 9–2.*

7 Piazza dei Cavalieri. The piazza, with its fine Renaissance **Palazzo dei Cavalieri, Palazzo dell'Orologio,** and **Santo Stefano dei Cavalieri,** was laid out by Giorgio Vasari in about 1560. The square was the seat of the Ordine dei Cavalieri di San Stefano (Order of the Knights of St. Stephen), a military and religious institution meant to defend the coast from possible invasion by the Turks. Also in this square is the prestigious **Scuola Normale Superiore,** founded by Napoléon in 1810 on the French model. Here graduate students pursue doctorates in literature, philosophy, mathematics, and science. In front of the school is a large statue of Ferdinando I de' Medici dating from 1596. On the extreme left is the tower where the hapless Ugolino della Gherardesca (died 1289) was imprisoned with his two sons and two grandsons; legend holds that he ate them. Dante immortalized him in Canto XXXIII of his *Inferno.* Duck into the **Church of Santo Stefano** and check out Bronzino's *Nativity of Christ* (1564–65).

8 Santa Maria della Spina. Originally an oratory dating from the 13th century, this gem of a church has been restored several times, most recently in 1996–98, owing to flood damage. It's a delicate, tiny church, and a fine example of Tuscan Gothic architecture. ⊠ *Lungarno Gambacorti* ☎ *No phone* ✆€2.50 ⊘ *Apr.–Oct., Tues.–Fri. 10–1:15 and 2:30–5:45; Nov.–Mar., Thurs. and Fri. 10–2, Sat. and 2nd Sun. of month 10–5.*

OFF THE
BEATEN
PATH

La Certosa di Pisa. A *certosa* is a monastery whose monks belong to the strict Carthusian order. This vast and sprawling complex, begun in 1366, was suppressed by Napoléon in the early 1800s, and then again in 1866. Most of the art and architecture you see dates from the 17th and 18th centuries. The Carthusians returned here, only to leave it permanently in 1969. Also within it is the **Museo di Storia Naturale e del Territorio.** This museum of natural history contains fossils, 24 whale skeletons that serve to trace the mammal's development over the millennia, and some exhibits of local minerals. ✛ *10 km (6 mi) east of Pisa via road north of Arno, through Mezzana and then toward Calci and Montemagno* ☎050/938430 ✆€4 ⊘ *Tues.–Sat. 8:30–6:30, Sun. 8:30–12:30, with tours on the half hour.*

San Piero a Grado. This 11th-century basilica, located 8 km (5 mi) southwest of Pisa along the Arno, was built over the remains of two earlier churches. According to legend, it was here that Peter the Apostle stepped off the boat in AD 42—his first step on Italian soil. (It would have made more sense for him to land on the Adriatic Coast, as he was coming from Antioch.) The structure is a lovely example of Romanesque architecture, and it's not without its quirks: it has two apses, one at each end. On the walls are some crumbling, but still vibrant, frescoes dating from the 12th and 13th centuries. Thirty-one of these frescoes depict scenes from the lives of Saints Peter and Paul, an uncommon subject in Tuscan wall painting. ⊠ *Via Vecchia di Marina, San Piero a Grado* ☎050/960065 ✆*Free* ⊘ *Daily 8-7.*

WHERE TO EAT

$$–$$$ ✕**Beny.** Apricot walls hung with etchings of Pisa make this small, single-room restaurant warmly romantic. Husband and wife Damiano and Sandra Lazzerini have been running the place for two decades, and it shows in their obvious enthusiasm while talking about the menu and daily specials. Beny specializes in fish: its *ripieno di polpa di pesce a pan grattato con salsa di seppie e pomodoro* (fish-stuffed ravioli with tomato-octopus sauce) is a delight. Another flavorful dish is the *sformato di verdura* (a flan with Jerusalem artichokes), which comes embellished with sweet *gamberoni* (shrimp). ⊠ *Piazza Gambacorti 22* ☎ *050/25067* ═ *AE, DC, MC, V* ⊘ *Closed Sun. and 2 wks in mid-Aug. No lunch Sat.*

$$ ✕**La Mescita.** Tall, vaulted ceilings and stenciled walls lined with wine bottles provide the simple background at this trattoria. Young chef Giovanni Marchi spent some time cooking in the United States, and he brings a fresh perspective to Tuscan fare. His ravioli stuffed with mozzarella and topped with oven-roasted tomatoes is superb. ⊠ *Via Cavalca 2, Santa Maria* ☎ *050/544294* ═ *AE, DC, MC, V* ⊘ *Closed Sun. No lunch Tues.*

$$ ✕**La Pergoletta.** On an old-town street named for its beautiful towers, this small, simple restaurant is in one such tower itself. There's also a shady garden for outdoor dining. Emma Forte, the proprietor and chef, cooks such Tuscan classics as *minestra di farro* (spelt soup) and choice interpretations of *grigliata* (grilled beef, veal, or lamb). Her sense of whimsy accounts for some of the non-Italian ingredients such as ginger that find their way into her dishes. Parents with small children may be pleased to find there's a children's menu. ⊠ *Via delle Belle Torri 40* ☎ *050/542458* ═ *AE, DC, MC, V* ⊘ *Closed Mon. and 1 wk in Aug. No lunch Sat.*

$$ ✕**Osteria dei Cavalieri.** This charming white-wall restaurant, a few steps
★ from Piazza dei Cavalieri, is reason enough to come to Pisa. They can do it all here—serve up exquisitely grilled fish dishes, please vegetarians, and prepare *tagliata* (thin slivers of rare beef) for meat lovers. Three set menus, from the sea, garden, and earth, are available, or you can order à la carte. For dinner there's an early seating (around 7:30) and a later one (around 9); opt for the later one if you want time to linger over your meal. ⊠ *Via San Frediano 16* ☎ *050/580858* ✍ *Reservations essential* ═ *AE, DC, MC, V* ⊘ *Closed Sun., 2 wks in Aug., and Dec. 29–Jan. 7. No lunch Sat.*

$ ✕**Il Re di Puglia.** In winter at "The King of Puglia," in the countryside 15 minutes outside of Pisa, you can enjoy Tuscan favorites in a large room with a fireplace. In summer you sit outside on a covered terrace. Beef, sausage, vegetables, and bruschetta are prepared on a very large grill, and all are well executed. Paired with the formidable wine list and friendly service, they make for a memorable meal. ⊠ *Via Aurelia Sud 7* ☎ *050/960157* ✍ *Reservations essential* ═ *No credit cards* ⊘ *Closed Mon. and Tues. No lunch Wed.–Sat.*

WHERE TO STAY

$$$$ ⛄ **Hotel Relais dell'Orologio.** What used to be a private family palace opened as an intimate hotel in spring of 2003. Eighteenth-century antiques fill the rooms and public spaces; some rooms have stenciled walls and wood-beam ceilings. On the third floor, sloped ceilings add romance. A large shared sitting room, complete with fireplace, provides a relaxing spot to read or sip a glass of wine. **Pros:** Location—in the center of town, but on a quiet side street. **Cons:** Breakfast costs extra. ⊠ *Via della Faggiola 12/14, off Campo dei Miracoli, Santa Maria, 56126* ☎ *050/830361* 🖷 *050/551869* ⊕ *www.hotel relaisorologio.com* ⤳ *16 rooms, 5 suites* 🖐 *In-room: safe, refrigerator, dial-up. In-hotel: restaurant, room service, bar, concierge, laundry service, parking (fee), some pets allowed, no-smoking rooms, minibar* ⊟ *AE, DC, MC, V* ⊚|*EP.*

$$ ⛄ **Royal Victoria.** In a pleasant palazzo facing the Arno, a 10-minute walk from the Campo dei Miracoli, this comfortably furnished hotel has been in the Piegaja family since 1837. That continuity may help explain why such notables as Charles Dickens and Charles Lindbergh enjoyed staying here. Antiques and reproductions are in the lobby and in some rooms, whose style ranges from the 1800s, complete with frescoes, to the 1920s. Ask for a room in the charming old tower. There's also a pretty rooftop garden where you can order cocktails. **Pros:** Friendly staff, free use of a Lancia that seats five—a great vehicle for tooling around Pisa. **Cons:** Rooms vary significantly in size; all are a little worn. ⊠ *Lungarno Pacinotti 12, 56126* ☎ *050/940111* 🖷 *050/940180* ⊕ *www.royalvictoria.it* ⤳ *48 rooms, 40 with bath* 🖐 *In-room: no a/c (some), dial-up. In-hotel: room service, bicycles, concierge, laundry service, parking (fee), some pets allowed* ⊟ *AE, DC, MC, V* ⊚|*BP.*

$–$$ ⛄ **Fattoria di Migliarino.** Martino Salviati and his wife, Giovanna, have
★   turned their working *fattoria* (farm)—on which they raise soybeans, corn, and sugar beets—into an inn. The charming, spacious apartments accommodate anywhere from two to eight people and are rustically furnished, many of them with fireplaces. There's also a farmhouse that has been converted into a B&B. The pool is framed by fields, and the only sound you're likely to hear is the clucking of the hens they keep for eggs. The surrounding woods can be explored on horseback or with a mountain bike. During high season, a one-week stay at the apartments is mandatory. **Pros:** Near Pisa airport, a good choice for a tranquil last night in Italy. **Cons:** Mandatory one-week apartment stay during high season. ⊠ *Via dei Pini 289* ✛ *10 km (6 mi) northwest of Pisa, Migliarino 56010* ☎ *050/803046 or 335/6608411* 🖷 *050/803170* ⊕ *www.fattoriadimigliarino.it* ⤳ *10 rooms in B&B, 7 apartments* 🖐 *In-room: no a/c (some), kitchen, no TV. In-hotel: pool, no elevator* ⊟ *MC, V* ⊚|*BP.*

NIGHTLIFE & THE ARTS

The **Luminaria** feast day, on June 16, is Pisa at its best. The day honors Saint Ranieri, the city's patron saint. Palaces along the Arno are lit with white lights, and there are plenty of fireworks.

Pisa has a lively performing-arts scene, most of which happens at the 19th-century Teatro Verdi. Music and dance performances are presented from September through May. Contact **Fondazione Teatro di Pisa** (⊠ *Via Palestro 40, Lungarni* ☎ *050/941111* ⊕ *www.teatrodipisa. pi.it*) for schedules and information.

THE ROAD FROM FLORENCE TO LUCCA

The cities along the route between Florence and Lucca are primarily industrial—and they've been that way for a long time. Prato has been producing textiles since the Middle Ages; Renaissance art lovers should pay a visit to the Duomo, with its magnificent Filippo Lippi frescoes. Farther northwest, Pistoia's historic center abounds with artistic treasures. If you're looking for a spa treatment, or if you want to experience a bit of kitsch, Italian style, visit Montecatini Terme, where the clock seems to have stopped some time in the 1950s.

PRATO

19 km (12 mi) northwest of Florence, 60 km (37 mi) east of Lucca.

GETTING HERE

Prato is a quick train ride from Florence. By car it's a 45-minute trip on the A11/E76 toll road.

VISITOR INFORMATION

Prato tourism office (⊠ *Piazza delle Carceri 15* ☎ *0574/24112*).

EXPLORING

The wool industry in this city, one of the world's largest producers of cloth, was known throughout Europe as early as the 13th century. Business was further stimulated in the 14th century by a local cloth merchant, Francesco di Marco Datini, who built his business, according to one of his surviving ledgers, IN THE NAME OF GOD AND OF PROFIT. One thing that distinguishes Prato from other Italian towns of its size is the presence of modern public art—most notably Henry Moore's mammoth, marble *Square Form with Cut* in Piazza San Marco.

Prato's Romanesque **Duomo**, reconstructed from 1211, is famous for its **Pergamo del Sacro Cingolo** (Chapel of the Holy Girdle), to the left of the entrance, which enshrines the sash of the Virgin Mary. It is said that the girdle was given to the apostle Thomas by the Virgin Mary when she miraculously appeared after her Assumption into heaven. The Duomo also contains 15th-century frescoes by Prato's most famous son, Fra Filippo Lippi. His scenes from the life of Saint Stephen are on the left wall of the **Cappella Maggiore** (Main Chapel); those from the life of

John the Baptist are on the right. ⊠*Piazza del Duomo* ☎*0574/26234* ⊙*Mon.–Sat. 7–noon and 3:30–7, Sun. 7–12:30 and 3:30–8.*

NEED A BREAK?

Prato's *biscotti* (literally "twice-cooked" cookies) have an extra-dense texture, lending themselves to submersion in your caffè or vin santo. The best biscotti in town are at Antonio Mattei (⊠ *Via Ricasoli 20/22* ☎*0574/25756* ⊕*www.antoniomattei.it*).

A sculpture by Donatello (circa 1386–1466) that originally adorned the Duomo's exterior pulpit is now on display in the **Museo dell'Opera del Duomo.** The museum also includes such 15th-century gems as Fra Filippo Lippi's *Madonna and Child,* Giovanni Bellini's (circa 1432–1516) *Christ on the Cross,* and Caravaggio's (1571–1610) *Christ Crowned with Thorns.* ⊠*Piazza del Duomo 49* ☎*0574/29339* ⊠*€4, combination ticket €6 (includes Museo di Pittura Murale and il Castello)* ⊙*Mon. and Wed.–Sat. 9:30–12:30 and 3–6:30, Sun. 9:30–12:30.*

The permanent collection in the **Museo di Pittura Murale** *(Museum of Mural Painting)* contains frescoes removed from sites in and around Prato such as those by Agnolo Gaddi, Nicolo Gerini, and Il Volterrano. ⊠*Piazza San Domenico 8* ☎*0574/440501* ⊠*€4, combination ticket €6 (includes Museo dell'Opera del Duomo and il Castello)* ⊙*Mon., Wed., and Thurs. 9–1; weekends 9–1 and 3–6.*

Prato's **Centro per l'Arte Contemporanea Luigi Pecci** *(Luigi Pecci Center of Contemporary Art)* contains works of artists from around the world completed after 1965. The exhibitions constantly change and often feature debut presentations. ⊠ *Viale della Repubblica 277* ☎*0574/5317* ⊕*www.centropecci.it* ⊠*€5* ⊙ *Wed.–Mon. 10–6:30.*

Preserved in the **Museo del Tessuto** *(Textile Museum)* is what made this city a Renaissance economic powerhouse. The collection includes clothing, fabric fragments, samples, and the machines used to make them from the 14th to the 20th centuries. Check out the 15th-century fabrics with pomegranate prints, a virtuoso display of Renaissance textile wizardry. ⊠*Piazza del Commune* ☎*0574/611503* ⊠*€6; free Sun.* ⊙ *Weekdays 10–6, Sat. 10–2, Sun. 4–7. Tours by appointment.*

The church of **Santa Maria delle Carceri** was built by Giuliano Sangallo in the 1490s and is a landmark of Renaissance architecture. ⊠*Piazza Santa Maria delle Carceri, off Via Cairoli and southeast of the cathedral* ☎*0574/27933* ⊠*Free* ⊙*Daily 7–noon and 4–7.*

The formidable **Castello** *(Castle),* near Santa Maria delle Carceri, is an impressive sight. The Lombard Emperor Frederick II (1194–1250) built the seat of his authority in Tuscany. Frederick's castles were designed to echo imperial Rome, and the many columns, lions, and porticoes testify to his ambition. This is the only castle he built outside of Sicily and Puglia in southern Italy. ⊠*Piazza Santa Maria delle Carceri* ☎*0574/38207* ⊠*€2.50, combination ticket €6.50 (includes Museo dell'Opera del Duomo and Museo di Pittura Murale)* ⊙*Nov.–Mar., Wed.–Mon. 9–1; Apr.–Oct., Wed.–Mon. 9–1 and 4–7.*

Poggio a Caiano. For a look at gracious country living Renaissance style, take a detour to the Medici villa in Poggio a Caiano. Lorenzo "il Magnifico" (1449–92) commissioned Giuliano da Sangallo (circa 1445–1516) to redo the villa, which was lavished with frescoes by important Renaissance painters such as Pontormo (1494–1556), Franciabigio (1482–1525), and Andrea del Sarto (1486–1531). You can walk around the austerely ornamented grounds while waiting for one of the hourly villa tours, which start on the half hour. ✉*Piazza dei Medici 14* ✛ *7 km (4½ mi) south of Prato (follow signs)* ☎*055/877012* ✏*€2 (includes villa and garden)* ☉*Sept. and Oct., daily 8:15–5:30; Nov.–Feb., daily 8:15–3:30; Mar., daily 8:15–4:30; Apr. and May, daily 8:15–5:30; June–Aug., daily 8:15–6:30.*

Carmignano. Pontormo's *Visitation* is in this small village, a short car ride from Poggio a Caiano. The Franciscan church of **San Michele,** dedicated in 1211, houses the work. The painting dates from 1527–30, and it may well be Pontormo's masterpiece. The luminous colors, flowing drapery, and steady gaze shared between the Virgin and Saint Elizabeth are breathtaking. The church's small cloister, shaded by olive trees, is always open and offers a quiet place to sit. ✛*15 km (9 mi) south of Prato, through Poggio a Caiano, up Mt. Albano* ☎*055/8712046* ✏*Free* ☉*Oct.–Apr., daily 7:30–5; May–Sept., daily 7:30–6.*

OFF THE BEATEN PATH

In the small town of **Artimino,** next door to Carmignano, is the **Villa Medicea La Ferdinanda di Artimino.** Built by Ferdinando I de' Medici (1549–1609) in the 1590s, it was originally used as a hunting lodge. ✛*11 km (7 mi) south of Prato (head east from Carmignano or south from Poggio a Caiano, up Mt. Albano)* ☎*055/871124* ✏*Free* ☉*Nov.–Jan., Thurs.–Sat. by reservation, Sun. 10–noon; Feb.–Oct., Mon., Tues., and Thurs.–Sat. 9:30–12:30, Wed. by reservation, Sun. 10–noon.*

WHERE TO STAY & EAT

$$–$$$ ✗**Baghino.** In the heart of the historic center, Baghino serves the typical Tuscan classics. Primi such as ribollita (minestrone with bread and beans) can be had, as well as an array of great grilled meats. The *ravioli alla Senese* (with spinach sauce and pecorino cheese) should not be missed. ✉*Via dell'Accademia 9* ☎*0574/27920* ▤*AE, DC, MC, V* ☉*Closed Aug. No lunch Mon. No dinner Sun.*

$$ ✗**Da Delfina.** Delfina Cioni began cooking many years ago for hungry ★ hunters in the town of Artimino, 20 km (12 mi) south of Prato; now her son Carlo maintains the culinary legacy. Dishes celebrate Tuscan food, with an emphasis on fresh local ingredients. Secondi such as *coniglio con olive e pignoli* (rabbit sautéed with olives and pine nuts—the house specialty) are a real treat. The seasonal menu is complemented by a fine wine list, and service is gracious. From the restaurant's four comfortably rustic rooms (and outside terrace when it's warm) you have a glorious view of the Tuscan countryside, including a Medici villa. ✉*Via della Chiesa 1, Artimino* ☎*055/8718074* ✎*Reservations essential* ▤*No credit cards* ☉*Closed Mon. and 3 wks in Aug. No lunch Tues. No dinner Sun.*

$–$$ ✕**Biagio Pignatta.** Biagio Pignatta was Ferdinando I's chef, and was so beloved that he was admitted into a select knightly order: check out his coat of arms on the outside wall of the restaurant—it includes a heraldic crest and a pot of beans. The menu here, just south of Prato, is Tuscan, with some unexpected twists like a truffled artichoke or the *spiedino di capretto* (roast kid kebab). The compact wine list offers many Tuscan favorites, including some made very locally. Save room for the stellar desserts—they steal the show here. ✉ *Viale Papa Giovanni XXIII 1, Artimino* ☎ *055/8751406* ✁ *AE, DC, MC, V* ⊘ *No lunch Wed. or Thurs.*

¢   ✕**La Vecchia Cucina di Soldano.** This place could be mistaken for an Italian grandmother's kitchen: it's completely unpretentious, tablecloths are red-and-white checked, and the servers are like old friends. Local Pratesi specialties include the odd but tasty *sedani ripieni* (stuffed celery), in which celery is pressed and stuffed with a minced veal and mortadella filling, then coated in flour and egg before being fried in olive oil and served with a meat sauce. Or you might enjoy the superb *tagliolini sui fagioli* (thin noodles with beans). The restaurant teems with locals. Clearly they, too, like the rock-bottom prices. ✉ *Via Pomeria 23* ☎ *0574/34665* ✁ *No credit cards* ⊘ *Closed Sun.*

$$–$$$ ⌂**Hotel Paggeria Medicea.** Ferdinando I loved to hunt, and so erected his villa to accommodate this whim. His servants bunked in what is now this lovely, tranquil hotel in the middle of lush countryside. Some of the simply but elegantly furnished rooms look out on a view that doesn't quit; others face flowers and a pool. If you're contemplating a longer stay, consider renting one of the apartments in centuries-old buildings dotting the surrounding area. **Pros:** Peace and tranquillity, spectacular views. **Cons:** A car is vital. ✉ *Viale Papa Giovanni XXIII 1, 59015* ☎ *055/875141* 🖷 *055/8751470* ⊕ *www.artimino.com* ⟳ *37 rooms* ⌂ *In-room: safe, refrigerator, dial-up. In-hotel: bar, pool, concierge, laundry service, parking (fee), some pets allowed, no-smoking rooms* ✁ *AE, DC, MC, V.*

$ ⌂**Albergo Giardino.** In the center of Prato's historic district and a stone's throw from the cathedral, this simple and clean hotel has friendly service. The rooms are nothing special, but the location is ideal. **Pros:** A bargain for town center location. **Cons:** Rooms can feel sterile. ✉ *Via Magnolfi, 2/4/6, 59100* ☎ *0574/26189* 🖷 *0574/606591* ⊕ *www. giardinohotel.com* ⟳ *28 rooms* ⌂ *In-room: safe, refrigerator, Wi-Fi. In-hotel: bar, laundry service, public Internet, public Wi-Fi, parking (no fee), some pets allowed* ✁ *AE, DC, MC, V* ⌾*BP.*

PISTOIA

18 km (11 mi) northwest of Prato, 43 km (27 mi) east of Lucca, 37 km (23 mi) northwest of Florence.

GETTING HERE

From Florence or Lucca, Pistoia is an easy train ride; trains run frequently. By car, take the A11/E76.

VISITOR INFORMATION

Pistoia tourism office (⊠*Palazzo dei Vescovi* ☎0573/21622).

EXPLORING

Founded in the 2nd century BC as a support post for Roman troops, Pistoia grew over the centuries into an important trading center. In the Middle Ages it was riven by civic strife and eventually fell to the Florentines, who imposed a pro-Guelf government in 1267; it lost its last vestiges of independence to Florence in 1329.

Reconstructed after heavy bombing during World War II, it has preserved some fine Romanesque architecture. Modern-day Pistoia's major industries include the manufacture of rail vehicles (including the cars for Washington, D.C.'s Metro) and tree and plant nurseries, which flourish on the alluvial plain around the city.

The Romanesque **Duomo,** the Cattedrale di San Zeno, dates from as early as the 5th century. It houses a magnificent silver altar dedicated to Saint James. The two half-figures on the left are by Filippo Brunelleschi (1377–1446), the first Renaissance architect (and designer of Florence's magnificent Duomo cupola). The octagonal **Battistero,** with green-and-white-stripe marble cladding, dates from the middle of the 14th century. Three of its eight sides have doorways; the main door facing the piazza is crowned with a rose window. Note the lovely little lantern crowning the top of the building. ⊠*Piazza del Duomo* ☎*0573/25095* 🎫*Free; access to altarpiece €2* ⊘*Church: Oct.–Apr., Mon.–Sat. 8–12:30 and 3:30–7, Sun. 8–1 and 3:30–7; May–Sept., daily 8–1 and 3:30–7. Altar: Mon.–Sat. 10–12:30 and 3–5:30, Sun. 8–9:30, 11–11:30, and 4–5:30.*

The Palazzo del Comune, begun around 1295, houses the **Museo Civico,** containing works by local artists from the 13th to 19th centuries. ⊠*Piazza del Duomo 1* ☎*0573/371296* 🎫*€3.50, combination ticket €6.50 (includes Palazzo Rospigliosi and Fondazione Marino Marini)* ⊘ *Mon., Tue., and Thurs.–Sat. 10–6, Wed. 4–7, Sun. 11–6.*

The **Antico Palazzo dei Vescovi** *(Old Bishop's Palace)* and **Museo della Cattedrale di San Zeno** contain spectacular treasures from Pistoia's cathedral—including ornate pieces in gold, rings with jewels the size of small eggs, and solemn, powerful statuary. Below, however, are Roman, medieval, and even Etruscan archaeological sites uncovered in a 1970s renovation. The warren of corridors and caves below and the plain, spare rooms above both show off their treasures with simple elegance. ⊠*Piazza del Duomo* ☎*0573/369272* 🎫*€4* ⊘*Tues., Thurs., and Fri. 10–1 and 3–5.*

Founded in the 13th century and still a functioning hospital, the **Ospedale del Ceppo** has a facade with a superb early-16th-century exterior terra-cotta frieze. It was begun by Giovanni della Robbia (1469–1529) and completed by the workshop of Santi and Benedetto Buglioni between 1526 and 1528. Don't miss the 17th-century graffiti on the columns outside. ⊠*Piazza Giovanni XIII, down Via Pacini from Piazza del Duomo* ⊘*Closed to the public.*

Pistoia's medieval skyline.

In the 12th-century church of **Sant'Andrea**, the fine pulpit by Giovanni Pisano (circa 1250–1314) depicts scenes from the life of Christ in a series of high-relief richly sculpted marble panels. ⊠ *Piazzetta Sant'Andrea, Via Sant'Andrea* ☎*0573/21912* ✆*Free* ☉ *Daily 7:30– 12:30 and 3:30–6.*

The 16th-century mannerist-style **Palazzo Rospigliosi** houses the **Museo Rospigliosi** and the **Museo Diocesano,** with a collection of mostly 16th- and 17th-century works. The Museo Rospigliosi contains a room referred to as Pope Clement IX's (1600–69) apartment, although there's no evidence that the Pistoian native, born Giulio Rospigliosi, actually stayed there. The Museo Diocesano has liturgical objects and furnishings from the diocese of Pistoia. Many date from the 13th, 14th, and 15th centuries. ⊠ *Via Ripa del Sale 3* ☎*0573/28740* ✆*€3.50, combination ticket €6.50 (includes both museums and Museo Civico and the Fondazione Marino Marini)* ☉*Tues.–Sat. 10–1 and 3–6.*

Lest you think that Tuscany produced only Renaissance artists, the **Fondazione Marino Marini** presents many works from its namesake modern native Pistoian (1901–80). Sculpture, etchings, paintings, engravings, and mixed media have all been installed in the elegantly renovated 14th-century Convento del Tau. ⊠ *Corso Silvano Fedi 30* ☎*0573/30285* ☏*0473/31332* ✆*€3.50, combination ticket €6.50 (includes Palazzo Rospigliosi and Museo Civico)* ☉*Oct.–Mar., Mon.–Sat. 10–5; Apr.– Sept., Mon.–Sat. 10–6.*

An architectural gem in green-and-white marble, the medieval church of **San Giovanni Fuorcivitas** holds a *Visitation* by Luca della Robbia (1400–82), a painting attributed to Taddeo Gaddi, and a holy-water font that may have been made by Fra Guglielmo around 1270. ⊠ *Via Cavour* ☎ *0573/24784* ⊙ *Daily 7:30–12 and 5–6:30.*

3

A 20-minute drive out of town brings you to the **Giardino Zoologico**, a small zoo laid out to accommodate the wiles of both animals and children. ⊠ *Via Pieve a Celle 160/a, take Bus 29 from train station* ☎ *0573/911219* 🎫 *€9.50* ⊙ *Oct.–Mar., daily 9–5, Apr.–Sept., daily 9–7.*

WHERE TO STAY & EAT

$$ ✕ **S. Jacopo.** This charming restaurant minutes from the Piazza del Duomo has white walls, tile floors, and tasteful prints and photographs on the walls that contrast nicely with the rustic blue table linens. The menu has mostly regional favorites, such as the *maccheroni S. Jacopo* (wide ribbons of house-made pasta in a duck sauce), but the restaurant can turn out perfectly grilled squid as well. Save room for dessert, especially the apple strudel. ⊠ *Via Crispi 15* ☎ *0573/27786* ▭ *AE, DC, MC, V* ⊙ *Closed Mon. and 2 wks in July/Aug.*

$ ✕ **La BotteGaia.** Jazz plays softly in the background as patrons sip wine at rustic tables in rooms with exposed brick-and-stone walls. In warm weather you can also dine alfresco with a splendid view of the Piazza del Duomo. Typical wine-bar fare, such as plates of cured ham and cheese, shares the menu with a surprisingly sophisticated list of daily specials. For example, you might try *insalatina con foie gras condita con vinaigrette* (foie gras with dressed greens). ⊠ *Via del Lastrone 17* ☎ *0573/365602* ⌗ *Reservations essential* ▭ *AE, DC, MC, V* ⊙ *Closed Mon. and last 3 wks in Aug. No lunch Sun.*

$ ✕ **Trattoria dell'Abbondanza.** Entering from a quiet side street, you walk into a small place with cream-color walls that's busy but not noisy, its staff attentive but never pushy. Traditional dishes include, for first courses, *minestra di farro* (a hearty soup made with farro) and *maccheroni all'anatra* (pasta in a duck sauce). For seconds, there's *baccalà alla Livornese* (salt cod in a tomato sauce), roast rabbit, and tripe. *Torta rustica*, a cake of cornmeal and cream, makes a fine dessert. ⊠ *Via dell'Abbondanza 10/14, off Via degli Orafi* ☎ *0573/368037* ▭ *MC, V* ⊙ *Closed Wed. No lunch Thurs.*

$ ⌂ **Hotel Leon Bianco.** Most everything you want to see in Pistoia is only a few minutes' walk from this small hotel. Here you'll find a somewhat utilitarian lobby decorated in chintz, a small bar at which to enjoy an *aperitivo* (aperitif), and lively innkeepers who speak perfect English. **Pros:** Numerous triple rooms make it good for families. **Cons:** A Fodor's reader reports, "rooms are spotless, though not very cosy." ⊠ *Via Panciatichi 2, 51100* ☎ *0573/26675 or 0573/26676* 🖷 *0573/26704* ⊕ *www.hotelleonbianco.it* ⋙ *26 rooms* ♿ *In-room: no* *a/c (some), Wi-Fi. In-hotel: bar, laundry service, public Internet, some pets allowed, no-smoking rooms* =*AE, DC, MC, V* IOIBP.

NIGHTLIFE & THE ARTS

★ In mid-July **Pistoia Blues** (☎*0573/994659* ⊕*www.pistoiablues.com*) brings international blues artists and rock-and-rollers to town for performances in the main square. **La Giostra dell'Orso** *(Bear Joust)*, on July 25, celebrates Saint James, Pistoia's patron saint. During the staged event, three knights from each section of the city fight a "bear" (actually a target shaped like a bear that they strike, on horseback). The visitor center has more information on the event.

MONTECATINI TERME

15 km (9 mi) west of Pistoia, 49 km (30 mi) west of Florence, 29 km (18 mi) northeast of Lucca.

GETTING HERE

Montecatini Terme is one of the stops on the Florence–Lucca train line, and getting to the centro storico is an easy walk from the station. The A11/E76 will get you here by car.

VISITOR INFORMATION

Montecatini Terme tourism office (⊠*Viale Verdi 66–68* ☎*0572/772244*).

EXPLORING

Immortalized in Fellini's film *8½*, Montecatini Terme is the home of Italy's premier *terme* (spas). Known for their curative powers—and, at least once upon a time, for their great popularity among the wealthy—the mineral springs flow from five sources and are taken for a variety of ailments, including liver and skin disorders. Those "taking the cure" report each morning to one of the town's *stabilimenti termali* (thermal establishments) to drink their prescribed cupful of water. Afterward, guests can enjoy a leisurely breakfast, read the newspaper, recline and listen to music, or walk in the parks that surround these grand old spas.

The umbrella group **Terme di Montecatini** (⊠*Viale Verdi 41* ☎*0572/778487* ⊕*www.termemontecatini.it*) has information on the town's nine thermal spas.

For more traditional beauty treatments, there's the **Excelsior** (⊠*Viale Verdi 61* ☎*0572/778518, 0572/778541 for appointments*), which offers manicures, facials, and massage therapies with mud, algae, and oils.

The town's wealth of art-nouveau buildings went up during its most active period of development, at the beginning of the 20th century. Like most other well-heeled resort towns, Montecatini attracts the leisured traveler, conventioneer, and senior citizen on a group tour; it's trimmed with a measure of neon and glitz; aside from taking the waters and people-watching in Piazza del Popolo, there's not a whole lot to do here. There are, however, plenty of places to stay, making the town a good base from which to explore the region.

The most attractive art-nouveau structure in town, **Terme Tettuccio,** has lovely colonnades. Here fountains set up on marble counters dispense mineral water, bucolic scenes painted on tiles decorate walls, and an orchestra plays under a frescoed dome. ⌧*Viale Verdi 71* ☎*0572/778501* 🎫*€13* ⊙*Daily 7:30–noon and 4:30–7.*

Piazza del Popolo, the main square in town, teems with cafés and bars. It's an excellent spot for people-watching; in the evening and on weekends

it seems like everyone is out walking, seeing, and being seen.

Piazza del Popolo offers a view of the basilica of **Santa Maria Assunta.** The church and bell tower, completed in 1962, have bold geometric lines that are a little incongruous among its more ornate neighbors. ⌧*Piazza del Popolo* ☎*No phone* 🎫*Free* ⊙*Daily 8–noon and 3–5:30.*

NEED A BREAK? *Cialde,* a local specialty, are circular wafers made with flour, sugar, eggs, and almonds from Puglia. The Bargilli family has been serving them with their terrific ice cream since 1936. Try them at Bargilli (⌧*Viale Grocco 2* ☎*0572/79459*), the family's shop and probably the best *gelateria* in town.

The older town, **Montecatini Alto,** sits atop a hill nearby and is reached by a funicular from Viale Diaz. Though there isn't much to do once you get up there, the medieval square is lined with restaurants and bars, the air is crisp, and the views of the Nievole, the valley below, are gorgeous.

WHERE TO STAY & EAT

$$–$$$ ✕**La Cascina.** Just off the Piazza del Popolo, and on the way to the *terme,* this restaurant offers seafood specialties in a relaxed setting. If you're hankering for a well-made cocktail with great nibbles, stop at their American bar before proceeding either to the sushi bar—done up in Japanese style—or to the dining room. Start with the raw seafood antipasto and finish with the chocolate sponge-cake dessert. There's plenty of outdoor seating for summer and live music on weekends. ⌧*Viale Verdi 43* ☎*0572/78474* ⊕*www.incascina.it* 🖃*AE, DC, MC, V* ⊙*Closed Mon.*

$$$ 🏨**Croce di Malta.** Taste and sophistication have been the calling cards of this hotel since 1911. It's a short walk on tree-lined streets from the center of town; it's even closer to the thermal baths. Rooms are spacious, with high ceilings; many have deep bathtubs with water jets. You can enjoy an aperitivo in the majestic lobby before dining at either of the guests-only restaurants . The menus change daily and offer Tuscan specialties as well as other options; the food is as elegant as the hotel. **Pros:** Good location, attentive staff. **Cons:** Attracts many tour groups.

Viale IV Novembre 18, 51016 ☎*0572/9201* 🖷*0572/767516*
⊕*www.crocedimalta.com* ⇱*122 rooms, 22 suites* &*In-room: refrig-erator, dial-up. In-hotel: 2 restaurants, room service, bar, pools, gym, concierge, laundry service, parking (fee), some pets allowed, no-smok-ing rooms* ▤*AE, DC, MC, V* ☺*BP.*

PESCIA

8 km (5 mi) west of Montecatini Terme, 19 km (12 mi) northeast of Lucca, 61 km (38 mi) northwest of Florence.

GETTING HERE
If you want to visit Pescia, do not take the train, as the station stop is a solid 25-minute, dull walk from the center of town. By car, take the A11/E76. Lazzi bus lines will get you to Pescia; they have offices in Florence, Lucca, Pistoia, and Viareggio.

VISITOR INFORMATION
Pescia tourism office (✉ *Via Fratelli Rosselli 2* ☎*0574/24112*).

EXPLORING
This sleepy little town has a large flower market and some lesser-known Renaissance art. During the early Middle Ages it was dominated by Lucca, but by 1339 it had come under Florence's influence, where it remained throughout the Renaissance. Pescia has long been a center for coppersmithing. The town is justly proud of its white beans. The best are grown in the dry gravel riverbeds of Sorana, a village just over the hills north of Pescia.

The **Santuario della Madonna di Pie di Piazza,** a little chapel built in 1447 and designed by Andrea Cavalcanti, the adopted son of Filippo Brunelleschi, is one of the few examples of Brunelleschi's style outside of Florence. Inside is a 15th-century *Madonna and Child* on a wood panel that was transported to the church in a solemn procession in 1605. ✉*Piazza Mazzini* ☎*No phone* ✉*Free* ☺*Daily 8–1 and 4–6.*

The church of **Santi Stefano e Nicolao** is an odd combination of Roman-esque and baroque. It dates from as early as the 11th century and had alterations as late as the 18th century. A *Madonna and Child with Angels,* by the school of Andrea Orcagna (active 1343/44–1368), and a panel painting of the *Madonna and Child with Sts. Nicholas and John the Baptist* (circa 1400) are among the more interesting works in the church, but because they hang on side walls in the presbytery, they are difficult to see. ✉*Piazza Stefano* ☎*No phone* ✉*Free* ☺*Daily 10–12:30 and 4–6.*

The **Museo Civico** contains Tuscan paintings, a Lorenzo Monaco trip-tych, Etruscan objects, and works attributed to the school of Fra Angelico and Fra Bartolommeo. At this writing, the museum is closed for restoration. Contact the tourist office (☎*0574/24112*) for further information. ✉*Piazza Santo Stefano* ☎*0572/490057* ✉*Free* ☺*Nov.–Mar., Wed., Fri., and Sat. 10–1 and 3–6; Apr.–Oct., Wed., Fri., and Sat. 10–1 and 4–7.*

Sant'Antonio Abate, a tiny oratory, has an amazing wood sculpture of the *Deposition,* popularly known as the "Ugly Saints." In seven pieces, it dates from the second half of the 12th century. Early-15th-century frescoes depict scenes from the life of Saint Anthony Abbot and include what is considered the oldest view of Pescia. If the door is locked, nearby businesses may know where to get the key. ⊠ *Via Battisti* ☎ *No phone* ✆ *Free* ⊗ *Daily 7–7.*

The church of **San Francesco** has a wood-panel painting by Bonaventura Berlinghieri (active 1228–43) that dates from 1235; it depicts scenes from the life of Saint Francis. ⊠ *Piazza San Francesco* ☎ *No phone* ✆ *Free* ⊗ *Daily 8:30–noon and 4–5:45.*

Unless you're a great fan of late baroque, the **Duomo** is a disappointment compared to Pescia's other churches. ⊠ *Piazza del Duomo* ☎ *No phone* ✆ *Free* ⊗ *Daily 8–7:30.*

OFF THE
BEATEN
PATH

Museo della Carta *(Paper Museum).* Handmade Italian paper is becoming rarer and rarer, although only two generations ago more than 15 small paper factories operated on the banks of the Pescia River. Used paper and cloth were broken up in great stone basins, the soggy masses poured onto forms, and the water drained out. The sheets were then stacked, hung to dry, pressed, and pressed again. This small museum in Pietrabuona, with two informative videos (narrated in Italian), a room of old paper-making machinery, and the nearby remains of an old factory, attempts to preserve the knowledge, even if it cannot forestall the decline of the industry. ⊠ *Piazza la Croce, 3 km (2 mi) north of Pescia, Pietrabuona* ☎ *0572/476252* ✆ *Free* ⊗ *Tues., Thurs., and Sat., 9:30–noon.*

Parco di Pinocchio. In a little village 4 km (2½ mi) west of Pescia, once the summer home of Carlo Lorenzini (1826–90), author of *Pinocchio,* is a theme park devoted to the fictional marionette, where sculptures illustrate various characters and scenes from the story. It's a fine place to bring children and to have a picnic. The park makes more sense if the story is fresh in your mind—so you might want to reread it or watch the 1940 Disney film beforehand. Collodi, the name of the village, was also Lorenzini's pen name. His mother was born in the village, and he spent summers here as a child. ⊠ *Via San Gennaro 2, Collodi* ☎ *0572/429342* ✆ *€10* ⊗ *Daily 8:30–sunset.*

Garzoni Gardens. Just around the corner from Parco di Pinocchio are the Garzoni Gardens, one of Italy's best-restored 17th-century gardens, with a long cascading fountain, a park with hidden statuary, and a maze. ⊠ *Piazza della Vittoria* ☎ *0572/429590* ✆ *€7* ⊗ *Mar. 16–Nov. 14, daily 8:30–sunset, Nov. 15–Mar. 15, weekends 8:30–sunset.*

LUCCA

Ramparts built in the 16th and 17th centuries enclose a charming fortress town filled with churches (99 of them), terra-cotta-roofed buildings, and narrow cobblestone streets, along which local ladies maneuver bikes to do their daily shopping. Here Caesar, Pompey, and Crassus agreed to rule Rome as a triumvirate in 56 BC; Lucca was later the first Tuscan town to accept Christianity. The town still has a mind of its own, and when most of Tuscany was voting communist as a matter of course, Lucca's citizens rarely followed suit. The famous composer Giacomo Puccini (1858–1924) was born here; he is celebrated during the summer Opera Theater and Music Festival of Lucca. The ramparts circling the centro storico are the perfect place to stroll, bicycle, or just admire the view.

GETTING HERE
You can reach Lucca easily by train from Florence; the historic center is a short walk from the station. If you're driving, take the A11/E76.

VISITOR INFORMATION
Lucca tourism office (⊠ *Piazza Santa Maria 35* ☎ *0583/91991* ⊕ *www. lucca.turismo.toscana.it*).

EXPLORING LUCCA

Traffic (including motorbikes) is restricted in the walled historic center of Lucca. Walking is the best, most enjoyable way to get around. Or you can rent a bicycle; getting around on bike is easy, as the center is quite flat.

MAIN ATTRACTIONS

8 **Duomo.** The round-arch facade of the cathedral is a fine example of the
★ rigorously ordered Pisan Romanesque style, in this case happily enlivened by an extremely varied collection of small carved columns. Take a closer look at the decoration of the facade and that of the portico below; they make this one of the most entertaining church exteriors in Tuscany. The Gothic interior contains a moving Byzantine crucifix—called the Volto Santo, or Holy Face—brought here, according to legend, in the 8th century (though it probably dates from between the 11th and early-13th centuries). The masterpiece of the Sienese sculptor Jacopo della Quercia (circa 1371–1438) is the marble *Tomb of Ilaria del Carretto* (1407–1408). ⊠ *Piazza del Duomo* ☎ *0583/490530* 🎫 *€2* ⊙ *Duomo: weekdays 7–5:30, Sat. 9:30–6:45, Sun. 11:30–11:50 and 1–5:30. Tomb: Nov.–Mar., weekdays 9:30–4:45, Sat. 9:30–6:45, Sun. 11:30–11:50 and 1–5; Apr.–Oct., weekdays 9:30–5:45, Sat. 9–6:45, Sun. 9–10 and 1–5:45.*

NEED A BREAK?
Stella Polare (⊠ *Via Vittorio Veneto 21* ☎ *0583/496332*) bills itself as a "classic bar and bistrot." In this case, that means expertly mixed cocktails, wines by the glass, and light meals at lunch and dinner. It's right on Piazza Napoleone, and so it's a great spot for people-watching. On weekends they offer an English breakfast, which means bacon and eggs.

★ **Passeggiata delle Mura.** Any time of day when the weather is clement, you can find the citizens of Lucca cycling, jogging, strolling, or kicking a soccer ball in this green, beautiful, and very large park—neither inside nor outside the city but rather right on the ring of ramparts that defines Lucca. Sunlight streams through two rows of tall plane trees

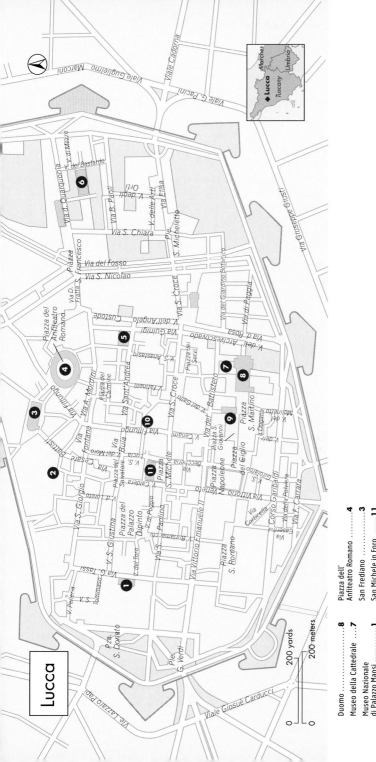

Lucca

3

to dapple the *passeggiata delle mura* (walk on the walls), which is 4.2 km (2½ mi) in length. Ten bulwarks are topped with lawns, many with picnic tables, and some with play equipment for children. Be aware at all times of where the edge is—there are no railings and the drop to the ground outside the city is a precipitous 40 feet.

❹ Piazza dell'Anfiteatro Romano. Here's where the ancient Roman amphitheater once stood; some of the medieval buildings built over the amphitheater retain its original oval shape and brick arches. ⊠*Off Via Fillungo, near north side of old town.*

❸ San Frediano. The church of San Frediano, just steps from the Anfiteatro, has a 14th-century mosaic decorating its facade and contains works by Jacopo della Quercia (circa 1371–1438) and Matteo Civitali (1436–1501), as well as the lace-clad mummy of Saint Zita (circa 1218–78), the patron saint of household servants. ⊠*Piazza San Frediano* 🕾*No phone* 🎫*Free* ☉*Mon.–Sat. 8:30–noon and 3–5, Sun. 10:30–5.*

⓫ San Michele in Foro. In the middle of the centro storico is this church with a facade even more fanciful than that of the Duomo. The upper levels of the facade have nothing but air behind them (after the front of the church was built, there were no funds to raise the nave), and the winged Archangel Michael, who stands at the very top, seems precariously poised for flight. The facade, heavily restored in the 19th century, displays busts of 19th-century Italian patriots such as Garibaldi and Cavour. Check out the superb Filippino Lippi (1457/58–1504) panel painting of Saints Girolamo, Sebastian, Rocco, and Helen in the right transept. ⊠*Piazza San Michele* 🕾*No phone* 🎫*Free* ☉*Daily 9–noon and 3–6.*

❺ Torre Guinigi. The tower of the medieval Palazzo Guinigi contains one ☺ of the city's most curious sights: a grove of ilex trees has grown at the top of the tower and their roots have pushed their way into the room below. From the top you have a magnificent view of the city and the surrounding countryside. (Only the tower is open to the public, not the palazzo.) ⊠*Palazzo Guinigi, Via Sant'Andrea* 🕾*No phone* 🎫*€3.50* ☉*Mar. and Apr., daily 9:30–6; May–Sept., daily 9–midnight; Oct.–Feb., daily 9–5.*

ALSO WORTH SEEING

❼ Museo della Cattedrale. The cathedral museum exhibits many items too precious to be in the church, most notably the finely worked golden decorations of the Volto Santo, the Byzantine crucifix that remains in the Duomo. ⊠*Piazza Antelminelli* 🕾*0583/490530* 🎫*€4, combination ticket €5.50 (includes tomb in Duomo and San Giovanni's baptistery and archaeological works)* ☉*Mid-Mar.–mid-Nov., daily 10–6; mid-Nov.–mid-Mar., weekdays 10–2, weekends 10–5.*

❶ Museo Nazionale di Palazzo Mansi. Highlights here include the lovely *Portrait of a Youth* by Pontormo; portraits of the Medici painted by Bronzino (1503–72); and paintings by Tintoretto, Vasari, and others. ⊠*Palazzo Mansi, Via Galli Tassi 43, near west walls of old city* 🕾*0583/55570* 🎫*€4, combination ticket €6.50 (includes Museo Nazionale di Villa Guinigi)* ☉*Tues.–Sat. 8:30–7, Sun. 8:30–1:30.*

6 **Museo Nazionale di Villa Guinigi.** On the eastern end of the historic center, this museum has an extensive collection of local Romanesque and Renaissance art. The museum represents an overview of Lucca's artistic traditions from Etruscan times until the 17th century, housed in the former 15th-century villa of the

3

Guinigi family. ⊠ *Villa Guinigi, Via della Quarquonia* ☎ *0583/496033* 🎫 *€4, combination ticket €6.50 (includes Museo Nazionale di Palazzo Mansi)* ⊗ *Tues.–Sat. 8:30–7, Sun. 8:30–1:30.*

2 **Palazzo Pfanner.** Here you can rest your feet and let time pass, surrounded by a harmonious arrangement of sun, shade, blooming plants, water, and mysterious statuary. The palazzo's well-kept formal garden, which abuts the city walls, centers on a large fountain and pool. Allegorical statues line pebbled paths that radiate outward. The palazzo, built in the 17th century, was purchased in the 19th century by the Pfanners, a family of Swiss brewers. The family, which eventually gave the town a mayor, still lives here. ⊠ *Via degli Asili 33* ☎ *0583/954029* 🎫 *Garden €3, palazzo €3.50, garden and palazzo €4.50* ⊗ *Mar.–mid-Nov., daily 10–6; mid-Nov.–Feb., by appointment only.*

9 **Ss. Giovanni e Reparata.** The baptistery of this church, one piazza over from the Duomo, is lovely enough, but the unusual element here is an archaeological site, discovered in 1969, where five layers of Luccan history were uncovered. As you walk the paths and catwalks suspended above the delicate sites in the grottoes under the church, you move from era to era—from the 2nd-century-BC site of a Roman temple through the 5th, 8th, 9th, and 11th centuries. When seen after coming up the stairs from underground, the 12th-century church feels almost modern. ⊠ *Piazza San Giovanni* ☎ *0583/490530* 🎫 *Baptistery and archaeological site €2.50, combination ticket €6 (includes tomb in Duomo and Museo della Cattedrale)* ⊗ *Mid-Mar.–mid-Nov., daily 10–6; mid-Nov.–mid-Mar., weekdays 10–2, weekends 10–5.*

NEED A BREAK? Gelateria Veneta (⊠ *Via V. Veneto 74* ☎ *0583/467037*) makes outstanding gelato, sorbet, and ices (some sugar-free). They prepare their confections three times a day using the same recipes with which the Brothers Arnoldo opened the place in 1927. The pièces de résistance are frozen fruits stuffed with creamy filling: don't miss the apricot-sorbet-filled apricot. Note that they close shop in October and reopen around Easter.

10 **Torre delle Ore** *(Tower of the Hours).* The highest spot in Lucca is the top of this tower, which had its first mechanical clock in 1390. It's since contained several clocks over the centuries; the current timepiece was installed in 1754. The reward for the climb to the top is a panoramic view of the town. ⊠ *Via Fillungo at Via dell'Arancio* ☎ *Contact tourist office, 0583/91991 for information* 🎫 *€3.50* ⊗ *Apr.–Nov. by appointment only.*

OFF THE
BEATEN
PATH

Villa Reale. Eight kilometers (5 mi) north of Lucca in Marlia, this villa was once the home of Napoléon's sister, Princess Elisa. Restored by the Counts Pecci-Blunt, the estate is celebrated for its spectacular gardens, laid out in the 16th century and redone in the middle of the 17th. Gardening buffs adore the legendary *teatro di verdura*, a theater carved out of hedges and topiaries; concerts are occasionally held here. During the summer, concerts are held in the gardens of other famous Lucca villas as well. Contact the Lucca tourist office (☎0583/91991) for details. ✉*North of Lucca along the river Serchio, in the direction of Barga and Bagni di Lucca, Marlia* ☎*0583/30108* 💶*€7* ☉ *Guided visits: Mar.–Nov., Tues.–Sun. at 10, 11, noon, 3, 4, and 5.*

WHERE TO EAT

$$$ ✕**La Mora.** Detour to this former stagecoach station, now a gracious, rustic country inn 9 km (5½ mi) north of Lucca, for local specialties—from minestra di farro to homemade *tacconi* (a thin, short, wide pasta) with rabbit sauce and lamb from the nearby Garfagnana mountains. You might be tempted by the varied *crostini* (toasted bread) and delicious desserts. ✉*Via Sesto di Moriano 1748, Ponte a Moriano* ☎*0583/406402* ▭*AE, DC, MC, V* ☉*Closed Wed., Jan. 1–15, and June 15–30.*

$$ ✕**Buca di Sant'Antonio.** The staying power of Buca di Sant'Antonio—
★   it's been around since 1782—is the result of superlative Tuscan food brought to the table by waitstaff that doesn't miss a beat. The menu includes the simple-but-blissful, like *tortelli lucchesi al sugo* (meat-stuffed pasta with a tomato-and-meat sauce), and more daring dishes such as roast *capretto* (kid) with herbs. A white-wall interior hung with copper pots and brass musical instruments creates a classy but comfortable dining space. ✉*Via della Cervia 3* ☎*0583/55881* ▭*AE, DC, MC, V* ☉*Closed Mon., 1 wk in Jan., and 1 wk in July. No dinner Sun.*

$$ ✕**Il Giglio.** Just off Piazza Napoleone, this restaurant has quiet, late-19th-century charm and classic cuisine. It's a place for all seasons, with a big fireplace for chilly weather and an outdoor patio in summer. If mushrooms are in season, try the *tacchonni con funghi*, a homemade pasta with mushrooms and a local herb called *niepitela*. A local favorite during winter is the *coniglio con olive* (rabbit stew with olives). ✉*Piazza del Giglio 2* ☎*0583/494508* ▭*AE, DC, MC, V* ☉*Closed Wed. and 15 days in Nov. No dinner Tues.*

$$ ✕**i Santi.** This intimate little wine bar, just outside the Piazza dell'Anfiteatro Romano, offers a perfect place to have a light meal and a fine glass of wine. The extensive wine list has first-rate local and foreign (French) selections, and the menu has tasty things to go with it, such as *carpaccio di manzo affumicato* (thin slices of smoked beef served with celery and a young cheese). Specials include a pasta of the day. In summer it is open throughout the day, meaning if you're hungry at 4 in the afternoon or at 11:30 at night (when just about everywhere else is closed), you're in luck. ✉*Via dell'Anfiteatro 29/a* ☎*0583/496124* ▭*AE, DC, MC, V* ☉*Closed Wed. Nov.–Mar.*

$ ✕**Trattoria da Leo.** A few short turns away from the facade of San Michele, this noisy, informal, traditional trattoria delivers *cucina alla casalinga* (home cooking) in the best sense. Try the typical minestra di farro to start or just go straight to *secondi piatti* (entrées); in addition to the usual roast meats, there's excellent chicken with olives and a good cold dish of boiled meats served with a sauce of parsley and pine nuts. Save some room for a dessert, such as the rich, sweet, fig-and-walnut torte or the lemon sorbet brilliantly dotted with bits of sage, which tastes almost like mint. ⊠ *Via Tegrimi 1, at corner of Via degli Asili* ☎*0583/492236* ⊟*No credit cards* ⊘*No lunch Sun. Closed Sun. Nov.–Mar.*

3

WHERE TO STAY

$$$$ ⌂**Locanda l'Elisa.** When Napoléon's sister, Elisa Baciocchi, arrived in Lucca to preside over it as a princess, she came with an entourage. One member built this delightful indigo villa 3 km (2 mi) south of Lucca. Surrounded by rosemary, lavender, and azaleas, the hotel preserves the intimacy of a well-furnished home; it's decorated in Empire style, with 19th-century furniture, prints, and fabrics. The attached restaurant elevates Lucchesi specialties such as *tordelli lucchese con sfoglia di farina di farro integrale al ragù d'anatra* (tortelli with farro in a duck sauce) to new heights. **Pros:** Multilingual staff, top-notch restaurant. **Cons:** A car is vital. ⊠ *Via Nuova per Pisa 1952, 55050 Massa Pisana* ☎*0583/379737* 🖷*0583/379019* ⊕*www.locandalelisa.it* ↝*3 rooms, 7 suites* ⌂*In-room: safe, refrigerator, dial-up. In-hotel: restaurant, bar, pool, concierge, laundry service, public Internet, parking (no fee)* ⊟*AE, DC, MC, V* ⊘*Closed Jan. 7–Feb. 11* ⦿*EP.*

$$$$ ⌂**Villa La Principessa.** A circular sweeping driveway brings you to this luxe villa 3 km (2 mi) outside Lucca. Some rooms in this exquisitely decorated 19th-century structure have handsome beamed ceilings, and doors are individually decorated. Antique furniture and portraits impart an aura of gracious living; the dramatic sitting room with its splendid chandelier, marbled floors, and damask wallpaper is the perfect place to write a postcard while enjoying a cocktail. A stay here evokes the time of Napoléon's court, when many of his retinue built their summer pleasure palaces outside the city. The restaurant is open for dinner only (and closed Tuesday). **Pros:** Large pool, well-manicured grounds. **Cons:** Rooms are nicer in the main villa, a car is vital. ⊠ *Via Nuova per Pisa 1616, 55050 Massa Pisana* ☎*0583/370037* 🖷*0583/379136* ⊕*www.hotelprincipessa.com* ↝*34 rooms, 7 suites* ⌂*In-room: safe, refrigerator, dial-up, Wi-Fi. In-hotel: restaurant, room service, bar, pool, concierge, laundry service, some pets allowed* ⊟*AE, DC, MC, V* ⊘*Closed Nov.–Mar.* ⦿*BP.*

$$$–$$$$ ⌂**Hotel Ilaria.** The former stables of the Villa Bottini have been transformed into a modern hotel within the historic center. A second-floor terrace, overlooking the villa, makes a comfortable place to relax, and there's a hot tub for the adventurous. Rooms are done in a warm wood veneer with blue and white fittings. The availability of free bicycles is a nice bonus in this bike-friendly city, and the sumptuous buffet breakfast could see you through dinner. Residenza dell'Alba, the hotel's annex

across the street, was originally part of a 14th-century church; now it's a luxe accommodation with in-room hot tubs. **Pros:** A Fodor's reader sums it up as a "nice modern small hotel," free bicycles. **Cons:** Though in city center, it's a little removed from main attractions. ⊠ *Via del Fosso 26, 55100* ☎*0583/47615* 🖷*0583/991961* ⊕*www.hotelilaria. com* ↘*36 rooms, 5 suites* ⌂*In-room: safe, refrigerator. In-hotel: bar, bicycles, concierge, laundry service, public Internet, parking (no fee), some pets allowed (fee)* ⊟*AE, DC, MC, V* �[○|*BP.*

$$$ 🖼 **Alla Corte degli Angeli.** This charming hotel with a friendly staff is right off the main shopping drag, Via Fillungo. Terra-cotta floors and stenciled walls impart a cozy feeling, while the high brick and timbered ceilings create a sense of spaciousness. The sitting room, with its fireplace and bar, provides a lovely place to relax. Breakfast is served in a cheery room with sponged-painted walls. **Pros:** Many rooms are connecting, making them good for families. **Cons:** Some rooms have tubs but no showers. ⊠ *Via degli Angeli 23, 55100* ☎*0583/469204* 🖷*0583/991989* ⊕*www.allacortedegliangeli.com* ↘*12 rooms* ⌂*In-room: refrigerator, Wi-Fi. In-hotel: bar, laundry service, public Internet, parking (fee), some pets allowed* ⊟*AE, DC, MC, V* ⏹○⏹*BP.*

$$$ 🖼**Palazzo Alexander.** This small, elegant boutique hotel is on a quiet side street a short walk from San Michele in Foro. The building, dating from the 12th century, has been restructured to create the ease common to Lucchesi nobility: timbered ceilings, warm yellow walls, and brocaded chairs adorn the public rooms, and the motif continues into the guest rooms, all of which have high ceilings and that same glorious damask. Top-floor suites have sweeping views of the town. One suite is on the mezzanine floor, but also has city views. **Pros:** Intimate feel, gracious staff. **Cons:** Some Fodor's readers complain of too-thin walls. ⊠ *Via S. Giustina 48, 55100* ☎*0583/583571* 🖷*0583/583610* ⊕*www. palazzo-alexander.com* ↘*9 rooms, 3 suites, 1 apartment* ⌂*In-room: safe, refrigerator, dial-up. In-hotel: bar, bicycles, concierge, laundry service, public Internet, parking (fee)* ⊟*AE, DC, MC, V* ⏹○⏹*BP.*

$$ 🖼 **Albergo San Martino.** Down a narrow street facing a quiet, sun-sprinkled *piazzale* (small square) stands this small hotel. The brocade bedspreads are fresh and crisp, the proprietor friendly. Although around the corner from the Duomo, the busy Corso Garibaldi, and the great walls of Lucca, the inn, tucked away as it is, feels private—a place to retreat to when you have seen all the church facades you can stand. Two of the eight rooms are wheelchair accessible. In the cheerful apricot breakfast room, filled with framed prints, you can get a more-than-solid breakfast. A little terrace with wicker chairs provides a lovely place to unwind. **Pros:** Comfortable bed, great breakfast. **Cons:** Breakfast costs €20. ⊠ *Via della Dogana 9, 55100* ☎*0583/469181* 🖷*0583/991940* ⊕*www.albergosanmartino.it* ↘*6 rooms, 2 suites* ⌂*In-room: refrigerator. In- hotel: bar, bicycles (fee), no elevator, laundry service* ⊟*AE, DC, MC, V* ⏹○⏹*EP.*

$$ 🖼 **La Luna.** On a quiet, airy courtyard close to the Piazza del Mercato, this hotel, run by the Barbieri family for more than four decades, occupies two renovated wings of an old building. The bathrooms are modern, but some rooms still have the flavor of Old Lucca. One of

the suites has high frescoed ceilings and a chandelier, an echo of a nobler age. **Pros:** Professional staff, the annex has wheelchair-accessible rooms. **Cons:** Some of the rooms feel dated. ✉*Corte Compagni 12, at Via Fillungo, 55100* ☎*0583/493634* 🖷*0583/490021* ⊕*www. hotellaluna.com* ⌇*27 rooms, 2 suites* ⌂*In-room: safe (some), refrigerator. In-hotel: bar, parking (fee)* ▤*AE, DC, MC, V* ☉*Closed Jan. 7–31* ⭗*EP.*

$ 🍴**Fattoria di Fubbiano.** Lucca is famous for producing some of the world's finest olive oil, and it could be argued that the best of all is produced here at this agriturismo 10 minutes outside Lucca's *centro storico*. In addition to oil, the firm also makes wine and has lodging available. There's a villa that sleeps up to 12; a small house reached by a narrow road often dotted with horses grazing at the side; and three apartments. The apartments have kitchenettes; the house and villa both have kitchens. During high season, management prefers to rent for weeklong stays. **Pros:** Very much a rural experience. **Cons:** A car is a necessity. ✉No street address, just name, postal code, and city *55010 San Gennaro* ☎*0583/978011* 🖷*0583/978344* ⊕*www.fattoriadifubbiano.com* ⌇*3 apartments, 1 farmhouse, 1 villa* ⌂*In-room: no a/c, kitchen (some). In-hotel: pools, laundry facilities* ▤*MC, V* ⭗*EP.*

$ 🍴**Piccolo Hotel Puccini.** Steps away from the busy square and church of San Michele, this little hotel is quiet and calm—and a great deal. Wallpaper, hardwood floors, and throw rugs are among the handsome decorations. Paolo, the genial manager, speaks fluent English and dispenses great touring advice. **Pros:** Cheery, English-speaking staff. **Cons:** Breakfast costs extra, some rooms are on the dark side. ✉*Via di Poggio 9, 55100* ☎*0583/55421* 🖷*0583/53487* ⊕*www.hotelpuccini.com* ⌇*14 rooms* ⌂*In-room: no a/c, safe. In-hotel: bar, laundry service, some pets allowed, no-smoking rooms* ▤*AE, MC, V* ⭗*EP.*

NIGHTLIFE & THE ARTS

The **Estate Musicale Lucchese,** one of many Tuscan music festivals, runs throughout the summer in Lucca. Contact the Lucca tourist office for details. The **Opera Theater and Music Festival of Lucca,** sponsored by the Opera Theater of Lucca and the music college of the University of Cincinnati, runs from mid-June to mid-July; performances are staged in open-air venues. Call the Lucca tourist office or the Opera Theater of Lucca (☎*0583/46531*) for information.

Throughout summer there are jazz, pop, and rock concerts in conjunction with the **Estate Musicale Lucchese** music festival. The **Lucca Tourist Office** (✉*Piazza Santa Maria Verdi 35, San Michele* ☎*0583/91991*) has schedule and ticket information for many local events, including the Opera Theater and Estate Musicale Lucchese festivals.

From September through April you can see operas, plays, and concerts staged at the **Teatro del Giglio** (✉*Piazza del Giglio, Duomo* ☎*0583/46531* ⊕*www.teatrodelgiglio.it*).

Lucca Comics and Games (☎*0583/48522* ⊕*www.luccacomicsandgames. com*) takes place the first weekend of November. The city's piazzas are

filled with tents featuring exhibitions and games, and the streets are invaded with comic book fans and gamesters. During the last week of October, and continuing through the Comics festival, a Mostra Mercato (market show) takes place as well.

SPORTS & THE OUTDOORS

A good way to spend the afternoon is to go biking around the large path atop the city's ramparts. There are two good spots right next to each other where you can rent bikes. The prices are about the same (about €12.50 for the day and €2.50 per hour for city bikes) and they are centrally located, just beside the town wall.

The people are friendlier and speak English at **Berutto Cicli** (⊠ *Via dei Gaspari 83/r, Anfiteatro* ☎*0583/517073*), which rents bikes near the Piazza di Anfiteatro. **Poli Antonio Biciclette** (⊠*Piazza Santa Maria 42, Lucca East* ☎*0583/493787*) is the option for bicycle rental on the east side.

SHOPPING

CHOCOLATE

Chocolate lovers will be pleased with the selection at **Caniparoli** (⊠ *Via San Paolino 96* ☎*0583/53456*), a small stylish shop specializing in artisanal chocolates. They are so serious about their sweets that they do not make them from June to August, because of the heat.

CLOTHING

Bargain hunters won't want to miss **Benetton Stock Outlet** (⊠ *Via Roma 19, Anfiteatro* ☎*0583/464533*), with its brightly colored garments at reduced prices.

Mode Mignon (⊠*Piazza Bernardini 1-2-3* ☎*0583/491217*) provides one-stop high-end designer shopping. Prada, Miu-Miu, Gucci, Dolce e Gabbana, Jil Sander, and Tod's—among others—can be found here.

FOOD

Lucca is known for its farro, an ancient barleylike grain that has found its way into regional specialties such as *zuppa* (or *minestra*) *di farro* (farro soup). It's available in food shops all over the city. Lucca is most famous for its olive oil, however, which is exported throughout the world. Look for extra-virgin oil whose label clearly indicates that it is entirely from Tuscany or, better yet, entirely from a local *fattoria*, or farm. *Olio nuovo* (new oil) is available for a few weeks in November, when the olive-picking season begins. This new oil is strong-flavored and peppery—great for drizzling on soup, pasta, and bread—and it's also nearly impossible to find in North America. Wine from small Lucca producers is also difficult to find abroad.

Antica Bottega di Prospero (⊠ *Via San Lucia 13* ☎*No phone*)sells top-quality local products, including farro, dried porcini mushrooms, olive oil, and wine.

Visit **Enoteca Vanni** (✉*Piazza del Salvatore 7* ☎*0583/491902* ⊕*www. enotecavanni.com*), which has a huge selection of wines, as well as an ancient cellar worth seeing. For the cost of the wine only, tastings can be organized through the shopkeepers and held in the cellar. Not far away is a smaller shop, **Massei Ugo** (✉*Via S. Andrea 19* ☎*0583/467656*), with great wine prices and assorted local delicacies. The store's owner, Ugo Massei, doesn't speak English, but he's friendly and helpful.

MARKETS

On the third weekend of the month there's an **antiques market** in Piazza San Martino. Vendors unveil their wares around 8:30 and start packing up around dusk. There's something for everyone, including old-fashioned glassware, ancient coins, and furniture—some antique, some just old. Check out the 19th-century tools and collections of fascist memorabilia.

Looking for old prints? Old postcards? Old comic books? Just behind the church of San Giusto (off Via Beccheria, which runs for about two blocks between Piazza Napoleone and Piazza San Michele) are **bookstalls** that open their cupboard doors on clement days (including Sunday), from about 10 to 7. You may discover anything from hand-tinted prints of orchids to back issues of *Uomo Ragno* (Spider-Man looks and acts just the same even when he's speaking Italian).

PASTRIES

A particularly delicious version of *buccellato*—the sweet, anise-flavor bread with raisins that is a specialty of Lucca—is baked at **Pasticceria Taddeucci** (✉*Piazza San Michele 34* ☎*0583/494933*). For a broad selection of scrumptious pastries, visit **Pasticceria Pinelli** (✉*Via Beccheria 28* ☎*0583/496119*). It's a favorite of Lucca's senior citizens, who frequently stop in after Sunday Mass.

THE GARFAGNANA

In the heart of the Alpi Apuane, the Garfagnana is one of the most visually stunning regions in all of Tuscany. Roads wind around precipitous, jagged peaks and through old stone villages. Cool mountain air tempers even the sultriest summer. Most of the major cities and towns are found along the Serchio, Italy's third-largest river, which runs north–south. The Val di Lima (Lima Valley), formed by the Lima River, has for centuries been known for its curative thermal waters and its lush chestnut groves.

As you plan your travels through the area, keep in mind that you'll encounter winding two-lane mountain roads—driving 10 miles may take longer than you'd expect. Pass through in October, though, and you'll be rewarded with bursts of yellow and splashes of red as the leaves change color.

SAN MARCELLO PISTOIESE

33 km (21 mi) northwest of Pistoia, 66 km (41 mi) northwest of Florence.

GETTING HERE

By car, you're likely to approach San Marcello Pistoiese from Pistoia; take the SS435 to the SS66, which takes you right into town (follow the signs). Copit provides frequent bus service as well. There is no train service.

VISITOR INFORMATION

Pistoia tourism office (⊠ *Palazzo dei Vescovi* ☎ *0573/21622*).

EXPLORING

This small town—small, but still the largest in the area—bustles in summer and winter (when it's one of Tuscany's few ski destinations), but calms down during spring and fall. It's set amid spectacular scenery; you can drive across a dramatic suspension bridge over the Lima River.

The **Museo Ferrucciano** has exhibits on the history of the area, as well as on the 1530 battle, waged in the nearby village of Gavinana, in which the Republic of Florence resisted the troops of Charles V of Spain. Note that at this writing the museum was closed indefinitely. ⊠ *Piazza Francesco Ferrucci* ☎ *0573/621289* 🖶 *055/630623* 💶 *€1.55* ⊘ *July and Aug., daily 10–noon and 5–7; Sept.–June, Thurs. and Sat. 3–6.*

The **Pieve di San Marcello** church dates from the 12th century. The interior was redone in the 18th century, and most of the art inside is from that period. ⊠ *Piazza Arcangeli* ☎ *No phone* 💶 *Free* ⊘ *Daily 9–1 and 3–6.*

SPORTS & THE OUTDOORS

You can rent mountain bikes and equipment for paragliding from **Nonsolovolo** (⊠ *Via XXIV Maggio 10, Lizzano Pistoiese* ☎ *0573/677700* ⊕ *www.nonsolovolo.it*). The Web site is in Italian only.

ABETONE

20 km (12 mi) northwest of San Marcello Pistoiese, 53 km (33 mi) northwest of Pistoia, 86 km (53 mi) northwest of Florence.

GETTING HERE

By car from Pistoia, take the SS435/SR436 and follow signs for Abetone-Modena. You'll exit onto the SS66/SR66; continue for some 30 km (18 mi) to the SS12, which will take you into Abetone. Copit buses run to Abetone, but there is no train service.

VISITOR INFORMATION

Abetone tourism office (⊠ *Via Pescinone 15* ☎ *0573/607811*).

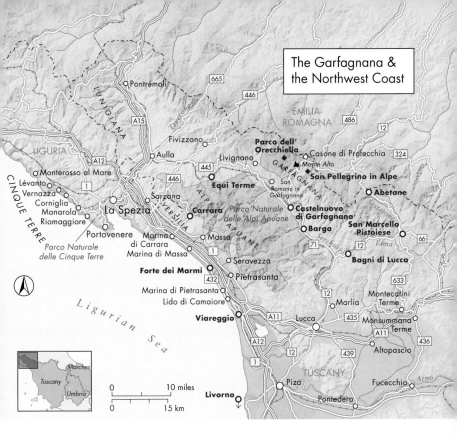

The Garfagnana &
the Northwest Coast

EXPLORING

Abetone is one of the most-visited vacation spots in the Apennine Mountains, where Tuscans, Emilia-Romagnans, and others come to ski. Set above two valleys, the resort town is on the edge of a lush and ancient forest of more than 9,000 acres. The numerous ski trails are mostly for beginner and intermediate levels (the entire area has only two expert slopes). Summer is the time to trek or mountain bike in and around the beautiful hills and mountains.

WHERE TO STAY & EAT

$–$$ ✕ **La Locanda dello Yeti.** Stop at this restful osteria after a day on the slopes or a trek through the forest. The specialty of the house is mushrooms—on *crostini* (toasted bread), polenta, or pasta. Mushrooms also garnish the fine grilled meats. They also do a fine *lombatina di capriolo* (a type of venison steak). The local house wine is refreshing. ✉ *Via Brennero 324* ☎*0573/606974* ⏵*Reservations essential* ▭*MC, V* ☉*Closed Tues., 20 days in June, and 10 days in Sept.*

$ ✕ **La Capannina.** Fresh local ingredients—chestnuts, mushrooms, freshwater fish, cheeses, olive oil, and herbs—are the keys to the fabulous cooking of husband-and-wife owners Duccio Ugolini and Miriam Manni. The traditional, rustic Tuscan soups and pastas are filling, but save room for dessert, especially anything made with the local chestnuts. This mountainside restaurant also has seven rooms for rent (€70 nightly). ⊠ *Via Brennero 256* ☎*0573/60562* ⊟*AE, DC, MC* ⊘*Closed Mon. and 2 wks in May and Oct.*

WORD OF MOUTH

"If you are going to be in Lucca then you should definitely plan on touring the Garfagnana area. It is beautiful, unspoiled, not heavily trafficked and lots of trees."
–janelp

$ 🖻 **Hotel Bellavista.** Originally a 19th-century villa belonging to Marchesa Guendalina Strozzi—her ancestors were powerful bankers in Renaissance Florence—this is now a contemporary inn. Some of the public rooms have a quaint Victorian charm to them, but the guest rooms have more contemporary decor, with basic wooden furniture and no frills. Ask for one of the eight with a whirlpool tub. In winter you can use this as a base to ski to the slopes; in summer the Bellavista is perfectly situated for trekking and mountain biking. **Pros:** Can ski from hotel to chairlift. **Cons:** Attracts a younger, sometimes rowdy crowd. ⊠ *Via Brennero 383, 51021* ☎*0573/6002451* 🖷*0573/60028* ⊕*www.bellavista-abetone.it* ⚲*40 rooms, 2 suites* ⚴*In-room: no a/c, safe. In-hotel: restaurant, bar, minibar* ⊟*AE, MC, V* ⊘*Closed May, Oct., and Nov.* ⦿*BP.*

SKIING

The area has 37 ski slopes, amounting to about 50 km (31 mi) of ski surface, all accessible through the purchase of a single Multipass. You can check the Abetone section of the **Pistoiese ski area** (⊕*www. lamontagnapistoiese.it*) Web site for details on the Multipass. **Consorzio Impianti** (⊠ *Via Brennero 429* ☎*0573/60557*), the group that manages ski facilities, has information on the Multipass, as well as maps, directions, and area information. **F. Ballantini** (⊠ *Via Brennero 615* ☎*0573/60482*) rents skis.

EN ROUTE Stop at the **San Pellegrino in Alpe** monastery en route from Abetone to Castelnuovo di Garfagnana to see the staggering view and the large wooden cross. Story has it that a 9th-century Scot, Pellegrino by name, came to this spot to repent. Inside the monastery, the **Museo Etnografico** is devoted to rural life and has over 4,000 items on display. ⊠ *Via del Voltone 14, San Pellegrino in Alpe* ✚*Off SR12, 16 km (10 mi) northeast of Castelnuovo di Garfagnana, 28 km (17 mi) northwest of Abetone;* ☎*0573/649072* 🖻*Monastery free, museum €2.60* ⊘*June–Sept., daily 9:30–1 and 2:30–7; Oct.–May, Tues.–Sun. 9–noon and 2–5.*

BAGNI DI LUCCA

36 km (22 mi) southwest of Abetone, 27 km (17 mi) north of Lucca, 101 km (63 mi) northwest of Florence.

GETTING HERE

By car from Florence, take the A11 and exit at Capannori. Take the SS439 in the direction of Lucca. From Lucca, take the SS12/Via del Brennero. This leads to the SP18, which takes you directly into Bagni di Lucca. Lazzi bus lines also operate from Lucca and Florence. Trains run nearly every hour from Lucca and take about 25 minutes.

VISITOR INFORMATION

Bagni di Lucca tourism office (⊠ *Via Umberto I 139* ☎ *0583/805754* ⊕ *www.prolocobagnidilucca.it*).

EXPLORING

Pretty Bagni di Lucca was a fashionable spa town in the early 19th century—in part because of its thermal waters. The Romantic poet Percy Bysshe Shelley (1792–1822) installed his family here during the summer of 1818. He wrote to a friend in July of that year that the waters here were exceedingly refreshing: "My custom is to undress and sit on the rocks, reading Herodotus, until perspiration has subsided, and then to leap from the edge of the rock into this fountain." In 1853, Robert and Elizabeth Browning spent the summer in a house on the main square. Its heyday behind it, the town is now a quiet, charming place where elegant thermal spas still soothe on temperate summer days.

OFF THE BEATEN PATH

The **Centro Termale Bagni di Lucca** has two natural steam-room caves, as well as spa services such as mud baths, massage, hydrotherapy, and facials. ⊠ *Piazza San Martino 11* ☎ *0583/87221* ⊕ *www.termebagnidilucca.it* ⊠ *€10 for thermal pool; spa services vary* ☯ *May–Sept., daily 9–6; Oct.–Jan., daily 9–12:30.*

Il Ponte della Maddalena *(The Magdalen's Bridge)* is, oddly, also known as the Devil's Bridge. Commissioned in all likelihood by Matilde di Canossa (1046–1115), it was restructured by the petty despot Castruccio Castracani in the early 14th century. It's worth the climb to the middle—the bridge is narrow, steep, and pedestrians-only—to check out the view. Despite 1836 flood damage and early-20th-century alterations, it seems little changed from the Middle Ages. If you're heading north along the Serchio from Lucca to Bagni di Lucca, you will see the bridge on your left.

WHERE TO EAT

$ ★ ✕ **Osteria i Macelli.** Honest Tuscan cooking prevails at this simple trattoria next to a large parking lot. No matter that there's no view: the terrific food and pleasing service—all of it served in a typical Tuscan dining room with high timbered ceilings—make a stop here well worth the detour. Locals swear by the *affettati misti* (sliced cured meats), which include the stellar *biroldo* (cured pork from nearby Garfagnana). The *ravioli di castagne* (ravioli stuffed with chestnut puree, sauced with radicchio and pancetta bits) should not be missed. ⊠ *Piazza i Macelli, Borgo a Mozzano* ✛ *21 km (13 mi) north of Lucca on the SS12;* ☎ *0583/88700* ▭ *AE, DC, MC, V* ☯ *Closed Jan. 1–15 and Sept. 1–15.*

¢–$ ✕ **La Ruota.** About 3 km (2 mi) west of Bagni di Lucca in the tiny village of Fornoli, La Ruota is known for dishes that are traditional in the region along the Serchio River, such as smoked trout, and fried frogs' legs. Their lasagne is scrumptious, and the *novelline alla lucchese* (a breaded veal cutlet topped with tomato sauce) tasty. Lunch specials are a steal, and pizza on the menu is bound to please the fussiest of palates.

✉ *Via Giovanni XXIII 29/b, Fornoli* ☎*0583/805627* ▭*AE, DC, MC, V* ⊘*No dinner Mon. or Tues.*

BARGA

17 km (11 mi) northwest of Bagni di Lucca, 111 km (69 mi) northwest of Florence.

GETTING HERE
By car from Lucca, take the SS12/Via del Brennero directly to Barga. Though there is train service to Barga, the station is far away from the centro storico. The only bus option is the small CLAP line (✉ Via Roma 7 ☎ 0583/723050), which runs between here and Castelnuovo di Garfagnana.

VISITOR INFORMATION
Barga tourism office (✉ *Via di Mezzo 45* ☎ *0583/724745* ⊕*www.commune.barga.lu.it*).

EXPLORING
Barga is a lovely little hill town with a finely preserved medieval core. It produced textiles—particularly silk—during the Renaissance and wool in the 18th century. You won't find textiles here today; now the emphasis is on tourism. Here the black American squadrons, known as the Buffalo Soldiers, are remembered by the locals for their bravery defending this mountainous area during World War II.

Walking around Barga is not for the faint of heart: it's one steep uphill after another to get to the tiny centro storico, and more steps to get to Piazza del Duomo.

The **Duomo,** dedicated to Saint Christopher, is a Romanesque cathedral, made from elegant limestone (quarried from nearby caves), which saw four separate building campaigns. The first began in the 9th century, and it was only finished in the 15th. Inside, the intricately carved pulpit, one of the finest examples of mid-12th-century Tuscan sculpture, commands center stage. The view from the Duomo is incredible: to the west, gaze upon the Alpi Apuane; to the east, the Appennines. ✉ *Via del Duomo* ☎*No phone* ▭*Free* ⊘*Daily 9–7.*

OFF THE BEATEN PATH

Grotta del Vento. About 14 km (9 mi) southwest of Barga, after following a winding road flanked by both sheer cliffs and fabulous views, you come to Tuscany's Cave of the Wind. As the result of a steady internal temperature of 10.7°C (about 51°F), the wind is sucked into the cave in the winter and blown out in the summer. It has a long cavern with stalactites, stalagmites, "bottomless" pits, and subterranean streams. One-, two-, and three-hour guided tours of the cave are given. (From November through March only the one-hour tour is offered.) ✉*SP 39, west at Galliciano, Fornovolasco* ☎*0583/722024* 🖷*0583/722053* ⊕*www.grottadelvento.com* ▭*€7.50 for 1 hr, €12 for 2 hrs, €17 for 3 hrs* ⊘*Daily 10–6.*

WHERE TO STAY

$$ **Il Ciocco.** A huge resort and convention center, Il Ciocco has its own soccer stadium, basketball court, and equestrian center. Most rooms have balcony views of the surrounding pine-forested hills and the distant Alpi Apuane. Furnishings include dark-wood desks, some chandeliers, and some wood paneling. Apartments and chalets are available for rental by the week; half and full board are available. **Pros:** A great place for kids. **Cons:** Public spaces are characterless. ✥ *Off SP7, 7 km (4½ mi) north of Barga, Castelvecchio Pascoli 55051* ☎*0583/7191* 🖷*0583/723197* ⊕*www.ciocco.it* ⤳*220 rooms, 15 suites, 56 apartments, 12 chalets* ⚄*In-room: no a/c (some), kitchen (some), refrigerator, Wi-Fi (some). In-hotel: restaurant, tennis courts, pool, gym, bicycles, children's programs (ages 6–17), laundry service, public Internet, Wi-Fi, some pets allowed*⊟*AE, DC, MC, V* ⋆❍⋆*BP.*

> ## WORD OF MOUTH
>
> "Barga is a lovely hill town, with a beautiful Romanesque style Duomo on the top of the hill, the view of…the surrounding mountains is breathtaking." –JudyC

NIGHTLIFE & THE ARTS

From mid-July to mid-August, the stony streets of Barga come alive as opera fans come to **Opera Barga** (✉*Teatro dell'Accademia dei Differenti, Piazza Angelio 4* ⊕*www.barganews.com/operabarga*). This highly regarded opera festival takes place at the **Teatro dell'Accademia dei Differenti** (Theater of the Academy of the Different). The Opera Barga began in 1967 as a workshop for young singers and musicians. Now it stages lesser-known baroque operas, as well as contemporary works. Check their Web site for current information.

Listen to the newest music during **Barga Jazz** (✉*Teatro dell'Accademia dei Differenti, Piazza Angelio 4* ⊕*www.barganews.com/barga-jazz*), a jazz orchestra competition (in July and August). The scores presented each year are selected by a special committee and a winner is selected by an international jury.

CASTELNUOVO DI GARFAGNANA

13 km (8 mi) northwest of Barga, 47 km (27 mi) north of Lucca, 121 km (75 mi) northwest of Florence.

GETTING HERE

By car from Lucca, take the SS12/Via del Brennero, follow signs to Borgo a Mozzano; then take the SS445, which leads directly into town. CLAP buses (✉ *Piazza della Repubblica* ☎ *0583/62039*) run between Castelnuovo di Garfagnana and Barga. There is no train service.

VISITOR INFORMATION

Castelnuovo di Garfagnana tourism office (✉ *Piazza della Erbe* ☎ *0583/641007*).

EXPLORING

Castelnuovo di Garfagnana might be the best base for exploring the Garfagnana, because it's central with respect to the other towns. During the Renaissance the town's fortunes were frequently tied to those of the powerful Este family of Ferrara. It's now a bustling town with a lovely historic center.

La Rocca *(The Fortress)* dates from the 13th century and has a plaque commemorating writer Ludovico Ariosto's brief tenure here as commissar general for the Este. Ariosto (1474–1533) wrote the epic poem *Orlando Furioso* (1516), among other works. You can only see the impressive walls and great entryway of the fort from the outside—at this time entry into La Rocca is not allowed. ⊠ *Piazza Umberto I.*

The **Duomo,** a cathedral dedicated to Saint Peter, was begun in the 11th century and was reconstructed in the early 1500s. Inside is a crucifix dating from the 14th to 15th century. There's also an early-16th-century terra-cotta attributed to the school of the della Robbia. ⊠ *Piazza del Duomo* ☎ *0583/62170* 🎫 *Free* ⊙ *Daily 9–7.*

Preserved ancient forests and barren rocky peaks create dramatic scenery in the **Parco Naturale delle Alpi Apuane,** a national park that encompasses several towns. Its highest peak, Monte Pisanino, rises more than 6,000 feet and towers over an artificial lake, Lago di Vagli, which covers the submerged village of Fabbricca. The tiny stone villages of Vagli di Sotto and Vagli di Sopra sit alongside the lake. Plan on a half or full day of hiking in the Natural Park of the Apuane Alps. Remember to wear comfortable sports shoes or hiking boots and bring plenty of drinking water. A two-lane winding road through the park (SP13) connects Castelnuovo di Garfagnana to the sea. To get to Vagli di Sotto and Vagli di Sopra, go north of Castelnuovo di Garfagnana on SR445 to Poggio and then turn west on SP50. ☎ *0583/644478* ⊕ *www.parcapuane.toscana.it* 🎫 *€1.50.*

WHERE TO STAY & EAT

$$ ✕ **Giaccò.** A beautiful ride along winding, tree-lined mountain roads brings you to this little gem in the middle of nowhere. A simple interior provides the perfect backdrop for Tuscan classics. Start with the antipasto della casa, a delightful mix of sliced, cured meats, truffled polenta, and an exquisite farro salad. The grill takes center stage here, and all the usual fare's on hand; the bistecca fiorentina is particularly good. The wine list isn't exceptional, but there are some well-priced bottles that pair nicely with the food. ⊠ *Via Provinciale di Arni 2,* ☎ *0583/667048* ▭ *V* ⊙ *Closed Tues. and 3 wks in Nov.*

$ ✕ **Osteria Vecchio Mulino.** "The old mill" has an antique marble serving counter filled with free nibbles and two large wooden tables in a room lined with wine bottles. The enthusiastic host, Andrea Bertucci, proudly touts local products on his simple menu, which usually consists of superior cheese and affettati misti (mixed sliced cured meats). Traditional local dishes with farro grain, polenta, pecorino cheese, and salami round out the selections. Finish your meal with their famous *caffè al vetro con miele di castagno* (coffee in a glass with chestnut honey). This osteria keeps deli hours (7:30 AM to 8 PM). ⊠ *Via Vittorio Emanuele 12* ☎*0583/62192* ⊕*www.ilvecchiomulino.com* ⊟*AE, DC, MC, V* ⊗*Closed Mon. and 3 wks in Oct. or Jan.*

$ ✕⊡ **La Lanterna.** Take a few minutes' drive up a long, winding road from the center of town to this modern inn with beautiful mountain views. Wall-to-wall carpeting complements neutral color schemes and fairly motel-like furnishings. The restaurant serves bountiful regional specialties; the menu, featuring farro in several guises, is fantastic and inexpensive. The chef has a gift for sauces—try the pork in a radicchio sauce and anything (pasta or meat) with a porcini mushroom sauce. Half board is available. **Pros:** Location just off the main drag, fine restaurant. **Cons:** Unexceptional decor. ⊠*Località le Monache,* ⊹*1½ km (1 mi) southwest of Castelnuovo di Garfagnana, Piano Pieve55032* ☎*0583/62272* 🖷*0583/641418* ⊕*www.hotellalanterna.com* 🖙*42 rooms* ⚂*In-hotel: restaurant, some pets allowed* ⊟*AE, DC, MC, V* ⊗*Restaurant closed Tues.* ⦿*BP.*

SPORTS & THE OUTDOORS

HIKING & CLIMBING   The **Centro Accoglienza Parco** (⊠*Piazza Erbe 1* ☎*0583/644242* ✎*garfagnana@tin.it*) can help you with hiking information, particularly for the Parco Naturale delle Alpi Apuane.

For detailed maps and information about trekking in the mountains surrounding Castelnuovo di Garfagnana, contact the **Club Alpino Italiano** (*Italian Alpine Club* ⊠*Via Vittorio Emanuele* ☎*0583/65577* ⊕*www.cai.it*)

PARCO DELL'ORECCHIELLA

15 km (9 mi) north of Castelnuovo di Garfagnana, 64 km (40 mi) north of Lucca, 121 km (72 mi) northwest of Florence.

GETTING HERE

A car is your only option in this part of the world. The southeastern boundary of the park is accessible via SR324, a pretty 30-minute drive on the winding two-lane road from Abetone. To get here from Lucca, take the SS12/Via del Brennero to the SP2, which leads to the SP20; from there take the SS445/SR445 to the SS324/SP72. Continue on the winding SP16 to the SP47, which leads to the SP48, which leads to the park.

EXPLORING

Orecchiella Park is 52 square km (21 square mi) of protected land dedicated to the preservation of local flora and fauna, including eagles, mouflon, and deer. There is a botanical garden and, for avid hikers, many trails marked with the length of time necessary to complete them—anywhere from 2½ to 5 hours. To find the visitor center, drive to Castiglione Garfagnana, follow signs to Corfino, then go 7 km (4 mi) on SP48, and then follow the sign to turn into the park—the visitor center is just inside the gate. The botanical garden is 2 km (1¼ mi) from the visitor center. ⊹*7 km (4 mi) north of Corfino* ☎*0583/619098 for information, 0583/955525 National Forest Administration* ✒*Park*

€1.50, garden €2 ⊘ *Apr. and May, Sun. 9* AM–sunset; June, weekends 9–7; July and Aug., daily 9–7; Sept., daily 9* AM–sunset; Oct.–Nov. 1, weekends 9* AM–sunset.

WHERE TO EAT

$ ✕**Bar Ristorante Orecchiella.** Signora Ilda presides in the kitchen, serving grilled meats—*cinghiale* (wild boar) is often on the menu—and rich pasta dishes. This little place is quite rustic, set in the woods in San Romano in Garfagnana, near the main parking lot at Parco dell'Orecchiella. ⊠*Parco dell'Orecchiella,* ✛ *7 km (4 mi) north of Corfino on SP48, San Romano in Garfagnana* ☎*0583/619010* ▭*No credit cards* ⊘*Closed Mon.–Sat. Nov.–Mar. and Fri. Apr.–mid-June and mid-Sept.–Oct.*

THE NORTHWEST COAST

Livorno has been a port town since the 16th century, and continues to host countless cruise and cargo ships from around the world. It has a gritty, lively feel. Heading up the coast you'll pass lots of beaches (both sandy and rocky, but none all that inviting) until you hit the popular destinations of Viareggio and swank, expensive Forte dei Marmi. The air gets clearer if you head up the hills toward Carrara, a lively, beautiful, rarely visited town.

On the Ligurian coast west of Tuscany are the five seaside villages that make up the Cinque Terre. They're a hugely popular side trip for visitors to northwest Tuscany.

LIVORNO

24 km (15 mi) south of Pisa, 187 km (116 mi) west of Florence.

GETTING HERE

Livorno is easily reached by rail; trains from Florence run hourly. By car it's about an hour east of Florence on the Fi-Pi-Li.

VISITOR INFORMATION

Livorno tourism office (⊠ *Piazza Cavour 6* ☎*0586/204611* ⊕*www. prolocobagnidilucca.it*).

EXPLORING

Livorno is a gritty city with a long and interesting history. In the early Middle Ages it alternately belonged to Pisa and then to Genoa. In 1421 Florence, seeking access to the sea, bought it. Cosimo I (1519–74) started construction of the harbor in 1571, putting Livorno on the map. After Ferdinando I de' Medici (1549–1609) proclaimed Livorno a free city, it became a haven for people suffering from religious persecution; Roman Catholics from England and Jews and Moors from Spain and Portugal, among others, settled here. The *Quattro Mori* (Four Moors), also known as the Monument to Ferdinando I, commemorates this. (The statue of Ferdinand I dates from 1595, the bronze Moors by Pietro Tacca from the 1620s.)

In the following centuries, and particularly in the 18th, Livorno boomed as a port. In the 19th century, the town drew a host of famous Britons passing through on their grand tours. Its prominence continued up to World War II, when it was heavily bombed. Much of the town's architecture, therefore, postdates the war, and it's somewhat difficult to imagine what it might have looked liked before. Livorno has recovered from the war, however, as it's become a huge point of departure for container ships, as well as a spot for cruise ships to dock for the day.

Most of Livorno's artistic treasures date from the 17th century and aren't all that interesting unless you dote on obscure baroque artists. Livorno's most famous native artist, Amedeo Modigliani (1884–1920), was of much more recent vintage. Sadly, there's no notable work by him in his hometown.

There may not be much in the way of art, but it's still worth strolling around the city. The **Mercato Nuovo,** which has been around since 1894, sells all sorts of fruits, vegetables, grains, meat, and fish. Outdoor markets nearby are also chock-full of local color. The presence of Camp Darby, an American military base just outside of town, accounts for the availability of many American products.

If you have time, Livorno is worth a stop for lunch or dinner at the least.

WHERE TO EAT

$$ ✕**Ristorante Gennarino.** Lovers of seafood fill this unpretentious trattoria. The unremarkable decor (yellowed walls, fluorescent lights) can be taken as a testament to the singular focus here on high-quality cuisine. Start with the *insalata di mare tiepida* (seafood antipasti), and follow with the flavorful spaghetti *all'ammiraglia* (admiral-style, laden with mussels, baby clams, squid, and fresh tomatoes). ⊠ *Via Santa Fortunata 11* ☎ *0586/888093* ⌂ *Reservations essential* ▭ *AE, DC, MC, V* ⊙ *Closed Wed. and 15 days in June.*

$ ✕**Cantina Nardi.** It's only open for lunch, and it's well off the beaten tourist path (even if it is in the center of Livorno's shopping district). But getting here is worth the trouble: this tiny place, lined with bottles of wine, has a small menu that changes daily, a superb wine list, and gregarious staff. Their *baccalà alla livornese* (deep-fried salt cod served with chickpeas) is succulently crisp; soups, such as ribollita, are very soothing. ⊠ *Via Cambini 6/8* ☎ *0586/808006* ▭ *AE, MC, V* ⊙ *Closed Sun. No dinner.*

VIAREGGIO

8 km (5 mi) south of Pietrasanta, 25 km (15 mi) northwest of Lucca, 97 km (60 mi) northwest of Florence.

GETTING HERE

Trains run frequently from Florence on the Lucca line. By car from Lucca, take the A11 and follow the signs for Viareggio. Exit at Massarosa and take the SS439 to the SP5, which goes into the center of town.

VISITOR INFORMATION

Viareggio tourism office (✉ *Vialle Carducci 10* ☎*0584/962233* ⊕*www. comune.viareggio.lu.it*).

EXPLORING

Tobias Smollett (1721–71), the English novelist, wrote in the 1760s that Viareggio was "a kind of sea-port on the Mediterranean.… The roads are indifferent and the accommodation is execrable." Much has changed here since Smollett's time. For one, this beach town becomes very crowded in summer, so accommodations are plentiful. It can also be loud and brassy at the height of the season, though there's peace and quiet in the autumn and early spring.

Viareggio has numerous buildings decorated in the 1920s Liberty style, characterized by colorful wood and some with ornate exterior decoration. Locals and tourists alike stroll along the town's wide seaside promenade lined with bars, cafés, and some very fine restaurants. If you can't make it to Venice for *Carnevale* (Carnival), come here, where the festivities are in some ways more fun than in Venice. The city is packed with revelers from all over Tuscany, taking part in the riot of colorful parades with giant floats. Book lodging far in advance, and be aware that hotels charge top prices during Carnevale.

WHERE TO STAY & EAT

$$$$
★
✕**Romano.** The Franceschini family has been running this swank fish eatery since the 1970s. Ebullient host Romano Franceschini is justifiably proud of the food produced by his wife and daughter, Franca and Cristina; son Roberto, an accomplished sommelier, presides over the floor. Don't miss the *fantasia di pesce crudo* (fantasy of raw fish), which arrives at the table with an aroma redolent of the sea, and follow up with any of the marvelous fish seconds. Or you can leave everything in the Franceschinis' hands and order the tasting menu (€85 without wine). ✉ *Via Mazzini 122* ☎*0584/31382* ⚞*Reservations essential* ▤*AE, DC, MC, V* ⊗*Closed Mon. and Jan. No lunch Tues. in July and Aug.*

$$$–$$$$
🏨**Hotel President.** A quiet elegance pervades here. The rooms have somewhat formal decor, high ceilings, and pastel walls; some look directly out at the sea, across the promenade. Others have an extra bed, making it easier for those traveling with children (who stay for free under age six). The hotel restaurant, Ristorante Gaudi, has panoramic views of the sea; the bar is on an outdoor terrace with furniture from the early 1900s. Half board is available. **Pros:** Sea views. **Cons:** A touch stuffy. ✉ *Viale Carducci 5, 55049* ☎*0584/962712* ⚞*0584/963658* ⊕*www.hotelpresident.it* ⚞*50 rooms* ⚞*In-room: safe, refrigerator, dial-up. In-hotel: restaurant, bar, bicycles, some pets allowed* ▤*AE, DC, MC, V* ⧀*BP.*

The outrageous is the rule at Viareggio's Carnevale festivities.

$$$ ⊞**Grand Hotel Royal.** In operation since 1899, the Grand Hotel Royal looks majestic from the outside, and sweepingly high ceilings maintain the feeling inside. In cooler months, enjoy dinner served in the romantic salon—with arched windows, French Empire–style chairs, and soft pink tablecloths—which doubled as a ballroom in the past. Dine in the garden during summer. The restaurant changes its menu daily. There's also a yellow breakfast room flooded with sunlight. Rooms have tile floors and elegant wood-and-upholstery furniture. Some have balconies overlooking the sea (for an additional charge). In high season a three-day minimum stay is required. **Pros:** Sea views. **Cons:** Three-day minimum stay in high season. ⊠ *Viale Carducci 44, 55049* ☎*0584/45151* 🖷*0584/31438* ⊕*www.hotelroyalviareggio.it* ➷*102 rooms, 2 suites* ⌂*In-room: refrigerator, dial-up. In-hotel: restaurant, pool, public Wi-Fi, bicycles (fee)*🚬*AE, DC, MC, V* ⊗*Closed Nov.* ⧖*BP.*

NIGHTLIFE & THE ARTS
For four Sundays and Shrove Tuesday preceding Lent, this little seaside town produces its world-famous **Carnevale** (☎*0584/962568* ⊕*www. viareggio.ilcarnevale.com*), with intricate floats, or *carri*, representing Italy's most influential celebrities and politicians and sometimes the famous and infamous from around the world. Started in the late 1800s, the Viareggio Carnevale differs from the carnival held in Venice because of its parades of huge and fantastical floats. Traditionally, they were put together by Viareggio's shipbuilders, and in the beginning the masked celebrants were civil and political protesters, and the floats were, and

often still are, used as a vehicle to lampoon popular figures of the day. Other events—music, parties, and art displays—also take place during Carnevale. The crowds are huge, with many attending in costume.

SPORTS & THE OUTDOORS

Club Nautico Versilia (⊠*Piazza Artiglio* ☎*0584/31444*) can assist sailors who wish to tour the coastal waters with maps, port and docking information, charter and craft-rental resources, and information about craft repair and refueling.

FORTE DEI MARMI

8 km (5 mi) south of Massa, 37 km (27 mi) northwest of Lucca, 106 km (66 mi) northwest of Florence.

GETTING HERE

By car from Florence, take the A11, following signs for Viareggio. From there, take the A12/E80 following signs for Genova. Exit at Versilia, and take the SP70 directly into town. Coming by train isn't a good option; the station is far from the center of town, and the taxi ride in is expensive.

VISITOR INFORMATION

Forte dei Marmi tourism office (⊠*Via A. Franceschi 8b* ☎*0584/80091* ⊕*www.comune.forte-dei-marmi.lucca.it*)

EXPLORING

Forte dei Marmi is a playground for wealthy Italians and equally well-heeled tourists. Its wide, sandy beaches—strands are 6 km (4 mi) long—have the Alpi Apuane as a dramatic backdrop. The town was, from Roman times, the port for marble quarried in Carrara. In the 1920s, it became the fashionable seaside resort it remains today. During the winter the town's population is about 10,000; in the summer, it swells to seven or eight times that.

WHERE TO STAY & EAT

$$$$ ✕**Bistrot.** For beachside dining, this seafood restaurant can't be beat. The delicious *carpaccio di branzino* (thin slices of sea bass) is quickly seared and then served with fragrant local olive oil, basil, and tomatoes. The regal champagne risotto with lobster is a house favorite. Pastas are homemade, and the *sauté di frutti di mare,* a cross between a soup and stew, has *vongole* (clams), tomatoes, and garlic in a heavenly broth. Adventurous sorts can put themselves into the chef's hands and try the €85 tasting menu. For dessert have the hot flan made with *gianduia* chocolate and pieces of white chocolate. ⊠*Viale Franceschi 14* ☎*0584/89879* ▭*AE, DC, MC, V* ⊙*Closed Tues. Oct.–May. No lunch Aug.*

$$$–$$$$ ✕**Lorenzo.** The affable Lorenzo Viani has presided here for more than 20 years, and his restaurant still draws a crowd. Start with the chilled raw oysters before moving on to seafood pasta, sea bass with chopped tomatoes, or a fish tartare. Or request the *menu degustazione* (tasting menu) and let chef Gioacchino Pontrelli prepare the freshest items

of the day. You can also choose vegetarian and *terra* (meat) tasting menus. ⊠*Via Carducci 61* ☎*0584/84030* ⚐*Reservations essential* ▤*AE, DC, MC, V* ⊗*Closed mid-Dec.–Jan. and Mon. No lunch July and Aug.*

$$$$ ⚏**Byron.** The pale yellow exterior only hints at the elegance inside the ★ hotel created by joining two Liberty villas from 1899 and 1902. Refined furnishings include gem-color fabrics and dark wood. Many rooms have balconies that face the sea or the mountains. The billiard room and bar overlook a garden of pine trees and flowers. Walk across the street to get to the beach. The restaurant, La Magnolia, serves regional cuisine poolside during the summer. A one-week minimum stay and half board are mandatory June 1 to September 15. The rest of the year continental breakfast is included in the price. Full board is always available. **Pros:** Cutting-edge chef Andrea Mattei at the hotel restaurant, golf and tennis privileges, sunny staff. **Cons:** One-week minimum stay. ⊠*Viale Arthur-Jules Morin 46, 55042* ☎*0584/787052* ⊟*0584/787152* ⊕*www.hotel-byron.net* ⇱*23 doubles, 3 suites* ⚐*In-room: kitchen (some). In-hotel: restaurant, bar, pool, concierge, laundry service, public Internet, Wi-Fi* ▤*AE, DC, MC, V* ⅋◍*BP, MAP.*

$$$$ ⚏**Hotel Ritz.** Late artist Henry Moore found inspiration for a few of his sculptures while residing at this 1930s Beaux-Arts villa. Here there's none of the stuffiness associated with some upscale hotels. Rooms are simple but elegant, with modern-art prints on the walls, art deco–esque furniture, and large marble bathrooms. At least half board is required from June 1 to August 31; in other months a continental breakfast is included in the room price. Full board is available year-round. The hotel is one block from the area's beach clubs and a short walk from the center of town. **Pros:** Multilingual staff, nearness to the beach. **Cons:** Beach costs extra (you have to join a beach club) ⊠*Via Flavio Gioia 2, 55042* ☎*0584/787531* ⊟*0584/787522* ⊕*www.ritzfortedeimarmi.com* ⇱*32 rooms* ⚐*In-room: safe, VCR, Wi-Fi (some). In-hotel: restaurant, room service, bar, pool, bicycles (fee), concierge, laundry service, public Internet* ▤*AE, DC, MC, V* ⅋◍*FAP, MAP.*

NIGHTLIFE & THE ARTS

After a day at the beach, the place to see and be seen is **Alma Rosa Art Music and Bar** (⊠*Viale Morin 89/a* ☎*0584/82503*). The clientele during high season frequently includes Italian national soccer players and other young, good-looking celebs and politicos. A champagne tasting and a happy "hour" runs from 6 PM to 10 PM daily. Leonardo, the charming owner-bartender, speaks English. On Saturday night there's a DJ.

SPORTS & THE OUTDOORS

BIKING **Claudio Maggi Cicli** (⊠*Viale Morin 85* ☎*0584/89529* ⊟*0584/81699* ⊕*www.ciclimaggi.it*), which is near the beach, has been selling bicycle equipment and renting bikes since 1906. From May through September it's open daily 8 to 1 and 3 to 8; from October through April it's closed Wednesday and Sunday. **Maggi-Coppa** (⊠*Via A. Franceschi 4/d* ☎*0584/83528*), which rents bicycles, is right on the beach and keeps late hours: 8 AM to midnight daily from May through August, 8 to 8 daily the rest of the year.

HIKING & CLIMBING The **Forte dei Marmi Club Alpino Italiano** (✉ *Via Buonarroti 47* ☎ *0584/89808* ⊕ *www.caifortedeimarmi.it*) can provide information on area hiking and rock climbing, and about guided tours. The club itself is open only on Friday from 9 PM to 11 PM, and their Web site is in Italian.

SCUBA DIVING For information about the best places to scuba dive on the Versilian and Ligurian coasts, contact the **Associazione Subacquei Versilia** (✉ *Via S. Allende 38* ☎ *0584/82070*).

CARRARA

45 km (28 mi) southeast of Riomaggiore, 126 km (79 mi) northwest of Florence.

GETTING HERE
By car, take the A11, following signs for Lucca, then at Viareggio take the A12. Trains run frequently from Florence, but a change of trains is almost always required, and the Carrara station is not centrally located. Coming from Lucca, you usually have to change trains at Viareggio.

VISITOR INFORMATION
Carrara tourism office (✉ *Lungomare A. Vespucci 24, Marina di Massa* ☎ *0585/240063*).

EXPLORING
Carrara, from which the famous white marble takes its name, lies in a beautiful valley midway up a spectacular mountain in the Apuane Alps. The surrounding peaks are free of foliage and white as snow, even in summer, because they are full of marble stone. Marble has been quarried in the area for the past 2,000 years. The art historian Giorgio Vasari (1511–74) recorded that Michelangelo came to Carrara with two apprentices to quarry the marble for the never-completed tomb of Julius II (1443–1513). According to Vasari, Michelangelo spent eight months among the rocks conceiving fantastical ideas for future works.

The area around Carrara has a lot of still-active quarries—well over 100 at last count. Most of them are not open to the public for safety reasons. However, it is possible to tour specific marble caves. The **Carrara visitor information center**, 7 km (4½ mi) away in Marina di Massa, has details about which areas you can visit. ✉ *Lungomare A. Vespucci 24, Marina di Massa* ☎ *0585/240063*.

Carrara's history as a marble-producing center is well documented in the **Museo del Marmo** *(Marble Museum)*, beginning with early works from the 2nd century. Exhibits detail the working of marble, from quarrying and transporting it to sculpting it. At this writing, the museum was closed for restoration, with tentative plans to reopen sometime in 2008. ✉ *Viale XX Settembre 85* ☎ *0585/845746* 🎟 *€4.50* 🕐 *May–Sept., Mon.–Sat. 10–6; Oct.–Apr., Mon.–Sat. 9–5.*

Work began on the **Duomo** in the 11th century, and continued into the 14th. The cathedral, dedicated to Saint Andrew, is the first church of the Middle Ages constructed entirely of marble. Most of it comes from the area (the white, light blue-gray, black, and red). The tremendous facade is a fascinating blend of Pisan Romanesque and Gothic architecture. Note the human figures and animals on Corinthian capitals. ⊠*Piazza del Duomo* ☎*No phone* ☑*Free* ☉*Daily 9–7.*

The lovely baroque church of **San Francesco** is a study in understated elegance. It dates from the 1620s to 1660s, and even though it was built during the peak years of the baroque, the only excess can be found in the twisting marble columns that embellish the altars. ⊠*Piazza XXVII Aprile* ☎*No phone* ☑*Free* ☉*Daily 9–7.*

During the 19th and 20th centuries Carrara became a hotbed for anarchism, and during World War II it put up fierce resistance to the Nazis. The town is still lively thanks to its art institute. The **Accademia di Belle Arti,** founded by Maria Teresa Cybo Malaspina d'Este in 1769, draws studio art students from all over Italy. Their presence explains the energetic and artistically eclectic presence in some of the piazzas.

WHERE TO STAY

$ ⛺**Hotel Carrara.** Although this quiet hotel isn't actually in Carrara, it is right across the street from the Avenza-Carrara train station. Distinctive wall hangings—copies of Renaissance masterworks—complement red lamp shades and bedspreads in guest rooms. The dinner-only restaurant ($–$$) serves seafood specialties and regional pastas and grilled meats. The included breakfast buffet is extensive. **Pros:** Proximity to train station. **Cons:** Rooms are somewhat utilitarian. ⊠*Via Petacchi 21, 4 km (2½ mi) southeast of Carrara, Avenza 54031* ☎*0585/857616* ☎*0585/50344* ⊕*www.hotelcarrara.it* ⌨*32 rooms* ⌂*In-room: safe, refrigerator, Wi-Fi (fee). In-hotel: restaurant, public Internet, Wi-Fi (fee), some pets allowed* ⊟*AE, DC, MC, V* ⏻*BP.*

THE CINQUE TERRE

FIVE REMOTE VILLAGES MAKE ONE MUST-SEE DESTINATION

"Charming" and "breathtaking" are adjectives that get a workout when you're traveling in Italy, but it's rare that both apply to a single location. The Cinque Terre is such a place, and this combination of characteristics goes a long way toward explaining its tremendous appeal.

The area is made up of five tiny villages (Cinque Terre literally means "Five Lands") clinging to the cliffs along a gorgeous stretch of the Ligurian coast. The terrain is so steep that for centuries footpaths were the only way to get from place to place. It just so happens that these paths provide beautiful views of the rocky coast tumbling into the sea, as well as access to secluded beaches and grottoes.

Backpackers "discovered" the Cinque Terre in the 1970s, and its popularity has been growing ever since. Despite summer crowds, much of the original appeal is intact. Each town has maintained its own distinct charm, and views from the trails in between are as breathtaking as ever.

Monterosso

Corniglia

Terracing around Corniglia

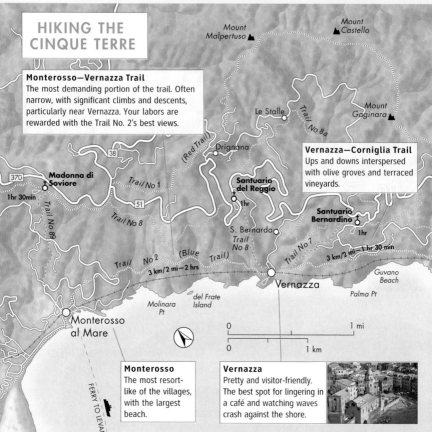

HIKING THE CINQUE TERRE

Monterosso—Vernazza Trail
The most demanding portion of the trail. Often narrow, with significant climbs and descents, particularly near Vernazza. Your labors are rewarded with the Trail No. 2's best views.

Vernazza—Corniglia Trail
Ups and downs interspersed with olive groves and terraced vineyards.

Mount Malpertuso

Mount Castello

Le Stalle

Trail No 8a

Mount Gaginara

Drignana

(Red Trail)

38

Madonna di Soviore
1hr 30min

370

Trail No 1

Santuario del Reggio
1hr

51

Trail No 89

Trail No 8

S. Bernardo
Trail No 8

Trail No 7

Santuario Bernardino
1hr

3 km/2 mi–1 hr 30 min

Trail No 2 (Blue Trail)
3 km/2 mi–2 hrs

Vernazza

Guvano Beach

Palma Pt

del Frate Island

Molinara Pt

Monterosso al Mare

0   1 mi

0   1 km

FERRY TO LEVANTO

Monterosso
The most resort-like of the villages, with the largest beach.

Vernazza
Pretty and visitor-friendly. The best spot for lingering in a café and watching waves crash against the shore.

THE CLASSIC HIKE

Hiking is the most popular way to experience the Cinque Terre, and Trail No. 2, the Sentiero Azzurro (Blue Trail), is the most traveled path. To cover the entire trail is a full day: it's approximately 13 km (8 mi) in length, takes you to all five villages, and requires about five hours, not including stops, to complete. The best approach is to start at the eastern-most town of Riomaggiore and warm up your legs on the easiest segment of the trail. As you work your way west, the hike gets progressively more demanding. For a less strenuous experience, you can choose to skip a leg or two and take the ferry (which provides its own beautiful views) or the inland train running between the towns instead.

Manarola

Along Trail No.2

Via dell'Amore

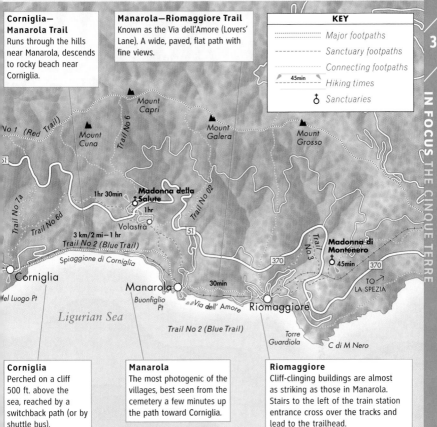

Corniglia– Manarola Trail
Runs through the hills near Manarola, descends to rocky beach near Corniglia.

Manarola–Riomaggiore Trail
Known as the Via dell'Amore (Lovers' Lane). A wide, paved, flat path with fine views.

KEY

··········	*Major footpaths*
- - - - -	*Sanctuary footpaths*
— — —	*Connecting footpaths*
45min	*Hiking times*
⚲	*Sanctuaries*

3

IN FOCUS THE CINQUE TERRE

Mount Capri

No 1 (Red Trail)

Mount Cuna

Trail No 6

Mount Galera

Mount Grosso

51

Trail No 7a

Trail No 6d

1hr 30min

Madonna della Salute ⚲

1hr

Trail No 02

Volastra

3 km/2 mi—1 hr
Trail No 2 (Blue Trail)

51

Madonna di Montenero ⚲ 45min

Trail No 3

370

370

Spiaggione di Corniglia

TO LA SPEZIA

⚲ **Corniglia**

Manarola

30min

Riomaggiore

el Luogo Pt

Buonfiglio Pt

Via dell' Amore

Ligurian Sea

Trail No 2 (Blue Trail)

Torre Guardiola

C di M Nero

Corniglia
Perched on a cliff 500 ft. above the sea, reached by a switchback path (or by shuttle bus).

Manarola
The most photogenic of the villages, best seen from the cemetery a few minutes up the path toward Corniglia.

Riomaggiore
Cliff-clinging buildings are almost as striking as those in Manarola. Stairs to the left of the train station entrance cross over the tracks and lead to the trailhead.

BEYOND TRAIL NO.2

Trail No. 2 is just one of a network of trails crisscrossing the hills. If you're a dedicated hiker, spend a few nights and try some of the other routes. Trail No. 1, the Sentiero Rosso (Red Trail), climbs from Portovenere (east of Riomaggiore) and returns to the sea at Levanto (west of Monterosso al Mare). To hike its length takes from 9 to 12 hours; the ridge-top trail provides spectacular views from high above the villages, each of which can be reached via a steep path. Other shorter trails go from the villages up into the hills, some leading to religious sanctuaries. Trail No. 9, for example, starts from the old section of Monterosso and ends at the Madonna di Soviore Sanctuary.

FODOR'S FIRST PERSON

Angelo Benvenuto
Fisherman,
Monterosso al Mare

Angelo Benvenuto is a 10th-generation fisherman from Monterosso who organizes special boating excursions along the Cinque Terre in his *lampara* (wooden anchovy fishing boat).

Q: Although hiking the Cinque Terre has become a favorite with travelers, you and others maintain that the "way of life" in the Cinque Terre is really that of the sea....

A: For nearly one thousand years Monterosso has been a fishing village. We eat, live, and breathe the sea. In fact, when the barbarians invaded Italy during the middle ages, they did not come down to Monterosso because they were afraid of the sea. Because of this Monterosso as well as the other villages were protected and untouched. Everyday life is always connected to the sea.

Yet, the *sentiri* (trails) were also essential to our livelihood. They provided access to the elements we needed on land such as produce, animals, and of course wine! Now

they are a source of entertainment and beauty for our visitors.

Q: How has the Cinque Terre changed over the past 20 years?

A: There are obviously more people visiting, but everyday life has remained the same. I still go out to fish for the majority of our meals, and my wife works in the garden to provide us with fresh vegetables, fruit, even eggs. It is this way for most of the Cinque Terre.

Of course, many of us have gone into the tourism business—hotels, restaurants, cafes. The tourists have brought us opportunity and some financial stability which is very good for us, for all of the villages.

Q: What is your perfect day in the Cinque Terre?

A: Take a hike up to the garden (located on the slopes above town) or maybe even to Vernazza to visit friends. Then after a nice fresh seafood lunch, glass of *Sciacchetra'* (local dessert wine) and a short *pisolino* (nap), I would then head out to sea on my lampara and enjoy the silence of the sea and the beautiful landscape, and catch some fish for dinner!

PRECAUTIONS

If you're hitting the trails, you'll want to carry water with you, wear sturdy shoes (hiking boots are best), and have a hat and sunscreen handy. ⚠ Check weather reports before you start out; especially in late fall and winter, thunderstorms can send townspeople running for cover and make the shelterless trails slippery and dangerous. Rain in October and November can cause landslides and close the trails. Note that the lesser-used trails aren't as well maintained as Trail No. 2. If you're undertaking the full Trail No.

1 hike, bring something to snack on as well as your water bottle.

ADMISSION

Entrance tickets for use of the trails are available at ticket booths located at the start of each section of Trail No. 2, and at information offices in the Levanto, Monterosso, Vernazza, Corniglia, Manarola, Riomaggiore, and La Spezia train stations.

A one-day pass costs €5, which includes a trail map and a general information leaflet. Information about local train and boat schedules is also available from the information offices.

Working Cinque Terre's vertical vineyards

GETTING THERE & GETTING AROUND

The local train on the Genoa–La Spezia line stops at each of the Cinque Terre, and runs approximately every 30 minutes. Tickets for each leg of the journey (€1.30) are available at the five train stations. In Corniglia, the only one of the Cinque Terre that isn't at sea level, a shuttle service (€1) is provided for those who don't wish to climb (or descend) the hundred-or-so steps that link the train station with the cliff-top town.

Along the Cinque Terre coast two ferry lines operate. From June to September, Golfo Paradiso runs from Genoa and Camogli to Monterosso al Mare and Vernazza. The smaller, but more frequent, Golfo dei Poeti stops at each village from Portovenere (east of Riomaggiore) to Monterosso, with the exception of Corniglia, four times a day. A one-day ticket costs €22.

WHEN TO GO

The ideal times to see the Cinque Terre are September and May, when the weather is mild and the summer tourist season isn't in full swing.

SWIMMING & BEACHES

Each town has something that passes for a beach, but there are only two options where you'll find both sand and decent swimming. The more accessible is in Monterosso, opposite the train station; it's equipped with chairs, umbrellas, and snack bars. The other is the secluded, swimwear-optional Guvano Beach, between Corniglia and Vernazza. To reach it from the Corniglia train station, bypass the steps leading up to the village, instead following signs to an abandoned train tunnel. Ring a bell at the tunnel's entrance, and the gate will automatically open; after a dimly lit 10-minute walk, you'll emerge at the beach. Both beaches have a nominal admission fee.

Monterosso al Mare

THE TOWNS

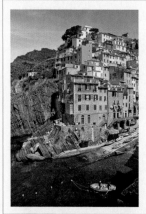

Riomaggiore

At the eastern end of the Cinque Terre, Riomaggiore is built into a river gorge (thus the name, which means "river major") and is easily accessible from La Spezia by train or car. It has a tiny harbor protected by large slabs of alabaster and marble, which serve as as tanning beds for sunbathers, as well as being the site of several outdoor cafes with fine views. According to legend, settlement of Riomaggiore dates far back to the 8th century, when Greek religious refugees came here to escape persecution by the Byzantine emperor.

Manarola

The enchanting pastel houses of Manarola spill down a steep hill overlooking a spectacular turquoise swimming cove and a bustling harbor. The whole town is built on black rock. Above the town, ancient terraces still protect abundant vineyards and olive trees. This village is the center of the wine and olive oil production of the region, and its streets are lined with shops selling local products.

Corniglia

The buildings, narrow lanes, and stairways of Corniglia are strung together amid vineyards high on the cliffs; on a clear day views of the entire coastal strip are excellent. The high perch and lack of harbor make this farming community the most remote of the Cinque Terre. On a pretty pastel square sits the 14th-century church of **San Pietro**. The rose window of marble imported from Carrara is impressive, particularly considering the work required to get it here. ⊠ *Main Sq.* ☎ *0187/3235582* ☉ *Wed. 4–6, Sun. 10–noon.*

Vernazza

With its narrow streets and small squares, Vernazza is arguably the most charming of the five towns. Because it has the best access to the sea, it became wealthier than its neighbors—as evidenced by the elaborate arcades, loggias, and marblework. The village's pink, slate-roof houses and colorful squares contrast with the remains of the medieval fort and castle, including two towers, in the old town. The Romans first inhabited this rocky spit of land in the 1st century.

Today Vernazza has a fairly lively social scene. It's a great place to refuel with a hearty seafood lunch or linger in a café between links of the hike on Trail No. 2.

Monterosso al Mare

Beautiful beaches, rugged cliffs, crystal-clear turquoise waters, and plentiful small hotels and restaurants make Monterosso al Mare, the largest of the Cinque Terre villages (population 1,730), the busiest in midsummer. The village center bustles high on a hillside. Below, connected by stone steps, are the port and seaside promenade, where there are boats for hire. The medieval tower, Aurora, on the hills of the Cappuccini, separates the ancient part of the village from the more modern part. The village is encircled by hills covered with vineyards and olive groves, and by a forest of scrubby bushes and small trees.

Monterosso has the most festivals of the five villages, starting with the Lemon Feast on the Saturday preceding Ascension Sunday, followed by the Flower Festival of Corpus Christi, celebrated yearly on the second Sunday after Pentecost. During the afternoon, the streets and alleyways of the *centro storico* (historic center) are decorated with thousands of colorful flower petals set in beautiful designs that the evening procession passes over. Finally, the Salted Anchovy and Olive Oil Festival takes place each year during the second weekend of September.

Thursday, the **market** attracts mingled crowds of tourists and villagers from along the coast to shop for everything from pots and pans and underwear to fruits, vegetables, and fish. Often a few stands sell local art and crafts as well as olive oil and wine. ⊠ *Old town center* ☉ *Thurs. 8–1.*

The **Chiesa di San Francesco,** was built in the 12th century in the Ligurian Gothic style. Its distinctive black stripes and marble rose window make it one of the most photographed sites in the Cinque Terre. ⊠ *Piazza Garibaldi* ☎ *No phone* 🎫 *Free* ☉ *Daily 9–1 and 4–7.*

Main Square, Vernazza

WHERE TO STAY & EAT

From June through September, reservations are essential if you plan to stay in a hotel or B&B here. *Affitacamere* (rooms for rent in private homes) are a more modest alternative, often indicated by a simple sign on the front door. At agencies in Riomaggiore and Monterosso you can book officially licensed affitacamere. These rooms vary considerably in comfort, amenities, and cost; arrive early for a good selection.

Riomaggiore

$$–$$$ ✕ **La Lanterna.** Colorful chalkboards out in front of this small trattoria by the harbor list the day's selection of fresh fish; the set-up might sound modest, but this is arguably the finest restaurant in the Cinque Terre. Over the winter, Chef Massimo serves as a teacher at the Culinary Academy in Switzerland, and he always returns with new ideas for his menu. When available, their *cozze ripiene* (stuffed mussels) shouldn't be missed. Other offerings may be a touch exotic, such sting ray with ligurian herbs and white wine. ⊠ *Via San Giacomo* 10 ☎ *0187/920589* ▤ *AE, DC, MC, VC* ◔ *Closed Jan and 2 wks in Nov.*

$ ⌂ **Due Gemelli.** Set above the sea, this small hotel has fabulous views of the turquoise water. The rooms have simple, mismatched furnishings, but they all have balconies, making them bright and airy. ⊠ *Via Litoranea 1, 19017* ☎ *0187/920111* 🖷 *0187/920678* ⊕ *www.duegemelli.it* ➹ *14 rooms* ⌂ *Restaurant, bar; no a/c* ▤ *AE, DC, MC, V* ⑩ *BP.*

Manarola

$ ⌂ **Ca' d'Andrean.** If you want to stay in one of the less crowded of the Cinque Terre, this tiny, simple hotel is one of your best options. White-tile floors cool off the rooms, some of which have balconies. In summer, breakfast, an optional extra at €6 per person, is served in a flower garden. ⊠ *Via Discovolo 101, 19010* ☎ *0187/920040* 🖷 *0187/920452* ⊕ *www.cadandrean.it* ➹ *10 rooms* ⌂ *Bar; no a/c* ▤ *No credit cards* ◔ *Closed mid-Nov.–mid-Dec.*

Corniglia

$–$$ ✕⌂ **Cecio.** On the outskirts of Corniglia, many of the spotless rooms at the family-run Cecio have spectacular views of the town clinging to the cliffs above the bay. The same memorable vista can be enjoyed from the hotel's restaurant, which serves inexpensive and well-prepared local seafood dishes. Try the delicious lasagna with pesto sauce as a first course. ⊠ *Via Serra 58, 19010, toward Vernazza* ☎ *0187/812043* 🖷 *0187/812138* ➹ *12 rooms* ⌂ *Restaurant; no a/c, no room phones, no TV in some rooms* ▤ *DC, MC, V* ⑩ *BP.*

Vernazza

$$–$$$ ✕ Gambero Rosso. Relax on Vernazza's main square at this fine trattoria looking out at a church. Enjoy such delectable dishes as shrimp salad, vegetable torte, and squid-ink risotto. The creamy pesto, served atop spaghetti, is some of the best in the area. End your meal with Cinque Terre's own *sciacchetrà,* a dessert wine served with semisweet biscotti. Don't drink it out of the glass—dip the biscotti in the wine instead. ⊠ *Piazza Marconi 7* ☎ *0187/812265* ⊟ *AE, DC, MC, V* ⊗ *Closed Mon. Jan. and Feb.*

$–$$ ✕⌷ Trattoria Gianni Franzi. Order your pesto with *fagiolini* (green beans), a Ligurian specialty that somehow tastes better when you're eating it outside in a beautiful *piazzetta* (small square) with a view of the port, as you can here. Above the restaurant, a number of simply furnished, economical rooms are available. Your choice here is between the smaller, older rooms without private bathrooms, but with tiny balconies and great views of the port, or those in the newer section, with bathrooms but no view. ⊠ *Via G. Marconi 1, 19018* ☎ *0187/821003* 🖷 *0187/812228* ⊕ *www.giannifranzi.it* ⇔ *20 rooms, 12 with bath* ⌂ *Restaurant, bar* ⊟ *AE, DC, MC, V* ⊗ *Closed Jan. 8–Feb.; restaurant closed Wed. early Mar.–mid-July and mid-Sept.–early Jan.* †◯† *BP.*

$$$ ✕⌷ La Malà. A cut above other lodging options in the Cinque Terre, this family-run B&B has only four rooms, and they fill up quickly. The rooms are small but well equipped, with flat screen TVs, a/c, marble showers, and comfortable bedding. Two of the rooms have sea views; the other two face the port of Vernazza. There's a shared terrace literally suspended over the Mediterranean. Book early! ⊠ *Giovanni Battista 29, 19018* ☎ *334/2875718* ⊕ *www.lamala.*

it ⇔ *4 rooms* ⌂ *In-room: safe, refrigerator, satellite TV, hairdryer, tea & coffee maker.* ⊟ *AE, DC, MC, V* ⊗ *Closed Jan. 10–Mar.*

Monterosso al Mare

★ $$$ ✕ Miki. Specialties here are anything involving seafood. The *insalata di mare* (seafood salad), with squid and fish, is more than tasty; so are the grilled fish and any pasta with seafood. If you're in the mood for a pizza, you can order that here as well. Miki has a beautiful little garden in the back, perfect for lunch on a sunny day. ⊠ *Via Fegina 104* ☎ *0187/817608* ⊟ *AE, DC, MC, V* ⊗ *Closed Nov. and Dec., and Tues. Sept.–July.*

$ ✕ Enoteca Internazionale. Located on the main street in centro, this wine bar offers a large variety of vintages, both local from further afield, plus delicious light fare; its umbrella-covered patio is a perfect spot to recuperate after a day of hiking. The owner, Susanna, is a certified sommelier who's always forthcoming with helpful suggestions on local wines. ⊠ *Via Roma 62* ☎ *0187/817278* ⊟ *AE, MC, V* ⊗ *Closed Tues., Jan–Mar.*

$$ ✕⌷ Il Giardino Incantato. This small B&B in the historic center of Monterosso oozes comfort and old-world charm. The building dates back to the 16th century and still maintains its wood beam ceiling and stone walls. Each room has been impeccably restored with modern amenities. Breakfast is served either in your room on request or in their lovely private garden under the lemon trees. The owner, Maria Pia, goes out of her way to make you feel at home and whips up a fabulous frittata for breakfast. ⊠ *Via Mazzini 18, 19016* ☎ *0185/818315* ⊕ *www.ilgiardinoincantato.net* ⇔ *3 rooms, 1 junior suite* ⌂ *In-room: safe, refrigerator, satellite TV, hairdryer, tea & coffee maker. In-hotel: private garden.* ⊟ *AE, DC, MC,*

Chianti, Siena & Central Tuscany

WORD OF MOUTH

"Siena is not for a daytime, 'hit the highlights' tour. It is deeper than that. I think it is Italy's most enchanting medieval city. Give it a go!"

—jtrandolph

WELCOME TO CENTRAL TUSCANY

TOP REASONS TO GO

★ **Wine tasting in Chianti:** Sample the fruits of the region's many vineyards, at either the wineries or the wine bars found in just about every town.

★ **The Piazza del Campo, Siena:** Sip a cappuccino or enjoy some gelato as you take in this spectacular shell-shaped piazza.

★ **San Gimignano:** Grab a spot at sunset on the steps of the Collegiata as flocks of swallows swoop in and out of the famous medieval towers.

★ **Buying alabaster in Volterra:** Watch the carving of this softly luminous milk-white stone at the shops belonging to local craftspeople.

★ **Cheering the Palio in Siena:** Vie for a spot among thousands to salute the winners of this race, which takes over Siena's main square twice each year.

1 Chianti. The heart of Italy's most famous wine region is dotted with appealing towns. The largest, **Greve**, comes alive with a bustling local market in its town square every Saturday, while **Radda** sits on a hilltop in classic Tuscan style, ringed by a 14th-century walkway. Cutting through the region is the **Strada Chiantigiana**, one of Italy's great drives.

2 Siena. Throughout the Middle Ages, Siena competed with Florence for regional supremacy. Today it remains one of Italy's most enchanting medieval towns, with an exceptional Gothic cathedral and a main square, **il Campo,** that has an almost magical charm.

3 Monteriggioni & Colle di Val d'Elsa. These two sleepy hill towns are pleasing, laid-back stops on the road between Siena and San Gimignano.

4 San Gimignano. From miles away you can spot San Gimignano's soaring medieval "skyscrapers"— towers that were once the ultimate status symbol of the aristocracy.

San Gimignano

5 **Volterra.** Etruscan artifacts and Roman ruins are highlights of this city set in a rugged moonscape of a valley.

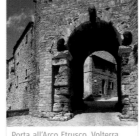

Porta all'Arco Etrusco, Volterra

GETTING ORIENTED

Undulating hills blanketed with vineyards, groves of silver-green olive trees, and enchanting towns perched on hilltops are the essence of central Tuscany. Siena, with its extraordinary piazza and magnificent cathedral, anchors the southern end of the region. Cypress-lined roads wind their way west to San Gimignano and Volterra, and north through the Chianti district.

Piazza del Campo, Siena

CENTRAL TUSCANY PLANNER

Making the Most of Your Time

Central Tuscany has an enticing landscape, one that invites you to follow its meandering roads to see where they might lead. Perhaps you'll come to a farmhouse selling splendid olive oil or one of the superb wines produced in the region; or perhaps you'll arrive at a medieval *pieve* (country church), an art-filled abbey, a *castello* (castle), or a restaurant where a flower-bedecked terrace looks out on a spectacular panorama.

Whatever road you take, **Siena**, Italy's most enchanting medieval city, is the one stop that's mandatory. The perfectly preserved *centro storico*, with its medieval palaces, is a delight to walk around; vehicle traffic is banned. Once in the region, however, there are plenty of other places to explore: **San Gimignano** is known as the "medieval Manhattan" because of its enormous towers, built by rival families, that still stand today. Like Siena, it benefited from commerce and trade along the pilgrimage routes, as the wonderful art in its churches and museums attests. With additional time, consider venturing farther afield to **Volterra**, with a stop in **Colle di Val d'Elsa** along the way.

The Tourist Offices

The tourist information office in Greve is an excellent source for general information about the Chianti wine region and its hilltop towns. In Siena the centrally located tourist office, in Piazza del Campo, has information about Siena and its province. Both offices book hotel rooms for a nominal fee. Offices in smaller towns can also be a good place to check if you need last-minute accommodations.

Tourist bureaus in larger towns are typically open from 8:30 to 1 and 3:30 to 6 or 7; bureaus in villages are generally open from Easter until early November, but usually remain closed on Saturday afternoon and Sunday.

Finding a Place to Stay

Siena, San Gimignano, and Volterra are among the most-visited towns in Tuscany, so there's no lack of choice for hotels across the price range. You can often stay right on the main square. The best accommodations, however, are often a couple of miles outside town. If you're staying a week, you have enough time to rent out an *agriturismo* (working farm) apartment. Stock up your refrigerator with local groceries and wines, go for hikes in the hills, and take more leisurely day trips to the main towns of the region.

DINING & LODGING PRICE CATEGORIES (IN EUROS)

	¢	$	$$	$$$	$$$$
RESTAU-RANTS	under €15	€15–€25	€25–€35	€35–€45	over €45
HOTELS	under €70	€70–€110	€110–€160	€160–€220	over €220

Restaurant prices are for a first course (*primo*), second course (*secondo*), and dessert (*dolce*). Hotel prices are for two people in a standard double room in high season, including tax and service.

GETTING AROUND

By Car

The best way to discover central Tuscany is by car, as its beauty often reveals itself along the road less traveled. The Certosa exit from the A1 highway (the Autostrada del Sole, running between Rome and Florence) provides direct access to the area. The Florence–Siena Superstrada (no number) is a four-lane, divided road with exits onto smaller country roads. The Via Cassia (SR2) winds its way south from Florence to Siena, along the western edge of the Chianti region. The superstrada is more direct, but much less scenic, than the SR2, and it can have a lot of traffic, especially on Sunday evenings. The Strada Chiantigiana (SR222) cuts through Chianti, east of the superstrada, in a curvaceous path past vineyards and countryside.

From Poggibonsi, a modern town to the west of the superstrada, you can quickly reach San Gimignano and then take the SR68 toward Volterra. The SR68 continues westward to join the Via Aurelia (SR1), linking Pisa with Rome.

By Train

Traveling between Florence and Siena by train is quick and convenient; trains make the 80-minute trip several times a day, with a change in Empoli sometimes required. Train service also runs between Siena and Chiusi–Chianciano Terme, where you can make Rome–Florence connections. Siena's train station is 2 km (1 mi) north of the centro storico, but cabs and city buses are readily available.

Other train service within the region is limited. For instance, the nearest station to Volterra is at Saline di Volterra, 10 km (6 mi) to the west. From Siena, trains run north to Poggibonsi and southeast to Sinalunga. Trains run from Chiusi–Chianciano Terme to Siena (1 hour) with stops in Montepulciano, Sinalunga, and Asciano. There are no trains to San Gimignano, Monteriggioni, or the Chianti wine region.

You can check the Web site of the state railway, the **Ferrovie dello Stato** (☎ *892021 toll-free within Italy* ⊕ *www. trenitalia.com*), for information. You can also get information and tickets at most travel agencies.

By Bus

Buses are a reliable but time-consuming means of getting around the region because they often stop in every town. There are two primary bus services: **Tra-In** (☎ *0577/204111* ⊕ *www.trainspa.it*) covers much of the territory south of Florence and has several runs a day between Rome and Siena (2½ hours). **SITA** (☎ *0577/204270* ⊕ *www.sita-on-line.it*) has regular service between Florence and Siena (1 hour) as well as to numerous towns in Chianti. A third line, **CPT** (☎ *050/502564* ⊕ *www.cpt.pisa.it*), has infrequent buses between Volterra and Colle di Val d'Elsa, and also connects Volterra with the nearest train station in Saline.

By Bicycle

In spring, summer, and fall, cyclists dot the landscape. Many are on weeklong tours, but it's also possible to rent bikes for jaunts in the countryside or to join afternoon or day tours. I **Bike Italy** (⊠ *Borgo degli Albizi 11, Florence* ☎☎ *055/2342371* ⊕ *www.ibikeitaly.com*) leads one-day rides through Chianti. **Marco Ramuzzi** (⊠ *Via Stecchi 23, Greve in Chianti* ☎ *055/853037* ⊕ *www.ramuzzi.com*) rents bikes from his shop in Greve in Chianti. Most Tuscan roads are in excellent condition, though often narrow, winding, and steep.

4

Updated
by Peter
Blackman

COUNTRY ROADS WIND AROUND CYPRESS trees on hilltops that often appear to catch and hold on to the clouds. Planted vineyards, fields, and orchards turn those curving hills into a patchwork of colors and textures that have inspired artists and delighted travelers for centuries. Sitting majestically in the midst of all this natural splendor is Siena, longtime rival of Florence, and one of Italy's best-preserved medieval cities. Other hilltop towns will beckon you as well: San Gimignano, with its lofty towers; the ancient city of Volterra, once capital of a flourishing Etruscan state; and a myriad of charming villages dotting the rolling hills of Chianti.

The rolling hills are the region's most famous geographic feature, and you can expect to do a lot of winding up and down on the beautifully panoramic roads that link the area's hill towns. The narrow medieval streets of these old town centers are mostly closed to traffic. Park outside the city walls and walk in. Keep in mind that roads often lack shoulders in these parts and that gas stations are rarely open on Sunday.

Siena fills to the brim in the weeks surrounding the running of the Palio on July 2 and August 16, when prices, crowds, and commotion are at their highest. Between May and late September, hotels and restaurants throughout the region fill up and foreign license plates and rental cars cram the roads. There's a reason for the crush: summer is a glorious time to be driving in the hills and sitting on terraces. If you want fewer crowds, try visiting during the spring or fall. Spring can be especially spectacular, with blooming poppy fields, bursts of yellow broom, and wild irises growing by the side of the road. Fall is somewhat more soothing, when all those colors typically associated with Tuscany—burnt sienna, warm ocher, mossy forest greens—predominate.

In the winter months you may have towns mostly to yourself, although the choices for hotels and restaurants can be a bit more limited than when the season is in full swing. From November through mid-March it's fairly difficult to find a room in San Gimignano and Volterra: plan accordingly.

CHIANTI

This is the heartland: both sides of the Strada Chiantigiana, or SR222, are embraced by glorious panoramic views of vineyards, olive groves, and castle towers. Traveling south from Florence, you first reach the aptly named one-street-town of Strada in Chianti. Farther south, the number of vineyards on either side of the road dramatically increases—as do the signs inviting you in for a free tasting of wine. Beyond Strada lies Greve in Chianti, completely surrounded by wineries and filled with wineshops. There's art to be had as well: Passignano, west of Greve, has an abbey that shelters a 15th-century *Last Supper* by Domenico and Davide Ghirlandaio. Farther still, along the Strada Chiantigiana, are Panzano and Castellina in Chianti, both hill towns. It's from near Panzano and Castellina that branch roads head

The classic rolling hills of central Tuscany.

to the other main towns of eastern Chianti: Radda in Chianti, Gaiole in Chianti, and Castelnuovo Berardenga.

The Strada Chiantigiana gets crowded during the high season, but no one is in a hurry. The slow pace gives you time to soak up the beautiful scenery.

GREVE IN CHIANTI

40 km (25 mi) north of Siena, 28 km (17½ mi) south of Florence.

GETTING HERE
Driving from Florence or Siena, Greve is easily reached via the Strada Chiantigiana (SR222). SITA buses travel frequently between Florence and Greve. Tra-In and SITA buses connect Siena and Greve, but a direct trip is virtually impossible. There is no train service to Greve.

VISITOR INFORMATION
Greve in Chianti tourism offices (✉ *Via Giovanni da Verrazzano 59* ☎ *055/8546287* ✉ *Via Giovanni da Verrazzano 33* ☎ *055/8546299*).

EXPLORING
If there is a capital of Chianti, it is Greve, a friendly market town with no shortage of cafés, *enoteche* (wine bars), and crafts shops along its pedestrian street.

CENTRAL TUSCANY, PAST & PRESENT

It may be hard to imagine that much of central Tuscany was once the battleground of warring Sienese and Florentine armies, but until Florence finally defeated Siena in 1555, the enchanting walled cities of this gentle area were strategic-defensive outposts in a series of seemingly never-ending wars.

Since the 1960s many British and northern Europeans have relocated here: they've been drawn to the unhurried life, balmy climate, and old villages. They've bought and restored farmhouses, many given up by the young heirs who decided not to continue life on the farm and instead found work in cities. There are so many Britons, in fact, that the area has been nicknamed Chiantishire. But don't let this be a deterrent to a visit: the whole area still proudly exerts its strongly Tuscan character.

The gently sloping, asymmetrical **Piazza Matteotti** is an attractive arcade whose center holds a statue of the discoverer of New York harbor, Giovanni da Verrazano (circa 1480–1527). Check out the lively market held here on Saturday morning.

The church of **Santa Croce** has a triptych by Bicci di Lorenzo (1373–1452) and an Annunciation painted by an anonymous Florentine master that dates from the 14th century. ⊠*Small end of Piazza Matteotti* ☎*No phone* ☑*Free* ⊙*Daily 9–1 and 3–7.*

About 2 km (1 mi) west of Greve in Chianti is the tiny hilltop hamlet of **Montefioralle.** This is the ancestral home of Amerigo Vespucci (1454–1512), the mapmaker, navigator, and explorer who named America. (His niece Simonetta may have been the inspiration for Sandro Botticelli's *Birth of Venus,* painted sometime in the 1480s.)

Chiesa di San Donato a Lamole. The tiny village of Lamole contains this Romanesque church that was greatly modified in 1860; the only remnant of its earlier incarnation can be found in its simple facade. Inside is a 14th-century altarpiece, as well as a curious side chapel on the right that is decorated with rather garish 20th-century religious works. From Greve in Chianti, drive south on SR222 for about 1 km (½ mi); take a left and follow signs for Lamole. It's about 10 km (6 mi) southeast of Greve. ⊠*Località Lamole in Chianti* ☎*055/8547015* ☑*Free* ⊙*Daily 9–12:30 and 4–6:30.*

The terrace at **Ristoro di Lamole,** with its sweeping views of valleys and a glimpse of Panzano in the distance, makes the drive to Lamole via a maddeningly twisting road worth it. The bar–restaurant serves superb *panini* (sandwiches) and more-substantial fare ($). The primi, particularly any featuring game, are excellent. The desserts are made in-house and are some of the best in the area. Try the simple and delicious *torta della nonna* (grandmother's cake) topped with pine nuts and filled with rich yellow cream. ⊠*Via di Lamole 6,, 50022* ☎*055/8547050* ⊙*Closed Wed. and Nov.–Apr.*

WHERE TO STAY & EAT

$$–$$$ ✕**Il Caminetto.** The pasta is all homemade at this small, cozy country restaurant; the *gnocchi ripieno ai funghi porcini* (potato dumplings stuffed with porcini mushrooms) are a real treat. There's a terrace for summer dining under the shade of lime trees. ⊠ *Via della Montagnola 52 ✛ 11 km (7 mi) north of Greve, Località Strada in Chianti, 50027* ☎*055/8588909* ▤*MC, V* ⊗*Closed Tues. No lunch Mon.–Sat.*

$–$$ ✕**Locanda il Gallo.** Terrific thin-crust pizzas come out of the wood-burning oven here. The large, informal, country dining rooms have stone walls and wood-beam ceilings, and there's a veranda for dining outside in summer. The restaurant is about 4 km (2½ mi) north of Greve in Chianti. ⊠ *Via Lando Conti 16, Località Chiocchio, 50027* ☎*055/8572266* ▤*AE, DC, MC, V* ⊗*Closed Tues.*

$$–$$$ ✕▥**Castello Vicchiomaggio.** Stay in a fortified castle built more than a millennium ago (and rebuilt during the Renaissance). Today, in addition to being a charming inn, it is a prestigious wine estate where you can taste local vintages. The restaurant ($$–$$$$) serves homemade pastas and specialties such as *stracotto,* beef cooked in the farm's own prize-winning Chianti Classico. Throughout the main building and two nearby farmhouses you'll find wonderful heavy wooden furniture. **Pros:** Spacious rooms, spectacular views, very helpful staff. **Cons:** Some rooms lack a/c, you need a car to get around. ⊠ *Via Vicchiomaggio 4, Località Vicchiomaggio, 50022* ☎*055/854079* ⊕*www.vicchiomaggio.it* ⇙*7 rooms, 8 apartments, 2 houses* ⌂*In-room: no a/c (some), safe, kitchen (some), refrigerator. In-hotel: restaurant, pool, no elevator, public Internet* ▤*MC, V* .

$$$$ ▥**Villa Bordoni.** David and Catherine Gardner, Scottish expats, have transformed a ramshackle 16th-century villa into a stunning little hotel nestled in the hills above Greve. Much care has been taken in decorating the rooms, no two of which are alike. All have stenciled walls; some have four-poster beds, others small mezzanines. Bathrooms are a riot of color, with tiles from Vietri. A sitting room on the second floor, with a cozy fireplace, is the perfect place for a cup of tea or a glass of wine. The hotel's restaurant has a talented young chef who gives cooking lessons in the modern kitchen. **Pros:** Splendidly isolated, beautiful decor, wonderful hosts. **Cons:** On a long and bumpy dirt road, need a car to get around. ⊠ *Via San Cresci 31/32, Località Mezzuola, 50022* ☎*055/8547453* ⊕*www.villabordoni.com* ⇙*8 rooms, 3 suites* ⌂*In-room: safe, dial-up, Wi-Fi. In-hotel: restaurant, pool, bicycles, laundry service, public Wi-Fi, parking (no fee)* ▤ *AE, DC, MC, V* ⊗*Closed 3 wks in Jan. and Feb.* ⦿*BP.*

Fodor's Choice ★

$$ ▥**Villa Vignamaggio.** Reputed to be the birthplace of the woman made famous by Leonardo da Vinci's *Mona Lisa,* the Villa Vignamaggio has origins in the 14th century. This historic estate, which includes the main building and two small cottages, is surrounded by manicured classical Italian gardens. Some rooms have exposed beams, whereas others have the genuine ancient plaster walls that faux-paint treatments attempt to replicate. The villa also produces some very fine wines; ask about tastings at the reception desk. Fodors.com users report that the villa is in a "good location for day trips in northern Tuscany." A minimum stay of

4

two nights is required. **Pros:** Unbeatable views, informative wine tastings. **Cons:** No elevator to third floor, the staff seems less than attentive. ✉ *Via Petriolo 5, Località Vicchiomaggio, 50022* ☎*055/854661* ⊕*www.vignamaggio.com* ➟*3 rooms, 4 suites, 13 apartments, 2 cottages* ⌂*In-room: kitchen (some). In-hotel: tennis court, pools, no elevator, laundry service, public Internet, some pets allowed,* ⊟*AE, DC, MC, V* ☉*Closed mid-Nov.–mid-Mar.* ❧*BP.*

$ 🏨 **Albergo del Chianti.** At a corner of the Piazza Matteotti, the Albergo del Chianti has rooms with views of the square or out over the tile rooftops toward the surrounding hills. Plain modern cabinets and wardrobes stand near wrought-iron beds. The swimming pool, sunny terrace, and grassy lawn behind the hotel are a nice surprise. **Pros:** Central location, best value in Greve. **Cons:** Rooms facing the piazza can be noisy, lobby is run-down, small bathrooms. ✉*Piazza Matteotti 86, 50022* ☎*055/853763* ⊕*www.albergodelchianti.it* ➟*16 rooms* ⌂*In-room: refrigerator. In-hotel: restaurant, bar, pool, public Wi-Fi* ⊟*MC, V* ☉*Closed Jan.* ❧*BP.*

$ 🏨 **La Camporena.** The farmhouse of La Camporena, 3 km (2 mi) south of Greve, dates from the 1200s. The rooms are rustic, with hand-hewn wood furnishings. Here you can discover the joys of country living with none of the hard farm work involved: your hosts will point out the numerous walking paths in the surrounding countryside. Then you can discuss your day's adventures at dinner, over farm-fresh produce. **Pros:** Peaceful surroundings, splendid views, extremely helpful hosts. **Cons:** No a/c, need a car to get around. ✉*Via Convertoie 27, 50022* ☎*055/853184* ⊕*www.lacamporena.com* ➟*17 rooms* ⌂*In-room: no a/c. In-hotel: restaurant, bar, no elevator, public Internet, some pets allowed* ⊟*AE, DC, MC, V* ❧*BP.*

PASSIGNANO

8 km (5 mi) south of Mercatale, 29 km (18 mi) south of Florence.

GETTING HERE

By car, take the Tavernelle exit from the Florence–Siena Superstrada. Direct bus or train service is not available.

EXPLORING

One of the finest and best-preserved works of art in Italy is in the dining hall of the towering 11th-century **Badia a Passignano** *(Abbey of Passignano)*: a stunningly massive, 21-foot-wide *Last Supper* (1476) by Domenico and Davide Ghirlandaio. The monastery's church of San Michele Arcangelo has a 13th-century sculpture of Saint Michael slaying the dragon. At this writing the abbey was closed for restoration, but even if you can't get in to see the *Last Supper,* it's worth the drive to walk on the beautiful hillsides. ✉*Via Passignano* ☎*055/8071622.*

WHERE TO EAT

$$$$ ✕**Osteria di Passignano.** In an ancient wine cellar owned by the Anti-
★   nori family—who also happen to own much of what you see in these parts—is a sophisticated restaurant ably run by chef Marcello Crini and his attentive staff. The menu changes seasonally; traditional Tus-

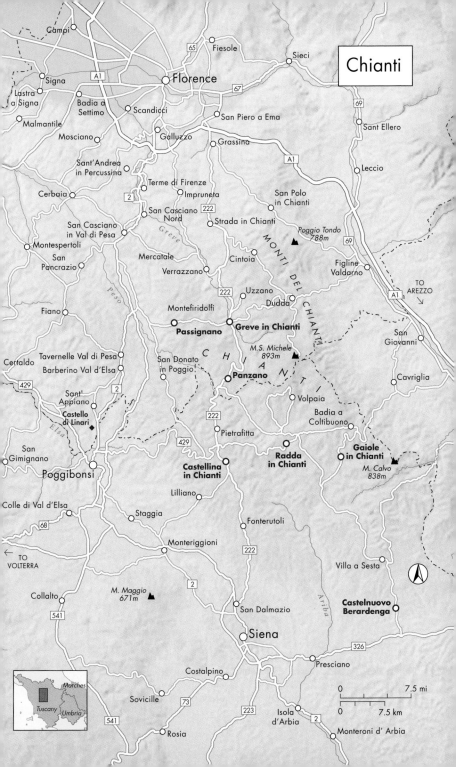

EATING WELL IN CENTRAL TUSCANY

Chianti restaurants serve Tuscan dishes similar to those in Florence, but they also have local specialties, such as pasta creations made with *pici* (a long, thick, hand-rolled spaghetti). You'll find other pasta dishes, like *pappardelle alla lepre* (a long, flat type of pasta noodle with hare sauce), and soups, such as *pappa al pomodoro* (a thick tomato soup) and *ribollita* (Tuscan bread soup), on most menus.

Panzanella, a salad of tomato, basil, bread, and onion, is a common first course on summer menus. Many recipes are from the *nonna* (grandmother) of the restaurant's owner, handed down through time but never written down.

The so-called *tonno del Chianti* (Chianti tuna) is really a dish of tender flakes of rabbit meat that look and, believe it or not, taste like tuna—it's actually delicious. Pecorino, a soft sheep's-milk cheese, makes it onto many menus in pasta dishes and appetizers.

The Sienese often add a subtle flair of extra herbs and garlic to their rendition of traditional Tuscan fare. Antipasti (usually made of the simplest ingredients) are extremely satisfying.

A typical starter might be a plate of excellent locally cured meats, such

as those made from *cinta senese*, a species of domestic pig rescued from near extinction. *Verdure sott'olio* (marinated vegetables) are usually artichokes, red peppers, carrots, celery, cauliflower, olives, and capers marinated in olive oil. Second courses are traditionally game meats and *piccione* (pigeon), served either roasted or stuffed and baked, is commonly on the menu.

After your meal, try some delicious amber-color *vin santo*, a sweet dessert wine with *cantuccini* (hard almond cookies), which are dunked once or twice in the glass. It's made from choice white Trebbiano Toscano or Malvasia del Chianti grapes and is aged in small, partially filled oak barrels. Other favorite Sienese sweets include *ricciarelli*, succulent almond-flavor cookies.

Excellent extra-virgin olive oil is produced throughout the region, and the best way to taste it is in the form of a *fett'unta* (greasy slice), a thick slice of toasted Tuscan bread rubbed with garlic, sprinkled with salt, and dripping with olive oil. Asking for a plate or bowl to sample olive oil with bread before a meal is a dead giveaway that you're a tourist—it's the invention of American restaurateurs.

can cuisine is given a delightful twist through the use of unexpected herbs. Particularly tantalizing is the *filetto di vitello alle spezie* (spiced veal fillet), served with roast tomatoes and beans flavored with sage. The extensive wine list includes local vintages as well as numerous international labels. Daylong cooking courses are also available. ⊠ *Via Passignano 3350028* ☎*055/8071278* ▤*AE, D, MC, V* ⊗*Closed Sun., 3 wks in Jan., and 1 wk in Aug.*

$-$$ ✕**La Cantinetta di Rignana.** On Sunday afternoons this old-fashioned
★ trattoria is teeming with lively Italian families. Grilled meats are the specialty of the house. If you have room for dessert, the kitchen whips up a mean tiramisu. Enjoy the farmhouse feel of the dining room, or

Continued on page 227

GRAPE ESCAPES
THE PLEASURES OF TUSCAN WINE

The vineyards stretching across the landscape of Tuscany may look like cinematic backdrops, but in fact they're working farms, and they produce some of Italy's best wines. No matter whether you're a wine novice or a connoisseur, there's great pleasure to be had from exploring this lush terrain, visiting the vineyards, and uncorking a bottle for yourself.

GETTING TO KNOW TUSCAN WINE

Most of the wine produced in Tuscany is red (though there are some notable whites as well), and most Tuscan reds are made primarily from one type of grape, sangiovese. That doesn't mean, however, that all wines here are the same. God (in this case Bacchus) is in the details: differences in climate, soil, and methods of production result in wines with several distinct personalities.

Chianti

Chianti is the most famous name in Tuscan wine, but what exactly the name means is a little tricky. It once identified wines produced in the region extending from just south of Florence to just north of Siena. In the mid-20th century, the official Chianti zone was expanded to include a large portion of central Tuscany. That area is divided into eight subregions. **Chianti Classico** is the name given to the original zone, which makes up 17,000 of the 42,000 acres of Chianti-producing vineyards.

Classico wines, which bear the *gallo nero* (black rooster) logo on their labels, are the most highly regarded Chiantis (with **Rùfina** running second), but that doesn't mean Classicos are always superior. All Chiantis are strictly regulated (they must be a minimum 75% to 80% sangiovese, with other varieties blended in to add nuance), and they share a strong, woodsy character that's well suited to Tuscan food. It's a good strategy to drink the local product—**Colli Senesi Chianti** when in Siena, for example. The most noticeable, and costly, difference comes when a Chianti is from *riserva* (reserve) stock, meaning it's been aged for at least two years.

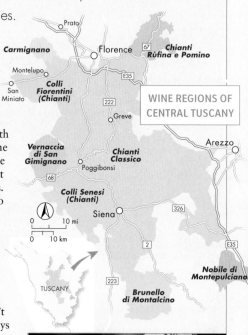

WINE REGIONS OF CENTRAL TUSCANY

DOC & DOCG The designations "DOC" and "DOCG"—Denominazione di Origine Controllata (e Garantita)—mean a wine comes from an established region and adheres to rigorous standards of production. Ironically, the esteemed Super Tuscans are labeled *vini da tavola* (table wines), the least prestigious designation, because they don't use traditional grape blends.

Brunello di Montalcino

The area surrounding the hill town of Montalcino, to the south of Siena, is drier and warmer than the Chianti regions, and it produces the most powerful of the sangiovese-based wines. Regulations stipulate that Brunello di Montalcino be made entirely from sangiovese grapes (no blending) and aged at least four years. **Rosso di Montalcino** is a younger, less complex, less expensive Brunello.

The Super Tuscans

Beginning in the 1970s, some winemakers, chafing at the regulations imposed on established Tuscan wine varieties, began blending and aging wines in innovative ways. Thus were born the so-called Super Tuscans. These pricey, French oak–aged wines are admired for their high quality, led by star performers as **Sassicaia**, from the Maremma region, and **Tignanello**, produced at the Tenuta Marchesi Antinori near Badia a Passignano. Purists, however, lament the loss of local identity resulting from the Super Tuscans' use of nonnative grape varieties such as cabernet sauvignon and merlot.

Vino Nobile di Montepulciano

East of Montalcino is Montepulciano, the town at the heart of the third, and smallest, of Tuscany's top wine districts.

Blending regulations aren't as strict for Vino Nobile as for Chianti and Brunello, and as a result it has a wider range of characteristics. Broadly speaking, though, Vino Nobile is a cross between Chianti and Brunello—less acidic than the former and softer than the latter. It also has a less pricey sibling, **Rosso di Montepulciano.**

The Whites

Most whites from Tuscany are made from **trebbiano** grapes, which produce a wine that's light and refreshing but not particularly aromatic or flavorful—it may hit the spot on a hot afternoon, but it doesn't excite connoisseurs.

Golden-hewed **Vernaccia di San Gimignano** is a local variety with more limited production but greater personality—it's the star of Tuscan whites. Winemakers have also brought chardonnay and sauvignon grapes to the region, resulting in wines that, like some Super Tuscans, are pleasant to drink but short on local character.

TOURING & TASTING IN TUSCAN WINE COUNTRY

Strade del Vino di Toscana Tuscany has visitor-friendly wineries, but the way you go about visiting is a bit different here from what it is in California or France. Many wineries welcome drop-ins for a tasting, but for a tour you usually need to make an appointment a few days in advance. There are several approaches you can take, depending on how much time you have and how serious you are about wine:

PLAN 1: FULL IMMERSION. Make an appointment to tour one of the top wineries (see our recommendations on the next page), and you'll get the complete experience: half a day of strolling through vineyards, talking grape varieties, and tasting wine, often accompanied by food. Groups are small; in spring and fall, it may be just you and the winemaker. The cost is usually €10 to €15 per person, but can go up to €40 if a meal is included. Remember to specify a tour in English.

PLAN 2: SEMI-ORGANIZED. If you want to spend a few hours going from vineyard to vineyard, make your first stop one of the local tourist information offices—they're great resources for maps, tasting itineraries, and personalized advice about where to visit. The offices in **Greve, Montalcino,** and **Montepulciano** are the best equipped. **Enoteche** (for more about them, turn the page) can also be good places to pick up tips about where to go for tastings.

PLAN 3: SPONTANEOUS. Along Tuscany's country roads you'll see signs for wineries offering **vendita diretta** (direct sales) and **degustazioni** (tastings). For a taste of the local product with some atmosphere thrown in, a spontaneous visit is a perfectly viable approach. You may wind up in a simple shop or an elaborate tasting room; either way, there's a fair chance you'll sample something good. Expect a small fee for a three-glass tasting.

THE PICK OF THE VINEYARDS

Within the Chianti Classico region, these wineries should be at the top of your to-visit list, whether you're dropping in for a taste or making a full tour. (Tours require reservations unless otherwise indicated.)

CHIANTI CLASSICO

Badia a Coltibuono

(✉ Gaiole in Chianti ☎ 0577/749498 ⊕ www.coltibuono. com). Along with an extensive prelunch tour and tasting, there are shorter afternoon tours, no reservation required, starting on the hour from 2 to 5. (See "Gaiole in Chianti" in this chapter.)

Castello di Fonterutoli

(✉ Castellina in Chianti ☎ 0577/73571 ⊕ www. fonterutoli.it). Hour-long tours include a walk through the neighboring village.

Castello di Volpaia

(✉ Radda in Chianti ☎ 0577/738066 ⊕ www. volpaia.com). The castle is part of the tiny town of Volpaia, perched above Radda.

Castello di Verrazzano

(✉ Via S. Martino in Valle 12, Greve in Chianti ☎ 055/854243 ⊕ www. verrazzano.com). Tours here take you down to the cellars, through the gardens, and into the woods in search of wild boar.

Villa Vignamaggio (✉ Via Petriolo 5, Greve in Chianti ☎ 055/854661 ⊕ www. vignamaggio.com). Along with a wine tour, you can spend the night at this villa where Mona Lisa is believed to have been born. (See "Where to Stay" under "Greve in Chianti" in this chapter.)

Rocca delle Màcie

(✉ Località Le Macie 45, Castellina in Chianti ☎ 0577/732236 ⊕ www.rocca dellemacie.com). A full lunch or dinner can be incorporated into your tasting here.

Castello di Brolio

(✉ Gaiole in Chianti ☎ 0577/730220 ⊕ www.ricasoli.it). One of Tuscany's most impressive castles also has a centuries-old winemaking tradition. (See "Gaiole in Chianti" in this chapter.)

REMEMBER ⚠

Always have a designated driver when you're touring and tasting. Vineyards are usually located off narrow, curving roads. Full sobriety is a must behind the wheel.

MORE TUSCAN WINE RESOURCES

Enoteche: Wine Shops

The word *enoteca* in Italian can mean "wine store," "wine bar," or both. In any event, *enoteche* (the plural, pronounced "ay-no-*tek*-ay") are excellent places to sample and buy Tuscan wines, and they're also good sources of information about local wineries. There are scores to choose from. These are a few of the best:

Enoteca Italiana, Siena (Fortezza Medicea, Viale Maccari ☎ 0577/288497 ⊕ www. enoteca-italiana.it). The only one of its kind, this *enoteca* represents all the producers of DOC and DOCG wines in Italy and stocks over 400 labels. Wine by the glass and snacks are available.

Enoteca Osticcio, Montalcino (✉ Via Matteotti 23 ☎ 0577/848271 ⊕ www. osticcio.com). There are more than one thousand labels in stock. With one of the best views in Montalcino, it is also a very pleasant place to sit and meditate over a glass of Brunello.

Enoteca del Gallo Nero, Greve in Chianti (✉ Piazzetta S. Croce 8 ☎ 055/853297). This is one of the best stocked *enoteche* in the Chianti region.

Palazzo Avignonesi, Montepulciano (Via di Gracciano nel Corso 91 ☎ 0578/757872). The streets of Montepulciano are lined with *enoteche,* but these 12th-century cellars of the Avignonesi winery merit special mention.

Wine on the Web

Tuscan wine country is well represented on the Internet. A good place for an overview is ⊕ www.terreditoscana.regione.-toscana.it. (Click on "Le Strade del Vino"; the page that opens next will give you the option of choosing an English-language version.) This site shows 14 *strade del vino* (wine roads) that have been mapped out by consortiums representing major wine districts (unfortunately, Chianti Classico isn't included), along with recommended itineraries. You'll also find links to the consortium Web sites, where you can dig up more detailed information on touring. The Chianti Classico consortium's site is ⊕ www.chianticlassico.com. The Vino Nobile di Montepulciano site is ⊕ www.vinonobiledimontepulciano.it, and Brunello di Montalcino is ⊕ www. consorziobrunellodimontalcino.it. All have English versions.

choose a table in the garden overlooking the vineyards. The restaurant is *4 km (2 mi) west of Passignano.* ⊠ *Via di Rignana 15, Località Rignana 450028* ☎055/852601 ═*AE, D, MC, V* ⊗*Closed Tues.*

PANZANO

7 km (4½ mi) south of Greve in Chianti, 36 km (22 mi) south of Florence.

GETTING HERE

From Florence or Siena, Panzano is easily reached by car along the Strada Chiantigiana (SR222). SITA buses travel frequently between Florence and Panzano. From Siena, the journey by bus is extremely difficult because SITA and Tra-In do not coordinate their schedules. There is no train service to Panzano.

EXPLORING

The magnificent views of the valleys of the Pesa and Greve rivers easily make Panzano one of the prettiest stops in Chianti. The triangular Piazza Bucciarelli is the heart of the new town. A short stroll along Via Giovanni da Verrazzano brings you up to the old town, Panzano Alto, which is still partly surrounded by medieval walls. The town's 13th-century castle is now almost completely absorbed by later buildings (its central tower is now a private home).

In the church of **Santa Maria Assunta** you can see an Annunciation attributed to Michele di Ridolfo del Ghirlandaio (1503–77). ⊠*Panzano Alto* 🎫*Free* ⊗*Daily 7–noon and 4–6.*

An ancient church even by Chianti standards, the hilltop **San Leolino** probably dates from the 10th century, but it was completely rebuilt in the Romanesque style sometime in the 13th century. It has a 14th-century cloister worth seeing. The 16th-century terra-cotta tabernacles are attributed to Giovanni della Robbia, and there's also a remarkable triptych (attributed to the Master of Panzano) that was executed sometime in the mid-14th century. Open days and hours are unpredictable; check with the tourist office in Greve in Chianti for the latest. ✛*3 km (2 mi) south of Panzano, Località San Leolino* ☎*No phone* 🎫*Free.*

WHERE TO STAY & EAT

$$–$$$ ✕**Montagliari.** This ancient stone farmhouse is the place to go for very tasty Tuscan food. Enjoy your meal in the courtyard, or, when the temperature drops, the main dining room with a farm-style fireplace. The *peposo* (beef stew laced with black pepper) is particularly piquant; the *papardelle al cinghiale* (flat noodles with a wild boar sauce) delightfully fragrant. The wine list, particularly strong on local varieties, includes the farm's own Chianti Classico. ⊠ *Via Montagliari 29, 50020* ☎055/852014 ⚖*Reservations essential* ═*AE, MC, V* ⊗*Closed Mon. and early Jan.–late Feb.*

$$ ✕**Solociccia.** "Abandon all hope, ye who enter here," announces the menu, "you're in the hands of a butcher." Indeed you are, for this restaurant is the creation of Dario Cecchini, Panzano's local merchant of meat. Served at communal tables, the set meal consists of no less

FODOR'S FIRST PERSON

Dario Cecchini
Butcher, Panzano

Dario Cecchini loves meat. At the half-century mark and standing more than 6 feet tall, he could be a poster boy for the beef industry. He breathes health, vitality, vigor.

By trade, Dario is a butcher, but his Antica Macelleria Cecchini is not your typical butcher shop. From its intimate confines at Via XX Luglio 11 in Panzano, he holds forth behind a counter teeming with luscious meats. Opera plays in the background; sometimes customers sing along. Dario quotes Dante as he offers up samples of his wares.

Dario calls himself *un artigiano* (an artisan)—an indication of the pride he takes in his work. His shop has been in the family since the late 1700s, and his father trained Dario in the craft. "At 13," he says, "my grandmother made me a butcher's jacket. My mother began to cry. I guess she hoped I'd choose something else." The same grandmother is responsible for Dario's habit of offering wine to his customers.

"She said a glass of wine brings people together, and I like to bring people together."

Dario is perhaps the world's greatest devotee of *bistecca fiorentina*, the definitive Tuscan steak. To get one of his *bistecche*, you must request it seven days in advance. Ask him to halve its width, and you will incur this genial man's scorn. About its preparation, Dario brooks no compromises. "It must be very thick, seared on both sides, and very, very rare in the middle." If you prefer your steak well done? "You shouldn't order it." This is not to say that Dario is an unwavering traditionalist. One of his prized creations is sushi del Chianti, which took him five years to develop. After a taste of the coarsely ground raw beef, it can be difficult to stop eating.

What wine does Dario pair with his bistecca? "A young, simple, unstructured Chianti." If—heaven forbid—such a Chianti is not on the wine list? "Any young, honest red will do—no dallying in oak casks. Anything disliked by the *Wine Spectator*."

than six meat courses, chosen at Dario's discretion. They are accompanied by seasonal vegetables, white beans with olive oil, and focaccia bread. Though Cecchini emphasizes that steak is never on the menu, this lively, crowded place is definitely not for vegetarians. The entrance is on Via XX Luglio. ⊠ *Via Chiantigiana 5, 50022* ☎ *055/852727* ⌂ *Reservations essential* ▤ *AE, DC, MC, V* ☉ *Closed Mon.–Wed. No dinner Sun.*

¢–$ ✕**Enoteca Baldi.** Sample the local vino while satisfying your appetite with simply prepared and presented bruschetta, soups, and pastas. In summer a few tables are set in the shade under the trees in the town's main square. ⊠ *Piazza Bucciarelli 26, 50022* ☎ *055/852843* ▤ *MC, V.*

$$$$ 🏨 **Villa Le Barone.** Once the home of the Viviani della Robbia family,
Fodor'sChoice this 16th-century villa in a grove of ancient cypress trees retains many
★ aspects of a private country dwelling. It feels like a "second home," according to some fodors.com users. The honor bar allows you to enjoy an *aperitivo* on the terrace while admiring the views of the pool

to the rose gardens, across the hills to the town. Guest rooms have white-plaster walls, timber ceilings, and some tile floors. The restaurant uses fresh produce from the owner's farm in western Tuscany. Though the hotel staff may recommend it, the full, three-meal plan is not mandatory. **Pros:** Beautiful location, wonderful restaurant, great base for exploring the region. **Cons:** Noisy a/c, 20-minute walk to nearest town. ✉ *Via San Leolino 19, 50022* ☎ *055/852621* ⊕ *www.villalebarone.it* ⇗ *30 rooms* ⌂ *In-room: no a/c (some), no TV. In-hotel: restaurant, bar, tennis court, pool, no elevator, concierge, laundry service, public Internet* ⊟ *AE, MC, V* ⊘ *Closed Nov.–Easter* ⵔⵀ*BP.*

$$ ⛏ **Villa Sangiovese.** On the town's main square, this simple, well-run hotel has rooms that look out to the hillside or face the piazza. An enclosed courtyard is used for summer dining, and a terraced garden has numerous shady resting places that lead down to the pool. Country-style rooms with terra-cotta tile floors are furnished with antiques. The hotel's restaurant serves regional dishes. A minimum stay of three nights is required. **Pros:** Immaculate rooms, pool area great for kids, great location for exploring Chianti. **Cons:** Front rooms can be noisy, lots of stairs to climb. ✉ *Piazza Bucciarelli 5, 50022* ☎ *055/852461 www.villasangiovese.it* ⇗ *17 rooms, 2 suites* ⌂ *In-room: no a/c (some), no TV. In-hotel: restaurant, pool, no elevator* ⊟ *MC, V* ⊘ *Closed mid-Dec.–mid-Mar. Restaurant closed Wed.* ⵔⵀ*BP.*

SHOPPING

★ **Antica Macelleria Cecchini** (✉ *Via XX Luglio 5* ☎ *055/852020*) may be the world's most dramatic butcher shop. Here, amid classical music and lively conversation, owner Dario Cecchini holds court: while quoting Dante, he serves samples of his very fine *sushi di Chianina* (raw slices of Chianina beef gently salted and peppered). He has researched recipes from the 15th century and sells pâtés and herb concoctions found nowhere else. Serious food enthusiasts should not miss the place.

CASTELLINA IN CHIANTI

13 km (8 mi) south of Panzano, 59 km (35 mi) south of Florence, 22 km (14 mi) north of Siena.

GETTING HERE

As with all the towns along the Strada Chiantigiana (SR222), Castellina is an easy drive from either Siena or Florence. From Siena, Castellina is well served by the local Tra-In bus company. However, only one bus a day travels here from Florence. The closest train station is at Castellina Scalo, some 15 km (9 mi) away.

VISITOR INFORMATION

Castellina in Chianti tourism office (✉ *Piazza del Comune 1* ☎ *0577/741392*).

EXPLORING

Castellina in Chianti—or simply Castellina—is on a ridge above three valleys: the Val di Pesa, Val d'Arbia, and Val d'Elsa. No matter what direction you turn, the panorama is bucolic. The strong 15th-century medieval walls and fortified town gate give a hint of the history of this village, which was an outpost during the continuing wars between Florence and Siena. In the main square, the Piazza del Comune, there's a 15th-century palace and a 15th-century fort constructed around a 13th-century tower. It now serves as the town hall.

Treat yourself to one of the terrifically fragrant ice creams at **L'Antica Delizia** (⊠ *Via Fiorentina 4* ☎*0577/741337*). The fruit flavors—*fragola* (strawberry), *melone* (cantaloupe), and *limone* (lemon)—are particularly good.

WHERE TO STAY & EAT

$$$$ ✗**Albergaccio.** The fact that the dining room can seat only 35 guests makes a meal here an intimate experience. The ever-changing menu mixes traditional and creative dishes. In late September and October *zuppa di funghi e castagne* (mushroom and chestnut soup) is a treat; grilled meats and seafood are on the list throughout the year. There's also an excellent wine list. When the weather is warm make sure you dine on the terrace. ⊠ *Via Fiorentina 25, 53011* ☎*0577/741042* ⌛*Reservations essential* ⊟*No credit cards* ⊘*Closed Sun. No lunch Wed. and Thurs.*

$$-$$$ ✗**Osteria alla Piazza.** Relax amid vineyards on a countryside terrace with one of Chianti's most spectacular views of the vineyards in the valley of the River Pesa. Enjoy the sophisticated menu: the *girasole ai quattro sapori*, a giant vegetable-filled ravioli flavored with fresh tomato sauce and a few drops of cream, arrives at the table looking much like a *girasole* (sunflower). And certainly, try any of the delicious desserts. It's in La Piazza, 15 km (8 mi) north of Castellina. ⊠*Località La Piazza53011* ☎*0577/733580* ⌛*Reservations essential* ⊟*MC, V* ⊘*Closed Mon. and Jan. and Feb.; closed weekdays Mar., Nov., and Dec.*

$-$$ ✗**Ristorante Le Tre Porte.** The specialty of the house, a thick slab of beef called *bistecca alla fiorentina*, is usually served very rare. Paired with grilled fresh porcini mushrooms when in season (in spring and fall), it's a heady dish. The main floor of the restaurant has a small dining room serving full-course meals. In the evening a second room is opened downstairs where you can order pizzas from the wood-burning oven. Reservations are essential in July and August. ⊠*Via Trento e Trieste 453011* ☎*0577/741163* ⊟*AE, DC, MC, V* ⊘*Closed Tues.*

$$-$$$ ⌂**Locanda Le Piazze.** This old farmhouse has been transformed into a marvelous hotel tucked in among vineyards. The three common rooms are cozy but elegant, filled with well-stuffed upholstered couches and chairs; the breakfast room looks out on a sweeping panorama of hills. The chirping of birds is about the only noise you'll hear on the grounds awash in flowers. Timbered ceilings hang above beds covered with floral comforters. **Pros:** Pastoral setting, fun cooking classes, luxurious bathrooms. **Cons:** No a/c, need a car to get around. ⊠*Locanda Le Piazze, Località Le Piazze, 53011* ☎*0577/743190* ⊕*www.locandale-piazze.it* ⇩*20 rooms* ⌂*In-room: no a/c, no TV (some). In-hotel: restaurant, bar, pool, no elevator, laundry service, public Internet* ⊟*AE, DC, MC, V* ⊘*Closed Nov.–Apr.* ⌷*BP.*

$-$$$ ⌂**Palazzo Squarcialupi.** In the center of Castellina, this 15th-century
palace is a tranquil place to stay. Rooms are spacious, with high ceil-

ings, tile floors, and 18th-century furnishings; bathrooms are tiled in local stone. Many of the rooms have views of the valley below, some look toward the town's main pedestrian street. Common areas are elegant, with deep, plush couches that invite you to recline. There's an ample breakfast buffet throughout the year, and you can arrange for a light lunch in the warmer months. The multilingual staff goes out of its way to be helpful. Users of fodors.com praised the "lovely room, fantastic views," and "friendly staff." **Pros:** Great location, elegant public spaces. **Cons:** On a street with no car access, across from a noisy restaurant. ⊠ *Via Ferruccio 22, 53011* ☎*0577/741186* 🖷*0577/740386* ⊕*www.palazzosquarcialupi.com* 🖙*17 rooms* 🛆*In room: refrigerator. In-hotel: bar, pool, laundry service, public Wi-Fi, some pets allowed* ▤*AE, DC, MC, V* ⊗*Closed Nov.–Mar.* ⚏*BP.*

$$ 🖼**Hotel Belvedere di San Leonino.** Stroll around the wonderful gardens in this restored country estate dating from the 14th century. The guest rooms, with arched windows and oak-beam ceilings, are in two houses that look out on vineyards to the north and Siena to the south. The homey furnishings include antique wardrobes and ladder-back chairs. The dining room, open to guests only, has a prix-fixe menu. In summer you can enjoy dinner by the pool surrounded by rolling green lawn. **Pros:** Great family atmosphere, lovely old house, central location. **Cons:** Stairs to climb, need a car to get around. ⊠*Località San Leonino, 53011* ☎*0577/740887* 🖷*0577/740924* ⊕*www.hotelsanleonino.com* 🖙*28 rooms* 🛆*In-room: no a/c, safe. In-hotel: restaurant, pool, no elevator, public Internet* ▤*AE, MC, V* ⊗*Closed mid-Nov.– mid-Apr.* ⚏*BP.*

$ 🖼**Hotel Salivolpi.** The family that owns this farmhouse took special care not to change too much when they began accepting guests: faded family photos, mementos of long-past journeys, and bric-a-brac of all kinds decorate the common areas. Each room is simply furnished with antiques that are typical of the late 18th and early 19th centuries in Chianti—heavy wooden wardrobes, marble-top chests, and woven straw–seat chairs. There's a large pool and splendid views of the valley to the south of Castellina from the garden. **Pros:** Tranquil location, 10-minute walk to nearest town. **Cons:** Run-down rooms, some stairs to climb, no a/c in some rooms. ⊠*Via Fiorentina 89, 53011* ☎*0577/740484* 🖷*0577/740998* ⊕*www.hotelsalivolpi.com* 🖙*19 rooms* 🛆*In-room: no a/c (some). In-hotel: pool, no elevator, public Wi-Fi* ▤*AE, MC, V* ⚏*BP.*

SHOPPING

Castellina is a small town, with most of its shops located either along Via Ferruccio or on the Piazza del Comune. But don't miss the specialty stores hidden away on Via delle Volte, which runs inside the eastern medieval walls of the town—you can reach it from either end of Via Ferruccio.

Antiquario Mario Cappelletti (⊠*Via Ferruccio 34* ☎*0577/740980*) carries interesting prints and reproductions of well-known Renaissance artworks. **Cappelletti** (⊠*Via Ferruccio 39–43* ☎*0577/740420*) has been producing quality leather goods since 1893. The reasonably priced briefcases are especially nice. **La Giravolta** (⊠*Via delle Volte 32*

☎*0577/742004*) sells nothing but *i prodotti biologici* (organic products). The merchandise includes wines, candles, and pasta sauces. Lucia Volentieri has a delightful selection of delicately hand-painted ceramics in her **Laboratorio di Ceramica** (⊠ *Via Trento e Trieste 24* ☎*0577/741133*). **Le Volte Enoteca** (⊠ *Via Ferruccio 12* ☎*0577/741314*) stocks an ample and well-chosen supply of local wines produced by small estates.

RADDA IN CHIANTI

10 km (6 mi) east of Castellina in Chianti, 55 km (34 mi) south of Florence.

GETTING HERE
Radda can be reached by car from either Siena or Florence along the SR222 (Strada Chiantigiana), and from the A1 highway. Three Tra-In buses make their way from Siena to Radda. One morning SITA bus travels from Florence to Radda. There is no train service convenient to Radda.

VISITOR INFORMATION
Radda in Chianti tourism office (⊠*Piazza Ferrucci 1* ☎*0577/738494*).

EXPLORING
Radda in Chianti sits on a hill stretching between the Val di Pesa and Val d'Arbia. It is easily reached by following the SR429 from Castellina. It's another one of those tiny villages with steep streets for strolling; follow the signs that point you toward the *camminamento medioevale,* a covered 14th-century walkway that circles part of the city inside the walls.

Palazzo del Podestà, or Palazzo Comunale, the city hall for more than four centuries, has 51 coats of arms imbedded in the facade. An extensive restoration project means the building is closed to visitors until at least the end of 2008. ⊠*Piazza Ferrucci.*

Volpaia, with a population of fewer than 50 people, is a small town perched on a hill 10 km (6 mi) north of Radda. During the wars between Florence and Siena, it served as a key military outpost, but lost its importance when the Florentines defeated Siena in 1555. There's a small enoteca on Piazza della Torre where you can sample and purchase the fine wines, olive oil, and flavored vinegars made by **Castello di Volpaia** (⊠*Piazza della Cisterna 1* ☎*0577/738066*). Tours of the winery are also available.

WHERE TO STAY & EAT

$–$$ ✕**Osteria Le Panzanelle.** Silvia Bonechi's experience in the kitchen—and Fodor'sChoice a few precious recipes handed down from her grandmother—is one
★ of the reasons for the success of this small restaurant. The other is the front-room hospitality of Nada Michelassi. These two *panzanelle* (women from Panzano) serve a short menu of tasty and authentic dishes at what the locals refer to as *prezzi giusti* (the right prices). Both the *pappa al pomodoro* (tomato soup) and the *peposo* (peppery beef stew)

Tuscany in its autumn gold.

are exceptional. Whether you are eating inside or under large umbrellas on the terrace near a tiny stream, the experience is always congenial. "The best food we had in Tuscany," writes one user of fodors.com. Reservations are essential in July and August. ⊠*Località Lucarelli 29* ✛ *8 km (5 mi) northwest of Radda on road to Panzano, 53017* ☎*0577/733511* ▤*MC, V* ⊘*Closed Mon. and Jan. and Feb.*

$$$–$$$$
Fodor'sChoice
★
✕⌗ **Relais Fattoria Vignale.** On the outside it's a rather plain manor house with an annex across the street. Inside it's a refined and comfortable country house with numerous sitting rooms that have terra-cotta floors and nice stonework. Guest rooms have exposed-brick walls and wood beams and are filled with simple wooden furnishings and handwoven rugs. The grounds, flanked by vineyards and olive trees, are equally inviting, with lawns, terraces, and a pool. The sophisticated Ristorante Vignale ($–$$$) serves excellent wines and local specialties like *cinghiale in umido con nepitella e vin cotto* (wild boar stew flavored with catmint and wine). **Pros:** Intimate public spaces, excellent restaurant, helpful and friendly staff. **Cons:** North-facing rooms blocked by tall cypress trees, single rooms are small, annex across a busy road. ⊠*Via Pianigiani 9, 53017* ☎*0577/738300 hotel, 0577/738094 restaurant, 0577/738012 enoteca* ⊕*www.vignale.it* ↴*37 rooms, 5 suites* &*In-room: safe, refrigerator. In-hotel: restaurant, bar, pool, concierge, laundry service, public Internet* ▤*AE, DC, MC, V* ⊘*Closed Nov.–Mar. 15.* †◎†*BP.*

$$$–$$$$
⌗ **Il Borgo di Vescine.** At this former Etruscan settlement, a series of low-slung medieval stone buildings with barrel-tile roofs are connected by

cobbled paths and punctuated by cypress trees. Unfussy rooms have terra-cotta tile floors, attractive woodwork, and comfortable elegant furnishings. The fire-lit reading room and bar is particularly inviting. **Pros:** Set in a lovely park, cozy public rooms. **Cons:** Long walk to nearest town, isolated location. ✛*5 km (3 mi) west of Radda in Chianti 53017, Località Vescine* ☎*0577/741144* ⊕*www.vescine.it* ⧉*16 rooms, 7 suites* ᵬ *In-room: refrigerator. In-hotel: tennis court, pool, no elevator, public Internet, some pets allowed* ▤*AE, MC, V* ⊘*Closed Nov.–Apr., except Christmastime* ¶⊙¶*BP.*

$$$–$$$$ ⛺**La Locanda.** At an altitude of more than 1,800 feet, this converted farmhouse is probably the loftiest luxury inn in Chianti. Its views are breathtaking, looking down on Volpaia and Radda, with Siena and the hills of southern Tuscany as a backdrop. The infinity pool, set on the hillside, takes full advantage of the magnificent panorama. Hosts Guido and Martina Bevilacqua are on hand to pamper you. Guest rooms are simple but tasteful, with high beamed ceilings, painted, as was once the tradition in these parts, in pale pastels. To get here, take the bumpy gravel road 2 km (1 mi) northwest from Volpaia. **Pros:** Idyllic setting, panoramic views, wonderful hosts. **Cons:** On a very rough gravel access road, isolated location, need a car to get around. ✉*Località Montanino Nord, off Via della Volpaia* ✛ *13 km (8 mi) northwest of Radda in Chianti, 53017* ☎*0577/738833* ⊕*www.lalocanda.it* ⧉*6 rooms, 1 suite* ᵬ*In-room: no a/c. In-hotel: pool, public Internet* ▤*MC, V* ⊘*Closed 2 wks mid-Aug. and mid-Nov.–mid-Mar.* ¶⊙¶*BP.*

$–$$ ⛺**Podere Terreno.** People come from all over the world to enjoy the quiet country life in this 16th-century farmhouse. Seven double rooms are furnished with unadorned wood furniture. Dinners, which are included in rates along with breakfast, are inventive. The friendly owners, who speak English, enjoy cooking local dishes, serving wine they made themselves, and sparking conversation at the dinner table. **Pros:** Historic setting, comfortable accommodations, great home-cooked meals. **Cons:** Isolated location, need a car to get around. ✉*Via della Volpaia* ✛ *5 km (3 mi) north of Radda in Chianti, Volpaia53017* ☎*0577/738312* ⊕*www.podereterreno.it* ⧉*7 rooms* ᵬ*In-room: no a/c. In-hotel: restaurant, no elevator, public Internet, some pets allowed* ▤*AE, MC, V* ⊘*Closed Christmas wk* ¶⊙¶*MAP.*

¢   ⛺**La Bottega di Giovannino.** The name is actually that of the wine bar run by Giovannino Bernardoni and his daughter Monica, who also rent rooms in the house next door. This is a fantastic place for the budget-conscious traveler, as rooms are immaculate. Most have a stunning view of the surrounding hills. All have their own bath, though most of them necessitate taking a short trip outside one's room. **Pros:** Great location in the center of town, close to restaurants and shops, super value. **Cons:** Some rooms are small, some bathrooms are down the hall, basic decor. ✉*Via Roma 6–8, 53017* ☎*0577/738056* ⊕*www.labottegadigiovannino.it* ⧉*10 rooms, 2 apartments* ᵬ*In-room: no a/c, no phone. In-hotel: bar, no elevator* ▤*AE, MC, V* ¶⊙¶*EP.*

SHOPPING

Like its sister shop in Florence, **Ceramiche Rampini** (✉ *Casa Beretone, Località Beretone di Vistarenni* ☎ *0577/738043* ⊕ *www.rampiniceramics.com*), 5 km (3 mi) south of Radda in Chianti, produces exquisite (and expensive) hand-painted ceramic objects, including plates, bowls, and candlesticks. The firm ships anywhere in the world and keeps its customers' information on file. If you break a plate or want to buy more, they'll know exactly what your pattern is.

Locals come here to buy their nuts, bolts, and small tools, but **Tecno-Casa** (✉ *Via Roma 20/22* ☎ *0577/738613*) also has a surprisingly varied assortment of traditional household items, including coffeemakers and cups, wine decanters, and decorative bottle stoppers.

La Bottega delle Fantasie (✉ *Via Roma 47* ☎ *0577/738978*) sells colorful pillows and carefully crafted linens in sun-drenched Tuscan hues.

GAIOLE IN CHIANTI

9 km (5½ mi) southeast of Radda in Chianti, 69 km (43 mi) south of Florence.

GETTING HERE

To get here by car from the A1, take the Montevarchi exit and follow signs for Gaiole on the SR408. Gaiole is relatively well connected to Siena by Tra-In buses. Gaiole cannot be reached by train.

EXPLORING

A market town since 1200, Gaiole is now a central destination for touring southern Chianti. A stream runs through its center and flowers adorn many of its window boxes. The surrounding area is dotted with castles perched on hilltops (the better to see the approaching enemy): they were of great strategic importance during the Renaissance and still make dazzling lookout points.

It's a pretty drive up winding and curving roads to **Castello di Meleto,** a fortress from the 13th century. Attached is an 18th-century villa; more importantly, there's a wineshop that serves tastes of the locally produced wine as well as honeys and jams. It's worth touring the castle if you want to get a sense of how 18th-century aristocrats lived; if that doesn't interest you, proceed directly to the enoteca for a tasting. Six apartments clustered near the castle are available for rent. ✉ *Località Meleto ✛ 5 km (3 mi) south of Gaiole* ☎ *0577/749496 castle, 0577/749129 enoteca* ⊕ *www.castellomeleto.it* 💶 *€8* 🕐 *Tours: Mon. 3 and 4:30; Tues.–Sat. 11:30, 3, and 4:30; Sun. 11:30, 4, and 5. Wineshop: mid-Mar–mid-Nov., daily 9–7; mid-Nov.–mid-Mar., weekends 9–7.*

★ If you have time for only one castle, visit the stunning **Castello di Brolio.** At the end of the 12th century, when Florence conquered southern Chianti, Brolio became Florence's southernmost outpost, and it was often said, "When Brolio growls, all Siena trembles." Brolio was built about AD 1000 and owned by the monks of the Badia Fiorentina; the "new" owners, the Ricasoli family, have been in possession since 1141. Bettino Ricasoli (1809–80), the so-called Iron Baron, was one of the founders of modern Italy and is said to have invented the original formula for Chianti wine. Brolio, one of Chianti's best-known labels, is still justifiably famous. Its cellars may be toured by appointment. There's a sign at the Brolio gate that translates as RING BELL AND BE PATIENT. You pull a rope and the bell above the ramparts peals, and in a short time, the caretaker arrives to let you in. The grounds are worth visiting, even though the 19th-century manor house is not open to the public. (The current baron is very much in residence.) There are two apartments here available for rent by the week. ⊠ *Località Brolio ✛ 2 km (1 mi) southeast of Gaiole* ☎*0577/730227* 🖅*€5* ⊙*June–Sept., daily 9–noon and 2–6:30; Oct.–May, Sat.–Thurs. 9–noon and 2–6:30.*

Vertine, 2 km (1 mi) to the west of Gaiole, is a charming hamlet that dates as far back as the 10th century. The walled town is oval in shape and has a tall watchtower guarding the city gate. A walk along the still unspoiled streets gives you a glimpse of life in a Tuscan hill town as it once was, and the views of the undulating countryside from the occasional opening in the walls are spectacular. Stop for a snack after your stroll around town: **Bar Blu** (⊠ *Località Vertine 38* ☎*0577/749029*) makes sandwiches to order and serves plates of cheese and cold cuts.

North of Gaiole a turnoff leads to the **Badia a Coltibuono** *(Abbey of the Good Harvest)*, which has been owned by Lorenza de' Medici's family for more than a century and a half (the family isn't closely related to the Renaissance-era Medici). Wine has been produced here since the abbey was founded by Vallombrosan monks in the 11th century. Today the family continues the tradition, making Chianti Classico and other wines, along with cold-pressed olive oil and various flavored vinegars and floral honeys. A small Romanesque church with campanile is surrounded by 2,000 acres of oak, fir, and chestnut woods threaded with walking paths—open to all—that pass two small lakes. Though the abbey itself, built between the 11th and 18th centuries, serves as the family's home, parts are open for tours (in English, German, or Italian). Visit the jasmine-draped main courtyard, the inner cloister with its antique well, the musty old aging cellars, and the Renaissance-style garden redolent of lavender, lemons, and roses. In the shop, **L'Osteria,** you can taste wine and honey, as well as pick up other items like homemade beeswax hand lotion in little ceramic dishes. The Badia is closed on public holidays. ⊠ *Località Badia a Coltibuono ✛ 4 km (2½ mi) north of Gaiole* ☎*0577/749498 for tours, 0577/749479 for shop* 🖅*0577/749235* ⊕*www.coltibuono.com* 🖅*Abbey €3* ⊙*Tours: May–July and Sept. and Oct., weekdays 2:30, 3, 3:30, 4; shop: Mar.–mid-Jan., daily 9–1 and 2–7.*

WHERE TO STAY & EAT

$$–$$$ ✕**Badia a Coltibuono.** Outside the walls of Badia a Coltibuono is the abbey's pleasant restaurant, with seating on a terrace or in soft-yellow rooms divided by ancient brick arches. The *crema di peperoni e patate* (a creamless red pepper and potato soup) arrives at the table accompanied by homegrown olive oil; the *lasagnette agli asparagi al forno* (lasagna with asparagus and pecorino) is fragrant. It all pairs marvelously with the abbey's own wines. Between 2:30 and 7:30 you can order from a bistro menu that has sandwiches, salads, and desserts. ✉*Località Badia a Coltibuono* ✛ *4 km (2½ mi) north of Gaiole,53013* ☎*0577/749424* ▬*MC, V* ✆*Closed Mon. and Nov.–Feb.*

$$–$$$ ✕**Osteria del Castello.** South African–born chef Seamus de Pentheny ★ O'Kelly trained extensively in Paris and uses sophisticated techniques for his up-to-the-minute takes on Italian food. His *insalata di prosciutto con aceto balsamico* (mixed greens with blanched prosciutto drizzled with aged balsamic vinegar) is a delight, as is just about everything else on the menu. "Our three hour lunch was heavenly," writes a user of fodors.com. The wine list has some of Brolio's best offerings. The restaurant is nestled within a forest a stone's throw from the Castello di Brolio. ✉*Località Brolio* ✛ *2 km (1 mi) southeast of Gaiole, 53013* ☎☎*0577/747277* ✍*Reservations essential* ▬*AE, DC, MC, V* ✆*Closed Thurs.*

$–$$$ ✕**La Grotta della Rana.** A perfect stop for lunch while you're exploring the region's wineries, this trattoria offers *cucina casalinga* (home cooking) that can be eaten in the dining room or on a lovely outdoor patio. (If you time dinner right, you might get to watch a memorable sunset.) Outstanding primi include *maccheroni alla nonna* (macaroni with asparagus in a light cream sauce dotted with truffle oil). The *misto alla griglia* (mixed grilled meats) includes succulent pork. Also notable is the *filetto al pepe verde* (Chianina beef in a creamy green-peppercorn sauce). ✉*Località San Sano* ✛ *8 km (5 mi) south of Gaiole, 53013* ☎*0577/746020* ▬*AE, MC, V* ✆*Closed Wed. and Feb.–mid-Mar.*

$ ✕**Lo Sfizio di Bianchi.** A pleasant restaurant with outdoor seating in ★ Gaiole's main square, this spot is as popular with the locals as it is with travelers. The menu, presented on small blackboards, has the occasional unexpected item, like the plate of perfectly grilled vegetables that is listed as an antipasto but almost makes a meal in itself. The kitchen also makes its own delicious pastries and ice cream, so skipping dessert is difficult. Reservations are essential weekends. ✉*Via Ricasoli 44/4653013* ☎*0577/749501* ▬*AE, MC, V* ✆*Closed Tues. No dinner Mon.*

$$$$ ✕▦**Castello di Spaltenna.** This rustic yet elegant lodging includes ★ a former convent (dating to the 1300s) and a Romanesque church. Sumptuous striped fabrics or silky sheers drape from canopy beds; chiseled-stone fireplaces and massage-jet tubs set the suites apart. Windows look out on the hills, woods, and vineyards. Dine by candlelight on sophisticated classics—*filetto di manzo con fungo porcino al vino rosso* (beef fillet topped by a grilled boletus mushroom in a red-wine sauce), for example—at the first-class restaurant ($$–$$$) with a courtyard. **Pros:** Romantic setting, excellent restaurant, discreet and professional service. **Cons:** Some rooms are reached via narrow stairways, some rooms look over the interior courtyard. ⊠*Pieve di Spaltenna, 53013* ☏*0577/749483* ⊕*www.spaltenna.it* ⇆*30 rooms, 8 suites, 1 apartment* ⚭*In room: refrigerator. In-hotel: restaurant, room service, bar, tennis court, pools, laundry service, public Internet* ▤*AE, DC, MC, V* ⊘*Closed early Jan.–mid-Mar.* ⦿|*BP.*

$$$–$$$$
Fodor's Choice
★

▥**Borgo Argenina.** Elena Nappa, a former interior designer, is now the consummate hostess at this centuries-old villa. The old-fashioned guest rooms are lovingly decorated with antique quilts and handmade wood furnishings (refrigerators are a nod to modern times). Elena is an authority on the surrounding area and happily draws maps and suggests wine-tasting and -touring routes. Follow signs for San Marcellino Monti to get here. **Pros:** Homemade buffet breakfasts, off-the-beaten-path feel. **Cons:** No pool, need a car to get around. ⊠*Località Borgo Argenina* ✛*15 km (9 mi) south of Gaiole, 53013* ☏*0577/747117* *www.borgoargenina.it* ⇆*6 rooms, 1 villa, 2 houses* ⚭*In-room: no a/c, refrigerator. In-hotel: no elevator, laundry service, parking (free)* ▤*AE, DC, MC, V* ⊘*Closed mid-Nov.–mid-Mar.* ⦿|*BP.*

$$–$$$
▥**Hotel Residence San Sano.** An open-hearth fireplace and hand-hewn stone porticoes hark back to a time when this was a 13th-century fortress. The small hotel also has modern amenities, including a beautiful outdoor pool. Shuttered windows and doors in the guest rooms bring in the sunlight. Bedsteads have unadorned, curving lines in dark wood. The scent of lavender and rosemary wafts from the gardens. **Pros:** Good base for exploring Chianti, great family atmosphere, warm and friendly hosts. **Cons:** Need a car to get around; furnishings, in true Tuscan style, are very plain. ⊠*Località San Sano* ✛*10 km (6 mi) south of Gaiole, 53013* ☏*0577/746130* ☒*0577/746156* ⊕*www.sansanohotel.it* ⇆*14 rooms* ⚭*In-room: safe, refrigerator. In-hotel: restaurant, pool, no elevator, laundry facilities, some pets allowed* ▤*AE, DC, MC, V* ⊘*Closed Jan.–Mar.* ⦿|*BP.*

CASTELNUOVO BERARDENGA

20 km (12 mi) southeast of Gaiole in Chianti, 90 km (56 mi) southeast of Florence, 23 km (14 mi) east of Siena.

GETTING HERE

Castelnuovo is easily reached by car from Siena via the SS73. Tra-In buses run infrequently from Siena. Castelnuovo's train station, Castelnuovo Berardenga Scalo, is 8 km (5 mi) away.

VISITOR INFORMATION
Castelnuovo Berardenga tourism office(⊠*Via Roma 8* ☏*0577/355500*).

EXPLORING

The southernmost village in Chianti has a compact center with hilly, curving streets. A plethora of piazzas invite wandering.

Peek at the gardens of **Villa Chigi,** a 19th-century villa built on the site of a 14th-century castle (actually the "new castle" from which Castelnuovo got its name). The villa is closed to the public, but its manicured gardens are open on Sunday and holidays. ✉ *Strada la Ragnaia* ☎ *No phone* 🎫 *Free* ⏲ *Apr.–Sept., Sun. 10–8; Oct.–Mar., Sun. 10–5.*

The neoclassical church of **San Giusto e San Clemente,** built in the 1840s on a Greek-cross plan, contains a Madonna and Child with angels by an anonymous 15th-century master. Also inside is the *Holy Family with St. Catherine of Siena,* attributed to Arcangelo Salimbeni (1530/40–79). ✉ *Piazza Matteotti 4* ☎ *0577/355133* 🎫 *Free* ⏲ *Daily 7:30–7.*

San Gusmè. Of the medieval villages that surround Castelnuovo Berardenga, hilltop San Gusmè is the oldest and most interesting. The village retains its original early 1400s layout, with arched passageways, gates topped with coats of arms, narrow squares, and steep streets. You can walk through the entire village in 20 minutes, but in those 20 minutes you may feel as if you have stepped back in time some 600 years. ✉ *SR484* ✣ *5 km (3 mi) north of Castelnuovo Berardenga.*

WHERE TO STAY

$$$$ **Borgo San Felice.** Spread across five buildings, this elegant lodging used to be a small medieval town. Now it's given over to luxury, which is immediately apparent upon entering the reception area: white walls, high vaulted ceilings, and furniture covered in exquisite chintz prints mingle with tasteful etchings and watercolors. Rooms have tile floors, spacious bathrooms, and windows that open out onto peace and tranquillity. The restaurant ($$$$), Poggio Antico, serves sophisticated versions of Tuscan classics. **Pros:** Beautiful buildings, romantic setting, heated pool. **Cons:** Service is sometime lax, need a car to get around. ✉ *Località San Felice* ✣ *8 km (5 mi) northwest of Castelnuovo Berardenga, 53019* ☎ *0577/359260* 🌐 *www.borgosanfelice.com* *43 rooms, 6 suites* *In-room: safe, refrigerator. In-hotel: restaurant, room service, bar, tennis courts, pool, gym, bicycles, no elevator, concierge, laundry service, public Internet, some pets allowed* 💳 *AE, DC, MC, V* ⏲ *Closed Nov.–Mar.* 🍽 *BP.*

SIENA

With its narrow streets and steep alleys, a stunning Gothic Duomo, a bounty of early Renaissance art, and the glorious Palazzo Pubblico overlooking its magnificent Campo, Siena is often described as Italy's best-preserved medieval city. It is also remarkably modern: many shops sell cutting-edge clothes by up-and-coming designers. Make a point of catching the *passeggiata* (evening stroll), when the locals throng the Via di Città, Banchi di Sopra, and Banchi di Sotto, the city's three main streets.

Sienese mythology holds that the city shares common ancestry with Rome: the legendary founder, Senius, was said to be the son of Remus, the twin brother of Rome's founder, Romulus. The city emblem—a she-wolf and suckling twins—promulgates the claim. Archaeological evidence suggests there were prehistoric as well as Etruscan settlements here, which undoubtedly made way for Saena Julia, the Roman town established by Augustus in the 1st century BC.

Siena's frenetic Palio.

Siena rose to prominence as an essential stop on that most important of medieval roads, the Via Francigena (or Via Romea), prospering from the yearly flow of thousands of Christian pilgrims coming south to Rome from northern Europe. Siena developed a banking system—one of Europe's oldest banks, the Monte dei Paschi, is still very much in business—and dominated the wool trade, thereby establishing itself as a rival to Florence. The two towns became regional powers and bitter enemies, each taking a different side in the struggle that divided the peninsula between the Guelphs (loyal to the Pope) and Ghibellines (loyal to the Holy Roman Emperor). Siena aligned itself with the latter.

Victory over Florence in 1260 at Montaperti marked the beginning of Siena's golden age. Even though the Florentines avenged the loss nine years later, Siena continued to prosper. During the following decades Siena erected its greatest buildings (including the Duomo); established a model city government presided over by the Council of Nine; and became a great art, textile, and trade center. All of these achievements came together in the decoration of the Sala della Pace in Palazzo Pubblico. It makes you wonder what greatness the city might have gone on to achieve had its fortunes been different, but in 1348 a plague decimated the population, brought an end to the Council of Nine, and left Siena economically weak and vulnerable. Siena succumbed to Florentine rule in the mid-16th century, when a yearlong siege virtually eliminated the native population. Ironically, it was precisely this decline that, along with the steadfast pride of the Sienese, prevented further development, to which we owe the city's marvelous medieval condition today.

But although much looks as it did in the early 14th century, Siena is no museum. Walk through the streets and you can see that the medieval *contrade,* 17 neighborhoods into which the city has been historically divided, are a vibrant part of modern life. You may see symbols of the *contrada*—Tartuca (turtle), Oca (goose), Istrice (porcupine), Torre (tower)—emblazoned on banners and engraved on building walls. The Sienese still strongly identify themselves by the contrada where they were born and raised; loyalty and rivalry run deep. At no time is this more visible than during the centuries-old Palio, a twice-yearly horse race held in the Piazza del Campo, but you need not visit during the wild festival to come to know the rich culture and enchanting pleasures of Siena; those are evident at every step.

GETTING HERE

From Florence, the quickest way to Siena is via the Florence–Siena Superstrada. Otherwise, take the Via Cassia (SR2), for a scenic route. Coming from Rome, leave the A1 at Valdichiana, and follow the Siena–Bettole Superstrada. SITA provides excellent bus service between Florence and Siena. Because buses are direct and speedy, they are preferable to the train, which sometimes involves a change in Empoli.

VISITOR INFORMATION

Siena tourism office (⊠*Piazza del Campo 56* ☎*0577/280551* ⊕*www.comune.siena.it*).

EXPLORING SIENA

If you come by car, you're better off leaving it in one of the parking lots around the perimeter of town. Driving is difficult or impossible in most parts of the city center. Practically unchanged since medieval times, Siena is laid out in a "Y" over the slopes of several hills, dividing the city into *terzi* (thirds). Although the most interesting sites are in a fairly compact area around the Campo at the center of town in the neighborhoods of Città, Camollìa, and San Martino, be sure to leave some time to wander into the narrow streets that rise and fall steeply from the main thoroughfares, giving yourself at least two days to really explore the town. At the top on the list of things to see is the Piazza del Campo, considered by many to be the finest public square in Italy. The Palazzo Pubblico sits at the lower end of the square and is well worth a visit. The Duomo is a must-see, as is the nearby Cripta.

Tra-In (☎*0577/204111* ⊕*www.trainspa.it*) buses also run frequently within and around Siena, including through the centro storico. Tickets cost €0.90 and should be bought in advance at tobacconists or newsstands. Routes are marked with signposts.

The **Association of Official Tour Guides** (⊠*Piazza del Campo 56* ☎*0577/288084* ⊕*www.terredisiena.it*) offers a two-hour walking tour that takes in most of the major sights, such as the Duomo, the

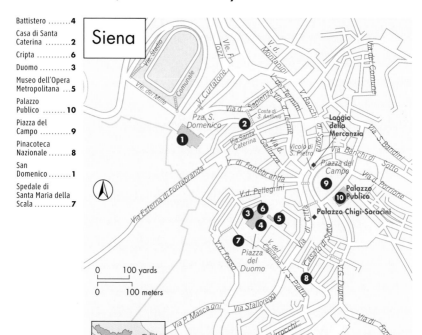

Campo, and the exterior of Palazzo Pubblico. You can arrange for English-speaking guides.

TIMING It's a joy to walk in Siena—hills notwithstanding—as it's a rare opportunity to stroll through a medieval city rather than just a town. (There is quite a lot to explore, in contrast to tiny hill towns that can be crossed in minutes.) The walk can be done in as little as a day, with minimal stops at the sights. But stay longer and take time to tour the church building and museums, and to enjoy the streetscapes themselves. Several of the sites have reduced hours on Sunday afternoon and Monday.

MAIN ATTRACTIONS

⑥ Cripta. After it had lain unseen for possibly 700 years, a crypt was rediscovered under the grand *pavimento* (floor) of the Duomo during routine excavation work and was opened to the public in 2003. An unknown master executed the breathtaking frescoes here sometime between 1270–80; they retain their original colors and pack an emotional punch even with sporadic damage. The *Deposition/Lamentation* gives strong evidence that the Sienese school could paint emotion just as well as the Florentine school—and did it some 20 years before Giotto. Guided tours in English take place more or less every

FodorśChoice
★

half hour and are limited to no more than 35 persons. ⊠*Piazza del Duomo, Città* ☎*0577/283048* ⚑*€6; €10 combined ticket includes the Duomo, Battistero, and Museo dell'Opera Metropolitana* ☉*June–Aug., daily 9:30–8; Sept.–May, daily 9:30–7.*

❸ **Duomo.** Siena's Duomo is beyond question one of the finest Gothic
Fodor'sChoice cathedrals in Italy. The multicolored marbles and painted decoration
★ are typical of the Italian approach to Gothic architecture—lighter and much less austere than the French. The amazingly detailed facade has few rivals in the region, although it's quite similar to the Duomo in Orvieto. It was completed in two brief phases at the end of the 13th and 14th centuries. The statues and decorative work were designed by Niccolo and Giovanni Pisano, although most of what we see today are copies, the originals having been removed to the nearby Museo dell'Opera Metropolitana. The gold mosaics are 18th-century restorations. The Campanile (no entry) is among central Italy's finest, the number of windows increasing with each level.

The Duomo's interior, with its black-and-white striping throughout and finely coffered and gilded dome, is simply striking. Step in and look back up at Duccio's (circa 1255–1319) panels of stained glass that fill the circular window. Finished in 1288, it's the oldest example of stained glass in Italy. The Duomo is most famous for its unique and magnificent inlaid-marble floors, which took almost 200 years to complete; more than 40 artists contributed to the work, made up of 56 separate compositions depicting biblical scenes, allegories, religious symbols, and civic emblems. The floors are covered for most of the year for conservation purposes, but are unveiled during September and October. The Duomo's carousel pulpit, also much appreciated, was carved by Nicola Pisano (circa 1220–84) around 1265; the *Life of Christ* is depicted on the rostrum frieze. In striking contrast to all the Gothic decoration in the nave are the magnificent Renaissance frescoes in the **Biblioteca Piccolomini,** off the left aisle. Painted by Pinturicchio (circa 1454–1513) and completed in 1509, they depict events from the life of native son Aeneas Sylvius Piccolomini (1405–64), who became Pope Pius II in 1458. The frescoes are in excellent condition and have a freshness rarely seen in work so old.

The Duomo is grand, but the medieval Sienese people had even bigger plans. They wanted to enlarge the building by using the existing church as a transept for a new church, with a new nave running toward the southeast, to make what would be the largest church in the world. But only the side wall and part of the new facade were completed when the Black Death struck in 1348, decimating Siena's population. The city fell into decline, funds dried up, and the plans were never carried out. (The dream of building the biggest church was actually doomed to failure from the start—subsequent attempts to get the project going revealed that the foundation was insufficient to bear the weight of the proposed structure.) The beginnings of the new nave, extending from the right side of the Duomo, were left unfinished, perhaps as a testament to unfulfilled dreams, and ultimately enclosed to house the adjacent ⇨**Museo dell'Opera Metropolitana.** The ⇨**Cripta** was discovered during routine preservation work on the church and has been opened to the public. ⊠*Piazza del Duomo, Città* ☎*0577/283048* 🎫*€3 Nov.– Aug.; €5 Sept. and Oct.; €10 combined ticket includes the Cripta, Battistero, and Museo dell'Opera Metropolitana* ⏱*Mar.–Oct., Mon.–Sat. 10:30–7:30, Sun. 1:30–6:30; Nov.–Feb., Mon.–Sat. 10:30–6:30, Sun. 1:30–5:30.*

⑤ Museo dell'Opera Metropolitana. Part of the unfinished nave of what was to have been a new cathedral, the museum contains the Duomo's treasury and some of the original decoration from its facade and interior. The first room on the ground floor displays weather-beaten 13th-century sculptures by Giovanni Pisano (circa 1245–1318) that were brought inside for protection and replaced by copies, as was a tondo of the *Madonna and Child* (now attributed to Donatello) that once hung on the door to the south transept. The masterpiece is unquestionably Duccio's *Maestà,* one side with 26 panels depicting episodes from the Passion, the other side with a *Madonna and Child Enthroned.* Painted between 1308 and 1311 as the altarpiece for the Duomo (where it remained until 1505), its realistic elements, such as the lively depiction of the Christ child and the treatment of interior space, proved an enormous influence on later painters. The second floor is divided between the treasury, with a crucifix by Giovanni Pisano and several statues and busts of biblical characters and classical philosophers, and La Sala della Madonna degli Occhi Grossi (the Room of the Madonna with the Big Eyes), named after the namesake painting it displays by the Maestro di Tressa, who painted in the early 13th century. The work originally decorated the Duomo's high altar, before being displaced by Duccio's *Maestà.* There is a fine view from the tower inside the museum. ⊠*Piazza del Duomo, Città* ☎*0577/283048* 🎫*€6; €10 combined ticket includes the Duomo, Cripta, and Battistero* ⏱*Mar.–May and Sept. and Oct., daily 9:30–7; June–Aug., daily 9:30 AM–10 PM; Nov.–Feb., daily 10–5.*

⑧ Pinacoteca Nazionale. The superb collection of five centuries of local painting in Siena's national picture gallery can easily convince you that the Renaissance was by no means just a Florentine thing—Siena was arguably just as important a center of art and innovation as its rival to the north, especially in the mid-13th century. Accordingly, the most interesting section of the collection, chronologically arranged, has several important "firsts." Room 1 contains a painting of the *Stories of the True Cross* (1215) by the so-called Master of Tressa, the earliest identified work by a painter of the Sienese school, and is followed in Room 2 by late-13th-century artist Guido da Siena's *Stories from the Life of Christ,* one of the first paintings ever made on canvas (earlier painters used wood panels). Rooms 3 and 4 are dedicated to Duccio, a student of Cimabue (circa 1240–1302) and considered to be the last of the proto-Renaissance painters. Ambrogio Lorenzetti's landscapes in Room 8 are the first truly secular paintings in Western art. Among later works in the rooms on the floor above, keep an eye out for the preparatory sketches used by Domenico Beccafumi (1486–1551) for the 35 etched marble panels he made for the floor of the Duomo. ⊠*Via San*

Pietro 29, Città ☎*0577/281161* 📷*€4* ⊙*Tues.–Sat. 8:15–7:15; Sun. 8:15–1:15; Mon. 8:30–1:30; last entrance ½ hr before closing.*

❼ Spedale di Santa Maria della Scala. For more than a thousand years, this complex across from the Duomo was home to Siena's hospital, but now it serves as a museum to display some terrific frescoes and other Sienese Renaissance treasures. Restored 15th-century frescoes in the Sala del Pellegrinaio (once the emergency room) tell the history of the hospital, which was created to give refuge to passing pilgrims and to those in need, and to distribute charity to the poor. Incorporated into the complex is the church of the Santissima Annunziata, with a celebrated *Risen Christ* by Vecchietta (also known as Lorenzo di Pietro, circa 1412–80). Down in the dark Cappella di Santa Caterina della Notte is where Saint Catherine went to pray at night. The subterranean archaeological museum contained within the *ospedale* (hospital) is worth seeing even if you're not particularly taken with Etruscan objects: the interior design is sheer brilliance—it's beautifully lighted, eerily quiet, and an oasis of cool on hot summer days. The displays—including the *bucchero* (dark, reddish clay) ceramics, Roman coins, and tomb furnishings—are clearly marked and can serve as a good introduction to the history of regional excavations. Don't miss della Quercia's original sculpted reliefs from the Fonte Gaia. Although the fountain has been faithfully copied for the Campo, there's something incomparably beautiful about the real thing. ✉*Piazza del Duomo, Città* ☎*0577/224811* 📷*€6* ⊙*Mar. 16–Jan. 9, daily 10:30–6:30; Jan. 10–Mar. 15, daily 10:30–4:30.*

ALSO WORTH SEEING

❹ Battistero. The Duomo's 14th-century Gothic Baptistery was built to prop up one side of the Duomo. There are frescoes throughout, but the highlight is a large bronze 15th-century baptismal font designed by Jacopo della Quercia (1374–1438). It's adorned with bas-reliefs by various artists, including two by Renaissance masters: the *Baptism of Christ* by Lorenzo Ghiberti (1378–1455) and the *Feast of Herod* by Donatello. ✉*Entrance on Piazza San Giovanni* ☎*No phone* 📷*€3; €10 combined ticket includes the Duomo, Cripta, and Museo dell'Opera del Duomo* ⊙*June–Aug., daily 9:30–8; Sept.–May, daily 9:30–7.*

❷ Casa di Santa Caterina. Caterina Benincasa was born here in 1347, and although she took the veil of the Dominican Tertiary order at age eight, she remained here, devoting her life to the sick and poor in the aftermath of the devastating plague of 1348. She had divine visions and received the stigmata, but is most famous for her words and her argumentative skills. Her letters—many of which are preserved in the Biblioteca Comunale—were dictated because she did not know how to write. She is credited with convincing Pope Gregory XI (1329–78) to return the papacy to Rome after 70 years in Avignon and French domination, ending the Western Schism. Caterina died in Rome in 1380 and was canonized in 1461. A few years later the city purchased the family house and turned it into a shrine, one of the first examples of its kind in Italy. The rooms of the house, including her cell and the kitchen, were converted into a series of chapels and oratories and decorated by noteworthy

Continued on page 250

Climbing the 400 narrow steps of the **Torre del Mangia** rewards you with unparalleled views of Siena's rooftops and the countryside beyond.

The **Palazzo Pubblico**, Siena's town hall since the 14th century.

Something about the fan-shaped, sloping design of **Il Campo** encourages people to sit and relax (except during the Palio, when they stand and scream). The communal atmosphere here is unlike that of any other Italian piazza.

PIAZZA DEL CAMPO

9 Fodor'sChoice ★

The fan-shaped **Piazza del Campo**, known simply as il Campo (The Field), is one of the finest squares in Italy. Constructed toward the end of the 12th century on a market area unclaimed by any contrada, it's still the heart of town. The bricks of the Campo are patterned in nine different sections—representing each member of the medieval Government of Nine. At the top of the Campo is a copy of the **Fonte Gaia,** decorated in the early 15th century by Siena's greatest sculptor, Jacopo della Quercia, with 13 sculpted reliefs of biblical events and virtues. Those lining the rectangular fountain are 19th-century copies; the originals are in the Spedale di Santa Maria della Scala. On Palio horse race days (July 2 and August 16), the Campo and all its surrounding buildings are packed with cheering, frenzied locals and tourists craning their necks to take it all in.

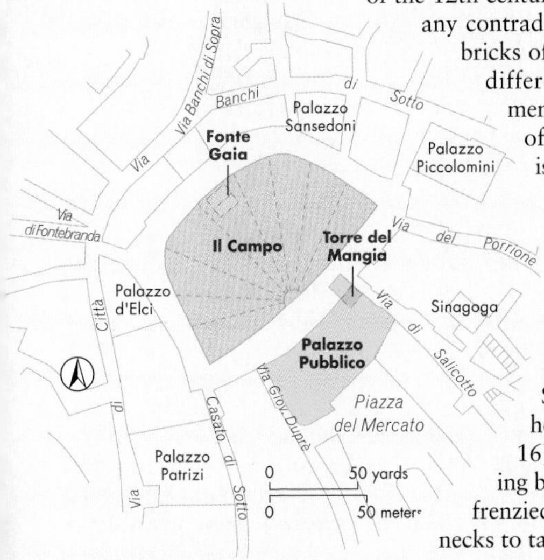

Map labels: Via Banchi di Sopra · Banchi · di · Sotto · Palazzo Sansedoni · **Fonte Gaia** · Palazzo Piccolomini · Via · Via di Fontebranda · **Il Campo** · **Torre del Mangia** · Via del Porrione · Sinagoga · Palazzo d'Elci · Via di Città · **Palazzo Pubblico** · Via di Salicotto · Via Giov. Duprè · Casato di Sotto · *Piazza del Mercato* · Palazzo Patrizi · Via · 0 50 yards · 0 50 meters

Margin (vertical): **4** IN FOCUS PIAZZA DEL CAMPO

10 The Gothic **Palazzo Pubblico,** the focal point of the Piazza del Campo, has served as Siena's town hall since the 1300s. It now also contains the **Museo Civico,** with walls covered in early Renaissance frescoes. The nine governors of Siena once met in the Sala della Pace, famous for Ambrogio Lorenzetti's frescoes called *Allegories of Good and Bad Government,* painted in the late 1330s to demonstrate the dangers of tyranny. The good government side depicts utopia, showing first the virtuous ruling council surrounded by angels and then scenes of a perfectly running city and countryside. Conversely, the bad government fresco tells a tale straight out of Dante. The evil ruler and his advisers have horns and fondle strange animals, and the town scene depicts the seven mortal sins in action. Interestingly, the bad government fresco is severely damaged, and the good government fresco is in terrific condition. The **Torre del Mangia,** the palazzo's famous bell tower, is named after one of its first bell ringers, Giovanni di Duccio (called Mangiaguadagni, or earnings eater). The climb up to the top is long and steep, but the view makes it worth every step. ⊠ *Piazza del Campo 1, Città* ☎ *0577/41169* ✆ *Museo €7, Torre €6, combined ticket €10* ☉ *Museo Nov.–Mar. 15, daily 10–6:30; Mar. 16–Oct., daily 10–7. Torre Nov.–Mar. 15, daily 10–4; Mar. 16–Oct., daily 10–7.*

THE PALIO

The three laps around a makeshift racetrack in Piazza del Campo are over in less than two minutes, but the spirit of Siena's Palio—a horse race held every July 2 and August 16—lives all year long.

The Palio is contested between Siena's contrade, the 17 neighborhoods that have divided the city since the Middle Ages. Loyalties are fiercely felt. At any time of year you'll see on the streets contrada symbols—Tartuca (turtle), Oca (goose), Istrice (porcupine), Torre (tower)—emblazoned on banners and engraved on building walls. At Palio time, simmering rivalries come to a boil.

It's been that way since at least August 16, 1310, the date of the first recorded running of the Palio. At that time, and for centuries to follow, the race went through the streets of the city. The additional July 2 running was instituted in 1649; soon thereafter the location was moved to the Campo and the current system for selecting the race entrants established. Ten of the contrade are chosen at random to run in the July Palio. The August race is then contested between the 7 contrade left out in July, plus 3 of the 10 July participants, again chosen at random. Although the races are in theory of equal importance, Sienese will tell you that it's better to win the second and have bragging rights for the rest of the year.

The race itself has a raw and arbitrary character—it's no Kentucky Derby. There's barely room for the 10 horses on the makeshift Campo course, so falls and collisions are inevitable. Horses are chosen at random three days before the race, and jockeys (who ride bareback) are mercenaries hired from surrounding towns. Almost no tactic is considered too underhanded. Bribery, secret plots, and betrayal are commonplace—so much so that the word for "jockey," *fantino,* has come to mean "untrustworthy" in Siena. There have been incidents of drugging (the horses) and kidnapping (the jockeys); only sabotaging a horse's reins remains taboo.

Above: The tension of the starting line. Top left: The frenzy of the race. Bottom left: A solemn flag bearer follows in the footsteps of his ancestors.

17 MEDIEVAL CONTRADE

AQUILA

BRUCO

CHIOCCIOLA

Festivities kick off three days prior to the Palio, with the selection and blessing of the horses, trial runs, ceremonial banquets, betting, and late-night celebrations. Residents don their contrada's colors and march through the streets in medieval costumes. The Campo is transformed into a racetrack lined with a thick layer of sand. On race day, each horse is brought to the church of the contrada for which it will run, where it's blessed and told, "Go little horse and return a winner." The Campo fills through the afternoon, with spectators crowding into every available space until bells ring and the piazza is sealed off. Processions of flag wavers in traditional dress march to the beat of tambourines and drums and the roar of the crowds. The *palio* itself—a banner for which the race is named, dedicated to the Virgin Mary—makes an appearance, followed by the horses and their jockeys.

The race begins when one horse, chosen to ride up from behind the rest of the field, crosses the starting line. There are always false starts, adding to the frenzied mood. Once underway, the race is over in a matter of minutes. The victorious rider is carried off through the streets of the winning contrada (where in the past tradition dictated he was entitled to the local girl of his choice), while winning and losing sides use television replay to analyze the race from every possible angle. The winning contrada will celebrate into the night, at long tables piled high with food and drink. The champion horse is guest of honor.

Reserved seating in the stands is sold out months in advance of the races; contact the Siena Tourist Office (✉ Piazza del Campo 56 ☎ 0577/280551) to find out about availability, and ask your hotel if it can procure you a seat. The entire area in the center is free and unreserved, but you need to show up early in order to get a prime spot against the barriers.

CIVETTA

DRAGO

GIRAFFA

ISTRICE

LEOCORNO

LUPA

NICCHIO

OCA

ONDA

PANTERA

SELVA

TARTUCA

TORRE

VALDIMONTONE

artists over the following centuries with scenes from Caterina's life. In 1939 she was made a patron saint of Italy, along with Saint Francis of Assisi. In 1970 she was elevated to Doctor of the Church, the highest possible honor in Christendom. She has been named a patron saint of Europe but, strangely enough, never of her hometown. ⊠ *Entrance on Costa di San Antonio, off Via della Sapienza, Camollìa* 🕾 *0577/280801* 🎟 *Free* 🕒 *Daily 9–1 and 3–5:30.*

Orto Botanico. Siena's botanical garden is a great place to relax and enjoy views onto the countryside below. Guided tours in English are available by reservation. ⊠ *Via Pier Andrea Mattioli 4, Città* 🕾 *0577/232874* 🎟 *€8* 🕒 *Weekdays 8–12:30 and 2:30–5, Sat. 8–noon.*

❶ San Domenico. Although the Duomo is celebrated as a triumph of 13th-century Gothic architecture, this church, built at about the same time, turned out to be an oversize, hulking brick box that never merited a finishing coat in marble, let alone a graceful facade. Named for the founder of the Dominican order, the church is now more closely associated with Saint Catherine of Siena. Just to the right of the entrance is the chapel in which she received the stigmata. On the wall is the only known contemporary portrait of the saint, made in the late 14th century by Andrea Vanni (circa 1332–1414). Farther down is the famous **Cappella di Santa Caterina,** the church's official shrine. Catherine, or bits and pieces of her, was literally spread all over the country—a foot is in Venice, most of her body is in Rome, and only her head and finger are here (kept in a reliquary on the altar). She was revered throughout the country long before she was officially named a patron saint of Italy in 1939. On either side of the chapel are well-known frescoes by Sodoma (aka Giovanni Antonio Bazzi, 1477–1549) of *St. Catherine in Ecstasy.* Don't miss the view of the Duomo and town center from the apse-side terrace. ⊠ *Costa di Sant'Antonio, Camollìa* 🕾 *0577/280893* 🎟 *Free* 🕒 *Mid-Mar.–Oct., daily 7–1 and 2:30–6:30; Nov.–mid-Mar., daily 9–1 and 3–6.*

Not far from San Domenico, the **Enoteca Italiana** (⊠ *Fortezza Medicea, Viale Maccari, Camollìa* 🕾 *0577/288497*) is a fantastically stocked wine cellar in the bastions of the Fortezza Medici. It serves wines by the glass and various small dishes. Take some time to peruse the labels that are on the shelves (the wines of more than 400 wineries are stocked here). It's open daily from noon to 1 AM. On Friday evenings in winter there's also a piano bar.

Sinagoga. Down a small street around the corner from Il Campo, this synagogue is worth a visit simply to view the two sobering plaques that adorn its facade. One commemorates June 28, 1799, when 13 Jews were taken from their homes by a fanatic mob and burned in the

Ricciarelli, delicate almond cookies native to Siena.

square. The other memorializes the Sienese Jews who were deported during World War II. Guided tours in English are available by arrangement. ⊠ *Vicolo delle Scotte 14, San Martino* ☎ *0577/284647* ☉ *Sun. 10–1 and 2–5.*

WHERE TO EAT

$$$–$$$$
★
✕ **Antica Trattoria Botteganova.** Along the road that leads to Chianti is arguably the best restaurant in Siena. Chef Michele Sorrentino's cooking is all about clean flavors, balanced combinations, and inviting presentation. Look for inspiring dishes such as spaghetti *alla chitarra in salsa di astice piccante* (with a spicy lobster sauce), or ravioli di ricotta con ragù d'agnello (with sheep's-milk cheese and lamb sauce). The interior, with high vaulting, is relaxed yet elegant, and the service is first-rate. ⊠ *Strada per Montevarchi 29* ✛ *2 km (1 mi) northeast of Siena, 53100* ☎ *0577/284230* ✍ *Reservations essential* ☰ *AE, DC, MC, V* ☉ *Closed Sun.*

$$$–$$$$
✕ **Le Logge.** Bright flowers provide a dash of color at this classic Tuscan dining room, and stenciled designs on the ceilings add some whimsy. The wooden cupboards (now filled with wine bottles) lining the walls recall its past as a turn-of-the-19th-century grocery store. The menu, with four or five *primi* (first courses) and *secondi* (second courses) changes regularly, but almost always includes their classic *malfatti all'osteria* (ricotta and spinach dumplings in a cream sauce). Desserts such as *coni con mousse al cioccolato e gelato allo zafferano* (two diminutive ice-

cream cones with chocolate mousse and saffron ice cream) provide an inventive ending to the meal. When not vying for one of the outdoor tables, make sure to ask for one in the main downstairs room. ⊠ *Via del Porrione 33, San Martino53100* ☎*0577/48013* ⚐*Reservations essential* ⊟*AE, DC, MC, V* ✆*Closed Sun. and 3 wks in Jan.*

$$–$$$ ✕**Osteria Castelvecchio.** On the daily menu you're likely to find both Sienese standards, such as spaghetti *saporiti con gli aromi* (with tomatoes and herbs), as well as more offbeat selections like *bocconcini di pollo alla mediterranea* (tender chicken cooked in a robust tomato-and-olive sauce). Husband-and-wife team Simone Romi and Sabrina Fabi are committed to including *piatti di verdura* (vegetarian dishes) among the choices, and they've put together a great wine list. A tasting menu allows you to sample just about all the daily specials. The little restaurant with high vaulted ceilings is in the oldest part of town. ⊠ *Via Castelvecchio 65, Città53100* ☎*0577/49586* ⊟*AE, DC, MC, V* ✆*Closed Tues.*

$–$$ ✕**Hosteria il Carroccio.** Angle for one of the few seats here to have an intimate meal and to try dishes both creative and deliciously simple. The *palline di pecorino con lardo e salsa di pere* (pecorino cheese balls wrapped with pork fat and briefly grilled), for instance, are sublime. So, too, are the amply portioned primi—the *pici* (a local pasta specialty resembling a thick spaghetti) is especially good. Sit at tables outside in summer. ⊠ *Via Casato di Sotto 32, Città53100* ☎*0577/41165* ⊟*MC, V* ✆*Closed Wed., 2 wks in Jan., and 2 wks in July.*

$–$$

Fodor'sChoice

★ ✕**Osteria del Coro.** Chef-owner Stefano Azzi promotes local produce, uses age-old Sienese recipes, and backs it all up with a stellar wine list. His *pici con le briciole al modo mio* (thick spaghetti with breadcrumbs), liberally dressed with fried *cinta senese* (a bacon made from a long-snouted pig), dazzles. The place was once a pizzeria, and it retains its unadorned, unpretentious air—you certainly wouldn't come because of the decor. ⊠ *Via Pantaneto 85/87, Città, 53100* ☎*0577/222482* ⊟ *DC, MC, V* ✆*Closed Mon.*

$–$$

★ ✕**Trattoria Papei.** The menu hasn't changed for years, and why should it? The *pici al cardinale* (handmade spaghetti with a duck and bacon sauce) is wonderful, and all the other typically Sienese dishes are equally delicious. Tucked away behind the Palazzo Pubblico in a square that serves as a parking lot for most of the day, the restaurant's location isn't great, but the food is. ⊠*Piazza del Mercato 6, Città, 53100* ☎*0577/280894* ⊟*MC, V* ✆*Closed Mon.*

¢–$ ✕**Osteria Il Grattacielo.** Wiped out from too much sightseeing? Consider a meal at this hole-in-the-wall restaurant where locals congregate for a simple lunch over a glass of wine. There's a collection of *verdure sott'olio* (marinated vegetables), a wide selection of *affettati misti* (cured meats), and various types of frittatas. All off this can be washed down with the cheap, yet eminently drinkable, house red. A couple of bench tables provide outdoor seating in summer. Don't be put off by the absence of a written menu. All the food is displayed at the counter, so you can point if you need to. ⊠ *Via Pontani 8, Camollìa53100* ☎*0577/289326* ⊟*No credit cards* ✆*Closed Sun.*

WHERE TO STAY

$$$$ ⚑ **Certosa di Maggiano.** A 14th-century monastery has been converted into this upscale country hotel. Rooms have the style and comfort of an aristocratic villa, with classic prints and bold colors such as daffodil yellow. Common rooms are luxurious, with fine woods and leather upholstery. Fodors.com users describe this as "a great romantic hotel." In warm weather, breakfast is served on the patio next to the garden ablaze with flowers. **Pros:** Elegant service, luxurious rooms. **Cons:** Some find the atmosphere too formal, located outside of town. ✉ *Siena Sud exit off Superstrada, Strada di Certosa 82* ✚ *½ km (¼ mi) east of Siena, 53100* ☎ *0577/288180* ⊕ *www.certosadimaggiano. it* ⇙ *9 rooms, 8 suites* ♿ *In-room: refrigerator. In-hotel: restaurant, tennis court, pool, concierge, laundry service, no kids under 12* ⊟ *AE, MC, V* ⦿ *MAP.*

$$$$ ⚑ **Grand Hotel Continental.** Pope Alexander VII of the famed Sienese Chigi family gave this palace to his niece as a wedding present in 1600; through the centuries it has been a private family home as well as a grand hotel. It exudes elegance, from the stately pillared entrance to the crisp-linen sheets. Some guest rooms take in panoramic views, whereas others have 18th-century frescoes and massive chandeliers. The excellent staff is reason enough to consider a stay here. **Pros:** Luxurious accommodations, great location on the main drag, first-rate concierge. **Cons:** Sometimes stuffy atmosphere, rooms show signs of wear. ✉ *Banchi di Sopra 85, Camollìa, 53100* ☎ *0577/56011* ⊕ *www. royaldemeure.com* ⇙ *40 rooms, 11 suites* ♿ *In-room: safe, refrigerator, VCR (some), Wi-Fi. In-hotel: restaurant, room service, bar, concierge, laundry service, public Wi-Fi, parking (fee), some pets allowed,* ⊟ *AE, DC, MC, V* ⦿ *BP.*

$$$ ⚑ **Borgo Pretale.** A small hamlet hidden in the hills to the south of
★   Siena has been converted into this delightful hotel. Surrounded by open fields and rolling woodlands, Borgo Pretale is an amazingly tranquil place to stay, but close enough to Siena to be a base of exploration. Rooms vary in size, but all are filled with elegant furnishings, including some canopy beds. One room of the restaurant (closed Monday) has a wall of windows looking out into the countryside. **Pros:** Bucolic location, lots of walking trails, lovely rooms. **Cons:** Few restaurant options nearby, need a car to get around. ✉ *Località Pretale* ✚ *11 km (7 mi) east of Siena, 53018, Sovicille* ☎ *0577/345401* 🖷 *0577/345625* ⊕ *www.borgopretale.it* ⇙ *27 rooms, 7 suites* ♿ *In-hotel: restaurant, bar, tennis court, pool, gym, bicycles, no elevator, public Internet* ⊟ *AE, D, MC, V* ⊘ *Closed Nov.–Easter* ⦿ *BP.*

$$$ ⚑ **Hotel Santa Caterina.** Manager Lorenza Capannelli and her fine staff
★   are welcoming, hospitable, enthusiastic, and go out of their way to ensure a fine stay. Dark, straight-lined wood furniture stands next to beds with floral spreads; some have upholstered headboards. Rooms in the back look out onto the garden or the countryside in the distance. When it's warm, breakfast is served in the flower-filled garden with a view of the Siena countryside, providing a gorgeous start to the day. The well-run hotel is outside Porta Romana—a 15-minute walk south of Piazza del Campo. **Pros:** Friendly staff, a short walk to center of

town, breakfast in the garden. **Cons:** On a busy intersection, outside city walls. ⊠ *Via Piccolomini 7, San Martino, 53100* ☏*0577/221105* ⊕*www.hscsiena.it* ⤴*22 rooms* ⚘*In-room: refrigerator, dial-up. In-hotel: concierge, laundry service, public Internet, parking (fee), some pets allowed* ▤*AE, DC, MC, V* ⑩*BP.*

$$$ ⌂ **Palazzo Ravizza.** This romantic palazzo exudes a sense of genteel
★ shabbiness. Rooms have high ceilings, antique furnishings, and bathrooms decorated with hand-painted tiles. The location is key: from here it's just a 10-minute walk to the Duomo. Il Capriccio ($$–$$$), ably run by chef Fabio Tozzi, specializies in traditional Tuscan fare. In warm weather, enjoy your meal in the garden with a trickling fountain. "We have only positive things to say about Palazzo Ravizza ...from the amazing Tuscan view, to the proximity to Il Campo this hotel was by far the best one we stayed at throughout our Italy vacation," says one traveler on fodors.com. **Pros:** 10-minute walk to the center of town, pleasant garden with a view beyond the city walls, professional staff. **Cons:** Not all rooms have views, some of the rooms are a little cramped. ⊠ *Pian dei Mantellini 34, Città, 53100* ☏*0577/280462* ⊕*www.palazzoravizza.it* ⤴*38 rooms, 4 suites* ⚘*In-room: safe, refrigerator, Wi-Fi (some). In-hotel: restaurant, bar, concierge, laundry service, public Internet, public Wi-Fi, parking (no fee), some pets allowed* ▤*AE, DC, MC, V* ⑩*BP.*

$$ ⌂ **Antica Torre.** The cordial Landolfo family has carefully evoked a private home with their eight guest rooms inside a restored 16th-century tower. Simple but tastefully furnished rooms have ornate wrought-iron headboards, usually atop twin beds. The old stone staircase, large wooden beams, wood shutters, and original brick vaults here and there are reminders of the building's great age. Antica Torre is in a southeast corner of Siena, a 10-minute walk from Piazza del Campo. **Pros:** Near the town center, charming atmosphere. **Cons:** Narrow stairway up to the rooms, low ceilings, cramped bathrooms. ⊠ *Via Fieravecchia 7, San Martino, 53100* ☏*0577/222255* ⊕*www.anticatorresiena.it* ⤴*8 rooms* ⚘*In-hotel: no elevator* ▤*AE, DC, MC, V* ⑩*BP.*

$$ ⌂ **Chiusarelli.** Caryatids stud the grounds of this well-kept neoclassical villa; a small garden invites reading. Guest rooms are functional, airy, and reasonably quiet, but the handy location—near the long-distance bus terminal and parking area, and minutes away from the main sights—is the big plus here, that and the pleasant staff. Single rooms are not the usual monastic-cell size. Head downstairs to the restaurant for inexpensive meals. **Pros:** Next to the main bus terminal, spacious rooms, quiet garden. **Cons:** On a busy street, bland furnishings. ⊠ *Viale Curtatone 15, Camollia, 53100* ☏*0577/280562* ⊕*www.chiusarelli.com* ⤴*48 rooms, 1 suite* ⚘*In-room: safe, Wi-Fi. In-hotel: restaurant, bar, public Internet, public Wi-Fi, parking (no fee), some pets allowed* ▤*AE, MC, V* ⑩*BP.*

NIGHTLIFE & THE ARTS

THE ARTS

Performances by local and national classical musicians take place during a series of concerts held in churches and courtyards during the **Settimane Musicali Senesi festival** in mid-July.

Estate Musicale Chigiana (⊠*Accademia Musicale Chigiana, Via di Città 89, Città* ☎*0577/22091* ⊕*www.chigiana.it*) sponsors master classes and workshops during July and August, and concerts are held from June through August. Age-old venues such as Santa Maria della Scala and the church of Sant'Agostino provide wonderful stages.

NIGHTLIFE

Join the locals for *aperitivi* (apertifs) at **Caffè del Corso** (⊠*Banchi di Sopra 22, Camollìa* ☎*No phone*), where aspiring artists and savvy students hobnob until 3 AM. A happening local hangout, **L'Officina** (⊠*Piazza del Sale 3, Camollìa* ☎*0577/286301*) has live music on Thursday. The other nights, DJs spin sounds ranging from Latin-inspired rhythms to dance and rock. The wine bar at **Sapordivino** (⊠*Grand Hotel Continental, Banchi di Sopra 85, Città* ☎*0577/56011*) has live piano music most evenings. A well-stocked liquor collection includes a well-thought-out list of whiskeys.

SPORTS & THE OUTDOORS

Siena's thrilling **Palio** (⊠*Siena tourist office, Piazza del Campo 56, Città* ☎*0577/280551*) horse race takes place every year on July 2 and August 16. Three laps around the track in the Piazza del Campo earn participants of the Palio the respect or scorn of the other 16 contrade. Tickets usually sell out months in advance; call the Siena tourist office for more information. Note that some hotels reserve a number of tickets for guests. It's also possible you might luck out and get an unclaimed seat or two. The standing-room center of the piazza is free to all on a first-come, first-served basis, until just moments before the start.

SHOPPING

Siena is known for a delectable variety of cakes and cookies with recipes dating to medieval times. Some Sienese sweets are *cavallucci* (sweet spice biscuits), *panforte* (a traditional Christmas delicacy, literally "strong bread," with honey, hazelnuts, almonds, and spices), *ricciarelli* (almond-paste cookies), and *castagnaccio* (a baked Tuscan flat cake made in the fall and winter from a batter of chestnut flour topped with pine nuts and rosemary).

ARTS & CRAFTS

Embroidered linens, curtains, and sheets are among the housewares sold at **Antiche Dimore** (⊠*Via di Città 115, Città* ☎*0577/45337*). The products are made by Sienese artisans. If you've always wanted a 14th- or 15th-century painting to hang on your wall, but cost of acquiring one is prohibitive, consider purchasing one of the superb copies at

Bottega dell'Arte (⊠ *Via Stalloreggi 47, Città* ☎*0577/40755*) made by Chiara Perinetti Casoni. Her work in tempera and in gold leaf is of the highest quality.

At **Fioretta Bacci** (⊠ *Via San Pietro 7, Città* ☎*0577/282200*), wool, mohair, silk, linen, and cotton are woven on-site, and turned into sweaters and jackets in the colors of the rainbow. **Siena Ricama** (⊠ *Via di Città 61, Città* ☎*0577/288339*) has been famous for centuries for its fine embroidery work, and Bruna Brizza continues the tradition in her tiny shop. Hand stitching, usually on simple white and cream-color linen, adorns lamp shades, tablecloths, and other housewares.

Tapestries, kilims, and Oriental rugs—both contemporary and ancient—fill **Tappezzerie Lippi** (⊠ *Via dei Termini 21–25, Camollìa* ☎*0577/280633*). The store also has upholstered sofas and chairs. Stained-glass artists create and sell contemporary secular and religious works at **Vetrate Artistiche Toscane** (⊠ *Via della Galluzza 5, Camollìa* ☎*0577/48033*).

FOOD & DRINK

Antico Pizzicheria (⊠ *Via di Città 93–95, Città* ☎*0577/289164*) has been a *salumeria* (delicatessen) since 1889. The cheeses, cured meats, and made-to-order panini are top-notch. Bruno De Miccoli stocks an impressive array of verdure sott'olio, local wines, and dried herbs at **La Bottega dei Sapori Antichi** (⊠ *Via delle Terme 39–41, Camollìa* ☎*0577/285501*). Locals flock to **Nannini** (⊠ *Banchi di Sopra 24, Camollìa* ☎*0577/236009*) to quaff a cappuccino and to pick up panforte (the chocolate panforte is a real treat) and ricciarelli to go.

Enoteca Italiana (⊠ *Fortezza Medicea, Camollìa* ☎*0577/288497*), Italy's only state-sponsored enoteca, has a vast selection of wines from all parts of the country. Housed in the fortress that the Florentines built to dominate Siena after they conquered the town in 1555, it's a must for any lover of Italian wines.

MONTERIGGIONI & COLLE DI VAL D'ELSA

From Siena the Via Cassia (SR2) heading north passes through two pretty towns, Monteriggioni and Colle di Val d'Elsa. Both are well worth visiting: Monteriggioni, for its spectacularly well-preserved ring of medieval walls, and Colle di Val d'Elsa for the elegance of its 15th-century upper town.

MONTERIGGIONI

19 km (12 mi) northwest of Siena, 55 km (34 mi) south of Florence.

GETTING HERE

You can reach Monteriggioni by car on either the SR2 or the Florence–Siena Superstrada. Buses run frequently to and from Siena. With frequent service to and from Siena, the closest train station to Monteriggioni is in Castellina Scalo. You will then have to reach Monteriggioni on foot—it's a 4 km (2½ mi) walk.

VISITOR INFORMATION

Monteriggioni tourism office (⊠*Piazza Roma 23* ☎*0577/304810*).

EXPLORING

Tiny Monteriggioni makes a nice stop on the way north to Colle di Val d'Elsa, San Gimignano, or Volterra. It's hard to imagine that this little town surrounded by poppy fields was ever anything but sleepy, but in the 13th century Monteriggioni served as Siena's northernmost defense against impending Florentine invasion. (It's likely that the residents of the town spent many a sleepless night.) The town's formidable walls are in good condition, although the 14 square towers are not as tall as in Dante's (1265–1321) time, when the poet likened them to the four giants who guarded the horrifying central pit of hell. The town empties of day-trippers at sundown, and this hamlet becomes very tranquil.

WHERE TO STAY & EAT

$$–$$$ ✗**Il Pozzo.** Famous for its preparation of a 16th-century recipe of *cinghiale al cioccolato* (wild boar stewed in chocolate sauce), this restaurant is a popular spot. Tamer specialties include a range of homemade fresh pastas, *filetto alla boscaiola* (fillet of beef with porcini mushrooms), *piccione ripieno* (stuffed squab), and a long list of homey desserts. ⊠*Piazza Roma 2* ☎*0577/304127* ▤*AE, DC, MC, V* ⊗*Closed Mon., last 3 wks in Jan.–mid-Feb. No dinner Sun.*

$$$ 🏨**Borgo San Luigi.** This 17th-century villa lined with lavender bushes and cypress trees sits just outside Monteriggioni. The guest rooms in the villa and the adjacent workers' quarters—converted into 10 apartments—have wood-beam ceilings and terra-cotta floors. Festive striped fabrics in yellows, oranges, and reds cover iron canopies in some rooms. The facilities, such as the health club and the tennis courts, are those of a four-star establishment. A poolside restaurant is open in summer. **Pros:** Good base for exploring Siena, some rooms have kitchens, excellent gym and pool. **Cons:** Somewhat isolated, few restaurants are located within walking distance. ⊠*Strada della Cerreta 7, 4 km (2½ mi) southwest of Monteriggioni, Località San Luigi Strove, 53035* ☎*0577/301055* ⊕*www.borgosanluigi.it* ⇗*54 rooms, 10 apartments* ⌂*In-room: safe, kitchen (some), VCR. In-hotel: restaurant, room service, bar, tennis courts, pool, gym, concierge, public Internet, public Wi-Fi, some pets allowed* ▤*AE, DC, MC, V* ⦿*BP.*

$$$ 🏨**Hotel Monteriggioni.** A sense of freshness comes from the terra-cotta floors, high wood-beamed ceilings, and soothing whitewashed walls in the hotel's guest rooms. The serene garden, facing a town wall, is filled with oleanders, geraniums, and olive trees. **Pros:** Great location inside town walls, well-appointed rooms, peaceful setting. **Cons:** No views beyond the walls, no nightlife to speak of. ⊠*Via il Maggio 4, 53035* ☎*0577/305009* ⊕*www.hotelmonteriggioni.net* ⇗*12 rooms* ⌂*In-room: safe, dial-up. In-hotel: restaurant, pool, laundry service, public Internet, some pets allowed,* ▤*AE, DC, MC, V* ⊗*Closed Jan. 9–Feb. 28* ⦿*BP.*

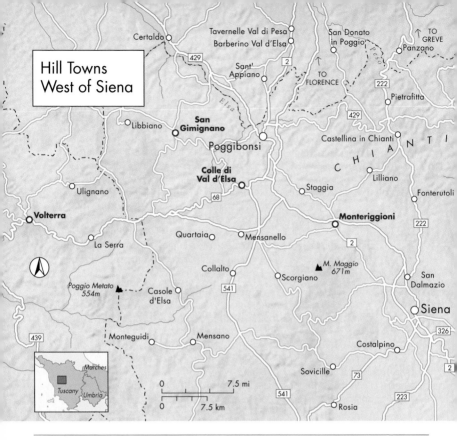

COLLE DI VAL D'ELSA

12 km (7 mi) west of Monteriggioni, 25 km (16 mi) northwest of Siena, 51 km (32 mi) south of Florence.

GETTING HERE
You can reach Colle di Val d'Elsa by car on either the SR2 from Siena or the Florence–Siena Superstrada. Bus service to and from Siena and Florence is frequent.

VISITOR INFORMATION
Colle di Val d'Elsa Tourism Office (⊠ *Via Campana 43* ☎ *0577/922791*).

EXPLORING
Most people pass through on their way to and from popular tourist destinations Volterra and San Gimignano—a shame, since Colle di Val d'Elsa has a lot to offer. It's another town on the Via Francigena that benefited from trade along the pilgrimage route to Rome. Colle got an extra boost in the late 16th century when it was given a bishopric, probably related to an increase in trade when nearby San Gimignano was cut off from the well-traveled road. The town is arranged on two levels, and from the 12th century onward the flat lower portion was given over to a flourishing paper-making industry; today the area is

mostly modern, and efforts have shifted toward the production of fine glass and crystal.

Make your way from the newer lower town (Colle Bassa) to the prettier, upper part of town (Colle Alta); the best views of the valley are to be had from Viale della Rimembranza, the road that loops around the western end of town, past the church of San Francesco. The early-16th-century Porta Nuova was inserted into the pre-existing medieval walls, just as several handsome Renaissance palazzos were placed into the medieval neighborhood to create what is now called the Borgo. The Via Campana, the main road, passes through the facade of the surreal Palazzo Campana, an otherwise unfinished building that serves as a door connecting the two parts of the upper town. Via delle Volte, named for the vaulted arches that cover it, leads straight to Piazza del Duomo. There is a convenient parking lot off the SS68, with stairs leading up the hill. Buses arrive at Piazza Arnolfo, named after the town's favorite son, Arnolfo di Cambio (circa 1245–1302), the early-Renaissance architect who designed Florence's Duomo and Palazzo Vecchio (but sadly nothing here).

WORD OF MOUTH

"What Tuscany has to offer is beautiful vistas and winding roads that take you to small towns and villages—like Monteriggioni. We found it on the way to Siena from Florence. It was a charming walled village. When we got home, we found out that Dante described the well in the center of the piazza as the entrance to hell in his *Divine Comedy*." –tony

The 15th-century **Chiesa di Santa Caterina** has a stained-glass window in the apse executed by Sebastiano Mainardi (circa 1460–1513), as well as a haunting *Pietà* created by local artist Zacchia Zacchi (1473–1544). ⊠ *Via Campana* 🕾 *No phone* 🖅 *Free* 🕘 *Daily 8–noon and 3–6.*

Several reconstructions have left little to admire of the once-Romanesque **Duomo.** Inside is the **Cappella del Santo Chiodo** (Chapel of the Holy Nail), built in the 15th century to hold a nail allegedly from the cross upon which Christ was crucified. (Perhaps it inspired the locals to go into the nail-making business, which became another of the town's flourishing industries.) ⊠ *Piazza del Duomo* 🕾 *No phone* 🖅 *Free* 🕘 *Daily 8–noon and 4–6.*

The **Museo Civico e d'Arte Sacra** displays religious relics as well as triptychs from the Sienese and Florentine schools dating from the 14th and 15th centuries. It also contains the town's tribute to Arnolfo di Cambio, with photos of the buildings he designed for other towns. Down Via del Castello, at No. 63, is the house-tower where Arnolfo was born in 1245. (It's not open to the public.) Note that despite the posted opening times, winter hours are highly variable. ⊠ *Via del Castello 33* 🕾 *0577/923888* 🖅 *€3* 🕘 *Apr.–Oct., Tues.–Sun. 10:30–12:30 and 4:30–7:30; Nov.–Mar., weekends 10:30–noon and 3:30–6:30.*

WHERE TO STAY & EAT

$$$$ ✕ **L'Antica Trattoria.** Residents of Colle di Val d'Elsa hold this trattoria in high esteem, even though it's a little overpriced. Tuscan classics fill the large menu, which concentrates on game, particularly pheasant, pigeon, and quail. Some of the pastas, such as *tortelli di sedano in purea di fagioli* (stuffed pasta with creamy celery and topped with a light bean puree) differ from the usual fare. The decor is simple; in warmer months outdoor seating on a square is a possibility. The service is first-rate. ⊠ *Piazza Arnolfo di Cambio 23, 53034* ☎ *0577/923747* ⛴ *Reservations essential* ▭ *AE, DC, MC, V* ⊘ *Closed Tues. and last wk in Aug.*

$$$$ ✕ **Ristorante Arnolfo.** Food lovers should not miss Arnolfo, one of Tus-
Fodor's Choice cany's most highly regarded restaurants. Chef Gaetano Trovato sets
★ high standards of creativity; his dishes daringly ride the line between innovation and tradition, almost always with spectacular results. The menu changes frequently and has a fixed-price option, but you are always sure to find fish and lots of fresh vegetables in the summer. You're in for a special treat if the specials include *carrè di agnello al vino rosso e sella alle olive* (rack of lamb in a red wine sauce and lamb saddle with olives). ⊠ *Piazza XX Settembre 52, 53034* ☎ *0577/920549* ▭ *AE, DC, MC, V* ⊘ *Closed Tues. and Wed., last wk in Jan.–Feb., and last wk in Aug.*

✕ **Molino il Moro.** The early-12th-century grain mill, now a romantic restaurant, is perched over a rushing river. The chef concocts sophisti-cated spins on traditional dishes, such as the divine *filetto di coniglio in crosta con purè di pruge* (rabbit loin with a prune puree). The wine list is short but sweet, the service note-perfect. ⊠ *Via della Ruota 2, 53034* ☎ *0577/920862* ▭ *AE, DC, MC, V* ⊘ *Closed Mon. No lunch Tues.*

¢ ✕ **L'Angolo di Sapia.** A short and simple set menu that changes with the seasons is one of the reasons to eat here. The other is the sweeping view from the terrace of the countryside below. You might want to start with the *piatto misto* (mixed plate, which in this case includes a slice of vegetable tart and mozzarella and tomatoes) and then continue with one of the house specialties like the *topini della torre* (gnocchi in a vibrant saffron sauce). Every evening there's a cocktail hour with an ample free buffet. ⊠ *Via del Castello 4, 53034* ☎ *0577/921453* ▭ *DC, MC, V* ⊘ *Closed Mon.–Wed. Oct.–Apr. No lunch.*

$$$$ ⌂ **La Suvera.** Pope Julius II once owned this luxurious estate in the
★ valley of the River Elsa. The papal villa and an adjacent building have magnificently furnished guest rooms and suites appointed with antiques. A wall-size tapestry depicting the Roman army hangs beside a red canopy bed in the Angels Room. La Suvera's first-rate facili-ties include drawing rooms, a library, an Italian garden, a park, and the Oliviera restaurant (serving organic estate wines). **Pros:** Luxuri-ous accommodations, historic setting, far from the madding crowd. **Cons:** Out-of-the-way location, showing its age, some bristle at the extremely formal service. ⊠ *Off SS541* ✛ *15 km (9 mi) south of Colle di Val d'Elsa, Pievescola, 53030* ☎ *0577/960300* ⊕ *www.lasuvera.it* ⤶ *36 rooms, 12 suites* ♿ *In-room: safe, refrigerator. In-hotel: restau-rant, room service, bar, tennis court, pool, bicycles, concierge, laundry*

service, public Internet, no kids under 12 ⊟AE, DC, MC, V ⊗Closed Nov.–Easter †◎|BP.

$–$$ ⊞**Villa Belvedere.** The Conti-Iannone family has been running this place since 1984, and a visit here feels like you've dropped in on friends. The 17th-century villa has lovely guest rooms, some of which have three beds (with an option for adding a fourth), making this a good spot for families. A classic garden provides a place to read or enjoy a drink, and the two on-site restaurants serve local specialties. On a good day you can glimpse San Gimignano in the distance. A fair amount of traffic passes the hotel, so ask for a room that does not face the street. Half board is available. **Pros:** Family-friendly environment, spacious rooms, good restaurants. **Cons:** Traffic noise can be a problem, no a/c. ⊠Località Belvedere ✛ 1½ km (1 mi) south on SS2, 53034 ☎0577/920966 ⊟0577/924128 ⊕www.villabelvedere.com ⤶15 rooms △In-room: no a/c. In-hotel: restaurants, bar, tennis court, pool, parking (no fee), some pets allowed ⊟AE, DC, MC, V.

SHOPPING

The crystal at **Cristalleria Ceramica Artistica** (⊠Via Castello 40 ☎0577/959666) runs the gamut from conventional to inspired: particularly gorgeous are the opaque-glass vases, which look as if they'd just been dug up, intact, from Etruscan tombs. Art meets contemporary design in the glass objects at **La Molleria Gelli** (⊠Via delle Romite 26 ☎0577/920163). The slanted champagne flutes are a marvel of engineering, as are the wine carafes, shaped like a child's top, that perfectly balance and gently spin.

SAN GIMIGNANO

Fodor's Choice
★
14 km (9 mi) northwest of Colle di Val d'Elsa, 38 km (24 mi) northwest of Siena, 54 km (34 mi) southwest of Florence.

When you're on a hilltop surrounded by soaring medieval towers silhouetted against the sky, it's difficult not to fall under the spell of San Gimignano. Its tall walls and narrow streets are typical of Tuscan hill towns, but it's the medieval "skyscrapers" that set the town apart from its neighbors. Today 14 towers remain, but at the height of the Guelph–Ghibelline conflict there was a forest of more than 70, and it was possible to cross the town by rooftop rather than by road. The towers were built partly for defensive purposes—they were a safe refuge and useful for pouring boiling oil on attacking enemies—and partly for bolstering the egos of their owners, who competed with deadly seriousness to build the highest tower in town.

The relative proximity of San Gimignano, arguably Tuscany's best-preserved medieval hill town, to Siena and Florence also makes it one of Italy's most visited. But the traffic is hardly a new thing; the Etruscans were encamped here, and the Romans made it an outpost. With the yearly flow of pilgrims to and from Rome in the Middle Ages, the town—then known as Castel di Selva—became a prosperous market center. When locals prayed to a martyred bishop from Modena for

relief from invading barbarians, relief they got, and in gratitude they rechristened the town in his honor as San Gimignano. Devastated by the Black Death of 1348, the town subsequently fell under Florentine control. Things got going again in the Renaissance, with some of the best and brightest painters in the area—Ghirlandaio (1449–94), Benozzo Gozzoli (1420–97), and Pinturicchio (circa 1454–1513)—coming to work, but soon after, the main road was moved, cutting San Gimignano off from the main trade route and sending it into decline.

Today San Gimignano isn't much more than a gentrified walled city, touristy but still very much worth exploring because, despite the profusion of cheesy souvenir shops lining the main drag, there's some serious Renaissance art to be seen here. Tour groups arrive early and clog the wine-tasting rooms—San Gimignano is famous for its light white Vernaccia—and art galleries for much of the day, but most sights stay open through late afternoon, when all the tour groups have long since departed.

GETTING HERE
You can reach San Gimignano by car from the Florence–Siena Superstrada. Exit at Poggibonsi Nord and follow signs for San Gimignano. Although it involves changing buses in Poggibonsi, getting to San Gimi-

gnano by bus is a relatively straightforward affair. SITA operates the service between Siena or Florence and Poggibonsi, while Tra-In takes care of the Poggibonsi to San Gimignano route. You cannot reach San Gimignano by train.

VISITOR INFORMATION
San Gimignano tourism office (✉ *Piazza Duomo 1* ☎ *0577/940008* ⊕ *www.sangimignano.com*).

EXPLORING SAN GIMIGNANO

The center of San Gimignano is closed to traffic. If you arrive by car, there are parking lots next to the Parco della Rimembranza, near Porta San Giovanni, the main pedestrian entrance into town. Buses from Florence and Siena all stop at Porta San Giovanni. Follow Via San Giovanni a short way to the center of town. Souvenir shops lining the way leave no doubt about the lifeblood of the town, but better things lie ahead. Pass under Arco dei Becci, a leftover from the city's Etruscan walls, to Piazza della Cisterna, a square named for the cistern at its center. The Piazza del Duomo, where you'll find the Museo Civico, lies just beyond the two towers built by the Ardinghelli family. Continue along Via San Matteo and turn right just before Porta San Matteo to reach Sant'Agostino.

TIMING You can see all of San Gimignano's main sights in a single day. But, if you arrive in the morning and leave in the afternoon, you miss the town at its best. From 9 to 5 tourists on jaunts from Florence and Siena swarm San Gimignano's streets, filling the shops and museums. In the evening, when all the day-trippers have departed, the town is transformed. Reclaiming its serenity, San Gimignano takes on a magically medieval air that, if you can possibly stay the night in or near town, is not to be missed.

MAIN ATTRACTIONS

❷ The town's main church is not officially a *duomo* (cathedral) because San Gimignano has no bishop. Behind the simple facade of the Romanesque **Collegiata** lies a treasure trove of fine frescoes, covering nearly every part of the interior. Bartolo di Fredi's 14th-century fresco cycle of Old Testament scenes extends along one wall. Their distinctly medieval feel, with misshapen bodies, buckets of spurting blood, and lack of perspective, contrasts with the much more reserved scenes from the *Life of Christ* (attributed to 14th-century artist Lippo Memmi), painted on the opposite wall just 14 years later. Taddeo di Bartolo's otherworldly *Last Judgment* (late 14th century), with its distorted and suffering nudes, reveals the great influence of Dante's horrifying imagery in *The Inferno* and was surely an inspiration for later painters. Proof that the town had more than one protector, Benozzo Gozzoli's arrow-riddled *St. Sebastian* was commissioned in gratitude after the locals prayed to the saint for relief from plague. The Renaissance **Cappella di Santa Fina** is decorated with a fresco cycle by Domenico Ghirlandaio illustrating the life of Saint Fina. A small girl who suffered from a terminal disease, Fina repented for her sins—among them having accepted an orange from a boy—and in penance lived out the rest of her short life on a wooden board, tormented by rats. The scenes depict the arrival of Saint Gregory, who appeared to assure her that death was near; the flowers that miraculously grew from the wooden plank; and the miracles that accompanied her funeral, including the healing of her nurse's paralyzed hand and the restoration of a blind choirboy's vision. ⊠ *Piazza Duomo* ☎ *0577/940316* ⌗ *€3.50; €5.50 includes the Museo d'Arte Sacra* ⊙ *Apr.–Oct., weekdays 9:30–7:10, Sat. 9:30–5:10, Sun. 12:30–5:10; Nov. 1–15, Dec. 1–Jan. 15, and Feb. 1–Mar., Mon.–Sat. 9:30–4:40, Sun. 12:30–5:10. Closed Nov. 16–30 and Jan. 16–31.*

❺ The impressive **Museo Civico** occupies what was the "new" Palazzo del
★ Popolo; the Torre Grossa is adjacent. Dante visited San Gimignano for only one day as a Guelph ambassador from Florence to ask the locals to join the Florentines in supporting the pope—just long enough to get the main council chamber, which now holds a 14th-century *Maestà* by Lippo Memmi, named after him. Off the stairway is a small room containing the racy frescoes by Memmo di Filippuccio (active 1288–1324), depicting the courtship, shared bath, and wedding of a young, androgynous-looking couple. That the space could have been a private room for the commune's chief magistrate may have something to do with the work's highly charged eroticism.

Upstairs, paintings by famous Renaissance artists Pinturicchio (*Madonna Enthroned*), and Benozzo Gozzoli (*Madonna and Child*), and two large *tondi* (circular paintings) by Filippino Lippi (circa 1457–1504) attest to the importance and wealth of San Gimignano. Also worth seeing are Taddeo di Bartolo's *Life of San Gimignano*, with the saint holding a model of the town as it once appeared; Lorenzo di Niccolò's gruesome martyrdom scene in the *Life of St. Bartholomew* (1401); and scenes from the *Life of St. Fina* on a tabernacle that was designed to hold her head. Admission includes the steep climb to the top of the Torre Grossa, which on a clear day has spectacular views. ⊠ *Piazza Duomo* ☎ *0577/990312* ⌗ *€5* ⊙ *Mar.–Oct., daily 9:30–7; Nov.–Feb., daily 10–5:30.*

There's no shortage of places to try Vernaccia di San Gimignano, the justifiably famous white wine with which San Gimignano would be singularly associated—if it weren't for all those towers. At **Enoteca Gustavo** (⊠ *Via San Matteo 29* ☎ *0577/940057*) you can buy a glass of Vernaccia di San Gimignano and sit down with a cheese plate or with one of the fine crostini served up in this tiny wine bar.

❶ Make a beeline for Benozzo Gozzoli's superlative frescoes inside the
★ church of **Sant'Agostino**. This Romanesque–Gothic church contains Benozzo's stunning 15th-century fresco cycle depicting scenes from the life of Saint Augustine. The saint's work was essential to the early development of church doctrine. As thoroughly discussed in his autobiographical *Confessions* (an acute dialogue with God), Augustine, like many saints, sinned considerably in his youth before finding God. But unlike the lives of other saints, where the story continues through a litany of deprivations, penitence, and often martyrdom, Augustine's

life and work focused on philosophy and the reconciliation of faith and thought. Benozzo's 17 scenes on the choir wall depict Augustine as a man who traveled and taught extensively in the 4th and 5th centuries. The 15th-century altarpiece by Piero del Pollaiolo (1443–96) depicts *The Coronation of the Virgin* and the various protectors of the city. On your way out of Sant'Agostino, stop in at the **Cappella di San Bartolo,** with a sumptuously elaborate tomb by Benedetto da Maiano (1442–97). ⊠*Piazza Sant'Agostino, off Via San Matteo* ☎*0577/907012* ✆*Free* ⊗*Apr.–Oct., daily 7–noon and 3–7; Nov. and Dec. and Mar., daily 7–noon and 3–6; Jan. and Feb., Mon. 3–6, Tues. –Sun. 10–noon and 3–6.*

ALSO WORTH SEEING

❹ Proving that the Middle Ages were about more than walled towns, intricate mosaics, and illuminated manuscripts, the private **Museo di Criminologia Medioevale** exhibits what was once the cutting edge in torture technology. Though some scholars dispute the historical accuracy of many of the instruments, the final, very contemporary object—an electric chair imported from the United States—is real. ⊠*Via del Castello 1–3* ☎*0577/942243* ✆*€8* ⊗*Nov.–mid-Mar., Mon.–Sat. 10–6, Sun. 10–7; mid-Mar.–July, daily 10–8; Aug., daily 10–midnight; Sept. and Oct., daily 10–8.*

❻ Even with all the decoration in the Collegiata, the fine collection of various religious articles at the **Museo d'Arte Sacra,** through the pretty courtyard, is still worth a look. The highlight is a *Madonna and Child* by Bartolo di Fredi. Other pieces include several busts, wooden statues of Christ and the Virgin Mary and the angel Gabriel, and several illuminated songbooks. ⊠*Piazza Pecori 4* ☎*0577/940316* ✆*€3; €5.50 includes the Collegiata* ⊗*Apr.–Oct., weekdays 9:30–7:10, Sat. 9:30–5:10, Sun. 12:30–5:10; Nov. 1–15, Dec. 1–Jan. 15, and Feb. and Mar., Mon.–Sat. 9:30–4:40, Sun. 12:30–4:40. Closed Nov. 16–30 and Jan. 16–31.*

❸ Across the piazza from the Collegiata is the **Palazzo del Podestà,** the "old" town hall built in 1239. Its tower was erected by the municipality in 1255 to settle the raging "my-tower-is-bigger-than-your-tower" contest—as you can see, a solution that just didn't last long. ⊠*Piazza Duomo.*

❼ If you want to see more of that quintessential Tuscan landscape, walk up to the **Rocca di Montestaffoli.** Built after the Florentine conquest to keep an eye on the town, and dismantled a few centuries later, it's now a public garden. ⊠*Off Porta Quercecchio* ☎*No phone* ✆*Free* ⊗*Daily dawn–dusk.*

❽ From the Rocca take the steps down to get to the **Museo Ornitologico,** housed in a former church. It contains a 19th-century collection of more than 300 birds. ⊠*Via Quercecchio* ☎*0577/941388* ✆*€1.50* ⊗*Apr.–Sept., daily 11–5:30.*

WHERE TO EAT

$–$$ ✕**La Mangiatoia.** Multicolored gingham tablecloths provide an interesting juxtaposition with rib-vaulted ceilings dating from the 13th century. The lighthearted touch might be explained by the influence of chef Susi Cuomo, who has been presiding over the kitchen for more than 20 years. The menu is seasonal—in autumn, don't miss her *sacottino di pecorino al tartufo* (little packages of pasta stuffed with pecorino and seasoned with truffles). In summer eat lighter fare on the intimate, flower-bedecked terrace in the back. ⊠ *Via Mainardi 5, off Via San Matteo, 53037* ☏ *0577/941528* ▭ *MC, V* ⊗ *Closed Tues., 3 wks in Nov., and 1 wk in Jan.*

¢–$ ✕**Osteria del Carcere.** Though it calls itself an *osteria* (a tavern), this place much more resembles a wine bar, with a bill of fare that includes several different types of pâtés and a short list of seasonal soups and salads. The sampler of goat cheeses, which can be paired with local wines, should not be missed. Operatic arias play softly in the background, and service is courteous. ⊠ *Via del Castello 1353037* ☏ *0577/941905* ▭ *No credit cards* ⊗ *Closed Wed. and early Jan.–Mar. No lunch Thurs.*

WHERE TO STAY

The **Cooperativa Hotels Promotion** (⊠ *Via di San Giovanni 125* ☏ *0577/940809* ⊕ *www.hotelsiena.com*) provides commission-free booking for local hotels and farmhouses.

$$$$ ⌂ **La Collegiata.** After serving as a Franciscan convent and then the residence of the noble Strozzi family, the Collegiata has been converted into a fine hotel, with no expense spared in the process. Arched, multi-pane windows look out on the surrounding park. All the guest rooms (some with private balconies) are furnished with a mix of wood and upholstered antiques in warm browns and reds, and precious tapestries. Bathrooms have large whirlpool baths. A summer restaurant occupies the deconsecrated church, with tables set out near the entrance. **Pros:** Gorgeous views from terrace, elegant rooms in main building. **Cons:** Long walk into town, service can be impersonal, some rooms are dimly lit. ⊠ *Località Strada 27* ⊹ *1 km (½ mi) north of San Gimignano town center, 53037* ☏ *0577/943201* ⊕ *www.lacollegiata.it* ☞ *20 rooms, 1 suite* ⌂ *In-room: safe. In-hotel: restaurant, room service, bar, pool, public Internet, parking (no fee), some pets allowed* ▭ *AE, DC, MC, V* ⊗ *Closed Jan. and Feb.* ⦿ *BP.*

$$ ⌂ **Bel Soggiorno.** If you're looking for a place within the town walls, this is a fine choice. Contemporary furnishings in the guest rooms are softened by warm, umber-color walls and floral artwork. A major draw here is the restaurant ($$$). One wall is glass, revealing a sweeping view of a Tuscan hillside. The dining room itself is simple and rustic; the food, however, is not: the *petto di faraona con mele condite, salsa*

4

al miele e pecorino di fossa (breast of guinea fowl with apples, honey, and aged pecorino) is a real treat. The same family has run both the hotel and the restaurant since 1886. **Pros:** Inside the ancient walls of San Gimignano, magnificent views, some rooms have small terraces facing the countryside. **Cons:** Plain decor, sombre public spaces. ⊠ *Via San Giovanni 91, 53037* ☎*0577/940375* ⊕*www.hotelbelsoggiorno. it* ⤶*21 rooms* △*In-room: refrigerator. In-hotel: restaurant, laundry service, public Internet, parking (fee)* ⊟*AE, DC, MC, V* ⊘*Closed late Nov.–late Dec. and 2 wks in Feb. Restaurant closed Wed.* ⦿*BP.*

$-$$ 🏠**Pescille.** A rambling farmhouse has been transformed into a handsome hotel with understated contemporary furniture in the bedrooms and country-classic motifs such as farm implements hanging on the walls in the bar. From this charming spot you get a splendid view of San Gimignano's towers. **Pros:** Splendid views, quiet atmosphere, 10-minute walk to town. **Cons:** Furnishings a bit austere, there's an elevator for luggage but not for guests. ⊠ *Strada Provinciale Castel San Gimignano, Località Pescille* ⤢*4 km (2½ mi) south of San Gimignano town center, 53037* ☎*0577/940186* ⊕*www.pescille.it* ⤶*38 rooms, 12 suites* △*In-room: refrigerator, Wi-Fi. In-hotel: bar, tennis court, pool, gym, no elevator, public Internet, public Wi-Fi, parking (no fee)* ⊟*AE, DC, MC, V* ⊘*Closed Nov.–Mar.* ⦿*BP.*

NIGHTLIFE & THE ARTS

San Gimignano is one of the few small towns in the area that make a big deal out of **Carnevale** festivities, with locals dressing up in colorful costumes and marching through the streets from 3:30 to 6:30 on the four Sundays preceding Shrove Tuesday.

If you visit in summer, check with the tourist office about concerts and performances related to the **Estate San Gimignanese** (⊠*Piazza Duomo 1* ☎*0577/940008* ⊕*www.sangimignano.com*), one of Tuscany's oldest summer arts festivals. It's held mid-June to August each year.

SHOPPING

Antica Latteria di Maurizio e Tiziana (⊠ *Via San Matteo 19* ☎*0577/941952*) has an arresting collection of cheeses, and perhaps the best array of verdure sott'olio in town. It also makes top-notch panini.

As everywhere else, the town brightens on **open-air market** mornings, every Thursday and Saturday, in Piazza del Duomo. It's the place to pick up fresh fruits and other snacks.

VOLTERRA

30 km (18 mi) southwest of San Gimignano.

As you approach the town through bleak, rugged terrain, you can see that not all Tuscan hill towns rise above rolling green fields. Volterra stands mightily over Le Balze, a stunning series of gullied hills and valleys formed by erosion that has slowly eaten away at the foundation of the town—now considerably smaller than it was during its Etruscan glory days 25 centuries ago. The town began as the northernmost city of the 12 that made up the Etruscan League, and excavations in the 18th century revealed a bounty of relics, which are on exhibit at the impressively overstocked Museo Etrusco Guarnacci. The Romans and later the Florentines laid siege to the town to secure its supply of minerals and stones, particularly alabaster, which is still worked into handicrafts on sale in many of the shops around town.

GETTING HERE

By car, the best route from San Gimignano follows the SP1 south to Castel San Gimignano and then the SS68 all the way to Volterra. Coming from the west, take the SS1, a coastal road to Cecina, then follow the SS68 to Volterra. Either way, there's a long, winding climb at the end of your trip. Traveling to Volterra by bus or train is complicated; avoid it if possible, especially if you have lots of luggage. From Florence or Siena, the journey is best made by bus and involves a change in Colle di Val d'Elsa. From Rome or Pisa, it is best to take the train to Cecina and then take a bus to Volterra or a train to the Volterra-Saline station. The latter is 10 km (6 mi) from town.

VISITOR INFORMATION

Volterra tourism office (✉ *Piazza dei Priori 20* ☎ *0588/87257* ⊕ *www. volterratur.it*).

EXPLORING VOLTERRA

Driving in the old town is forbidden. There are several parking lots around the perimeter of the city walls, the most convenient of which is the underground parking lot at Piazza Martiri della Libertà. Begin your exploration of Volterra from Piazza Martiri della Libertà and take Via Marchesi to Piazza dei Priori. It's lined with an impressive collection of medieval buildings, including the imposing Palazzo dei Priori, the seat of city government for more than seven centuries. Across the piazza is the Palazzo Pretorio topped by the Torre del Porcellino, named after the sculpted little boar mounted at the upper window. Walk down Via Turazza along the side of the Duomo to the triangular Piazza San Giovanni, and head out the left corner of the piazza to steal a look at the ancient Porta all'Arco Etrusco.

TIMING   Allow at least three hours to see the town. Off-season, it's best to make an early start in order to have time in the museums before they close. The whole town can easily be seen in a day, although its distance from everything else makes it a good stopover as well.

MAIN ATTRACTIONS

6 **Duomo.** Behind the textbook 13th-century Pisan–Romanesque facade is proof that Volterra counted for something during the Renaissance, when many important Tuscan artists came to decorate the church. Three-dimensional stucco portraits of local saints are on the gold, red, and blue ceiling (1580) designed by Francesco Capriani, including

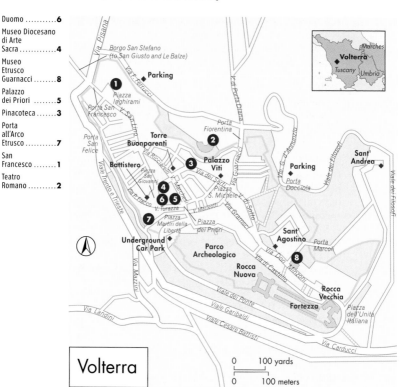

Volterra

0   100 yards
0   100 meters

Saint Linus, the successor to Saint Peter as pope and claimed by the Volterrans to have been born here. The highlight of the Duomo is the brightly painted 13th-century wooden life-size *Deposition* in the chapel of the same name. The unusual Cappella dell'Addolorata (Chapel of the Grieved) has two terra-cotta Nativity scenes; the depiction of the arrival of the Magi has a background fresco by Benozzo Gozzoli. The 16th-century pulpit in the middle of the nave is lined with fine 14th-century sculpted panels, attributed to a member of the Pisano family. Across from the Duomo in the center of the piazza is the **Battistero,** with stripes that match the Duomo. Evidently this baptistery got a lot of use, as the small marble baptismal font carved by Andrea Sansovino in 1502 was moved to the wall to the right of the entrance in the mid-18th century to make room for a larger one. ⊠*Piazza San Giovanni* ☎*0588/86192* ⊡*Free* ☉*Daily 7–7.*

❽ **Museo Etrusco Guarnacci.** An extraordinarily large and unique collection of Etruscan relics is made all the more interesting by clear explanations in English. The bulk of the collection is comprised of roughly 700 carved funerary urns: the oldest, dating from the 7th century BC, were made from tufa (volcanic rock); a handful are made of terra-cotta; and the vast majority—from the 3rd to 1st century BC—are from alabaster. The urns are grouped by subject and taken together form a fascinating testimony about Etruscan life and death. Some illustrate domestic scenes, others the funeral procession of the deceased. Greek gods and mythology, adopted by the Etruscans, also figure prominently. The sculpted figures on many of the covers may have been made in the image of the deceased, reclining and often holding the cup of life overturned. Particularly well known is *Gli Sposi (Husband and Wife)*, a haunting, elderly duo in terra-cotta. Also on display are Attic vases, bucchero ceramics, jewelry, and household items. ⊠ *Via Don Minzoni 15* ☎ *0588/86347* ⊕ *www.comune.volterra.pi.it* 🖃 *€8, includes admission to Museo Diocesano di Arte Sacra and Pinoteca* ☉ *Mid-Mar.–early Nov., daily 9–6:45; early Nov.–mid-Mar., daily 9–1:15.*

❸ Pinacoteca. One of Volterra's best-looking Renaissance buildings contains an impressive collection of Tuscan paintings arranged chronologically on two floors. Head straight for Room 12, with Luca Signorelli's (circa 1445–1523) *Madonna and Child with Saints* and Rosso Fiorentino's *Deposition*. Both are masterpieces, and though painted just 30 years apart, they serve to illustrate the shift in style from the early-16th-century Renaissance ideals to full-blown mannerism: the balance of Signorelli's composition becomes purposefully skewed in Fiorentino's painting, where the colors go from vivid but realistic to emotively bright. Other important paintings in the small museum include Ghirlandaio's *Apotheosis of Christ with Saints* and a polyptych of the *Madonna and Saints* by Taddeo di Bartolo, which once hung in the Palazzo dei Priori. ⊠ *Via dei Sarti 1* ☎ *0588/87580* ⊕ *www.comune. volterra.pi.it* 🖃 *€8, includes admission to Museo Etrusco Guarnacci and Museo Diocesano di Arte Sacra* ☉ *Mid-Mar.–early Nov., daily 9–7; early Nov.–mid-Mar., daily 9–1:45.*

❼ Porta all'Arco Etrusco. Even if a good portion of the arch was rebuilt by the Romans, the three dark, weather-beaten, 3rd-century BC heads carved in basaltic rock (thought to represent Etruscan gods) still face outward, greeting those who enter. A plaque recalls the efforts of the locals who saved the arch from destruction by filling it with stones during the German withdrawal at the end of World War II.

❷ Teatro Romano. Just outside the walls past Porta Fiorentina are the ruins of the 1st-century BC Roman theater, one of the best-preserved in Italy, with adjacent remains of the Roman *terme* (baths). ⊠ *Viale Francesco Ferrucci* ☎ *0586/260837* 🖃 *€2* ☉ *Mar.–May and Sept.–Nov., daily 10–1 and 2–4; June–Aug., daily 10–6:45; Dec.–Feb., weekends 10–1 and 2–4.*

ALSO WORTH SEEING

❹ Museo Diocesano di Arte Sacra. The religious-art collection housed in the Bishop's Palace was collected from local churches and includes an unusual reliquary by Antonio Pollaiolo with the head of Saint Octavian in silver resting on four golden lions. There's also a fine terra-cotta bust of Saint Linus by Andrea della Robbia (1435–1525/28). Two paintings are noteworthy: Rosso Fiorentino's (1495–1540) *Madonna di Villamagna* and Daniele da Volterra's (1509–66) *Madonna di Ulignano*, named for the village churches in which they were originally placed.

⊠*Palazzo Vescovile, Via Roma 1* ☎*0588/86290* ⊕*www.comune. volterra.pi.it* ☞*€8, includes admission to Museo Etrusco Guarnacci and Pinoteca* ⊙*Mid-Mar.–early Nov., daily 9–1 and 3–6; early Nov.–mid-Mar., daily 9–1.*

❺ Palazzo dei Priori. Tuscany's first town hall was built between 1208 and 1254, with a no-nonsense facade, fortresslike crenellations, and a five-sided tower. Such fortifications were commonplace at the time; these served as a model for other similar structures throughout the region, including Florence's Palazzo Vecchio. The Florentine medallions that adorn the facade here were added after the Florentines conquered Volterra. The town leaders still meet on the first floor in the Sala del Consiglio; the room is open to the public and has a mid-14th-century fresco of the *Annunciation.* ⊠*Piazza dei Priori* ☎*0588/87257* ☞*€1* ⊙*Mid-Mar.–Oct., daily 10:30–5:30; Nov.–mid-Mar., weekends 10–5.*

❶ San Francesco. Look inside the church for the celebrated early-15th-century frescoes of the *Legend of the True Cross* by a local artist. It traces the history of the wood used to make the cross upon which Christ was crucified. From Piazza San Giovanni, take Via Franceschini (which becomes Via San Lino) to the church. ⊠*Piazza Inghirami, off Via San Lino* ☎*No phone* ☞*Free* ⊙*Daily 8–noon and 3–6.*

OFF THE BEATEN PATH

Le Balze. Walk along Via San Lino, through Porta San Franceso, and out Borgo Santo Stefano into Le Balze—a desolate, undulating landscape of yellow earth drawn into crags and gullies as if worn down by a desert torrent long past. This area was originally part of the Etruscan town (called Vlathri; as usual, the current name is closer to the Roman name, Volaterrae), as evidenced by walls that extend 1 km (½ mi) toward the old Porta Menseri. Toward the end of the road, on the right, is the church of San Giusto (with terra-cotta statues of the town's patron saints). The church was built to replace an earlier church under which the earth had eroded. The haunting landscape is thought to have been created when rainwater collected and wore down the soil substructure. The bus for Borgo San Giusto, leaving from Piazza Martiri, goes through Le Balze (about 10 runs per day).

WHERE TO EAT

$–$$$ ✕**Il Sacco Fiorentino.** Start with the *antipasti del Sacco Fiorentino*—a
★ medley of sautéed chicken liver, porcini mushrooms, and polenta drizzled with balsamic vinegar. The meal just gets better when you move on to the *tagliatelle del Sacco Fiorentino*, a riot of curried spaghetti with chicken and roasted red peppers. The wine list is a marvel, as it's long and very well priced. White walls, tile floors, and red

Volterra's Porta all'Arco Etrusco.

tablecloths create an understated tone that is unremarkable, but once the food starts arriving, it's easy to forgive the lack of decoration. ✉ *Piazza XX Settembre 18, 56048* ☎ *0588/88537* ▭ *AE, DC, MC, V* ⊘ *Closed Wed.*

$–$$ ✕ **Da Badò.** This is the best place in town to eat traditional food elbow-to-elbow with the locals. Da Badò is family-run, with Lucia in the kitchen and her sons Giacomo and Michele waiting tables. Lucia likes to concentrate on just a few dishes, so it won't take long to decide between the standards, all prepared with a sure hand: *zuppa alla volterrana* (a soup made with vegetables and bread), *pappardelle alla lepre* (wide fettuccine with rabbit sauce), and a stew of either rabbit or wild boar. A slice of homemade almond tart is a must. ✉ *Borgo San Lazzaro 9, 56048* ☎ *0588/86477* ▭ *AE, DC, MC, V* ⊘ *Closed Wed.*

WHERE TO STAY

$ ▤ **San Lino.** Within the town's medieval walls, this convent-turned-hotel has wood-beam ceilings, graceful archways, and terra-cotta floors in public spaces. The furnishings are contemporary wood laminate and straight-line ironwork. Sip a beverage or write a postcard on the small terrace filled with potted geraniums; the pool area is framed on one side by a church with a stained-glass window of the Last Supper. The restaurant ($–$$) serves Tuscan classics and local specialties such as *zuppa alla volterrana,* a thick vegetable soup. Half board is available. **Pros:** Steps away from center of town, friendly and helpful staff, convenient parking. **Cons:** A little run-down; elevators are noisy; breakfast is adequate, but nothing to write home about. ⊠ *Via San Lino 26, 56048* ☎ *0588/85250* 🖷 *0588/80620* ⊕ *www.hotelsanlino.com* ⇆ *43 rooms* ⚭ *In-room: refrigerator, dial-up. In-hotel: restaurant, bar, pool, concierge, laundry service, public Internet, parking (fee), some pets allowed* ☰ *AE, DC, MC, V* ⊗ *Closed Nov.–Jan.* ⦿ *BP.*

NIGHTLIFE & THE ARTS

On the first Sunday in September the **Astiludio festival** celebrates a flag-throwing tradition that dates to 1406. Performances and processions are part of the activities.

SHOPPING

A large loom dominates in the tiny workshop/showroom where **Anna Maria Molesini** (⊠ *Via Gramsci 45* ☎ *0588/88411*) weaves scarves, shawls, throws, and jackets. Her work, mostly in mohair, is done in lively hues. At **Camillo Rossi** (⊠ *Via Lungo le Mura del Mandorlo 7* ☎ *0588/86133*) you can watch the artisans create household items in alabaster, and then buy their wares.

At **Cooperativa Artieri Alabastro** (⊠ *Piazza dei Priori 5* ☎ *0588/87590*) two large showrooms in medieval buildings contain a large number of alabaster objects for sale, including bookends, ashtrays, and boxes. In a former medieval monastery, **Galleria Agostiniane** (⊠ *Piazza XX Settembre 3* ☎ *0588/86868*) showcases alabaster objects. There's also a video demonstrating how the mineral is quarried and shaped.

Volterra's **mercato** *(market)* is held on Saturday morning from November to April in Piazza dei Priori, and on Viale Ferrucci (just outside the city walls) from May through October. On hand are a selection of fresh fruits and vegetables, as well as vendors selling everything from corkscrews to *intimi* (underwear).

It may be hard to imagine that much of central Tuscany was once the battleground of warring Sienese and Florentine armies, but until Florence finally defeated Siena in 1555, the enchanting walled cities of this gentle area were strategic-defensive outposts in a series of seemingly never-ending wars.

Arezzo, Cortona
& Eastern Tuscany

WORD OF MOUTH

"My wife and I spent two nights in Cortona several years ago.
It is a beautiful little hill town with few tourists."

—Padgett

WELCOME TO EASTERN TUSCANY

Arezzo

TOP REASONS TO GO

★ **Driving through the Parco Nazionale Casentino:** The vistas along the winding road of this park in the Casentino will not disappoint.

★ **Piero della Francesca's** *True Cross* **frescoes:** If your holy grail is great Renaissance art, seek out these 12 silently enigmatic scenes in Arezzo's Basilica di San Francesco.

★ **Santa Maria del Calcinaio:** The interior of this Cortona church is much like that of Florence's Duomo, and it's a prime example of Renaissance architecture.

★ **Shopping for jewelry in Arezzo:** Gold has been part of Arezzo's past since Etruscan times, and today the town is well known worldwide for jewelry design.

1 Arezzo. Tuscany's third-largest city feels a touch more cosmopolitan than the neighboring hill towns—meaning among other things that it has the best shopping in the region. The real draw, though, is the **Basilica di San Francesco**, adorned with frescoes by Piero della Francesca.

2 Cortona. This ancient stone town, made famous by the book *Under the Tuscan Sun*, sits high above the perfectly flat Valdichiana valley, offering great views of beautiful countryside.

3 Sansepolcro. Lovers of Renaissance painting make pilgrimages to out-of-the-way Sansepolcro, birthplace of Piero della Francesca. He often worked in, or near, his hometown, finding inspiration for the landscapes in his often enigmatic paintings.

Shop window, Arezzo

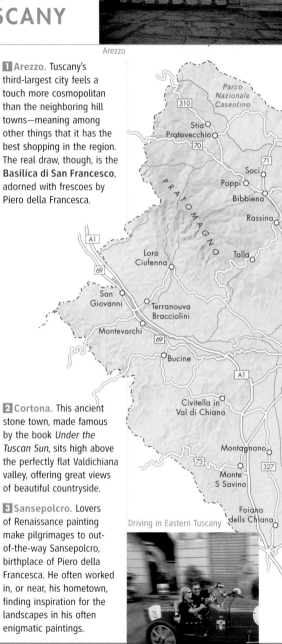

Driving in Eastern Tuscany

Via Colcitrone, Arezzo

4 The Casentino. A short distance north of Arezzo, the Casentino region is highlighted by the **Parco Nazionale Casentino**—a drive through the park reveals one gorgeous view after another. Dante, exiled here from Florence, recorded his love of the countryside in *The Divine Comedy*.

GETTING ORIENTED

The hill towns of Arezzo and Cortona are the main attractions of eastern Tuscany; despite their appeal, this part of the region gets less tourist traffic than its neighbors to the west. You'll truly escape the crowds if you venture north to the Casentino, which is backwoods Tuscany—tiny towns and abbeys are sprinkled through beautiful forestland, some of which is set aside as a national park.

Rooftops of Cortona

EASTERN TUSCANY PLANNER

Italy's National Parks

Parco Nazionale Casentino is one of Tuscany's finest "off the beaten path" experiences—the beautiful mountain scenery has been maintained and safeguarded by monks for eight centuries. It's also an example of Italy's burgeoning national parks system. There are currently 22 parks covering a total of around 1.5 million hectares (58,000 square miles), or about 5% of the country—more than twice as much as 25 years ago. And a new park is added or an existing park is expanded every few months (in 2008, three new parks were in line to join the list). The trend is a boon for nature lovers, who can enjoy huge expanses of unspoiled territory.

Statue of Ferdinando I, in Arezzo's Piazza della Libertà

Making the Most of Your Time

The lovely hill towns of **Arezzo** and **Cortona** serve as introductions to the region. They carry on age-old local traditions—each September Arezzo's beautiful Franciscan, Gothic, and Romanesque churches are enlivened by the Giostra del Saracino, a costumed medieval pageant. Since ancient times, Arezzo has been home to important artists: from the Etruscan potters who produced those fiery-red vessels to the poet Petrarch and Giorgio Vasari, writer, architect, and painter. Cortona, magnificently situated, with olive groves and vineyards creeping up to its walls, commands sweeping views over Lago Trasimeno and the plain of the Valdichiana. The delightful medieval streets are a pleasure to wander, and the town has two fine galleries and a scattering of churches that are worth a visit.

Plan on spending a good four days to tour the area. Arezzo and Cortona each merit a full day, and if you stay in the vicinity you'll have a good base from which to explore the countryside. Both towns are close to the A1 (Autostrada del Sole) and are on main train lines.

Finding a Place to Stay

A visit to Tuscany is a trip to the country. There are good hotels in Arezzo and Cortona, but for a classic experience stay in one of the rural accommodations—often converted villas, sometimes working farms or vineyards (known as *agriturismi*).

DINING & LODGING PRICE CATEGORIES (IN EUROS)

	¢	$	$$	$$$	$$$$
RESTAURANTS	under €15	€15–€25	€25–€35	€35–€45	over €45
HOTELS	under €70	€70–€110	€110–€160	€160–€220	over €220

Restaurant prices are for a first course (*primo*), second course (*secondo*), and dessert (*dolce*). Hotel prices are for two people in a standard double room in high season, including tax and service.

GETTING AROUND

By Car

The best way to travel within the region, making it possible to explore tiny hill towns and country restaurants, is by car. The roads are better north–south than east–west, so allow time for excessively winding roads when heading east or west. Sometimes it's faster to go a little out of your way and get on one of the bigger north–south routes.

The A1 (Autostrada del Sole), which runs from Florence to Rome, passes close to Arezzo. Cortona is just off the highway linking Perugia to the A1, and Sansepolcro can be reached from Arezzo on the SR73, with Monterchi a short 3-km (1½-mi) detour along the way.

Though Arezzo is the third-largest city in Tuscany (after Florence and Pisa), the old town is pretty small, and is on a low hill almost completely closed to traffic. Look for parking along the roads that circle the lower part of town, near the train station, and walk into town from there.

Just as in Arezzo, in Cortona the city center is completely closed to traffic, and the few parking areas sprinkled outside the city walls don't make it easy to park. The majority of Cortona's streets are very steep. Fortunately, most of the main sights are grouped near the Duomo in the lower part of town, but if you want to visit the upper town, be prepared for a stiff climb.

For visits to the mountainous National Park of the Casentino, and the smaller towns and villages farther to the east, such as Sansepolcro and Monterchi, a rental car is almost a necessity: bus schedules can be difficult to plan around, and train service is either infrequent or nonexistent. All make for rewarding day trips, though a fair part of your time will be spent on winding, beautiful, country roads. If you want time to explore, plan to stay the night.

By Bus

Bus service between Florence and Arezzo is provided three times daily by **SITA** (☎ 055/47821 in Florence, 0575/74361 in Sansepolcro, 800/373760 toll free in Italy ⊕ www.sitabus.it), which also offers a regular service between Arezzo and Cortona. Both SITA and the bus company **Baschetti** (☎ 0575/749816 in Sansepolcro ⊕ www.baschetti.it) provide service between Arezzo, Monterchi, and Sansepolcro.

All bus service in the province of Arezzo is coodinated by **Etruria Mobilità** (☎ 0575/39881 in Arezzo ⊕ www.etruriamobilita.it), a cooperative of eight different transport companies, including SITA and Baschetti; it's the best source for information about bus service to outlying towns in the region.

By Train

The national railway service, **Ferrovia dello Stato** (☎ 892021 in Italy ⊕ www.trenitalia.com), has frequent trains between Florence and Arezzo. A regular service links Arezzo with Cortona, and with Poppi and the Casentino, but between Arezzo and the coast, train service is scarce or nonexistent.

Updated
by Peter
Blackman

CLOSER TO ITALY'S RUGGED APENNINES than any other part of the region, eastern Tuscany hides its secrets in the deep valleys of the upper Arno and Tiber rivers, and among mountains covered with thick forests of chestnut, fir, and beech: it was here, at La Verna, that Saint Francis founded a sanctuary and received the signs of Christ's wounds, and here that Michelangelo first saw the light of day. This part of Tuscany invites those who seek a more contemplative approach to travel, away from the madding crowd.

AREZZO

Arezzo is today best known for the magnificent Piero della Francesca frescoes in the church of San Francesco. It's also the birthplace of the poet Petrarch (1304–74), the Renaissance artist and art historian Giorgio Vasari, and Guido d'Arezzo, the inventor of musical notation. Arezzo dates from pre-Etruscan times, when around 1000 BC the first settlers—who continue to puzzle scholars today—erected a cluster of huts. Arezzo thrived as an Etruscan capital from the 7th to the 4th centuries BC, and was one of the most important cities in the Etruscans' anti-Roman 12-city federation, resisting Rome's rule to the last.

The city eventually fell and in turn flourished under the Romans. In 1248 Guglielmino degli Ubertini, a member of the powerful Ghibelline family, was elected bishop of Arezzo. This sent the city headlong into the enduring conflict between the Ghibellines (pro-emperor) and the Guelphs (pro-pope). In 1289 Florentine Guelphs defeated Arezzo in a famous battle at Campaldino. Among the Florentine soldiers was Dante Alighieri (1265–1321), who often referred to Arezzo in his *Divine Comedy.* Guelph–Ghibelline wars continued to plague Arezzo until the end of the 14th century, when Arezzo lost its independence to Florence.

GETTING HERE

Arezzo is easily reached by car from the A1 (Autostrada del Sole), the main highway running between Florence and Rome. Direct trains connect Arezzo with Rome (2½ hours) and Florence (1 hour). Direct bus service is available from Florence, but not from Rome.

VISITOR INFORMATION

Arezzo tourism office (✉*Piazza della Repubblica 28* ☎*0575/377678* ⊕*www.apt.arezzo.it*).

EXPLORING AREZZO

Sitting on a low hill in a wide plain, Arezzo, especially the clock tower of its Duomo, is visible from afar. Surrounding the older town is an extensive area of urban and industrial sprawl, but once you begin to walk along the narrow, gently climbing pedestrian streets inside the walls, all sense of the surrounding confusion disappears. As you climb, the standard stores of the lower town are gradually replaced by the exclusive antiques and jewelry shops for which Arezzo is famous, and

the anonymous modern buildings of the new town give way to elegant Renaissance town palaces, fine Gothic and Romanesque churches, and the charming medieval squares of the upper town—all of which is crowned, quite naturally, by the Duomo itself.

MAIN ATTRACTIONS

❻ Basilica di San Francesco. The famous Piero della Francesca frescoes depicting *The Legend of the True Cross* (1452–66) were executed on the three walls of the Capella Bacci, the main apse of this 14th-century church. What Sir Kenneth Clark called "the most perfect morning light in all Renaissance painting" may be seen in the lowest section of the right wall, where the troops of Emperor Maxentius flee before the sign of the cross. The view of the frescoes from the nave of the church is limited, but a much closer look is available from the Capella Bacci by reservation. Call ahead or consult the Web site; admission is limited to 25 people every ½ hour. ⊠ *Piazza San Francesco* ☎ *0575/20630 church, 0575/352757 Capella Bacci reservations* ⊕ *www.pierodellafrancesca.it* ⊠ *Church free, Capella Bacci €6* ⊗ *Church: daily 8:30–6:30. Capella Bacci: Apr.–Oct., weekdays 9–6:30, Sat. 9–5:30, Sun. 1–5:30; Nov.–Mar., weekdays 9–5:30, Sat. 9–5, Sun. 1–5.*

❶ Duomo. Arezzo's medieval cathedral at the top of the hill contains an eye-level fresco of a tender *Magdalene* by Piero della Francesca (1420–

Fodor's Choice
★

DID YOU KNOW

Arezzo's Piazza Grande is the site of a major antiques fair on the first weekend of every month, as well as a medieval joust on the first Sunday in September.

92); look for it in the north aisle next to the large marble tomb near the organ. Construction of the Duomo began in 1278, but twice came to a halt, and the church wasn't completed until 1510. The facade, designed by Arezzo's Dante Viviani, was added later (1901–14). ⊠*Piazza del Duomo 1* ☎*0575/23991* ⊙*Daily 6:30–12:30 and 3–6:30.*

❹ Piazza Grande. With its irregular shape and sloping brick pavement, framed by buildings of assorted centuries, Arezzo's central piazza echoes Siena's Piazza del Campo. Though not quite so magnificent, it's lively enough during the outdoor antiques fair the first Sunday of the month and when the **Giostra del Saracino** (Saracen Joust), featuring medieval costumes and competition, is held here on the first Sunday of September.

❺ Santa Maria della Pieve *(Church of Saint Mary of the Parish).* The curving, tiered apse on Piazza Grande belongs to a fine Romanesque church that was originally Paleo-Christian, built on the remains of an old Roman temple. It was redone in Romanesque style in the 12th century. The facade dates from the early 13th century, but it includes granite columns from the Roman period. Interior frescoes by Piero della Francesca, Lorenzo Ghiberti (1378–1455), and Pietro Lorenzetti (circa 1290–1348) were sadly lost in the 16th, 17th, and 18th centuries. To the left of the altar there is a 16th-century episcopal throne by Vasari. ⊠*Corso Italia 7* ☎*0575/22629* ⊙*May–Sept., daily 8–1 and 3–7; Oct.–Apr., daily 8–noon and 3–6.*

ALSO WORTH SEEING

❽ Anfiteatro Romano. Periodic excavations since 1950 have brought to light segments of Arezzo's Roman amphitheater, which was probably built during the early 2nd century AD. The entire perimeter has been exposed, and you can see some of the entrance passages and the structures that supported the amphitheater's central arena. ⊠*Via Crispi* ☎*0575/20882 museum* 🎟*Free* ⊙*Daily 8:30–7:30.*

❸ Casa di Giorgio Vasari. Giorgio Vasari (1511–74), the region's leading mannerist artist, architect, and art historian, designed and decorated this house after he bought it in 1540. He ended up not spending much time there, since he and his wife moved to Florence in 1554. Today the building houses archives on Vasari, and underwhelming works by the artist and his peers are on view. In the first room, which Vasari called the "Triumph of Virtue Room," a richly ornamented wooden ceiling shows Virtue combating Envy and Fortune in a central octagon. Frescoes on the walls depict, among other things, Extravagance, Charity, the Fire of Troy, and a panorama of a Rome cow field. ⊠*Via XX Settembre 55* ☎*0575/409040* 🎟*€2* ⊙*Mon.–Sat. 8:30–7:30, Sun. 8:30–1.*

❼ Museo Archeologico. The Archaeological Museum in the **Convento di San Bernardo,** just outside the **Anfiteatro Romano,** exhibits a fine collection of Etruscan bronzes. ⊠*Via Margaritone 10* ☎*0575/20882* 🎟*€4* ⊙*Daily 8:30–7.*

② **San Domenico.** Inside the northern city walls, this church was begun by Dominican friars in 1275 and completed in the 14th century. The walls were once completely frescoed and decorated with niches and chapels. Very little remains of the original works: a famous 13th-century crucifix by Cimabue (circa 1240–1302), frescoes by Spinello Aretino (1350–1410), and some 14th- and 15th-century paintings. ⊠*Piazza San Domenico* ☎*0575/23255* ᐁ*Free* ☉*Daily 8–7.*

NEED A BREAK?
The old-fashioned-looking Pasticceria Gli Svizzeri (⊠*Corso Italia 61* ☎*0575/355757*) has scrumptious pastries and cappuccino, plus a tiny restaurant in the back. It's a good place for an Italian-style breakfast, a coffee and pastry on the go, or a leisurely mid-afternoon pick-me-up during a long day of sightseeing.

WHERE TO EAT

$$–$$$ ✕**Antica Trattoria da Guido.** Owned by a southern Italian, this small trattoria serves tasty adaptations of Calabrian dishes, such as homemade pasta served with *salsa ai pomodori secchi* (a spicy sauce of sun-dried tomatoes, capers, and red peppers). The display of homemade pastries makes decisions difficult at the end of the meal. The dining room is a pleasant mix of rustic and modern, and the service is friendly. ⊠*Via di San Francesco 1* ☎*0575/23271* ═*MC, V* ☉*Closed Sun. and 2 wks in mid-Aug.*

$–$$ ✕**La Torre di Gnicche.** Wine lovers shouldn't miss this wine bar/eatery with more than 700 labels on the list, located just off Piazza Grande. Seasonal dishes of traditional fare, such as *acquacotta del casentino* (porcini mushroom soup) and *baccalà in umido* (salt-cod stew), are served in the simply decorated, vaulted dining room. You can accompany your meal with one, or more, of the almost 30 wines that are available by the glass. Limited outdoor seating is available in warm weather. ⊠*Piaggia San Martino 8* ☎*0575/352035* ═*AE, MC, V* ☉*Closed Wed., Jan., and 2 wks in July.*

WHERE TO STAY

$$ ▨**Castello di Gargonza.** Enchantment reigns at this tiny 13th-century countryside hamlet, part of the fiefdom of the aristocratic Florentine Guicciardini. The modern Count Roberto Guicciardini reinvented the place as an agriturismo to rescue a dying village. A castle, church, and cobbled streets set the stage. Guest rooms vary in style; some are decidedly more basic than others. However, high wood-beam ceilings, terra-cotta floors, and modern bathrooms are the rule throughout. Apartments have three to eight rooms each, sleeping as many as 10 people, and have as many as four baths. A minimum three-night stay is required for most rooms; a minimum one-week stay for the apartments. **Pros:** Romantic, one-of-a-kind accommodation in a medieval castle; peaceful, isolated setting. **Cons:** Standard rooms are extremely basic, a little out-of-the-way for exploring the region, private transportation is a necessity. ⊠*SR73* ✛ *28 km (17 mi) southwest of Arezzo, Monte*

5

San Savino 52048 ☎*0575/847021* 📠*0575/847054* ⊕*www.gargonza.
it* 🗢*37 rooms, 8 apartments* ⌂*In-room: no a/c, kitchen (some), refrigerator, no TV. In-hotel: restaurant, bar, pool, public Internet, public
Wi-Fi* ⊟*AE, DC, MC, V* ⊘*Closed last 3 wks in Jan.–Feb.* ¶⌷*BP.*

$$ 🏨**Cavaliere Palace Hotel.** On a quiet backstreet in the old town, the
Cavaliere is moments away from the main sights. The carpeted rooms
in the restored 19th-century town house are small but comfy, with con-
temporary furnishings. **Pros:** Location, location, location. **Cons:** Some
complain of noise from nearby disco, very plain decor. ⊠*Via Madonna
del Prato 83, Arezzo 52100* ☎*0575/26836* 📠*0575/21925* ⊕*www.
cavalierehotels.com* 🗢*27 rooms* ⌂*In-room: refrigerator, WI-Fi. In-
hotel: public Wi-Fi, parking (fee)* ⊟*AE, D, MC, V* ¶⌷*CP.*

$ 🏨**Calcione Country and Castle.** The elegant Marchesa Olivella Lotter-
Fodor'sChoice   inghi della Stufa has turned her six-centuries-old family estate (circa
★   1483) into a top-notch agriturismo. Think sophisticated rustic: many
of the apartments have open fireplaces, and the stone houses have a
private pool (the rest share the estate pool). Explore the grounds, which
include olive groves, vineyards, and private lakes for fishing and wind-
surfing. "We hated leaving," says one user of fodors.com. To make up
for the absence of room phones, mobile phones are made available to
guests. From June to mid-September, a minimum one-week stay is man-
datory. **Pros:** Houses can sleep up to 17; large swimming pools; quiet,
beautiful, remote setting. **Cons:** Private transportation is a must: near-
est village is 8 km (5 mi) away, some complain about insects in summer,
no a/c. ⊠*Calcione, 26 km (15 mi) southwest of Arezzo, Lucignano
52046* ☎*0575/837100* 📠*0575/837153* ⊕*www.calcione.com* 🗢*2
houses, 1 cottage, 6 apartments* ⌂*In-room: no a/c, no phone, kitchen,
no TV (some). In-hotel: tennis court, pools, laundry facilities, some
pets allowed* ⊟*No credit cards* ⊘*Closed Nov.–Mar.* ¶⌷*EP.*

SHOPPING

Ever since Etruscan goldsmiths set up their shops here more than 2,000
years ago, Arezzo has been famous for its jewelry. Today the town lays
claim to being one of the world's capitals of jewelry design and manu-
facture, and you can find an impressive display of big-time baubles in
the town center's shops. Arezzo is also famous, at least in Italy, for its
antiques dealers.

ANTIQUES

Antique silver and jewelry are the specialization at **Alma Bardi Antichità**
(⊠*Corso Italia 97* ☎*0575/20640*).

Grace Gallery (⊠*Via Cavour 30* ☎*0575/354963*) deals in antique fur-
niture and paintings.

Come to **La Belle Epoque** (⊠*Piazza San Francesco 18* ☎*0575/355495*)
to look for antique lace and embroidered linens.

The first weekend of every month, between 8:30 and 5:30 each day,
Piazza Grande, a colorful flea market selling antiques and not-so-
antiques takes place here in the town's main square.

GOLD

Among the lovely pieces at **Borghini's** (⊠ *Corso Italia 130* ☎*0575/24678*) are beautiful gold bracelets with matching necklaces.

As the name suggests, diamonds are the specialty at **Il Diamante** (⊠ *Via Guido Monaco 69* ☎*0575/353450*).

CORTONA

Cortona is called "Mother of Troy and Grandmother of Rome" in popular speech, and so may be one of Italy's oldest towns. Tradition claims that it was founded by Dardanus, the founder of Troy (after whom the Dardanelles are named). He was fighting a local tribe, so the story goes, when he lost his helmet (*corythos* in Greek) on Cortona's hill. In time a town grew up that took its name (Corito) from the missing headgear. By the 4th century BC the Etruscans had built the first set of town walls, the cyclopean traces of which can still be seen in the 3-km (2-mi) sweep of the present fortifications. As a member of the Etruscans' 12-city league, Cortona became one of the federation's leading northern cities. The area's important consular road, the Via Cassia, passed the foot of Cortona's hill, maintaining the town's importance under the Romans. Medieval fortunes waned, however, as the plain below reverted to marsh. After holding out against such neighbors as Perugia, Arezzo, and Siena, the *commune* was captured by King Ladislas of Naples in 1409 and sold to the Florentines two years later.

GETTING HERE
Cortona is easily reached by car from the A1 (Autostrada del Sole): take the Valdichiana exit toward Perugia, then follow signs for Cortona. Regular bus service, provided by Etruria Mobilità, is available between Arezzo and Cortona (1 hour). Train service to Cortona is made inconvenient by the location of the train station, in the valley 3 km (2 mi) steeply below the town itself. From there, you have to rely on bus or taxi service to get up to Cortona.

VISITOR INFORMATION
Cortona tourism office (⊠ *Via Nazionale 42* ☎*0575/630352* ⊕*www.apt.arezzo.it*).

EXPLORING CORTONA

Brought into the limelight by Frances Mayes's book *Under the Tuscan Sun,* and a subsequent movie, Cortona is no longer the destination of just a few specialist art historians, and of those seeking reprieve from busier tourist venues. The main street, Via Nazionale, is now lined with souvenir shops and thronged with people during the summer. Though the main sights of Cortona certainly make braving the crowds worthwhile, much of the town's very considerable charm still lies in its maze of quiet and narrow backstreets. It's here that you will see laundry hanging from high windows, and children playing, and catch the

Duomo **2**
Museo Diocesano **3**
Palazzo Casali **1**
San Domenico **4**
San Francesco **5**
San Niccolò **6**
Santa Margherita **7**
Santa Maria del Calcinaio **8**

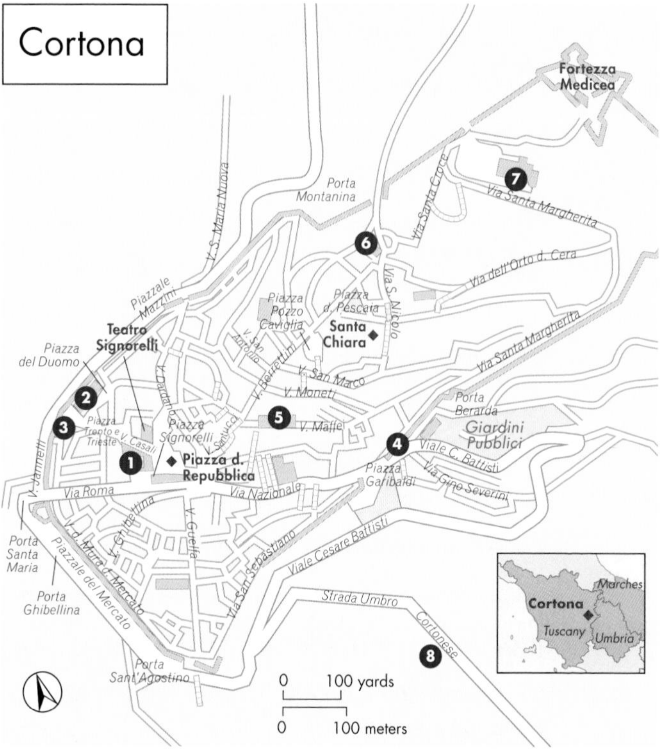

delightful smell of slowly simmering pasta sauce wafting on the breeze. Wander off the beaten track and you won't be disappointed.

MAIN ATTRACTIONS

2 **Duomo.** Cortona's cathedral stands on an edge of the city, next to what's left of the Etruscan and medieval walls running from Porta Santa Maria to Porta Colonia. It was built on the site of an old Romanesque church, but the present Renaissance church was begun in 1480 and finished in 1507. An arcade along the outside wall was erected in the 16th century. Inside, the Duomo is a mixture of Renaissance and baroque styles featuring an exquisite 1664 baroque tabernacle on the high altar by Francesco Mazzuoli. ✉ *Piazza Duomo* ☎ *0575/62830* 🎟 *Free* ⏲ *Daily 10–12:30 and 3–5.*

3 **Museo Diocesano.** The Diocesan Museum houses an impressive number of large, splendid paintings by native son Luca Signorelli (1445–1523), as well as a beautiful *Annunciation* by Fra Angelico (1387/1400–1455), which is a delightful surprise in this small town. The former oratory of the Compagnia del Gesù, reached by descending the 1633 staircase opposite the Duomo, is part of the museum. The church was built between 1498 and 1505 and restructured by Giorgio Vasari in 1543. Frescoes depicting sacrifices from the Old Testament by Doceno

(1508–56), based on designs by Vasari, line the walls. ⊠*Piazza Duomo* ☎*0575/62830* 🖾*€5* 🕘*Tues.–Sun. 10–5.*

❽ Santa Maria del Calcinaio. Legend has it that the image of the Madonna
★ appeared on a wall of a medieval *calcinaio* (lime pit used for curing leather), the site on which the church was then built between 1485 and 1513. The linear gray-and-white interior recalls Florence's Duomo. Sienese architect Francesco di Giorgio (1439–1502) most likely designed the sanctuary: the church is a terrific example of Renaissance architectural principles. ⊠*Località Il Calcinaio 227* ✛ *3 km (2 mi) southeast of Cortona's center on Via Guelph* ☎*0575/604830* 🖾*Free* 🕘*Mon.–Sat. 3:30–6, Sun. 10–12:30.*

ALSO WORTH SEEING

❶ Palazzo Casali. Built originally by the Casali family, who lived here until 1409, this palace combines 13th- to 17th-century architectural styles. Today the palace contains the Accademia Etrusca, which has an extensive library; **La Biblioteca Comunale;** and the **Museo dell'Accademia Etrusca e della Città di Cortona (aka MAEC).** An eclectic mix of Egyptian objects, Etruscan and Roman bronzes and statuettes, and paintings are on display in the museum. In the basement, sections of the Etruscan and Roman buildings that form the foundations of the palace have been exposed. Look for work by Renaissance artists such as Luca Signorelli and Pinturcchio (circa 1454–1513). From May through September, guided tours are available in English with prior arrangement. Accompanied visits, but only with Italian guides, to the Etruscan tombs on the slopes below Cortona may also be booked. ⊠*Piazza Signorelli 9* ☎*0575/637235* 🖾*Museo €7, Biblioteca free* 🕘*Tues.–Sun. 10–5.*

❹ San Domenico. Inside this rather anonymous-looking 14th-century church, just outside Cortona's walls, is an altarpiece depicting the Coronation of the Virgin against a sparkling gold background by Lorenzo di Niccolò Gerini (active late 14th–early 15th centuries). Among the other works is a Madonna and Child by Luca Signorelli. ⊠*Largo Beato Angelico* ☎*0575/62246* 🖾*Free* 🕘*Daily 10–12:30 and 4–5:30.*

NEED A BREAK?
Caffe degli Artisti (⊠ *Via Nazionale 18* ☎*0575/601237*) is a pleasant place to stop for a cappuccino, sandwiches at lunchtime, or the array of appetizers set out during the cocktail hour. During the summer months, a few outdoor tables are set up directly on Via Nazionale, Cortona's main pedestrian street, and provide a great perch for those who love to people-watch.

❺ San Francesco. In the mid-13th century, this Gothic-style church was built on the site of Etruscan and Roman baths. It's closed for reconstruction at this writing, but it contains frescoes dating from 1382, a big crucifix by Giuseppe Piamontini of Florence, and the Relic of Santa Croce, a vestige from the True Cross given to Brother Elia when he served as an envoy for Federico II in Constantinople. The church has a beautiful organ, built in 1466 and, fortunately, it was only partially damaged during World War II. ⊠*Piazza San Francesco* ☎*0575/603205* 🕘*Daily 9–7.*

Piazza Signorelli, Cortona.

San Niccolò. A small, cypress-lined courtyard and porch stand in front of the delightful San Niccolò, a Renaissance church. On the main altar is a fresco by Luca Signorelli, the *Deposition of Christ*, painted around 1510. On the left wall is another fresco by Signorelli of the Madonna and Child, which was plastered over in 1768 and rediscovered in 1847. To visit the church, ring the custodian's doorbell on the left-hand side of the building. ⊠ *Via S. Niccolò* ☎ *0575/604591* 💵 *A minimum donation of €1 is requested* ⊙ *Daily 9–12 and 3–5.*

❼ Santa Margherita. The large 1897 basilica was constructed over the foundation of a 13th-century church dedicated to the same saint. What makes the 10-minute uphill walk worthwhile is the richly decorated interior. The body of the 13th-century Saint Margherita—clothed but with skull and bare feet clearly visible—is displayed in a case on the main altar. ⊠ *Piazzale Santa Margherita* ☎ *0575/603116* 💵 *Free* ⊙ *Daily 8–12 and 3–6.*

WHERE TO STAY & EAT

$$ – $$$ ✕ **Osteria del Teatro.** Photographs from theatrical productions spanning many years line the walls of this tavern off Cortona's large Piazza del Teatro. The food is simply delicious—try the *filetto al lardo di colonnata e prugne* (beef cooked with bacon and prunes); service is warm and friendly. ⊠ *Via Maffei 2* ☎ *0575/630556* ▤ *AE, DC, MC, V* ⊙ *Closed Wed. and 2 wks in Nov. and in Feb.*

$$$$ ✕⌂ **Il Falconiere.** Choose here from ★ rooms in an 18th-century villa, suites in the *chiesetta* (chapel, or little church), or for more seclusion, Le Vigne del Falco suites at the far end of the property. Husband-and-wife team Riccardo and Silvia Baracchi run the show, serving an almost exclusively American

and British clientele. Their restaurant's ($$$$) inventive seasonal menu includes *pici alla carbonara con lo zafferano di Centoia e pancetta croccante* (homemade thick spaghetti with carbonara sauce), over which, if your heart desires, you can add shaved white truffles. Cooking classes and guided wine tastings are available, and a small shop sells estate-produced olive oil and wine. **Pros:** Attractive setting, in the valley beneath Cortona; excellent service; elegant, but relaxed. **Cons:** A car is a must, some find rooms in main villa a little noisy, lacks full 24-hour service. ⊠*Località San Martino 370* ✛ *3 km (1½ mi) north of Cortona, 52044* ☎*0575/612679* ⧠*0575/612927* ⊕*www.ilfalconiere. com* ⌂*13 rooms, 7 suites* ⌂*In-room: safe, refrigerator, dial-up. In-hotel: restaurant, room service, bar, pools, concierge, laundry service, public Internet, parking (no fee), some pets allowed (fee)* ⊟*AE, MC, V* ⊗ *No lunch in restaurant Tues. Nov.–Mar. Hotel closed last 3 wks in Jan.–mid-Feb.* ❘◎❘*BP.*

SHOPPING

Il Cocciaio. For nice ceramics, with many pieces depicting the brilliant sunflowers that blanket local fields, check here. ⊠*Via Nazionale 54* ☎*0575/604405.*

SANSEPOLCRO & THE CASENTINO

Sansepolcro, as far east as you can go in Tuscany without entering either Umbria or the Marches, sits in the Valtiberina, the upper valley of the Tiber River. Once a provincial Roman town, and then a busier medieval city, Sansepolcro has now developed an extremely unappealing urban sprawl that almost completely masks its real treasures. Pass the 'burbs, enter the ancient walls, and you'll find narrow pedestrian streets, Romanesque and Gothic churches, elegant Renaissance *palazzi* (the Florentines conquered Sansepolcro in 1441), and charming city squares. All roads in Sansepolcro eventually lead to the small Museo Civico, where works by Piero della Francesca, the town's most famous artist, adorn the walls—a must-visit for any lover of Italian Renaissance art.

The sparsely populated region of the Casentino—defined as the upper valley of the Arno, the Val d'Arno, which originates here as a spring on Mt. Falterona—contains enough castles, Romanesque parish churches, and unspoiled villages to keep you happily exploring for days. But the jewels in its crown are contained within the Parco Nazionale Casentino, an 89,000-acre preserve of great beauty. The heart of the park, on an Apennine ridge between the Arno and the Tiber, straddling Tuscany and Emilia-Romagna, is the antique forest tended as a religious duty for eight centuries by the monks of the Abbazia Camaldoli, designers of the world's first forestry code. Every year they have planted 4,000–5,000 saplings, resulting in large tracts of early-growth forest. Although they began by maintaining the mix of silver firs and beeches, eventually they planted only firs, creating vast, majestic stands of the deep green trees whose 150-foot, straight black trunks were once floated down the Arno to be used for the tallest masts of warships.

SANSEPOLCRO

40 km (25 mi) east of Arezzo.

GETTING HERE
Traveling to Sansepolcro by either car or bus from Arezzo will be much preferred over the journey by train, which can take up to four hours. By car, follow the SS73; if traveling by bus (1 hour), check with Etruria Mobilità for the schedule, though service is infrequent.

VISITOR INFORMATION
Sansepolcro tourism office (⊠ *Via Matteotti 8* ☎ *0575/740536* ⊕ *www. apt.arezzo.it*)

EXPLORING
Originally called *Borgo San Sepolcro* (City of the Holy Sepulchre), this sprawling, largely agricultural town, takes its name from relics brought here from the Holy Land by two pilgrims in the 10th century. Today, inside a circle of 15th-century walls, the gridlike street plan hints at the town's even more ancient Roman origins. Known, foremost, as the birthplace of Piero della Francesca—several of his paintings are displayed in the town's Civic Museum—the old center of Sansepolcro retains a distinctly medieval air, with narrow streets lined with medieval churches and 15th-century palaces.

Piero della Francesca is the star at the small provincial **Museo Civico.** Three—possibly four—of his works are on display: the reassembled altarpiece of the *Misericordia* (1445–62), and frescoes depicting the *Resurrection* (ca. 1460), *Saint Julian,* and the disputed *Saint Louis of Toulouse,* which is possibly the work of a close follower of the artist. Other works of interest are those by Santi di Tito (1536–1603), also from Sansepolcro, and Pontormo's *San Quintino* (1517–18). ⊠ *Via Aggiunti 65* ☎ *0575/732218* 🎫 *€6* ⏰ *June 15–Oct. 15, daily 9:30–1:30 and 2:30–7; Oct. 16–June 14, daily 9:30–1 and 2:30–6.*

OFF THE BEATEN PATH

Monterchi. This sleepy town, sitting on a small knoll about 15 km (9 mi) south of Sansepolcro, would probably attract little attention, if it were not for the fact that Piero della Francesca stopped here to paint one of his greatest masterpieces in the 1450s. And, not surprisingly, Monterchi's **Museo "Madonna del Parto"** displays only one painting, Piero's *Madonna del Parto* (ca.1455), a fresco depicting the expectant Virgin flanked by two angels. The fresco, originally painted for the small chapel of Santa Maria a Momentana in Monterchi's cemetery, was restored in 1992–93 and moved, shortly thereafter, into the museum. The iconography of the image is extremely rare and, emphasized by its static atmosphere and studied symmetry, the fresco achieves an extraordinary sense of enigmatic and monumental spirituality. ⊠ *Via Reglia 1* ☎*0575/70713* 🖻*€3.10; pregnant women are admitted free of charge* ☉*Apr.–Sept., Tues.–Sun. 9–1 and 2–7; Oct.–Mar., Tues.–Sun. 9–1 and 2–6.*

WHERE TO EAT

$–$$ ✕**Taverna Toscana.** An exceptionally fresh and tasty *panzanella* (Tuscan bread salad) might start off your meal at this deliciously authentic trattoria in the center of Sansepolcro. Follow it with a homemade pasta, accompanied by a glass of house wine, a Banfi Cabernet Sauvignon from Montalcino, and you can't go wrong. A complimentary glass of *vin santo* is offered with your choice of dessert. ⊠ *Via Luca Pacioli 50/a* ☎*0575/742017* ▤*MC, V* ☉*Closed Tues.*

PARCO NAZIONALE CASENTINO

★ *Pratovecchio: 55 km (34 mi) north of Arezzo, 50 km (31 mi) east of Florence.*

GETTING HERE

You'll need a car to explore this area: getting here by bus, though surprisingly easier from Florence than it is from Arezzo, is a complicated and time-consuming process; it's impossible by train.

VISITOR INFORMATION

Park information office (⊠ *Via Guido Brocchi 7 Pratovecchio* ☎*0575/50301* ⊕ *www.parcoforestecasentinesi.it*) There are branch offices at **Camaldoli** (☎*0575/556130*)and **Chiusi della Verna** (☎*0575/532098*).

EXPLORING

A drive through the park, especially on the very winding 34-km (21-mi) road between the Monastero di Camaldoli and Santuario della Verna, passing through the lovely abbey town of Badia Prataglia, reveals one satisfying vista after another, from walls of firs to velvety pillows of pastureland where sheep or white cattle graze. In autumn the beeches add a mass of red-brown to the palette, and in spring torrents of bright golden broom pour off the hillsides with an unforgettable profusion and fragrance. Walking the forests—which also include sycamore, lime, maple, ash, elm, oak, hornbeam, and chestnut trees and abundant brooks and impressive waterfalls—is the best way to see some of the wilder creatures, from deer and mouflon (wild sheep imported from Sardinia starting in 1872) to eagles and many other birds, as well as 1,000 species of flora, including many rare and endangered plants and an orchid found nowhere else. The **Grande Escursione Apenninica** (GEA) hiking route, which is accessible from both the Monastero di Camaldoli and the Sanutario della Verna, runs along a winding ridge.

The park organizes theme walks in summer and provides English-speaking guides anytime with advance notice.

WHERE TO STAY

$ ⊞ **Fattoria di Celli.** Set on a gentle rise in the countryside outside the castle town of Poppi, this former *fattoria*—a dormitory housing farm workers—is a tranquil place with lawns punctuated by flowers and modern sculptures, play areas for children, and picnic tables placed to appreciate mountain views. Apartments and villas have working fireplaces and exposed beams; some rooms have original stone walls. Look for hand-painted details—flowers on an armoire, a stenciled border at ceiling height, a mural on a wall. The Fattoria di Celli has a required one-week minimum stay. **Pros:** Great for kids, peaceful and beautiful location. **Cons:** No a/c; 5 km (3 mi) to nearest town—a car is a must; simple, rustic accommodations. ⊠*Località Celli, Poppi52013* ☎*0575/583860* 🖷*0575/500191* ⊕*www.fattoriadicelli.com* ➭*16 apartments* 🖧*In-room: no a/c, kitchen (some), no TV. In-hotel: restaurant, tennis court, pools, no elevator, laundry facilities, some pets allowed* ▤*No credit cards* ⏱⃝*EP.*

MONASTERO DI CAMALDOLI

20 km (12 mi) northeast of Pratovecchio, 55 km (34 mi) north of Arezzo.

GETTING HERE

As with the Casentino National Park in general, the only practical way to reach the monastery is by car: take SP71 to Serravalle, then follow the signs. Bus service is infrequent and the schedule is tortuous; train service is nonexistent.

EXPLORING

In 1012 Saint Romualdo, scion of a noble Ravenna family, came upon the forests of the Casentino and found their remoteness, their beauty, and their silence conducive to religious contemplation. He stayed and founded a hermitage, Monastero Camaldoli (named for Count Maldoli, who donated the land), which became the seat of a new, reformed Benedictine order. Four centuries after the order's founding by Saint Benedict, Romualdo felt it had become too permissive. An important requirement of the order was preserving its ascetic atmosphere: "If the hermits are to be true devotees of solitude, they must take the greatest care of the woods." When the flow of pilgrims began to threaten that solitude, Romualdo had a monastery and hospital built 1 km (½ mi) down the mountain to create some distance. Today the hermitage, **Sacro Eremo di Camaldoli**—where the monks live in complete silence in 20 separate little cottages, each with its own walled garden—can be seen through gates, and the church and original cell of Romualdo, the model for all the others, can be visited. The church, rebuilt in the 13th century and transformed in the 18th to its present appearance, strikes an odd note in connection with such an austere order and the simplicity of the hermits' cells, because it's done up in gaudy baroque style, complete with gilt cherubs and a frescoed vault. Its most appealing artwork is the glazed terra-cotta relief *Madonna and Child with Saints* (including a large figure of Romualdo and a medallion depicting his fight with the devil) by Andrea della Robbia.

Within the monastery is the church (repeatedly restructured) containing 14th-century frescoes by Spinello Aretino, seven 16th-century panel paintings by Giorgio Vasari, and a quietly lovely monastic choir. The choir has 18th-century walnut stalls, more Vasari paintings, and a serene fresco (by Santi Pacini) of Saint Romualdo instructing his white-robed disciples. In a hospital built for sick villagers in 1046 is the 1543 **Antica Farmacia** (Old Pharmacy), with original carved walnut cabinets. Here you can buy herbal teas and infusions, liqueurs, honey products, and toiletries made by the monks from centuries-old recipes as part of their daily routine balancing prayer, work, and study (the monastery is entirely self-supporting). In the back room is an exhibit of the early pharmacy's alembics, mortars, and other equipment with which the monks made herbs into medicines. You can attend short spiritual retreats organized by the monks throughout the year: contact the *foresteria* (visitors lodge) for details. ⊠ *SP 67, Camaldoli 52010* ☎ *0575/556021 Monastero, 0575/556013 Foresteria* ✉ *0575/556001* ⊕ *www.camaldoli.it* ✏ *Free* ⊗ *Daily 9–1 and 3:30–6.*

SANTUARIO DELLA VERNA

34 km (21 mi) southeast of Monastero di Camaldoli and of Pratovecchio.

GETTING HERE
The only practical way to reach the sanctuary is by car—it's 21 km (13 mi) east of Bibbiena on SP208. There is no direct bus service, and train service is nonexistent.

EXPLORING
A few hills away from the Monastero di Camaldoli, dramatically perched on a sheer-walled rock surrounded by firs and beeches, is La Verna, founded by Saint Francis of Assisi in 1214. Ten years later, after a 40-day fast, Saint Francis had a vision of Christ crucified, and when it was over, Francis had received the stigmata, the signs of Christ's wounds, on his hands, feet, and chest. A stone in the floor of the 1263 Chapel of the Stigmata marks the spot. A covered corridor through which the monks pass, chanting in a solemn procession each afternoon at 3, on the way to Mass is lined with simple frescoes of the *Life of St. Francis* by a late 17th-century Franciscan artist. The true artistic treasures of the place, though, are 15 della Robbia glazed terra-cottas. Most, like a heartbreakingly beautiful Annunciation, are in the 14th-

to 15th-century basilica, which has a 5,000-pipe organ that sings out joyously at masses.

Several chapels, each with its own story, can be visited, and some natural and spiritual wonders can also be seen. A walkway along the 230-foot-high cliff leads to an indentation where the rock is said to have miraculously melted away to protect Saint Francis when the devil tried to push him off the edge. Most touching is the enormous Sasso Spicco (Projecting Rock), detached on three sides and surrounded with mossy rocks and trees, where Saint Francis meditated. You can also view the Letto di San Francesco (Saint Francis's Bed), a slab of rock in a cold, damp cave with an iron grate on which he prayed, did penance, and sometimes slept. A 40-minute walk through the woods to the top of Mt. Penna passes some religious sites and ends in panoramic views of the Arno Valley, but those from the wide, cliff-edge terrace are equally impressive, including the tower of the castle in Poppi, the Prato Magno (great meadow), and the olive groves and vineyards on the lower slopes. Santuario della Verna's foresteria also has simple but comfortable rooms with or without bath. A restaurant ($) with basic fare is open to the public, and a shop sells souvenirs and the handiwork of the monks. ⊠ *SP208 east from Bibbiena* ✚ *21 km (13 mi) east of Bibbiena, La Verna 52010* ☎ *0575/534211* 🖷 *0575/599320* ⊕ *www. santuariolaverna.org* 🖻 *Free* ⊘ *Apr.–Oct., daily 7:30–9:30; Nov.–Mar. daily 7:30* AM–*7:30* PM.

As you leave La Verna, be glad you needn't do it as Edith Wharton (1862–1937) did on a 1912 visit during a drive across the Casentino. As she wrote, her car "had to be let down on ropes to a point about ¾ mi below the monastery, Cook [her chauffeur] steering down the vertical descent, and twenty men hanging on to a funa [rope] that, thank the Lord, didn't break."

OFF THE
BEATEN
PATH

Caprese Michelangelo. Some 10 km (6 mi) south of La Verna on SR54 is the small hilltop community of Caprese Michelangelo, where *the* Michelangelo was born on March 6, 1475. The **Museo Michelangelo,** which opened in 1964 to celebrate the 400th anniversary of Michelangelo's death, displays photographs, plaster casts, and documents relating to the artist's work. ⊠ *Via Capoluogo 3* ☎ *0575/793776* 🖻 *€5* ⊘ *Apr.–May, Mon.–Sat. 11–6, Sun. 11–7; June, July, and Sept., Mon.–Sat. 10–7, Sun. 9:30–7:30; Aug., daily 9:30–7:30; Oct. Mon.–Sat. 10:30–5:30, Sun. 10:30–6:30; Nov.–Mar., Mon.–Sat. 11–5, Sun. 11–6.* One weekend in mid-October, Caprese Michelangelo's very lively **Sagra della Castagna** *(Chestnut Festival)* takes place. Among the many other chestnut-based delights that feature in the fair, you can sample freshly made *castagnaccia* (a typically Tuscan dessert made with chestnut flour, pine nuts, and rosemary). *Tourist office* ⊠ *Via Capoluogo 10* ☎ *0575/791016* ⊕ *www.capresemichelangelo.net.*

Southern Tuscany

WORD OF MOUTH

"The best times of day to see the Val d'Orcia are in the early morning or late afternoon. When the shadows are long, the cypress trees & umbrella pines look more pronounced as they 'dance up the hill' (my wife's term)."

—StuDudley

WELCOME TO SOUTHERN TUSCANY

TOP REASONS TO GO

★ **Pienza's urban renewal:** A 15th-century makeover turned this otherwise un-pretentious village into a model Renaissance town.

★ **Saturnia's hot water:** The gods themselves re-portedly had a hand in creating the springs at this world-famous spa town.

★ **Napoléon's home in exile:** The island of Elba, where the French leader was once imprisoned, is the prettiest island in the Tuscan archipelago.

★ **Wine tastings in Mon-tepulciano:** This gorgeous town also happens to be the home of one of Italy's finest wines—Vino Nobile di Montepulciano.

★ **A stroll through Ab-bazia di Sant'Antimo:** This 12th-century Romanesque abbey shows French, Lombard, and even Spanish influences.

1 Val d'Orcia. In the area surrounding this lush valley you'll find some of southern Tuscany's most attractive towns. **Montalcino** and **Montepulciano** are famed for their wine, **Pienza** for its urban planning and its pecorino cheese.

2 Le Crete. South of Siena, the stark clay landscape and unassuming towns are inter-rupted by **Abbazia di Monte Oliveto Maggiore**, the most-visited abbey in Tuscany.

3 The Maremma. Tuscany's deep south may not con-form to your expectations for the region; it's best known for its cattle ranches and its coastline. "Discov-ering" the Maremma has become popular with off-the-beaten-path travelers, though you hardly have to rough it here—you'll find exceptional food and wine, and the spa town of **Satur-nia** is all about indulgence.

TUSCANY

UMBRIA

GETTING ORIENTED

Southeast of Siena, not far from the Umbrian border, the towns of Montepulciano, Montalcino, and Pienza are Tuscan classics—perched on hills, constructed during the Middle Ages and the Renaissance, and saturated with fine wine. Venture farther south and you encounter Tuscany with a rougher edge: the Maremma region is populated by cowboys, and a good portion of the landscape remains wild. But you won't forget you're in Italy here; the wine is still excellent, and some locals store their supply in Etruscan tombs.

6

Siena

326

A1

2

LE CRETE

Asciano

San Galgano

Buonconvento

Abbazia di Monte Oliveto Maggiore

2

223

Montepulciano

1

Montalcino

Pienza

UMBRIA

VAL D'ORCIA

San Quirico d'Orcia

Chiusi

73

Roccastrada

Sant'Antimo

71

Via Cassia

Monti Amiata

Radicofani

223

Arcidosso

Ombrone River

Castell' Azzara

2

A1

Acquapendente

Grossieto

322

3

Sorano

Saturnia

Sovana

Pitigliano

1

Monti dell'Uccellina

Manciano

LAZIO

THE MAREMMA

74

Albinia

Orbetello

1

GIANNUTRI

Montalcino

4 Elba & the Surrounding Islands. It's a short hop from the coast to the islands of the Tuscan archipelago. Several of them—most notably **Elba**—have long been vacation getaways.

Elba

SOUTHERN TUSCANY PLANNER

Life's a Beach

Apart from the occasional rocky promontory, the coast of southern Tuscany is virtually one long stretch of fine-sand beach. Private beach areas are common near the resort towns to the south of Livorno and just to the north of Monte Argentario, where there are chairs and umbrellas for rent, shower facilities, and bars. Along the rest of the coast, the beaches are public. They're particularly pleasant in the nature reserve at Monti dell'Uccellina and along the sandbars that connect Monte Argentario to the mainland. On the islands, rocky shores predominate, although Elba has sandy beaches on its southern side.

Making the Most of Your Time

The towns in southern Tuscany are fairly close together, so it's possible to pick one of them as your base and take day trips to almost everywhere else in the region. **Pienza,** in the middle of the **Val d'Orcia,** makes an excellent place to begin your trip. Other good choices include **Montepulciano** and **Montalcino.** From any of these it's only a short drive to all the other towns in the Val d'Orcia, as well as the famous abbeys in and around **Le Crete.**

If your main reason for visiting this region is a dip the hot springs, you should stay in **Saturnia** or one of the surrounding villages. (Because so many people go there for a soak, Saturnia has the most luxurious lodgings.)

If your destination is the Tuscan archipelago, you'd do best to choose one island, as there is no ferry service between them. **Elba** is more famous, but it's hard to find a place to lay your towel in the summer months. **Giglio** has less crowded beaches, and a few accessible on foot or by boat that you might have to yourself.

Finding a Place to Stay

Southern Tuscany is a great place to enjoy the *agriturismo* (agrotourism) lifestyle: if you have a week to stay in one of these rural farmhouses, pick someplace central, such as Pienza, and explore the region from that base. It may be so relaxing and the food so good that you might have trouble wandering away.

You will also find many hotels in this region: modern affairs in cities, surfside beach resorts, and timeworn villas.

The Island of Giglio

DINING & LODGING PRICE CATEGORIES (IN EUROS)				
¢	$	$$	$$$	$$$$
RESTAU-RANTS	under €15	€15–€25	€25–€35	€35–€45	over €45

Restaurant prices are for a first course (*primo*), second course (*secondo*), and dessert (*dolce*). Hotel prices are for two people in a standard double room in high season, including tax and service.

GETTING AROUND

By Car

The area is easily reached by car on the A1 highway (Autostrada del Sole), which runs between Rome and Florence—take the Chiusi–Chianciano Terme exit for Montepulciano, Pienza, and San Quirico Val d'Orcia. From Florence, the fastest route to southern Tuscany is via the Florence–Siena Superstrada and then the Via Cassia (SR2) from Siena, for Buonconvento and Montalcino. There is also a good road (SR223) linking Siena and Grosseto, for outings to the Parco Naturale della Maremma and Monte Argentario.

From Genoa or the northern Tuscan coast, follow the coastal highway (A12) to reach Livorno and its ferry service to Capraia. For direct ferry service to Elba, continue south on the SS1 (the Via Aurelia) to reach Piombino. Past Piombino, the SS1 passes Grosseto, the Parco Naturale della Maremma, and Monte Argentario, before continuing south toward Rome.

If you don't have a car but want to experience the region's beautiful back roads, you can hire a car and driver to get around. In Montalcino, reliable service is provided by **Mulinari** (☎ *0348/5175154*) and **Pierangeli** (☎ *0577/848656 or 0577/849113*). In Montepulciano, try **Paolo Cencini** (☎ *0330/7322723*) or **Stefano Bernardini** (☎ *0578/716081 or 0348/2868790*).

By Train

Train service within this region is slow; in many cases, buses are quicker. Trains run from Chiusi–Chianciano Terme to Siena (1 hour) with stops in Montepulciano and Asciano. You can check the Web site of the state railway, the **Ferrovie dello Stato** (☎ *892021 toll free within Italy* ⊕ *www.trenitalia.com*), for information, or stop in any travel agency, as many book and print train tickets and are likely to speak English.

By Bus

Although tortuous roads and circuitous routes make bus travel in southern Tuscany slow, it's a reliable way to get around if you don't have a car. Schedules are always changing, so plan your trip carefully with the aid of local tourist offices. (They're also more likely to have an English-speaking staff than are bus stations.) The major bus stations for the region are in Siena and Grosseto, but most towns have bus service even if they don't have actual bus stations.

The bus company **SITA** (☎ *0577/204270 in Siena, 055/47812 in Florence* ⊕ *www.sita-on-line.it*) covers most of the routes to towns south of Siena. **Tra-In** (☎ *0577/204111* ⊕ *www.trainspa.it*) also provides service to Montalcino and Montepulciano. **RAMA** (☎ *199/848787* ⊕ *www.rama-mobilita.it*) in Grosseto provides bus service through the Maremma region. On Elba, **ATL** (☎ *0565/914392*) buses take you around the island.

6

Updated
by Peter
Blackman

AS DIVERSE AS ITALY ITSELF, southern Tuscany ranges from the green knolls of the Val d'Orcia to the sandy beaches at Punta Ala. It contains the wildest parts of Tuscany—the Maremma, once a malaria-ridden swampland where the butteri, Italy's cowboys, rounded up their cattle, now a peaceful woodland fringed with beaches; Monte Amiata, a scruffy mountain landscape where goats gnaw at clumps of brown grass among scattered rocks; and the still-wild islands of the Tuscan archipelago. Some of Tuscany's best-kept secrets lie here in the south, among them the Abbazia di San Galgano, which is open to the sky, and the cool mountain enclaves of Monte Amiata. This is Etruscan country, where the necropolis near Sovana hints at a rich and somewhat mysterious pre-Roman civilization.

VAL D'ORCIA

The Val d'Orcia (Orcia Valley) is a sumptuous green valley with breathtaking views of the Orcia River, which runs through it. The area's long-standing agricultural tradition has left it utterly undeveloped, and so the vistas here are classic Tuscany—rolling hills topped by villages, wide plains, swaths of blooming fields punctuated by vineyards and olive groves. Picture-perfect Pienza, medieval San Quirico d'Orcia, and Bagno Vignoni are great photo-op stops; amateur archaeologists will enjoy pondering Chiusi's painted Etruscan tombs; and Chianciano Terme's thermal baths can provide a sybaritic treat during your stay. Hills near Montalcino border the valley in the west, and it's in that hilltop town that Siena chose to make a last desperate stand against the invading Florentines. Not to be missed is the superbly positioned Abbazia di Sant'Antimo to the south. Montepulciano, filled with town palaces and Renaissance churches—and fortified by some great red wine—is at the valley's boundary in the east.

CHIUSI

40 km (25 mi) south of Cortona, 84 km (50 mi) southeast of Siena, 126 km (78 mi) southeast of Florence.

GETTING HERE
Chiusi is easily reached by car on the A1 highway (Autostrada del Sole), which runs between Rome and Florence. Tra-In buses link Chiusi with Siena, but train service is faster and more frequent. Chiusi is on a main rail line between Florence and Rome, and can be reached from either city.

VISITOR INFORMATION
Chiusi tourism office (⊠ *Piazza Duomo 1* ☎ *0578/227667*).

EXPLORING
Chiusi was once one of the most powerful of the ancient cities of the Etruscan League, and it's now a valuable source of information about that archaic civilization. Fifth-century BC tombs found in the nearby hills have provided archaeologists with a wealth of artifacts. On the

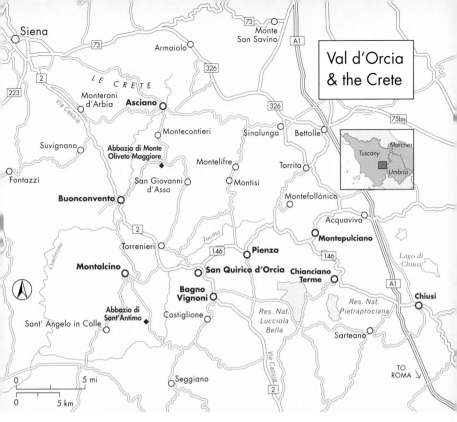

route of the ancient Via Cassia, Chiusi became a major Roman center and an important communication hub that linked Rome with the agriculturally rich Chiana Valley to the east, with Siena to the northwest, and to other major cities in central and northern Italy. When the Chiana Valley became a malaria-ridden swamp during the Middle Ages, Chiusi's importance declined, and it was not until the Medici devised a scheme to drain the valley (with plans supplied by Leonardo da Vinci) in the early 15th century that the town began to reestablish itself.

Most of the artifacts found during the excavations of Chiusi's Etruscan sites are now on display in the small but expertly laid out **Museo Nazionale Etrusco**. Relics include elegant Etruscan and Greek vases, carved Etruscan tomb chests, and a number of the strange canopic jars with anthropomorphic shapes that are particular to this area. The tombs themselves can be seen by arrangement with the museum; visits are accompanied by a member of the museum staff. These underground burial chambers are still evocative of ancient life, particularly in the Tomba della Scimmia (Tomb of the Monkey), where well-preserved frescoes depict scenes from ordinary life 2,500 years ago. The Tomba del Leone (Tomb of the Lion) and Tomba della Pellegrina (Tomb of the Pilgrim) are open by appointment during museum hours. ⊠ *Via Porsenna 93r* ☎ *0578/20177* ⌨ *Museum €4, with tombs €6* ☉ *Museum:*

daily 9–8 (last entrance 7:30). Tomba della Scimmia: by appointment Apr.–Oct., Tues., Thurs., and Sat. at 11 and 4; Nov.–Mar., Tues., Thurs., and Sat. at 11 and 2:30.

WHERE TO STAY & EAT

$$$$ ✕⌂ **La Frateria di Padre Eligio.** It's not
★ an overstatement to say that this former convent, founded in 1212 by Saint Francis himself, remains a spiritual place. Guest rooms, occupying the original pilgrims' quarters, are simple in the finest sense—with terra-cotta floors, stone walls, exposed ceiling beams, rustic wooden furniture, and museum-quality medieval artwork. The restaurant ($$$$) is one of the most sophisticated in southern Tuscany, serving eight-course set meals making full use of the gardens and wine cellar. The flowered courtyards and grounds, spread along a wooded hillside, are immaculately maintained by young recovering addicts who've found a higher path. **Pros:** Contemplative surroundings, excellent restaurant, small and intimate inn. **Cons:** No a/c, off-the-beaten-path location, need a car to get around. ⊠ *Off A1, Convento San Francesco* ✛*10 km (6 mi) southwest of Chiusi, Cetona 53040* ☎*0578/238261* ⊕*www.lafrateria.it* ⟿*5 rooms, 2 suites* ⌂*In-room: no a/c, no TV. In-hotel: restaurant, no elevator* ▤*AE, MC, V* ⊙*Closed early Jan.–mid-Feb. Restaurant closed Tues.*

CHIANCIANO TERME

11 km (7 mi) northwest of Chiusi, 73 km (44 mi) southeast of Siena.

GETTING HERE

From Rome or Florence, Chiusi is easily reached by car on the A1 highway (Autostrada del Sole). Tra-In buses link Chianciano with Siena. The closest train station to Chianciano Terme is in Chiusi, about 15 km (9 mi) away.

VISITOR INFORMATION

Chianciano Terme tourism office (⊠ *Via G. Sabatini 7* ☎*0578/63538* ⊟*0578/64623* ⊕*www.chianciano.com*).

EXPLORING

People from around the world come to the *città del fegato sano* (city of the healthy liver) to experience the curative waters. The area's innumerable mineral-water springs are reputed to restore and maintain the health of the skin, among other things. This is nothing new; as early as the 5th century BC, Chianciano Terme was the site of a temple to Apollo the Healer. It's no secret, either—the Terme di Chianciano spa alone claims to draw 120,000 visitors a year, and Italian state health insurance covers visits to the baths and springs for qualified patients. But you can test the waters yourself at a number of springs. If you're not here for the waters, probably the most interesting part of Chianciano is the old town, which lies to the north. The modern town, stretching along a hillside to the south, is a series of hotels, shops, and restaurants catering to spa aficionados.

Terme di Chianciano is an organization that represents three spas. The Terme Web site lists the varied spa treatments available (mornings only at Acqua Santa and Acqua Sillene). Perhaps to offset the clinical coldness of the actual treatment centers, each spa is surrounded by a large park filled with trees, flower gardens, and reflecting pools. There are facilities for such light sporting activities as tennis and boccie, and dance floors are available for musical events on summer evenings. The all-important water is served up at long counters, where the spa staff is always ready to refill your glass. Be warned: the mineral water can have a cleansing effect on your system that may come on suddenly. ⊠ *Via delle Rose 12* ☎ *0578/68292* ⊕ *www.termechianciano.it.*

The water at **Acqua Santa,** taken as a drinking cure, is known for curing liver and digestive ailments and for detoxifying in general. ⊠ *Piazza Martiri Perugini* ☎ *0578/68411* 🎫 *Jan.–May and Nov. and Dec., €7; June–Sept., €9; entrance includes the Acqua Fucoli spa until noon* ⊙ *Daily 8–noon.* The waters of **Acqua Fucoli** are usually taken as a drinking cure for all manner of intestinal disorders. ⊠ *Viale G. Bacelli* ☎ *0578/68430* 🎫 *Morning €9, entrance fee includes the Acqua Santa spa; afternoon €5* ⊙ *Apr. 16–Oct. 16, daily 8–7:30.* The steamy-hot waters at **Acqua Sillene** are used for private mineral and mud tub baths. The spa has nonaquatic activities including tennis, boccie, and miniature golf (all for additional fees). ⊠ *Piazza Marconi* ☎ *0578/68551* 🎫 *Varies according to the treatments chosen* ⊙ *Daily 8–noon and 4–7:30.*

At **Terme Sant'Elena,** the waters are said to help with kidney and urinary-tract ailments and all manner of digestive disorders; there are boccie courts and a pretty park to stroll in while you sip. On summer afternoons you can dance to live orchestra music in the park. ⊠ *Viale dell Libertà 112* ☎ *0578/31141* ⊕ *www.acquasantelena.it* 🎫 *June–Oct. 15, €6; Oct. 16–31, €5.50* ⊙ *Jun.–Oct., weekdays 8:30–noon and 3–6, Sat. 9–noon.*

The walled medieval town of **Chianciano,** 3 km (2 mi) northeast of Chianciano Terme, is best known for its proximity to the spa town; nevertheless, the well-preserved old town is appealing. The **Museo Civico Archeologico** contains a good collection of Etruscan and Roman sculpture and pottery excavated from around the area. ⊠ *Via Dante, Chianciano* ☎ *0578/30471* 🎫 *€4* ⊙ *Apr.–Oct., daily 10–1 and 4–7; Nov.–Mar., weekends 10–1 and 4–7.*

To the southeast of Chianciano, 10 km (6 mi) along SP19, lies **Sarteano,** a relatively unspoiled village that dates from the 12th and 13th centuries. The town's narrow streets, which wind slowly up toward an imposing fortress, now privately owned, make for very pleasant strolling. Don't miss the small church of **San Martino,** which houses a striking Annunciation by the important Sienese painter Domenico Beccafumi (1486–1551). ⊠ *Piazza San Martino* ☎ *No phone* 🎫 *Free* ⊙ *Daily 9–12:30 and 4–7:30.*

**OFF THE
BEATEN
PATH**

Cetona. Follow SP19 past Sarteano and continue on SP21 to reach the delightful village of Cetona. Time may seem to have stopped as you walk along the quiet, narrow, medieval lanes and back alleys of this village. Peer through the locked gate for a glimpse of the privately owned castle, and take in splendid views of olive orchards, cypress groves, and the quiet wooded slopes of Mt. Cetona from the town's terraced streets. ⊕ *20 km (12 mi) southeast of Chianciano Terme.*

MONTEPULCIANO

10 km (6 mi) northeast of Chianciano Terme, 65 km (40 mi) southeast of Siena, 114 km (70 mi) southeast of Florence.

GETTING HERE
From Rome or Florence, take the Chiusi–Chianciano exit from the A1 highway (Autostrada del Sole). From Siena, take the SR2 south to San Quirico and then the SP146 to Montepulciano. Tra-In offers bus service from Siena to Montepulciano several times a day. Montepulciano's train station is in Montepulciano Stazione, 10 km (6 mi) away.

VISITOR INFORMATION
Montepulciano tourism office (✉ *Via di Gracciano nel Corso 59r* ☎ *0578/757341* ⊕ *www.prolocomontepulciano.it*).

EXPLORING
Perched on a hilltop, Montepulciano is made up of a pyramid of red-brick buildings set within a circle of cypress trees. At an altitude of almost 2,000 feet, it is cool in summer and chilled in winter by biting winds sweeping down its spiraling streets. The town has an unusually harmonious look, the result of the work of three architects: Antonio Sangallo "il Vecchio" (circa 1455–1534), Vignola (1507–73), and Michelozzo (1396–1472). The group endowed it with fine palaces and churches in an attempt to impose Renaissance architectural ideals on an ancient Tuscan hill town.

★ Montepulciano's pièce de résistance is the beautiful **Piazza Grande**, filled with handsome buildings. On the Piazza Grande is the **Duomo**, which has an unfinished facade that doesn't measure up to the beauty of the neighboring palaces. On the inside, however, its Renaissance roots shine through. You can see fragments of the tomb of Bartolomeo Aragazzi, secretary to Pope Martin V (who reigned from 1417 to 1431); it was created by Michelozzo between 1427 and 1436, and pieces of it have been dispersed to museums in other parts of the world. ✉ *Piazza Grande* ☎ *0578/757761* ✉ *Free* ⊙ *Daily 9–12:30.*

Though sections of the **Palazzo Comunale** date from the late 13th century, it was restructured in the 14th century and again in the mid-15th century. Michelozzo oversaw this last phase. From the tower, a commanding view of Siena, Mt. Amiata (the highest point in Tuscany), and Lake Trasimeno (the largest lake on the Italian peninsula) can be enjoyed on a clear day. ✉ *Piazza Grande* ☎ *No phone* ✉ *Free* ⊙ *Daily 8–1.*

Summer in Valle d'Orcia.

Michelozzo had a hand in creating the beautiful travertine facade on the church of **Sant'Agostino**, which was built in 1285 and renovated in the early 1400s. He also sculpted the terra-cotta relief of the Madonna and Child above the door. ⊠*Piazza Michelozzo* ☎*0578/757761* 🎟️*Free* ⊙ *Daily 9–12:30 and 3:30–7:30.*

★ On the hillside below the town walls is the church of **San Biagio**, designed by Antonio Sangallo il Vecchio. A paragon of Renaissance architectural perfection, it's considered his masterpiece. Inside the church is a painting of a Madonna. According to legend, the painting was the only thing remaining in an abandoned church that two young girls entered on April 23, 1518. The two girls saw the eyes of the Madonna moving, and that same afternoon so did a farmer and a cow, who knelt down in front of the painting. In 1963 the image was proclaimed the Madonna del Buon Viaggio (Madonna of the Good Journey), the protector of tourists in Italy. ⊠*Via di San Biagio* ☎*0578/7577761* ⊙ *Daily 9–12:30 and 3:30–7:30.*

WHERE TO STAY & EAT

$$$–$$$$ ✕**La Grotta.** You might be tempted to pass right by the innocuous
★ entrance across the street from San Biagio, but you'd miss some fantastic food. Try the *tagliolini con carciofi e rigatino* (thin noodles with artichokes and bacon) or *tagliatelle di grano saraceno con asparagi e zucchine* (flat, buckwheat-flour noodles with asparagus and zucchini). Wash it down with the local wine, which just happens to be one of Italy's finest—Vino Nobile di Montepulciano. The desserts, such as an

EATING WELL IN SOUTHERN TUSCANY

In popular tourist towns such as Monte Argentino, Saturnia, and the villages sprinkled across the island of Elba, there are excellent upscale restaurants that serve elaborate dishes.

But to savor the diverse flavors of the cooking of this region, look for the family-run trattorias found in every town. The service and set-ting are often basic, but the food can be great.

Few places serve lighter fare at midday, so be prepared to face heavy meals at lunch and dinner, especially in out-of-the-way towns. Hours for meals are fairly standard: lunch between 12:30 and 2, dinner between 7:30 and 10.

extravagantly rich triple-chocolate flan, are prepared with particular flair. ⊠ *Via di San Biagio 16, 53045* ☎*0578/757479* ⊟*AE, MC, V* ⊗ *Closed Wed. and Jan. and Feb.*

$$$$ 🍴**Podere Dionora.** The cypress-lined drive to this secluded country retreat hints that you have found something special. The Dionora sits serenely on an estate surrounded by carefully manicured lawns, woodlands, and vineyards. Earth-tone fabrics complement antiques such as sleigh or iron beds in the individually decorated rooms, all of which have functioning fireplaces. Every bathroom has a sauna and massage tub. A separate building, where the buffet breakfast is served and international newspapers await you each morning, has large arched windows with delightful views of lawns and vineyards on all four sides. **Pros:** Secluded setting, great views, attentive service. **Cons:** Long walk to the nearest town, need a car to get around. ⊠ *Via Vicinale di Poggiano* ⊕ *3 km (2 mi) east of Montepulciano town center, 53045* ☎*0578/717496* ⊕*www.dionora.it* ⤴*4 rooms, 2 suites* ⚄*In-room: no phone, safe, refrigerator. In-hotel: pool, bicycles, no elevator* ⊟*AE, DC, MC, V* ⊗*Closed mid-Dec.–mid-Feb.* �🍽️*BP.*

$$$ 🍴**Relais San Bruno.** Alberto Pavoncelli converted his family's summer
★ home, just minutes from the town center, into a splendid inn. Set in extensive gardens with hammocks hidden here and there, the hotel's emphasis is on tranquillity and relaxation. The well-appointed rooms are located in four separate cottages; breakfast is served in a fifth. Reproductions of Columbian artist Fernando Botero's paintings add a touch of whimsy. A fodors.com user wrote: "the view of San Biagio and Montepulciano is stunning." **Pros:** King-size beds in most rooms, functioning fireplaces, relaxed but attentive service. **Cons:** Cottages can be chilly, need a car to get around. ⊠ *Via di Pescaia 5/7, 53045* ☎*0578/716222* ⊕*www.sanbrunorelais.com* ⤴*7 rooms, 1 suite* ⚄ *In-hotel: bar, pool, no elevator, public Internet* ⊟*AE, DC, MC, V* 🍽️*BP.*

$$ 🍴**San Biagio.** A five-minute walk from the church of the same name,
★ the San Biagio makes a great base for exploring the surrounding countryside. All the rooms are simply decorated, but the lack of luxurious appointments is more than made up for by the friendly and professional service. A buffet breakfast prepares you for your day's explo-

rations, and a dip in the indoor pool, no matter what the weather, provides a welcome finish. Several pleasant walking trails pass in front of the hotel: ask your hosts for details. **Pros:** Heated indoor pool, family-friendly atmosphere. **Cons:** Some rooms face a busy road, lots of tour groups. ⊠ *Via San Bartolomeo 2, 53045* ☎*0578/717233* ⊕*www. albergosanbiagio.it* ⌐*27 rooms* ⌂*In-hotel: restaurant, pool* ⊟*AE, DC, MC, V* ⓘ*BP.*

NIGHTLIFE & THE ARTS

The **Cantiere Internazionale d'Arte** (⊠*Piazza Grande 7* ☎*0578/757341*), held in July and August, is a festival of art, music, and theater ending with a dramatic production staged in the Piazza Grande.

PIENZA

★ *12 km (7 mi) west of Montepulciano, 52 km (31 mi) southeast of Siena, 120 km (72 mi) southeast of Florence.*

GETTING HERE

From Siena, drive south along the SR2 to San Quirico d'Orcia and then the SP146. The trip should take just over an hour. Tra-In shuttles passengers between Siena and Pienza. There is no train service to Pienza.

VISITOR INFORMATION

Pienza tourism office (⊠*Piazza Pio II* ☎*0578/749071* ⊕*www.porta-lepienza.it*).

EXPLORING

Pienza owes its appearance to Pope Pius II (1405–64), who had grand plans to transform his hometown of Corsignano—its former name—into a compact model Renaissance town. The man entrusted with the transformation was Bernardo Rossellino (1409–64), a protégé of the great Renaissance-architectural theorist Leon Battista Alberti (1404–72). His mandate was to create a cathedral, a papal palace, and a town hall that adhered to the vainglorious pope's principles. Gothic and Renaissance styles were fused, and the buildings were decorated with Sienese paintings. The net result was a project that expressed Renaissance ideals of art, architecture, and civilized good living in a single scheme: it stands as an exquisite example of the architectural canons that Alberti formulated in the early Renaissance and that were utilized by later architects, including Michelangelo, in designing many of Italy's finest buildings and piazzas. Today the cool nobility of Pienza's center seems almost surreal in this otherwise unpretentious village, known locally for *pienzino*, a smooth sheep's-milk pecorino cheese.

In 1459 Pius II commissioned Rossellino to design the perfect palazzo for his papal court. The architect took Florence's Palazzo Rucellai by Alberti as a model and designed the 100-room **Palazzo Piccolomini.** Three sides of the building fit perfectly into the urban plan around it, while the fourth, looking over the valley, has a lovely loggia uniting it with the gardens in back. Guided tours departing every 30 minutes take you to visit the papal apartments, including a beautiful library, the

Sala delle Armi—with an impressive weapons collection—and the music room, with its extravagant wooden ceiling forming four letter P's, for Pope, Pius, Piccolomini, and Pienza. The last tour departs 30 minutes before closing. ⊠*Piazza Pio II* ☎*0578/286300* ⊕*www. palazzopiccolominipienza.it* 🎫*€7* ⊘*Mid-Mar.–mid-Oct., Tues.–Sun. 10–6:30; mid-Oct.–mid-Mar., Tues.–Sun. 10–4:30.*

The 15th-century **Duomo** was also built by the architect Rossellino under the influence of Alberti. The facade is divided in three parts with Renaissance arches under the pope's coat of arms encircled by a wreath of fruit. Inside, the cathedral is simple but richly decorated with Sienese paintings. The Duomo's perfection didn't last long—the first cracks appeared immediately after the building was completed, and its foundations have shifted slightly ever since as rain erodes the hillside behind. You can see this effect if you look closely at the base of the first column as you enter the church and compare it with the last. ⊠*Piazza Pio II* ☎*No phone* 🎫*Free* ⊘*Tues.–Sun. 10–1 and 3–7.*

The **Museo Diocesano** sits to the left of the Duomo. It's small but has a few interesting papal treasures and rich Flemish tapestries. The most precious piece is a rare mantle woven in gold with pearls and embroidered religious scenes that belonged to Pope Pius II. ⊠*Corso Il Rossellino 30* ☎*0578/749905* 🎫*€4* ⊘*Mid-Mar.–Oct., Wed.–Mon. 10–1 and 3–6:30; Nov.–mid-Mar., weekends 10–1 and 3–6.*

Part of the acclaimed 1996 film *The English Patient* was filmed at **Sant'Anna in Camprena,** a former Benedictine monastery where you can view frescoes by Sodoma (1477–1549) in the dining hall and in the room where the eponymous patient lay in bed. It's best reached by car or bicycle, as public transportation isn't available. For the world-weary, extremely plain rooms are available in the austere silence of the monastery. Double rooms with private bathroom and breakfast are €75 per night; those without private bathroom are €60. To get here from Pienza, take the road to San Quirico for 1 km (½ mi), then turn right at the sign for the monastery. ⊠*Località Sant'Anna in Camprena* ☎*0578/748037 or 338/4079284* ⊕*www.camprena.it* 🎫*Free* ⊘*Weekends 9–6.*

WHERE TO STAY & EAT

$–$$ ✕**La Chiocciola.** Take the few minutes to walk from the old town for typical Pienza fare, including homemade *pici* (thick, short spaghetti) with hare or wild-boar sauce. The restaurant's version of *formaggio in forno* (baked cheese) with assorted accompaniments such as fresh porcini mushrooms is reason enough to venture here. ⊠ *Via dell'Acero 2* ☎*0578/748683* ▤*MC, V* ☉*Closed Wed. and 10 days in Feb.*

¢ ✕**Osteria Sette di Vino.** Tasty dishes based on the region's cheeses are the specialty at this simple and inexpensive *osteria* (tavern). Try versions of pici or the starter of radicchio baked quickly to brown the edges. The local pecorino cheese appears often on the menu—the pecorino *grigliata con pancetta* (grilled with cured bacon) is divine. Can't decide? Try the pecorino tasting menu. Osteria Sette di Vino is on a quiet, pleasant square in the center of Pienza. ⊠*Piazza di Spagna 1* ☎*0578/749092* ▤*No credit cards* ☉*Closed Wed., July 1–15, and Nov.*

$–$$ ⛨**Hotel Corsignano.** Just outside the old city walls, Hotel Corsignano is modern and comfortable. Two light-beige buildings, the older one right on the road, are connected by a hallway. Guest rooms are decorated with simple wooden furniture: those in the newer wing are quieter and larger than those in the front. The staff is exceptionally friendly and helpful. **Pros:** Steps away from center of town, helpful staff. **Cons:** Modern building lacks charm, some rooms face a busy street. ⊠*Via della Madonnina 11, 53026* ☎*0578/748501* ⊕*www.corsignano.it* ⇥*40 rooms* ⛨*In-room: safe, refrigerator. In-hotel: restaurant, laundry service, public Internet, parking (no fee), some pets allowed* ▤*AE, DC, MC, V* ⛨*BP.*

¢ ⛨**Camere di Pienza.** A Renaissance building on the main street houses this tiny hotel. The four rooms have pretty, if simple, decoration and particularly nice ceilings—three with wood beams and one with a fresco. **Pros:** Charming rooms, convenient location in center of town. **Cons:** No a/c, steps to climb. ⊠*Corso Il Rossellino 23, 53026* ☎*0578/748500* ⇥*4 rooms* ⛨*In-room: no a/c. In-hotel: no elevator* ▤*No credit cards* ⛨*EP.*

SAN QUIRICO D'ORCIA

9½ km (5½ mi) southwest of Pienza, 43 km (26 mi) southeast of Siena, 111 km (67 mi) southeast of Florence.

GETTING HERE

From Siena, San Quirico d'Orcia is an hour-long drive on the SR2. Tra-In provides buses from Siena to San Quirico. There is no train service to San Quirico.

VISITOR INFORMATION

San Quirico d'Orcia tourism office (⊠ *Via Dante Alighieri 33* ☎*0577/897211* ⊕*www.comunesanquirico.it*).

EXPLORING

San Quirico d'Orcia, on the modern Via Cassia (SR2) south from Siena toward Rome, has almost-intact 15th-century walls topped with 14 turrets. The pleasantly crumbling appearance of the town recalls days of yore, and it's well suited for a stop to enjoy a gelato in a local bar or a meal and to see its Romanesque church.

The 13th-century **Collegiata** church has three majestic portals, one possibly the work of Giovanni Pisano (circa 1245/48–1318). Behind the high altar are some fine examples of inlaid woodwork by Antonio Barilli (1482–1502). In the floor of the right aisle, look for the tomb slab of Henry of Nassau, a pilgrim knight who died here in 1451. ⊠*Piazza Chigi* ☎*No phone* 🖃*Free* ⊗*Daily 8:30–12:30.*

Near the Collegiata stands **Palazzo Chigi**, named after the family to whom the Medici gave San Quirico in 1667. Small art exhibitions are occasionally displayed in the palace courtyard, which is otherwise closed to the public. ⊠*Piazza Chigi.*

Against the walls of San Quirico d'Orcia is the **Horti Leonini**, a public park with Italian-style gardens that retain merely a shimmer of their past opulence. In the center, is an early-18th-century statue of Cosimo III, one of the last of the Medici dukes of Tuscany. ⊠*Off Piazza Libertà.*

WHERE TO STAY & EAT

$–$$ ✕**Trattoria al Vecchio Forno.** A meal here is always special. Don't miss the dishes accented with porcini mushrooms, such as the excellent mushroom soup. You might also try pici with tomato or boar sauce, and roast boar and game. The menu is rounded out by a varied wine selection. There's a nice garden out back. ⊠*Via Piazzola 8* ☎*0577/897380* ▤*MC, V* ⊗*Closed Wed., 10 days in mid-Nov., and 2 wks in mid-Jan.*

$$ 🛏**Palazzo del Capitano.** The guest rooms at this 14th-century palace are named for signs of the zodiac, but the astrological reference stops at the painted symbol on the door. Each elegant room is unique: an antique sewing-machine table serves as a nightstand; a medieval-looking chandelier with a forged-iron ring and a globe hangs from a ceiling; elegant striped silk covers a wood settee. Some rooms have ivory-color drapes hanging from baldachin beds—iron canopy beds with a painted medallion on the headpiece. A lovely garden opens behind the hotel. Five cheaper rooms, named for constellations, are available in an annex. **Pros:** Central location, elegant furnishings, secluded garden. **Cons:** Rooms are on the small side, some street noise, getting here by car is difficult. ⊠*Via Poliziano 18, 53027* ☎*0577/899028 or 0577/899421* ⊕*www.palazzodelcapitano.com* 🛏*14 rooms, 2 suites* &*In-room: safe. In-hotel: restaurant, bar* ▤*MC, V* ⊚*BP.*

BAGNO VIGNONI

5 km (3 mi) south of San Quirico d'Orcia, 48 km (29 mi) southeast of Siena, 116 km (70 mi) southeast of Florence.

GETTING HERE

Bagno Vignoni is off the SR2, about an hour from Siena. Tra-In provides bus service from Siena to Bagno Vignoni. There is no train station nearby.

VISITOR INFORMATION

Bagno Vignoni tourism office (⊠*Località Bagno Vignoni 2* ☎*0577/888975* ⊕*www.comunesanquirico.it*).

EXPLORING

Bagno Vignoni has been famous since Roman times for the sulfurous waters that come bubbling up into the large rectangular pool that forms the town's main square, Piazza delle Sorgenti (Square of the Springs). Medieval pilgrims and modern hikers alike have soothed their tired feet in the pleasantly warm water that flows through open channels on its way to the River Orcia. Of particular interest are the ruins of a medieval bathhouse on the edge of town and the Chapel of Saint Catherine, who, it seems, came here often.

Bagno Vignoni's public hot-spring pool, **Piscina Val di Sole,** provides warm-water relaxation for more than just your feet. Stand under the waterfall to massage and soothe weary shoulder muscles. Though the facility remains open, there's no swimming allowed between 1 and 2:30 from April to September. The last admission is one hour before closing. ⊠ *Via Ara Urcea 43* ☏ *0577/887112* ⊕ *www.piscinavaldisole.it* ⊠ *€12* ⊙ *Apr.–Sept., Fri.–Wed. 9:30–6; Oct.–Mar., Fri.–Wed. 10–5.*

OFF THE BEATEN PATH   **Vignoni Alto.** A steep gravel road leads north out of Bagno Vignoni for 2 km (1 mi) to the village of Vignoni Alto, a tiny grouping of buildings huddled at the base of a 13th-century tower. The tower, now a private home, was built to watch over the Via Francigena. A spectacular view of the entire Val d'Orcia opens up from the eastern gate.

WHERE TO EAT

$$ ✕ **Bottega di Cacio.** Lots of shaded outdoor seating makes this a very pleasant place for lunch on a warm day. Pecorino cheese, spicy salami, and grilled vegetables *sott'olio* (preserved in olive oil) are served cafeteria-style. And, if you want something even spicier, the stuffed hot peppers are delicious. There is a good selection of wine, but the choice of desserts is limited. ⊠ *Piazza del Moretto 31* ☏ *0577/887477* ▤ *No credit cards* ⊙ *Closed Thurs.*

MONTALCINO

19 km (12 mi) northeast of Bagno Vignoni, 41 km (25½ mi) south of Siena, 109 km (68 mi) south of Florence.

GETTING HERE

By car, follow the SR2 south from Siena, then follow the SP45 to Montalcino. Several Tra-In buses travel between Siena and Montalcino daily, making a tightly scheduled day trip possible. There is no train service available.

VISITOR INFORMATION

Montalcino tourism office (⊠ *Costa del Municipio 8* ☏ *0577/849331* ⊕ *www.prolocomontalcino.it*).

EXPLORING

Tiny Montalcino, with its commanding view from high on a hill, can claim an Etruscan past. It saw a fair number of travelers, as it was directly on the road from Siena to Rome. During the early Middle Ages it enjoyed a brief period of autonomy before falling under the orbit of Siena in 1201. Now Montalcino's greatest claim to fame is that it produces Brunello di Montalcino, one of Italy's most esteemed reds. Driving to the town, you pass through the Brunello vineyards. You can sample the excellent but expensive red in wine cellars in town or visit a nearby winery, such as Fattoria dei Barbi, for a guided tour and tasting; you must call ahead for reservations.

La Fortezza, a 14th-century Sienese fortress, has well-preserved battlements. Climb up the narrow, spiral steps for the 360-degree view of most of southern Tuscany. There's also an enoteca for tasting wines on-site. ⊠ *Via Panfilo dell'Oca* 🖀*0577/849211* 🎫*€3* ☉*Nov.–Mar., Tues.–Sun. 9–6; Apr.–Oct., daily 9–8.*

The **Museo Civico e Diocesano d'Arte Sacra** is in a building that belonged in the 13th century to the Augustinian monastic order. The ticket booth is in the glorious refurbished cloister, and the sacred art collection, gathered from churches throughout the region, is displayed on two floors in former monastic quarters. Though the art here might be called "B-list," a fine altarpiece by Bartolo di Fredi (circa 1330–1410), the *Coronation of the Virgin,* makes dazzling use of gold. In addition, there's a striking 12th-century crucifix that originally adorned the high altar of the church of Sant'Antimo. Also on hand are many wood sculptures, a typical medium in these parts during the Renaissance. ⊠ *Via Ricasoli 21* 🖀*0577/846014* 🎫*€4.50* ☉*Apr.–Oct., Tues.–Sun. 10–1 and 4–5:50; Nov.–Mar., Tues.–Sun. 10–1 and 2–5:40.*

The cellars of the venerable **Fattoria dei Barbi** date from the 17th century and hold almost 200 oak wine barrels. Some of Italy's most famous wines are produced here, including an excellent range of Brunellos, a fine Rosso di Montalcino, and the estate's special Super Tuscan brands: Brusco dei Barbi and Bruscone dei Barbi. Olive oil, salami, and pecorino cheese are made at the winery's organic farm. Guided tours of the cellars are followed by wine tastings, during which you can also sample the other products. ⊠*Località Podernovi 1* 🖀*0577/841111* ⊕*www.fattoriadeibarbi.it* 🎫*€7–€16, depending on wines tasted* ☉*Tours weekdays at 10:30, 11:30, 3:30, and 4:30.*

WHERE TO STAY & EAT

$$$$ ✕**Poggio Antico.** One of Italy's renowned chefs, Roberto Minnetti, abandoned his highly successful restaurant in Rome to move to the countryside outside Montalcino. Now he and his wife Patrizia serve in a relaxed dining room with regal arches and beamed ceilings. The Tuscan cuisine is masterfully interpreted: a frequent option on the changing menu is *pappardelle al ragù di agnello* (flat, wide noodles in a lamb sauce) or venison in a sweet-and-sour sauce. ⊠*On road to Grosseto* ✛ *4 km (2½ mi) south of Montalcino, Località I Poggi* 🖀*0577/849200* 🖃*AE, MC, V* ☉*Closed 3 wks in Dec. and Mon. Oct.–Mar.*

$$–$$$ ✕**Fattoria dei Barbi.** Set among the vineyards that produce excellent Brunello—as well as its younger cousin, Rosso di Montalcino—is this rustic taverna with a large stone fireplace. The estate farm produces many of the ingredients used in such traditional specialties as *stracotto nel brunello* (braised beef cooked with beans in Brunello wine).

This eatery is a few minutes south of Montalcino, in the direction of Sant'Antimo. ⊠*Località Podernuovi* 🕾*0577/847117* ⚔*Reservations essential* ⊟*AE, DC, MC, V* ⊗*Closed Wed. and mid-Jan.–mid-Feb.*

$ ✕**Il Grappolo Blu.** Any one of this restaurant's *piatti tipici* (typical plates) is worth trying: the local specialty, *pici all'aglione* (thick, long noodles served with sautéed cherry tomatoes and many cloves of garlic), is done particularly well. The chef also has a deft touch with vegetables; if there's fennel on the menu, make sure to try it. The interior, with white walls and an odd collection of prints, doesn't leave much of an impression, but the service is warm and friendly. ⊠*Scale di via Moglio 1* 🕾*0577/847150* ⚔*Reservations essential* ⊟*AE, DC, MC, V* ⊗*Closed Fri.*

¢–$ ✕**Enoteca Osteria Osticcio.** Tullio and Francesca Scrivano have beautifully remodeled this restaurant and wineshop. Upon entering, you descend a curving staircase to a tasting room filled with rustic wooden tables. Adjacent is a small dining area with a splendid view of the hills far below, and outside is a lovely little terrace perfect for sampling Brunello di Montalcino when the weather is warm. The menu is light and pairs nicely with the wines, which are the main draw. The *acciughe sotto pesto* (anchovies with pesto) is a particularly fine treat. ⊠*Via Matteotti 23* 🕾*0577/848271* ⊟*AE, DC, MC, V* ⊗*Closed Sun. No dinner.*

$ 🏠**La Crociona.** A quiet and serene family-owned farm, La Crociona is in the middle of a small vineyard with glorious views. The apartments, which can sleep up to six people, have antique iron beds and 17th-century wardrobes. There's a big terrace and a pool where guests tend to congregate. You are invited to use the family's barbecue grill, as well as sample the owner's own wine supply. **Pros:** Peaceful location, great for families. **Cons:** No a/c, need a car to get around. ⊠*Località La Croce, 53024* 🕾*0577/848007* ⊕*www.lacrociona.com* ⇋*7 apartments* &*In-room: no a/c, no phone, kitchen. In-hotel: pool, bicycles, no elevator, laundry facilities, laundry service, public Internet* ⊟*MC, V* ⦿*EP.*

ABBAZIA DI SANT'ANTIMO

FodorsChoice *10 km (6 mi) south of Montalcino, 51 km (32 mi) south of Siena, 119*
★ *km (74 mi) south of Florence.*

GETTING HERE
Abbazia di Sant'Antimo is a 15-minute drive from Montalcino. Tra-In bus service is extremely limited. The abbey cannot be reached by train.

EXPLORING
It's well worth your while to visit this 12th-century Romanesque abbey, as it's a gem of pale stone in the silvery green of an olive grove. The exterior and interior sculpture is outstanding, particularly the nave capitals, a combination of French, Lombard, and even Spanish influences. The sacristy (seldom open) forms part of the primitive Carolingian church (founded in AD 781), its entrance flanked by 9th-century pilasters. The small vaulted crypt dates from the same period. Above the nave runs a *matroneum* (women's gallery), an unusual feature once used to separate the congregation. Equally unusual is the ambulatory,

for which the three radiating chapels were almost certainly copied from a French model. Stay to hear the canonical hours celebrated in Gregorian chant. On the drive that leads up toward Castelnuovo dell'Abate is a small shop that sells souvenirs and has washrooms. A 2½-hour hiking trail (signed as #2)

leads to the abbey from Montalcino. Starting near Montalcino's small cemetery, the trail heads south through woods, along a ridge road to the tiny hamlet of Villa a Tolli, and then downhill to Sant'Antimo. ⊠*Località Sant'Antimo Castelnuovo dell'Abate* ☎*0577/835659* ⊕*www.antimo.it* ⊠*Free* ☉*Daily 6 AM–9 PM.*

LE CRETE

Van Gogh never saw the area south of Siena known as Le Crete (*creta* means "clay" in Italian), but in the bare, moonstone-color clay hills around Asciano—the rolling wheat fields, the warm light, the dramatic gullies and ravines cut by centuries of erosion—he would have perhaps found worthy subjects, as these landscapes seem carved into the earth much in the way that the furrows of paint layer his canvases.

BUONCONVENTO

27 km (17 mi) southeast of Siena, 80 km (50 mi) south of Florence.

GETTING HERE

By car, Buonconvento is a 30-minute drive south from Siena on the SR2. Tra-In buses travel daily between Siena and Buonconvento several times a day, making a carefully scheduled day trip quite possible. A train connects Siena with Buonconvento, Monte Amiato Scalo, Asciano, and Arbia.

VISITOR INFORMATION

Buonconvento tourism office (⊠*Via Soccini 41* ☎*0577/807181* ⊕*www. comune.buonconvento.siena.it*).

EXPLORING

Buonconvento reached the height of its importance when it served as a major outpost along the Roman road, Via Cassia, although it's also remembered by the history books as the place where Holy Roman Emperor Henry VII was poisoned by a Eucharist wafer.

Today quiet Buonconvento is worth a stop for a look at its tiny **Museo d'Arte Sacra**, a two-room picture gallery with more than its fair share of works by Tuscan artists such as Duccio and Andrea di Bartolo. The highlight is a triptych with the *Madonna and Saints Bernardino and Catherine* by Sano di Pietro. ⊠*Via Soccini 17* ☎*0577/807181* ⊠*€3.50* ☉*Mar.–Oct., Tues.–Sun. 10–1 and 3–7; Nov.–Feb., weekends 10–1 and 3–5.*

EN
ROUTE

If you're heading northwest to Siena, stray 9 km (5½ mi) west of the Via Cassia to Vescovado and follow the signs from here 2 km (1 mi) south to **Murlo**, a tiny fortified medieval *borgo* (village) that has been completely restored. An imposing bishop's palace holds the **Antiquarium Poggio Civitate**, a museum containing Etruscan relics. Although there are many beautiful pieces on display, the almost entirely complete roof and pediment from a 5th-century BC Etruscan house are especially rare. The museum is named after the nearby site from which most of the artifacts were excavated. ✉*Piazza della Cattedrale 4* ☎*0577/814099* 🖃*€3.20* ☉*Mar. and Oct., Tues.–Sun. 10–1 and 3–5; Apr–.June, and Sept., Tues.–Sun. 10–1 and 3–7; July and Aug., Tues.–Sun. 10–7; Nov.–Feb., Tues.–Fri. 10–1, weekends 10–1 and 3–5.*

ABBAZIA DI MONTE OLIVETO MAGGIORE

★ *9 km (5½ mi) northeast of Buonconvento, 37 km (23 mi) southeast of Siena.*

GETTING HERE

From Siena, the abbey is a 45-minute drive on the SR2 south to Buonconvento and then the SP451 to Monte Oliveto. Bus and train service are not available.

EXPLORING

Tuscany's most-visited abbey, Monte Oliveto Maggiore sits in an oasis of olive and cypress trees amid the harsh landscape of Le Crete. It was founded in 1313 by Giovanni Tolomei, a rich Sienese lawyer who, after miraculously regaining his lost sight, changed his name to Bernardo in homage to the Saint Bernard of Clairvaux, who is sometimes credited with the creation of medieval monasticism. Bernardo then founded a monastic order dedicated to the restoration of Benedictine principles. The name of the order—the White Benedictines—refers to a vision that Bernardo had in which Jesus, Mary, and his own mother were all clad in white. The monks are sometimes also referred to as Olivetans, which is the name of the hill where the monastery was built. Famous for maintaining extreme poverty—their feast-day meal consisted of two eggs—they slept on straw mats and kept a vow of silence. Although the monks look like they are eating a little better these days and are not afraid to strike up a conversation, the monastery still operates, and most of the area is off limits to visitors. One of Italy's most important book restoration centers is here, and the monks still produce a wide variety of traditional liqueurs (distilled from herbs that grow on the premises), which are available in the gift shop along with enough food products to fill a pantry, all produced by monks in various parts of Italy.

From the entrance gate, a tree-lined lane leads down to the main group of buildings, with paths veering off to several shrines and chapels dedicated to important saints of the order. The church itself is not particularly memorable, but the exquisite choir stalls (1503–05) by Fra Giovanni da Verona are among the country's finest examples of *intarsia* (wood inlay). Forty-eight of the 125 stalls have inlaid decoration, each set up as a window or arched doorway that opens onto a space

Continued on page 325

SIMPLY PERFECT
*The Basic Goodness
of Tuscan Food*

THE CUISINE OF TUSCANY ISN'T COMPLICATED. In fact, every dish follows the same basic recipe:

■ Begin with fresh, high-quality ingredients, preferably produced within walking distance of the kitchen.

■ Prepare them using techniques that have been refined over centuries, ideally by members of the chef's family.

■ Serve the finished dish unpretentiously ("plate" is not a verb here), accompanied by a glass of good local wine.

The recipe looks simple, but executing it is not so easy. Some of the staples of "fine dining" that chefs elsewhere depend upon are pointedly missing.

There's nothing exotic: it would violate the "walking distance" principle of fresh, local ingredients. There's nothing ostentatious: showiness would distract from the basic beauty of the food. And innovation is looked on with a skeptical eye: if a new recipe or a new technique were really so good, surely someone in the preceding ten generations would have already thought of it.

The result is a cuisine that's inextricably tied to the place where it's made. There may now be Tuscan restaurants all over the globe, but you can still only eat genuine Tuscan food in Tuscany. It's home cooking that's worth traveling halfway around the world to taste.

320 <

EXPLORING THE TUSCAN MENU

Menu Basics

A meal in Tuscany (and elsewhere in Italy) traditionally consists of five courses, and every menu you encounter will be organized along this five-course plan:

First up is the **antipasto** (appetizer), often consisting of cured meats or marinated vegetables. Next to appear is the **primo**, usually pasta or soup, and after that the **secondo**, a meat or fish course with, perhaps, a **contorno** (vegetable dish) on the side. A simple **dolce** (dessert) rounds out the meal.

This, you've probably noticed, is a lot of food. Italians have noticed as well—a full, five-course meal is an indulgence usually reserved for special occasions. Instead, restaurant meals are a mix-and-match affair: you might order a primo and a secondo, or an antipasto and a primo, or a secondo and a contorno.

■ TIP→ The crucial rule of restaurant dining is that you should **order at least two courses**. It's a common mistake for tourists to order only a secondo, thinking they're getting a "main course" complete with side dishes. What they wind up with is one lonely piece of meat.

After you've eaten at a couple of restaurants, you may feel you're experiencing déjà vu: many of the same dishes are served almost everywhere. This is a by-product of the devotion to local, traditional cuisine, and part of the pleasure of dining in Tuscany is seeing how preparations vary from region to region and restaurant to restaurant.

What follows is a rundown, course by course, of classic dishes. The ones highlighted as "quintessential" are the epitome of Tuscan cooking. They shouldn't be missed.

Clockwise from bottom left: A well-worn menu; preparing *ribollita*; a typical food shop.

ANTIPASTI: APPETIZERS

The quintessential antipasto
Affettati misti

The name, roughly translated, means "mixed cold cuts," and it's something Tuscans do exceptionally well. The platter of cured meats is sure to include ***prosciutto crudo*** (ham, cut paper thin) and ***salame*** (dry sausage, prepared in dozens of ways, some spicy, some sweet). The most distinctly Tuscan *affettati* are made from ***cinta senese*** (a once nearly extinct pig found only in the heart of the region) and ***cinghiale*** (wild boar, which roam all of central Italy). You can eat these delicious slices unadorned or layered on a piece of bread.

From left: A typical affettati misti plate; two butchers; artichokes cured in olive oil

Other classics

Crostini
Toasted slices of bread with toppings—most commonly *fegatini* (chicken liver pâté), though other meat and vegetable concoctions also appear

Verdure sott'olio
Peppers, carrots, artichokes, and other vegetables cured in olive oil

Lardo di Colonnata
Not to be confused with lard (rendered fat), *lardo* is pig back fat that's seasoned with herbs, soaked in brine, and cured for months. Sliced thin and served over bread, it's a melt-in-your-mouth delicacy.

A WELL-OILED CUISINE

Olive oil is far and away the most important ingredient in Tuscan kitchens: it's a condiment, a cooking oil, a marinade, a salad dressing, a bread spread—one way or another, it makes its way into every meal.

The oil from Tuscany is frequently lauded as the best in the world. Open a bottle and you'll immediately know why: the aroma reaches out and grabs you. Like wine connoisseurs, oil lovers struggle for words to describe the experience—"spicy," "fruity," "herby," "redolent of artichokes"—but the sensual character of Tuscan oils defies description.

Which area in Tuscany produces the best oil is the subject of a never-ending debate. Sample as you go and decide for yourself—or simply enjoy the fact that there is no right answer. It's all good.

PRIMI: FIRST COURSES

The quintessential primo

Ribollita

A vegetable soup thickened with cannellini beans and stale bread—a classic example of how Tuscans make great things from humble ingredients. *Cavolo nero* (black cabbage, sometimes called Tuscan kale in the U.S.) is another key element—it gives the flavor a little kick. Upon serving, the soup is "christened" with a generous swirl of olive oil. In southern Tuscany, ribollita sometimes comes with chopped red onions on the side.

Other classics

Panzanella
A summer salad made of bread, tomatoes, basil, cucumbers, and olive oil

Pappa al pomodoro
Pureed tomato soup, thickened with bread

Zuppa alla frantoiana
Another bean, bread, and vegetable soup, this time run through a food mill

Pappardelle col sugo di cinghiale
Fresh pasta cut in wide strips with wild boar sauce

Ravioli di ricotta e spinaci
Spinach and cheese ravioli

Local specialties
(and the town or region where they're found)

Pici all'aglione
Hand-rolled pasta with garlic sauce (Siena and Montalcino)

Linguine alla granseola
Linguine with stone crab (a staple on Elba)

Minestra al farro
Soup made with *farro*, a barley-like grain (Lucca and the Garfagnana)

Ignudi
"Naked" ravioli-spinach and cheese dumplings minus the pasta (Florence and Chianti)

Crespelle
Crepe-like pancakes, stuffed with spinach and cheese and topped with a bechamel sauce (Florence)

Polenta di castagne
Chestnut polenta (the Garfagnana)

Acquacotta
"Cooked water"—thick vegetable soup (a specialty of the Maremma)

Tordelli di carne al ragù
Meat-stuffed tortelli pasta with a meat sauce (Lucca, where they prefer the spelling with a "d")

SECONDI: SECOND COURSES

The quintessential secondo
Bistecca alla fiorentina

You can get grilled steak everywhere from Texas to Tokyo, but in Tuscany they've found a way to make it their own. *Bistecca alla fiorentina* is an extra-thick T-bone that comes from ox-like Chianina cattle, a carefully nurtured Tuscan breed. It's seasoned with salt, pepper, and olive oil, and always served rare; cooking it longer is considered a travesty. Maybe it's the high quality of the beef, maybe it's the wonderful oil—whatever the reason, *bistecca alla fiorentina* truly is exceptional.

Other classics

Arista di maiale
Roast pork with sage and rosemary

Calamari all'inzimino
Squid and spinach stew

Tagliata di manzo
Thin slices of roasted beef, drizzled with oil

Fritto di pollo e coniglio
Fried chicken and rabbit

Salsiccia e fagioli
Pork sausage with beans

Local specialties

Frittura di paranza
Mixed fish fry (found all along the coast, but best in Livorno)

Piccione
Pigeon—it can be roasted, stuffed, or baked (southern Chianti)

Baccalà con ceci
Salt cod with chickpeas (much beloved by the Livornesi)

Peposo
A peppery beef stew (Impruneta)

Trippa alla fiorentina
Trip stewed in a tomato sauce (Florence)

Ricotta cheese, Vitereta, Tuscany

A TASTE OF THE TYPICAL

While "typical" can be a disparaging term in English, its Italian equivalent, *"tipico,"* is high praise. Whether you're talking about a type of cheese, a variety of wine, or a particular cut of pasta, *"tipico"* indicates something that's traditional to the location where you find it. Which means it's been perfected over the course of centuries. And that means, whatever it is, you won't get it better anywhere else.

CONTORNI: VEGETABLES

The quintessential contorno
Fagioli all'olio

Tuscans are known among fellow Italians as *"mangiafagioli"* (bean eaters), and with good reason. White cannellini beans are the standard, usually boiled with fresh sage, drained, and liberally laced with olive oil. Another preparation is *fagioli all'uccelletto,* in which the beans are cooked with tomato and sage. *Fagioli al fiasco* are slow-cooked in a glass bottle.

Other classics

Virtually any fresh vegetable, either briefly boiled or sautéed in oil, possibly with a touch of garlic. Greens are especially popular—look for *cime di rape* (turnip greens) as well as *spinaci* (spinach). Other seasonal favorites are *carciofi* (artichokes), *asparagi* (asparagus) *piselli* (peas), *zucchini, peperoni* (peppers), and *fave* (fava beans).

DOLCI: DESSERTS

The quintessential dolce
Cantuccini con vin santo

These hard little almond cookies, also known as **biscotti di Prato**, are virtually inedible when dry, but dip them into sweet vin santo wine, and the result is delectable.

From left: Castagnaccio; cantucci and vin santo; buccellato

Other classics

Tuscan cuisine is not particularly noted for its desserts. Meals often end with an unadorned piece of fruit. Here and there, though, you'll find exceptions.

Local specialties

Buccellato	*Ricciarelli*	*Brigidini*
An anise-flavored sweet bun (Lucca)	Delicate almond cookies (Siena)	Sugary wafers, best when topped with gelato (Montecatini)
Castagnaccio	*Panforte*	
A flat chestnut-flour cake (Lucca)	Candied fruit and nut cake (Siena)	

(a town, a landscape) or an object (a musical instrument, a bird), rendered in marvelous perspective. Check at the entrance for the schedule of Masses, as the monks often chant the liturgy.

In the abbey's main cloister, frescoes by Luca Signorelli and Sodoma depict scenes from the life of St. Benedict. Signorelli began the cycle by painting scenes from the saint's adult life as narrated by Saint Gregory the Great, and although his nine scenes are badly worn, the individual expressions are fittingly austere and pensive, full of serenity and religious spirit, and as individualized as those he painted in the San Brizio chapel in Orvieto's Duomo. Later Sodoma filled in the story with scenes from the saint's youth and the last years of his life. The results are also impressive, but in this case what stands out are the use of color and earthier imagery. Note the detailed landscapes, the rich costumes, the animals (similar to those Sodoma was known to keep as pets), and the scantily clad boys he apparently preferred (for this he was called "the Sodomist" and described by Vasari as "a merry and licentious man…of scant chastity"). ⊠*SS451* ☎*0577/707611* ✉*By donation* ☉*Daily 9:15–noon and 3:15–5:45.*

WHERE TO STAY & EAT

6

$–$$ ✕**La Torre.** You can enjoy straightforward Tuscan fare in the massive tower at the abbey's entrance, or, when it's warm, on a flower-filled terrace. The *pici ai funghi* (extra-thick handmade spaghetti with mushroom sauce) or *zuppa di funghi* (mushroom soup) take the sting out of a crisp winter day, and the grilled meats are a good bet at any time of year. If you want lighter fare, there's a bar serving panini that has outdoor seating. ⊠*Abbazia di Monte Oliveto Maggiore* ✛ *8 km (5 mi) south of Asciano on SS451* ☎*0577/707022* ▭*AE, DC, MC, V* ☉*Closed Tues.*

$$$$ ✕▭**La Chiusa.** Daniela and Umberto Lucherini bought an old farmhouse in 1974 and turned it into a significant restaurant ($$$$) with emphasis on Tuscan classics. An impeccable staff serves exquisitely prepared food, such as the *pappardelle alla Dania* (wide noodles tossed with tomatoes, garlic, and two cheeses). The menu changes according to the seasons; the well-culled (and expensive) wine list complements the selections. "We had an outrageously good dinner," writes a user of fodors.com. Guest rooms live up to the high standards created in the kitchen, as the terra-cotta floors, crisp fabrics, and immense bathrooms (most with Jacuzzis) further a sense of luxurious well-being. **Pros:** Delightful setting, excellent restaurant, personal service. **Cons:** Standard rooms are on the small side, need a car to get around. ⊠ *Via della Madonnina 88* ✛ *25 km (15 mi) east of Abbazia di Monte Oliveto Maggiore, Montefollonico 53040* ☎*0577/669668* ⊕*www.ristorantelachiusa.it* ⌂*15 rooms* ⚑*In-room: no a/c, safe (some), refrigerator. In-hotel: restaurant, room service, no elevator, concierge, laundry service, public Internet, parking (no fee), some pets allowed* ▭*AE, DC, MC, V* ☉*Closed mid-Jan.–Mar.* ⦿*BP.*

$$$$ ✕▭**Locanda dell'Amorosa.** What was a self-sufficient hamlet with its
Fodor's Choice   own chapel in the 14th century is now a refined inn. Some rooms have
★   stunning views, others a private garden or terrace. All have sumptuous

fabrics flowing around windows and woven rugs on the terra-cotta floors. The grounds teem with rambling roses, thick lavender, and multicolor geraniums in spring and summer. The restaurant ($$$–$$$$) has candlelit tables next to stone walls and the Tuscan menu has flights of fantasy such as *risotto primavera in spuma di piselli e prosciutto croccante*, a rice-and–spring vegetable dish in a creamy pea sauce with fried prosciutto bits. **Pros:** Romantic setting, excellent restaurant, luxurious rooms. **Cons:** Standard rooms are small, need a car to get around. ⊠ *Località Amorosa j 23 km (14 mi) east of Abbazia di Monte Oliveto Maggiore, Sinalunga 53048* ☏ *0577/677211* ⊕ *www.amorosa.it* ⇥ *17 rooms, 8 suites* ⚭ *In-room: safe, refrigerator, dial-up. In-hotel: restaurant, room service, bar, pool, bicycles, no elevator, concierge, laundry service, public Internet* ⊟ *AE, DC, MC, V* ☉ *Closed Jan. and Feb.*

$ ⌂ **Fattoria del Colle.** Amid rolling vineyards and olive trees is this *fattoria* (farmhouse) that produces fine wine and olive oil. The main stone house retains its enormous stone fireplace and a 16th-century family chapel next door. Apartments (sleeping up to 14) and a separate house (sleeping up to 22) have traditional wood furniture—some antique—and full kitchens; some have fireplaces. Half board is available. **Pros:** Great for families, beautiful location. **Cons:** No a/c, no phones in rooms, 30-minute walk to nearest town. ⊠ *Off A1* ⊹ *10 km (6 mi) west of Valdichiana exit, 12 km (7 mi) east of Abbazia di Monte Oliveto Maggiore, Trequanda 53020* ☏ *0577/662108* 🖷 *0577/662202* ⊕ *www.cinellico-lombini.it* ⇥ *2 rooms, 19 apartments* ⚭ *In-room: no a/c, no phone, kitchen, no TV. In-hotel: restaurant, tennis court, pools, bicycles, no elevator, laundry service* ⊟ *MC, V* ¹⊚¹*BP.*

ASCIANO

8 km (5 mi) north of Abbazia di Monte Oliveto Maggiore, 25 km (16 mi) southeast of Siena, 124 km (77 mi) southeast of Florence.

GETTING HERE

From Siena, driving to Asciano on the SP438 takes about 40 minutes. Tra-In has limited bus service, making the train, with five or six daily departures, a better option.

VISITOR INFORMATION

Asciano tourism office (⊠ *Corso Matteotti 18* ☏ *0577/719510* ⊕ *www.comune.asciano.siena.it*).

EXPLORING

Founded by the Etruscans around the 5th century BC, Asciano is now a sleepy little town surrounded by 13th-century walls. The tiny centro storico (historic center) is eminently bike-friendly; any serious cyclists should consider a pit stop here.

Fodor's Choice
★

Palazzo Corboli, a magnificent palace dating from the 12th century, has been refurbished and houses the **Museo d'Arte Sacra e Archeologico.** The collection of Etruscan artifacts is displayed well, but the real highlight is the collection of lesser-known 13th- and 14th-century paintings from the Sienese school. ⊠*Corso Matteotti 122* ☎*0577/719524* ☑*€4.50* ☺*Mar.–Oct., Tues.–Sun. 10:30–1 and 3–6:30; Nov.–Feb., Tues.–Sun. 10:30–1 and 3:30–5:30.*

The basement of the local **Farmacia De Munari** holds the town's most important Roman artifact, a polychrome Roman mosaic from the 1st to 2nd centuries AD. To see the mosaic, you must ask for the keys at the tourist information office. ⊠*Corso Matteotti 80* ☎*0577/718124* ☑*Free* ☺*Weekdays 9–1 and 4–8, Sat. 9–1.*

THE MAREMMA

6

The wildest part of Tuscany is here in its southern heart. And it's here that you get a sense of what the region looked like before Tuscany became a must-see on the grand tour. The landscape alternates between rolling hills and tufa cliffs; hill towns abound, linked by narrow, winding roads. Saturnia—with its superior hotels, restaurants, and one-of-a-kind hot springs—makes a good base to explore and sample the best of what the south has to offer: ancient Etruscan tombs and caverns at Sovana and Sorano, the famous white wine of Pitigliano, and wild mushrooms and chestnut honey from the rugged slopes of Monte Amiata, which presides over Tuscany with views from Arezzo to the sea.

MONTE AMIATA

16 km (10 mi) south of Abbazia di Sant'Antimo, 86 km (52 mi) southeast of Siena, 156 km (94 mi) southeast of Florence.

GETTING HERE

Monte Amiata can be reached by car from Siena on the SR2 (Via Cassia). Bus service is extremely limited. There is a train station at Monte Amiata Scalo, but it is at the base of the mountain and not well served by local buses.

VISITOR INFORMATION

Monte Amiata tourism office (⊠ *Via Mentana 97, La Piazzetta, Abbadia San Salvatore* ☎*0577/778608* ⊕*www.webamiata.it*).

EXPLORING

At 5,702 feet, this benign volcano is one of Tuscany's few ski slopes, but it's no Mont Blanc. Come in warmer months to take advantage of an abundance of hiking trails that cross wide meadows full of wildflowers and slice through groves of evergreens. Panoramic views of all of Tuscany present themselves on the winding road up to the summit. Along the way, you pass through a succession of tiny medieval towns, including Castel del Piano, Arcidosso, Santa Flora, and Piancastagnaio, where you can pick up picnic supplies and sample the chestnuts and game for which the mountain is famous. The thousand-year-old village of **Abbadia San Salvatore** is worth a stop—skip the nondescript new town and head straight to the *centro storico* to explore winding stone streets with tiny churches around every corner. The abbey for which the town was named was founded in 743; its current appearance reflects an 11th-century renovation, but the original crypt remains intact. The tourist office in town has hiking trail maps for Monte Amiata. ⊠ *Tourist office, Via Mentana 97, La Piazzetta* ☎ *0577/778608.*

SORANO

38 km (23 mi) south of Abbadia San Salvatore on Monte Amiata, 138 km (86 mi) southeast of Siena, 208 km (130 mi) southeast of Florence.

GETTING HERE

Being in the southern part of Tuscany, Sorano is most easily reached from Rome. From the A1 highway, take the Orvieto exit. There are no practical ways to arrive here by bus or train.

EXPLORING

Sorano's history follows the pattern of most settlements in the area: it was an ancient Etruscan citadel, built up in the 15th century and fortified by one of the many warring families of Tuscany (in this case, the Orsini). It's the execution that sets it apart. With its tiny, twisted streets and stone houses connected by wooden stairways and ramps, Sorano looks as if it was carved from the tufa beneath it—and that's because it was. Underneath the town, visible as you approach, is a vast network of *colombari,* Etruscan-era rooms lined with hundreds of niches carved into stone walls, dating from the 1st century BC. The colombari aren't yet open to the public, but Sorano is worth a visit regardless, if only to walk its medieval alleyways and to watch old-style artisans at work. Views of the densely forested hills around town will have you reaching for your camera.

WHERE TO STAY

$$ **Della Fortezza.** From high above Sorano, all the rooms in the austere-looking 11th-century Orsini castle have spectacular views of the town and the surrounding countryside. Wood-beam ceilings hang above white and pastel walls in most rooms, and windows have dark-wood shutters. A careful mix of antique and modern furniture—rococo chairs and upholstered couches—makes for a pleasant and comfortable stay. The hotel closes for some time during the winter; the length and month of the closure vary annually. **Pros:** Rooms have great views of Sorano, romantic location. **Cons:** Very basic decor, no a/c in rooms. ⊠ *Piazza Cairoli 5, 58010* ☎ *0564/632010* ⊕ *www.hoteldellafortezza.it* ⤢ *14 rooms, 1 suite* ⌂ *In-room: no a/c, no phone (some), refrigerator. In-*

CLOSE UP

In Search of Etruscan Artifacts

To fully appreciate the strangely quixotic relationship that the ancient Etruscan culture had with the tufa rock that provided the fabric of the civilization, you must visit southern Tuscany. The houses and tombs, and sometimes even the roads, were carved from this soft volcanic stone, making it impossible to think about the Etruscans without also imagining the dark sandy tufa that surrounded them.

Some of the best-preserved, and most mysterious, of all their monumental tombs are in the area of Pitigliano, Sorano, and Sovana. In the necropolis of the latter, you can actually walk on a section of Etruscan road that is almost 2,500 years old.

Chiusi should not be missed if you are interested in things Etruscan: several tombs that still retain their brightly colored decorations and a particularly fine and thoughtfully organized archaeological museum await you there.

hotel: restaurant, bar, no elevator, public Internet, parking (no fee) ⊟*AE, DC, MC, V* ⦿|*BP.*

6

PITIGLIANO

10 km (6 mi) south of Sorano, 147 km (92 mi) southeast of Siena, 217 km (136 mi) southeast of Florence.

GETTING HERE

Pitigliano is best reached by car along the SR74 from either the Via Aurelia to the west or the A1 highway to the east. Plan on a journey of about an hour. Pitigliano cannot be reached by train or bus.

VISITOR INFORMATION
Maremma regional tourism office (⊠*Piazza Garibaldi 51* ☎*0564/617111* ⊕*www.lamaremmafabene.it*).

EXPLORING
From a distance, the medieval stone houses of Pitigliano look as if they melt into the cliffs upon which they are perched. Etruscan tombs, which locals use to store wine, are connected by a network of caves and tunnels. At the beginning of the 14th century, the Orsini family moved their base from Sovana to the better-fortified Pitigliano. They built up the town's defenses and fortified their home, Palazzo Orsini. Later, starting in 1543, Antonio da Sangallo the Younger added to the town's fortress, building bastions and towers throughout the town and adding the aqueduct as well.

Pitigliano has become a trendy locale for Italian vacation rentals, making the town center very lively in the summer. Restaurants serve up good meals that, as a result of the tourist boom, have inflated prices. Bianco di Pitigliano (Pitigliano white wine) is a fresh and light, dry wine produced from the vines that thrive in the tufa soil of the area.

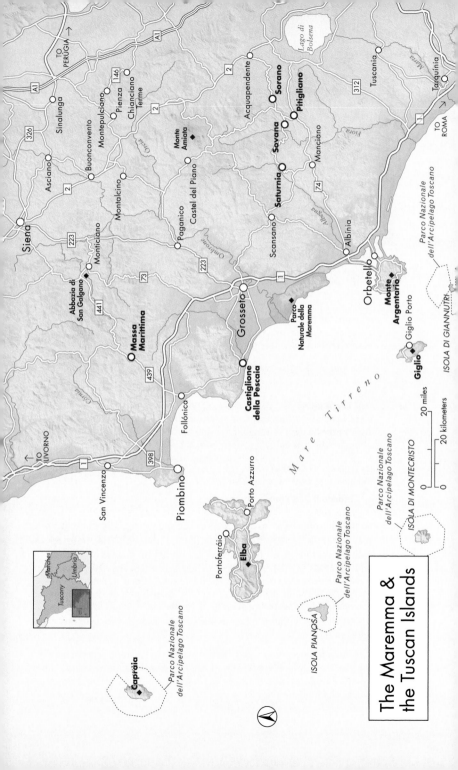

The Maremma & the Tuscan Islands

The 18th-century baroque **Duomo** has a single nave with chapels and paintings on the sides. There are two altarpieces by local artist Francesco Zuccarelli (1702–88), a rococo landscape artist and a founder of the British Royal Academy who was a favorite of George III. ⊠ *Piazza S. Gregorio* ☎ *0564/616090* ▨ *Free* ⊗ *Daily 9–7.*

Inside the **Palazzo Orsini** is the **Museo Zuccarelli,** featuring paintings by Zuccarelli as well as a Madonna by Jacopo della Quercia (1371/74–1438), a 14th-century crucifix, and other works of interest. ⊠ *Piazza della Repubblica* ☎ *0564/616074* ▨ *€2.50* ⊗ *Apr.–Oct., Tues.–Sun. 10–1 and 4–7; Nov.–Mar., Tues.–Fri. 10–1 and 3–6.*

Piccola Gerusaleme di Pitigliano is the ghetto where Jews took refuge from 16th-century Catholic persecution; a thriving community lived here until the beginning of World War II. Inside the precinct are the remains of ritual bathing basins, a wine cellar, a museum of Jewish culture, a kosher butchery and bakery, and the restored synagogue, where religious services are held on the Sabbath. ⊠ *Via Firenze 116a* ☎ *0564/616006* ▨ *€2.50* ⊗ *Apr.–Oct., Sun.–Fri. 10–12:30 and 4–7; Nov.–Mar., Sun.–Fri. 10–12:30 and 3–5:30.*

WHERE TO STAY & EAT

$$–$$$ ✕ **Il Tufo Allegro.** The name means Happy Tufa; you would be happy, too, if you ate at this fine restaurant cut directly into the tufa rock plateau upon which old Pitigliano sits. The cuisine is local and regional: *coniglio al finocchio selvatico* (rabbit with wild fennel) is particularly tasty, and fish also figures on the menu from time to time. ⊠ *Vicolo della Costituzione 5* ☎ *0564/616192* ▤ *AE, DC, MC, V* ⊗ *Closed Tues. and mid-Jan.–mid-Feb. No lunch Wed. Oct.–July.*

¢–$ 🛏 **Locanda Il Tufo Rosa.** The space for part of this tiny guesthouse has been carved out of the tufa rock beneath the aqueduct at the entrance to the old town. Rooms are small and simply decorated with painted armoires and wood dressing tables, but immaculately clean. Beds stand right up against walls with a floral print chair rail. Only one room, the smallest, has no air-conditioning. **Pros:** Excellent location, best value in town. **Cons:** Rooms are small, getting here is difficult, narrow stairways to climb. ⊠ *Piazza Petruccioli 97, 58017* ☎ *0564/617019* ⊕ *www.iltuforosa.com* ▤ *0564/617784* ➟ *6 rooms* & *In-room: no a/c (some), no phone, refrigerator. In-hotel: no elevator* ▤ *No credit cards* ⦿*|EP.*

SOVANA

5 km (3 mi) north of Pitigliano, 155 km (97 mi) southeast of Siena, 225 km (141 mi) southeast of Florence.

GETTING HERE

Like Sorano and Pitigliano, Sovana is best reached by car along the SR74, either from the Via Aurelia to the west or the A1 highway to the east. Sovana cannot be reached by train or bus.

EXPLORING

This town of Etruscan origin was once the capital of the area in southern Tuscany dominated by the Aldobrandeschi family, whose reign was at its height in the 11th and first half of the 12th centuries. One member of the family, Hildebrand, was the 11th-century Catholic reformer Pope Gregory VII (circa 1020–85). The 13th- to 14th-century Romanesque fortress known as the Rocca Aldobrandesca is now in ruins. Via di Mezzo, with stones arranged in a fish-scale pattern, is the main street running the length of the town.

The town extends from the Rocca Aldobrandesca on the eastern end to the imposing **Duomo,** built between the 10th and 14th centuries, on the edge of town to the west. ⊠*Piazza del Duomo* ☎*No phone* ☝*Free* ⊙*Daily 10–1 and 2:45–5:45.*

The central **Piazza del Pretorio** is where you'll find the 13th-century Palazzo Pretorio, which has a facade adorned with crests of Sovana's captains of justice; and the Renaissance Palazzo Bourbon dal Monte.

The little 14th-century church of **Santa Maria Maggiore** has frescoes from the late-15th-century Sienese Umbrian school. ⊠*Piazza del Pretorio* ☎*No phone* ☝*Free* ⊙*Daily 8:30–12:30 and 4–6:30.*

You can visit some of Italy's best-preserved monumental rock tombs, dating from the 2nd to the 3rd centuries BC, at the **Etruscan necropolis.** Some of the tombs, such as the so-called Tomba Sirena (Siren's Tomb), preserve clear signs of their original and elaborately carved decorations. Others, like the Tomba Ildebranda (Hildebrand Tomb), are spectacular evidence of the architectural complexity sometimes achieved. Don't forget to walk along the section of an Etruscan road carved directly into the tufa stone. ⊕ *1½ km (1 mi) west of town center* ☎*0564/614074* ☝*€5.50* ⊙*Daily 9–sunset.*

WHERE TO EAT

$$$–$$$$
Fodor's Choice
★

✕**La Taverna Etrusca.** Elaborately prepared Tuscan fare is served at this elegant restaurant on Sovana's central square. For your first course try the local specialty, *zuppa di ortiche con quadratini di ricotta* (nettle soup with ricotta cheese). Grilled meat and some fish dishes highlight the list of second courses. Service is prompt and highly professional. An outdoor terrace provides plenty of fresh air in the summer months. ⊠*Piazza del Pretorio 16* ☎*0564/616183* ▭*AE, DC, MC, V* ⊙*Closed Wed.*

SATURNIA

25 km (15 mi) east of Sovana, 129 km (77 mi) south of Siena, 199 km (119 mi) south of Florence.

GETTING HERE

Saturnia is a 30-minute drive from Pitigliano. Follow the SS74 to Manciano, then the SS322 to Montemerano, and then turn right onto the Strada Saturnia–La Croce. The RAMA bus company travels from Grosseto to Saturnia, but three changes make the journey particularly arduous. There is no train service to Saturnia.

EXPLORING

Saturnia was settled even before the Etruscan period, but nowadays it's best known not for what lies buried beneath the ground but for what comes up from it: hot, sulfurous water that supplies the town's world-famous spa. According to an oft-repeated legend, the thermal waters were created when Saturn, restless with earth's bickering mortals, threw down a thunderbolt and created a hot spring whose miraculously calming waters created peace among them. Today these magnesium-rich waters bubble forth from the clay, drawing Italians and non-Italians alike seeking relief for skin and muscular ailments as well as a bit (well, a lot) of relaxation. Unlike better-known spa centers such as Montecatini Terme, nature still has her place here.

Outside Saturnia, the hot, sulfurous waters cascade over natural limestone shelves at the **Cascate del Gorello** *(Gorello Falls)*, affording bathers a sweeping view of the open countryside. The falls are on public land and can be enjoyed 24 hours a day. They get extremely crowded—day and night—during August. ✛ *2 km (1 mi) south of Saturnia, on road to Montemerano* ☎*No phone* ▨*Free.*

The swimming pools and treatments at **Terme di Saturnia** spa and resort are open to nonguests. You might make an appointment for a thermal mud therapy or rent a lounge chair and umbrella to sit by the pools. ✛*3 km (2 mi) east of Saturnia on road to Montemerano, after Gorello Falls* ☎*0564/601061* ⊕*www.termedisaturnia.it* ▨*Full day €22, half day €17* ☉*May–Sept., daily 9:30–7:30; Oct.–Apr., daily 9:30–5:30.*

Pre-Etruscan tombs at the **Necropoli del Puntone** aren't kept up well, but they're interesting simply for their age, as they're even older than Saturnia's legendary baths. ✛*1 km (½ mi) north of Saturnia, on the road to Poggio Murello, turn left and follow signs* ☎*No phone* ▨*Free* ☉*Daily 24 hrs.*

WHERE TO STAY & EAT

$$$$ ✕**Da Caino.** At this excellent restaurant in the nearby town of Montem-
★ erano, specialties include tomatoes and peppers on crisp phyllo dough, lasagne with pumpkin, ravioli *ripieni di olio extra vergine di olive* (filled with extra-virgin olive oil, capers, anchovies, and tomatoes), and such hearty dishes as *cinghiale lardolato con olive* (wild boar larded with olives). Prices are among the highest in the region; locals consider it a serious splurge. ⊠*Via della Chiesa 4* ✛ *7 km (4½ mi) south of Saturnia on the road to Scansano, Montemerano* ☎*0564/602817*

CLOSE UP

Terme, Wrath of the Gods

In a country known for millennia as a hotbed of seismic activity, Tuscany seems to have gotten a lucky break. Although Campania and Sicily are famous for active volcanoes, and Umbria and the Marches stand on notoriously shaky ground, Tuscany's underground activity makes itself known in the form of steamy and sulfurous hot springs that have earned the region a name as a spa-goer's paradise.

Tuscany is dotted throughout with small *terme* (thermal baths) where hot waters flow from natural springs deep under the earth's surface. Since the time of the Etruscans, these hot springs have been valued for their curative properties. The Romans attributed the springs' origins to divine thunderbolts that split the earth open and let flow the miraculous waters. Regardless of their origin, their appeal endures, as the presence of thousands of people taking the waters in the Maremma attests.

Each of the springs has different curative properties, attributable to the various concentrations of minerals and gases that individual water flows pick up on their way to the surface. Carbon dioxide, for example, is said to strengthen the immune system, and sulfur, its characteristic rotten-egg smell notwithstanding, is said to relieve pain and aid in relaxation.

Although customs and conventions vary between spas, you generally pay an admission fee to swim in baths that range from hot natural lakes and waterfalls (with accompanying mud) to giant limestone swimming pools filled with cloudy, bright blue, steaming water. Larger establishments have treatments that can range from mineral mud baths to steam inhalations.

Believers swear that Tuscany's hot springs have a positive effect on everything from skin disorders to back pain to liver function to stress. Whatever your opinion, a good soak in a Tuscan spring is a relaxing way to take a break, and as far as geological phenomena go, it beats an earthquake or a volcanic eruption any day.

A few of the region's spas, notably the world-famous Montecatini Terme (see chapter 3), are well known outside of Tuscany. For the most part, however, the local establishments that run the springs are not well publicized, which can mean a more local flavor, lower prices, and fewer crowds: Terme di Bagni di Lucca is near Lucca; Terme di Chianciano is near Chiusi; Bagno Vignoni is just south of San Quirico d'Orcia; and Terme di Saturnia is not too far from Grosseto.

Local tourist offices have the most up-to-date information on smaller springs, many of which are open for only part of the year.

⚑*Reservations essential* ▤*DC, MC, V* ⊘*Closed Wed., Jan., and 2 wks in July. No lunch Thurs.*

$$$-$$$$ ✕**I Due Cippi–Da Michele.** Owner Michele Aniello captivates with a creative menu that emphasizes local ingredients like wild boar and duck. Try the *tortelli di castagne al seme di finocchio* (chestnut-stuffed pasta pillows with butter sauce and fennel seeds). In good weather you can enjoy your meal on a terrace overlooking the town's main square. ✉*Piazza Veneto 26a* ☎*0564/601074* ⚑*Reservations essential* ▤*AE, DC, MC, V* ⊘*Closed Dec. 20–26, Jan. 10–25, and Tues. Oct.–June.*

$$$$ 🏨**Terme di Saturnia.** Spa living might not get any more top-notch than this: roam the spa resort in a plush white bathrobe (waiting in your room) before dipping into the 37.5°C (100°F) sulfurous thermal pools. Seemingly every possible health and beauty treatment is available. Sleek elegance pervades public and private rooms: tall windows have floor-to-ceiling draperies in rich colors like steel blue and gray or burnt umber and sage;

floors are polished wood. Eclectic furniture includes some sleigh-shape benches and oval night tables. You can opt for half or full board to complete the experience. **Pros:** Luxurious setting, excellent service, wide range of treaments. **Cons:** On the pricey side, aseptic atmosphere. *⚓3 km (2 mi) east of Saturnia on road to Montemerano, past Gorello Falls, 58050 ☎0564/601061 ⊕www.termedisaturnia.it ⤳130 rooms, 10 suites ⚘In-room: safe, refrigerator, VCR. In-hotel: 3 restaurants, room service, bar, tennis courts, pools, gym, spa, concierge, laundry facilities, laundry service, public Internet, some pets allowed ▤AE, DC, MC, V ⓘBP.*

$–$$ 🏨**Villa Acquaviva.** An elegant villa painted antique rose appears at the end of a tree-lined driveway perched on top of a hill off the main road 1 km (½ mi) before Montemerano. It has expansive views and quintessential Tuscan charm. Tastefully decorated rooms—with curly ironwork or tapestries as bed headboards—are in both the main villa and a guesthouse. The farm that fans out around the villa produces fine wine and olive oil. **Pros:** Near the hot springs, lovely views, family-friendly atmosphere. **Cons:** Attendants can be hard to find during the day, need a car to get around. *⊠Strada Scansanese ⚓6 km (4 mi) south of Saturnia, Montemerano 58050 ☎0564/602890 ☎0564/602895 ⊕www.relaisvillaacquaviva.com ⤳22 rooms, 3 suites ⚘In-room: safe, refrigerator. In-hotel: restaurant, bar, tennis court, pool, no elevator, some pets allowed ▤MC, V ⓘEP.*

$
★ 🏨**Villa Clodia.** The villa in the oldest part of town has splendid views over the nearby hills and the steamy clouds coming from the hot springs. Inside it's just as nice, with hand-painted decoration in the rooms and a cozy library with a marble fireplace. Breakfast is served in a country-style room with gingham tablecloths, but early risers may be able to stake a claim on one of the terrace tables overlooking the valley. **Pros:** Excellent location on edge of town, great views, cozy environment. **Cons:** Some rooms are small, need a car to get around. *⊠Via Italia 43, 58050 ☎0564/601212 ☎0564/601305 ⊕www.hotelvillaclodia. com ⤳8 rooms, 2 suites ⚘In-room: safe. In-hotel: pool, parking (no fee) ▤MC, V ⊘Closed Dec. ⓘBP.*

$ 🏨**Villa Garden.** After seeing the floral curtains and bedspreads, you won't be surprised that the rooms at this small place are named for flowers. Just a few minutes from the center of town, it's a good place to

A field of sunflowers in the Maremma.

stay if you want to take the waters without breaking the bank. The buffet breakfast is filling and tasty, the staff courteous and efficient. **Pros:** Tranquil location, good value. **Cons:** No a/c in some rooms, a downhill walk from town center. ⊠ *Via Sterpeti 56, 58014* ☎ *0564/601182* ⊕*www.countryvillagarden.com* ⤶*10 rooms* ⌂*In-room: no a/c (some), safe, refrigerator. In-hotel: bar, no elevator, public Internet, parking (no fee), some pets allowed* ▭*AE, MC, V* ⓄⅠ*BP.*

EN ROUTE The largest town in southern Tuscany, **Grosseto** is the capital of the Maremma. First recorded in the 9th century as a *castellum* (castle) built to defend a bridge and a port on the nearby River Ombrone, Grosseto is now a thriving agricultural center. Badly damaged during World War II, most of the town has been rebuilt since the 1950s, but a small *centro storico* (historic center), protected defensive walls that follow a hexagonal plan, is worth a short visit on your way to the coast.

PARCO NATURALE DELLA MAREMMA

10 km (6 mi) south of Grosseto, 88 km (55 mi) southwest of Siena, 156 km (97 mi) south of Florence.

GETTING HERE
The park is best reached by car from the Via Aurelia (SS1), which runs between Rome and Pisa. Local bus service connects the park with the train station in nearby Grosseto.

VISITOR INFORMATION

Parco Naturale della Maremma tourism office (⊠ *Via del Bersgliere 7/9, Alberese* ☎ *0564/407098* ⊕ *www.parco-maremma.it*).

EXPLORING

The well-kept nature preserve at **Monti dell'Uccellina** is an oasis of green hills sloping down to small, secluded beaches on protected coastline. Wild goats and rabbits, foxes and wild boars, as well as horses and a domesticated long-horned white ox unique to this region, make their home among miles of sea pines, rosemary plants, and juniper bushes. The park also has scattered Etruscan and Roman ruins and a medieval abbey, the **Abbazia di San Rabano.** Enter from the south at Talamone (turn right 1 km [½ mi] before town) or from Alberese, both reachable from the SS1 (Via Aurelia). Daily limits restrict the number of cars that can enter, so in summer it's best to either reserve ahead or to leave your car in Alberese and use the regular bus service; contact the park's information office for bookings, and to secure English-language guides. ⊠ *Off Via Bersagliere, Alberese* ☎ *0564/407098* 🎫 *€3–€8* 🕙 *Daily 9–1 hr before sunset.*

MONTE ARGENTARIO

Porto Santo Stefano 60 km (37 mi) southeast of Saturnia, 118 km (74 mi) southwest of Siena, 186 km (116 mi) southwest of Florence.

GETTING HERE

The Monte Argentario peninsula lies just off the SS1 (Via Aurelia), which connects Rome and Pisa. It's a two-hour drive from either city. Intercity buses are not a viable option. The closest train station is in Orbetello Scalo, with local bus service available to both Porto Ercole and Porto Santo Stefano.

VISITOR INFORMATION

Monte Argentario tourism office (⊠ *Corso Umberto 55a, Porto Santo Stefano* ☎ *0564/814208* ⊕ *www.monteargentario.it*).

EXPLORING

Connected to the mainland only by three thin strips of land, Monte Argentario feels like an island. The north and south isthmuses, La Giannella and La Feniglia, have long sandy beaches popular with families, but otherwise the terrain is rugged, dotted with luxurious vacation houses (including Sophia Loren's). There are beautiful views from the panoramic mountain road encircling the promontory, and a drive here is a romantic sunset excursion. The mountain itself rises 2,096 feet above the sea, and it's ringed with rocky beaches and sheer cliffs that afford breathtaking views of the coast.

On the north side, busy and colorful **Porto Santo Stefano** is Monte Argentario's main center, with markets, hotels, restaurants, and ferry service to Giglio and Giannutri, two of the Tuscan islands.

To the south of Monte Argentario, **Porto Ercole** is the haunt of the rich and famous, with top-notch hotels and restaurants perched on the cliffs.

WHERE TO STAY & EAT

$$$–$$$$ ✕**Gambero Rosso.** Enjoy a seaside Italian classic right at Porto Ercole. Simple preparations of fresh fish have been drawn from local waters. Try the antipasto *sorpresa del Gambero* (surprise of the house), an ever-changing array of six, sometimes seven, different fish dishes (fried, chilled, or baked, for example). The chef lets his imagination run wild, and it's only to the benefit of the happy diners. It's even better if you enjoy it on the terrace with a view. ⊠*Lungomare Andrea Doria 62, Porto Ercole* ☎*0564/832650* ♨*Reservations essential* ⊟*AE, DC, MC, V* ⊗*Closed Wed. and mid-Nov.–mid-Jan.*

$$–$$$$ ✕**La Fontanina di San Pietro.** Grape vines climbing up a trellis, cherry trees in the countryside overlooking the port: the scene here is romantic. Dine on scampi with zucchini and spaghetti *allo scoglio* (with fresh clams and mussels in a light tomato sauce), while enjoying a fruity white from the well-matched wine list. The catch of the day can be prepared a number of ways and is priced by weight; the *pesce spada* (swordfish) is terrific. ⊠ *Via del Campone, outside Porto San Pietro* ☎*0564/825261* ⊟*AE, DC, MC, V* ⊗*Closed Wed. and Jan.*

$$–$$$ ✕**Armando.** The family-run restaurant is known for spaghetti *alle briciole* (literally, "with crumbs"), and the kitchen here conjures up a richly inventive version, dressed with garlic, olive oil, hot peppers, and anchovies. The *moscardini con fagioli* (similar to cuttlefish, served with beans) is tastily aromatic. This nautical-themed place may not be perfect for a romantic meal, but the food makes up for the lack of allure. ⊠ *Via Marconi 1/3, Porto Santo Stefano* ☎*0564/812568* ⊟*AE, DC, MC, V* ⊗*Closed Wed. and Nov.–Mar.*

$$$$ ⛱**Il Pellicano.** Worldly cares are softly washed away by the comforts of the rooms (some damask linens, tapestry-like canopies, marble highboys), the superlative attentiveness of the staff, and the hotel's magnificent garden setting. If you choose, a buffet lunch is served on a canopied terrace above the pool, with numerous smaller terraces tucked away on the sloping cliffs for a peaceful afternoon nap. Chaises and white umbrellas sit oceanside on the beach. Some rooms are in separate cottages. If absolute privacy, but not the cost, is your main concern, one suite has a private pool. **Pros:** Spectacular setting and gardens, superlative service, excellent dining options. **Cons:** Isolated location, on a long dirt road, beach is rocky. ⊠*Località Lo Sbarcatello* ✛ *5 km (3 mi) west of Porto Ercole, 58018* ☎*0564/858111* ☎*0564/833418* ⊕*www. pellicanohotel.com* ⌦*40 rooms, 10 suites* ♿*In-room: refrigerator. In-hotel: 2 restaurants, tennis courts, pool, gym, spa, laundry service, public Internet, parking (no fee), some pets allowed* ⊟*AE, DC, MC, V* ⊗*Closed Nov.–Mar.* ☉*BP.*

$$–$$$ ⛱**Hotel Don Pedro.** The private beach more than makes up for the lack of a pool at this hotel in Porto Ercole. As a guest you can enjoy the complimentary beach chairs and umbrellas, and there's a good restaurant and a bar on the beach. Rooms are spacious and spare, with tile floors and a few pieces of painted or dark-wood furniture with lathe-turned legs and simple curves. Some have French doors that open onto a terrace. **Pros:** Panoramic views of port, private beach, family-friendly atmosphere. **Cons:** Not all rooms have sea views, furnishings showing their age. ✉ *Via Panoramica 7, Porto Ercole 58018* ☎*0564/833914* 🖷*0564/833129* ⊕*www.hoteldonpedro.it* ⇙*60 rooms* ⌂*In-hotel: restaurant, bar, beachfront, laundry service* ▬*AE, MC, V* ⊘*Closed Nov.–Easter* ⓘⓄⓘ*EP.*

MASSA MARITTIMA

111 km (69 mi) southeast of Livorno, 48 km (30 mi) east of Piombino, 66 km (42 mi) southwest of Siena, 132 km (82 mi) southwest of Florence.

GETTING HERE

From Siena, the easiest way to reach Massa Marittima is to take the SP73bis, then the SP441. Bus service from Siena, provided by Tra-In, is not timed to make day trips feasible. Massa Marittima cannot be reached by train.

VISITOR INFORMATION

Massa Marittima tourism office (✉ *Via Todini 3/5* ☎*0566/902756* 🖷*0566/940095* ⊕*www.altamaremmaturismo.it*).

EXPLORING

Massa Marittima is a charming medieval hill town with a rich mining and industrial heritage—pyrite, iron, and copper were found in these parts. After a centuries-long slump (most of the minerals having been depleted), the town is now popular simply for its old streets.

The central Piazza Garibaldi, dating from the 13th to the early 14th centuries, contains the Romanesque **Duomo**, with sculptures of the life of patron saint Cerbone above the door. ✉*Piazza Garibaldi* ☎*0566/902237* ✉*Free* ⊘*Daily 8–noon and 3–6.*

The 13th-century Palazzo Pretorio, on the Piazza Garibaldi, is home to the **Museo Archeologico,** with plenty of Etruscan artifacts. A number of displays reconstruct the nature of daily life for the Etruscans who once inhabited the hills in this area. ✉*Piazza Garibaldi* ☎*0566/902289* ✉*€3 (includes both museums)* ⊘*Apr.–Oct., Tues.–Sun. 10–12:30 and 3:30–7; Nov.–Mar., Tues.–Sun. 10–12:30 and 3–5.*

In the converted convent church of San Pietro all'Orto, the **Museo di Arte Sacra** houses a large number of medieval paintings and sculptures gathered from churches in and around Massa Marittima. Perhaps the most important piece, Ambrogio Lorenzetti's early 14th-century *Maestà*, was discovered in the storage room of the church in 1866. ✉*Corso Diaz 36* ☎*0566/901954* ✉*€5* ⊘*Apr.–Sept., Tues.–Sun. 10–1 and 3–6; Oct.–Mar., Tues.–Sun. 11–1 and 3–5.*

The **Museo Arte e Storia della Miniera** *(Museum of the Art and History of Mining)*, in the upper part of town, shows how dependent Massa Marittima has been since Etruscan times on copper, lead, and silver. Exhibits trace the history of the local mining industry. You can even visit a real mine. ✉*Palazzetto delle Armi, Piazza Matteotti* ☎*0566/902289* ✉*Museum €1.50; museum and mine €5* ⊘*Museum:*

6

Apr.–Oct., Tues.–Sun. 3–5:30; Nov.–Mar. by appointment. Mine visits: Apr.–Oct., Tues.–Sun. at 10, 11, noon, 12:45, 3:30, 4:30, 5, and 5:45; Nov.–Mar. at 10, 11, noon, 12:45, 3, 4, and 4:30.

Built to both defend and control their new possession after the Sienese conquered Massa Marittima in 1335, the **Fortezza dei Senesi** crowns the upper part of town. Just inside the imposing Sienese gate is the so-called **Torre del Candeliere** *(Tower of the Candlemaker)*, a massive bastion that is connected to the outer walls by the **Arco Senese,** a high arched bridge. A visit to the tower gives access to the arch and to the upper city walls, where commanding views open before you. ⊠*Piazza Matteotti* ☎*0566/902289* ⌂*€2.50* ⊙*Apr.–Oct., Tues.–Sun. 10–1 and 3–6; Nov.–Mar., 11–1 and 2:30–4:30.*

You can see the **Antico Frantoio,** an old olive press, on a small street inside the walls of the **Fortezza dei Senesi**. Mules harnessed to the heavy stone wheel pulled it around, and as it rolled, the olives on the flat surface were crushed by its weight, extracting the precious oil—the same technique is used today (minus the mules). ⊠*Via Populonia 18* ☎*0566/902289* ⌂*€1.50* ⊙*Apr.–Oct., Tues.–Sun. 10:30–1; Nov.– Mar. by appointment.*

WHERE TO STAY

$$ **Rifugio Prategiano.** Horseback trail rides through Tuscany's cowboy country are an integral part of the experience at Rifugio Prategiano. Your hosts can organize picnics and suggest itineraries or organize weeklong tours. But nonriders don't have to mope at the bar—this agriturismo also has a pool and idyllic views. Rooms are plainly decorated with modern wooden wardrobes and desks; most are carpeted; some are enlivened by wood-beam ceilings. **Pros:** Great for families with children, plenty of outdoor sports activities, peaceful setting. **Cons:** Very simple furnishings, no a/c in rooms, need a car to get around. ⊠*Via dei Platani 3b, Località Prategiano* ✚ *17 km (11 mi) west of Abbazia San Galgano, Montieri 58026* ☎*0566/997700* ⊕*www. prategiano.com* ↝*24 rooms* ⌂*In-room: no a/c. In-hotel: restaurant, tennis court, pool, bicycles, no elevator, some pets allowed* ⊟*MC, V* ⊙*Closed Nov.–mid-Mar.* ⌂*BP.*

NIGHTLIFE & THE ARTS

On the first Sunday after May 22, and again on the first Sunday in August, Massa Marittima's three traditional neighborhood groups dress in medieval costumes, parade through the town, and compete in the **Balestro del Girifalco** *(Falcon Crossbow Contest)*, where contestants try to shoot down a toy falcon.

ABBAZIA DI SAN GALGANO

32 km (20 mi) northeast of Massa Marittima, 33 km (20 mi) southwest of Siena, 87 km (54 mi) south of Florence.

GETTING HERE

You'll need a car to get here, as bus and train service is not available. From Siena, follow the SP73bis, then take the SP441 south.

EXPLORING

Time has had its way with this Gothic cathedral without a rooftop, a hauntingly beautiful sight well worth a detour. The church was built in the 13th century by Cistercian monks, who designed it after churches built by their order in France. But starting in the 15th century it fell into ruin, declining gradually over centuries. Grass has grown through the floor, and the roof and windows are gone. What's left of its facade and walls makes a grandiose and desolate picture. In July and August the scene is enlivened by evening concerts arranged by the Accademia Musicale Chigiana in Siena. Contact the tourist information office at the abbey for details. ⊠*Off SP441* ☎*0577/756738 for tourist office* ⊕*www.prolocochiusdino.it* ⊠*Free* ⊙*Tourist office: daily 9–12:30 and 2–6, church: daily 24 hrs.*

Behind the church, a short climb brings you to the charming little **Chiesetta di Monte Siepi,** with frescoes by painter Ambrogio Lorenzetti (documented 1319–48), and a sword in a stone. Legend has it that Galgano, a medieval warrior and bon vivant, was struck by a revelation on this spot in which an angel told him to give up his fighting and frivolous ways forever. As token of his conversion, he plunged his sword into the rock, where it still remains today. ⊠*Above Abbazia di San Galgano* ☎*No phone* ⊠*Free* ⊙*Daily 9–sunset.*

ELBA & THE SURROUNDING ISLANDS

The Tuscan archipelago is a wide semicircle of islands that traces a path, in the crystal-clear sea, between Livorno and Monte Argentario. All of the larger islands in the group can be reached by ferry service from the mainland, whereas the smaller islands, like the charmingly named Formiche di Grosseto (Ants of Grosseto) and the Formica di Montecristo (Ant of Montecristo), can only be reached by private boat. The largest, and most famous, of the islands is Elba, with several large towns and its own airport. Equally popular as a summer destination is Giglio. Other islands, like Capraia, Pianosa, and Montecristo, more closely guard their natural beauty, offering visitors few or no hotels or restaurants. The peak season is in July and August—book your ferry journey well in advance.

GIGLIO

GETTING HERE

To get to Giglio, take one of the Toremar car ferries that run between Porto Santo Stefano on the Monte Argentario peninsula and Giglio Porto. The trip, which costs €6.30 for passengers and €28.80 for cars, takes about an hour.

VISITOR INFORMATION

Giglio tourism office (⊠*Via Provinciale 9, Giglio Porto* ☎*0564/809400* ⊕*www.isoladelgiglio.it*).

EXPLORING

Rocky, romantic Isola del Giglio (Island of the Lily) is an hour by ferry from Porto Santo Stefano—but a world away from the mainland's hustle and bustle. The island's three towns—**Giglio Porto,** the charming harbor where the ferry arrives; **Giglio Castello,** a walled village at Giglio's highest point; and **Giglio Campese,** a modern town on the west side of the island—are connected by one long, meandering road. But to really explore Giglio you need a good pair of hiking boots. A network of rugged trails climbs up the steep hills through clusters of wild rosemary and tiny daffodils, and once you leave town, chances are your only company will be the goats who thrive on Giglio's sun-baked hills.

The island's main attraction, however, is at sea level—a sparkling array of lush coves and tiny beaches, most accessible only on foot or by boat. With the exception of Giglio Campese, where the sandy beach is as popular in summer as any mainland resort, most of the little island's coastline is untouched, leaving plenty of room for peaceful sunning for those willing to go off the beaten path.

WHERE TO STAY

$$$$ **Pardini's Hermitage.** This ultraprivate hotel is free from noise except **★** for the lapping of waves on the rocks. Terraces and flowering gardens spill down a rocky cliff to private beaches below. On the hill above, the owners raise purebred donkeys that you can ride over the mountain and goats that produce fresh yogurt and cheese for breakfast. Rooms feel more like those of a private home than a hotel; to complete your sense of relaxation, hydromassages and mud baths are available at the hotel's spa. You can only get here via the hotel's private boat. Pros: Pure pampering, spectacular views, homey accommodations. Cons: Isolation makes the hotel a poor base from which to tour the island, no a/c. ⊠ *Località Cala degli Alberi, Giglio Porto 58013* 🕾 *0564/809034* ⊕ *www.hermit.it* ⤶ *12 rooms* ⚟ *In-room: no a/c, no TV (some). In-hotel: restaurant, beachfront, no elevator, laundry service, public Internet, some pets allowed* ⊟ *V* ⊗ *Closed Oct.–Mar.* ⭐| *FAP.*

$$ **Hotel Arenella.** Sitting above the sea, this isolated hotel has a private rocky beach reachable by a steep 60-foot descent. Rooms in the main building are large and airy; rooms in the other building are smaller, but have verandas. All are simply but comfortably filled with contemporary Italian furnishings. The property is on the mountain road leading away from Giglio Porto, 3 km (2 mi) out of town. Unfortunately, it's not on the bus route to Giglio Castello—to get here you need to rent a car, or ask the hotel to send one to pick you up at the ferry. Pros: Magnificent views, peaceful location, shuttle service to the port. Cons: Long walk to nearest restaurants, modern decor geared to a business clientele. ⊠ *Via Arenella 5, Giglio Porto 58013* 🕾 *0564/809340* ⊕ *www.hotelarenella.com* ⤶ *26 rooms* ⚟ *In-room: refrigerator. In-hotel: beachfront, no elevator, laundry service, public Internet* ⊟ *AE, MC, V* ⊗ *Closed Nov.–Easter* ⭐| *MAP.*

SPORTS & THE OUTDOORS

HIKING For day-trippers, the best hike is the 1,350-foot ascent from Giglio Porto to Giglio Castello. It's a 4-km (2½- mi) trek that takes about an hour and affords marvelous views of the island's east coast. Frequent bus service to and from Castello allows the option of walking just one way. The rest of the island's trails are reasonably well marked. Pick up maps at the tourist office in Giglio Porto.

WATER SPORTS **Dimensione Mare** (⊠ *Via Thaon de Revel 28, Giglio Porto 0564/809558* ⊕ *www.dimensionemare.it*) runs scuba courses and can help arrange dives. Rent motorboats for exploring the island's innumerable coves through **Giglio Noleggio** (⊠ *On the port, Giglio Porto* ☎ *0347/0547755* ⊕ *www.boatmen.it*). You can charter your own snorkeling or beach excursion and let someone else do the driving through **Marco Bartoletti** (⊠ *Località Arenella* ⊹ *2½ km (1 mi) north of Giglio Porto* ☎ *0336/535054*).

ELBA

GETTING HERE
Torremar car ferries make the one-hour trip between Portoferraio and Piombino on the mainland. The cost is €7.10 for passengers, €36 for cars.

VISITOR INFORMATION
For information about the flora and fauna to be found on Elba, as well as throughout the Tuscan archipelago, contact the **Parco Nazionale dell'Arcipelago Toscano.** The tourism office also has detailed walking and hiking maps.

Elba tourism office (⊠ *Calata Italia 26, Portoferraio* ☎ *0565/914671* ⊕ *www.aptelba.it*).

Parco Nazionale dell'Arcipelago Toscano tourism office (⊠ *Via Guerrazzi 1, Portoferraio* ☎ *0565/919411* ⊕ *www.islepark.it*).

EXPLORING
Elba is the Tuscan archipelago's largest island, but it resembles nearby verdant Corsica more than it does its rocky Italian sisters, thanks to a network of underground springs that keep it lush and green. It's this combination of semitropical vegetation and dramatic mountain scenery—unusual in the Mediterranean—that has made Elba so prized for so long, and the island's uniqueness continues to draw boatloads of visitors throughout the warm months. A car is very useful for getting around the island, but public buses stop at most towns several times a day; the tourist office has timetables.

Lively **Portoferraio,** the port town where Victor Hugo (1802–85) spent his boyhood, makes a good base. Head right when you get off the ferry to get to the centro storico, fortified in the 16th century by the Medici grand duke Cosimo I (1519–74). Most of the pretty, multicolor buildings that line the old harbor date from the 18th and 19th centuries, when the boats in the port were full of mineral exports rather than tourists.

The **Museo Archeologico** reconstructs the island's ancient history through a display of Etruscan and Roman artifacts recovered from shipwrecks. ⊠*Calata Buccari, Portoferraio* ☎*0565/917338* ⌨*€2* ⊘*June 15–Sept. 15, daily 9:30–2:30 and 5–midnight; Sept. 16–June 14, Thurs. 10:30–1:30 and 4–8.*

Napoléon was famously exiled on Elba, in 1814–15, during which time he built the **Palazzina dei Mulini** out of two windmills. It still contains furniture from the period and Napoléon's impressive library, with the more than 2,000 volumes that he brought here from France. ⊠*Piazzale Napoleone 1, Portoferraio* ☎*0565/915846* ⌨*€3, €5 with admission to Villa San Martino* ⊘*Mon. and Wed.–Sat. 9–7, Sun. 9–1.*

A couple of miles outside Portoferraio, the **Villa San Martino** was Napoléon's summer residence during his 10-month exile on Elba. Temporary exhibitions are held in a gallery attached to the villa. The Egyptian Room, decorated with idealized scenes of the Egyptian campaign, may have provided Napoléon the consolation of glories past. The villa's classical facade was added by a Russian prince, Anatolia Demidoff, after he bought the house in 1852. ⊠*Località San Martino* ☎*0565/914688* ⌨*€3, €5 with admission to Palazzina dei Mulini* ⊘*Tues.–Sat. 9–7 and Sun. 9–1.*

On the south side of Elba, **Marina di Campo** is a classic summer vacationer's town, with a long sandy beach and a charming, laid-back marina full of bars, boutiques, and restaurants.

The waters of **Porto Azzurro** are noticeably *azzurro* (sky-blue). It's worth a stop for a walk and a gelato along the rows of yachts harbored here.

The island of Elba's quietest town is old-fashioned **Rio Marina,** with a pebble beach, an old mine, a leafy public park, and ferry service to Piombino.

The slopes of **Monte Capanne** are crossed by a twisting road that provides magnificent vistas at every turn; the tiny towns of **Poggio** and **Marciana** have enchanting little piazzas full of flowers and trees. You can hike to the top of Monte Capanne, or take an unusual open-basket cable car from just above Poggio.

The most famous prisoner on the island of **Montecristo,** about 50 km (30 mi) south of Elba, was fictional: Alexandre Dumas's legendary count. Today the island is a well-protected nature preserve with wild Montecristo goats and vipers, peregrine falcons, and rare Corsican seagulls who make their home amid rosemary bushes and stunted pine trees. Scientific-research teams are given priority for permission to land on the island, and an annual quota of 1,000 visitors strictly limits even their number. Montecristo is in the custody of the **Corpo Forestale,** which has plenty of information about visits to the island. ⊠*Follonica* ☎*0566/40019* ⊕*www.corpoforestale.it*

A cove on Elba.

WHERE TO STAY & EAT

$$$–$$$$ ✕**La Canocchia.** In the center of Rio Marina sits this breezy restaurant. Seafood takes center stage: specialties include ravioli *scampi e asparagi o calamari* (stuffed with large shrimp or squid, in light asparagus sauce) and saffron-perfumed catches of the day. The *frittura di paranza* (mixed fried fish) is crisp and light, and the *involtini di pesce spada* (swordfish rolls) melt in your mouth. Book ahead in summer, as it can get very crowded. ⊠*Via Palestro 3, Rio Marina* ☎*0565/962432* ▭*MC, V* ⊘*Closed Mon. and Nov.–mid-Feb.*

$$–$$$ ✕**Trattoria da Lido.** Come here for commendable *gnocchetti di pesce* (bite-size potato-and-fish dumplings) with a white cream sauce and fresh *pesce all'elbana* (whitefish baked with vegetables and potatoes). The bustling, casual trattoria is in the old center of Portoferraio, at the beginning of the road to the old Medici walls. ⊠*Salita del Falcone 2, Portoferraio* ☎*0565/914650* ▭*AE, DC, MC, V* ⊘*Closed mid-Dec.–mid-Feb.*

$ ✕**Il Cantuccio.** This small, simple eatery is a standout in the touristy
★ Marina di Campo. Shady outdoor tables on a backstreet keep diners cool on warm nights. If the long menu seems daunting, focus on the list of specials, which often includes such local delicacies as spaghetti *alle uova di pesce* (with sea-bream caviar). The staff is friendly and well informed, particularly about wine. ⊠*Via Largo Garibaldi 2, Marina di Campo* ☎*0565/976775* ▭*AE, DC, MC, V.*

$ ✕**Il Mare.** Homemade pastas and fresh seafood are served here with
★ a dash of style. The young chef puts a creative spin on the classics,

Getting Here & Around: Tuscany's Islands

Passenger and car ferries link the Tuscan islands with the mainland. From Piombino, **Moby Lines** (⊠ *Nuova Stazione Marittima, Piombino* ☎ *0565/221212* ⊕ *www.mobylines.it*) sails to Portoferraio on Elba. **Toremar** (⊠ *Nuova Stazione Marittima, Piombino* ☎ *0565/31100* ⊕ *www.toremar.it*), which provides ferry service between Piombino and Elba's main ports, also offers service to the smaller islands: from Livorno to Capraia; from Piombino to Pianosa; and from Porto Santo Stefano to Giglio. Prices can differ drastically, so comparison shop before buying your tickets. Reserve your seat ahead of time during in the peak season months of July and August.

On Elba there are numerous places to rent bikes, scooters, motorcycles, or cars: at **Baby Rent** (⊠ *Piazza Marinai d'Italia 9, Portoferraio* ☎ *0565/918883*) you can choose, among other things, BMW convertibles for touring the island in style; **BW's Rent** (⊠ *Via Manganaro 98, Elba, Portoferraio,* ☎ *0565/930491 or 0347/7371790*) has everything from mopeds to Yamaha touring bikes; **Chiappi** (⊠ *Calata Italia 30, Elba, Portoferraio* ☎ *0565/916779*) rents Honda and Yamaha scooters.

coming up with such delights as homemade vegetable gnocchi with scampi in a butter and saffron sauce. The *semifreddi* (literally, "half cold"; chilled or partially frozen desserts) are particularly good. Just a few steps from Rio Marina's pretty port, this is an easy stop on your way to or from the ferry. ⊠ *Via del Pozzo 16, Rio Marina* ☎ *0565/962117* ⊟ *V.*

$$$$ ⚏ **Hermitage.** You have private access to a white sandy beach at this hotel on a private bay. The bar and restaurant stand beachside, which means you never need to leave your spot on the sand. A central building and several surrounding cottages contain guest rooms with simple white-wood desks and beds with ironwork insets. Some rooms have balconies. During high season half board is mandatory. **Pros:** Wide range of sports equipment, several good restaurants, on a private beach and bay. **Cons:** Half board is mandatory in high season, can get very crowded. ⊹ *8 km (5 mi) west of Portoferraio, La Biodola 57037* ☎ *0565/974811* ⊕ *www.hotelhermitage.it* ⇦ *114 rooms, 16 suites* ⚏ *In-room: refrigerator. In-hotel: 3 restaurants, bars, golf course, 9 tennis courts, 3 pools, public Internet, some pets allowed* ⊟ *AE, MC, V* ⊗ *Closed Nov.–Mar.* ⦿ *MAP.*

$$$$ ⚏ **Park Hotel Napoleone.** A late-19th-century villa stands in a park next to Napoléon's Villa San Martino. Hand-painted medallions form the centerpieces of scrolled ironwork beds and chairs that are painted in colors coordinating with the draperies—some deep reds and blues. The rather high price reflects the fact that breakfast and dinner are included. Full board is also available. Buses run often from the hotel to the port in Portoferraio; it's only 5 km (3 mi) west to the sandy beach of Biodola. **Pros:** In a gorgeous park, excellent restaurant, a great base for exploring the island. **Cons:** Hour-long walk to the beach and nearest town, half board is mandatory, some furnishings are showing their age. ⊠ *Località San Martino* ✚ *5 km (3 mi) west of Portoferraio's center, Portoferraio 57037* ☎ *0565/918502* ✆ *www.parkhotel napoleone.com* ⤳ *64 rooms, 1 suite* ♿ *In-room: refrigerator. In-hotel: restaurant, bar, tennis courts, pools, bicycles, laundry service, public Internet, parking (no fee), some pets allowed* ⊟ *DC, MC, V* ☉ *Closed Nov.–Easter* ⭕ *MAP*.

$$$ ⭐ 🏨 **Hotel Riva del Sole.** A short walk from the center of lively Marina di Campo, this bright, pleasant hotel caters to a loyal Italian and German clientele. Breezy rooms with tile floors provide cool relief from the hot sun, and some have terraces facing the ocean. Marble bathrooms are an elegant touch. On warm nights the scent of oleander growing next to the hotel will truly give you sweet dreams. The spacious restaurant, which specializes in elegantly prepared seafood, is an added bonus. **Pros:** Caters to families with children, the beach is steps away, very close to town center. **Cons:** Standard rooms lack balconies, not all rooms have sea views. ⊠ *Viale degli Eroi 11, Marina di Campo 57034* ☎ *0565/976316* ✆ *www.hotel-rivadelsole.com* ⤳ *60 rooms* ♿ *In-room: safe, refrigerator. In-hotel: restaurant, bar, laundry service, public Internet, parking (no fee)* ⊟ *AE, DC, MC, V* ☉ *Closed Nov.–Apr.* ⭕ *EP*.

$$ 🏨 **Hotel Rio sul Mare.** Convenient to Rio Marina's charming town center and gravel beach, this comfortable hotel has pretty sea views. Ask for one of the five rooms that have terraces facing the sea. Use of beach chairs and umbrellas is complimentary. **Pros:** Close to town center, very attractive sea views from all rooms. **Cons:** Not all rooms have a/c, the nearby beach is rocky. ⊠ *Via Palestro 34, Rio Marina 57038* ☎ *0565/924225* ✆ *www.hotelriomarina.it* ⤳ *35 rooms* ♿ *In-room: no a/c (some), refrigerator. In-hotel: restaurant, beachfront, laundry service, public Internet, parking (no fee), some pets allowed* ⊟ *AE, DC, MC, V* ☉ *Closed Nov.–Mar.* ⭕ *BP*.

SPORTS & THE OUTDOORS

BEACHES Elba's most celebrated beaches are the sandy stretches at **Biodola, Procchio,** and **Marina di Campo,** but the entire island—and particularly the westernmost section, encircling Monte Capanne—is ringed with beautiful coastline. Indeed, it seems that every sleepy town has its own perfect tiny beach. Try **Cavoli** and **Fetovaia** anytime but July and August, when all the car-accessible beaches on the island are packed (there are also some accessible only by boat, such as the black-sand beach of **Punta Nera**).

WATER SPORTS **Subnow** (⊠ *Ville degli Ulivi Camping, Località La Foce, Marina di Campo* ☎ *0565/976048* ✆ *www.subnow.it*) organizes daily diving excursions, for experts and beginners, into the waters of Elba's National Marine Park.

Spaziomare (✉ *Via Vittorio Veneto, Porto Azzurro* ☎ *0565/95112 or 348/6017862* ⊕ *www.spaziomare.it*) has motorboats available for half- and full-day rentals and sailboats to rent by the week. Adventurous types can rent sea kayaks and mountain bikes from **Il Viottolo** (✉ *Via Pietri 6, Marina di Campo* ☎ *0565/978005* ⊕ *www.ilviottolo. it*), which also organizes three-day guided excursions on land and sea.

CAPRAIA

GETTING HERE
Car ferry service from Livorno is provided by Toremar. The trip takes 2½ hours.

EXPLORING
Only a handful of people actually live on the island of Capraia, which is frequented mainly by sailors. It's a rocky and hilly unspoiled national park, with only one sandy beach, **Cala della Mortola,** on the northern end of the island; the rest of the coast is a succession of cliffs and deep green coves with pretty rock formations. The 2½-hour ferry trip departs from Livorno and pulls in at the town of **Capraia Isola,** dominated by the Fortezza di San Giorgio up above. Nearby, an archway leads to an area that was once a prison.

The **Cooperativa Parco Naturale Isola di Capraia** (✉ *Via Assunzione 42, Capraia Isola* ☎ *0586/905071*) can help with villa rentals and ferry schedules.

Capraia's clear waters and undersea life draw raves from scuba divers. **Capraia Diving Service** (✉ *Via Assunzione 100/B, Capraia Isola* ☎ *0586/905137* ⊕ *www.capraiadiving.it*) has scuba-diving equipment and boats.

Perugia, Assisi & Northern Umbria

WITH THE MARCHES

WORD OF MOUTH

"The towns in Umbria have kind of an urban flair to them. It's the unique coexistence of urban and cultivated landscape that makes Umbria very, very special; where else do you have merely five minutes to go by foot from the urban theater to the next vineyard?"

—Franco

WELCOME TO NORTHERN UMBRIA

Basilica of Saint Francis

TOP REASONS TO GO

★ **Assisi's shrine to Saint Francis:** Recharge your soul in this rose-color hill town with a visit to the gentle saint's majestic basilica, adorned with memorable frescoes.

★ **Palazzo Ducale, Urbino:** It's one of Italy's finest examples of Renaissance architecture, so admire the facade before going inside to see works by Titian and Piero della Francesca.

★ **Corso Vanucci, Perugia:** Take a stroll down this palace-lined road, where residents of Umbria's capital stretch their legs before dinner.

★ **Gubbio:** Take part in the Corsa dei Ceri, the most spectacular of the region's festivals, then try truffles in one of the town's restaurants.

1 Perugia. Umbria's largest town is easily reached from Rome, Siena, or Florence. Home to some of Perugino's great frescoes and a hilltop centro storico (historic center), it's also favored by chocolate lovers, who celebrate their passion at October's Eurochocolate Festival.

2 Around Perugia. The quiet towns lying around Perugia include **Deruta**, which produces exceptional ceramics, and **Torgiano**, where you can tour the Wine Museum and taste the wines from the surrounding valley. **Lago Trasimeno** is the place for water sports and waterfront dining.

3 Assisi. The city of Saint Francis is a major pilgrimage site, crowned by one of Italy's greatest churches. Despite the throngs of visitors, it still maintains its medieval hill-town character.

TUSCANY

Sansepolcro
San Giustino
Fraccan
Citta di Castello
Trestina
Montecastelli
Umbertide
Passignano sul Trasimeno
Lago di Trasimeno Magione
Castiglione
Monte Buono
Panicale

E45
73
E78
257
73
416
71
75
71
75
599
220

Perugia

4 North Toward Urbino.
A trip through the rugged terrain of northeast Umbria takes you to **Gubbio**, where from the Piazza della Signoria you can admire magnificent views of the countryside below.

5 The Marches. East of Umbria, the steep, twisting roads of this region lead to well-preserved medieval towns before settling down to the sandy beaches of the Adriatic. The main attraction is **Urbino**, the best surviving example of the ideal Renaissance city.

GETTING ORIENTED

Central Italy doesn't begin and end with Tuscany; Umbria picks up where its more famous neighbor leaves off. Divided by the Apennine Mountain range, the region is studded with medieval and Renaissance villages and fortresses—a landscape hallowed by Saint Francis and immortalized in the works of Raphael and Perugino.

7

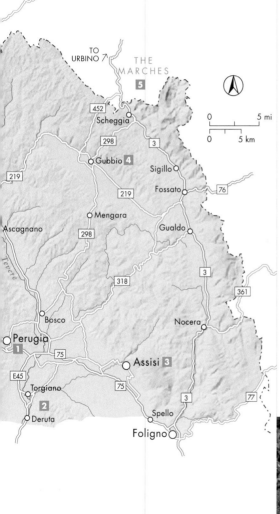

Grape harvesting

NORTHERN UMBRIA PLANNER

Festivals to Plan a Trip Around

Perugia is the place to be every July, when it hosts **Umbria Jazz,** one of the continent's biggest jazz festivals. For 10 days there are free concerts around the city center, treating listeners to everything from gospel to funk. The biggest names in jazz, from Dizzy Gillespie to Wynton Marsalis, have all played in Perugia. It's also a great chance to be among the first to hear up-and-coming performers. But the festival is not just about jazz. In recent years icons from the world of pop, such as Elton John, Eric Clapton, Carlos Santana, and Sting, have all performed at Umbria Jazz..

If you're feeling blue after Umbria Jazz, stick around. The weeklong **Trasimeno Blues,** held at Lake Trasimeno immediately after Umbria Jazz, attracts performers from New Orleans and beyond. Open-air concerts are held in the towns that surround lovely Lago Trasimeno.

If you've got a sweet tooth, head to Perugia during the third week of October for **Eurochocolate,** when the town is almost entirely dedicated to cacao and its various derivatives. Huge chocolate sculptures are surrounded by crowds eager to sample all sorts of varieties from around the world.

Making the Most of Your Time

The region's largest and liveliest city, **Perugia,** is a logical place to start your tour of northern Umbria, and is an excellent base for day trips to other towns—including **Assisi,** the region's top attraction. If you prefer to stay somewhere more peaceful, opt for a smaller town such as **Torgiano** or **Corciano,** both of which are within easy reach of the main roads that link the major points of interest. Allow a day for **Gubbio,** northeast of Perugia, and another for **Urbino,** in the Marches. Both are worth the effort it takes to reach them. Although Umbria is landlocked, you can find secluded beaches on the islands on **Lake Trasimeno.**

Finding a Place to Stay

Virtually all the old towns in northern Umbria have somewhere to stay, even if it's just an inn with a few rooms. Such places are usually reasonably priced and perfectly comfortable. Larger towns provide a complete range of hotels, from spartan to luxurious, but prices tend to be higher.

Agriturismi are scattered throughout the countryside. These working farms range from rustic establishments to luxury resorts. They're ideal if you're traveling by car and appreciate the quiet beauty of the country more than the conveniences of towns. You can find listings at **Agriturist Umbria** (⊠ *Via Savonarola 38, Perugia 06121* ☎ *075/36665* ⊕ *www.agrituristumbria.com*)and **Turismo Verde** (⊠ *Via Maria Angeloni 1, Perugia 06124* ☎*075/5002953* ⊕ *www.turismoverde.it*).

DINING & LODGING PRICE CATEGORIES (IN EUROS)

	¢	$	$$	$$$	$$$$
RESTAURANTS	under €15	€15–€25	€25–€35	€35–€45	over €45
HOTELS	under €70	€70–€110	€110–€160	€160–€220	over €220

Restaurant prices are for a first course (*primo*), second course (*secondo*), and dessert (*dolce*). Hotel prices are for two people in a standard double room in high season, including tax and service.

GETTING AROUND

By Car

Umbria has a good road network. SR75bis links Perugia to Tuscany (to Siena via SR326 and E76) and to the Florence–Rome Autostrada del Sole (A1), Italy's main north–south highway; SR75bis also goes right by Lago Trasimeno. The E45 crosses from one side of Umbria to the other, and is the one to take for most of your visits. However, driving through the mountains to Urbino can be a bit treacherous because of the winding roads; plan for plenty of travel time.

The A14 superhighway travels southeast from Bologna and follows the Adriatic coast through the entire length of the Marches; branches lead to Urbino, Ancona, Loreto, and Ascoli Piceno. SS San Marino, a state highway, takes you to the Republic of San Marino from Rimini.

Northern Umbria is a mountainous region divided by the Apennine range, which runs down the center of Italy. Umbria's valleys run north–south, so travel is much easier if you're headed in one of those directions. Crossing east–west often involves winding, occasionally treacherous roads.

By Bus

Perugia's bus station is in Piazza Partigiani, which you can reach by taking the escalators from the town center. Perugia is served by the **Sulga Line** (☎075/5009641 ⊕ *www. sulga.it*), which has daily departures to Rome's Stazione Tiburtina and to Florence's Piazza Adua. Connections between Rome, Spoleto, and the Marches are provided by the bus companies **Bucci** (☎0721/32401 ⊕ *www.auto-lineebucci.com*) and **Soget** (☎0721/371318).

Local bus services between all the major and minor towns of Umbria are good. Some of the routes in rural areas are designed to serve as many places as possible and are, therefore, quite roundabout and slow. Schedules change often, so consult with local tourist offices before setting out.

By Train

Several direct daily trains run by the Italian state railway, **Ferrovia dello Stato** (☎892021 *toll free in Italy* ⊕ *www.trenitalia. com*), link Florence and Perugia. The Florence–Chiusi train stops at Castiglione del Lago, on Lago Trasimeno, and sometimes at Città della Pieve as well. Daily direct service between Perugia and Rome is available, but this service isn't frequent and a change at Foligno, from the main Rome–Ancona line, is often required. Main rail lines, with fast Intercity and Eurocity trains, link Ancona with Bologna and Rome. A small, privately owned railway, **Ferrovia Centrale Umbra** (☎075/5729121), runs south from Città di Castello to Terni via Perugia. Gubbio and San Marino have no train service.

If you're catching a train in Perugia, go first to the information office on your right as you enter. If you don't know what ticket you want, the ticket-sales staff tend to send you to the information office.

7

Updated
by Jonathan
Willcocks

NORTHERN UMBRIA IS RICH IN history, art, tradition, and breath-taking landscapes. It's squeezed between eastern Tuscany—notably Arezzo and Cortona—and the Marches, where the Renaissance architecture of the Palazzo Ducale in Urbino beckons. The landscapes are the same as what you see in the paintings of Renaissance master Perugino: gentle hills, a few large lakes, and the Tiber River meandering across the plains.

Perugia, the largest and richest of Umbria's cities, owes its elegance to the 3,000 years of history concentrated in a town that, neither too big nor too small, was clearly designed to fit the human scale. Gubbio, Perugia's neighbor to the north, climbs straight up a mountain, filling the bottom half with its houses and churches. Every May, costumed runners ascend to the top, to the church of Sant'Ubaldo, during the bizarre Festa dei Ceri, or Festival of the Candles. From Gubbio, you can travel across to Urbino or up to the Republic of San Marino, which claims to be the oldest and smallest independent state in the world.

The steep hills and deep valleys that make Umbria so picturesque also make it difficult to explore. Driving routes must be chosen carefully to avoid tortuous mountain roads. But Perugia is a convenient base from which to explore the region, and you can get around fairly quickly by car. You might want to combine your trip with a southern Tuscany itinerary that includes Arezzo and Cortona or with visits to Assisi, Spoleto, and southern Umbria. You can reasonably visit the area around Perugia, see Gubbio and Città di Castello, and take a side trip to Urbino in four days. You would be shortchanging a trip to this region if you skipped Urbino and its storybook palace.

Northern Umbria is fairly free of the great masses of visitors that descend upon the other regions, even in summer, when you might welcome the lush greenness of these interior tracts. In August much of the local population shifts to Adriatic resorts such as Rimini and Parco del Conero for vacation. The forested Umbrian hills also ensure a stunning autumnal landscape and an explosion of greenery in the spring. In both spring and fall the number of visitors is especially low and the temperatures are usually moderate, but keep in mind that April and November may be rainy.

The predominantly hilly terrain of northern Umbria means that winters can be bitterly cold, and snow is common. Because many destinations here are hilltop towns, including Perugia itself, you should be prepared for harsh conditions and possible hazardous driving if you're traveling at this time of year.

PERUGIA

Perugia is a majestic, handsome, wealthy city, and with its trendy boutiques, refined cafés, and grandiose architecture, it doesn't try to hide its affluence. A student population of more than 30,000 means that the city is abuzz with activity throughout the year. Umbria Jazz, one of the region's most important music festivals, attracts music lovers from

Perugia's Fontana Maggiore by night.

around the world, and Eurochocolate, the international chocolate festival, is an irresistible draw for anyone with a sweet tooth.

GETTING HERE
The best approach to the city is by train. The area around the station doesn't attest to the rest of Perugia's elegance, but buses running from the station to Piazza d'Italia, the heart of the old town, are frequent. If you are driving to Perugia and your hotel doesn't have parking facilities, leave your car in one of the lots close to the center. Electronic signs indicate the location of lots and the number of spaces free. If you park in the Piazza Partigiani, take the escalators that pass through the fascinating subterranean excavations of the Roman foundations of the city and lead to the town center.

VISITOR INFORMATION
Umbria's regional tourism office (⌧ *Piazza Matteotti 18* ☎ *075/5736458* 🖷 *075/5720988* ⊕ *www.perugia.umbria2000.it*) .is in Perugia. The staff is well informed about the area, and can give you a wide selection of leaflets and maps to assist you during your trip. It's open Monday to Saturday 8:30 to 1:30 and 3 to 6:30, and Sunday 8:30 to 1.

NORTHERN UMBRIA THROUGH THE AGES

In Etruscan times, Perugia and Gubbio were among the last to bow to Roman rule. The Romans eventually conquered the cities in the 3rd century BC. Perugia was caught in the middle of a power struggle between two Roman rulers and was burned, sacked, and destroyed in 140 BC. The city was slowly rebuilt, and during the medieval period gave its allegiance to the popes.

After winning a war with Assisi in 1202, Perugia flourished. Churches and government buildings were erected, and a university was founded in 1308. In the 15th century the city's noblemen became more powerful. The Baglioni family briefly ruled the city, but power quickly returned to the Church. In 1540 the Perugians rebelled against a salt tax imposed by Pope Paul III (1468–1549), winning the so-called

Salt War, but one of the pope's three sons, Pier Luigi Farnese (1503–47), fathered before his spiritual conversion in 1519, quickly reconquered the area. Perugia didn't become independent of the Church's rule until 1860, when the troops of Victor Emmanuel II of Savoy (1820–78) conquered it and unified the entire Italian peninsula.

Gubbio, which during Roman times was home to a theater that held 12,000 spectators, followed a different path. Its destiny, intertwined with that of Urbino in the Marches, was to be decided by the Montefeltro and Della Rovere families of Urbino during the Renaissance. Like Perugia, in 1631 it fell under the rule of the Papal States, and didn't become part of Umbria until 1861, after the unification of Italy.

EXPLORING PERUGIA

Thanks to Perugia's hilltop position, the medieval city remains almost completely intact. It is the best-preserved hill town of its size, and few other places in Italy better illustrate the model of the self-contained city-state that so shaped the course of Italian history.

MAIN ATTRACTIONS

⓫ **Arco di Augusto** *(Arch of Augustus)*. Dating from the 3rd century BC, this arch was the entrance to the Etruscan and Roman acropolis. In the same square is the Università per Stranieri (University for Foreigners). ✉*Piazza Fortebraccio.*

❹ **Collegio del Cambio** *(Bankers' Guild Hall)*. These elaborate rooms, on
★ the ground floor of the **Palazzo dei Priori,** served as the meeting hall and chapel of the guild of bankers and money changers. Most of the frescoes were done by the most important Perugian painter of the Renaissance, Pietro Vannucci, better known as Perugino. He included a remarkably honest self-portrait on one of the pilasters. The iconography includes common religious themes, such as the Nativity and the Transfiguration seen on the end walls. On the left wall are female figures representing the virtues, beneath them the heroes and sages of antiquity. On the right wall are figures presumed to have been painted in part by Perugino's most famous pupil, Raphael. (His hand, experts say, is most apparent in the figure of Fortitude.) The *cappella* (chapel)

of San Giovanni Battista has frescoes painted by Giannicola di Paolo, another student of Perugino. ⊠*Corso Vannucci 25* ☎*075/5728599* 🎫*€4.50, €5.50 with Collegio della Mercanzia* ⊙*Mon.–Sat. 9–12:30 and 2:30–5:30, Sun. 9–1.*

❻ Collegio della Mercanzia *(Merchant's Meeting Hall).* This room of carved wood, two doors away from the **Palazzo dei Priori** entrance of the Collegio del Cambio, dates back to the 1300s. It was the original meeting room for merchants, especially fabric traders. Trading didn't actually take place here, but merchants met to set prices and to standardize trade practices. ⊠*Corso Vannucci 15* ☎*075/5730366* 🎫*€1.50, €5.50 with Collegio del Cambio* ⊙*Mar.–Oct. and Dec. 20–Jan. 6, Tues.–Sat. 9–1 and 2:30–5:30, Sun. 9–1; Nov.–Dec. 19 and Jan. 7–Feb., Tues., Thurs., and Fri. 8–2, Wed. and Sat. 8–4, Sun. 9–1.*

❶ Corso Vannucci. A string of elegantly connected *palazzi* (palaces) expresses the artistic nature of this city center, the heart of which is concentrated along Corso Vannucci. Stately and broad, this pedestrians-only street runs from Piazza d'Italia to Piazza IV Novembre. Along the way, the entrances to many of Perugia's side streets might tempt you to wander off and explore. But don't stray too far as evening falls, when Corso Vannucci fills with Perugians out for their evening *passeggiata*, a pleasant pre-dinner stroll that may include a pause for an aperitif at one of the many bars that line the street.

NEED A BREAK? You can enjoy the lively comings and goings on Corso Vannucci from the vantage point of the Bar Sandri (⊠*Corso Vannucci 32* ☎*075/5724112*). The 19th-century bar has wood paneling and ceiling frescoes that date from 1860. Red-vested waiters serve homemade chocolates, pastries, and ice creams, along with *tavola pronta*, a daily selection of fast first and second courses, to Sandri's lunch crowd. If you notice students steering clear of the bar, it's because superstition dictates that if they go there they won't finish their degree.

❷ Duomo. Severe yet mystical, the Duomo, also called the Cathedral of San Lorenzo, is most famous for being the home of the wedding ring of the Virgin Mary, stolen by the Perugians in 1488 from the nearby town of Chiusi. The ring, kept high up in a red-curtained vault in the chapel immediately to the left of the entrance, is kept under lock—15 locks, to be precise—and key most of the year. It's shown to the public on July 30 (the day it was brought to Perugia) and the second-to-last Sunday in January (Mary's wedding anniversary). The cathedral itself dates from the Middle Ages and has many additions from the 15th and 16th centuries. The most visually interesting element is the altar to the Madonna of Grace; an elegant fresco on a column at the right of the entrance of the altar depicts *La Madonna delle Grazie* and is surrounded by prayer benches decorated with handwritten notes to the Holy Mother. Around the column are small amulets—symbols of gratitude from those whose prayers were answered. There are also elaborately carved choir stalls, executed by Giovanni Battista Bastone in 1520. The altarpiece (1484), an early masterpiece by Luca Signorelli

Perugia

0   300 yards

0   300 meters

(circa 1441–1523), shows the Madonna with Saint John the Baptist, Saint Onophrius, and Saint Lawrence. Sections of the church may be closed to visitors during religious services.

The **Museo Capitolare** displays a large array of precious objects associated with the cathedral, including vestments, vessels, and manuscripts. Outside the Duomo is the elaborate **Fontana Maggiore,** which dates from 1278. It is adorned with zodiac figures and symbols of the seven arts. ⊠*Piazza IV Novembre* ☎*075/5724853* ⌂*Duomo free, museum €3.50* ☉*Duomo: Mon.–Sat. 7–12:30 and 4–6:45, Sun. 8–12:30 and 4–6:45; museum: daily 10–1 and 2:30–5:30; last admission ½ hr before closing.*

❺   **Galleria Nazionale dell'Umbria.** The region's most comprehensive art gal-
FodorśChoice   lery is housed on the fourth floor of the **Palazzo dei Priori.** Enhanced
★   by skillfully lit displays and computers that allow you to focus on the works' details and background information, the collection includes work by native artists—most notably Pintoricchio (1454–1513) and Perugino (circa 1450–1523)—and others of the Umbrian and Tuscan schools, among them Gentile da Fabriano (1370–1427), Duccio (circa 1255–1318), Fra Angelico (1387–1455), Fiorenzo di Lorenzo (1445–1525), and Piero della Francesca (1420–92). In addition to paintings,

the gallery has frescoes, sculptures, and some superb examples of crucifixes from the 13th and 14th centuries. Some rooms are dedicated to Perugia itself, showing how the medieval city evolved. ✉ *Corso Vannucci 19, Piazza IV Novembre* ☎ *075/5721009* ⊕ *www.gallerianazionaleumbria.it* 💶 *€6.50* ⏰ *Tues.–Sun. 8:30–7:30; last admission ½ hr before closing.*

WORD OF MOUTH

"Two things you must not fail to do in Perugia are to (a) join the evening walk on the Corso Vannucci beginning at about 5 pm and (b) take the escalators that go up and down and through the historic city walls. Also: Hang out as often as you dare at Sandri's, one of Italy's most marvelous cafe/pastry shops, on the Corso Vanucci." –nessundorma

❸ **Palazzo dei Priori** *(Palace of Priors).*
★ A series of elegant connected buildings, the palazzo serves as Perugia's city hall and houses three of the city's museums. The buildings string along Corso Vannucci and wrap around the Piazza IV Novembre, where the original entrance is located. The steps here lead to the **Sala dei Notari** (Notaries' Hall). Other entrances lead to the **Galleria Nazionale dell'Umbria**, the **Collegio del Cambio**, and the **Collegio della Mercanzia**. The Sala dei Notari, which dates back to the 13th century and was the original meeting place of the town merchants, had become the seat of the notaries by the second half of the 15th century. Wood beams and an interesting array of frescoes attributed to Maestro di Farneto embellish the room. Coats of arms and crests line the back and right lateral walls; you can spot some famous figures from Aesop's *Fables* on the left wall. The palazzo facade is adorned with symbols of Perugia's pride and past power: the griffin is the city symbol, and the lion denotes Perugia's allegiance to the Guelph (or papal) cause. ✉ *Piazza IV Novembre* 💶 *Free* ⏰ *June–Sept., Tues.–Sun. 9–1 and 3–7.*

Rocca Paolina. A labyrinth of little streets, alleys, and arches, this underground city was originally part of a fortress. It was built at the behest of Pope Paul III between 1540 and 1543 to confirm papal dominion over the city. Parts of it were destroyed after the end of papal rule, but much still remains. Begin your visit by taking the escalators from Piazza Italia and Via Masi. In the summer this is the coolest place in the city. ⏰ *Daily 8–7.*

ALSO WORTH SEEING

❼ **Museo Archeologico Nazionale.** The museum, next to the imposing church of San Domenico, contains an excellent collection of Etruscan artifacts from throughout the region. Perugia was a flourishing Etruscan city long before it fell under Roman domination in 310 BC. Little else remains of Perugia's mysterious ancestors, although the Arco di Augusto, in Piazza Fortebraccio, the northern entrance to the city, is of Etruscan origin. ✉ *Piazza G. Bruno 10* ☎ *075/5727141* ⊕ *www.archeopg.arti.beni culturali.it* 💶 *€4* ⏰ *Mon. 2:30–7:30, Tues.–Sun. 8:30–7:30.*

❿ **Oratorio di San Bernardino.** Agostino di Duccio (circa 1418–81) designed this lovely little Renaissance church with a pink-and-blue lacy stone facade in 1457–61. It honors the memory of Saint Bernard, who often preached in

Perugia and became one of the city's most important saints. ⊠ *Piazza San Francesco* ☎ *075/5733957* ✆ *Free* ⊙ *Daily 8–12:30 and 3:30–6.*

❽ San Filippo Neri. With its grandiose facade dating from 1663, this church is an interesting piece of baroque architecture. Inside are frescoes by various 18th-century artists, as well as a 1662 altarpiece by Pietro da Cortona (1596–1669) depicting the conception of Mary. ⊠ *Piazza Ferri* ☎ *075/5725472* ✆ *Free* ⊙ *Daily 7:30–noon and 4–7.*

⓬ San Severo. The only Raphael fresco in Perugia, painted in 1505–08, resides in this little church. The lower part (six saints) was added in 1521 by Raphael's teacher, Perugino. The admission ticket allows you also to visit the **Etruscan well** in Piazza Piccinino, behind the church. ⊠ *Piazza Raffaello* ☎ *075/5733864* ✆ *€2.50* ⊙ *Nov.–Mar., weekdays 10–1:30 and 2:30–4:30; Apr.–Oct., daily 10–1:30 and 2:30–6:30.*

❾ Torre degli Sciri *(Sciri Tower).* The tower, which dates from the 12th to 13th centuries, is the only one of its time still standing in Perugia. At a height of 151 feet, it proclaimed to the neighborhood the wealth of the family that built it. ⊠ *Via dei Priori.*

OFF THE BEATEN PATH

La Città della Domenica. This theme park is in the town of Montepulito, 8 km (5 mi) west of Perugia. The 500 acres of parkland can be toured on a train that runs through the grounds and takes visitors on a tour through fairy-tale landscapes including a castle, a toy village, and a labyrinth. There are also a reptile house, an aquarium, and several restaurants. ⊠ *Via Col di Tenda 140, Località Montepulito* ☎ *075/5054941* ✆ *€12* ⊙ *Apr.–mid-Sept., daily 10–6; mid-Sept.–Oct., weekends 10–7.*

WHERE TO EAT

$$–$$$ ✕ **Antica Trattoria San Lorenzo.** Brick vaults are not the only distinguishing feature of this small restaurant next to the Duomo, as both the food and the service are outstanding. Particular attention is paid to adapting traditional Umbrian cuisine to the modern palate. There is also a nice variety of seafood dishes on the menu. The *trenette alla farina di noce con pesce di mare* (flat noodles made with walnut flour topped with fresh fish) is a real treat. ⊠ *Piazza Danti 19-A* ☎ *075/5721956* ▤ *AE, D, MC, V* ⊙ *Closed Sun.*

$–$$$ ✕ **La Rosetta.** The restaurant, in the hotel of the same name, is a peaceful, elegant spot. In winter you dine inside under medieval vaults; in summer, in the cool courtyard. The food is simple but reliable and flawlessly served. The restaurant caters to the international hotel guests seeking to get away from the bustle of central Perugia. The delightful courtyard is just 10 meters off the main Corso Vannucci and a perfect spot to relax away from the noise. ⊠ *Piazza d'Italia 19* ☎ *075/5720841* ✎ *Reservations essential* ▤ *AE, DC, MC, V.*

$$ ✕ **La Taverna.** Medieval steps lead to a rustic two-story restaurant where wine bottles and artful clutter decorate the walls. Good choices from the regional menu include *caramelle al gorgonzola* (pasta rolls filled with red cabbage and mozzarella and topped with a Gorgonzola sauce) and grilled meat dishes, such as the *medaglioni di vitello al tartuffo* (grilled veal with truffles). ⊠ *Via delle Streghe 8, off Corso Vannucci* ☎ *075/5724128* ▤ *AE, DC, MC, V* ⊘ *Closed Mon.*

$–$$ ✗ **Il Falchetto.** Exceptional food at reasonable prices makes this Perugia's best bargain. Service is smart but relaxed in the two medieval dining rooms that put the chef on view. The house specialty is *falchetti* (homemade gnocchi with spinach and ricotta cheese). ⊠ *Via Bartolo 20* ☎ *075/5731775* ▤ *AE, DC, MC, V* ⊘ *Closed Mon. and last 2 wks in Jan.*

$ ✗ **Dal Mi' Cocco.** A great favorite with Perugia's university students, this
★ place is fun, crowded, and inexpensive. You may find yourself seated at a long table with other diners, but some language help from your neighbors could come in handy—the menu is in pure Perugian dialect. The fixed-price meals change with the season, and each day of the week brings some new creation *dal cocco* (from the "coconut," or head) of the chef. ⊠ *Corso Garibaldi 12* ☎ *075/5732511* ⚑ *Reservations essential* ▤ *No credit cards* ⊘ *Closed Mon. and July 25–Aug. 15*

WHERE TO STAY

$$$$ ⌂ **Brufani Palace.** This 19th-century palazzo has been turned into an elegant hotel. The public rooms and first-floor guest rooms have high ceilings and are decorated in grand belle-epoque style. The second-floor rooms are more modern; many on both floors have a marvelous view of either the countryside or the city. **Pros:** Great central position, fine views, nice bar. **Cons:** Fodor's reader's have complained of unexpected charges on the bill. ⊠ *Piazza d'Italia 12, 06121* ☎ *075/5732541* 🖷 *075/5720210* ⊕ *www.brufanipalace.com* ⇋ *63 rooms, 31 suites* △ *In-room: ethernet. In-hotel: restaurant, bar, pool, gym* ▤ *AE, DC, MC, V* ⌾ *BP*

$$$ ⌂ **Castello dell'Oscano.** A splendid neo-Gothic castle, a late-19th-century villa, and a converted farmhouse hidden in the tranquil hills north of Perugia offer a wide range of accommodations. Step back in time in the castle, where spacious suites and junior suites, all with high oak-beam ceilings, and some with panoramic views of the surrounding country, are decorated with 18th- and 19th-century antiques. The sweeping wooden staircase of the main lounge, and the wood-panel reading rooms and restaurant are particularly elegant. Rooms in the villa are smaller and more modern, and the apartments of the farmhouse, in the valley below the castle, have their own kitchens. The complex is in Cenerente, 5 km (3 mi) north of Perugia. **Pros:** Quiet elegance, fine gardens, Umbrian wine list. **Cons:** Distance from Perugia, not easy to find. ⊠ *Strada della Forcella 32, Cenerente 06070* ☎ *075/584371* 🖷 *075/690666* ⊕ *www.oscano.it* ⇋ *24 rooms, 8 suites, 13 apartments* △ *In-room: no a/c (some), ethernet. In-hotel: restaurant, bar, pool, gym, bicycles, no-smoking rooms* ▤ *AE, D, V* ⌾ *BP*

$$ ⌂ **Hotel Fortuna.** The elegant decor in the large rooms of this friendly hotel complements the frescoes, which date from the 1700s. Some rooms have balconies. The building itself, just out of sight of Corso Vannucci, dates to the 1300s. **Pros:** Central but quiet, homely atmosphere. **Cons:** Some small rooms, no restaurant. ⊠ *Via Bonazzi 19,*

7

06123 ☎*075/5722845* 📠*075/5735040* ⊕*www.umbriahotels.com* 🛏*51 rooms* &*In-hotel: restaurant, bar, parking (fee)* ⊟*AE, DC, MC, V* 🍴*BP*

$$ 🏨 **Il Cantico della Natura.** Don't let the rustic appearance of the buildings fool you, this is one of the plushest agriturismi in Umbria. The rooms are furnished in varying ethnic styles, with nice little extras thrown in such as bedside kettles and an array of teas and herbal infusions. The owners also organize a series of outdoor activities. Pros: Views of Lake Trasimeno and the surrounding countryside. Cons: Not easy to find, road poor in winter. ✉*Vocabolo Penna, Montesperello di Magione* ☎*075/841699* ⊕*www.ilcanticodellanatura.it* 🛏*12 rooms* &*In-hotel: restaurant, gym, bicycles* ⊟*AE, DC, MC, V* 🍴*BP*

$$ 🏨 **Locanda della Posta.** In the city's old district, this lodging is in an 18th-century palazzo. Renovations have left the lobby and other public areas rather bland, but the rooms are soothingly decorated in muted colors. Although facing busy Corso Vannucci and supposedly soundproof, they're still a bit noisy. Those on the upper floors at the back of the building are quieter and have great views. **Pros:** Some fine views, central position. **Cons:** Uninspiring lobby, some small rooms, no restaurant. ✉*Corso Vannucci 97, 06121* ☎*075/5728925* 📠*075/5732562* 🛏*38 rooms, 1 suite* &*In-hotel: bar, parking (fee)* ⊟*AE, DC, MC, V* 🍴*BP*

¢ 🏨 **Rosalba.** Scrupulously clean rooms put this budget lodging head and shoulders above the rest. Rooms at the back enjoy a view of Perugia's red-tile rooftops. On the top floor, Room 9 has a private terrace and sleeps up to five people, making it perfect for a family or group of friends. Although somewhat out of the way, the hotel is only a matter of minutes from Corso Vannucci by virtue of a nearby public escalator. **Pros:** Great prices, quiet location. **Cons:** Small rooms, no restaurant. ✉*Via del Circo 7, 06100* ☎*075/5728285* 📠*075/5720626* ⊕*www.hotelrosalba.com* 🛏*11 rooms* &*In-room: no TV. In-hotel: no elevator, parking (no fee)* ⊟*No credit cards* 🍴*EP*

NIGHTLIFE & THE ARTS

With its large student population, the city has plenty to offer in the way of bars and clubs. The best ones are around the city center, off Corso Vanucci. *Viva Perugia* is a good source of information about nightlife. The monthly, sold at newsstands, has a section in English.

THE OWNER OF BUSKERS (✉*Corso Cavour 46,* ☎*0755729202*) used to be a semiprofessional soccer player, but today you're more likely to find him near the dartboard. The decor is a little overwhelmingly pubby, but manages to blend in with the vaulted ceilings of the medieval cellars. In the small bar upstairs, unrequested plates of pasta and other foods begin to appear at 6 PM. This is happy hour, when students, locals, and in-the-know travelers can get themselves a free meal.

MUSIC FESTIVALS

Summer sees two music festivals in Perugia. **Umbria Jazz** (☎*075/5732432 ⊕www.umbriajazz.com*) is held for 10 days in July. Tickets are available starting at the end of April. The **Sagra Musicale Umbra** (☎*075/5721374 ⊕www.perugiamusicaclassica.com*), held from mid-August to mid-September, celebrates sacred music.

SHOPPING

Take a stroll down any of Perugia's main streets, including Corso Vannucci, Via dei Priori, Via Oberdan, and Via S. Ercolano, and you'll see many well-known designer boutiques and specialty shops.

The most typical thing to buy in Perugia is some Perugina chocolate, which you can find almost anywhere. The best-known chocolates made by Perugina are the chocolate-and-hazelnut-filled nibbles called Baci (literally, "kisses"). They're wrapped in silver paper that includes a sliver of paper, like the fortune in a fortune cookie, with multilingual romantic sentiments or sayings.

CRAFTS

Fragile (✉ *Via dei Priori 70* ☎*075/5736120*) makes and sells colorful handcrafted wood pieces, including fanciful decorations for children's bedrooms, or objects for the frivolous at heart.

FABRICS

Fabbri Antonio (✉*Via Oberdan 13* ☎*075/5726609*) offers beautiful, high-quality, traditionally patterned Umbrian napkins, tablecloths, and hand towels in delicate yellow, blue, and rust colors. The patterns are derived from regional Romanesque designs. **Il Telaio** (✉ *Via Rocchi 19* ☎*075/5726603*) sells woven traditional Umbrian fabrics. The name of the shop translates as "The Loom."

FOOD

Fans of Italian gastronomic specialties might like to stop by the **Casa del Parmigiano Reggiano** (✉ *Via Sant'Ercolano* ☎*0755731233/*) to buy some of the best local bounty: rich green olive oils, dried salami, cheeses, wines, cookies, and lentils.

LEATHER

Castagner (✉ *Via Calderini 3* ☎*075/5723236*) sells such well-heeled Italian brands as Hogan, Tod's, and Fratelli Rosetti. Belts and other accessories are also available.

AROUND PERUGIA

A simple drive or train ride through the hilly terrain that surrounds Perugia may make you feel as if you have traveled back to a time when life was gentler and less complex and land was respected for its beauty and the life it sustains. Hilltop towns, churches that peek out from behind screens of trees, fields of poppies and vineyards, expanses of green where animals contentedly graze—one pastoral scene after

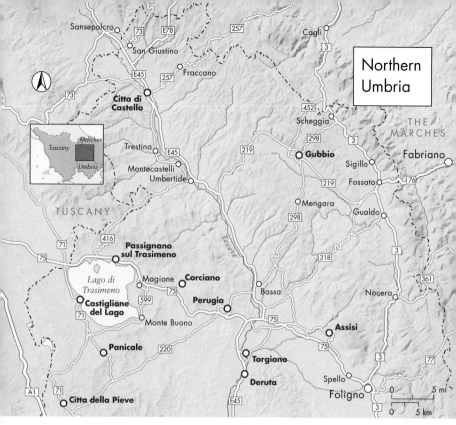

another passes before your eyes. South of Perugia, Torgiano is the center of Umbrian wine production and Deruta is the Umbrian ceramics center. A short distance east of Perugia you encounter the serene lake district of Trasimeno. The sleepy port of Passignano sul Trasimeno is on the northeast shore of the lake. Around Magione, also on the east side of the lake, the land once again becomes hilly and lush.

TORGIANO

16 km (10 mi) southeast of Perugia, 27 km (17 mi) southwest of Assisi.

GETTING HERE
From Perugia follow the directions for Rome and the E45 highway—Torgiano has its own exit. Buses run from Piazza Partigiani, the main bus terminal in Perugia.

EXPLORING
Torgiano rightly calls itself a town of wine, and the hilly area around it is carpeted with vineyards. Originally a small river port, it later played a role in local history as one of the towns that was fortified to help protect Perugia. The town itself is a quiet affair, and its two main streets, Corso Vittorio Emmanuele and Via Garibaldi, hold its most interesting sights.

Wine aficionados are certain to want to visit the winery **Cantine Lungarotti**, best known for its delicious Rubesco Lungarotti, San Giorgio, and Chardonnay wines. Tours are by appointment only. ⊠ *Via Mario Angeloni 12* ☎*075/988661* ⌂*Free* ⊘ *Weekdays 8–1 and 3–6.*

The fascinating **Museo del Vino** *(Wine Museum)* has a large collection of ancient wine vessels, presses, and tools that tell the story of viticulture in Umbria. The museum traces the history of wine in all its uses—for drinking, as medicine, and as part of religious rituals. Next door to the Museo del Vino, the **Osteria del Museo** (⊠*Corso Vittorio Emanuele 33* ☎*075/9880069*) is a local representative for the Lungarotti winery. You can taste and buy the winery's reds and whites here. The Osteria is small, so call in advance. ⊠*Corso Vittorio Emanuele 31* ☎*075/9880200* ⌂*€4.50* ⊘ *Apr.–Oct., daily 9–1 and 3–7; Nov.–Mar., daily 9–1 and 3–6.*

WHERE TO STAY & EAT

$$$

Fodor'sChoice

★

✕⊞ **Le Tre Vaselle.** Four charming stone buildings, linked underground, make up this hotel in the center of Torgiano. Its rooms are spacious, especially the suites, some of which have their own fireplaces. The floors are of typical Tuscan red-clay tiles; ceilings have wood beams. Olive groves surround the outdoor pool; a current pool and a whirlpool are indoors. The restaurant, Le Melagrane ($$$–$$$$), is a comfortable affair with red tablecloths, wood-beam ceilings, and exquisite local specialties. In summer you can dine alfresco on a terrace between two of the buildings. **Pros:** Plush furnishings, excellent service. **Cons:** Distance from Perugia, unexciting town. ⊠ *Via Garibaldi 48, 06089* ☎*075/9880447* ⊟*075/9880214* ⊕*www.3vaselle.it* ⇦*47 rooms, 13 suites* ⌂*In-room: ethernet. In-hotel: restaurant, bar, pools, gym* ⊟*AE, DC, MC, V* ⦿*BP*

$$$

★

✕⊞ **Posta dei Donini.** When the country's prime minister wanted a peaceful retreat, he chose the Posta dei Donini. In the center of this small village, it's known for privacy and exclusivity. As you wander the grounds, gardeners quietly go about their business. The guest rooms are beguilingly comfortable. For memorable ablutions don't miss the huge showerheads, commissioned from a Florentine artist. The hotel also has an excellent restaurant, Il Pantagruel ($$$$), where wine connoisseurs can complement their meals by choosing from a list of over 500 labels. **Pros:** Renaissance gardens, fabulous restaurant with extensive wine list. **Cons:** Uninteresting village, distance from Perugia. ⊠ *Via Deruta 43, 06079* ☎*075/609132* ⊕*www.postadonini. it* ⇦*33 rooms, 15 suites* ⌂*In-room: Wi-Fi. In-hotel: restaurant, bar, pool* ⊟*AE, DC, MC, V* ⦿*BP*

$$

⊞ **Castello Rosciano.** Dominating the vineyards above Torgiano, this lovingly restored castle has several apartments for travelers who want to relax close to the wine and ceramics area. Rooms have fine views, and the welcome is discreetly classy. The owners live on the estate and manage everything personally. The reception is a delightfully improvised affair, with a large fireplace and old furniture and paintings. Pros: Close to Torgiano and Deruta. Cons: Poor road in winter, not easy to find. ⊠ *Vocabolo di Signoria, Signoria di Torgiano 06089* ☎ *328/1357600*

⊕*www.castellodirosciano.com* ↩*5 rooms* ⌂ *In-room: no a/c. In-hotel: pool.* ═*No credit cards* ¶⨂✉☎

¢–$$ ⌂**Borgo Laurice.** The friendly and laid-back owners will pamper you at this small agriturismo in the valley near Torgiano. The cottage contains two spacious flats, one with a rooftop terrace with views of Torgiano and Monte Subasio. You may wake up to find that local produce from the surrounding farms has miraculously appeared on your doorstep. The farmer across the way takes pride in showing you around his small winery and letting you taste his potent white wine. The pool is right on the edge of corn and sunflower fields. **Pros:** Spectacular views, bucolic countryside. **Cons:** No restaurant, no a/c. ⨂*Madonna del Piano 14/13, 06079* ☎☎*075/6099222* ⊕*www.borgolaurice.it* ↩*2 apartments* ⌂*In-room: no a/c. In-hotel: pool, bicycles*═*MC, V* ¶*EP*

DERUTA

7 km (4½ mi) south of Torgiano, 19 km (11 mi) southeast of Perugia.

GETTING HERE
From Perugia follow the directions for Rome and the E45 highway; Deruta has its own exits. There are also trains from the smaller St. Anna train station in Perugia. Take the train in the direction of Terni, and get off at Deruta.

VISITOR INFORMATION
Deruta tourism office (⨂*Piazza dei Consoli 4* ☎*075/9711559*).

EXPLORING
This 14th-century medieval hill town is most famous for its ceramics. A drive through the countryside to visit the ceramics workshops is a good way to spend a morning, but be sure to stop in the town itself.

The notable sights in Deruta include the **Museo Regionale della Ceramica** *(Regional Ceramics Museum)*, part of which extends into the adjacent 14th-century former convent of San Francesco. Half the museum tells the history of ceramics, with panels in Italian and English explaining artistic techniques and production processes. The museum also holds the country's largest collection of modern Italian ceramics—nearly 8,000 pieces are on display. The most notable are the Renaissance vessels using the lustro technique, which originated in Arab and Middle Eastern cultures some 500 years before coming into use in Italy in the late 1400s. Lustro, as the name sounds, gives the ceramics a rich finish, which is accomplished with the use of crushed precious materials, such as gold, and silver. ⨂*Largo San Francesco* ☎*075/9711000* ⊕*www. museoceramicaderuta.it* 🎫*€5, includes admission to Pinoteca Comunale* ⊙*Apr.–June, daily 10:30–1 and 3–6; July–Sept., daily 10–1 and 3:30–7; Oct.–Mar., Wed.–Mon. 10:30–1 and 2:30–5.*

The **Pinacoteca Comunale**, the town museum, is housed in the Palazzo Comunale and displays religious paintings from the surrounding area. The most important works are those painted by the Umbrian master Niccolò di Liberatore (circa 1430–1502), known as L'Alunno, and a fresco attributed to Perugino. ✉ *Piazza Consoli 13* ☎ *075/9711000* ☑ *€5, includes admission to Museo Regionale della Ceramica* ⊘ *Weekends 10:30–1 and 3–6.*

WHERE TO STAY

$ 🏠 **Antica Fattoria del Colle.** Two structures from the early 1800s make up this pleasant lodging, which includes furnishings of the same era. The English-speaking owners make your stay relaxing and peaceful. A minimum stay of two nights is required in high season. **Pros:** Great position for ceramics and wine, delightful gardens. **Cons:** Distance from Perugia, no a/c. ✉ *Colle delle Forche 6, 06053* ☎ *075/972201* ⊕ *www.anticafattoriadelcolle.it* ⇗ *5 rooms, 2 apartments* ⚭ *In-room: no a/c, no TV. In-hotel: restaurant, pool, bicycles* ⊟ *No credit cards* ⊘ *Closed Jan. 15–Mar. 15* ¶⊙| *MAP.*

$ 🏠 **Melody.** The comfortable modern hotel just outside the center of ★ Deruta has commodious rooms; the newer ones have nice wood floors and wood furniture. All have balconies, but those in the back are quieter and have pleasant views of the surrounding hills. There's a reasonably priced restaurant on the premises. **Pros:** Easy access and parking for tired drivers, close to the best ceramics shops. **Cons:** Close to the highway, basic service. ✉ *SS E45 (south side of Deruta), 06053* ☎ *075/9711022* ☎ *075/9711018* ⊕ *www.hotelmelody.it* ⇗ *47 rooms* ⚭ *In-room: refrigerator, ethernet. In-hotel: restaurant, bar* ⊟ *AE, DC, MC, V* ¶⊙| *BP.*

SHOPPING

Deruta is home to more than 70 ceramics shops. They offer a range of ceramics, including extra pieces from commissions for well-known British and North American tableware manufacturers. If you ask, most owners will take you to see where they actually throw, bake, and paint their wares. A drive along Via Tiberina Nord takes you past one shop after another.

Ubaldo Grazia (✉ *Via Tibertina 181* ☎ *075/9 9710201*), on the outskirts of town, has a large selection of seconds in a wide range of styles. **Ceramiche El Frate** (✉ *Piazza dei Consoli 29* ☎ *075/9710729*) sells unusual tiles and jugs. **Fabbrica Maioliche Tradizionali** (✉ *Via Tiberina Nord 37* ☎ *075/9711220*) is one of the largest shops in the area. **Fratelli Mari** (✉ *Via Circonvallazione Nord 1* ☎ *075/9710400*), one of the oldest ceramics manufacturers in Deruta, produces a variety of pieces ranging in style from the steadfastly classical to the ultramodern.

Maioliche Cynthia (✉ *Via Umberto I 1* ☎ *075/9711255*), in Deruta's central Piazza dei Consoli, specializes in reproductions of antique designs and offers a good selection. Four generations of the Veschini family have operated **Maioliche Fidia** (✉ *Piazza Consoli 25* ☎ *075/972121*), which produces elegant and highly crafted ceramics in traditional designs. The factory is in the valley below town.

Traditional patterns are the focus at **Maioliche Fima di Picchiotti Piero** (✉ *Via Tiberina Nord 111* ☎*075/9711285*).

CORCIANO

21 km (13 mi) northwest of Deruta, 13 km (8 mi) northwest of Perugia, 97 km (60 mi) east of Siena.

GETTING HERE
From Perugia, follow the directions for the Firenze highway, and take the Corciano exit. Then follow the SS75bis until you reach the town. The trip takes about 20 minutes.

EXPLORING
A nicely preserved medieval hilltop village, Corciano has a view of the valley that stretches as far as Lago Trasimeno. Supposedly founded by Coragino, the companion of Ulysses, it was one of many towns that helped guard Perugia during the Middle Ages. Today you can still see the thick fortified walls, which now protect a far more peaceful environment. Pleasant breezes sweep through its immaculately kept streets, from which you can see, on a clear day, Monte Amiata and Todi.

At the **Museo della Casa Contadina** *(Farmhouse Museum)*, you can see what a typical Corciano home was like before the industrial era. It's only open late afternoon on weekends. ✉ *Via Tarragone 16* ☎*No phone* 💰*€1* 🕐*Apr.–Oct., weekends 4–8).*

Over the main altar of the **Chiesa di Santa Maria Assunta** *(Church of the Assumption of Mary)* hangs the *Assunta* (Assumption) which, having been rather energetically restored, is attributed to Perugino. ✉*Piazza della Vittoria 1* ☎*No phone* 💰*Free* 🕐*Daily 9–12:30 and 3:30–6:30.*

LAGO TRASIMENO

Passignano sul Trasimeno: 16 km (10 mi) northwest of Corciano, 30 km (18 mi) northwest of Perugia. Castiglione del Lago: 22 km (13 mi) southwest of Passignano, 52 km (31 mi) west of Perugia.

GETTING HERE
If you're driving, follow the signs for the highway in the direction of Firenze. It will take you about 20 minutes to reach the Passignano exit. There are trains from the main Perugia train station; get off at Passignano.

VISITOR INFORMATION
Lago Trasimeno tourism office (✉*Piazza Mazzini 10, Castiglione del Lago* ☎*075/9652484).*

EXPLORING
Passignano sul Trasimeno is a picturesque town on the northern shore of Lago Trasimeno, complete with castle ruins and medieval walls. During World War II an airplane factory was located here, so the area was

generously bombed by the Allies. Miraculously, much of the old center survived. Along the lakefront are a number of good restaurants and some bars with outdoor seating that are the gathering places for the town's younger set. There are some grass and sand beaches around Passignano sul Trasimeno, but these are often crowded with large families in the summer (with regrettable consequences for the water quality).

In **Castiglione del Lago,** on the western shore, evidence of Etruscan origins, castle ruins, and medieval city walls lend a mysterious, elegant air. The **Palazzo della Corgna** (⊠ *Piazza A. Gramsci 1* 🕾 *No phone*) is worth a visit for its Renaissance frescoes. The palace is open daily April to October, but only on weekends the rest of the year. Admission is €3.

> ## WORD OF MOUTH
>
> "The northern shore of Lake Trasimeno is where over 2,200 years ago the Carthaginian general Hannibal destroyed a Roman army. Although it isn't described in any guidebooks, Dad suggests we detour to see the battle site. (Uh-oh.) Sure enough, a village on the lake shore, Tuoro sul Trasimeno, has a small museum dedicated to Hannibal and the battle above its tourist information office." –MRand

From both towns you can take an hourly ferry to **Isola Maggiore** (🕾🖶 *075/827157* 🌐 *www.apmperugia.it*). This small island is the permanent home of just 15 people, and they live in houses dating from the 15th century. The black-and-white postcards sold everywhere confirm that the island's single street has changed little over the years. A few old ladies sit outside the semi-deserted buildings, working at intricate lace patterns they learned from their great-grandmothers. The secluded pebble beaches are great for a dip in the cold, clear water. Don't swim out too far, as the lake is famous for its treacherous undercurrents.

WHERE TO STAY & EAT

$$–$$$$ ✕ **Cacciatori–Da Luciano.** The fresh fish here comes straight from the lake, and is exceptional. The entire menu is sumptuous, with a wide range of meat and seafood courses and fine wines. Ask for a table near the windows overlooking the lake. ⊠ *Via Pompili 11, Passignano sul Trasimeno* 🕾 *075/827210* 🖃 *AE, DC, MC, V* ⊗ *Closed Wed. and 3 wks in Jan.*

$ ✕🖭 **Kursaal.** Each of the simply decorated rooms at this resort hotel has a balcony, most with views of Lago Trasimeno. With extensive gardens and a large pool next to the private beach, the hotel is ideal for family vacations. The restaurant ($$–$$$), also overlooking the lake, has a veranda that's especially nice in summer. As you might guess, it features fish from the lake. The hotel is about 1 km (½ mi) east of Passignano sul Trasimeno. **Pros:** Views of the lake, low prices for the area. **Cons:** Simple service, outside the town center. ⊠ *Viale Europa 24, Passignano sul Trasimeno 06065* 🕾 *075/828085* 🖶 *075/827182* 🌐 *www.kursaalhotel.net* 🛏 *16 rooms, 2 suites* 🛋 *In-room: refrigerator. In-hotel: restaurant, bar, pools, beachfront* 🖃 *MC, V* ⊗ *Closed Jan. and Feb.* ⦿ *BP.*

$ ✕🖭 **Locanda del Galluzzo.** Sitting 2,145 feet above lake level, this small hotel has beautiful views of the lake and the surrounding countryside.

You can stroll though the olive groves that surround the pool. Rooms and apartments are simply furnished with dark-wood furniture. The restaurant ($–$$) turns out delicious meals, and in summer you can dine on a roofed terrace with great views of the sunset over the water. The hotel is 5 km (3 mi) east of Passignano sul Trasimeno. **Pros:** Wonderful lake views, attentive service. **Cons:** Not easy to find, breakfast is insubstantial. ⊠ *Via Castel Rigone 12-A, Passignano sul Trasimeno 06060* ☎ *075/845352* 🖷 *075/845312* ⊕ *www.locandadelgalluzzo. it* ⟳ *4 rooms, 6 apartments* ⌂ *In-room: no a/c, no phone, kitchen (some). In-hotel: restaurant, bar, pool* ▬ *AE, DC, MC, V* ¶ *BP.*

$ 🏨 **Casal de' Cucchi.** This impeccably maintained complex of holiday flats has great food and its own fine wines, and the management organizes a number of outdoor activities around the lake area. Pros: Wine tasting, views. Cons: Distance from major Umbrian towns. ⊠ *Vocabolo i Cucchi, Petrignano del Lago* 🖷 *075/9528116* ⊕ *www.agriturismofanini.it* ⟳ *10 apartments, 10 rooms* ⌂ *In-room: refrigerator. In-hotel: restaurant, pool, bicycles* ▬ *V* ¶ *BP.*

$–$$ 🏨 **Hotel Lido.** On the shore of Lake Trasimeno, this hotel has views of the islands and, on clear days, Castiglione del Lago. The rooms are simple but comfortable. The restaurant, which serves a robust selection of meat and fish, is built on a jetty that reaches out across the water. It's a pleasant place to take in the panorama. **Pros:** Views of the lake, central location in Passignano. **Cons:** Simple service, uninspiring lobby. ⊠ *Via Roma, 06065* 🖷 *075/827219* 🖷 *075/827251* ⊕ *www.umbria hotels.com* ⟳ *53 rooms* ⌂ *In-hotel: restaurant, pool* ▬ *AE, DC, MC, V* ⊘ *Closed Jan. and Feb.* ¶ *BP.*

CITTÀ DELLA PIEVE

26 km (16 mi) south of Castiglione del Lago, 43 km (26 mi) southwest of Perugia.

GETTING HERE

From Perugia follow the directions for the SS220, and then merge onto the SS71 which leads up to Città della Pieve. The trip will take you about 50 minutes.

EXPLORING

Perugino was born in this small Etruscan town of plain brick buildings and flat-top towers, so it makes sense that the churches here are chock-full of his frescoes, some in better condition than others. Worth a peek are the churches of Santa Maria dei Servi and San Pietro, outside the city walls.

Perugino's *Baptism of Christ* and *Madonna in Glory* in the 17th-century **Duomo**, a Roman structure that was transformed by Gothic and baroque renovations, are examples of the artist's later works. ⊠ *Piazza Plebiscito* 🖷 *No phone* 🎫 *Free* ⊘ *Daily 9–noon and 3–6.*

In **Santa Maria dei Bianchi** the *Adoration of the Magi*, painted in 1504, is particularly well restored. It depicts the Nativity scene in perfect Renaissance court style on a spring day, with the Perugian countryside in the background. At a time when Leonardo da Vinci (1452–1519) and Michelangelo (1475–1564) were exploring new scientific and religious territory, Perugino reaffirmed a classical, humanistic Renaissance style. ⊠*Via Vannucci* ☎*075/8299696* ✉*Free* ⊙*Daily 9–12:30 and 3:30–6:30.*

PANICALE

21 km (13 mi) northeast of Città della Pieve, 34 km (20 mi) southwest of Perugia.

GETTING HERE

From Perugia follow the directions for the SS220. After about 20 kms. take the SP306 which leads into Panicale. The trip will take you about 50 minutes.

EXPLORING

The small town of Panicale, with a population of just over 5,000, sits on a low hill about 8 km (5 mi) from Lago Trasimeno. On the drive from Città della Pieve to Panicale, a wide-open view of Lago Trasimeno reveals the islands on the lake and the mountains on its far shore. The town has preserved some of its original medieval walls and gateways, making it a pleasant place to explore. The region is known in the area for its handcrafted lace and needlework.

Outside the city walls, the church of **San Sebastiano** is where Perugino painted his famous fresco the *Martyrdom of St. Sebastian.* Although it was executed in 1505, only one year later than the *Adoration of the Magi* in Città della Pieve, it is much more abstract. The painting is almost dreamlike, with Saint Sebastian on a strange classical terrace and God appearing fatherlike above. The landscape in the background, however, is the same Perugian countryside found in many of the master's pieces. Visits start from the tourist office in Piazza Umberto. ⊠*Off Piazza Vittoria* ☎*0758/37602* ✉*Free* ⊙*Daily 10–noon and 3–6.*

ASSISI

The small town of Assisi is one of the Christian world's most important pilgrimage sites and home of the Basilica di San Francesco—built to honor Saint Francis (1182–1226) and erected in swift order after his death. The peace and serenity of the town is a welcome respite after the hustle and bustle of some of Italy's major cities.

Like most other towns in the region, Assisi began as an Umbri settlement in the 7th century BC and was conquered by the Romans 400 years later. The town was Christianized by Saint Rufino, its patron saint, in the third century, but it is the spirit of Saint Francis, a patron saint of Italy and founder of the Franciscan monastic order, that is felt throughout its narrow medieval streets. The famous 13th-century basilica was decorated by the greatest artists of the period.

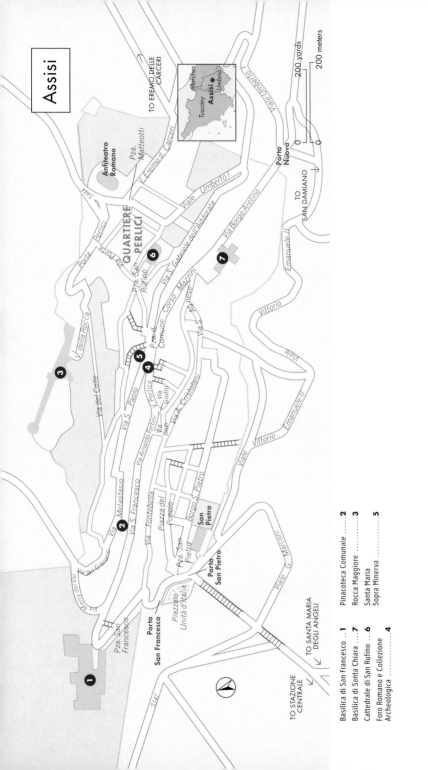

Assisi

TO EREMO DELLE
CARCERI

Anfiteatro
Romano

Pza.
Matteotti

V. Eremo d. Carceri

QUARTIERE
PERLICI

Porta Perlici

Via di Porta Perlici

Pza. San
Rufino

Via S. Gabriele dell'Addolorata

Viale Umberto I

Viale Umberto I

Porta
Nuova

TO
SAN DAMIANO

Via Borgo Aretino

Corso Mazzini

Via S. Agnese

Pza. d.
Comune

Via
Giotto

Via A. Cristofani

Via S. Paolo

Via del Colle

V. della Rocca

Via Metastasio

Via S. Francesco

Via Arnaldo Fortini

Via Poltica

Via
Base

Vittorio Emanuele II

Vittorio Emanuele II

Viale Vittorio

Viale G. Marconi

Pza. San
Pietro

Piazza del
Popolo

Borgo S. Pietro

Via Fontebella

Via San Giacomo

Via Metri del Val

Pza. San
Francesco

Porta
San Francesco

Piazzale
Unità d'Italia

Porta
San Pietro

San
Pietro

TO SANTA MARIA
DEGLI ANGELI

TO STAZIONE
CENTRALE

Marches
Tuscany
Assisi
Umbria

Viale Umberto I

0   200 yards
0   200 meters

Basilica di San Francesco ..**1**
Basilica di Santa Chiara **7**
Cattedrale di San Rufino ...**6**
Foro Romano e Collezione
Archeologica **4**

Pinacoteca Comunale **2**
Rocca Maggiore **3**
Santa Maria
Sopra Minerva **5**

GETTING HERE

Assisi lies on the Terontola–Foligno rail line, with almost hourly connections to Perugia and direct trains to Rome and Florence several times a day. The Stazione Centrale is 4 km (2½ mi) from town, with a bus service about every half hour. Assisi is easily reached from the A1 Motorway (Rome–Florence) and the S75b highway. The walled town is closed to traffic, so cars must be left in the parking lots at Porta San Pietro, near Porta Nuova, or beneath Piazza Matteotti. (Pay your parking fee at the *cassa* [ticket booth] before you return to your car to get a ticket to insert in the machine that will allow you to exit.) It's a short but sometimes steep walk into the center of town; frequent minibuses (buy tickets from a newsstand or tobacco shop near where you park your car) make the rounds for weary pilgrims.

VISITOR INFORMATION

Assisi tourism office (✉ *Piazza del Commune 22* ☎ *075/812534* ⊕ *www. assisi.umbria2000.it*).

EXPLORING ASSISI

Assisi is pristinely medieval in architecture and appearance, owing in large part to relative neglect from the 16th century until 1926, when the celebration of the 700th anniversary of Saint Francis's death brought more than 2 million visitors. Since then, pilgrims have flocked here in droves, and today several million arrive each year to pay homage. But not even the constant flood of visitors to this town of just 3,000 residents can spoil the singular beauty of this significant religious center, the home of some of the Western tradition's most important works of art. The hill on which Assisi sits rises dramatically from the flat plain, and the town is dominated by a medieval castle at the very top.

Even though Assisi can become besieged with sightseers disgorged by tour buses, who clamor to visit the famous basilica, it's difficult not to be charmed by the tranquillity of the town and its medieval architecture. Once you've seen the basilica, stroll through the town's narrow winding streets to see beautiful vistas of the nearby hills and valleys peeking through openings between the buildings.

MAIN ATTRACTIONS

❼ Basilica di Santa Chiara. The lovely, wide piazza in front of this church is reason enough to visit. The red-and-white-striped facade of the church frames the piazza's panoramic view over the Umbrian plains. Santa Chiara is dedicated to Saint Clare, one of the earliest and most fervent of Saint Francis's followers and the founder of the order of the Poor Ladies—or Poor Clares—which was based on the Franciscan monastic order. The church contains Clare's body, and in the **Cappella del Crocifisso** (on the right) is the cross that spoke to Saint Francis. A heavily veiled nun of the Poor Clares order is usually stationed before the cross in adoration of the image. ✉ *Piazza Santa Chiara* ☎ *075/812282* ☺ *Nov.–mid-Mar., daily 6:30–noon and 2–6; mid-Mar.–Oct., daily 6:30–noon and 2–7.*

6 **Cattedrale di San Rufino.** Saint Francis and Saint Clare were among those baptized in Assisi's Cattedrale, which was the principal church in town until the 12th century. The baptismal font has since been redecorated, but it is possible to see the crypt of Saint Rufino, the bishop who brought Christianity to Assisi and was martyred on August 11, 238 (or 236 by some accounts). Admission to the crypt includes the small **Museo Capitolare,** with its detached frescoes and artifacts. ✉ *Piazza San Rufino* ☎ *075/812283* ⊕ *www.sistemamuseo.it* 🎟 *Crypt and Museo Capitolare €2.50* ⊙ *Cattedrale: daily 7–noon and 2–6; crypt and Museo Capitolare: mid-Mar.–mid-Oct., daily 10–1 and 3–6; mid-Oct.–mid-Mar., daily 10–1 and 2:30–5:30.*

ALSO WORTH SEEING

4 **Foro Romano e Collezione Archeologica.** Assisi didn't begin and end with Saint Francis. Five meters (16 feet) below the medieval town is an archaeological collection of Umbrian artifacts, housed in the crypt of a former 11th-century church of Saint Nicholas (destroyed in 1929). The collection is all the more interesting for its incongruity in this medieval–Renaissance town. The *foro* (forum) may have been linked with a sacred site joined to the Tempio di Minerva. Before you walk through, be sure to request the English-language text guide—artifacts are numbered but not labeled. The admission ticket also gives admission to the Pinacoteca Communale. ✉ *Via Portica 2* ☎ *075/813053* ⊕ *www.sistemamuseo.it* 🎟 *€3.50* ⊙ *Nov.–Feb., 10:30–1 and 2:30–6; Mar.–May, Sept., and Oct., 10–1 and 2:30–6; June–Aug., 10–1 and 2:30–7.*

2 **Pinacoteca Comunale.** The city art gallery houses a collection of early paintings by mostly local Umbrian masters and provides a glimpse of some of Giotto's contemporaries as well as a fresco attributed to him. ✉ *Palazzo Vallemani, Via San Francesco, next to no. 12* ☎ *075/8155234* ⊕ *www.sistemamuseo.it* 🎟 *€3.50* ⊙ *Nov.–Feb., 10:30–1 and 2:30–6; Mar.–May, Sept., and Oct., 10–1 and 2:30–6; June–Aug., 10–1 and 2:30–7.*

3 **Rocca Maggiore.** Your walk to the peak of this 14th-century fortress is rewarded with great views. On the way, pass through the Quartiere Perlici, a little neighborhood with narrow streets that follow a symmetrical Roman layout; in one part the houses and street trace the elliptical plan of the 1st-century Anfiteatro Romano (Roman amphitheater) that stood on the site. ✉ *At the end of Via della Rocca* ☎ *075/815292* ⊕ *www.sistemamuseo.it* 🎟 *€2* ⊙ *Daily 10–6.*

5 **Santa Maria Sopra Minerva.** Dating from the time of the Emperor Augustus (27 BC–AD 14), this structure was originally dedicated to the Roman goddess of wisdom, in later times used as a monastery and prison before being converted into a church in the 16th century. The expectations raised by the perfect classical facade are not met by the interior, which was subjected to a thorough baroque transformation in the 17th century. ✉ *Piazza del Comune* ☎ *075/812268* ⊙ *Weekdays 7:15 AM–7:30 PM, weekends 8–7:30.*

Continued on page 379

ASSISI'S BASILICA DI SAN FRANCESCO

The legacy of St. Francis, founder of the Franciscan monastic order, pervades Assisi. Each year the town hosts several million pilgrims, but the steady flow of visitors does nothing to diminish the singular beauty of one of Italy's most important religious centers. The pilgrims' ultimate destination is the massive Basilica di San Francesco, which sits halfway up Assisi's hill, supported by graceful arches.

The basilica is not one church but two. The Romanesque **Lower Church** came first; construction began in 1228, just two years after St. Francis's death, and was completed within a few years. The low ceilings and candlelit interior make an appropriately solemn setting for St. Francis's tomb, found in the crypt below the main altar. The Gothic **Upper Church,** built only half a century later, sits on top of the lower one, and is strikingly different, with soaring arches and tall stained-glass windows (the first in Italy). Inside, both churches are covered floor to ceiling with some of Europe's finest frescoes: the Lower Church is dim and full of candlelit shadows, and the Upper Church is bright and airy.

VISITING THE BASILICA

THE LOWER CHURCH

The most evocative way to experience the basilica is to begin with the dark Lower Church. As you enter, give your eyes a moment to adjust. Keep in mind that the artists at work here were conscious of the shadowy environment—they knew this was how their frescoes would be seen.

In the first chapel to the left, a superb fresco cycle by Simone Martini depicts scenes from the life of St. Martin. As you approach the main altar, the vaulting above you is decorated with the *Three Virtues of St. Francis* (poverty, chastity, and obedience) and *St. Francis's Triumph*, frescoes attributed to Giotto's followers. In the transept to your left, Pietro Lorenzetti's *Madonna and Child with St. Francis and St. John* sparkles when the sun hits it. Notice Mary's thumb; legend has it Jesus is asking which saint to bless, and Mary is pointing to Francis. Across the way in the right transept, Cimabue's *Madonna Enthroned Among Angels and St. Francis* is a famous portrait of the saint. Surrounding the portrait are painted scenes from the childhood of Christ, done by the assistants of Giotto. Nearby is a painting of the crucifixion attributed to Giotto himself.

You reach the crypt via stairs midway along the nave—on the crypt's altar, a stone coffin holds the saint's body. Steps up from the transepts lead to the cloister, where there's a gift shop, and the treasury, which contains holy objects.

THE UPPER CHURCH

The St. Francis fresco cycle is the highlight of the Upper Church. (See facing page.) Also worth special note is the 16th-century choir, with its remarkably delicate inlaid wood. When a 1997 earthquake rocked the basilica, the St. Francis cycle sustained little damage, but portions of the ceiling above the entrance and altar collapsed, reducing their frescoes (attributed to Cimabue and Giotto) to rubble. The painstaking restoration is ongoing. ⚠**The dress code is strictly enforced—no bare shoulders or bare knees.** Piazza di San Francesco, 075/819001, Lower Church Easter–Oct., Mon.–Sat. 6 ⊦ –6:45 ⊙ , Sun. 6:30 ⊦ –7:15 ⊙ ; Nov.–Easter, daily 6:30–6. Upper Church Easter–Oct., Mon.–Sat. 8:30–6:45[1] Sun. 8:30–7:15; Nov.–Easter, daily 8:30–6.

FRANCIS, ITALY'S PATRON SAINT

PREGANDO ASPETTERO' CHE TORNI

St. Francis was born in Assisi in 1181, the son of a noblewoman and a well-to-do merchant. His troubled youth included a year in prison. He planned a military career, but after a long illness Francis heard the voice of God, renounced his father's wealth, and began a life of austerity. His mystical embrace of poverty, asceticism, and the beauty of man and nature struck a responsive chord in the medieval mind; he quickly attracted a vast number of followers. Francis was the first saint to receive the stigmata (wounds in his hands, feet, and side corresponding to those of Christ on the cross). He died on October 4, 1226, in the Porziuncola, the secluded chapel in the woods where he had first preached the virtue of poverty to his disciples. St. Francis was declared patron saint of Italy in 1939, and today the Franciscans make up the largest of the Catholic orders.

THE UPPER CHURCH'S ST. FRANCIS FRESCO CYCLE

The 28 frescoes in the Upper Church depicting the life of St. Francis are the most admired works in the entire basilica. They're also the subject of one of art history's biggest controversies. For centuries they thought to be by Giotto (1267-1337), the great early Renaissance innovator, but inconsistencies in style, both within this series and in comparison to later Giotto works, have thrown their origin into question. Some scholars now say Giotto was the brains behind the cycle, but that assistants helped with the execution; others claim he couldn't have been involved at all.

Two things are certain. First, the style is revolutionary—which argues for Giotto's in-

volvement. The tangible weight of the figures, the emotion they show, and the use of perspective all look familiar to modern eyes, but in the art of the time there was nothing like it. Second, these images have played a major part in shaping how the world sees St. Francis. In that respect, who painted them hardly matters.

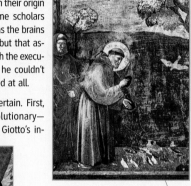

Starting in the transept, the frescoes circle the church, showing events in the saint's life (and afterlife). Some of the best are grouped near the church's entrance—look for the nativity at Greccio, the miracle of the spring, the death of the knight at Celano, and, most famously, the sermon to the birds.

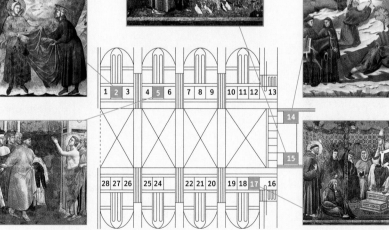

The St. Francis fresco cycle

1. Homage of a simple man
2. Giving cloak to a poor man
3. Dream of the palace
4. Hearing the voice of God
5. Rejection of worldly goods
6. Dream of Innocent III
7. Confirmation of the rules
8. Vision of flaming chariot
9. Vision of celestial thrones
10. Chasing devils from Arezzo
11. Before the sultan
12. Ecstasy of St. Francis
13. Nativity at Greccio
14. Miracle of the spring
15. Sermon to the birds
16. Death of knight at Celano
17. Preaching to Honorius III
18. Apparition at Arles
19. Receiving the stigmata
20. Death of St. Francis
21. Apparition before Bishop Guido and Fra Agostino
22. Verification of the stigmata
23. Mourning of St. Clare
24. Canonization
25. Apparition before Gregory IX
26. Healing of a devotee
27. Confession of a woman
28. Repentant heretic freed

FODOR'S FIRST PERSON

Sister Marcellina,
Order of St. Bridget

Sister Marcellina of the Order of St. Bridget talks about her life in Assisi, where she and 11 other sisters live in a convent and guesthouse on the outskirts of the town:

"Before coming to Assisi, I lived in various countries. I've lived in India, and in England, and been to Holland, to Sweden, and to Finland, as well as lived in Rome. But Assisi is the place that I would never want to change for any other. I don't know, I think there is something very special about this place. I've been here 13 years now, and each year I pray that I won't be sent somewhere else. I'm very happy here.

"I like the atmosphere of Assisi, it's very friendly, and of course with St. Francis and St. Claire, but especially St. Francis, there is a simplicity to life that I like very much. Even though I'm in the Order of St. Bridget, living here I feel very much a part of Franciscan spirituality. There is also a very strong ecumenical feeling to Assisi and this is very nice. There are over 60 different religious communities, with people from all over the world. And even though they come from different religious backgrounds they still feel a part of Assisi. Living here, you don't see the people of Assisi, you see people who have come from all over the world.

"There is something you feel when you come to Assisi, something you feel in your heart that makes you want to come back. And people do return! They feel the peacefulness and tranquility. Not that there aren't other aspects, like the commercialism—but these things happen. People return for the simplicity of this place. People feel attracted to Assisi. There's always something that people feel when they come here—even the hard-hearted ones!"

Asked if she thinks Assisi is changing, Sister Marcellina answers, with laughter in her voice, "When they wanted to make all the changes in the year 2000, the Jubilee Year, our Lord said, 'I must stop everything.' They had lots of projects to build new accommodations to house the people coming for the Jubilee Year, but the Lord said, 'No!'"

**OFF THE
BEATEN
PATH**

Eremo delle Carceri. About 4 km (2½ mi) east of Assisi is a monastery set in a dense wood against Monte Subasio. The "Hermitage of Prisons" was the place where Saint Francis and his followers went to "imprison" themselves in prayer. The only site in Assisi that remains essentially unchanged since Saint Francis's times, the church and monastery are the kinds of tranquil places that Saint Francis would

have appreciated. The walk out from town is very pleasant, and many trails lead from here across the wooded hillside of Monte Subasio (now a protected forest), with beautiful vistas across the Umbrian countryside. True to their Franciscan heritage, the friars here are entirely dependent on alms from visitors. ✉ *Via Santuario delle Carceri* ✚ *4 km (2½ mi) east of Assisi* ☎ *075/812301* ⊕ *www.eremocarceri.it* ✉ *Donations accepted* ⊗ *Nov.–Mar., daily 6:30–6; Apr.–Oct., daily 6:30 AM–7:15 PM.*

San Damiano. Dating to at least 1030, this was the church that Francis decided to restore in 1205. Nestled in an olive grove, it seems much more in keeping with the spirit of Saint Francis and his followers than the great basilica across town. This is where the crucifix (now in Santa Chiara) spoke to him: "*Vade, Francisce, et repara domum meam*" ("Go, Francis, and repair my house"). Francis took the command literally: he not only restored the building, but later set out to reform the Church. Saint Francis composed his *Canticle of the Creatures* here. Saint Clare, after taking the Franciscan vows, lived out her life in the convent of this church, attracting a wide following and fame for her piety. In a Papal bull in 1253, Pope Innocent IV (died 1254) confirmed her order, the Poor Clares; she died the next day. Shortly before her death, she reported having "seen" Masses held in the Basilica di San Francesco. For this reason she was designated the patron saint of television in the 1950s. ✉ *Località San Damiano* ✚ *1½ km (1 mi) south, outside the walls of Assisi* ☎ *075/812273* ✉ *Free* ⊗ *Daily 10–noon and 2–6.*

Santa Maria degli Angeli. Down by the train station, 8 km (5 mi) south of Assisi, this hulking baroque church restored in the 19th century was built over the **Porziuncola,** the church said to have been taken over by Saint Benedict in 576 and one of the first churches restored by Saint Francis. His little chapel in the forest is much venerated: it was in the adjacent **Cappella Transito,** then a humble cell, that Saint Francis died on the bare earth, wearing a borrowed tunic. Look for the fresco of the Crucifixion painted in 1486 by Pietro Vanucci, Raphael's master, better known as Perugino. ✉ *Località Santa Maria degli Angeli* ☎ *075/80511* ⊗ *Daily 6:15–12:50 and 2:30–7:30.*

7

WHERE TO EAT

Assisi is not a late-night town, so don't plan on any midnight snacks. What you can count on is the ubiquitous *stringozzi* pasta, as well as the local specialty *piccione all'assisana* (roasted pigeon with olives and liver). The locals eat *torta al testo* (a dense flat bread, often stuffed with vegetables or cheese) with their meals.

$$$-$$$$ ✕ **San Francesco.** An excellent view of the Basilica di San Francesco is the primary reason to come here. Locals consider this the best restaurant in town, where creative Umbrian dishes are made with aromatic locally grown herbs. The seasonal menu might include gnocchi topped with a sauce of wild herbs and *oca stufata di finocchio selvaggio* (goose stuffed with wild fennel). Appetizers and desserts are especially good. ⊠ *Via di San Francesco 52* ☎ *075/812329* ▤ *AE, DC, MC, V* ☺ *Closed Wed. and July 15–30.*

$$-$$$ ✕ **Osteria Piazzetta dell'Erba.** Hip service and sophisticated presentations
★ attract locals to this trattoria. The owners carefully select wine at local vineyards, buy it in bulk, and then bottle it themselves, resulting in high quality and reasonable prices. Choose from the wide selection of appetizers, including smoked goose breast, and from four or five types of pasta, plus various salads and a good selection of torta al testo fillings. For dessert, try the homemade biscuits, which you dunk in sweet wine. Outdoor seating is available. ⊠ *Via San Gabriele dell'Addolorata 15b* ☎ *075/815352* ▤ *AE, V* ☺ *Closed Mon. and a few wks in Jan. or Feb.*

$-$$$ ✕ **Buca di San Francesco.** In summer, dine in a cool green garden; in winter, under the low brick arches of the restaurant's cozy cellars. The unique settings and the first-rate fare make this central restaurant Assisi's busiest. Try homemade spaghetti *alla buca,* served with a roasted mushroom sauce. ⊠ *Via Brizi 1* ☎ *075/812204* ▤ *AE, DC, MC, V* ☺ *Closed Mon. and July 20–30.*

$-$$$ ✕ **La Fortezza.** Partially enclosed by Roman walls, this family-run restaurant has excellent service and reliably good food. A particular standout is *anatra al finocchio selvatico* (duck with wild fennel). ⊠ *Vicolo della Fortezza 2b* ☎ *075/812993* ⌂ *Reservations essential* ▤ *AE, DC, MC, V* ☺ *Closed Thurs. and Feb.*

$-$$$ ✕ **La Pallotta.** At this homey, family-run trattoria with a crackling fire-
Fodor'sChoice place and stone walls, the women do the cooking and the men serve the
★ food. Try the stringozzi *alla pallotta* (with a pesto of olives and mushrooms). Connected to the restaurant is an inn whose eight rooms have firm beds and some views across the rooftops of town. Hotel guests get a discount if they dine here. ⊠ *Vicolo della Volta Pinta 06081* ☎ *075/812649 or 075/812307* ▤ *AE, DC, MC, V* ☺ *Closed Tues. and 2 wks in Jan. or Feb.*

WHERE TO STAY

Advance reservations are essential at Assisi's hotels between Easter and October and over Christmas. Latecomers are often forced to stay in the modern town of Santa Maria degli Angeli, 8 km (5 mi) away. As a last-minute option, you can also inquire at restaurants to see if they are renting out rooms.

Until the early 1980s, pilgrim hostels outnumbered ordinary hotels in Assisi, and they present an intriguing and economical alternative to conventional lodgings. They are usually called *conventi* or *ostelli* ("convents" or "hostels") because they're run by convents, churches, or Catholic organizations. Rooms are spartan but peaceful. Check with the tourist office for a list.

$$$ ⊡**Hotel Subasio.** The converted monastery close to the Basilica di San Francesco is well past its prime, when guests included celebrities like Marlene Dietrich and Charlie Chaplin. If you can get past the kitschy hangings on the walls, you'll notice such vestiges of glamour as Venetian chandeliers. The hotel does have splendid views, comfortable sitting rooms, and flower-decked terraces, and it's a stone's throw from all those Giotto frescoes. Some rooms are grand in size and overlook the valley, whereas others are small and rough around the edges. The restaurant has a nice view, but the food could be better. **Pros:** Perfect location, views of the Assisi plain. **Cons:** Lobby a bit drab, some small rooms, service can be spotty. ⊠ *Via Frate Elia 2, 06082* ☎ *075/812206* 🖷 *075/816691* 🛏 *54 rooms, 8 suites* ⚑ *In-room: no a/c. In-hotel: restaurant, bar, parking (fee)* ⊟ *AE, DC, MC, V* ⦿ *BP.*

$–$$$ ⊡**San Francesco.** You can't beat the location—the roof terrace and some of the rooms look out onto the Basilica di San Francesco, which is opposite the hotel. Rooms and facilities range from simple to dreary, but you may be reminded that looks aren't everything by the nice touches like slippers, a good-night piece of chocolate, and soundproofing. Fruit, homemade tarts, and fresh ricotta make for a first-rate breakfast. **Pros:** Excellent location, great views. **Cons:** Simple rooms, sometimes noisy in peak season. ⊠ *Via San Francesco 48, 06082* ☎ *075/812281* 🖷 *075/816237* ⊕ *www.hotelsanfrancescoassisi.it* 🛏 *44 rooms* ⚑ *In-room: refrigerator, ethernet. In-hotel: restaurant, bar, public Internet, some pets allowed* ⊟ *AE, DC, MC, V* ⦿ *BP.*

$$ ⊡**Castello di Petrata.** Built as a fortress in the 14th century, the Castello di Petrata rightfully dominates the area, with Monte Subasio, Assisi, and the distant hills and valleys of Perugia all in view. Every room is different from the last: wood beams and sections of exposed medieval stonework add character, and comfortable couches turn each room into a delightful retreat. **Pros:** Great views of Assisi hills, gardens, and walks. **Cons:** Slightly isolated, far from Assisi town center. ⊠ *Via Petrata 25, Località Petrata, 06081* ☎ *075/815451* 🖷 *075/8043026* ⊕ *www.castellopetrata.com* 🛏 *22 rooms, 1 suite* ⚑ *In-room: no a/c, ethernet. In-hotel: restaurant, bar, pool, some pets allowed* ⊟ *AE, DC, MC, V* ⊗ *Closed Jan.–Mar.* ⦿ *BP.*

FodorśChoice
★

$$ ⊡**Hotel Il Palazzo.** An inn during the 12th and 13th centuries, this building was returned to its original purpose in 1996. Very near the Basilica di San Francesco, the location makes it a good base for sightseeing. The hotel has a dozen rooms—each different, some with wood beams and three with views of the valley. **Pros:** Good location without being too close to the crowds. **Cons:** No parking, no Internet. ⊠ *Via San Francesco 8, 06081* ☎ *075/816841* 🖷 *075/812370* ⊕ *www.hotelilpalazzo. it* 🛏 *12 rooms* ⚑ *In-room: refrigerator. In-hotel: restaurant* ⊟ *AE, MC, V* ⊗ *Closed Jan. and Feb.* ⦿ *BP.*

7

EATING WELL IN NORTHERN UMBRIA

Crossed by the Apennine range, the slopes of northern Umbria curve into graceful, hilly landscapes. The "green heart of Italy" produces a hearty cuisine. Pasta, rice, and soups (and in this region especially, lentils) are often laden with rich *tartufi neri o bianchi* (black or white truffles). The local pasta specialty, a thick spaghetti, goes by two names, *strin- gozzi* (also spelled *strangozzi*) and *ombrichelli*, and most often is served *al tartufo*, with a truffle sauce.

A meal of fresh fish pulled from Lake Trasimeno is enough to warrant a detour. Otherwise there are no real Umbrian seafood dishes. Once you leave Umbria and head to the coastal Marches region, however, seafood becomes more plentiful. One characteristic dish from Ancona, *brodetto*, is a savory fish soup full of the latest catch from the Adriatic. Ascoli Piceno, farther inland, takes credit for a particular gastronomic specialty worth noting: olive *ascol- ane*, stuffed green olives rolled in breading, deep fried, and served as an appetizer.

$ ⛲ **Fontebella.** Between Piazza del Popolo and the Basilica di San Fran- cesco, the Fontebella has spacious lounges and comfortable rooms (with rather small bathrooms), decorated with cheerful tapestries. The breakfast is especially ample, and the welcome is warm. **Pros:** Friendly service, full in-room Internet. **Cons:** Difficult parking, uninteresting lobby. ⊠ *Via Fontebella 25, 06081* ☎*075/812883* 🖷*075/812941* ⊕*www.fontebella.com* ⇥*44 rooms* ♿*In-room: ethernet. In-hotel: restaurant, bar, parking (fee)* ⊟*AE, DC, MC, V* ❍❘*BP.*

$ ⛲ **Hotel Umbra.** A 16th-century town house is the setting for this charm- ing hotel near Piazza del Comune. Ask for an upper room with a view over the Assisi rooftops to the valley below. The restaurant, closed for lunch on Tuesday and Wednesday, has a charming vine-covered ter- race leading to a secluded garden. **Pros:** Friendly welcome, pleasant small garden. **Cons:** Difficult parking, some small rooms. ⊠ *Via degli Archi 6, 06081* ☎*075/812240* 🖷*075/813653* ⊕*www.hotelumbra.it* ⇥*6 suites, 19 rooms* ♿*In-hotel: restaurant, bar* ⊟*AE, DC, MC, V* ☾*Closed mid-Jan.–mid-Mar.* ❍❘*BP.*

THE ARTS

Concerts are occasionally held in Assisi's various churches; check with the **tourist office** (⊠*Piazza del Comune 12* ☎*075/812534* ⊕*www. assisi.umbria2000.it*) or look for signs around town.

SHOPPING

If you're in the market for a Saint Francis cigarette lighter, you've come to the right place. You can sort through mountains of kitsch embla- zoned with the saint's image, from key chains to rope sandals to tiny blessed olive trees.

Look for some nice card shops with quality stationery and paper products. If you will not be passing through Deruta, near Perugia, Assisi has a number of shops that sell ceramics from the town; the selection is not as good but the prices are comparable. You can also pick up Umbrian truffles and all their aromatic and costly derivatives in Assisi's *alimentari* (local grocery shops) and gift shops.

Assisi is well known for white-and-blue *ricamo a punto,* a traditional style of embroidery kept alive by religious institutions over the centuries. A good shop for *ricamo* items is **Rossi** (⊠ *Via Frate Elia 1* ☎075/812555).

Assisi doesn't have any bakeries—the bread comes from surrounding towns—but there are several pastry shops, featuring, of course, *pane di San Francesco* (an egg bread sweetened with raisins and sugar). Thanks to the Lombard influence, strudels pop up, such as *rocciata di Assisi* (filled with apples, nuts, raisins, and dried fruit). A tantalizing display of these tasty treats can be found in the town center at **Bottega del Pasticcere** (⊠ *Via Portica 9* ☎075/812392).

NORTH TOWARD URBINO

The trip north from Perugia to Città di Castello and Gubbio, and across to Urbino, passes through rugged, mountainous terrain. Città di Castello can be combined with San Sepolcro in an itinerary, possibly also including Arezzo.

CITTÀ DI CASTELLO

54 km (32 mi) north of Perugia, 42 km (26 mi) east of Arezzo.

GETTING HERE

From Perugia take the E45 highway in the direction of Cesena, and exit at either Umbertide or Città di Castello. The last stretch of the highway needs resurfacing, so drive carefully. There are several signposted public car parks outside the city walls. Trains also run from Perugia on the Central Umbrian line.

VISITOR INFORMATION

Città di Castello tourism office (⊠ *Piazza Fanti* ☎075/8554922).

EXPLORING

This noble-looking town is still surrounded in part by 16th-century walls. At its center is the Piazza Matteotti, dominated by the 14th-century **Palazzo del Podestà,** which today houses the town's administrative offices and courts.

The **Duomo** dates from the 6th century, but was renovated between 1466 and 1529; in the 17th century it received an unfinished baroque face-lift. ⊠*Piazza del Duomo* ☎0758/521647 ⊠*Free* ☉*Daily 10– noon and 4–5:30.*

The **Palazzo Albizzini** displays some 130 works by Alberto Burri (1915–95), perhaps the town's most famous native son. Trained as a doctor, Burri began painting while held in a World War II detention camp in the United States. The collection reflects his work as one of Italy's most important proponents of art *informel* ("unformed" art, sometimes referred to as lyrical abstraction) in the 1950s and 1960s. ⊠ *Via Albizzini 1* ☎ *0758/554649* 🎟*€5* ⏱ *Tues.–Sat. 9–12:30 and 2:30–6, Sun. 9–1 and 3–8.*

Inside the 16th-century **Palazzo Vitelli alla Cannoniera,** built by Antonio da Sangallo the Younger (1483–1546) and with a facade by Giorgio Vasari (1511–74), is the **Pinacoteca Comunale,** second only to Perugia's art gallery for Umbrian painting. It houses paintings by Raphael—including *The Creation of Eve*—Luca Signorelli (1441–1523), and Ghirlandaio (1449–94). ⊠ *Via della Cannoniera 22/a* ☎ *0758/5206565* 🎟*€5* ⏱ *Tues.–Sun. 10–1 and 3–6.*

WHERE TO STAY & EAT

$$$ ✕**Il Postale di Marco e Barbara.** The friendly owners turned an old bus
★ depot into this stellar restaurant, creating a pleasant environment while retaining such elements as old wood beams and an antique gas pump. Every two weeks the kitchen presents a new selection of dishes using the freshest local vegetables, fish, and meat. Artistic and tasty antipasti might include roasted pigeon and lemon cream, or little tarts of mussels and vegetables. Look for entrées such as roasted quail with cherry tomatoes and beans. Throughout the year you can order a delicious *degustazione* (tasting) menu; the chef chooses your four courses. ⊠ *Via De Cesare 8* ☎ *075/8521356* 🍴 *Reservations essential* ▤*AE, DC, MC, V* ⏱ *Closed Mon. and 2 wks in Jan. No dinner Sun.*

$ 🏨**Hotel Le Mura.** Built in the early 1990s, this hotel just inside the old city walls has guest rooms that are bright and comfortable, with functional furnishings. A good buffet breakfast awaits you in the morning. One of the best parts of staying here is the friendly and efficient staff. **Pros:** Good location, good restaurant. **Cons:** Uninteresting furnishings, no Internet in rooms. ⊠ *Via Borgo Farinario 24/26, 06012* ☎ *075/8521070* 🖷*075/8521350* ⊕*www.hotellemura.it* 🛏*35 rooms* 🛎 *In-hotel: restaurant, bar, parking (fee)* ▤*AE, DC, MC, V* ⑩*BP.*

NIGHTLIFE & THE ARTS

Music lovers should schedule the **Festival delle Nazioni di Musica da Camera** (*International Chamber Music Festival* ⊠*S3bis j 80 km [50 mi] north of Perugia* ☎ *075/8522823* ⊕*www.festivalnazioni.com*), a two-week event held in late August and early September.

GUBBIO

35 km (22 mi) southeast of Città di Castello, 39 km (24 mi) northeast of Perugia, 92 km (57 mi) east of Arezzo.

GETTING HERE

The closest train station is Fossato di Vico, about 12 mi from Gubbio. Ten daily buses connect the train station with the city, a 30-minute trip.

If you are driving from Perugia take the SS298, which rises steeply up toward the Gubbio hills. The trip will take you one hour. There are also 10 buses a day that leave from Perugia's Piazza Partigiani, the main Perugia bus terminal.

VISITOR INFORMATION

Gubbio tourism office (⊠ *Piazza Oderisi 6* ☎ *075/9220693*).

EXPLORING

There is something otherworldly about this jewel of a medieval town tucked away in a mountainous corner of Umbria. Even at the height of summer, the cool serenity and quiet of Gubbio's streets remain intact. The town is perched on the slopes of Monte Ingino, meaning the streets are dramatically steep. Gubbio's relatively isolated position has kept it free of hordes of high-season visitors, and most of the year the city lives up to its Italian nickname, *La Città del Silenzio* (City of Silence). Parking in the central Piazza dei Quaranta Martiri—named for 40 hostages murdered by the Nazis in 1944—is easy and secure, and it is wise to leave your car in the piazza and explore the narrow streets on foot.

At Christmas, kitsch is king. From December 7 to January 10, colored lights are strung down the mountainside in a shape resembling an evergreen. Why? The town is proud to be the home of the world's largest Christmas tree.

The **Duomo,** on a narrow street on the highest tier of the town, dates from the 13th century, with some baroque additions—in particular, a lavishly decorated bishop's chapel. ⊠ *Via Ducale* ⊙ *Daily 8–12:45 and 3–7:30.*

★ The striking Piazza Grande is dominated by the medieval **Palazzo dei Consoli,** attributed to a local architect known as Gattapone, who is still much admired by today's residents. Studies have suggested that the palazzo was in fact the work of another architect, Angelo da Orvieto. In the Middle Ages the Parliament of Gubbio assembled in this palace, which has become a symbol of the town.

The Palazzo dei Consoli houses a museum, famous chiefly for the Tavole Eugubine, seven bronze tablets written in the ancient Umbrian language, employing Etruscan and Latin characters and providing the best key to understanding this obscure tongue. Also in the museum is a fascinating miscellany of rare coins and earthenware pots. The museum has exhilarating views over Gubbio's roofscape and beyond from the lofty loggia. For a few days at the beginning of May, the palace also displays the famous *ceri,* the ceremonial wooden pillars at the center of Gubbio's annual festivities. ⊠ *Piazza Grande* ☎ *075/9274298* ⊕ *www.comune.gubbio.pg.it* ⊠ *€5* ⊙ *Apr.–Oct., daily 10–1 and 3–6; Nov.–Mar., daily 10–1 and 2–5.*

The **Palazzo Ducale** is a scaled-down copy of the Palazzo Ducale in Urbino. (Gubbio was once the possession of that city's ruling family, the Montefeltro.) Gubbio's palazzo contains a small museum and a courtyard. Some of the public rooms offer magnificent views. ⊠ *Via Ducale* ☎075/9275872 ⌦*€2* ☉*Tues.–Sun. 8:30–7.*

Just outside the city walls at the eastern end of town is a **funicular** that provides a bracing ride to the top of Monte Ingino. (It's definitely not for those who suffer from vertigo.) ⊠*Follow Corso Garibaldi or Via XX Settembre to the end* ⌦*€4, €5 round-trip* ☉*Sept.–June 10–1:15 and 2:30–6, July and Aug., daily 8:30–7:30*

At the top of Monte Ingino is the **Basilica di Sant'Ubaldo,** repository of Gubbio's famous *ceri*—three 16-foot-tall pillars crowned with statues of Saints Ubaldo, George, and Anthony. The pillars are transported to the Palazzo dei Consoli on the first Sunday of May, in preparation for the Festa dei Ceri. ⊠*Monte Ingino* ☎075/9273872 ⌦*Free* ☉*Daily 8:30–noon and 4–7.*

WHERE TO STAY & EAT

$$$–$$$$

Fodor'sChoice

★

✕**Taverna del Lupo.** One of the city's most famous taverns, this popular place gets hectic on weekends and during the high season. Lasagne made in the Gubbian fashion, with ham and truffles, is an unusual indulgence, and the *suprema di faraono* (guinea fowl in a delicately spiced sauce) is a specialty. The restaurant has two fine wine cellars and an extensive wine list. Save room for the excellent desserts. ⊠ *Via Ansidei 21 06024* ☎075/9274368 ▤*AE, DC, MC, V* ☉*Closed Mon.*

$$–$$$$ ✕**Fornace di Mastro Giorgio.** The building dates to the 1300s, and its original stone-and-wood structure has been kept intact. (In the 1400s the space housed an important ceramics factory.) The menu, with seasonal changes, includes traditional but creative fare: *tagliatelle al tartuffo* (tagliatelle in a truffle sauce), *gnochetti al finocchio selvatico* (potato dumplings with wild fennel), *raviolini di faro con asparagi* (small ravioli with spelt and asparagus), and *filetto alle prugne* (filet mignon with prune sauce). ⊠*Via Mastro Giorgio 2* ☎075/9221836 ▤*AE, DC, MC, V* ☉*Closed Tues. No lunch Wed.*

$$$ ✕**Bosone Garden.** As the stone arches inside indicate, this space once served as the stables of the palace that now houses the Hotel Bosone. The menu includes a two-mushroom salad with truffles; risotto with porcini mushrooms, sausage, and truffles; and leg of pork. The garden, open in summer, seats 200. ⊠*Via Mastro Giorgio 1* ☎075/9220246 ▤*AE, MC, V* ☉*Closed Wed. Oct.–May and 2 wks in Jan.*

$–$$ ✕**Grotta dell'Angelo.** The rustic trattoria sits in the lower part of the old town near the main square. The menu features simple local specialties, including *capocollo* (a type of salami), *stringozzi* (very thick spaghetti), and lasagne *tartufata* (with truffles). The few outdoor tables are in high demand in the summer. The restaurant also offers a few small, basically furnished guest rooms, which should be booked in advance. ⊠*Via Gioia 47* ☎075/9273438 ⌂*Reservations essential* ▤*AE, DC, MC, V* ☉*Closed Tues. and Jan. 10–31.*

$–$$ ⊞**Hotel Bosone Palace.** A former palace is now home to this elegant hotel. Elaborate frescoes grace the ceilings of the two enormous suites,

St. Ubaldo Wins Again

Since 1160, the citizens of Gubbio have gathered in mid-May on the eve of the day celebrating the town's patron saint, Saint Ubaldo, for the **Festa dei Ceri** (⊕ *www.festadeiceri. it*). An expectant crowd gathers in the main square for the first important moment: the raising of the *ceri* (candles). Three teams of men in colorful costumes haul up three enormous wooden pillars, each one a tribute to the saint that protects their part of the town. Each of the pillars weighs nearly 900 pounds and is carried vertically with the aid of special frames.

After they parade up and down the streets, the main event begins: a race during which the teams carry the candles at breakneck speed to the top of Monte Ingino and the Basilica of St. Ubaldo. Running with the pillars is an honor, and locals vie for the chance to be one of the bearers, called *ceraioli*. Tradition often dictates which members of a family will participate. Teams accomplish the arduous task while surrounded by throngs of townspeople and visitors who come to absorb some of the fascinating, mystical emotion that defines the "race." Don't place any bets, though—the pillar capped with Saint Ubaldo always wins.

A note of caution: make sure you stand well back as the runners pass, because they won't stop for anyone, unless they fall themselves, in which case the pillars come crashing down.

7

which are furnished with painted antiques, and the hotel's small and delightful breakfast room. Standard rooms are comfortably, though more soberly, decorated with heavy wooden furniture. Ask for a room facing away from the sometimes-noisy street. **Pros:** Friendly welcome, excellent location. **Cons:** Some noise in tourist season, simple lobby. ⊠ *Via XX Settembre 22, 06024* ☎*075/9220688* 🖷*075/9220552* ⊕*www.mencarelligroup.com* 🛏*28 rooms, 2 suites* ♿*In-room: no a/c. In-hotel: restaurant, bar* ▤*AE, DC, MC, V* ⊗*Closed 3 wks in Jan.* ¶◎¶*BP.*

$ ▦**Castello Cortevecchio.** The centerpiece of this lodging is a 19th-century castle, which sits amid a 40-acre wooded park. Guest rooms are simple but elegant, with beamed ceilings, tile floors, and furnishings in wood and marble. You can stay in the castle itself or in one of a number of houses on the grounds. **Pros:** Walks in the park, sports facilities. **Cons:** Distance from Gubbio, not easy to find. ⊠*Località Nogna, 06020* ☎*075/9241017* 🖷*075/9241079* ⊕*www.castellocortevecchio.it* 🛏*10 rooms, 18 apartments, 4 suites* ♿*In-room: no a/c. In-hotel: restaurant, bar, tennis courts, pool, bicycles* ▤*AE, DC, MC, V* ⊗*Closed mid-Jan.–Feb. 10* ¶◎¶*EP.*

$ ▦**Hotel Gattapone.** The views from this family-run hotel in the center of Gubbio are of a sea of rooftops. Rooms are a good size, modern, and comfortable; some have wood beams on the ceilings. **Pros:** Central location, close to La Taverna del Lupo restaurant. **Cons:** Tight security can make entering difficult. ⊠*Via Ansidei 6, 06024* ☎*075/9272489* 🖷*075/9272417* ⊕*www.mencarelligroup.com* 🛏*16 rooms, 2 suites* ♿*In-room: no a/c. In-hotel: bar, parking (fee)* ▤*AE, DC, MC, V* ⊗*Closed Jan. 8–Feb. 8* ¶◎¶*BP.*

☾ A costumed medieval pageant with its roots in Gubbio's warring past, the **Palio della Balestra** (*Crossbow Tournament* ☎075/9220693) takes place on the last Sunday in May in the Piazza Grande.

THE MARCHES

An excursion from Umbria into the Marches region allows you to see a part of Italy rarely visited by foreigners. Not as wealthy as Tuscany or Umbria, the Marches has a diverse landscape of mountains and beaches, and marvelous views. Like that of neighbors to the west, the patchwork of rolling hills of Le Marche (as it is known in Italian) is stitched with grapevines and olive trees, bearing luscious wine and olive oil.

Traveling here isn't as easy as in Umbria or Tuscany. Beyond the narrow coastal plain and away from major towns, the roads are steep and twisting. An efficient bus service connects the coastal town of Pesaro to Urbino. Train travel in the region is slow, however, and stops are limited—although you can reach Ascoli Piceno by rail.

San Marino, perched high on the upper slopes of Monte Titano, is best reached from Rimini, on the southern coast of Emilia-Romagna. A main highway connects the two; a regular bus service to San Marino is available from Rimini's train station, airport, and city center.

URBINO

75 km (47 mi) north of Gubbio, 116 km (72 mi) northeast of Perugia, 230 km (143 mi) east of Florence.

GETTING HERE
Take the SS3bis from Perugia, and follow the directions for Gubbio and Cesena. Exit at Umbertide and take the SS219, then the SS452, and at Calmazzo the SS73bis to Urbino.

VISITOR INFORMATION
Urbino tourism office (⌧*Piazza Duca Federico 35* ☎0722/2613 ⊕*www.comune.orvieto.tr.it*).

EXPLORING
Majestic Urbino, atop a steep hill with a skyline of towers and domes, is something of a surprise to come upon. Although quite remote, it was once a center of learning and culture almost without rival in western Europe. The town looks much as it did in the glory days of the 15th century, a cluster of warm brick and pale stone buildings, all topped with russet-color tile roofs. The focal point is the immense and beautiful Palazzo Ducale.

The city is home to the small but prestigious Università di Urbino—one of the oldest in the world—and the streets are usually filled with students. Urbino is very much a college town, with the usual array of

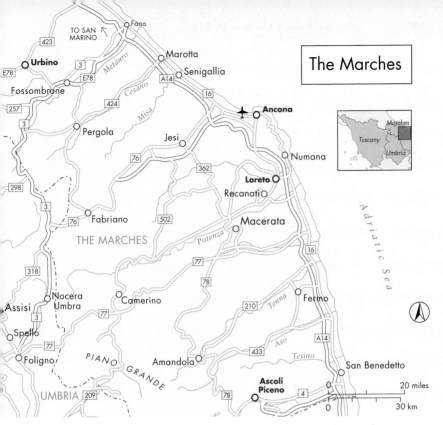

The Marches

bookshops, bars, and coffeehouses. In summer the Italian student population is replaced by foreigners who come to study Italian language and arts at several prestigious private fine-arts academies.

Urbino's fame rests on the reputation of three of its native sons: Duke Federico da Montefeltro (1422–82), the enlightened warrior-patron who built the Palazzo Ducale; Raffaello Sanzio (1483–1520), or Raphael, one of the most influential painters in history and an embodiment of the spirit of the Renaissance; and the architect Donato Bramante (1444–1514), who translated the philosophy of the Renaissance into buildings of grace and beauty. Unfortunately there is little work by either Bramante or Raphael in the city, but the duke's influence can still be felt strongly.

The **Casa Natale di Raffaello** (House of Raphael) is the house in which the painter was born and where he took his first steps in painting, under the direction of his artist father. There is some debate about the fresco of the Madonna here; some say it's by Raphael, whereas others attribute it to the father—with Raphael's mother and the young painter himself standing in as models for the Madonna and Child. ⊠ Via Raffaello 57 ☎ 0722/320105 ✍ €3 ⊘ Mon.–Sat. 9–1 and 3–7, Sun. 10–1.

Fodor'sChoice   The **Palazzo Ducale** *(Ducal Palace)*
★   holds a place of honor in the city. If
the Renaissance was, ideally, a celebration of the nobility of man and
his works, of the light and purity
of the soul, then there is no place in
Italy, the birthplace of the Renaissance, where these tenets are better
illustrated. From the moment you
enter the peaceful courtyard, you
know you're in a place of grace and
beauty, the harmony of the build-

WORD OF MOUTH

"I would suggest the Marches as a
great, off-the-beaten-path region
to visit. It has a very beautiful
landscape and is just as central
as Tuscany and Umbria (although,
unlike Umbria, it has a coastline,
and a nice one at that)." –Jackie
in Italy

ing reflecting the high ideals of the time. Today the palace houses the
Galleria Nazionale delle Marche (National Museum of the Marches),
with a superb collection of paintings, sculpture, and other objets d'art.
Some works were originally the possessions of the Montefeltro family;
others were brought here from churches and palaces throughout the
region. Masterworks in the collection include Paolo Uccello's *Profa-
nation of the Host,* Titian's *Resurrection* and *Last Supper,* and Piero
della Francesca's *Madonna of Senigallia.* But the gallery's highlight
is Piero's enigmatic work long known as *The Flagellation of Christ.*
Much has been written about this painting, and few experts agree on
its meaning. Legend had it that the figures in the foreground represent
a murdered member of the Montefeltro family (the barefoot young
man) and his two killers. However, Sir John Pope-Hennessy—the preeminent scholar of Italian Renaissance art—argues that they represent
the arcane subject of the vision of Saint Lawrence. Academic debates
notwithstanding, the experts agree that the work is one of the painter's masterpieces. Piero himself thought so: it is one of the few works
he signed (on the lowest step supporting the throne). ⊠*Piazza Duca
Federico* ☎*0722/322625* ⊕*www.comune.urbino.ps.it* 🎟€8 ⊗ *Mon.
8:30–2, Tues.–Sun. 8:30–7:15.*

WHERE TO STAY & EAT

$$$–$$$$ ✕**Vecchia Urbino.** In the center of town is this simple yet elegant wood-
panel restaurant with views of the hills. Recommended pasta dishes
include *vincisgrassi* (a meat lasagne), named after an Austrian cap-
tain who brought the recipe to Urbino more than a century ago, and
spaghetti *alla Vecchia Urbino* (with bacon and pecorino cheese). A
particularly good second course is the *coniglio al coccio* (literally, rab-
bit in earthenware); the rabbit is cooked in milk on the stovetop in an
earthenware casserole and then baked. Note: prices are higher when
fresh truffles are involved in the preparation. ⊠ *Via dei Vasari 3/5*
☎*0722/4447* ⊟*AE, DC, MC, V* ⊗*Closed Tues.*

$–$$ ✕**La Vecchia Fornarina.** Locals often crowd the small, two-room trattoria near the Piazza della Repubblica. The specialty is meaty country
fare, such as *coniglio* (rabbit) and *vitello alle noci* (veal cooked with
walnuts) or *ai porcini* (with mushrooms). There's also a good selection
of pasta dishes. ⊠ *Via Mazzini 14* ☎*0722/320007* ✍*Reservations
essential* ⊟*AE, DC, MC, V.*

Urbino's Palazzo Ducale.

¢–$ ✕**Angolo Divino.** At this *osteria* (informal restaurant) in the center of Urbino tradition reigns supreme: the menu is written in local dialect, flanked by Italian and English translations. Dishes range from the deliciously simple *spaghetti col pane grattugiato* (spaghetti with bread crumbs) to the temptingly rich *filetto al tartuffo* (beef fillet with truffles). ⊠ *Via S. Andrea 14* ☎*0722/327559* ▤*AE, D, MC, V* ☾*Closed Mon. and mid-Oct.–mid-Nov. No dinner Sun.*

$$–$$$ ▦**Hotel Bonconte.** This classic hotel, dating from the beginning of the 20th century, is just inside the city walls and close to the Palazzo Ducale. Rooms are pleasant and include some antiques; those at the front of the hotel have views of the valley below Urbino, although they also face the street. A terrace in the tranquil garden to the rear of the hotel adjoins the cozy breakfast room and bar. **Pros:** Some nice views, away from the bustle. **Cons:** Slightly overpriced, service is sleepy. ⊠ *Via delle Mura 28, 61029* ☎*0722/2463* ⊟*0722/4782* ⊕*www.viphotels. it* ⇆*23 rooms, 2 suites* ⚭*In-room: ethernet. In-hotel: bar* ▤*AE, DC, MC, V* ¶⭕*EP.*

¢ ▦**Hotel San Giovanni.** This hotel in the old town is housed in a renovated medieval building. The rooms are basic, clean, and comfortable—with a wonderful view from Rooms 24 to 30. There's a handy pizzeria below. **Pros:** Good budget option, excellent location. **Cons:** Basic service, no a/c. ⊠ *Via Barocci 13, 61029* ☎*0722/2827* ⊟*0722/329055* ⇆*31 rooms, 17 with bath* ⚭*In-room: no a/c. In-hotel: restaurant* ▤*No credit cards* ☾*Closed July* ¶⭕*BP.*

ANCONA

87 km (54 mi) southeast of Urbino, 139 km (86 mi) northeast of Perugia, 262 km (163 mi) east of Florence.

GETTING HERE

If you're driving from Perugia, take the SS318, which merges onto the SS76 highway to Fabriano and then on to Ancona. The drive takes around two hours. Trains leave from Perugia station several times a day.

VISITOR INFORMATION

Ancona tourism office (⊠ *Via Thaon de Revel 4* ☎*071/358991* ⊕*www. comune.ancona.it*).

EXPLORING

Ancona was probably once a lovely city. It's on an elbow-shape bluff (hence its name: *ankon* is Greek for "elbow") that juts out into the Adriatic. But Ancona was the target of serious aerial bombing during World War II—it was, and is, an important port city—and was reduced to rubble. The city was rebuilt in the unfortunate postwar poured-concrete style: practical and inexpensive but not aesthetically pleasing.

Unless you're waiting for one of the many ferries to Albania, Croatia, Greece, or Turkey, there is little reason to visit the city—with a few exceptions. The 2nd-century **Arco di Traiano** (Trajan's Arch) was part of Emperor Trajan's plan to enclose the harbor. Today it has a rather forlorn beauty, marking a greatness that Ancona no longer possesses. The **Duomo San Ciriaco** stands on a peak above Ancona, and is an interesting blend of Romanesque and Gothic architecture. If you look up you can see its painted wooden roof. The **Loggia dei Mercanti** is an exceptional example of Venetian–Gothic architecture, with its rows of arches and beguiling decorations.

WHERE TO STAY & EAT

$$ ✕**La Moretta.** This family-run trattoria is on the central Piazza del Plebiscito, and in summer there's dining outside in the square. Among the specialties here are *stoccafisso all'Anconetana* (cod baked with capers, anchovies, potatoes, and tomatoes) and the famous *brodetto* (fish stew). For a great deal, try the tasting menu, which will satisfy every imaginable taste bud. ⊠*Piazza del Plebiscito 52* ☎*071/202317* ▤*AE, DC, MC, V* ⊗*Closed Sun., Jan. 1–10, and Aug. 13–18.*

$$$ ▦**Grand Hotel Palace.** Widely held to be the best hotel in town, it's the extras here—slippers, bath salts, and shaving kits—that earn the ranking. Rooms are on the small side but beautifully furnished with French beds dressed in yellow damask, and half have a view directly over the port. Public rooms are grand and elegant, and the breakfast room is on the top floor with a panoramic view. **Pros:** Some decent views, attentive service. **Cons:** Slightly overpriced, some noise. ⊠*Lungomare Vanvitelli 24, 60100* ☎*071/201813* ▤*071/2074832* ⊕*palace.ancona@libero. it* ⏎*39 rooms, 1 suite* ⌂*In-room: ethernet. In-hotel: restaurant, bar, public Internet* ▤*AE, DC, MC, V* ⊗*Closed Dec. 23–Jan. 1* ⏉*BP.*

CLOSE UP

San Marino, a Country on a Cliff

The world's smallest and oldest republic, as San Marino dubs itself, is landlocked entirely by Italy. It consists of three ancient castles perched high on cliffs of sheer rock rising implausibly out of the flatlands of north Urbino, and a tangled knot of cobblestone streets below, lined with tourist boutiques, cheesy hotels and restaurants, and gun shops. The 45-minute drive from Rimini is easily justified, however, by the castle-top view of the countryside far below. The 1,000-meter-plus (3,300 feet and more) precipices will make jaws drop and acrophobes quiver.

San Marino was founded in the 4th century AD by a stonecutter named Marino who settled with a small community of Christians, escaping persecution by pagan emperor Diocletian. Over the millennia, largely because of the logistical nightmares associated with attacking a fortified rock, San Marino was more or less left alone by Italy's various conquerors, and continues to this day to be an independent country (population 26,000), supported almost entirely by its 3-million-visitors-per-year tourist industry.

San Marino's headline attractions are its **tre castelli** *(three castles)* —medieval architectural wonders that appear on every coat of arms in the city. Starting in the center of town, walk a few hundred yards past the trinket shops, along a paved cliff-top ridge, from the 10th-century **Rocca della Guaita** to the 13th-century **Rocca della Cesta** (which contains a museum of ancient weapons that's worthwhile mostly for the views from its terraces and turrets), and finally to the 14th-century **Rocca Montale** (closed to the public), the most remote of the castles. Every step of

the way affords spectacular views of Romagna and the Adriatic; it is said that on a clear day you can see Croatia. The walks make for a good day's exercise but are by no means arduous. Even if you arrive after visiting hours, they're supremely worthwhile. ☎ *0549/882670* ⊕ *www.museidistato. sm* ✉ *Rocca della Guaita and Rocca della Cesta €4.50* ☉ *Jan.–June 9, daily 9–5; June 10–Sept. 15, daily 8–8; Sept. 16–Dec. 30, daily 9–5.*

A must-see is the **Piazza della Libertà,** whose Palazzo Pubblico is guarded by soldiers in green uniforms. As you'll notice by peering into the shops along the old town's winding streets, the republic is famous for crossbows—and more: shopping for fireworks, firearms, and other items illegal for sale elsewhere is another popular tourist activity.

Visiting San Marino in winter—off-season—increases the appeal of the experience, as tourist establishments shut down and you more or less have the castles to yourself. In August every inch of walkway on the rock is mobbed with sightseers.

To get to San Marino by car, take highway SS72 west from Rimini. From Borgo Maggiore, at the base of the rock, a cable car whisks you up to the castles and town. Alternatively, you can drive all the way up the winding road; public parking is available in the town itself. Don't worry about changing money, showing passports, and the like (although the tourist office will stamp your passport for €1)—San Marino is, for all practical purposes, Italy, except, that is, for its majestic perch, its gun laws, and its reported 99% national voter turnout rate.

7

LORETO

31 km (19 mi) south of Ancona, 118 km (73 mi) southeast of Urbino.

GETTING HERE

If you're driving from Perugia, take the SS318 and then the SS76 highway to Fabriano and then on to Chiaravalle, where it merges with the A14 autostrada. The drive takes around 2½ hours. Trains also go to Loreto, but the station is about a mile outside the town center. Regular buses leave from the station to the center.

VISITOR INFORMATION

Loreto tourism office (⌷ *Via Solari 3* ☎*071/970276* ⊕*www.turismo. marche.it*).

EXPLORING

★ Loreto is famous for one of the best-loved shrines in the world, that of the **Santuario della Santa Casa** (House of the Virgin Mary), within the **Basilica della Santa Casa.** Legend has it that angels moved the house from Nazareth, where the Virgin Mary was living at the time of the Annunciation, to this hilltop in 1295. The reason for this sudden and divinely inspired move was that Nazareth had fallen into the hands of Muslim invaders, whom the angelic hosts viewed as unsuitable keepers of this important shrine. Excavations made at the behest of the Catholic Church have shown that the house did once stand elsewhere and was brought to the hilltop—by either crusaders or a family named Angeli—around the time the angels (*angeli*) are said to have done the job.

The house itself consists of three rough stone walls contained within an elaborate marble tabernacle. Built around this centerpiece is the giant basilica of the Holy House, which dominates the town. Millions of visitors come to the site every year (particularly at Easter and on the December 10 Feast of the Holy House), and the little town of Loreto can become uncomfortably crowded with pilgrims. Many great Italian architects, including Bramante, Antonio da Sangallo the Younger (1483–1546), Giuliano da Sangallo (circa 1445–1516), and Sansovino (1467–1529), contributed to the design of the basilica. It was begun in the Gothic style in 1468 and continued in Renaissance style through the late Renaissance. The bell tower is by Luigi Vanvitelli (1700–73). Inside the church are a great many mediocre 19th- and 20th-century paintings but also some fine works by Renaissance masters such as Luca Signorelli and Melozzo da Forlì (1438-94).

If you're a nervous air traveler, you can take comfort in the fact that the Holy Virgin of Loreto is the patron saint of air travelers and that Pope John Paul II has composed a prayer for a safe flight—available in the church in a half-dozen languages. ⌷*Piazza della Madonna* ☎*071/970104* ⊕*www.santuarioloreto.it* ☉*June–Sept., daily 6:45* AM–8 PM*; Oct.–May, daily 6:45* AM–7 PM*. Santuario della Santa Casa closed daily 12:30–2:30.*

Ascoli Piceno's Palazzo del Popolo.

ASCOLI PICENO

88 km (55 mi) south of Loreto, 105 km (65 mi) south of Ancona.

GETTING HERE

From Perugia take the SS75 to Foligno, then merge onto the SS3 to Norcia. From here take the SS4 to Ascoli Piceno. There are also trains, but the journey would be quite long, taking you from Perugia to Ancona before changing for Ascoli Piceno.

VISITOR INFORMATION

Ascoli Piceno tourism office (⊠*Piazza del Popolo 1* ☎*0736/257288* ⊕*www.comune.ascolipiceno.it*).

EXPLORING

Ascoli Piceno isn't a hill town but sits in a valley ringed by steep hills and cut by the fast-racing Tronto River. In Roman times it was one of central Italy's most important market towns, and today, with almost 60,000 residents, it's a major fruit and olive producer, making it one of the most important towns in the region. Despite the growth Ascoli Piceno saw during the Middle Ages and at other times, the streets in the town center continue to reflect the grid pattern of the ancient Roman city. You'll even find the word *rua*, from the Latin *ruga*, used for "street" instead of the Italian *via*. Now largely closed to traffic, the city center is a great place to explore on foot.

★ The heart of the town is the majestic **Piazza del Popolo,** dominated by the Gothic church of **San Francesco** and the **Palazzo del Popolo,** a 13th-century town hall that contains a graceful Renaissance courtyard. The square itself functions as the living room of the entire city. At dusk each evening the piazza is packed with people strolling and exchanging news and gossip—the sweetly antiquated ritual called the *passeggiata,* performed all over the country.

☾ Ascoli Piceno's **Giostra della Quintana** *(Joust of the Quintana)* is held on the first Sunday in August. Children love this medieval-style joust and the processions of richly caparisoned horses that wind through the streets of the old town. ✉ *Piazza del Popolo 1* ☎ *0736/253045.*

WHERE TO STAY & EAT

$–$$ ✕**Ristorante Tornasacco.** You won't find nouvelle cuisine at this, one
★ of Ascoli Piceno's oldest restaurants. The owners pride themselves on meaty local specialties such as *olive ascolane* (olives stuffed with minced meat, breaded and deep-fried), *maccheroncini alla contadina* (homemade short pasta in a lamb, pork, and veal sauce), and *bistecca di toro* (bull steak). ✉ *Piazza del Popolo 36* ☎ *0736/254151* ▤ *AE, DC, MC, V* ☾ *Closed Fri., and July 15–31 and Dec. 23–28.*

$ ▦**Il Pennile.** Look for this modern, family-run hotel in a quiet residential area outside the old city center, amid a grove of olive trees. Some rooms have views of the city. **Pros:** Peaceful, a good budget option. **Cons:** Distance from town center, basic rooms. ✉ *Via G. Spalvieri, 63100* ☎ *0736/41645* 🖷 *0736/342755* ⤶ *33 rooms* ⚭ *In-room: ethernet. In-hotel: bar, gym, public Internet* ▤ *DC, MC, V* ⭐ *BP.*

Spoleto, Orvieto & Southern Umbria

WORD OF MOUTH

"The Signorelli frescoes inside the Orvieto Duomo are stunning. Bring binoculars so you can get good closeup views, as many of them are high up."

—nonnafelice

WELCOME TO SOUTHERN UMBRIA

Spoleto

TOP REASONS TO GO

★ **Spoleto's Festival dei Due Mondi:** Crowds may descend and prices ascend here during summer's must-see music festival, but Spoleto's hushed charm enchants throughout the year.

★ **Orvieto's Duomo:** Arresting visions of heaven and hell on the facade and brilliant frescoes within make this Gothic cathedral a dazzler.

★ **Dining in Spello:** Treat yourself in one of Spello's fine restaurants, and complement your meal with the deep red glory of a Montefalco Rosso.

★ **Tantalizing truffles:** Are Umbria's celebrated "black diamonds" coveted for their pungent flavor, their rarity, or their power in the realm of romance?

Duomo, Orvieto

1 The Valle Umbra. The valley running from Assisi to Spoleto is a great area for indulging the pleasures of exceptional food (particularly in **Spello**) and fine wine (particularly in **Monte-falco**). From there you can follow the Sagrantino trail across some of Umbria's gentlest hills and plains.

2 Spoleto. Though it's known to the world for its annual performing-arts festival, Spoleto offers much more than Puccini in its Piazza del Duomo. There are Filippo Lippi frescoes in the cathedral, a massive castle towering over the town, and a bridge across the neighboring valley that's an engineering marvel.

3 East of Spoleto. The town of **Norcia,** renowned for its talented butchers and its black truffles, is a lovely day trip from Spoleto. Farther off the beaten path, the **Valnerina** area is rich in natural wonders, including mountain trails leading to spectacular views.

Piazza Duomo in Orvieto

TUSCANY

UMBRIA

GETTING ORIENTED

A trip through southern Umbria will take you to a succession of sleepy hill-top towns, each one with its own historical attractions and culinary flavors. Spello and Spoleto give you a full immersion in the history and culture of the area, following the traces of Saint Francis and Il Perugino. Farther south you can visit the Marmore waterfalls or the peaceful shores of the lake at Piediluco.

Assisi
75

Spello
Foligno
1
Bevagna
Montefalco
Bastardo
Trevi
VALLE UMBRA
Bruna
MONTE MARTANI
316
2 Spoleto
418
Acquasparta
biz
3
Terni
Nera
Narni

THE MARCHES
77
3
Triponzo
209
3
Piedipaterno
VALNERINA
395
3
471
209

3 Norcia
396
Cascia

0   5 mi
0   5 km

8

Druso roman arch, Spoleto

4 Southwest Umbria. Between Spoleto and Orvieto there's a collection of quiet, laid-back towns, including Umbria's oldest, **Amelia.** The jewel of the area is charming **Todi.**

5 Orvieto. Of central Italy's many hill towns, none has a more impressive setting than Orvieto, perched on a plateau 1,000 feet above the surrounding valley. Its cathedral ranks with Assisi's as the most spectacular in Umbria.

SOUTHERN UMBRIA PLANNER

Making the Most of Your Time

Southern Umbria is particularly well suited to touring in a limited time—you can hop from one town to the next with minimal difficulty. Alternatively, any of the towns, with the exception of **Norcia** to the east, can be covered in day trips from Perugia. You can arrange your itinerary around some themes specific to Umbria: the paintings of Perugino, Raphael's master; the spiritual towns and places of Saint Francis; the Sagrantino Wine Road; sniffing around for truffles; castles and fortresses; bicycle routes; Umbria on horseback; or local festivals.

Travelers tend to fall in love with a particular tiny town and swear their allegiance to it. It's difficult, though, to anticipate which town will capture your heart. Every one we list has its charms, and much depends on circumstances—if a friendly local takes you under his wing, or you arrive on a perfect sunny afternoon, you're likely to be hooked. That said, the two "don't miss" towns in the region are **Spoleto** and **Orvieto**, simply because their sights are the most exceptional.

Tourist Information & Tours

In recent years tourism officials have opened many local offices, most of which are well staffed and open every day of the week. There is a wide range of publications in several languages, together with maps and leaflets explaining the local sights. The Spoleto office is particularly helpful and can provide information for the city and beyond.

Fully licensed English-speaking guides are available for groups or for individuals in many towns throughout Umbria. Full- and half-day tours may be booked with fixed rates through the regional tourist guide association, **Associazione Guide Turistiche dell'Umbria** (☎075/815228 ⊕*www.assoguide.it*).

Finding a Place to Stay

Your lodging options in southern Umbria can range from elegant hotels in the major town centers to restored country mansions and monasteries in the surrounding hills. The country lodgings are often cheaper than staying in a town, and provide better service and more facilities, especially for those looking for a swimming pool. As many of the towns are perched on hilltops, parking can also be a problem, with town centers frequently closed to traffic. Some of the rural accommodations close from November to January.

DINING & LODGING PRICE CATEGORIES (IN EUROS)

	¢	$	$$	$$$	$$$$
RESTAURANTS	under €15	€15–€25	€25–€35	€35–€45	over €45
HOTELS	under €70	€70–€110	€110–€160	€160–€220	over €220

Restaurant prices are for a first course (*primo*), second course (*secondo*), and dessert (*dolce*). Hotel prices are for two people in a standard double room in high season, including tax and service.

GETTING AROUND

By Car

The region is easily reached via the Rome–Florence auto-strada (A1), which has exits at Orte, Orvieto, and Perugia. Despite the hilly terrain, driving around southern Umbria is actually a snap. Highways run through or near the main towns, and distances are relatively short from one town to the next. The main highways within the region run south from Perugia (E45) to Todi and Terni or southeast from Perugia to Assisi, Spello, Foligno, and Spoleto (via S75) and Terni (via S3). Orvieto lies above the Rome–Florence autostrada (A1) and is also connected to Todi by a country road (79 bis).

Try to find time to follow an ancient consular road, such as Via Flaminia, built more than 2,000 years ago to transport Romans and even today offers lovely vistas as it connects some of the towns.

If you don't arrive in the area with a rental car from a major airport or town elsewhere in Italy, the best places to pick up a rental vehicle are probably Orvieto and Perugia, accessible by train and by bus from both Florence and Rome.

By Train

Although three train lines connect most of the towns, the stations are often a couple of miles from the towns themselves. Slow trains on the Rome–Ancona line make stops in Narni-Amelia, Terni, Spoleto, Trevi, and Foligno, whereas the Terontola–Foligno line connects Foligno, Spello, Assisi, and Perugia. Slow trains on the Rome–Florence line stop in Orvieto. **Ferrovia dello Stato** (FS ☎ 848/888088 ⊕ www.trenitalia.it), the Italian state railway, has information about train schedules and fares, including a prebooking service.

By Bus

A number of private bus lines operate within the region and offer service to and from major cities in Tuscany and Lazio. The Perugia-based line **Sulga** (✉ Strada dei Cappucinelli 4d, Perugia ☎ 075/5009641 ⊕ www.sulga.it) runs between Rome's international airport and Perugia.

Sena (✉ Piazza Gramsci, Siena ☎ 0577/283203 ⊕ www.sena.it) makes city connections between Tuscany, Umbria, and Lazio, and Florence, Siena, Perugia, Orvieto, and Rome.

Spoletina (✉ SS Flaminia Km 127.7, Spoleto ☎ 0743/212208 ⊕ www.spoletina.com) operates buses both within the city of Spoleto and between a number of the main towns of the region, including Perugia, Assisi, Norcia, Terni, and Foligno.

8

Updated
by Jonathan
Willcocks

SOUTHERN UMBRIA'S LUSH LANDSCAPES MIGHT have been painted by Perugino, Raphael's teacher. Here you'll find green hills with trees that seem sculpted in place, cascading slopes with vineyards and groves of olive trees, and forests cloaked in the same bluish haze that you see in Renaissance paintings. Here you can explore towns settled by ancient peoples: the mysterious and sophisticated Etruscans; the simpler Umbri (who gave the region its name); and the Romans, the great engineers who built temples, bridges, theaters, and roads—the last of which are still in use today. The absence of the overwhelming wealth of art and architecture that you find in Florence and Rome allows you to absorb the enchanting towns and local cultures at a relaxing pace.

To the south and west of the Umbrian Valley is a succession of lovely hill towns: Spello and Trevi spill down slopes; Montefalco enjoys a lofty vantage point; and Bevagna and Foligno occupy the valley floor. La Rocca, a medieval fortress, announces the sophisticated hillside town of Spoleto, known for its annual summer Festival dei Due Mondi, a world-famous musical extravaganza.

The drive between Norcia and Terni takes you through some beautiful forested hills past Ferentillo, with its medieval abbey, Abbazia di San Pietro in Valle, up on the hilltop. Down below, near the Nera River, is one of Umbria's more offbeat sights: 30 or so mummies preserved in a crypt.

To the west of Terni are the walled towns of Narni and Amelia, with their architectural walks and surprising archaeological treasures. To the northwest, majestic Orvieto rises dramatically above the cliffs on which it rests like a crown, with forests, vineyards, olive groves, medieval abbeys, and Etruscan archaeological sites.

THE VALLE UMBRA

Running through the heart of Umbria is the Valle Umbra, a fertile strip populated with small, often ancient towns. Assisi is at the northern end, Spoleto at the southern; between them, you won't encounter an abundance of A-list sights. The beautiful landscape, the relaxed pace of life, and some fabulous food are the reasons to visit here.

SPELLO

12 km (7 mi) southeast of Assisi, 33 km (21 mi) north of Spoleto.

GETTING HERE
Spello is an easy half-hour drive from Perugia. From the E45 highway, take the exit toward Assisi and Foligno. Merge onto the SS75 and take the Spello exit. There are also regular trains on the Perugia–Assisi. line.

VISITOR INFORMATION
Spello tourism office (✉ *Piazza Matteotti 3* ☎ *0742/301009* ⊕ *www.foligno.umbria2000.it*).

EXPLORING

Spello is a gastronomic paradise, especially compared to Assisi. Only a few minutes from Assisi by car or train, this hilltop town at the edge of Mt. Subasio makes an excellent strategic and culinary base for exploring nearby towns. Its hotels are well appointed and its restaurants serve some of the best cuisine and wines in the region—sophisticated in variety, and of excellent quality. Spello's art scene includes first-rate frescoes by Pinturicchio and Perugino and contemporary artists who can be observed at work in studios around town. If antiquity is your passion, the town also has some intriguing Roman ruins. And the warm, rosy-beige tones of the local *pietra rossa* stone on the buildings brighten even cloudy days.

The Romans moved in after the Umbri people, and traces remain of their walls, gates, and amphitheater. Spello became a Roman colony just as Julius Caesar was riding the crest of power. Its city gates were constructed then or after, during the age of Augustus. The municipal building, or *palazzo comunale,* has an edict (carved in marble between AD 324 and 337) that describes Emperor Constantine's wishes for the colony. The town was later ruled by Lombards, the Baglioni family, and the Papal States. The church of Santa Maria Maggiore was built over a temple to the Roman goddesses Juno and Vesta. In that church Benardino di Betto, known as Pinturicchio (1454–1513), painted the splendid frescoes in the Baglioni Chapel in 1501 (in Rome he painted the frescoes for the Borgia apartments at the Vatican). The church of San Lorenzo dates from 1120; take a look behind the main altar at the 1533 carpenter's craftsmanship in the beautiful inlaid wood scenes in the choir. Walk uphill through town to the gate, Porta Venere, with its three arches and 12-sided towers where the goddess Venus once had a temple. The view of the valley below shows the remains of the nearby Roman amphitheater that dates back to the 1st century AD.

Spello is 1 km (½ mi) from the train station, and buses run every 30 minutes for Porta Consolare, the Roman gate at the south end of town—the best place to enter. From Porta Consolare continue up the steep main street that begins as Via Consolare and changes names several times as it crosses the little town, following the original Roman road. As it curves around, notice the winding medieval alleyways to the right and the more uniform Roman-era blocks to the left.

The basilica of **Santa Maria Maggiore** has vivid frescoes by Pinturicchio in the Cappella Baglioni (1501). Striking in their rich colors, finely dressed figures, and complex symbolism, the *Nativity, Dispute at the Temple* (on the far left side is a portrait of Troilo Baglioni, the prior who commissioned the work), and *Annunciation* (look for Pinturicchio's self-portrait in the Virgin's room) are among Pinturicchio's finest works. They were painted after the artist had already won great acclaim for his work on the Palazzi Vaticani in Rome for Borgia Pope Alexander VI. Two pillars on either side of the apse are decorated with frescoes by Perugino (circa 1450–1523), the other great Umbrian artist of the 16th century. ✉*Piazza Matteotti 18*

8

SOUTHERN UMBRIA THROUGH THE AGES

The earliest inhabitants of Umbria, the Umbri, were thought by the Romans to be the most ancient inhabitants of Italy. With the coming of the Etruscans, who founded many of the great cities in Umbria, the Umbri fled into the mountains to the east. The Etruscans were in turn supplanted by the Romans. During the Middle Ages, the major towns were ruled for a time by powerful families, such as the Trinci in Foligno, and the Baglioni in Perugia. However, the proximity of Rome ensured that the region would more or less fall under papal dominion for several centuries. It was only in 1860 that Piemontese troops finally entered Perugia, ending papal rule and incorporating the area into the new Italian state.

Founded as early as the 6th century BC, Assisi has always dominated the valley of Umbria. It grew in power and wealth, making it vulnerable to aggressive neighbors. Over the centuries it was occupied by the Goths, fell into Byzantine hands, and at the end of the 6th century AD it was part of the Duchy of Spoleto. After a series of wars against Perugia, it fell under papal dominion in the 13th century.

The Romans founded the town of Spoletium in 241 BC. It soon became strategically important due to its position on the Via Flaminia, the main road through the region. In 217 BC the Spoletans fought Hannibal, and delayed his march on Rome. In AD 570 Spoleto acquired renewed importance as the capital of the Longobard duchy. Ultimately Spoleto also fell under papal rule, until Italian unification in 1860.

☎0742/301792 ✉Free ⊙May–Sept., daily 8:30–12:30 and 3–7; Oct.–Apr., daily 8:30–12:30 and 3–6.

The **Pinacoteca Civica,** to the left of Santa Maria Maggiore, holds a rich assortment of art that once adorned the basilica, including several unusual polychrome wooden statues that were carried during Easter processions in centuries past. Look for the painting by Marcantonio Grecchi (1573–1651) showing the city of Spello. ⊠*Via Consolare* ☎0742/301497 ✉€2.60 ⊙*Tues.–Sun. 10:30–12:30 and 3:30–5:30.*

The Gothic church of **Sant'Andrea** has a painting of the *Madonna and Child with Saints* by Pinturicchio, as well as the mummified remains of the church's namesake, who was an early follower of Saint Francis. ⊠*Via Cavour* ☎*No phone* ✉*Free.*

WHERE TO STAY & EAT

In addition to hotels, apartments are available to rent in Spello. Furnished with simple rustic furniture, they have full kitchens that make them perfectly adequate for an inexpensive stay. For more information, contact **In Urbe** (⊠*Via Giulia 97, 06038* ☎*0742/301145* ⊕*www.inurbe.it*).

$$–$$$ ✕**Il Cacciatore.** Wild fowl and game—especially grilled or roasted—are served at this trattoria, the name of which means "the hunter." Truffles (in season) are a specialty, served in a variety of ways, perhaps on pasta, which is hand-rolled daily. Or try the *pappardelle con sugo d'oca* (ribbons of pasta dressed in goose sauce) or tagliatelle with peas and

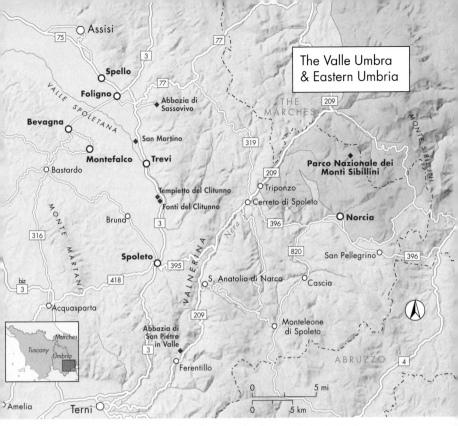

The Valle Umbra & Eastern Umbria

prosciutto. Though this place won't win awards for its looks, you may enjoy the view from the terrace, if weather permits. ⊠ *Via Giulia 42* ☏*0742/651141* 🖷*0742/301603* ▭*MC, V* ⊘*Closed Mon.*

$$–$$$
Fodor'sChoice
★

✕**Il Molino.** Almost a destination in itself, this former mill is one of the region's best restaurants. The sophisticated food showcases the bounty of Umbria. The types of olive oil used in the dishes and the names of the local farmers who grew the produce are noted on the menu. Appetizers are varied, and often highlight foods found only here, like the *risina*, a tiny white bean. Pasta sauces can vary from exquisitely rich to extremely delicate. The meat is first-rate, either elaborately prepared or grilled and topped with a signature sauce. The service is attentive, and the wine list has plenty of local and Italian options, including the pungent Sagrantino di Montefalco and fresh Orvieto whites. If you want something with a bit more depth, go for one of the Montepulciano wines, or even a Brunello di Montalcino, one of Italy's greatest reds. Outside seating lets you soak up the passing street scene; inside are a series of impressive 14th-century arches. ⊠*Piazza Matteotti 6/7* ☏*0742/651305* 🖷*0742/302235* ▭*AE, DC, MC, V* ⊘*Closed Tues.*

$–$$$
★

✕**Ristorante Il Pinturicchio.** For starters, don't miss the chef's flavorful focaccia, then continue with one of the truffles specialities or the spinach pasta with prosciutto and cheese. Your main dish might be lamb with wild fennel or chicken with pistachios. Dessert could be a chocolate soufflé or hazelnut-cream chantilly. The wine selection is excellent, and the service and atmosphere are refined. ⊠ *Via Largo G. Mazzini 8* ☎*0742/301003* ⊟*AE, MC, V.*

$$ ✕**La Cantina.** As its name implies, this is the place to sample wines from all over the country. The decor has a deliberately improvised feel, with a selection of old wooden furniture that blends in with the cellar location. The menu is seasonal and might include wild asparagus in spring and artichokes in fall and winter. The specialty of the house is grilled meat, especially the prized Tuscan Chianina beef and baby lamb chops. For dessert there's homemade apple *rocciata* (strudel). ⊠ *Via Cavour 2* ☎*0742/651775* ⊟*AE, DC, MC, V* ⊗*Closed Sun. No lunch.*

$ ✕**Bar Giardino Bonci.** The perfect place for a morning cappuccino, this coffee bar also does a delicious lunch, with simple panini and a platter with local cheeses and salami, perhaps buttressed by a glass of good local wine. Or you might stop by late afternoon to wind down with an aperitivo while you decide which of Spello's great restaurants you'll try for dinner. The large seating area in the back has a view of the valley as grand as that from La Bastiglia. ⊠ *Via Garibaldi 10* ☎*0742/651397* ⊟*No credit cards* ⊗*No dinner.*

$$ ✕⊡**La Bastiglia.** This cozy hotel is in a former grain mill, but polished
★ wood planks and handwoven rugs have replaced the rustic flooring. The comfortable sitting rooms and bedrooms are filled with a mix of antique and modern pieces. Rooms on the top floor—some with terraces—have views of the valley below, silvery green with olive trees. A separate building with additional rooms is surrounded by a garden. Pack light, as there are plenty of steps and you carry your bags. The hotel's wood-beamed restaurant ($$–$$$) serves refined international cuisine and unusual adaptations of traditional recipes. The menu changes with the seasons, so look for roasted pigeon or a sorbetto of wild berries in the summer; toward winter, truffles will appear. The regionally known sommelier dispenses advice about wines. **Pros:** Lovely terrace restaurant, cozy rooms, fine views. **Cons:** Some shared balconies, breakfast is underwhelming. ⊠ *Via Salnitraria 15, 06038* ☎*0742/651277* ⊕*www. labastiglia.com* ⊐*31 rooms, 2 suites* ⌂*In-hotel: restaurant, bar, pool* ⊟*AE, DC, MC, V* ⊗*Closed early Jan.–early Feb.* ⊙⏐*BP.*

$$–$$$ ⊡**Hotel Palazzo Bocci.** Quiet and elegant, this hotel is centrally located
★ on Spello's main street. The original building dates to the 14th century, but extensive restorations in the 18th and 19th centuries added bucolic ceiling and wall frescoes. You could settle in for a week and take a cooking course, or have the staff book you bicycle or horseback excursions through the countryside. The hotel has lovely sitting areas, a reading room, and a garden terrace off the bar. Several rooms have valley views. Consider splurging on the suite with the fireplace or reserving the room with the small terrace. **Pros:** Central location, splendid views of the valley. **Cons:** Noisy in summer months, not all rooms have views. ⊠ *Via Cavour 17, 06038* ☎*0742/301021* ⊕*www. palazzobocci.com* ⊐*23 rooms* ⌂*. In-room: safe, ethernet. In-hotel: restaurant, bar* ⊟*AE, DC, MC, V.*

SHOPPING

Spello is a good place to find excellent Umbrian olive oil and carved olive wood.

Try **Frantoio Cianetti** (✉ *Via Bulgarella 10* ☎*0742/652781*) for its own brand of cold-pressed, extra-virgin olive oil. **Angelo Passeri** (✉ *Via Giulia 18* ☎*0330/282104*) is a specialist in olive-wood carvings and produces works in an amazing variety of forms, such as animals and lamps.

Museo di Norberto (✉ *Via Cavour 61* ☎*0742/652044*) belongs to local painter Norberto, who was born in 1927 and at age 30 began to paint images of Spello in the naive style; his paintings are pricey now, but prints are available, too. Spello artist **Elvio Marchionni** (✉ *Via Consolare 78* ☎*0742/301153*) uses medieval techniques of mosaic and fresco that give his work the appearance of historic fragments—a technique so successful that his work adorns an altar in Santa Maria Maggiore. At his high-end shop you can commission a work or buy a painting.

At **L'Enoteca Il Pinturicchio** (✉ *Via Garibaldi 20* ☎*No phone*) you can pick up focaccia topped with local sausages, cheese, or greens. Try the local *ciauscolo* (fresh, spreadable pork salami) or *capocollo* or *lonzina* (both are cured pork meats). **Enoteca Properzio** (✉ *Via Torri di Properzio 8a* ☎*0742/301688*)) is one of Italy's top wineshops. Beware cool treatment if you're not a serious wine buyer. Oenophile or not, you can soberly request the €25 degustation menu. The wine bar closes at 9 PM.

FOLIGNO

8

5 km (3 mi) southeast of Spello, 18 km (11 mi) southeast of Assisi, 28 km (17 mi) north of Spoleto.

GETTING HERE

Foligno is a 45-minute drive from Perugia. From the E45 highway, take the exit toward Assisi and Foligno, then merge onto the SS75 and take the Foligno Nord exit. There are also regular trains on the Perugia-Assisi line. From the train station it's a 10-minute walk to the center.

VISITOR INFORMATION

Foligno tourism office (✉*Corso Cavour 126* ☎*0742/354459* ⊕*www.foligno.umbria2000.it*).

EXPLORING

The third-largest town in Umbria, Foligno has been an important commercial center since the 13th century (this is where Saint Francis came to sell his father's textiles before giving up all his worldly possessions). The town is divided into 10 *rioni,* or neighborhoods, that compete every year in an elaborately staged baroque festival.

Because Foligno was an industrial city, it was a target for severe Allied bombing in World War II; postwar reconstruction and flourishing light industry now obscure much of what must have once been a charming town. The town also suffered some of the worst damage wrought by

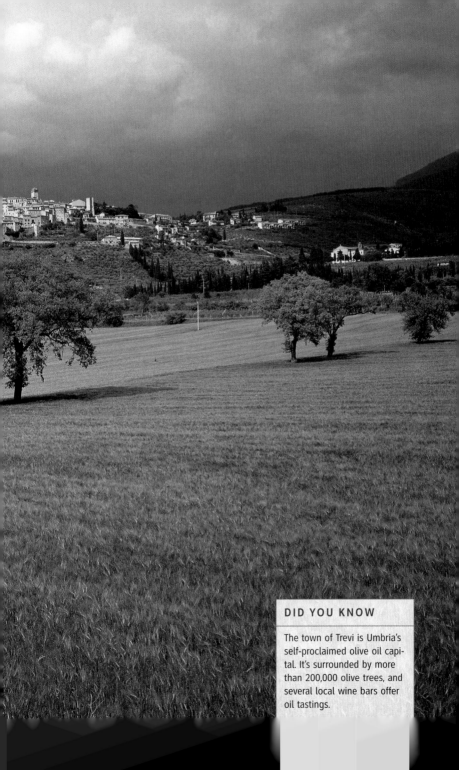

the 1997 earthquakes: it's not hard to imagine why the mayor broke out in tears at the sight of the collapsed 14th-century bell tower of the city hall. Facing that and handsomely restored, the enchanting—and puzzling—medieval facade of the Duomo survived intact.

The historic center of Foligno, which retains the old Roman street grid and some of its medieval heritage, has some Renaissance palaces and several churches worthy of a stop. Stroll along Via delle Conce (once the center for textile dyeing) and Via dei Molini for views of the canals. The main shopping street is Corso Cavour, where locals parade up and down during the evening hours, before and after dinner.

The 12th-century **Duomo** shows its better side to Piazza della Repubblica. Take some time to enjoy the elaborate marble carvings on the facade: the 12 signs of the zodiac are a curiously pagan feature over the main portal; underneath that are the symbols of the apostles; elsewhere the sun and the crescent moon appear; and on either side of the portal, fanciful animals appear, and elaborately carved grapes remind us that we are in the territory of Sagrantino. The bottom half of the facade is constructed of local stone and marble that form lovely horizontal stripes of pink and ivory; the upper half is lightened by the three bifurcated windows, and its rose window is formed of tiny columns that divide it like pie wedges. As you walk between the two ferocious lions and step inside past the bronze doors, note the geometric patterns of Cosmati mosaics that line the doorway. The interior reflects a variety of centuries of style. The two busts in the sacristy are attributed to Bernini; the *baldacchino,* with its tasseled canopy and four corkscrew columns entwined with rose tendrils, was commissioned in 1697 and looks as though it's copied from the one by Bernini in Saint Peter's in Rome. Look up in the cupola to see trompe-l'oeil rosettes painted to resemble carved marble. Exit the door that faces the Piazzetta Duomo to see the primary facade of the Duomo (it dates to around 1133 and was renovated in the early years of the 20th century). Across the street is an excellent restaurant called Sparafucile. ⊠ *Piazza della Repubblica* 🖀 *Free* ⊗ *Daily 8:30–noon.*

Palazzo Trinci on the north side of the Piazza della Repubblica was completed around 1407 for a Lombard overlord who combined his love of Roman antiquity with the humanistic craze. The mostly Gothic interior was built over and around Roman ruins, including a prize marble stele with a bas-relief of Amor and Psyche. An early-15th-century fresco cycle by Gentile da Fabriano unites ancient mythological themes with the world of chivalry and medieval courtly life. The details include depictions of Romulus and Remus. Pass through the hallway to see a Gothic stairway recycled from a previous building and a loggia that holds the *Story of the Foundation of Rome* and the Room of the Emperors. A small chapel was painted by Ottaviano Nelli in 1424.

Downstairs in the palazzo is the **Multimedia Museum of Tournaments, Matches, and Games,** a research center about jousting and other games from the Middle Ages to the 19th century; temporary exhibits have included a display of Renaissance costumes. On the second level you will find the Roman-era relics displayed in the **Museo Archeologico.** These pieces came mostly from the cemetery area of Capella di Santa Maria in Campis on the old Via Flaminia (once a major Roman consular road). It's hard to escape the theme of wine: note the three marble Dionysian panels complete with cavorting centaur, one of which still has traces of red paint—a reminder that ancient Greeks and Romans often painted their sculptures. Downstairs, the olive-oil lamp shows that the oil

WORD OF MOUTH

"Umbrian groceries are a joy for food addicts; almost every small village grocery is a true delicatessen shop. And if you happen to be in the Foligno area in late September, don't miss the 'Primi d'Italia' festival: a feast of pasta and risotto, with producers of all types (from industrial to small traditional manufacturers) from all over Italy—huge fun!" –franco

you toss on your salads has been vital to the economy for more than a few thousand years and a nearby bronze cornucopia pays tribute to the bounty of Umbria. Take a moment to look at the small bronze figurines dating to the 6th century BC: the Goddess Cupra, the two tiny figures of Mars in a Napoléon-style hat, and pottery that includes charming animal figures on a pot cover. The **Pinacoteca Civica,** an art gallery, has works by local painters who made Foligno an important art center during the Renaissance. ⊠*Piazza della Repubblica* ☎*0742/357989* ⊠*€6* ☺*Tues.–Sun. 10–7.*

Follow Via Mazzini to the Romanesque church of **Santa Maria Infraportas.** There are several cycles of votive frescoes in its three naves. The **Cappella dell'Assunta** has 12th-century, Byzantine-style frescoes. ⊠*Piazza San Domenico* ☎*0742/350517* ⊠*Free* ☺*Daily 8:30–noon and 3:30–6.*

8

WHERE TO STAY & EAT

$–$$
★ ✕**Il Bacco Felice.** The "Happy Bacchus" takes pride in its expert marriage of good food and good wine. The owner not only has an optimum wine selection, but also personally selects the best prosciutto and cheeses; the bread comes from the best bakeries in the valley. Hot vegetable soups (lentil, fava, barley) and rabbit casseroles are tasty standards here. The surprise? The owner raises his own free-range pigs, chickens, and rabbits as well as the seasonal tomatoes and peppers that wind up on your plate. Some outdoor seating is by the facade of the Duomo. ⊠*Via Garibaldi 73–75* ☎*393/8668407* ⊟*AE, DC, MC, V* ☺*Closed Mon.*

$–$$ ✕**Sparafucile Hostaria.** Look out over the facade of the Duomo from the outdoor seating at this enoteca. The daily changing menu often has good pork dishes or local homemade specialties like *frascarelli,* a tiny pasta that resembles rice. The friendly owner likes to showcase excellent local wines, like Sagrantino and Montefalco Rosso, while creating the kind of setting where diners often meet one another and join in ongoing conversations. ⊠*Piazzetta Duomo 30* ☎*0742/342602* ⊟*MC, V* ☺*Closed Wed. No lunch Sun.*

EATING WELL IN SOUTHERN UMBRIA

Truffles are the local delicacy. Try them—you'll see right away what all the fuss is about. Many Umbrian towns have their own excellent cured hams and salamis that go wonderfully well with the bread of the region. Lentils—for which the town of Castelluccio is best known—along with farro (an ancient grain used by the Romans, similar to wheat) and a variety of beans are popular in winter soups and in summer salads. Black celery comes from the Trevi area; look for it in local markets. Saffron, important to the area since medieval times, is raised around Cascia. It makes a fragrant appearance in many sauces.

Umbria's traditional pastas *ciriole* and *stringozzi* (also spelled *strangozzi*) are thicker versions of spaghetti, traditionally made using only flour and water. Pasta is a treat that in winter is accompanied by richer sauces, often with meat or game. In summer, sauces are lighter and include more vegetables.

Freshwater fish and even shrimp are featured in local dishes—a famous dish is the *carpa in porchetta*, made with giant 40-pound carps that are dressed and roasted like suckling pigs. Delicious *lumache* (snails) are smaller than the French escargots and might be sautéed with wild fen-nel and fresh rosemary, either on pasta or still in the shell.

The basic cheese of the region is a remarkably creamy pecorino (sheep's-milk cheese). Found in both hard and soft varieties, this cheese is often flavored with truffles or herbs and either eaten as a spread or grated into hot pasta. Cheeses from neighboring Tuscany and Lazio also make their way to the Umbrian table.

When it comes to wine, Sagrantino is not to be missed. Some experts consider it to be one of Italy's great reds, but prices are far more accessible than some of neighboring Tuscany's star wines. Another red to look for is Rosso di Montefalco, which combines the Sagrantino grape with other varieties to produce another full-bodied wine.

Try other Umbrian full-bodied reds, too, like Rubesco and Torgiano Rosso Riserva. Some of the Sagrantino winemakers also make whites, like Grechetto. Orvieto Classico is one of Italy's oldest varieties of white wine, but mass production has created some mediocre results, so take time to seek out some of the local winemakers. The monasteries and convents throughout the region produce various multicolor *rosolii* (sweet liqueurs) and digestive bitters, sold in all types of gift bottles.

$ ⌂ **Le Mura.** In the center of town, this quiet hotel has well-appointed rooms and cozy corners in which to read or sip a cup of tea. The restaurant has a good reputation even among locals, and breakfast includes freshly baked cakes. The main entrance is on Via Bolletta. **Pros:** Inexpensive rates, centrally located, tasty breakfast. **Cons:** Few in-room amenities, staff can seem unfriendly. ⊠ *Via Mentana 25, 06034* ☎*0742/357344* ⊕*www.lemura.net* ⇗*33 rooms, 3 suites* ⌂ *In-hotel: restaurant, bar, public Internet, parking (fee)* ▭*AE, D, MC, V* ⌊◎⌉*BP.*

$ ⛱**Villa Roncalli.** You won't have to put up with the creaking of old floors and the squealing of antique fixtures in this late-16th-century villa on the outskirts of town. The rooms have terra-cotta floors and modern furnishings. An ample buffet breakfast with homemade bread, jams, and cakes makes it hard to leave. Let the front desk know about any special needs when you check in, as you will be on your own after you get your key. **Pros:** Reasonable rates, restaurant is popular with locals. **Cons:** Front desk isn't always staffed, a 10-minute walk from central Foligno. ✉*Località Sant'Eraclio, Via Roma 25, 06034* ☎*0742/391091* ⤴*10 rooms* ⌂*In-room: no a/c (some). In-hotel: restaurant, bar, pool* ☰*AE, DC, MC, V* ⊘*Closed most of Jan. and last 3 wks in Aug.* ⏹*BP.*

THE ARTS

The 13th-century church of **San Domenico** (✉*Largo F. Frezzi 8* ☎*0742/344563*) is now an auditorium that hosts concerts and temporary exhibits.

BEVAGNA

9 km (5½ mi) west of Foligno, 27 km (17 mi) south of Assisi.

GETTING HERE

If you are driving from Perugia, follow the E45 toward Rome. Merge onto the SP318 and then the SP403, which leads you into Bevagna. The drive takes around 45 minutes. Trains run on the Perugia–Foligno line.

8

VISITOR INFORMATION

Bevagna tourism office (✉*Piazza Silvestri* ☎*0742/361667* ⊕*www.bevagna.it*).

EXPLORING

Bevagna's first building boom was probably around 220 BC, when the town—then called Mevania—was constructed on the ancient Roman consular road, Via Flaminia, 148 km (92 mi) from Rome. Part of the Forum was once at the intersection of what are now Via Crescimbeni and Via Santa Margherita. In the 3rd century AD, Via Flaminia was diverted through Spoleto and Terni, thus causing Bevagna's boom to bust. Later, medieval and Renaissance homes and shops covered Roman ruins, but the shapes of ancient Roman theaters and temples can be discerned from the medieval structures that you see today, as they were built using the Roman buildings' foundations.

Bevagna is divided into four distinct quarters (called *gaite* in the local dialect): San Giovanni, San Giorgio, San Pietro, and Santa Maria. The town is small and easily covered on foot. If you approach the town by car and park in the lot near Porta Todi, before you walk through the ancient gate look to your left to see a rectangular pool fed by the River Clitunno, where, until a few decades ago, local women brought their wash—an early self-service laundry.

★ Begin your visit in the center of town in the asymmetrical, medieval **Piazza Filippo Silvestri,** one of Umbria's most beautiful and harmonious squares, laid out in the 12th and 13th centuries. The square's Roman Corinthian column is known as San Rocco, and the 1896 fountain replaced an ancient octagonal cistern.

The 1195 church of **San Silvestro** is a fine example of Umbrian Romanesque architecture. The lower section of the church was constructed in travertine, and the upper section in local Subasio stone; the facade remains unfinished. Note the medieval animal heads sculpted on the cornice above. ⊠ *Piazza Silvestri* ☎ *No phone* ⊗ *Daily 10–12:30, 4–6:30.*

Inaugurated in 1886, the **Teatro Francesco Torti** has three tiers of boxes, each level in a different style. Domenico Braschi and Mariano Piervittori painted the wall and ceiling frescoes in the entrance, foyer, and theater during the same period; contemporary artist Luigi Frappi painted the stage curtain with the scene of the Clitunno River. If you come through in off-hours, ask at the Pro Loco tourist office (below Palazzo dei Consoli) for a tour. The theater is inside the **Palazzo dei Consoli,** which was the seat of local magistrates from at least 1187 until the 1832 earthquake. ⊠ *Piazza Silvestri* ☎ *0742/361667* ⊠ *€3.50, includes admission to Museo di Bevagna* ⊗ *Tues.–Sun. 3:30–6:30.*

The **Museo di Bevagna** has a small collection divided between archaeology and art. Among the artifacts is an ancient tablet in Umbrian writing that is read right to left, which is how it was done before locals had to conform to Roman ways. The art collection includes a wooden model of Santa Maria delle Grazie and paintings by lesser-known local artists from the Umbrian school. ⊠ *Palazzo del Municipio, Corso Matteotti 70* ☎ *0742/360031* ⊠ *€3.50, includes tour of Teatro Francesco Torti* ⊗ *Sept.–May, Tues.–Sun. 10:30–1 and 2:30–5; June–Aug., Tues.–Sun. 10:30–1 and 3:30–7.*

The **Roman marine mosaics** are from the 2nd century AD. Lively sea creatures made of black tiles adorn a white background. Lobsters, dolphins, and fanciful mythological figures face one another as if reflected in a mirror. You can track down other Roman ruins by using the free map available at the Pro Loco tourist office. You can only see the mosaics accompanied by a guide hired from Museo di Bevagna. ⊠ *Le Terme, San Giovanni quarter* ☎ *No phone* ⊠ *€2.60* ⊗ *Sept.–May, Tues.–Sun. 10:30–1 and 2:30–5; June–Aug., Tues.–Sun. 10:30–1 and 3–6:30.*

WHERE TO STAY & EAT

$$–$$$ ✕ **Enoteca Ristorante Piazza Onofri.** Local specialties are served in this medieval inn, which is run by the same folks who run the wineshop on Corso Matteotti. The attractive bar serves a good range of local vintages. It is also recommended by the Strada del Sagrantino tour-

ist office because of the excellent selection of Sagrantino wine from the Montefalco area. Some clean, rustic rooms are available upstairs. ✉ *Piazza Onofri 2* ☎ *0742/361926* ▭ *DC, MC, V* ⊘ *Closed Wed. No lunch weekdays.*

$ ✕ **La Bottega di Assù.** An improbable array of books, pots, jars, and other paraphernalia greets you as you walk into this tiny wine bar. The owner, Assunta Palmioli, is keen to help you try interesting wines from the Montefalco region and the rest of Umbria. She prepares simple but tasty dishes that you can eat in the tiny dining room or outside during the warmer months. The shop also sells olive oil, truffles, and other local specialties. In July and August the place is often open for dinner, so call ahead. ✉ *Corso Matteotti 102* ☎ *0742/360978* ▭ *MC, V* ⊘ *Closed Wed. No dinner.*

$ 🏨 **Hotel Palazzo Brunamonti.** This Renaissance-era palace is built over
★ Roman and medieval foundations, which are still visible. The hotel is very close to Piazza Silvestri, meaning it is only steps away from good restaurants and interesting museums. The decor in the guest rooms is simple—all the better for you to enjoy the architecture. On your way to the lovely breakfast room you can admire the 18th- and 19th-century frescoes in the halls. The owners and staff are exceptionally friendly and courteous. **Pros:** Central location, friendly staff. **Cons:** Very simple furnishings, no restaurant. ✉ *Corso Matteotti 79, 06031* ☎ *0742/361932* 🖷 *0742/361948* ⊕ *www.brunamonti.com* ↝ *16 rooms* ⚷ *In-room: refrigerator. In-hotel: restaurant, laundry service* ▭ *AE, DC, MC, V* ⊘ *Closed Jan. 7–mid-Feb.*

MONTEFALCO

8

6 km (4 mi) southeast of Bevagna, 34 km (21 mi) south of Assisi.

GETTING HERE

If you are driving from Perugia, take the E45 toward Rome. Take the Foligno exit, then merge onto the SP445 and follow it into Montefalco. The drive takes around 50 minutes. The nearest train station is in Foligno, about 7 km (4½ mi) away. From there you can take a taxi or a bus into Montefalco.

VISITOR INFORMATION

Montefalco tourism office (✉ *Via Ringhiera Umbra* ☎ *0742/379598* ⊕ *www.foligno.umbria2000.it*).

EXPLORING

Nicknamed the "balcony railing over Umbria" for its high, vantage point over the valley that runs from Perugia to Spoleto, Montefalco began as an important Roman settlement situated on the Via Flaminia. The town owes its current name—which means "Falcon's Mount"—to Emperor Frederick II (1194–1250). Obviously a greater fan of falconry than Roman architecture, he destroyed the ancient town, which was then called Coccorone, in 1249, and built in its place what would later become Montefalco. Aside from a few fragments incorporated in a private house just off Borgo Garibaldi, no traces remain of the old Roman center. However, Montefalco has more than its fair share of interesting art and architecture and is well worth the drive up the hill.

Three of the four original gates still provide a grand entrance to the town. The most majestic, the 14th-century Ghibelline **Porta Sant'Agostino** leads to the church of Sant'Agostino, which houses quite a curious artifact: a mummy of a 16th-century Spanish pilgrim who never made the journey home. From the church, Corso Goffredo Mameli (the main street) heads straight toward the 13th- to 14th-century Gothic church of Sant'Agostino, which reopened in 2004 after extensive renovation. At the end of the Corso is the **Piazza del Comune,** surrounded by several Renaissance buildings, including the 14th-century Palazzo Comunale.

At **La Strada del Sagrantino,** the tourist office in the piazza, the staff will advise you on selecting a wine, direct you to nearby enoteche for tastings, and give you free maps to find your way around Sagrantino Road and some remarkable wine territory. They can also book you a room in a hotel, at a vineyard, in a hillside apartment, or at an *agriturismo,* a working farm. ⊠*Piazza del Comune 17* ☎*0742/378490* ⊕*www.stradadelsagrantino.it.*

Montefalco's artistic highlight is the 14th-century **Chiesa-Museo di San Francesco,** a church-turned-museum that enshrines the masterworks of some of the region's finest Renaissance artists. In tribute to the Franciscan order and the religious significance of the region, Pietro Vannucci, known as Perugino, painted the 1503 *Annuciation and Nativity* in splendid colors. Look for a glimpse of the Umbrian landscape in the background. The highly original and vivid fresco cycle of the *Life of St. Francis,* painted in 1450–1452 by Benozzo Gozzoli, compares favorably with those by Giotto in Assisi. (Find the *Blessing of Montefalco,* one of the fresco scenes, for a look at the town during Gozzoli's time.) Upstairs are religious paintings and altarpieces by local artists. In the basement is a small collection of sculpture and fragments from various periods. ⊠*Via Ringhiera Umbra* ☎*0742/379598* 🎟*€4* ⊗*Nov.–Feb., Tues.–Sun. 10:30–1 and 2:30–5; Mar.– Oct., daily 10:30–1 and 2–6.*

If you like Gozzoli's work, there's some on display in the **Convento di San Fortunato,** though it's in less pristine condition than that in the Chiesa-Museo di San Francesco. The convent is a 15-minute walk outside the town walls: look for *Madonna with Saints and Angels* in the lunette over the doorway of the cloister chapel (left side) and the fresco of San Fortunato on the altar. Tiberio d'Assisi's *Life of St. Francis* (1512) is also in the cloister chapel. ⊠*Via San Fortunato 5* ☎*No phone* 🎟*Free* ⊗*Daily 9–noon and 3–6.*

**OFF THE
BEATEN
PATH**

Tessitura Pardi. Visit this factory to see how the cotton and linen textiles of Tessuti di Montefalco are woven. Call ahead to book an appointment. Bastardo is an easy stop between Todi or Spoleto and Montefalco, and not far from the Antonelli winery in San Marco. ⊠*SS316* ✥ *7 km (4½ mi) southwest of Montefalco; follow signs for Bastardo or Todi* ☎*0742/9975* 🎟*Free* ⊗ *Weekdays 9–1 and 2:30–5.*

WHERE TO STAY & EAT

Montefalco is a good stop for sustenance: here you need to go no farther than the main square to find a restaurant or bar with a hot meal, and most establishments—both simple and sophisticated—offer a splendid combination of history and small-town hospitality. Some of the wine producers, including Antonelli, have *casale,* or small apartments, near the vineyards that are usually rented by the week, but in low season are often available for a weekend. For information, contact the office of **Strada del Sagrantino** (☎*0742/378490* ⊕*www.stradadel-sagrantino.it*).

$–$$ ✕**Ristorante Il Coccorone.** This is a good place for a hearty meal. The local meats are outstanding, especially Chianina beef. The novel *pappardelle con sugo di Sagrantino* (wide noodles made with red wine) is very good. The wine list is the most comprehensive in the area and includes Sagrantino secco, Sagrantino passito, and Montefalco Rosso. Rub elbows here with local business executives and bon vivants. ⊠*Largo Tempestivi* ☎*0742/379535 or 0742/379016* ⊟*MC, V* ⊗*Closed Wed.*

¢–$ ✕**L'Alchemista.** "The Alchemist" is an apt name, as the chef's transformations are magical. Try the *fiore molle della Valnerina,* baked saffron cheese, bacon, and zucchini—served only here. In summer, cold dishes to try are *panzanella,* a local vegetable salad mixed with bread, or the barley salad tossed with vegetables. The *farro* (spelt) soup made with Sagrantino wine is a local specialty. The desserts are delicious: all are made on the premises and not too sweet. ⊠*Piazza del Comune 14* ☎*0742/378558* ⊟*DC, MC, V* ⊗*Closed Tues. Jan.–Mar.*

$$$
Fodor's Choice
★
Villa Pambuffetti. Zelda and F. Scott never had it so good. If you want to be pampered in the refined atmosphere of a private villa, this is the spot. Just outside the town walls, it's a short walk from all the town's sights. Guests appear to be part of the ambience, and dress on par with the elegance of the villa and of the excellent cuisine in the dining room. In winter you are greeted by the warmth of a fireplace as you enter the front door, in summer a pool cools you down, and cozy reading rooms beckon year-round. Cooking courses are given on the premises; horseback-riding and golf trips can be arranged; and shopping excursions for local textiles, cashmere, and ceramics are popular diversions. **Pros:** Peaceful gardens, refined furnishings. **Cons:** Outside the town center, can get crowded on weekends. ⊠*Viale della Vittoria 20* ☎*0742/379417* ⊕*www.villapambuffetti.com* ⇥*15 rooms, 3 suites* ⚙*In-room: safe, refrigerator. In-hotel: restaurant, bar, pool* ⊟*AE, D, MC, V.*

¢–$$ **Casale Satriano.** Stay in an apartment amid vineyards, olive groves, and oak forests belonging to the Antonelli family, a quality producer of Montefalco wines. Six small apartments sit near the swimming pool with a view of Monti Martani. Outside amenities include a shared wood-burning oven and playground; each apartment has a fireplace. **Pros:** Gorgeous views over the Martani hills, can enjoy the fine wines. **Cons:** Need a car to get around, a long way from main sights. ⊠*Azienda Agricola Antonelli San Marco, SS316, Località San Marco 59, between Montefalco and Bastardo, 06036* ☎*0742/379158* 🖷*0742/371063*

8

⊕*www.satriano.it* ↝*6 apartments* ⌂*In-room: kitchen. In-hotel: pool.* ⊟*DC, MC, V*

$ 🏨**Hotel Degli Affreschi.** Located just off Piazza del Comune, this hotel is named for frescoes that were discovered during a 2003 renovation. Not surprising, as part of the building dates to the 12th century. The rooms are simply furnished. **Pros:** Central location, good budget option. **Cons:** Front desk is not always staffed, simple furnishings. ✉*Corso Mameli 45, 06036* ☎*0742/379243* 🖷*0742/379 643* ↝*11 rooms* ⌂*In-hotel: no elevator* ⊟*AE, MC, V.*

SHOPPING

The local Sagrantino grape produces a dry ruby-red wine with plenty of body, called Sagrantino passito. Interest in this wine has revved area production. Another wine unique to this area is Montefalco Rosso, made from a blend of grapes that varies but mixes Sagrantino with Sangiovese, Cabernet, Merlot, or other grapes. If you would like to try a local white wine, Grechetto is far more interesting than most of the whites that are produced in Frascati near Rome

At **La Strada del Sagrantino** (✉*Piazza del Comune 17* ☎*0742/378490*) the staff can advise you on selecting a wine and give you free maps to find your way around Sagrantino Road and some remarkable wine territory. Wine can be purchased by the glass and by the bottle at **Federico II Enoteca** (✉*Piazza del Comune 1* ☎*0742/78902*).

TREVI

5 km (3 mi) southeast of Spello, 16 km (10 mi) southeast of Assisi.

GETTING HERE

Trevi is a 50-minute drive from Perugia. Follow the the E45 highway, taking the exit toward Assisi and Foligno. Merge onto the SS75 and choose the Foligno Est exit. Merge onto the SS3, then follow the SP425 to Trevi. There are regular trains on the Perugia-Assisi line. The station is outside the town center, but is served by regular shuttle buses.

VISITOR INFORMATION

Trevi tourism office (✉*Piazza Mazzini 5* ☎*0742/781150* ⊕*www.foligno.umbria2000.it*).

EXPLORING

Halfway between Assisi and Spoleto, the well-preserved town of Trevi cascades down the slope of a hill. The town—no relation to the famous fountain in Rome—calls itself the Olive Oil Capital, evidenced by its more than 200,000 olive trees. The best Umbrian olive oil is the extra-virgin variety from Trevi, chosen for the tables of the popes. Many *enoteche* (wine bars) now do double duty, offering olive-oil tastings to compare flavor and quality.

Most of the area's Roman ruins are in the Clitunno Valley below Trevi. The best artworks in town are found in the local churches: San Martino and Madonna delle Lacrime.

CLOSE UP

The Sagrantino Story

Sagrantino grapes have been used for the production of red wine for centuries. The wine began centuries ago as Sagrantino *passito*, a semisweet version in which the grapes are left to dry for a period after picking to intensify the sugar content. One theory traces the origin of Sagrantino back to ancient Rome in the works of Pliny the Elder, the author of the *Natural History* who referred to the Itriola grape that some researchers think may be Sagrantino. Others believe that in medieval times Franciscan friars returned from Asia Minor with the grape. ("Sagrantino" perhaps derives from sacramenti, the religious ceremony in which the wine was used.)

The passito is still produced today and is preferred by some. But the big change in Sagrantino wine production came in the past decades when Sagrantino *secco* (dry) came into the market. Both passito and secco have a deep ruby-red color that tends toward garnet highlights with a full body and rich flavor.

For the dry wines, producers not to be missed are Terre di Capitani, Antonelli, Perticaia, and Caprai. Try those labels for the passito as well, in addition to Ruggeri and Scacciadiavoli. Terre di Capitani is complex and has vegetable and mineral tones that join tastes of wild berries, cherries, and chocolate—this winemaker hand-pampers his grapes and it shows. Antonelli is

elegant, refined, and rich. The Ruggeri passito is one of the best, so don't be put off by its homespun label. Caprai is bold and rich in taste, and has the largest market share, including a high percentage exported to the United States. Perticaia has a full taste with a surprising "up" finish that suggested some divine presence other than Sagrantino.

Some wineries are small and not equipped to receive visitors. Arrange your winery visits at **La Strada del Sagrantino** (⊠ *Piazza del Comune 17* ☎ *0742/378490* ⊕ *www.stradadelsagrantino.it*) in Montefalco's main square. There you can pick up a map of the wine route and set up appointments, book accommodations, and then visit local enoteche. At the enoteche, ask the sommelier to guide you to some smaller producers you'll have difficulty finding elsewhere.

Sagrantino di Montefalco is celebrated twice yearly in the town of Montefalco, during September's Festa Della Vendemmia (Grape or Harvest Festival) and spring's Settimana Enologica (Wine Week), during which area grape farmers turn out for a parade through the streets and a tasting of past years' labors in the Piazza del Comune. Details can be obtained from the **Centro Agro-Alimentare dell'Umbria** (☎ *0742/344214* ⊕ *www.umbriadoc.com*) or the Strada del Sagrantino (⇨ *above*). Salute!

8

Raccolta d'Arte San Francesco, often called simply the Pinacoteca, was built in the 14th century on the site where a donkey lowered itself to its knees to listen to Saint Francis preach in 1213. The museum contains a good collection of paintings by local artists. See the duo of saints by Lo Spagna (circa 1450–1528): one shows Saint Cecilia (circa 1520), patron saint of musicians, holding pipes; nearby are a flute, tambourine, recorder, and at her feet, sheet music. Don't miss the vivid hues of Perugino's *Adoration of the Shepherds* (circa 1521) in the midst of an Umbrian landscape. There's also a collection of Etruscan artifacts. Off in one wing is the **Olive Oil Museum,** with an illustrated history of the various uses of the olive and its oil. ⊠ *Convento di San Francesco, Largo Don Bosco* ☏*0742/381628* ⊕*www.sistemamuseo. it* 🖅*€4* ⊘*Apr.–May and Sept., Tues.–Sun. 10:30–1 and 2:30–6; June and July, Tues.–Sun. 10:30–1 and 3:30–7; Aug., daily 10:30–1 and 3–7:30; Oct.–Mar., Fri.–Sun. 10:30–1 and 2:30–5.*

Halfway down the hill from Trevi is the **Madonna delle Lacrime** *(Church of Madonna of the Tears)*, built in 1487, with works by Lo Spagna and Perugino. Over the altar is a portrait of the Madonna that is said to have shed bloodstained tears on August 5, 1485, giving the church its name. To see the church, ring the bell at the convent next door. ✛ *1 km (½ mi) south of Trevi* ☏*0742/781150* ⊘*Daily 9–noon and 4–6:30.*

On the site of the church of **Sant'Emiliano,** a bishop is said to have knocked down a temple to the ancient Roman goddess Diana Trivia. The Romanesque structure, named for the Christian Armenian Emiliano who was martyred on January 28, 302, was constructed in the 11th century. Its dome is what you see as Trevi's "crown" from the valley below. A statue of Emiliano, the town's patron saint, is carried through town every January 27 in a torch-lit procession. ⊠ *Via Beato* ☏*0742/781150* 🖅*Free* ⊘*Daily 9–noon and 4–6.*

OFF THE BEATEN PATH

Tempietto e Fonti del Clitunno. South of Trevi is this tempietto (little temple), an early church built from bits and pieces of Roman temples. The badly worn frescoes, some of the earliest in Umbria, date from the 8th century. Farther down the road you'll find the Fonti del Clitunno (Springs of Clitunno), named after a Roman river god. The springs were famous in the ancient world partly because of the healing properties of water. Pliny the Younger mentions them in his writings, and Caligula visited on several occasions for the famous oracles. The remains of the Roman-era Tempio del Clitunno (Temple of Clitunno) are nearby. The springs were created when the Romans diverted several rivers upstream, although an earthquake in the 5th century AD greatly reduced the water supply; they were used until the 19th century to run the mills in the nearby town of Pissignano. ✛*2 km (1 mi) south of Trevi* 🖅*€2* ⊘*Apr.–Oct., daily 8:45–7:30; Nov.–Mar., daily 8:45–5:45.*

WHERE TO STAY & EAT

During Appuntamenti d'Autunno, held throughout October, temporary taverns are set up in courtyards and buildings, and local restaurants showcase historic menus.

$–$$
★

✕ **Taverna del Pescatore.** The unpromising location of this "fisherman's tavern," next to busy Via Flaminia, belies the tranquillity inside. Once you're seated on the terrace, the clear water of the Clitunno River flows just beyond your table. Sit back, listen for the birds in the trees, and keep an eye out for the occasional fish, on which the menu is based each day. Preparations are clean and simple and at times wonderfully eclectic: one springtime favorite is stringozzi with wild asparagus tips, trout fillet, and tiny tomatoes. ⊠*Statale Flaminia Km 139* ☏*0742/780920* ▤*AE, DC, MC, V* ⊘*Closed Wed. Sept.–July, and 2 wks in Jan.*

$$ ★ Antica Dimora alla Rocca. In a palazzo that dates back to 1650, this hotel has rooms with wood-beam ceilings, some elaborately painted, and tile floors. The penthouse suite has a sitting room with frescoes. Some rooms have lovely views of the rooftops. The restaurant, La Prepositura, is most dependable if you select one of the daily prix-fixe specials. **Pros:** Spacious rooms, central location. **Cons:** Not enough parking, reception area is dreary. ⊠*Piazza della Rocca, 06039* ☎*0742/38541 or 0742/78925* ⊕*www.hotelallarocca.it* ➮*38 rooms, 5 suites* ⌂*In-room: refrigerator, ethernet. In-hotel: restaurant, bar, laundry service, no-smoking rooms* ▤*AE, DC, MC, V.*

SPOLETO

For most of the year, Spoleto is one more in a pleasant succession of sleepy hill towns, resting regally atop a mountain. But for three weeks every summer the town shifts into high gear for a turn in the international spotlight for the Festival dei Due Mondi (Festival of Two Worlds), an extravaganza of theater, opera, music, painting, and sculpture. As the world's top artists vie for honors, throngs of art aficionados vie for hotel rooms. If you plan to spend the night in Spoleto during the festival, make sure you have confirmed reservations, or you may find yourself scrambling at sunset.

Spoleto has plenty to lure you during the rest of the year as well: the final frescoes of Filippo Lippi; the beautiful piazzas and streets with Roman and medieval attractions; and superb natural surroundings with rolling hills and a dramatic gorge. Spoleto makes a good base for exploring all of southern Umbria, as Assisi, Orvieto, and the towns in between are all within easy reach.

Umbri tribes were the first to settle here, probably taking advantage of the protection provided by the steep and narrow gorge that runs along the back of Spoleto's hill. As usual, the Romans were not far behind, fortifying the city walls and spanning the gorge with an aqueduct, which serves as a foundation for the breathtaking Ponte delle Torri. By all accounts an important city, Spoletum (as it was called in Latin) turned back Hannibal in the 2nd century BC. Ancient churches set in silvery olive groves below either side of town testify to Spoleto's importance in the early Christian period, when it ruled over a sizable independent duchy. During the Middle Ages the town had more than 100 towers, but they were toppled when the rebellious citizens refused to pay taxes. (As you walk around town, you can still see evidence of these towers in the walls of many houses.) In the 14th century the town fell under control of the Catholic Church, and La Rocca was built at its summit to enforce papal rule.

GETTING HERE

Spoleto is an hour's drive from Perugia. From the E45 highway, take the exit toward Assisi and Foligno, then merge onto the SS75 until you reach the Foligno Est exit. Merge onto the SS3, which leads to Spoleto. There are regular trains on the Perugia-Foligno line. From the train station it's a 15-minute uphill walk to the center, so you'll probably want to take a taxi.

VISITOR INFORMATION

Spoleto tourism office (⊠ *Piazza della Libertà 7* ☏ *0743/238921* ⊕ *www. spoleto.umbria2000.it*).

EXPLORING SPOLETO

The walled city is set on a slanting hillside, with the most interesting sections clustered toward the upper portion. Parking options inside the walls include Piazza Campello (just below the Rocca) on the southeast end, Via del Trivio to the north, and Piazza San Domenico on the west end. You can also park at Piazza della Vittoria farther north, just outside the walls. There are also several well-marked lots near the train station. If you arrive by train, you can walk 1 km (½ mi) from the station to the entrance to the lower town. Regular bus connections are every 15 to 30 minutes. You can also use the "trenino," as locals call the shuttle service added in 2004, from the train station to Piazza della Libertà, near the upper part of the old town, where you'll find the tourist office.

Like most other towns with narrow, winding streets, Spoleto is best explored on foot. Bear in mind that much of the city is on a steep slope, so there are lots of stairs and steep inclines. The well-worn stones can be slippery even when dry; wear rubber-sole shoes for good traction. Several pedestrian walkways cut across Corso Mazzini, which zigzags up the hill. A €2.60 combination ticket purchased at the tourist office allows you entry to the Pinacoteca Comunale, Casa Romana, and Galleria d'Arte Moderna. It's an excellent deal, since a combination ticket purchased directly from any one of these sights is €6.

MAIN ATTRACTIONS

❽ **Duomo.** The cathedral's 12th-century Romanesque facade received a
★ Renaissance face-lift with the addition of a loggia in a rosy pink stone. A stunning contrast in styles, the Duomo is one of the finest cathedrals in the region. The eight rose windows are especially dazzling in the late afternoon sun. Look under the largest rose window and you see two figures that appear to be holding up the structure; in the corners of the square surrounding the window, the four Evangelists are sculpted. Inside, the original tile floor dates from an earlier church that was destroyed by Frederick I (circa 1123–90).

Above the church's entrance is Bernini's bust of Pope Urban VIII (1568–1644), who had the rest of the church redecorated in 17th-century baroque; fortunately he didn't touch the 15th-century frescoes painted in the apse by Fra Filippo Lippi (circa 1406–69) between 1466–69. These immaculately restored masterpieces—the *Annunciation, Nativity,* and *Dormition*—tell the story of the life of the Virgin. The *Coronation of the Virgin,* adorning the half dome, is the literal and figurative high point. Portraits of Lippi and his assistants are on the right side of the central panel. The Florentine artist priest WHOSE

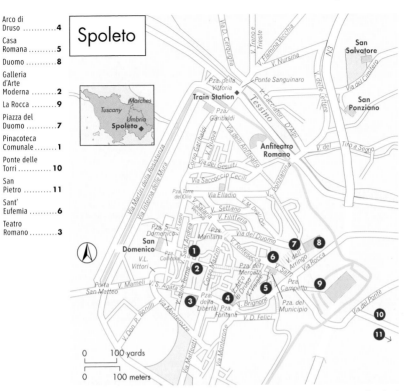

COLORS EXPRESSED GOD'S VOICE (the words inscribed on his tomb) died shortly after completing the work. His tomb, which you can see in the right transept (note the artist's brushes and tools), was designed by his son, Filippino Lippi (circa 1457–1504).

Another fresco cycle, including work by Pinturicchio, is in the Cappella Eroli, off the right aisle. Note the grotesques in the ornamentation, then very much in vogue with the rediscovery of ancient Roman paintings. The bounty of Umbria is displayed in vivid colors in the abundance of leaves, fruits, and vegetables that adorn the center seams of the cross vault. In the left nave, not far from the entrance, is the well-restored 12th-century crucifix by Alberto Sozio, the earliest known example of this kind of work, with a painting on parchment attached to a wood cross. To the right of the presbytery is the Cappella della Santissima Icona (Chapel of the Most Holy Icon), which contains a small Byzantine painting of a Madonna given to the town by Frederick Barbarossa as a peace offering in 1185, following his destruction of the cathedral and town three decades earlier. ⊠*Piazza del Duomo* ☎*0743/44307* ⊘*Mar.–Oct., daily 8:30–12:30 and 3:30–6; Nov.–Feb., daily 8:30–12:20 and 3:30–6.*

❾ **La Rocca.** Built in the mid-14th century for Cardinal Egidio Albornoz, this massive fortress served as a seat for the local pontifical governors,

A fresco by Fra Filippo Lippi in Spoleto's Duomo.

a tangible sign of the restoration of the Church's power in the area when the pope was ruling from Avignon. Several popes spent time here, and one of them, Alexander VI, in 1499 sent his capable teenage daughter Lucrezia Borgia (1480–1519) to serve as governor for three months. The Gubbio-born architect Gattapone (14th century) used the ruins of a Roman acropolis as a foundation and took materials from many Roman-era sites, including the Teatro Romano. La Rocca's plan is long and rectangular, with six towers and two grand courtyards, an upper loggia, and inside some grand reception rooms. In the largest tower, Torre Maestà, you can visit an apartment with some interesting frescoes. A small shuttle bus gives you that last boost up the hill from the ticket booth to the entrance of the fortress. If you phone in advance, you may be able to secure an English-speaking guide. ☒ *Via del Ponte* ☎ *0743/223055* ☒ *€6.50* ⊙ *Mid-Mar.–early June and mid-Sept.–Oct., weekdays 10–noon and 3–6:45, weekends 10–7; early June–mid-Sept., daily 10–7; Nov.–mid-Mar., weekdays 10–noon and 3–5, weekends 10–5.*

❼ Piazza del Duomo. The piazza is stage-set perfect, a harmonious square
★ enclosed on three sides by fine buildings, including the Duomo and the small Teatro Caio Melisso, one of the first theaters built in Italy. La Rocca stands behind and above it all. Try to arrive as the late afternoon sun catches the gold mosaics on the Duomo facade. In warm weather you can even dine outside on the square.

⑩ ★ Ponte delle Torri *(Bridge of the Towers).* Standing massive and graceful through the deep gorge that separates Spoleto from Monteluco, this 14th-century bridge is one of Umbria's most photographed monuments, and justifiably so. Built over the foundations of a Roman-era aqueduct, it soars 262 feet above the forested gorge—higher than the dome of St. Peter's in Rome. Sweeping views over the valley and a pleasant sense of vertigo make a walk across the bridge a must, particularly on a starry night. ⊠ *Via del Ponte.*

> **WORD OF MOUTH**
>
> "In Spoleto, be sure to take the walk up through the old city and on around the big castle at the top of the hill, so you can see, and walk along, the enormous ancient Roman aqueduct." –simpsonc510

ALSO WORTH SEEING

④ Arco di Druso *(Arch of Drusus).* Built in AD 23 by the Senate of Spoleto to honor the Roman general Drusus (circa 13 BC–AD 23), son of the emperor Tiberius, this arch once marked the entrance to the Foro Romano (Roman Forum). Excavations to the side reveal the original street level. ⊠ *Piazza del Mercato.*

⑤ Casa Romana. Spoleto became a Roman colony in the 3rd century BC, but the best excavated remains date from the 1st century AD. Excavated in the late 9th century, the Casa Romana was not a typical Roman residence. According to an inscription, it belonged to Vespasia Polla, the mother of Emperor Vespasian (one of the builders of the Coliseum and perhaps better known by the Romans for taxing them to install public toilets, later called "Vespasians"). The rooms, arranged around a large central atrium built over an *impluvium* (rain cistern), are decorated with black-and-white geometric mosaics. ⊠ *Palazzo del Municipio, Via Visiale 9* ☎ *0743/224656* 🖅 *€2.50, €6 combination ticket (includes Pinacoteca Comunale and Galleria d'Arte Moderna)* ☉ *Oct. 15–March 15, daily 10–6; March 16–Oct. 14, daily 10–8.*

② Galleria d'Arte Moderna. This five-room gallery contains the paintings and sculptures that from 1953 to 1968 won the Spoleto Prize, an honor given to significant works by renowned artists. Included are the original preparatory sketches for Alexander Calder's (1898–1976) *Teodelapio* (1962); the actual sculpture is near the train station. Don't miss one of Calder's portraits in wire, very different in style from his mobiles and heavier sculpture. Henry Moore is best known for his sculpture, but here you can also see some of his other mediums, including a collage. Other modern works are by contemporary Italian artists, such as Arnaldo Pomodoro, whose large golden globe sculpture, *Sphere Within a Sphere,* is on display in the Vatican. ⊠ *Palazzo Collicola* ☎ *0743/46434* 🖅 *€4, €6 combination ticket (includes Pinacoteca Comunale and Casa Romana)* ☉ *Oct. 16–Mar. 15, Wed.–Mon. 10:30–1 and 3:30–5:30; Mar. 16–Oct. 15, Wed.–Mon. 10:30–1 and 3:30–7.*

① Pinacoteca Comunale. This museum contains a small collection of works from the 12th to 18th centuries. Highlights include two 16th-century

8

frescoes by a local artist known as Lo Spagna, which were detached from La Rocca. ⊠*Palazzo Spada, Via delle Terme* ☎*0743/43722* 🖮*€3, €6 combination ticket(includes Casa Romana and Galleria d'Arte Moderna)* ⊙ *Wed.–Mon. 3:30–7.*

⓫ San Pietro. A walk to the church of San Pietro, at the foot of Monteluco, is a must. The dramas of life and death, and of good and evil, are the real attractions here, and are played out on the facade of this church that was rebuilt in the 13th century over earlier Christian, Roman, and Umbri holy sites. The carvings on the facade are among the best Romanesque carvings in the region, telling their story with simplicity and directness. Beneath the tympanum is a blank square that presumably once held a mosaic, flanked by reliefs of Saint Peter and Saint Andrew. Paired reliefs in the panels around the doors have peacocks mounted above allegories about work and of eternal life. The fates of two dying men, the just and the sinner, were sculpted on the church wall: the former being saved by Saint Peter, with the devil held at bay; the latter has the scales of justice tipped toward the devil and is abandoned by the Archangel Michael to a pair of demons. A man's struggle with a lion suggests that this is one he might not easily walk away from. The interior of the church can be visited, but the showstopper is the exterior, usually illuminated at night. ⊠*Strada di Monteluco* ✛ *1 km (½ mi) south of Spoleto* ☎*0743/44882* 🖮*Free* ⊙ *Daily 9–6:30.*

❻ Sant'Eufemia. In the courtyard of the archbishop's palace with a view of the Duomo over the back wall, this austere ancient church dates from the 12th century. Built on the site of a Roman-era *insula* (city block), the plain Romanesque interior has a Cosmati mosaic altar and frescoes on the pillars. Above the nave is a gallery where female worshippers were once required to sit—one of the few of its kind in this part of Italy. Admission to the church includes a visit to the **Museo Diocesano d'Arte Sacra,** which has a bronze bust by Bernini of Barberini Pope Urban VIII, who had been Bishop of Spoleto (1608–17) and donated this to the town in 1644. Have a look at some of the medieval painted wooden sculptures: a 14th-century Saint Cristina in her red dress or the 15th-century Saint Andrew draped in gold holding the church. The triptych of the Annunciation shows a peacock (once associated with the goddess Juno) on the roof above Mary. ⊠*Via Aurelia Saffi 13, between Piazza del Duomo and Piazza del Mercato* ☎*0743/23101* 🖮*€3* ⊙ *Oct.–Mar., Wed.–Sat. 10–1 and 3–5:30, Sun. 11–5; Apr.–Sept., weekdays10–6, weekends 10–6.*

❸ Teatro Romano. The Romans who had colonized the city in 241 BC, constructed this small theater in the 1st century AD; for centuries afterward it was used as a quarry for building materials. The most intact portion is the hallway that passes under the *cavea* (stands). The rest was heavily restored in the early 1950s and serves as a venue for Spoleto's Festival dei Due Mondi. The theater was the site of a gruesome episode in Spoleto's history: during the medieval struggle between Guelph (papal) and Ghibelline (imperial) forces, Spoleto took the side of the Holy Roman Emperor. Afterward, 400 Guelph supporters were massacred in the theater, their bodies burned in an enormous pyre. In the end, the Guelphs were triumphant, and Spoleto was incorporated into the states of the Church in 1354. Through a door in the west portico of the adjoining building is the **Museo Archeologico,** with assorted artifacts found in excavations primarily around Spoleto and Norcia. The collection contains Bronze Age and Iron Age artifacts from Umbrian and pre-Roman eras. Another section contains black-glaze vases from the Hellenistic period excavated from the necropolis of Saint Scolastica in Norcia. The highlight is the stone tablet inscribed on both sides with the Lex Spoletina (Spoleto Law). Dating from 315 BC, this legal document prohibited the desecration of the woods on the slopes of nearby Monteluco. ⊠ *Via Sant'Agata 18* ☎ *0743/223277* 🖅 *€4* ⊙ *Daily 8:30–7:30.*

OFF THE BEATEN PATH

San Salvatore. The church and cemetery of San Salvatore seem very much forgotten, ensconced in solitude and cypress trees on a peaceful hillside with the motorway rumbling below. One of the oldest churches in the world, it was built in the 4th century, largely of Roman-era materials. The highlight is the facade, with three exquisite marble doorways and windows, one of the earliest and best-preserved in Umbria; it dates from a restoration in the 9th century and has hardly been touched since. Inside is a 9th-century cross studded with gems. ⊠ *Via della Basilica di San Salvatore, off Via Flaminia* ⊙ *Nov.–Feb., daily 7–5; Mar., Apr., Sept., and Oct., daily 7–6; May–Aug., daily 7–7.*

WHERE TO EAT

Restaurants in Spoleto are generally of much better quality than those in Assisi. Local truffles are served with abandon in season, and are shipped all over the country. Dishes like *stringozzi alla spoletina* (with tomatoes, garlic, and red-pepper flakes) and the delicious *crescionda* (a spongy dessert, with a base of crushed almond cookies, eggs, milk, and bittersweet chocolate) stay closer to home. The tangy mix of wild greens that make up *insalata di campo* might include a seasonal assortment of dandelion leaves, wild arugula, fennel, borage, and sometimes edible flowers.

Aside from the many midsize hotels and small, family-run inns, Spoleto has *agriturismo* accommodations that range from the rustic to the downright luxurious. The **Spoleto tourism office** (⊠ *Piazza della Libertà 7* ☎ *0743/238920*) can advise you on different agriturismo options.

$$–$$$ ✕ **Apollinare.** Low wooden ceilings and flickering candlelight make this monastery from the 10th and 11th centuries Spoleto's most romantic spot. The kitchen serves sophisticated, innovative variations on local dishes. Sauces of cherry tomatoes, mint, and a touch of red pepper, or of porcini mushrooms, top the long, slender strangozzi. The *caramella* (light puff pastry cylinders filled with local cheese and served with a creamy Parmesan sauce) is popular. In warm weather you can dine under a canopy on the piazza across from the archaeological museum. ⊠ *Via Sant'Agata 14* ☎ *0743/223256* ▭ *AE, D, MC, V* ⊙ *Closed Tues.*

$$–$$$ ✕ **Il Pentagramma.** This stable-turned-restaurant has terra-cotta floors, stone walls, and a wood-burning oven. Its fresh local dishes change seasonally. The farro soup has a new twist here: it is pureed and served

8

CLOSE UP

Truffle Talk

More truffles are found in Umbria than anywhere else in Italy. The primary truffle areas are around Spoleto (signs warning against unlicensed truffle hunting are posted at the base of the Ponte delle Torri) and the hills around the tiny town of Norcia, which holds a truffle festival every February. Even though truffles grow locally, the rare delicacy can cost a small fortune—up to $200 for a quarter pound. In November 2004 a truffle that weighed just over two pounds brought in over $50,000 at the annual truffle auction, the highest price ever paid. Fortunately, the truffles that you eat will be more reasonable (and besides, a little goes a long way in most dishes). At the 2004 truffle festival in Valtopina (north of Assisi), truffles the size of cherries went for €8 to €12.

At such a price, there is great competition among the nearly 10,000 registered truffle hunters in the province, who use specially trained dogs to sniff them out among the roots of several trees, including oak and ilex. Although there have been incidents of inferior varieties being imported from China, you can be reasonably assured that the truffle shaved onto your pasta has been unearthed locally.

The kind of truffle you taste will depend on the season. In addition to the famous black and white truffles, there are at least seven or eight other local species. The mild summer truffle, called *scorzone estivo* (black outside and beige inside), is in season from May through December. The *scorzone autunnale* (smooth in appearance with a burnt brown color and visible veins inside) is picked from the beginning of October to the end of December. These two varieties are used especially for sauces. Norcia and Spoleto are ideal hunting territory for the *tartuffo nero* (reddish-black interior and fine white veins), winter's precious black truffle, prized for its extravagant flavor; it can grow to the size of an apple. Valtopina and Gubbio are stomping grounds for the white truffle, *tartuffo bianco*, which is shaved into omelets or over pasta, pounded into sauces, chopped and mixed with oil, or used to perfume meat.

Local residents have perfected freezing, drying, or preserving truffles in oil, so you can enjoy this delectable treat any time of year. Don't pass up the opportunity! The intense aroma of a dish perfumed with truffles is unmistakable and the flavor memorable.

inside a bread "bowl." Pastas might include *tortelli ai carciofi e noci* (artichoke-filled pasta with a hazelnut sauce) or, in summer, homemade fettucini served with sauce made from fresh vegetables and saffron. For your main course, you might try lamb in a truffle sauce. The stuffed zucchini flowers are lighter than usual, because they are baked (not fried) and filled with ricotta. The restaurant is off the Piazza della Libertà. ⊠ *Via Martani 4* ☎*0743/223141* ▤*DC, MC, V* ⊗*Closed Mon. and for about 2 wks after Christmas. No dinner Sun.*

$$–$$$ ✕**Il Tartufo.** As the name indicates, dishes prepared with truffles are the specialty here—don't miss the *risotto al tartufo*. But there are also dishes not perfumed with this expensive delicacy. Incorporating the ruins of a Roman villa, the restaurant's decor is rustic on the ground floor and more modern upstairs. In summer, tables appear outdoors and the traditional fare is spiced up to appeal to the cosmopolitan

crowd attending (or performing in) the Festival dei Due Mondi. ✉ *Piazza Garibaldi 24* ☎*0743/40236* ⚭*Reservations essential* ▤*AE, DC, MC, V* ✆*Closed Mon. and last 2 wks in July. No dinner Sun.*

$$–$$$ ✕**Ristorante Panciolle.** In the heart of Spoleto's medieval quarter, this
★ restaurant has one of the most appealing settings you could wish for: a small garden filled with lemon trees. Dishes change throughout the year, and may include pastas served with asparagus or mushrooms, as well as grilled meats. More expensive dishes prepared with fresh truffles are also available in season. ✉ *Via Duomo 3/5* ☎*0743/221241* ⚭*Reservations essential* ▤*DC, MC, V* ✆*Closed Wed.*

$–$$ ✕**Osteria del Trivio.** At this friendly trattoria everything is made on the premises. The menu changes daily, depending on what's in season. Dishes might include stuffed artichokes, pasta with local mushrooms, or chicken with artichokes. For dessert, try the homemade biscotti, made for dunking in sweet wine. There is a printed menu, but the owner can explain the dishes in a number of languages. A complete meal from appetizer to dessert with house wine is likely to cost no more than €25. ✉ *Via del Trivio 16* ☎*0743/44349* ▤*AE, DC, MC, V* ✆*Closed Tues.*

WHERE TO STAY

$$–$$$ 🏨**Cavaliere Palace Hotel.** An arched passageway off one of the city's
★ busy shopping streets leads to an elegant world through a quiet courtyard. Built in the 17th century for an influential cardinal, the rooms, particularly those on the second floor, retain their sumptuous frescoed ceilings; care has been taken to retain a sense of old-world comfort throughout. In warm weather enjoy breakfast on the terrace or in the peaceful garden at the back of the hotel. **Pros:** Quiet elegance, central position. **Cons:** Finding parking can be a problem, crowded in summer. ✉*Corso Garibaldi 49, 06049* ☎*0743/220350* ⊕*www.cavalierehotels. com* ⤶*29 rooms, 2 suites* ⚭*In-room: safe, refrigerator. In-hotel: restaurant, bar* ▤*AE, DC, MC, V* ✦*BP.*

8

$$ 🏨**Hotel dei Duchi.** This well-run hotel is a favorite among performers in the festival. It's in the center of town, near the Roman amphitheater. The spacious rooms, some looking out onto the gardens, have simple modern furniture. **Pros:** Central location, friendly staff. **Cons:** Unattractive building, parking can be difficult in summer months. ✉*Viale Matteotti 4, 06049* ☎*0743/44541* ⊕*www.hoteldeiduchi.com* ⤶*47 rooms, 2 suites* ⚭*In-hotel: restaurant, bar, parking (no fee), some pets allowed* ▤*AE, DC, MC, V* ✦*BP.*

$$ 🏨**Hotel Gattapone.** Lucky Gattapone—this small, secluded hotel sits on
★ the edge of the gorge separating the Rocca from Monteluco, overlooking the Ponte delle Torri. Wake up to wonderful views of the ancient bridge and the wooded slopes of Monteluco, then go for a morning walk around the Via del Ponte, which circles the base of La Rocca. Interiors are done in a modern style that's understated and tasteful, with beautiful wooden floors and comfortable leather furnishings. **Pros:** Lovely views, near many of the sights. **Cons:** Long walk to the shopping area, can feel a little crowded. ✉ *Via del Ponte 6, 06049*

☎0743/223447 ⊕*www.hotelgattapone.it* ↗*8 rooms, 8 suites* ♿*In-room: safe, refrigerator. In-hotel: bar, laundry service, parking (no fee)* ⊟*AE, DC, MC, V* ⊙|*BP.*

$$ 🏨 **Hotel San Luca.** The elegant San Luca is one of Spoleto's finest hotels,

Fodor's Choice   thanks to its commendable attention to detail, such as the hand-painted

★   friezes that decorate the walls of the spacious guest rooms and the generous selection of up-to-date magazines for your reading pleasure. The service is very gracious, and the prices are surprisingly modest. Enjoy an ample breakfast buffet, including homemade cakes, served in a cheerful room facing the central courtyard. You can sip afternoon tea in oversize armchairs by the fireplace, or take a walk in the hotel's sweet-smelling rose garden. The staff will give you route maps or help you book a guided bicycle tour. **Pros:** Very helpful staff, peaceful location. **Cons:** Outside the town center, a long walk to the main sights. ⊠*Via Interna delle Mura 19, 06049* ☎*0743/223399* ⊕*www.hotelsanluca.com* ↗*33 rooms, 2 suites* ♿*In-room: safe, refrigerator, ethernet. In-hotel: restaurant, laundry service, public Internet, parking (fee)* ⊟*AE, DC, MC, V* ⊙|*BP.*

$–$$ 🏨 **Hotel Clitunno.** A renovated 18th-century building in the center of town houses this pleasant hotel. Cozy guest rooms and intimate public rooms, some with timbered ceilings, have the sense of a traditional Umbrian home—albeit one with a good restaurant. The staff is glad to light the fireplace in Room 212 in advance of winter arrivals. Upper-floor rooms look over Spoleto's rooftops. The "older style" rooms, which have wood ceilings, iron beds, and nicer textiles, are more attractive. **Pros:** Friendly staff, good restaurant. **Cons:** Difficult to find a parking space, some small rooms. ⊠*Piazza Sordini 6, 06049* ☎*0743/223340* ⊕*www.hotelclitunno.com* ↗*45 rooms* ♿*In-hotel: restaurant, bar*⊟*AE, DC, MC, V* ⊙|*BP.*

$ 🏨 **Aurora.** This simple little hotel, facing Piazza della Libertà, is run by the owners of the downstairs Apollinare restaurant. The rooms are basic and clean. **Pros:** Cozy atmosphere, central location. **Cons:** Very basic rooms. ⊠*Via Apollinare 3, 06049* ☎*0743/220315* ⊕*www.hotelauroraspoleto.it* ↗*22 rooms* ♿*In-room: refrigerator. In-hotel: restaurant, bar* ⊟*AE, DC, MC, V* ⊙|*BP.*

$ 🏨 **Azienda Agrituristica Bartoli.** About 13 km (8 mi) southeast of Spoleto, this agriturismo offers simple rooms with private baths in a converted farmhouse. There is also an apartment that sleeps six. Rooms look out onto the green valleys below Monte di Patrico. Rent by the night or by the week, with half or full board. There are ample hiking trails in the area, and horses are available with or without guides. Ask about truffle hunting in fall or winter. **Pros:** Unforgettable views, great hiking. **Cons:** Very basic rooms, need a car to get around. ⊠*Località Patrico, 06049* ☎*0743/220058* ⊕*www.agriturismobartoli.it* ↗*11 rooms* ♿*In-room: no a/c, no TV* ⊟*No credit cards* ⊙|*MAP.*

THE ARTS

FodorsChoice
★

In 1958, composer Gian Carlo Menotti chose Spoleto for the first **Festival dei Due Mondi** (*Festival of Two Worlds* ✉*Piazza Duomo 8* ☎*0743/220320 or 800/565600* ⊕*www.spoletofestival.it*), a gathering of artists, performers, and musicians intended to bring together the "new" and "old" worlds of America and Europe. (A corresponding festival in South Carolina is no longer connected to this festival.) The annual event, held in late June to early July, is one of the most important cultural happenings in Europe, attracting big names in all branches of the arts, particularly music, opera, and theater. With so much activity, the small town gives itself over entirely to the festival—events are staged in every possible venue, from church cloisters to massive theaters. The closing concert, always free, takes place on the Piazza del Duomo.

You will notice the changes brought by the festival, as Spoleto has become one of the more cosmopolitan towns in the region. Undoubtedly you will see traces of past festivals: old promotional posters hung in virtually all the shops and hotels, and modern sculptures left to the city in its art gallery and on permanent display outdoors. These include Alexander Calder's enormous bronze *Teodelapio* sculpture in front of the train station, Anna Mahler's *Sitting* in Piazza della Signoria, and *Geodesic Dome* by Buckminster Fuller (1895–1983) in the Parco della Passeggiata. Tickets for all performances should be ordered in advance. Full program information is available beginning in February.

OUTDOOR ACTIVITIES & SPORTS

8

BIKING

The pretty countryside around Spoleto is well suited for bicycling, with terrain that ranges from flat country roads to steep mountain paths. The **Spoleto Tourist Office** (✉*Piazza della Libertà 7* ☎*0743/238920* ⊕*www.spoleto.umbria2000.it*) publishes an excellent pamphlet, *In Bicicletta nello Spoletino* (*Bicycling Around the Spoleto Area*), which details routes, distances, and levels of difficulty in Italian and English. You can get the pamphlet directly from the tourist office or from some hotels and bike shops. Bicycles can be rented at **Scocchetti Cicli** (✉*Via Marconi 82* ☎*0743/44728*). The shop is open Monday through Saturday 9–1 and 3:30–8. Call ahead to reserve.

HIKING

Pick up a map of local roads and trails from the **Spoleto Tourist Office** (✉*Piazza della Libertà 7* ☎*0743/238920* ⊕*www.spoleto.umbria2000.it*) and head out for a stroll in the country or a hike up the mountainside. Trails on **Monteluco**, a hill just across the Ponte delle Torri, wind steeply through the thick Bosco Sacro (Sacred Woods), passing caves and hermitages abandoned by spiritual seekers who have lived here since the time of Saint Francis.

HORSEBACK RIDING

Horses can be rented with English-speaking guides at the **Centro Ippico La Somma** (⊠ *Frazione Aiacugigli-Montebibico* ✛ *about 15 km [9 mi] south of Spoleto* ☎ *0743/54370* ⊕ *www.lasomma.it*), open daily 9:30–noon and 3:30–7.

SHOPPING

Spoleto's main shopping street begins as **Via Fontesecca** (near Piazza del Mercato) and continues down the hill, changing names several times. **Aracne** (⊠ *Vicolo Primo di Corso Mazzini 2* ☎*0743/46085*) specializes in fine lace and embroidery. **Mobilia** (⊠ *Via Filitteria 3* ☎*0743/45720*) is one of Spoleto's many antiques shops.

The second Sunday of every month sees the **Mercato delle Brisciole,** with antiques and crafts vendors taking over the streets of Spoleto's historic center. Down the road in Pissignano, the region's best **antiques fair** is held the first Sunday of each month.

EN ROUTE The road east from Spoleto (S395) goes 19 km (12 mi) to the Nera River, then turns north and becomes S209. As you climb higher, the olive groves that produce Spoleto's fine oil give way to chestnut trees and forests populated by wolves, porcupines, and owls. When you reach Cerreto di Spoleto, take the long way around to the S320, passing Triponzo, for the best views. Most minor roads are not in the best of shape, but they reward you with dramatic mountain scenery.

EAST OF SPOLETO

Spoleto is the obvious starting point for a visit to the eastern edges of Umbria, as few roads cut across the rugged mountainous terrain that quickly rises from the Valle Umbra. Roads narrow and the towns get smaller and farther apart as you break out off the well-traveled path between Assisi and Spoleto, but great rewards await. Spring brings milder weather with wildflowers at their finest, but truffle hunters should consider winter excursions. The main attractions are Norcia, a town known for black truffles and pork products, and for the road you take to get there, full of breathtaking views across unspoiled verdant mountain landscapes. To the east of Norcia, and extending into the Marches, is the Parco Nazionale dei Monti Sibillini, one of Italy's best nature reserves.

No less inviting is the Valnerina (Valley of the Nera River), which has its own protected nature area and stunning scenery. Lest any part of Italy be without an interesting church, the Abbazia di San Pietro della Valle sits like a gem amid the lush greenery of the valley.

NORCIA

48 km (31 mi) east of Spoleto, 99 km (62 mi) southeast of Perugia.

GETTING HERE

Norcia is a 1½-hour drive from Perugia. Follow the E45 highway toward Assisi and Cesena. Take the exit toward Assisi and Foligno, merge onto the SS75, then choose the Foligno Est exit. Merge onto the SS3 and take the exit toward Cascia/Norcia.

VISITOR INFORMATION

Norcia tourism office (⊠ *Via Solferino 22* ☎ *0743/828173* ⊕ *www.norcia.net*).

EXPLORING

A good day trip from Spoleto, Norcia is synonymous for most Italians with legendary sausages and prosciutto and the great tradition of butchers who have surgical precision with knives. (It's no coincidence that Norcia is also where one of Italy's first and most important schools for surgeons was founded.) In fact, from Rome to Rimini a *norcineria* is a place where sausages are made and sold, and a *norcino* is a pork butcher. (Under the circumstances, it is no wonder that the locals call themselves *nursiani*.) However, in recent years Norcia has produced fewer pigs, and Italians moan about imported pork. Other reasons to visit Norcia are the delicious cheeses, fine baked goods, and chocolate.

Norcia is the birthplace of Saint Benedict (San Benedetto), the founder of Christianity's first monastic order. The town is surrounded by stupendous, lush mountainous terrain, and one of the main reasons to visit Norcia is to enjoy the natural beauty or to go on a truffle hunt. The Sagra del Tartufo, the Black Truffle Festival, is usually held in late February.

The local sights are clustered around Piazza San Benedetto.

The 14th-century church of **San Benedetto** was built over the purported birthplace of the saint and his twin sister, Santa Scolastica. Both are represented in statues set into the facade. The remains of a Roman house are visible in the church crypt. Don't miss the fascinating set of nine medieval round stone vessels, once used to measure grain, that rest on a shelf under the portico on the Via Mazzini side. ⊠ *Piazza San Benedetto* ☎ *0743/817125* ▨ *Free* ☉ *Daily 9–12:30 and 3–6:30.*

Off to the side of San Benedetto, the **Duomo** bears the scars of repeated redecoration necessitated by frequent earthquakes over the centuries. ⊠ *Piazza San Benedetto.*

The superb **Castellina,** the sturdy papal palace, holds the **Museo Civico,** which offers more than the usual collection of local work. The della Robbia terra-cotta of the Madonna, a rare example in this region of the work of the masterful Florentine family, and a 13th-century *Deposition,* made up of several wooden statues, are worth the admission alone. Don't miss the Etruscan collection, acquired in 2002, that is displayed

8

on the ground floor; look for pottery with vivid geometric designs or the black-glaze pottery. ✉*Piazza San Benedetto* ☎*0743/817030* 💶€3 *museum, €4 with archaeological site* ⊙*Tues.–Sun. 10–1 and 4–6.*

SHOPPING

Pick up some cheese—or truffles, in season—at the **Boutique del Pecoraro** (✉*Via San Benedetto 7* ☎*0743/816453*). Local cheeses, salami, and truffle products are on plentiful, redolent display at **Norcineria Ercole Ulivucci** (✉*Via Mazzini 4* ☎*0743/816661*). It's closed Monday in even years, Tuesday in odd years. For cakes and pastries, head to the shop at **No. 13 Corso Sertorio** (☎*0744/816623*). As its name implies, **Norcineria Fratelli Ansuini** (✉*Via Anicia 105* ☎*0743/816643*), closed Tuesday, stocks a full range of the local pork products. Well worth a visit is **Tartufi Moscatelli** (✉*Corso Sertorio 42* ☎*0743/817388*), renowned for its truffles.

PARCO NAZIONALE DEI MONTI SIBILLINI

About 46 km (29 mi) east of Spoleto.

GETTING HERE

This is a vast park, with entrances from many different directions. Many visitors stay to the east in Norcia or to the west in Spoleto.

EXPLORING

Norcia lies within the boundaries of the Parco Nazionale dei Monti Sibillini, an unspoiled mountainous ridge that straddles the border between Umbria and the Marches. Southeast of Norcia is **San Pellegrino,** source of one of the country's most famous mineral waters. The main road that winds its way through the mountains, eventually crossing the border into Le Marche, passes through **Castelluccio,** a town known nationwide for its lentils and its spectacular fields of flowers in late spring. You're not here for the towns, though, but for the park, which, weather permitting, offers some of the country's best hiking. Ask about hiking to 2,173-meter (7,129-foot) Mt. Sibilla; it was on this mountain in ancient times that one of the famous prophetesses, or sibyls, for whom this park is named, lived in a cave. The maps issued by the Club Alpino Italiano (CAI), available at newsstands, are great for orienting yourself in the park. Note that the weather can change very quickly, one moment blue skies and the next a snowstorm. Unless you're used to these weather conditions, consider taking one of the many tours available.

The **Cooperativa Monte Patino** (✉*Casa del Parco Norcia, Via Solferino 22, Norcia* ☎*0743/817487* ⊕*www.montepatino.com*), open weekdays 9:30–1:30 and 3:30–6, offers guided tours in English, including excursions to villages and isolated churches and hiking in the Parco dei Sibillini. A full-day shopping tour focuses on visits to artisanal workshops and cheese and sausage producers.

If you prefer to travel without a guide, try the **Casa del Parco** (✉*Via Solferino 22, Norcia* ☎*0743/817090* ✉*Via Santa Caterina, Preci Alto*

Parco Nazionale dei Monti Sibillini.

☎0743/937000). Both offices, open daily 9:30–12:30 and 3–6, have free maps and brochures about the Umbrian side of the national park.

WHERE TO STAY

¢ ☖**Rifugio Perugia.** You won't have a private room in this *rifugio di montagna* (mountain refuge)—in fact, you'll have to share with three people and you'll likely be sleeping in a bunk bed. But if you enjoy the atmosphere of a cozy mountain retreat and of getting together over a last bottle of wine, do join in (and get the seat near the guy with the guitar). The restaurant is a modest affair, with plain wooden furniture. You can get simple, filling meals, ideal for refueling after a day hiking. The place is about 22 km (14 mi) southeast of Norcia. **Pros:** Mixing with other hikers, good budget option. **Cons:** Very basic facilities, dorm-style rooms. ✉*Località Canapine, 62039* ☎*0743/823019 or 368/646189* ✎*rifugioperugia@libero.it* ⇱*35 beds* ⚿*In-room: no a/c, no phone, no TV. In-hotel: restaurant, no elevator* ▭*MC, V* ☾*Closed Nov.–Easter.*

ABBAZIA DI SAN PIETRO IN VALLE

35 km (22 mi) southeast of Spoleto, 44 km (27 mi) southwest of Norcia.

GETTING HERE

The Abbazia di San Pietro in Valle is a 1½-hour drive from Perugia. Follow the E45 highway toward Assisi and Cesena, taking the exit toward Assisi and Foligno. Merge onto the SS75, then take the Foligno Est exit. Merge onto the SS3 and take the exit toward Cascia/Norcia. Merge onto the SS685, then the SS209.

EXPLORING

It's hard to believe that this remote building once served as one of the region's centers of Christianity, but the remnants of one of the fortresses that protected it, still visible in the distance, testify to its earlier importance. Column capitals in the apse and a 1st-century BC altar near the back door suggest that the 8th-century abbey was built over the ruins of a Roman temple. After it was sacked by the Saracens, Otto III began the restoration of the abbey in 996, which was completed by his successor, Henry II. The bell tower was built in the second half of the 11th century, the graceful cloister was added in the 12th century, and late in the 12th century frescoes were painted on the walls of the nave. Restored in 1995, the frescoes are considered important examples of Romanesque painting. The unknown artist who painted them preceded Giotto in trying to break away from the Byzantine style through realistic and vivid details. The main altar is a rare example of 8th-century Lombard bas-relief, which includes representations of the lord who commissioned the piece and the artist himself, called Ursus. To the right is a 3rd-century BC Roman sarcophagus containing the remains of Faroald II of Spoleto, the duke who built the abbey after having a vision of Saint Peter. If the abbey is closed, ring at the custodian's house, about 1 km (½ mi) south. Note that the southern road going up to the abbey is easier to navigate than the northern road, which is unpaved. ⊠*SS209* ✛ *3 km (2 mi) from Ferentillo* ☎*0744/780316* ✉*Donations accepted* ☉*Oct.–Apr., daily 10:15–12:30 and 2–5:30; May–Sept., daily 9–1 and 2–5:30.*

OFF THE BEATEN PATH

Down at the bottom of the Valmarino (SS209) is the town of Ferentillo, and next to it, the Nera River. Cross a little one-lane ancient bridge over the river and take a short walk up the hill to **Le Mummie di Ferentillo** *(The Mummies of Ferentillo)*, on the bottom level of the church of Saint Stefano. The mummies are the bodies of about 30 people who died between 1500 and 1871. They were buried in this cemetery and mummified by a rare natural occurrence—not by elaborate preparation—wherein a microfungus attacked the corpses, preserving the skin and some other bits. The odd mix of dead companions includes a lawyer who was punched to death, his killer on the other side of the room, and some Chinese pilgrims. This unlikely group is united in death in a single room, with lots of skulls in the background. ⊠*Chiesa di Santo Stefano a Precetto* ☎*0743/54395* ✉*€2.60* ☉*Nov.–Feb., daily 10–12:30 and*

2:30–5; Mar. and Oct., daily 9–12:30 and 2:30–6, Apr.–Sept., daily 9–12:30 and 2:30–7:30.

WHERE TO EAT

$$–$$$ ✕**Piermarini.** In the tiny town of Ferentillo, 4 km (2½ mi) south of the Abbazia di San Pietro in Valle, is the place to come for truffles. No-nonsense dishes include a truffle omelet, which allows the truffles to be enjoyed without competing flavors. Second courses include grilled kid, lamb, and roasted pork. There is a garden for outside dining in good weather. The owners also organize cookery courses. The eatery is 18½ km (11 mi) northeast of Terni, 28 km (19 mi) southeast of Spoleto. ⊠ *Via Ancaiano 23, Ferentillo* ☎*0744/780714* ▤*AE, D, MC, V* ⊘ *Closed Mon. and 1 wk in Jan.*

SOUTHWEST UMBRIA

It's a short drive from Spoleto to Terni, but tempting diversions along the way include one of central Italy's finest abbeys and the refreshing Lake Piediluco. Hold your breath while river rafting at the foot of the tallest falls in Europe, and then recover while driving through olive groves to sleepy Amelia—Umbria's oldest town—before stepping into the medieval past of Todi. Finish off your visit to the province in Orvieto, with its unforgettable Duomo and wine that has pleased locals for 3,000 years.

TERNI

33 km (21 mi) southwest of Spoleto, 70 km (45 mi) southeast of Orvieto.

GETTING HERE

From Perugia, take the E45 highway toward Rome. Exit at Terni Ouest. The drive will take about one hour. There are also regular trains from Perugia.

VISITOR INFORMATION

Terni tourism office (⊠ *Viale C. Battisti 7a* ☎*0744/423047* ⊕*www.terni.umbria2000.it*).

EXPLORING

Although a convenient jumping-off point for Lake Piediluco and the Marmore Falls, the attractions of Terni are less impressive, as the town was heavily bombed by the Allies in World War II. A church on the south side of town marks the burial place of Saint Valentine, who was born here about ad 175.

The local **Pinacoteca Comunale** has Benozzo Gozzoli's *The Marriage of St. Catherine,* as well as several noteworthy modern paintings. ⊠ *Via del Teatro Romano 13* ☎*0744/59421* ▤*€4.40* ⊘*Tues.–Sun. 10–1 and 4–7.*

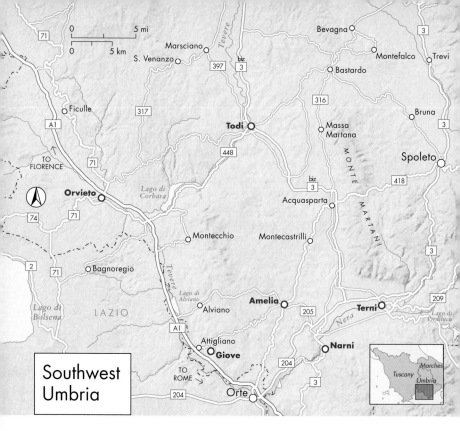

Just a few blocks from the Pinacoteca is the round church of **San Salvatore.** It is thought to have been a Roman temple, on account of its dome and oculus, a circular hole in the dome meant to represent the all-seeing eye of heaven. ⊠ *Via del Teatro Romano* ☎ *No phone* ▧ *Free* ⊙ *Daily 8:30–noon and 4–7.*

South of town, the basilica **San Valentino** is dedicated to the patron saint of lovers, of married couples, and of Terni. Valentine was beheaded on February 14, 273, in Rome—away from Terni to avoid a popular uprising. In 313 Constantine ordered a basilica constructed on the site of Valentine's tomb, later destroyed by the Goths. The present basilica was constructed from 1605 to 1618. A legend, which this church notes is "Anglo-Saxon in origin," is that Valentine would give lovers who visited him a flower from his garden—a symbol of the love that would consecrate their future marriage. ⊠ *Via Papa Zacaria 12* ☎ *0744/274508* ▧ *Free* ⊙ *Daily 8:30–noon and 4–7.*

**OFF THE
BEATEN
PATH**

Cascata delle Marmore. The road east of Terni (SS Valnerina) leads 10 km (6 mi) to the waterfalls at Marmore, which, at 541 feet, are the highest in Europe. A canal was dug by the Romans in the 3rd century BC to prevent flooding in the nearby agricultural plains. Nowadays the waters are often diverted to provide hydroelectric power for Terni, reducing the roaring falls to an unimpressive trickle, so check with the information office at the falls or with Terni's tourist office before heading here. On summer evenings, when the falls are in full spate, the cascading water is floodlit to striking effect. This is a good place for hiking, except in December and January, when most trails may be closed. ⊠*SP79* ⊹ *3 km (2 mi) east of Terni* ☎*0744/62982* ✉*€4* ⊙ *May, weekends noon–1 and 4–5; June–Aug., daily 11 AM–10 PM; mid-Mar.–Apr. and Sept., weekends noon–9; Jan.–mid-Mar., weekends noon–4.*

Lago di Piediluco. The road east from Terni (SS Valnerina) continues to Lake Piediluco, a nice spot to get your feet wet. The lake is the prettiest in the region, surrounded by steep, forested hillsides. There are facilities for boat and canoe rentals, as well as waterskiing and sailing, and a selection of bars offering snacks after your exertions.

OUTDOOR ACTIVITIES & SPORTS

Rapids near the Cascata delle Marmore make for good water rafting for all skill levels; inquire at the **Centro Rafting Le Marmore** (⊠*Belvedere Inferiore* ☎*0330/753420*), open daily from mid-March to October. A descent, with a brief class beforehand, takes about two hours.

NARNI

13 km (8 mi) southwest of Terni, 46 km (29 mi) southeast of Orvieto.

GETTING HERE

From Perugia, take the E45 highway toward Rome. Merge onto the SS675, then take the exit to San Gemini and follow signs for Narni Scalo. The drive takes around 1½ hours. There are also regular trains from Perugia.

VISITOR INFORMATION

Narni tourism office (⊠*Piazza del Popolo 18* ☎*0744/715362* ⊕*www.terni.umbria2000.it*).

EXPLORING

Once a bustling and important town at a major crossroads on the Via Flaminia, Narni is now a quiet backwater with only the occasional tourist invading its hilltop streets. Modern development is kept out of sight in the new town of Narni Scalo, below. This means that you will find the older neighborhood safely preserved behind, and in the case of Narni's subterranean Roman ruins, beneath, the town's sturdy walls.

You can take a unique tour of Narni's underground **Roman aqueduct—** the only one open to the public in all of Italy—but it's not for the claustrophobic. Contact Narni Sotterranea at least one week ahead to book a visit. ⊠*Narni Sotterranea, Via San Bernardo 12* ☎*0744/ 722292* ⊕*www.narnisotterranea.it* ✉*€15* ⊙ *Nov.–Mar., Sun. 11–1 and 3–5; Apr.–Oct., Sat. at 3 and at 6, Sun. 10–1 and 3–6; by appointment weekdays for groups.*

8

The **Duomo** originally had three aisles, but a fourth was added to the right of the church to incorporate a 6th-century shrine of San Giovenale, the patron saint of the town. As a result, the Via Flaminia passes through the church. A 9th-century mosaic over the shrine is partially visible. ⊠ *Piazza Cavour* ☎ *0744/722610* ⊕ *Free* ⊙ *Daily 8:30–1 and 3–7.*

Piazza Garibaldi, the town's main square, is built over the **Lacus**, a large late-medieval cistern with vaulting and remains of the Roman-era stone pavement. ⊠ *Below Piazza Garibaldi.*

The former **Monastero di San Domenico** is now the town library. Around the back, underneath the monastery, an entrance leads to a Romanesque church with frescoes from the 13th to 15th centuries. In the adjacent remains of a Roman building with a cistern is a cell used during the Inquisition. On its walls are graffiti left by prisoners. ⊠ *Via Mazzini* ☎ *0744/747203* ⊕ *Free* ⊙ *Weekdays 9–noon.*

The town's big artistic attraction is an altarpiece by Domenico Ghirlandaio (1449–94), *The Coronation of the Virgin,* in the Sala del Consiglio of the **Palazzo Comunale.** Opposite the altarpiece is a loggia by Gattapone. ⊠ *Piazza dei Priori* ☎ *0744/715362* ⊕ *Free* ⊙ *Daily 9–1 and 3–5.*

For centuries Narni was protected from invasion by its lofty perch above the Nera River and by its imposing **Rocca** *(fortress)* built by Cardinal Albornoz in the 14th century. Little now remains of the interior decoration of the castle, but the architecture and the views make the walk uphill worthwhile. ⊠ *Via del Monte* ☎ *0744/715362* ⊕ *Free* ⊙ *Apr.–Sept., Fri.–Sun. 10–7; Oct.–Mar., call ahead for hrs.*

The 12th-century church of **Santa Maria Impensole** is well worth a visit for its finely carved facade. Under the church, excavations have revealed an 8th-century church built over a Roman temple that was converted into a crypt for the church above. There are also two Roman cisterns, one of them in especially good condition. ⊠ *Via Mazzini* ☎ *0744/220097* ⊙ *Daily 9–noon and 4:30–6.*

WHERE TO EAT

$$–$$$ ✗ **Il Cavallino.** Run by the third generation of the Bussetti family, this trattoria is south of Narni on the Via Flaminia. The most dependable menu selections are the grilled meats. Rabbit roasted with rosemary and sage and juicy grilled T-bone steaks are house favorites; in the winter, phone ahead to request the wild pigeon. The wine has a limited selection of dependable local varieties. ⊠ *Via Flaminia Romana 220* ⊕ *3 km (2 mi) south of center* ☎ *0744/761020* ⊟ *AE, DC, MC, V* ⊙ *Closed Tues. and Dec. 20–26.*

AMELIA

50 km (31 mi) southeast of Orvieto.

GETTING HERE

From Perugia, take the E45 highway toward Rome. Merge onto the SS675, then take the exit to Amelia. The drive takes around 1½ hours. The nearest train station is Narni, with buses shuttling passengers to Amelia.

VISITOR INFORMATION

Amelia tourism office (⊠ *Via Orvieto 1* ☎*0744/981453* ⊕*www.terni.umbria2000.it*).

EXPLORING

Amelia has the distinction of being the oldest town in the region, with archaeological evidence from as far back as 1100 BC.

The main attraction, the bulky **town walls** that still surround it, shows that the Umbri knew a thing or two about fortifications—they are more than 20 feet thick at some points.

Admire the town walls from a path that leads from Porta Romana around the perimeter of the town, or walk up the main road to the brick **Duomo,** at the top of the town. The facade is made of travertine and pink terra-cotta. The interior, modified in the 19th century, is decorated with two Turkish flags won in the Battle of Lepanto. Although it now serves as the Duomo's bell tower, the unusual **Torre Civica** (circa 1050) was built before the church. Its 12 sides were thought originally to represent the signs of the zodiac, but were later designated as the Twelve Apostles. If the proportion speaks to you, perhaps it's because the height of the tower equals the sum of the widths of the sides. There are fine views from the top of the hill that look over vineyards and olive groves. ⊠*Piazza del Duomo* ☎*0744/981453* ☑*Free* ⊙*Daily 10–1 and 4–7.*

Don't miss **Museo Archeologico di Amelia,** one of Umbria's largest archaeological museums. A rare full-length bronze statue of Germanicus, brother of Claudius and father of Caligula, is the prize here. You can get another look at him from the floor above. The displays are attractive, but the descriptions are in Italian only. (English translations are in the works.) ⊠*Piazza Augusto Vera* ☎*0744/978120* ☑*€5* ⊙*Oct.–Mar., Fri.–Sun. 10:30–1 and 3:30–6; Apr.–Aug., Tues.–Sun. 10:30–1, 4:30–6:30.*

EN ROUTE The road northwest of Amelia (S205) passes first through **Lugnano in Teverina**, with its important Collegiata di Santa Maria Assunta. The facade is the region's best piece of Romanesque architecture. The interior is mostly undecorated, apart from a handsome Cosmati mosaic floor, which has complex geometric patterns. The road continues through Baschi, westward (13 km [8 mi]) toward Orvieto, and east (28 km [17 mi]) to Todi.

GIOVE

12½ km (8 mi) southwest of Amelia, 9½ km (6 mi) south of Lugnano in Teverina, 24 km (15 mi) west of Terni.

GETTING HERE

From Perugia, follow the E45 highway toward Rome. Merge onto the SS675, then take the exit to Amelia. Merge onto the SP28, then the SS205. Exit onto the SP31, which leads to Giove. The drive takes around 1½ hours. Trains on the Perugia–Terni line stop at the Narni–Amelia station.

EXPLORING

The little town of Giove was named for the Roman god Jupiter and for a famous temple in his honor that once stood here. Largo Macalle, next to the castle, has a beautiful view of the valley below, especially at sunset as you are looking west. Just outside the town is a convent with a Madonna by Perugino. The road continues to **Attigliano**, where the modern church of San Lorenzo the Martyr gives an idea of how all the churches in the region might look had they been built in the previous century.

Giove has an interesting 16th-century **Palazzo Ducale**, with 365 windows—one for each day of the year—and a peculiar spiral ramp large enough to allow horse-driven carts to enter the building through the front door and reach the upper floors. The castle is closed to the public. ⊠*Piazza XXIV Maggio.*

NEED A BREAK? If you arrive between September and May, head to Caffe di Notte (⊠*Largo Maccalle* 🖀*No phone*), an outdoor café that opens at 5:30 PM and serves into the wee hours; it has a lovely view of the valley below and serves simple sandwiches and drinks at very reasonable prices.

TODI

34 km (22 mi) south of Perugia, 34 km (22 mi) east of Orvieto.

GETTING HERE

Todi is best reached by car, as the town's two train stations are way down the hill and connected to the center by infrequent bus service. From Perugia, follow the E45 toward Rome. Take the Todi/Orvieto exit, then follow the SS79bis into Todi. The drive takes around 40 minutes.

VISITOR INFORMATION

Todi tourism office (⊠*Piazza del Popolo 38* 🖀*075/8945416* ⊕*www. todi.umbria2000.it*).

EXPLORING

As you stand on Piazza del Popolo, looking out onto the Tiber Valley below, it's easy to see how Todi is often described as Umbria's prettiest hill town. Legend has it that the town was founded by the Umbri, who followed an eagle who had stolen a tablecloth to this lofty perch. They liked it so much that they settled here for good. The eagle is now perched on the insignia of the medieval palaces in the main piazza. But historical evidence suggests that the Umbri didn't find an empty nest; Iron Age remains dating from 2700 BC make it the oldest settled area in the region. The usual Etruscan to Roman progression followed, and Todi rose to prominence in the 13th century, when it ruled over the *comune* (township) that included Amelia and Terni. Aside from the view and charm of the streets, there are also two small but worthwhile museums.

Built above the Roman Forum, **Piazza del Popolo** is Todi's high point, a model of spatial harmony with stunning views onto the surrounding countryside. In the best medieval tradition, the square was conceived to house both the temporal and the spiritual centers of power.

On one end of the Piazza del Popolo is the 12th-century Romanesque–Gothic **Duomo**, which was built over the site of a Roman temple. The simple facade is enlivened by a finely carved rose window. Look up at that window as you step inside and you will notice its peculiarity: each "petal" of the rose has a cherub's face in the stained glass. Take a close look at the capitals of the double columns with pilasters: perched between the acanthus leaves are charming medieval sculptures of saints—Peter with his keys, George and the dragon, and so on. You can see the rich brown tones of the wooden choir near the altar, but unless you have binoculars or request special permission in advance, you cannot get close enough to see all the exquisite detail in this Renaissance masterpiece of woodworking (1521–30). The severe, solid mass of the Duomo is mirrored by the Palazzo dei Priori (1595–97) across the way. ⊠*Piazza del Popolo* ☎*075/8943041* ✍*Free* ⊙*May–Sept., daily 9–12:30 and 2:30–6:30; Oct.–Apr., daily 9–4:30.*

8

A staircase on the Piazza del Popolo leads to the Palazzo del Popolo and the entrance to the **Pinacoteca di Todi.** The first room is devoted to the history of Todi; the collection includes religious garments, local coins, Roman relics, Etruscan pottery, and more recent ceramics from Deruta. The highlight of the Pinacoteca is the *Coronation of the Virgin* by Lo Spagna. ⊠*Palazzo del Popolo, Piazza del Popolo* ☎*075/8944148* ✍*€3.50* ⊙*Nov.–Mar., Tues.–Sun. 10:30–1 and 2:30–5; Apr.–Oct., Tues.–Sun. 10:30–1 and 3–6.*

Near Piazza Jacopone is the **Chiesa di San Fortunato.** Had the church been completed, it might have looked like a small version of the Duomo in Orvieto. But the project was never realized. Legend has it that Lorenzo Maitani (circa 1275–1330) was given the job but was murdered by the jealous Orvietani to ensure that no other Duomo could rival their own. Aside from the carved doorway and captivating angels attributed to Jacopo della Quercia (circa 1371–1438), the church remains more impressive for its sheer mass than its makeup. The whitewashed interior is remarkably free of any Gothic atmosphere. Under the main altar is the crypt of the local saint Jacopone da Todi (circa 1230–1306). ⊠*Piazza Umberti I* ☎*No phone* ✍*Free* ⊙*Oct.–Mar., Mon. 10–1, Tues.–Sun. 10–1 and 2:30–5; Apr.–Sept., Mon. 10–1, Tues.–Sun. 9:30–12:30 and 3–7.*

The lane to the left of the Chiesa di San Fortunato exit leads to a public garden, where you'll find a few benches and all that's left of the Rocca, the papal fortress. Follow the signs for the winding path that descends to an unexpected Renaissance treasure, the church of **Santa Maria della Consolazione.** Thought to have been inspired by designs by Bramante, it was begun in 1508 but not finished for another century. The perfect symmetry it has is heightened by an almost neoclassical purity of form and proportion. ⊠ *Piazza della Consolazione* ☎ *075/8943120* ✉ *Free* ⏰ *Apr.–Sept., daily 9–1 and 3–6; Oct.–Mar., daily 10–noon.*

WHERE TO STAY & EAT

$$–$$$ ✕ **Ristorante Umbria.** Todi's most popular restaurant for more than four decades, the Umbria is reliable for its sturdy country food and its wonderful view from the terrace. With just 16 tables outside, make sure you reserve ahead. In winter try legume soup, homemade pasta with truffles, or *palombaccio alla ghiotta* (roasted squab). Steaks, accompanied by a rich dark-brown wine sauce, are good as well. ⊠ *Via San Bonaventura 13* ☎ *075/8942737* ⊟ *AE, DC, MC, V* ⏰ *Closed Tues.*

$–$$ ✕ **La Mulinella.** If it weren't for all the other tables around, you'd think you were a guest at the home of Signora Irma, who has been making bread and pasta since she was a teenager. The generous *primi piatti* (first courses), which include dishes such as *tacchino farcito d'uva* (turkey stuffed with grapes) or stewed wild boar, may leave you little room to go on to the *secondi* (second courses). If you prefer, share a dish of her light-as-a-feather *gnocchetti* or tagliatelle in a goose sauce, and save room for the simple desserts. ⊠ *Località Pontenaia 29* ☎ *075/8944779* ⊟ *MC, V* ⏰ *Closed Wed. and Nov. 1–15.*

$$–$$$ 🏠 **Fattoria di Vibio.** This cluster of old stone farmhouses set on a ridge
★   has been converted into a lovely country inn. Painters' views of the vineyards and valleys below add to the gracious and relaxed atmosphere. Hike the country roads or relax poolside in summer; you can while the evening away at candlelit tables outside on the lawn or, on chilly nights, in front of the ample stone fireplace. For families or extended stays, the two cottages, with maid service and full use of hotel facilities, are a good deal. The inn is 12 km (7 mi) northwest of Todi. **Pros:** Lovely views, atmospheric lodgings, peace and quiet. **Cons:** Slow service, difficult to find. ⊠ *Località Buchella, 9 Doglio Montecastello di Vibio, 06057* ☎ *075/8749607* ⊕ *www.fattoriadivibio.com* ➥ *10 rooms, 3 suites, 2 cottages* ⏳ *In-room: no a/c, ethernet. In-hotel: restaurant, bar, pool, bicycles* ⊟ *AE, DC, MC, V* ⏰ *Closed Jan. and Feb.* �🍽 *MAP.*

$$–$$$ 🏠 **Tenuta di Canonica.** The affable hosts here, Daniele and Maria Fano,
★   have retained the architectural integrity of this brick farmhouse and medieval tower in the Tiber Valley. You're bound to marvel at the exposed stone walls, high-beam ceilings, brick floors, and terra-cotta tiles, all in soothing colors. Guest rooms are filled with family heirlooms and antique pieces. You can hike or ride on horseback through olive groves, orchards, and the forest on the grounds. The inn is 5 km (3 mi) northwest of center. **Pros:** Magnificent hilltop location. **Cons:** Remote location, long drive to Todi. ⊠ *Località La Canonica 75–76, 06059* ☎ *075/8947545* 🖨 *075/8947581* ⊕ *www.tenutadicanonica.com* ➥ *11*

rooms, 2 apartments &In-room: no a/c, no TV. In-hotel: restaurant, bar, pool, elevator ⊟MC, V ⏇BP.

$–$$ 🏨 **San Lorenzo 3.** Surrounded by antique furniture, paintings, and period knickknacks, you get a sense of a place more in tune with the 19th than the 21st century. This hotel doesn't pamper you with modern comforts; only three of the six rooms have private bathrooms, but all share a magnificent view over the valleys and hills to the north of the town. Don't be put off by the rather dark entrance to the building: climb the long flight of stairs that lead up to this intriguing guesthouse. **Pros:** Delightful old-world atmosphere, excellent central location. **Cons:** Few modern amenities, basic furnishings. ⊠ *Via San Lorenzo 3, 06059* ☏*075/8944555* ⊕*www.todi.net/lorenzo* ⇩*6 rooms, 3 with bath* &In-room: no a/c, no phone, no TV. In-hotel: no elevator ⊟No credit cards ⊘Closed Jan. and Feb. ⏇BP.

SHOPPING

Todi's local sweet, available in most pastry shops, is *panpolenta* (coffee cake made with corn flour and ground almonds). Local ceramics are available from several boutiques along Corso Cavour. The town also hosts one of Italy's most important annual antiques fairs (usually two weeks around Easter).

ORVIETO

The natural defenses of an enormous plateau rising 1,000 feet above the flat valley proved very attractive to settlers in central Italy as far back as the Bronze Age, making Orvieto among the oldest cities in the region. The Etruscans developed the town considerably, carving a network of 1,200 wells and storage caves out of the soft tufa (volcanic stone) of the mountain on which the city was built. By 283 BC the Romans had attacked, sacked, and destroyed the city, by then known as Volsinii Veteres. Perhaps they were attracted by the golden Orvieto Classico made from grapes grown in the rich volcanic soil of the valley below—a wine the town is still famous for today.

Charlemagne (742–814) changed the name to Urbs Vetus, from which the modern name derives. The town rose steadily as an independent commune in the late Middle Ages. When the Guelphs won decisively over the Ghibellines in the 14th century, Orvieto passed under the control of the papacy and was subsequently used by the popes as a refuge from enemies or the summer heat of Rome.

In addition to wine and some of the best restaurants in the region, Orvieto has much to offer: the celebrated Duomo, with Italy's finest Gothic facade, is alone worth the trip. Inside are masterly frescoes by Luca Signorelli (circa 1450–1523)—stunningly restored—perhaps the most underrated in the entire country. A couple of good museums and some excavations round out the sights.

The festival highlight of the year is the Festa della Palombella on Pentecost Sunday (the seventh Sunday after Easter). In this unique take on a fireworks show, a tabernacle with images of the Madonna and

8

the Apostles is set up on the steps in front of the central doorway of the Duomo. A white dove attached to a cable strung across the piazza slides down and ignites the fireworks.

A more traditional celebration is the Festa del Corpus Domini (the ninth Sunday after Easter), begun by Pope Urban IV in 1264, which may have its origin in the Miracle at Bolsena. Each year Bolsena's miraculous, bloodstained *corporale* (square linen cloth) is taken out of the chapel and led around town in a solemn procession, preceded by a rich court in sumptuous period costumes. Between Christmas and the first days of January, the Umbria Jazz Festival comes to Orvieto. Plan on big crowds, high-season rates in the hotels, and plenty of music flowing through the streets.

GETTING HERE

Orvieto is well connected by train to Rome, Florence, and Perugia. It's also adjacent to the A1 Superstrada that runs between Florence and Rome. Parking areas in the upper town tend to be crowded. A better idea is to follow the signs for the Porta Orvetiana parking lot, then take the free funicular that carries people up the hill.

VISITOR INFORMATION

Orvieto tourism office (⊠ *Piazza del Duomo 24* ☎*0763/341772* ⊕*www. orvieto.umbria2000.it*).

EXPLORING ORVIETO

If you are arriving by train, take the funicular that runs from the train station up the side of the hill and through the fortress to Piazzale Cahen. It runs every 20 minutes, daily 7:15 AM–8:30 PM, and costs €1. Although the workings have been modernized, there are a few pictures in each station of the old cog railcars, which were once run hydraulically. Keep your funicular ticket, as it will get you a discount on admission to the Museo Claudio Faina. Bus 1 makes the same trip from 8 AM to 11 PM. From Piazzale Cahen, Bus A runs to Piazza del Duomo in the town center.

A *Carta Orvieto Unica* (single ticket) is expensive but a great deal if you want to visit everything; for €18 you get admission to the four major sights in town—Cappella di San Brizio (at the Duomo), Museo Claudio Faina, Torre del Moro, and Orvieto Underground—plus a combination bus–funicular pass or five hours of free parking.

MAIN ATTRACTIONS

❺ Duomo. Orvieto's Duomo is, quite simply, stunning. The church was built to commemorate the Miracle at Bolsena. In 1263, a young priest who questioned the miracle of transubstantiation (in which the Communion bread and wine become the flesh and blood of Christ) was saying mass at nearby Lago di Bolsena. His doubts were put to rest, however, when a wafer he had just blessed suddenly started to drip blood, staining the linen covering the altar. The cloth and the host were taken to the pope, who proclaimed a miracle and a year later pro-

Fodor'sChoice
★

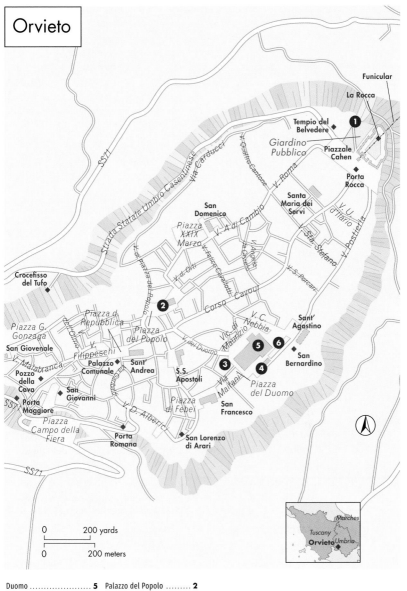

Orvieto

Funicular

La Rocca

Tempio del Belvedere

Giardino Pubblico

Piazzale Cahen

Porta Rocca

1

V. U. d'Itario

V. Postierla

SS71

Via Carducci

Strada Statale Umbro Casentinese

V. Quattro Cantone

V. Roma

San Domenico

Santa Maria dei Servi

Piazza XXIX Marzo

V. A di Cambio

Sta Stefano

V. Felice Cavallotti

V. degli Alberi

V. Angelo da Orvieto

V. di Piazza del Popolo

V. di Ofti

Crocefisso del Tufo

V. S. Porcari

Corso Cavour

2

Piazza d. Repubblica

Piazza del Popolo

V. C. Nebbia

Sant' Agostino

Piazza G. Gonzaga

San Giovenale

V. Malabranca

V. Filippeschi

Palazzo Comunale

Sant' Andrea

V. del Duomo

Vic. di Maurizio

San Bernardino

5 **6**

Pozzo della Cava

San Giovanni

S.S. Apostoli

3

4

Via Maitani

Piazza del Duomo

SS71

Porta Maggiore

V. D. Alberici

Piazza di Febei

San Francesco

Piazza Campo della Fiera

Porta Romana

San Lorenzo di Arari

SS71

V. del Olmo

Marches

Tuscany

Orvieto Umbria

| 0 | 200 yards |
| 0 | 200 meters |

8

vided for a new religious holiday—the Feast of Corpus Domini. Thirty years later, construction began on a *duomo* to celebrate the miracle and house the stained altar cloth.

It is thought that Arnolfo di Cambio (circa 1245–1302), the famous builder of the Duomo in Florence, was given the initial commission for the Duomo, but the project was soon taken over by Lorenzo Maitani (circa 1275–1330), who consolidated the structure and designed the monumental facade. Maitani also made the bas-relief panels between the doorways, which graphically tell the story of the Creation (on the left) and the Last Judgment (on the right). The lower registers, now protected by Plexiglas, succeed in conveying the horrors of hell as few other works of art manage to do, an effect made all the more powerful by the worn gray marble. Above, gold mosaics are framed by finely detailed Gothic decoration.

Inside, the cathedral is rather vast and empty; the major works are in the transepts. To the left is the **Cappella del Corporale,** where the square linen cloth (corporale) is kept in a golden reliquary that's modeled on the cathedral and inlaid with enamel scenes of the miracle. The cloth is removed for public viewing on Easter and on Corpus Domini (the ninth Sunday after Easter). In the right transept is the **Cappella di San Brizio,** or Cappella Nuova. In this chapel is one of Italy's greatest fresco cycles, notable for its influence on Michelangelo's *Last Judgment,* as well as for the extraordinary beauty of the figuration. In these works, the damned fall to hell, demons breathe fire and blood, and Christians are martyred. Some scenes are heavily influenced by the imagery in Dante's (1265–1321) *Divine Comedy.* ✉*Piazza del Duomo* ☎*0763/342477* ⛪*Church free, Cappella Nuova €5* ⊙*Nov.–Feb., daily 7:30–12:45 and 2:30–5:15; Mar. and Oct., daily 7:30–12:45 and 2:30–6:15; Apr.–Sept., daily 7:30–12:45 and 2:30–7:15.*

NEED A BREAK? Orvieto has plenty of spots to grab a quick bite—a boon in off-hours, when restaurants are closed and sightseers get peckish. Gastronomia Carraro (✉*Corso Cavour 101* ☎*0763/342870*) has an excellent selection of local sausages and cheeses. (Try the different kinds of pecorino.) It also has delicious pickled olives and tomatoes, perfect on a roll if the sightseeing has made you hungry. Alas, it's closed Sunday. For a snack or coffee on tables outside, check out Bar Sant'Andrea (✉*Piazza della Repubblica* ☎*0763/343285*). You can get simple, cheap food here, and in the summer sit on the small terrace. The service is quick and friendly, and if conversation is lacking you can always contemplate the rather odd-looking 12-sided bell tower of the church of Sant'Andrea across the piazza. Wonderful gelato in large scoops is to be had at ivy-shaded alfresco tables at L'Archetto (✉*Piazza del Duomo 14* ☎*0763/341034*). Try the delicately flavored pistachio and coconut ice cream while you admire the facade of the Duomo. It's closed mid-December through February.

The façade of Orvieto's Duomo.

❹ ★ Museo Archeologico Claudio Faina. This superb private collection, beautifully arranged and presented, goes far beyond the usual museum offerings of a scattering of local remains. The collection is particularly rich in Greek- and Etruscan-era pottery, from large Attic amphorae (6th–4th century BC) to Attic black- and red-figure pieces to Etruscan *bucchero* (dark, reddish clay) vases. Other interesting pieces in the collection include a 6th-century sarcophagus and a substantial display of Roman-era coins. ⊠*Piazza del Duomo 29* ☎*0763/341511* ⊕*www.museofaina.it* ⊡*€4.50* ☉*Oct.–Mar., Tues.–Sun. 11–3; Apr.–Sept., daily 9:30–6.*

❻ Museo Emilio Greco. Another medieval building built by a pope on leave here from Rome, 13th-century Palazzo Soliano was for many years the location of the Museo dell'Opera del Duomo, a fine collection that includes works by Signorelli and other notable names like Simone Martini and Arnolfo di Cambio. But the art treasures have been locked away during an interminable restoration. Meanwhile, the ground floor has been made into the Museo Emilio Greco, a good-looking space filled with sculpture and sketches from the prolific Sicilian artist Emilio Greco (born 1913)—who also made the doors for the Duomo in the 1960s. ⊠*Piazza del Duomo, Palazzo Soliano* ☎*0763/344605* ⊡*€2.50* ☉*Weekdays 10:30–4:30.*

Orvieto Underground. More than just about any other town, Orvieto has grown from its own foundations—if one were to remove from present-day Orvieto all the building materials that were dug up from below, there would hardly be a building left standing. The Etruscans, the Romans, and those who followed dug into the tufa (the same soft volcanic rock from which catacombs were made), and over the centuries created more than 1,000 separate cisterns, caves, secret passages, storage areas, and production areas for wine and olive oil. Some of the tufa removed was used as building blocks for the city that exists today, and some was partly

ground into *pozzolana*, which was made into mortar. The most thorough **Orvieto Underground tour** (⊠*Orvieto tourism office, Piazza del Duomo 24* ☎*0763/341772*) is run daily at 11, 12:15, 4, and 5:15. Admission for the hour-long English tour is €5.50. If you are short on time but still want a look at what it was like down there, head for the **Pozzo della Cava** (⊠*Via della Cava 28* ☎*0763/342373*), an Etruscan well for spring water. It's open Tuesday through Friday from 8 to 8, and costs €3.

ALSO WORTH SEEING

② **Palazzo del Popolo.** Built in tufa and basaltic rock, this was once the town hall. Restoration work in the late 1980s revealed the remains of an Etruscan temple underneath, and it now holds the state archives. ⊠*Piazza del Popolo.*

① **Pozzo di San Patrizio** *(St. Patrick's Well).* When Pope Clement VII (1478–1534) took shelter in Orvieto during the Sack of Rome in 1527, he had to ensure a safe water supply should Orvieto come under siege. Many wells and cisterns were built, and the pope commissioned one of the great architects of the day, Antonio da Sangallo the Younger (1493–1546), to build the well adjacent to the Rocca. After nearly a decade of digging, water was found at a depth of 203 feet. Two one-way spiral stairways allowed donkey-driven carts to descend and return without running into one another. Windows open onto the shaft, providing natural light in the stairwells. There are 248 steps down to the bottom, but you'll probably get the idea after just a few. The well was once compared to St. Patrick's Well in Ireland. The name stuck, and "pozzo di San Patrizio" has come to represent an inexhaustible source of wealth. ⊠*Viale Sangallo, off Piazzale Cahen* ☎*0763/343768* ⌂*€4.50* ☉*Oct.–Mar., daily 10–5:45; Apr.–Sept., daily 9:30–7:45.*

③ **Torre del Moro.** It's hard to imagine a simpler, duller affair than this tower in the center of town. It took on a little more character in the 19th century, when the large, white-face clock was added along with the fine 14th-century bell, marked with the symbols of the 24 arts and craft guilds then operating in the city. The views, however, are worth the climb. ⊠*Corso Cavour at Via del Duomo* ☎*0763/344567* ⌂*€2.80* ☉*May–Aug., daily 10–8; Mar., Apr., Sept., and Oct., daily 10–7; Nov.–Feb., daily 10–1 and 2:30–5.*

**OFF THE
BEATEN
PATH**

Crocefisso del Tufo. This 6th-century BC Etruscan necropolis, about 2 km (1 mi) down Viale Crispi, doesn't have the frescoes that other Etruscan tombs are famous for, and the relics that were buried within have long since been taken away (mostly to the Museo Claudio Faino). But the walk here is pleasant, and it can be interesting to see the type of site from which nearly all our knowledge of Etruscans comes. Names of the deceased are carved into the stone architraves above tomb chambers. ⊕ *2 km (1 mi) from Piazzale Cahen, down Viale F. Crispi (SS71)* ☎*0763/343611* ✎*€3* ⊙*Daily 8:30–7.*

WHERE TO EAT

The streets around the Duomo are lined with all types of bars and restaurants where you can eat simple or elaborate food and try the wines by the glass.

$$–$$$

Fodor'sChoice
★

✕**Il Giglio D'Oro.** A great view of the Duomo is coupled with superb food. Eggplant is transformed into an elegant custard with black truffles in the *sformatino di melenzane con vellutata al tartuffo nero.* Pastas, like *ombrichelli al pesto umbro,* are traditional, but perhaps with a new twist like fresh coriander leaves instead of the usual basil. Lamb roasted in a crust of bread is delicately seasoned with a tomato cream sauce. The wine cellar includes some rare vintages. ✉*Piazza Duomo 8* ☎*0763/341903* ▭*AE, MC, V* ⊙*Closed Wed.*

$$–$$$

✕**Le Grotte del Funaro.** If you can't do the official hour tour of Underground Orvieto, dine here instead, inside tufa caves under central Orvieto, where the two windows have splendid views of the hilly countryside during the day. The traditional Umbrian food is average, but with good, simple grilled meats and vegetables and pizzas. Oddly, the food is outclassed by an extensive wine list with top local and Italian labels and quite a few rare vintages. ✉*Via Ripa Serancia 41* ☎*0763/343276* ✎*Reservations essential* ▭*AE, DC, MC, V* ⊙*Closed Mon. and 1 wk in July.*

$–$$$
★

✕**Trattoria La Grotta.** The owner has been in this location for more than 20 years, and locals are still fond of him. He has attracted a steady American clientele without losing his touch with homemade pasta, perhaps with a duck or wild-boar sauce. Roast lamb, veal, or pork are all good, and the desserts are homemade. Franco knows the local wines well and has a carefully selected list, including some from smaller but excellent wineries, so ask about them. ✉*Via Luca Signorelli 5* ☎*0763/341348* ▭*AE, DC, MC, V* ⊙*Closed Tues.*

WHERE TO STAY

Orvieto has a wide choice of lodging options, so if you haven't reserved a hotel in advance, take the time to wander around and choose your favorite.

$$$
★

Hotel La Badia. One of the region's best-known country hotels occupies a 12th-century monastery. Vaulted ceilings and exposed stone walls establish the rustic elegance in the guest rooms, which have beamed ceilings and polished terra-cotta floors covered with rugs. The

8

rolling park around the hotel provides wonderful views of the valley. It's 4 km (2½ mi) south of Orvieto. **Pros:** Elegant atmosphere, fine views. **Cons:** Slightly overpriced, need a car to get around. ⊠*Località La Badia, Orvieto Scalo 05018* ☎*0763/301959* ⊕*www.labadiahotel. it* ⌗*18 rooms, 9 suites* ⌂*In-room: refrigerator. In-hotel: restaurant, bar, tennis courts, pool, parking (no fee)* ⊟*AE, MC, V* ⊗*Closed Jan. and Feb.* ⦶*BP.*

$$ ⛱**Hotel Palazzo Piccolomini.** This hotel is often preferred by local wine-makers and other professionals for its updated look with inviting lobby areas and a convenient location near the church of San Giovanni. From here it's a lovely short walk past Piazza della Repubblica to the Duomo. **Pros:** Peaceful atmosphere, efficient staff, good location. **Cons:** Unattractive building, slightly overpriced. ⊠*Piazza Ranieri 36 ,05018* ☎*0763/341743* ⊕*www.hotelpiccolomini.it* ⌗*28 rooms, 3 suites* ⌂*In-room: refrigerator, ethernet. In-hotel: bar, laundry service, parking (fee), no-smoking rooms* ⊟*AE, MC* ⦶*BP.*

$ ⛱**Gran Hotel Reale.** The best feature of this hotel is its location in the center of Orvieto, across a square that hosts a lively market. Facing the impressive Gothic–Romanesque Palazzo del Popolo, rooms are spacious and adequately furnished, with a traditional accent. **Pros:** Good budget option, friendly staff. **Cons:** Can be noisy, very basic rooms. ⊠*Piazza del Popolo 27, 05018* ☎*0763/341247* ⌗*31 rooms* ⌂*In-hotel: bar* ⊟*MC, V* ⊗*Closed Jan. and Feb.* ⦶*BP.*

WINE BARS

Orvieto has been known for white wine since its beginnings. There is evidence that the Etruscans grew grapes in the rich volcanic soil in the valley below and then fermented their wine in the cool caverns dug out of the tufa atop the hill. The Romans made special efforts to bring the local wine, which they blended with water and spices, back to Rome with them. Things had not changed by the early 16th century, when Signorelli was paid in part with wine for his work on the Cappella di San Brizio.

Although Orvieto Classico is the best-known wine in the region, it is no longer one of Italy's best. However, it is pleasantly drinkable and light. You will also have the chance to taste different types of Orvieto, from the well-known dry Orvieto Classico to the less-commercialized *abboccato* (semisweet) and the intensely flavored, sweeter *muffato*.

Begin your tastings at these *enoteche* (wine bars), *cantine* (wineshops), and *vinerie* (wineries).

At **Cantina Foresi** (⊠*Piazza del Duomo 2* ☎*0763/341611*), a light lunch of cheese, salami, bread, and salad is hard to beat. Hundreds of bottles are stored in the cool earth of the cellar, which was built in 1290 and is worthy of a visit. The few outdoor tables are a great place for a light snack while sipping.

At **La Bottega del Buon Vino** (⊠*Via della Cava 26* ☎*0763/342373*), a window in the floor looks down into the caves. It's closed Monday.

Many area wine producers create excellent variations of the standard Orvieto Classico wine. Close to town and highly recommended is **Azienda Agricola Palazzone** (⊠*Località Rocca Ripesana* ✚ *5 km [3 mi] from Orvieto* ☎*0763/344166*), where you can sample Muffa Nobile—a warm, golden, sweet wine with a rich taste caused by the fungus that is cultivated—Grechetto, and Orvieto Classico Superior that has been aged longer than most and has a richer taste than the mass-produced Orvietos. This vintner has also won awards for his Armaleo, a rich ruby red.

Castello della Sala (✚ *20 km [12 mi] north of Orvieto, Località Sala* ☎*0763/86051*), owned by the Antinori group, produces white wines of high quality. Housed in a 14th-century castle, this is an especially interesting place to try out some of Orvieto's new-style wines—Cervaro della Sala, Grechetto, and chardonnay—all aged in oak barrels.

SHOPPING

Orvieto has a few shops selling Orvietan-style pottery, bright-white vessels with hand-painted motifs. **La Torreta** (⊠*Corso Cavour 283* ☎*0763/340248*) has a kiln right in the shop and will custom paint something for you on the spot. For copies of ancient Etruscan and Greek ceramics, try **L'Arte del Vasaio** (⊠*Via Pedota 3* ☎*0763/342022*).

Established in 1907 to provide work for impoverished women, the tradition of lace-making, or *ars wetana,* has flourished in Orvieto. Using designs inspired by the reliefs on the facade of the Duomo, the patterns of Orvietan lace are unique and distinctive.

Specializing in *merletto* (lace) products, **Duranti** (⊠*Corso Cavour 107* ☎*No phone*) maintains the high standards set by one of the sustainers of the tradition during the last century, Eleonora Duranti. The Moretti family has long been associated with lace-making in Orvieto. Their products can be admired at **Ditta Moretti Merletti** (⊠*Via Duomo 55* ☎*0763/41714*).

Orvieto is a center for woodworking, particularly fine inlays and veneers. Corso Cavour is lined with a number of artisan woodworking shops, the best known being the **Michelangeli Family Studio** (⊠*Via Michelangeli 3, at Corso Cavour* ☎*0763/342377*). The imaginatively designed objects range in size from a giant *armadio* (wardrobe) to a simple wooden spoon. If all those Michelangeli flourishes don't quite suit you, head over to **Patrice** (⊠*Via Michelangeli 4* ☎*No phone*), who has a shop full of imaginative items that he has made, from crafts for children to trompe-l'oeil intarsia windows in wood.

8

ITALIAN VOCABULARY

ENGLISH	ITALIAN	PRONOUNCIATION
BASICS		
Yes/no	Sí/No	see/no
Please	Per favore	pear fa-vo-ray
Yes, please	Sí grazie	see grah-tsee-ay
Thank you	Grazie	grah-tsee-ay
You're welcome	Prego	pray-go
Excuse me, sorry	Scusi	skoo-zee
Sorry!	Mi dispiace!	mee dis-spee-ah-chay
Good morning/afternoon	Buongiorno	bwohn-jor-no
Good evening	Buona sera	bwoh-na say-ra
Good-bye	Arrivederci	a-ree-vah-dare-chee
Mr. (Sir)	Signore	see-nyo-ray
Mrs. (Ma'am)	Signora	see-nyo-ra
Miss	Signorina	see-nyo-ree-na
Pleased to meet you	Piacere	pee-ah-chair-ray
How are you?	Come sta?	ko-may stah
Very well, thanks	Bene, grazie	ben-ay grah-tsee-ay
Hello (phone)	Pronto?	proan-to
NUMBERS		
one	uno	oo-no
two	due	doo-ay
three	tre	tray
four	quattro	kwah-tro
five	cinque	cheen-kway
six	sei	say
seven	sette	set-ay
eight	otto	oh-to
nine	nove	no-vay
ten	dieci	dee-eh-chee
twenty	venti	vain-tee

thirty	trenta	train-ta
forty	quaranta	kwa-rahn-ta
fifty	cinquanta	cheen-kwahn-ta
sixty	sessanta	seh-sahn-ta
seventy	settanta	seh-tahn-ta
eighty	ottanta	o-tahn-ta
ninety	novanta	no-vahn-ta
one hundred	cento	chen-to
one thousand	mille	mee-lay
ten thousand	diecimila	dee-eh-chee-mee-la

USEFUL PHRASES

Do you speak English?	Parla inglese?	par-la een-glay-zay
I don't speak Italian	Non parlo italiano	non par-lo ee-tal-yah-no
I don't understand	Non capisco	non ka-peess-ko
Can you please repeat?	Può ripetere?	pwo ree-pet-ay-ray
Slowly!	Lentamente!	len-ta-men-tay
I don't know	Non lo so	non lo so
I'm American	Sono americano(a)	so-no a-may-ree-kah-no(a)
I'm British	Sono inglese	so-no een-glay-zay
What's your name?	Come si chiama?	ko-may see kee-ah-ma
My name is…	Mi chiamo…	mee kee-ah-mo
What time is it?	Che ore sono?	kay o-ray so-no
How?	Come?	ko-may
When?	Quando?	kwan-doe
Yesterday/today/ tomorrow	Ieri/oggi/domani	yer-ee/o-jee/ do-mah-nee
This morning/	Stamattina/Oggi	sta-ma-tee-na/o-jee
afternoon	pomeriggio	po-mer-ee-jo
Tonight	Stasera	sta-ser-a
What?	Che cosa?	kay ko-za
Why?	Perché?	pear-kay
Who?	Chi?	kee

Where is...	Dov'è...	doe-veh
the bus stop?	la fermata dell'autobus?	la fer-mah-tadel ow-toe-booss
the train station?	la stazione?	la sta-tsee-oh-nay
the subway	la metropolitana?	la may-tro-po-lee-tah-na
the terminal?	il terminale?	eel ter-mee-nah-lay
the post office?	l'ufficio postale?	loo-fee-cho po-stah-lay
the bank?	la banca?	la bahn-ka
the...hotel?	l'hotel...?	lo-tel
the store?	il negozio?	eel nay-go-tsee-o
the cashier?	la cassa?	la kah-sa
the...museum?	il museo...?	eel moo-zay-o
the hospital?	l'ospedale?	lo-spay-dah-lay
the elevator?	l'ascensore?	la-shen-so-ray
the restrooms?	Dov'è il bagno?	do-vay eel bahn-yo

Here/there	Qui/là	kwee/la

Left/right	A sinistra/a destra	a see-neess-tra/ a des-tra

Straight ahead	Avanti dritto	a-vahn-tee dree-to

Is it near/far?	È vicino/lontano?	ay vee-chee-no /lon-tah-no

I'd like...	Vorrei...	vo-ray
a room	una camera	oo-na kah-may-ra
the key	la chiave	la kee-ah-vay
a newspaper	un giornale	oon jor-nah-lay
a stamp	un francobollo	oon frahn-ko-bo-lo

I'd like to buy...	Vorrei comprare...	vo-ray kom-prah-ray

How much is it?	Quanto costa?	kwahn-toe coast-a

It's expensive/ cheap	È caro/economico	ay car-o/ ay-ko-no-mee-ko

A little/a lot	Poco/tanto	po-ko/tahn-to

More/less	Più/meno	pee-oo/may-no

Enough/too (much)	Abbastanza/troppo	a-bas-tahn-sa/tro-po

I am sick	Sto male	sto mah-lay

Call a doctor	Chiama un dottore	kee-ah-mah oondoe-toe-ray

Help!	Aiuto!	a-yoo-toe

Stop!	Alt!	ahlt

Fire!	Al fuoco!	ahl fwo-ko

Caution/Look out!	Attenzione!	a-ten-syon-ay

DINING OUT

A bottle of…	Una bottiglia di…	oo-na bo-tee-lee-ahdee
A cup of…	Una tazza di…	oo-na tah-tsa dee
A glass of…	Un bicchiere di…	oon bee-key-air-ay dee
Bill/check	Il conto	eel cone-toe
Bread	Il pane	eel pah-nay
Breakfast	La prima colazione	la pree-ma ko-la-tsee-oh-nay
Cocktail/aperitif	L'aperitivo	la-pay-ree-tee-vo
Dinner	La cena	la chen-a
Fixed-price menu	Menù a prezzo fisso	may-noo a pret-sofee-so
Fork	La forchetta	la for-ket-a
I am diabetic	Ho il diabete	o eel dee-a-bay-tay
I am vegetarian	Sono vegetariano/a	so-no vay-jay-ta-ree-ah-no/a
I'd like…	Vorrei…	vo-ray
I'd like to order	Vorrei ordinare	vo-ray or-dee-nah-ray
Is service included?	Il servizio è incluso?	eel ser-vee-tzee-o ay een-kloo-zo
It's good/bad	È buono/cattivo	ay bwo-no/ka-tee-vo
It's hot/cold	È caldo/freddo	ay kahl-doe/fred-o
Knife	Il coltello	eel kol-tel-o
Lunch	Il pranzo	eel prahnt-so
Menu	Il menù	eel may-noo
Napkin	Il tovagliolo	eel toe-va-lee-oh-lo
Please give me…	Mi dia…	mee dee-a
Salt	Il sale	eel sah-lay
Spoon	Il cucchiaio	eel koo-kee-ah-yo
Sugar	Lo zucchero	lo tsoo-ker-o
Waiter/Waitress	Cameriere/ cameriera	ka-mare-yer-ay/ ka-mare-yer-a
Wine list	La lista dei vini	la lee-sta day-ee vee-nee

Florence, Tuscany & Umbria Essentials

PLANNING TOOLS, EXPERT INSIGHT, GREAT CONTACTS

There are planners and there are those who, excuse the pun, fly by the seat of their pants. We happily place ourselves among the planners. Our writers and editors try to anticipate all the issues you may face before and during any journey, and then they do their research. This section is the product of their efforts. Use it to get excited about your trip to Florence, Tuscany & Umbria, to inform your travel planning, or to guide you on the road should the seat of your pants start to feel threadbare.

GETTING STARTED

We're really proud of our Web site: Fodors.com is a great place to begin any journey. Scan Travel Wire for suggested itineraries, travel deals, restaurant and hotel openings, and other up-to-the-minute info. Check out Booking to research prices and book plane tickets, hotel rooms, rental cars, and vacation packages. Head to Talk for on-the-ground pointers from travelers who frequent our message boards. You can also link to loads of other travel-related resources.

▍RESOURCES

ONLINE TRAVEL TOOLS

All About Florence, Tuscany & Umbria For **general information about Italy** go to ⊕www.dreamofitaly.com ⊕www.initaly. com ⊕ www.italiantourism.com and ⊕www. slowtrav.com.**Florence** ⊕www.aboutflorence. com, ⊕www.florenceby.com and ⊕www. yourwaytoflorence.com **Tuscany** ⊕www.dis-covertuscany.com ⊕www.theflorentine.net and ⊕www.turismo.toscana.it **Umbria** ⊕www.bel-laumbria.net, ⊕ www.umbria.org and ⊕www. umbriaonline.com.

Food and Wine www.chianticlassico.com ⊕www.divinacucina.com ⊕ www.great winecapitals.com.

Currency Conversion Google (⊕www. google.com) does currency conversion. Just type in the amount you want to convert and an explanation of how you want it converted (e.g., "14 Swiss francs in dollars"), and then voilà. **Oanda.com** (⊕www.oanda.com) also allows you to print out a handy table with the current day's conversion rates. **XE.com** (⊕www.xe.com) is a good currency conversion Web site.

Safety Transportation Security Administration (TSA ⊕www.tsa.gov).

Time Zones Timeanddate.com (⊕www. timeanddate.com/worldclock) can help you figure out the correct time anywhere in the world.

Weather Accuweather.com (⊕www.accu weather.com) is an independent weather-fore-casting service with especially good coverage of hurricanes. **Weather.com** (⊕www.weather. com) is the Web site for the Weather Channel.

Other Resources CIA World Factbook (⊕www.odci.gov/cia/publications/factbook/index.html) has profiles of every country in the world. It's a good source if you need some quick facts and figures.

VISITOR INFORMATION

Contacts At Home Italian Government Tourist Board (ENIT ⊠New York ☎212/245–4822 🖷212/586–9249 ⊠Chicago ☎312/644–0990 🖷312/644–3019 ⊠Los Angeles ☎310/820–0098 🖷310/820–6357).

Tourist Offices in Florence, Tuscany & Umbria Florence (☎055/290832 ⊕www. firenzeturismo.it). Gubbio 075/9220693, www. umbriaonline.com. **Lucca** (☎0583/491205 ⊕www.turismo.provincia.lucca.it). **Perugia** (☎075/5723327 ⊕www.perugiaonline.it). **Pisa** (☎050/560464 ⊕www. pisaturismo.it). **Siena** (☎0577/280551 ⊕ www.siena.turismo. toscana.it). **Tuscany** (☎0583/644354 ⊕www. welcometuscany.it). **Umbria** (☎ 075/5736458 ⊕www.umbria-turismo.it).

▍THINGS TO CONSIDER

SHIPPING LUGGAGE AHEAD

Imagine globetrotting with only a carry-on in tow. Shipping your luggage in advance via an air-freight service is a great way to cut down on backaches, hassles, and stress—especially if your packing list includes strollers, child car seats, etc. There are some things to be aware of, though. First, research carry-on restrictions; if you absolutely need something that isn't practical to ship and isn't allowed in carry-ons, this strategy isn't for you. Second, plan to send your bags as much as two weeks in advance to some international destinations. Third, plan to spend some money: it will cost least $100 to send a small piece of luggage, a golf bag, or a pair of skis to a domestic destination, much more to places overseas. Some people use Federal Express to ship their bags, but this can cost even more than air-freight services. All these services insure your bag (for most, the limit is $1,000, but you should verify that amount); you can, however, purchase additional insurance for about $1 per $100 of value.

Contacts **Luggage Concierge** (☎800/288–9818 ⊕www.luggageconcierge.com). **Luggage Free** (☎800/361–6871 ⊕www.luggagefree.com). **Sports Express** (☎800/357–4174 ⊕www.sportsexpress.com) specializes in shipping golf clubs and other sports equipment, as well as luggage.

PASSPORTS & VISAS

Travelers need only a valid passport to enter Italy for stays of up to 90 days.

PASSPORTS

We're always surprised at how few Americans have passports—only 25% at this writing. This number is expected to grow in coming years, when it becomes impossible to re-enter the United States from trips to neighboring Canada or Mexico without one. Remember this: A passport verifies both your identity and nationality—a great reason to have one.

U.S. passports are valid for 10 years. You must apply in person if you're getting a passport for the first time; if your previous passport was lost, stolen, or damaged; or if your previous passport has expired and was issued more than 15 years ago or when you were under 16. All children under 18 must appear in person to apply for or renew a passport. Both parents

must accompany any child under 14 (or send a notarized statement with their permission) and provide proof of their relationship to the child.

There are 13 regional passport offices, as well as 7,000 passport acceptance facilities in post offices, public libraries, and other governmental offices. If you're renewing a passport, you can do so by mail. Forms are available at passport acceptance facilities and online.

The cost to apply for a new passport is $97 for adults, $82 for children under 16; renewals are $67. Allow six weeks for processing, both for first-time passports and renewals. For an expediting fee of $60 you can reduce this time to about two weeks. If your trip is less than two weeks away, you can get a passport even more rapidly by going to a passport office with the necessary documentation. Private expediters can get things done in as little as 48 hours, but charge hefty fees for their services.

■TIP➔ Before your trip, make two copies of your passport's data page (one for someone at home and another for you to carry separately). Or scan the page and e-mail it to someone at home and/or yourself.

VISAS

U.S. citizens who plan to travel or live in Italy or the E.U. for longer than 90 days must acquire a valid visa from the Italian consulate serving their state before leaving the U.S. Plan ahead, because the process of obtaining a visa will take at least 30 days and the Italian government does not accept visa applications submitted by visa expediters.

U.S. Passport Information **U.S. Department of State** (☎877/487–2778 ⊕http://travel.state.gov/passport).

U.S. Passport Expediters **American Passport Express** (☎800/455–5166 or 603/559–9888 ⊕www.americanpassport.com). **Passport Express** (☎800/362–8196 or 401/272–4612 ⊕www.passportexpress.com).

Travel Document Systems (☎800/874–5100 or 202/638–3800 ⊕www.traveldocs.com).

TRIP INSURANCE

What kind of coverage do you honestly need? Do you even need trip insurance at all? Take a deep breath and read on.

We believe that comprehensive trip insurance is especially valuable if you're booking a very expensive or complicated trip (particularly to an isolated region) or if you're booking far in advance. Who knows what could happen six months down the road? But whether or not you get insurance has more to do with how comfortable you are assuming all that risk yourself.

Comprehensive travel policies typically cover trip-cancellation and interruption, letting you cancel or cut your trip short because of a personal emergency, illness, or, in some cases, acts of terrorism in your destination. Such policies also cover evacuation and medical care. Some also cover you for trip delays because of bad weather or mechanical problems as well as for lost or delayed baggage. Another type of coverage to look for is financial default—that is, when your trip is disrupted because a tour operator, airline, or cruise line goes out of business. Generally you must buy this when you book your trip or shortly thereafter, and it's only available to you if your operator isn't on a list of excluded companies.

If you're going abroad, consider buying medical-only coverage at the very least. Neither Medicare nor some private insurers cover medical expenses anywhere outside of the United States besides Mexico and Canada (including time aboard a cruise ship, even if it leaves from a U.S. port). Medical-only policies typically reimburse you for medical care (excluding that related to pre-existing conditions) and hospitalization abroad, and provide for evacuation. You still have to pay the bills and await reimbursement from the insurer, though.

■TIP➜ Expect comprehensive travel insurance policies to cost about 4% to 7% of the total price of your trip (it's more like 12% if you're over age 70). A medical-only policy may or may not be cheaper than a comprehensive policy. Always read the fine print of your policy to make sure that you are covered for the risks that are of most concern to you. Compare several policies to make sure you're getting the best price and range of coverage available.

BOOKING YOUR TRIP

Unless your cousin is a travel agent, you're probably among the millions of people who make most of their travel arrangements online. But have you ever wondered just what the differences are between an online travel agent (a Web site through which you make reservations instead of going directly to the airline, hotel, or car-rental company), a discounter (a firm that does a high volume of business with a hotel chain or airline and accordingly gets good prices), a wholesaler (one that makes cheap reservations in bulk and then re-sells them to people like you), and an aggregator (one that compares all the offerings so you don't have to)? Is it truly better to book directly on an airline or hotel Web site? And when does a real live travel agent come in handy?

ONLINE

You really have to shop around. A travel wholesaler such as Hotels.com or Hotel-Club.net can be a source of good rates, as can discounters such as Hotwire or Priceline, particularly if you can bid for your hotel room or airfare. Indeed, such sites sometimes have deals that are unavailable elsewhere. They do, however, tend to work only with hotel chains (which makes them just plain useless for getting hotel reservations outside of major cities) or big airlines (so that often leaves out upstarts like jetBlue and some foreign carriers like Air India). Also, with discounters and wholesalers you must generally prepay, and everything is nonrefundable. And before you fork over the dough, be sure to check the terms and conditions, so you know what a given company will do for you if there's a problem and what you'll have to deal with on your own.

■ **TIP →** To be absolutely sure everything was processed correctly, confirm reservations made through online travel agents, discounters, and wholesalers directly with your hotel before leaving home.

Booking engines like Expedia, Travelocity, and Orbitz are actually travel agents, albeit high-volume, online ones. And airline travel packagers like American Airlines Vacations and Virgin Vacations—well, they're travel agents, too. But they may still not work with all the world's hotels.

An aggregator site will search many sites and pull the best prices for airfares, hotels, and rental cars from them. Most aggregators compare the major travel-booking sites such as Expedia, Travelocity, and Orbitz; some also look at airline Web sites, though rarely the sites of smaller budget airlines. Some aggregators also compare other travel products, including complex packages—a good thing, as you can sometimes get the best overall deal by booking an air-and-hotel package.

WITH A TRAVEL AGENT

If you use an agent—brick-and-mortar or virtual—you'll pay a fee for the service. And know that the service you get from some online agents isn't comprehensive. For example Expedia and Travelocity don't search for prices on budget airlines like jetBlue, Southwest, or small foreign carriers. That said, some agents (online or not) *do* have access to fares that are difficult to find otherwise, and the savings can more than make up for any surcharge.

A knowledgeable brick-and-mortar travel agent can be a godsend if you're booking a cruise, a package trip that's not available to you directly, an air pass, or a complicated itinerary including several overseas flights. What's more, travel agents that specialize in a destination may have exclusive access to certain deals and insider information on things such as charter flights. Agents who specialize in types of travelers (senior citizens, gays and lesbians, naturists) or types of trips (cruises, luxury travel, safaris) can also be invaluable.

A top-notch agent planning your trip to Russia will make sure you get the correct visa application and complete it on time; the one booking your cruise may get you a cabin upgrade or arrange to have bottle of champagne chilling in your cabin when you embark. And complain about the surcharges all you like, but when things don't work out the way you'd hoped, it's nice to have an agent to put things right.

■ **TIP→** Remember that Expedia, Travelocity, and Orbitz are travel agents, not just booking engines. To resolve any problems with a reservation made through these companies, contact them first.

If you opt not to use a travel agent, Florence, Tuscany, and Umbria are easy destinations to plan without one. Booking flights, making hotel reservations, and reserving museum tickets are all things that can be done online or by telephone before you leave home. Reviews of hotels and restaurants by fellow travelers are also readily available.

If you are traveling during peak times and wish to make train reservations, these may be more difficult to manage online and a travel agent can be of assistance. Train passes, such as the Eurail Pass, can be purchased online.

Agent Resources American Society of Travel Agents (☎703/739–2782 ⊕www.travelsense.org).

Florence, Tuscany & Umbria Travel Agents Ciao Bambino (☎866/802-0300 ⊕www.ciaobambino.com). **Select Italy** (☎800/877-1755 ⊕www.selectitaly.com). **Zurer Travel** (☎202/210-6975 ⊕www.zurer.com).

■ ACCOMMODATIONS

Florence, Tuscany and Umbria have a varied and abundant number of hotels, B&Bs, *agriturismi,* and rental properties. In both the cities and the country you can find very sophisticated, luxurious palaces and villas as well as rustic farmhouses and small hotels.

Depending on your personal taste, you can find 600-year-old palazzos and converted monasteries restored as luxurious hotels while retaining the original atmosphere. On the other hand, modern Italian design has swept the world and boutique hotels have inhabited historic buildings using chic, stylish interior furnishings. Increasingly, the famed Tuscan and Umbrian wineries are creating rooms and apartments for three-day to week-long stays. Tuscan and Umbrian establishments are generally run with pride and are very clean. Although Italy has a star system for rating hotels, it is not always your best guide, since accommodation likes and dislikes differ from person to person.

Go online to find feedback from other travelers who have stayed at the hotels, apartments, B&Bs, and agriturismi you are considering.

Most hotels and other lodgings require you to give your credit-card details before they will confirm your reservation. If you don't feel comfortable e-mailing this information, ask if you can fax it (some places even prefer faxes). However you book, get confirmation in writing and have a copy of it handy when you check in.

Be sure you understand the hotel's cancellation policy. Some places allow you to cancel without any kind of penalty— even if you prepaid to secure a discounted rate—if you cancel at least 24 hours in advance. Others require you to cancel a week in advance or penalize you the cost of one night. Small inns and B&Bs are most likely to require you to cancel far in advance.

Most hotels allow children under a certain age to stay in their parents' room at no extra charge, but others charge for them as extra adults; find out the cutoff age for discounts.

■ **TIP→** Assume that hotels operate on the European Plan (**EP**, no meals) unless we specify that they use the Breakfast Plan (**BP**, with full breakfast), Continental Plan (**CP**, Continental breakfast), Full American Plan (**FAP**, all meals), or Modified American Plan (**MAP**, breakfast and dinner) or are **all-inclusive** (**AI**, all meals and most activities).

APARTMENT & HOUSE RENTALS

Italy gave birth to the Slow Food movement and it appears to be at the start of the Slow Travel phenomenon also. More and more travelers are turning away from the three-countries-in-two-weeks style of touring and choosing to spend a week in one city or a month in the countryside.

The most economical way to spend time in one place is to rent an apartment, a farmhouse, or a villa, depending on the number of people in your group and your budget.

These are readily available in Tuscany and Umbria. Most are owned by individuals and managed by rental agents who advertise available properties on the Internet. Many properties are represented by more than one rental agent and thus, the same property is frequently renamed ("Chianti Bella Vista" and "Tuscan Sun Home" and "Casa Toscana Sole," all names of the same farmhouse) on the various Internet rental sites. The rental agent may meet you at the property for the initial check-in or the owner may be present, while the rental agent only handles the online reservation and financial arrangements.

Issues to keep in mind when renting an apartment in a city or town for three nights to one month are the neighborhood (street noise and ambience), the availability of an elevator or number of stairs, the furnishings (including pots and pans and linens) and the cost of utilities (included in the rental cost, or not). Inquires about countryside properties should include those questions and also how isolated the property is (Do you have to drive for forty-five minutes to reach the nearest town?).

BED & BREAKFASTS

You can find cozy B&Bs in Florence, Perugia, Assisi, and Siena as well as in more rural areas. In towns and villages, B&Bs tend to be personal, homey, simple, and clean. In the Tuscan countryside you can find private villas that offer B&B accommodations; many are very upscale.

Reservation Services Bed & Breakfast.com (☎512/322–2710 or 800/462–2632 ⊕www.bedandbreakfast.com) also sends out an online newsletter. Bed & Breakfast Inns Online (☎310/280-4363 or 800/215–7365 ⊕www.bbonline.com). BnB Finder.com (☎212/432–7693 or 888/469-6663 ⊕www.bnbfinder.com).

CONVENTS & MONASTERIES

Throughout Tuscany and Umbria, tourists looking for lodging at a reasonable price seek out convents, monasteries, and religious houses. Religious orders usually charge from 30 to 60 euros per person per night for rooms that are clean, comfortable, and convenient. Most have private bathrooms; spacious lounge areas and secluded gardens or terraces are standard features. A continental breakfast ordinarily comes with the room. Sometimes, for an extra fee, family-style lunches and dinners are available.

Be aware of three issues when considering a convent or monastery stay: most have a curfew of 11 PM or midnight; you need to book in advance, because they fill up quickly; and your best means of booking is usually e-mail or fax—the person answering the phone may not speak English. For a list of convents in most cities in Tuscany and Umbria, go to ⊕www.hospites.it.

Religious Guest Houses in Florence Casa Santo Nome di Gesù (✉Piazza del Carmine 21, 50124 ☎055/213856 ᴃ 055/281835 |info@fmmfirenze.it). Istituto Gould/Foresteria Valdese di Firenze (✉Via dei Serragli 49, 50124 ☎055/212576 🖨 055/280274 ✍foresteriafirenze@diaconiavaldese.org ⊕www.istitutogould.it/foresteria). Istituto Oblate Dell'Assunzione (✉Borgo Pitti 15,

50121 ☎055/2480582 🖶 055/2346291 ✉info@fmmfirenze.it).

Religious Guest Houses in Assisi
Albergo Ancajani (✉Via Ancajani 16, 06081 ☎075/815128 🖶 075/815129 ✉albergoancajani@libero.it). **St. Anthony Guest House** (✉Via Galeazzo Alessi 10, 06081 ☎075/812542 B 075/813723 ✉atoneassisi@tiscalinet.it).

FARM HOLIDAYS & AGRITOURISM
Rural accommodations in the *agriturismo* (agricultural tourism) category are increasingly popular with both Italians and visitors to Italy; you stay on a working farm or vineyard.

Accommodations vary in size and range from luxury apartments, farmhouses, and villas to very basic facilities. Agriturist has compiled *Agriturismo,* which is available only in Italian but includes more than 1,600 farms in Italy; pictures and the use of international symbols to describe facilities make the guide a good tool. Local APT tourist offices also have information.

Agencies Agriturismo.net ⊕www.agriturismo.net). **Italy Farm Holidays** (☎914/631–7880 🖶914/631–8831 ⊕www.italyfarmholidays.com). **Agriturist** (☎06/685–2342 ⊕www.agriturist.it). **Italy Tourist: Farm Holiday** ⊕www.italytourist.it). .

HOME EXCHANGES
With a direct home exchange you stay in someone else's home while they stay in yours. Some outfits also deal with vacation homes, so you're not actually staying in someone's full-time residence, just their vacant weekend place.

Exchange Clubs Home Exchange.com (☎800/877–8723 ⊕www.homeexchange.com); $99.95 for a 1-year online listing. **HomeLink International** (☎800/638–3841 ⊕www.homelink.org); $110 yearly for Web-only membership; $170 includes Web access and two catalogs. **Intervac U.S** (☎800/756–4663 ⊕www.intervacus.com).; $95 for Web-only international membership; $140 includes Web access and a catalog.

HOSTELS
Hostels offer bare-bones lodging at low, low prices—often in shared dorm rooms with shared baths—to people of all ages, though the primary market is young travelers, especially students. Most hostels serve breakfast; dinner and/or shared cooking facilities may also be available. In some hostels you aren't allowed to be in your room during the day, and there may be a curfew at night. Nevertheless, hostels provide a sense of community, with public rooms where travelers often gather to share stories. Many hostels are affiliated with Hostelling International (HI), an umbrella group of hostel associations with some 4,500 member properties in more than 70 countries. Other hostels are completely independent and may be nothing more than a really cheap hotel.

Membership in any HI association, open to travelers of all ages, allows you to stay in HI-affiliated hostels at member rates. One-year membership is about $28 for adults; hostels charge about $15–$40 per night. Members have priority if the hostel is full; they're also eligible for discounts around the world, even on rail and bus travel in some countries.

Hostels in Florence, Tuscany, and Umbria run the gamut of low-end hotels to beautiful villas. In Florence, the campground and hostel near Piazzale Michelangelo has a better view of the city than any luxury hotel in town. Hostels in these two regions are not just for student travelers, but are good budget accommodations for couples and families.

Hostels In Italy Hostelling International—USA (☎301/495–1240 (national office, check online for the phone number of the office in your state ⊕www.hiusa.org). **Hostel World** (⊕www.hostelworld.com). **Ostelli on Line** (☎06/489 07740 ⊕www.ostellionline.org).

HOTELS

Italian hotels are awarded stars (one to five) based on their facilities and services. Keep in mind, however, that these are general indications and that a charming three-star might make for a better stay than a more expensive four-star. In the major cities, room rates are on a par with other European capitals: deluxe and four-star rates can be downright extravagant. In those categories, **ask for one of the better rooms,** because the less-desirable rooms—and there usually are some—don't give you what you're paying for. Except in deluxe and some four-star hotels, rooms may be very small by U.S. standards, and bathrooms usually have showers rather than bathtubs. Hotels with three or more stars always have bathrooms in all rooms.

In all hotels a rate card inside the door of your room or inside the closet door tells you exactly the maximum rate that can be legally charged for that particular room (rates in the same hotel may vary according to the location and type of room). On this card, breakfast and any other options must be listed separately. Any discrepancy between the basic room rate and that charged on your bill is cause for complaint to the manager and to the police.

High season in Italy, when rooms are at a premium, generally runs from Easter through the beginning of November, and then for two weeks at Christmas time. During low season and whenever a hotel isn't full, it's often possible to negotiate a discounted rate. Major cities have no official off-season as far as hotel rates go, but some hotels do offer substantial discounts during the slower parts of the year and on weekends. Always **inquire about special rates.** Major cities have hotel-reservation service booths in train stations. It's always a good idea to **confirm your reservation, dates, and rate by fax or e-mail.**

Although by law breakfast is supposed to be optional, most hotels quote room rates including breakfast. When you book a room, specifically **ask whether the rate includes breakfast** (*colazione*). You are under no obligation to take breakfast at your hotel, but in practice most hotels expect you to do so. The trick is to "offer" guests "complimentary" breakfast and have its cost built into the rate. However, it's encouraging to note that many of the hotels we recommend provide generous buffet breakfasts instead of simple, even skimpy, "continental" breakfasts. Remember, if the latter is the case, you can eat for less at the nearest coffee bar.

Hotels in the $$ and $ categories may charge extra for optional air-conditioning. In older hotels the quality of the rooms may be very uneven; if you don't like the room you're given, request another. This applies to noise, too. Front rooms may be larger or have a view, but they also may have a lot of street noise. If you're a light sleeper, request a quiet room when making reservations. Rooms in lodgings listed in this guide have a shower and/or bath, unless noted otherwise. (All hotels listed have private bath unless otherwise noted.) Remember to specify whether you care to have a bath or shower—not all rooms have both.

▮ AIRLINE TICKETS

Most domestic airline tickets are electronic; international tickets may be either electronic or paper. With an e-ticket the only thing you receive is an e-mailed receipt citing your itinerary and reservation and ticket numbers. The greatest advantage of an e-ticket is that if you lose your receipt, you can simply print out another copy or ask the airline to do it for you at check-in. You usually pay a surcharge (up to $50) to get a paper ticket, if you can get one at all. The sole advantage of a paper ticket is that it may be easier to endorse over to another airline if your flight is canceled and the airline with which you booked can't accommodate you on another flight.

■TIP➡ Discount air passes that let you travel economically in a country or region must often be purchased before you leave home. In some cases you can only get them through a travel agent.

■ RENTAL CARS

When you reserve a car, ask about cancellation penalties, taxes, drop-off charges (if you're planning to pick up the car in one city and leave it in another), and surcharges (for being under or over a certain age, for additional drivers, or for driving across state or country borders or beyond a specific distance from your point of rental). All these things can add substantially to your costs. Request child car seats and extras, such as GPS, when you book. Rates are sometimes—but not always—better if you book in advance or reserve through a rental agency's Web site. There are other reasons to book ahead, though: for popular destinations, during busy times of the year, or to ensure that you get certain types of cars (vans, SUVs, exotic sports cars).

■TIP➡ Make sure that a confirmed reservation guarantees you a car. Agencies sometimes overbook, particularly for busy weekends and holiday periods.

Florence, Tuscany, and Umbria have an intricate network of autostrade routes, good highways, and secondary roads, making renting a car a better but expensive alternative (because of high gas prices and freeway tolls) to public transportation. A rental car can be a good investment for carefree countryside rambles, offering time to explore more remote towns.

Having a car in major cities, however, often leads to parking and traffic headaches, plus the additional expense of garage and parking fees. In major cities, such as Florence, Siena, and Perugia,

there are restricted zones for cars. These areas are monitored by camera. If you drive to your hotel in the city center of these cities, inquire at the front desk of your hotel as to whether your rental car's license tag number must be submitted by the hotel to the police or traffic authority. Failure to do this may result in a large fine being levied on your car rental company and passed on to you.

Major car-rental companies offer Ford-type cars (such as Ford Fusion) and Fiats in various sizes and in good condition, all with air-conditioning. The local rental companies provide good service, and depending on the time of year, they may have greater availability than the well-known international companies. Because most Italian cars have standard transmissions, automatics are more expensive and must be reserved in advance. Mileage is usually unlimited, although certain offers limit included mileage to 150 km a day, after which you must pay for additional miles.

Most major U.S. car-rental companies have offices or affiliates in Italy, but the rates are generally better if you make a reservation from abroad rather than from within Italy. Each company's rental prices are uniform throughout Italy, so you won't save money by, for example, picking up a vehicle from a city rental office rather than from an airport location.

In Italy a U.S. driver's license is acceptable to rent a car, but you might also want to consider getting an International Driver's Permit (IDP). Italy, by law at least, requires non-Europeans to carry an IDP along with their domestic license because the IDP states in Italian (and a dozen other languages) that your license is valid. In practice, it depends on the police officer who pulls you over whether you will be penalized for not carrying the IDP.

In Italy you must be 18 years old to drive a car. Most rental companies will not rent to someone under age 21 and also refuse to rent any car larger than an economy or subcompact car to anyone under age 23, and further require customers under age 23 to pay by credit card. Additional drivers must be identified in the contract and must meet age requirements. There may be an additional daily fee for more than one driver. Upon rental, all companies require credit cards as a warranty; to rent bigger cars (2,000 cc or more), you must often show two credit cards. There are no special restrictions on senior citizen drivers. Book car seats, required for children under age 3, in advance. The cost is generally about €36 for the duration of the rental.

Hiring a car with a driver can come in handy, particularly if you plan to do some wine tasting. Ask at your hotel for recommended drivers, or inquire at the local tourist-information office. Typically, drivers are paid by the day, and are usually rewarded with a tip of about 15% on completion of the journey.

CAR-RENTAL INSURANCE

Italy requires car-rental companies to include Collision Damage Waiver (CDW) coverage in quoted rates. Ask your rental company about other coverage when you reserve the car and /or pick it up.

Everyone who rents a car wonders whether the insurance that the rental companies offer is worth the expense. No one has a simple answer. It all depends on how much regular insurance you have, how comfortable you are with risk, and whether or not money is an issue.

If you own a car, your personal auto insurance may cover a rental to some degree, though not all policies protect you abroad. If you don't have auto insurance, then seriously consider buying the CDW or loss-damage waiver (LDW) from the car-rental company, which eliminates your liability for damage to the car. Some credit cards offer CDW coverage, but it's usually supplemental to your own insurance and rarely covers SUVs, mini-

vans, or luxury models. If your coverage is secondary, you may still be liable for loss-of-use costs from the car-rental company. But no credit-card insurance is valid unless you use that card for *all* transactions, from reserving to paying the final bill. All companies exclude car rental in some countries, so be sure to find out about your destination.

■TIP➡ Diners Club offers primary CDW coverage on all rentals reserved and paid for with the card. This means that Diners Club's company—not your own car insurance—pays in case of an accident. It *doesn't* mean your car-insurance company won't raise your rates once it discovers you had an accident.

■ VACATION PACKAGES

Packages *are not* guided excursions. Packages combine airfare, accommodations, and perhaps a rental car or other extras (theater tickets, guided excursions, boat trips, reserved entry to popular museums, transit passes), but they let you do your own thing. During busy periods packages may be your only option, as flights and rooms may be sold out otherwise. Packages can save you time and money, particularly in peak seasons, but—and this is a really big "but"—you should price each part of the package separately. Also, be aware that prices advertised on Web sites and in newspapers rarely include service charges or taxes.

■TIP➡ Some packages and cruises are sold only through travel agents. Don't always assume that you can get the best deal by booking everything yourself.

Each year consumers are stranded or lose their money when packagers—even large ones with excellent reputations—go out of business. How can you protect yourself? First, always pay with a credit card; if you have a problem, your credit-card company may help you resolve it. Second, buy trip insurance that covers default. Third, choose a company that belongs to the United States Tour Operators Association, whose members must set aside funds to cover defaults. Finally, choose a company that also participates in the Tour Operator Program of the American Society of Travel Agents (ASTA), which will act as mediator in any disputes. You can also check on the tour operator's reputation among travelers by posting an inquiry on one of the Fodors.com forums.

Organizations **American Society of Travel Agents** (ASTA ☎703/739–2782 or 800/965–2782 ⊕www.asta.org). **United States Tour Operators Association** (USTOA ☎212/599–6599 ⊕www.ustoa.com). ■TIP➡ Local tourism boards can provide information about lesser-known and small-niche operators that sell packages to only a few destinations.

▌ GUIDED TOURS

Guided tours are a good option when you don't want to do it all yourself. You travel along with a group (sometimes large, sometimes small), stay in prebooked hotels, eat with your fellow travelers (the cost of meals is sometimes included, sometimes not), and follow a schedule. But not all guided tours are an if-it's-Tuesday-this-must-be-Belgium experience. A knowledgeable guide can take you places that you might never discover on your own. Tours aren't for everyone, but they can be just the thing for trips to places where making travel arrangements are difficult or time-consuming. Whenever you book a guided tour, find out what's included and what isn't. A "land-only" tour includes all your travel (by bus, in most cases) in the destination, but not necessarily your flights to and from or even within it. Also, in most cases prices in tour brochures don't include fees and taxes. And remember that you'll be expected to tip your guide (in cash) at the end of the tour.

SPECIAL-INTEREST TOURS

ART
Abercrombie & Kent (☎800/554-7016 ⊕www.abercrombiekent.com)

BIKING
■**TIP➡** Most airlines accommodate bikes as luggage, provided they're dismantled and boxed.

Backroads (☎800/462-2848 ⊕www.backroads.com). **Butterfield & Robinson** (☎866/551-9090 ⊕www.butterfield.com). **Ciclismo Classico** (☎800/866-7314 ⊕www.ciclismoclassico.com)

CULTURE
Elderhostel (☎800/454-5768 ⊕www.elderhostel.com). **Travcoa** (☎866/591-0070 ⊕www.travcoa.com)

CULINARY
Epiculinary (☎888/380-9010 ⊕www.epiculinary.com). **Joanne Weir** (☎415/262-0260 ⊕www.joanneweir.com). **Tuscan Women Cook** (☎815/717-7295 ⊕www.tuscanwomencook.com)

GOLF
Rosso Soave (☎039/055-230-5210 ⊕www.rossosoave.com)**Tuscany Golf & Tourism** (☎039/0574-600269 ⊕www.tuscanygolftourism.com)

HIKING
Backroads (☎800/462-2848 ⊕www.backroads.com)

SHOPPING
Shopping Safaris Tuscany (☎039/339/574-8922 ⊕www.shoppingsafaristuscany.com)**Take My Mother Please** (☎323/737-2200 ⊕www.takemymotherplease.com)

VOLUNTEER PROGRAMS
Elderhostel (☎800/454-5768 ⊕www.elderhostel.com)

WINE
Cellar Tours (☎034/915-213-939 ⊕www.cellartours.com). **Food & Wine Trails** (☎800/367-5348 ⊕www.foodandwinetrails.com)

TRANSPORTATION

▮ BY AIR

Flying time is 8½ hours from New York, 10–11 hours from Chicago, 11½ hours from Dallas (via New York), and 11½ hours from Los Angeles.

Airlines & Airports **Airline and Airport Links.com** (⊕www.airlineandairportlinks.com) has links to many of the world's airlines and airports, but for airports in Italy it is often more effective to Google the city name and "airport" (i.e., "Florence + airport" or "Pisa + airport").

Airline Security Issues **Transportation Security Administration** (⊕www.tsa.gov) has answers for almost every question that might come up.

AIRPORTS

The major gateways to Italy include Rome's Aeroporto Leonardo da Vinci (airport code FCO), better known as Fiumicino, and Milan's Aeroporto Malpensa (MIL). Flights to Florence make connections at Fiumicino and Malpensa.

Florence is serviced by Aeroporto A. Vespucci (FLR), also called Peretola, and by Aeroporto Galileo Galilei (PSA), which is about a mile outside the center of Pisa and about one hour from Florence.

Perugia is serviced by Aeroporto S. Egidio (PEG), a small airport that receives connecting flights from Milan's Malpensa airport and London's Stansted airport. Italy's airports are not known for being new, fun, or efficient. All have restaurants and snack bars and there is Internet access. Each airport has at least one nearby hotel, but in the case of Florence and Pisa, the city centers are only a fifteen-minute taxi ride away–so if you encounter a long delay, spend it in town.

Airports in Italy have been ramping up security measures, which include random baggage inspection and bomb-detection dogs.

Airport Information **Aeroporto A. Vespucci** (FLR, also called Peterola ☎055/3061300 ⊕www.aeroporto.firenze.it). **Aeroporto Galileo Galilei** (PSA ☎050/849300 ⊕www.pisa-airport.com). **Aeroporto Leonardo da Vinci** (FCO, also called Fiumicino ☎06/65951 ⊕www.adr.it). **Aeroporto Malpensa** (MIL ☎02/74852200 ⊕www.sea-aeroportimilano.it). **Aeroporto S. Egidio** (PEG ☎ 075/592141 ⊕www.airport.umbria.it).

▮**TIP→** Ask the local tourist board about hotel and local transportation packages that include tickets to major museum exhibits or other special events.

GROUND TRANSPORTATION

It takes about twenty minutes to get from **Aeroporto A. Vespucci** into Florence. Taxis are readily available, charging a fixed price of €20 with a €1 surcharge for each bag and a €3 surcharge for nighttime trips. Outside the main terminal, to the right is a bus stop where the SITA bus leaves every thirty minutes with a final destination near the main Florence train station (Santa Maria Novella)—a ticket costs €8.

There is a train from **Aeroporto Galileo Galilei** into the Central Pisa train station (Cost: €1.50). Thereafter, trains are available to all parts of Tuscany and Umbria. A train from Pisa to Florence takes just over an hour (Cost: €5.40). Taxis from the airport to central Pisa charge about €15. The cost from the airport to Florence by taxi is about €180. The Terravision bus runs from the Pisa airport to the train station in Florence (70 minutes)—one way €13.

The train from **Aeroporto Leonardo da Vinci** stops at five stations in Rome and takes one hour (Cost: €10) to get to the city. A taxi from the airport to the central train station costs about €60.

Metered taxis are available outside both Arrivals and Departures areas of **Aero-**

porto Malpensa. The journey time to central Milan is around 50 minutes and the taxi fare will be €75–90. For bus service to the Milan central train station, the Malpensa Shuttle departs every twenty minutes, 5:30–midnight. The journey time is about one hour (Cost: €6).

FLIGHTS

TO FLORENCE, TUSCANY & UMBRIA

Air travel to Italy is frequent and virtually problem-free. Sometimes, however, airport- or airline-related union strikes may cause delays of a few hours. These delays are usually reported in advance. Alitalia, Italy's national flag carrier, has the most nonstop flights to Rome and Milan. Frequent flights are available from the United States aboard Lufthansa, Air France, United, US Airways, or Continental; these stop once in Europe before they or their code-sharing partners continue on to Florence or Pisa.

WITHIN ITALY

Alitalia—in addition to other major European airlines and smaller, privately run companies such as Ryanair, Meridiana, and Air One—also has an extensive network of flights within Italy. Ask your domestic or Italian travel agent about discounts.

Information: Air One (☎ 06/488800 in Rome, 800/900966 elsewhere in Italy ⊕www.flyairone.it). **Alitalia** (☎800/223-5730 in the U.S., 06/65641 in Rome, 848/865641 elsewhere in Italy ⊕www.alitalia.it). **American Airlines** (☎800/433-7300 ⊕www.aa.com). **Continental Airlines** (☎800/523-3273 for U.S, 800/231-0856 for international reservations ⊕www.continental.com). **Delta Airlines** (☎800/221-1212 for U.S. reservations, 800/241-4141 for international reservations ⊕www.delta.com). Meridiana (☎199/111333 in Italy ⊕wwwmeridiana.it). **Ryanair** (☎800/223-5730 in Italy ⊕www.ryanair.com). **United Airlines** (☎800/864-8331 for U.S. reservations, 800/538-2929 for international reservations ⊕www.united.com). **USAirways** (☎800/428-4322 for U.S. and Canada reservations, 800/622-1015 for international reservations ⊕www.usairways.com).

▊ BY BOAT & FERRY

Ferries connect the mainland with the Tuscan islands, including Elba, Capraia, Pianosa, Giglio, and Giannutri. To many destinations there is also hydrofoil (*aliscafo*) service, which is generally twice as fast as ferries and double the price. Service is considerably more frequent in summer months. Passenger and car ferries travel to Elba. If you're traveling in July or August, try to make reservations at least a month ahead. The Toremar and Moby Lines ferry (*traghetti*) companies accept major credit cards and cash, but not traveler's checks.

Two ferry lines operate along the coast of Cinque Terre: Golfo Paradiso, which operates from June to September from Genoa and Camogli to the Cinque Terre villages of Monterosso al Mare and Vernazza; and the smaller, but more frequent, Golfo dei Poeti, which stops at each village (from Portovenere to Riomaggiore, except for Corniglia) four times a day.

The easiest place to find a schedule and fare information for ferries in Tuscany is on their Web sites. If you are already in the area, local tourist information offices, tourist agencies and the ticket offices at the port will have printed schedules. Payment may be made by credit card or cash (no traveler's checks).

Information **Golfo Paradiso** (☎0185/772091 ⊕www.golfoparadiso.it). **Golfo dei Poeti** (☎0187/732987 ⊕www.navigazionegolfodeipoeti.it). **Moby Lines** (☎199/303040 ⊕www.mobylines.it). **Toremar** (☎081/071998 ⊕www.toremar.it).

▊ BY BUS

Italy's bus network is extensive, although buses aren't as attractive an option as in other European countries, partly because of the low cost and convenience of train travel. Schedules are often drawn up with commuters and students in mind, and may be sketchy on weekends. Regional bus companies often provide the only means (not including car travel) of getting to out-of-the-way places. Even when this isn't the case, buses can be faster and more direct than local trains, so it's a good idea to **compare bus and train schedules.**

CLASSES

Both public and private buses offer only one class of service. Cleanliness and comfort levels are high on private buses, which have plenty of legroom and comfortable seats, but no toilets.

CUTTING COSTS

Public bus lines offer student and monthly passes. Private lines offer one-, three-, and six-month passes. Children under 3 feet in height ride free if they're traveling with an adult and don't require their own seat. Infant car seats are permitted on private bus lines. Bassinets are not made available by the bus companies.

Discount Passes None of the cities in Tuscany and Umbria are big enough to make the various discount bus pass schemes that appear and disappear with regularity worth the trouble. Most weeklong tourists to Florence, the largest city, will ride the city buses no more than four times at a cost of €1.20 per ticket. There is a 24-hour pass (€5) and a three-day pass (€12). A month-long pass is available for €34. Students staying for a semester in Florence may wish to look into an ATAF Student Pass, a month-long pass, costing €23. Passes are available at the central bus station located at the side of the train station and are renewable at newsstands. See www.ataf.net for information.

ATAF has an arrangement with Firenze City SightSeeing, a red open-top sightseeing bus in Florence. For €20 (€10 for children under 15) you can get off and on both it and all of the city buses during a 24-hour period. Pisa also has a City SightSeeing hop-on/off tour bus (€15 adults/€17 children).

In Perugia the public bus system is operated by APM, with the fare of €1 for a 70-minute ticket.

FARES& SCHEDULES

You may purchase tickets for city buses with cash at newsstands or at tobacco shops. The Florence public bus service ATAF is now allowing customers to buy tickets, with a surcharge, in cash (€2), on the bus from the driver–exact fare is necessary, as no change is given. You must validate the bus ticket in the machine on the bus. For the private lines, tickets may be purchased with cash at the bus station or at travel agencies bearing the bus line's logo. Be sure to validate the ticket either at the bus station or on the bus as soon as you board. Bus schedules for private lines may be obtained online or at the bus station; city bus schedules for Florence (ATAF) are available online at www.ataf.net.

PAYING

Credit cards and traveler's checks are generally not accepted for private-line bus tickets (some travel agencies may accept them) and public bus tickets purchased at newsstands and tobacco shops must be paid for in cash.

RESERVATIONS

Public bus lines do not issue reservations. For some private bus line direct routes (i.e. during commute hours) reservations are required.

Bus Information **APM Perugia** (☎075/5004530 ⊕www.apmperugia.it). **ATAF** (✉Stazione Centrale di Santa Maria Novella, Florence ☎055/5650642 or 055/5650222 ⊕www.ataf.net).**Firenze City SightSeeing** (⊕www.city-sightseeing.com). **Lazzi Eurolines** (✉Via Mercadante 2, Florence ☎055/363041 ⊕www.lazzi.it). **SITA** (✉Via Santa Caterina da Siena 17/r, Florence ☎055/214721 ⊕www.sitabus.it).

▌BY CAR

Tuscany and Umbria have an extensive network of *autostrade* (toll highways), complemented by equally well maintained but free *superstrade* (expressways). The ticket you are issued upon entering an autostrada must be returned when you exit and pay the toll; on some shorter autostrade, mainly connecting highways, the toll is paid upon entering. Viacards, debit payment cards on sale at many autostrada locations (€25 at toll booths), make paying tolls easier and faster by avoiding the hunt for change to pay the toll. Pass through the Viacard lane at toll booths, slipping the card into the designated slot. A *raccordo* is a ring road surrounding a city. *Strade regionale* and *strade provinciale* (regional and provincial highways, denoted by *S, SS, SR,* or *SP* numbers) may be two-lane roads, as are all secondary roads; directions and turnoffs on toll roads and expressways are frequent and clear; secondary roads aren't always clearly marked. Be prepared for fast and impatient fellow drivers.

GASOLINE

Gas stations are located at frequent intervals along the main highways and autostrade. In case you run out of gas along the toll roads or the main free *superstrade,* emergency telephones are provided. To find the phone, look on the pavement at the shoulder of the highway where painted arrows and the term "SOS" point in the direction of the nearest phone.

Gas stations on autostrade are open 24 hours. Gas stations in towns and cities are usually located on the periphery; they're rarely found in the center of municipalities. These stations are generally open Monday through Saturday 7–7 with a break at lunchtime.

Many stations have automatic self-service pumps that accept only bills of 5, 10, 20, and 50 euros and **don't give change** or a receipt (*ricevuta*). Full-service stations or those with an attendant take both cash and credit cards. It's not customary to tip the attendant when full service is provided.

As of this writing, gas (*benzina*) costs about €1.40 a liter. It's available in unleaded (*verde*) and super unleaded (*super*). Many rental cars in Italy take only diesel (*gasolio*), which costs about €1.10 a liter; **ask about the fuel type before you leave the rental place.**

PARKING

Parking space is at a premium in most towns and cities, but especially in the *centri storici* (historic centers), which are filled with narrow streets and restricted circulation zones. It's advisable to **leave your car only in guarded parking areas.** In Florence such indoor parking costs €23–€30 for 12–24 hours; outside attended parking costs about €10–€20. Parking in an area signposted ZONA DISCO (disk zone), usually found only in small towns, is allowed for limited periods (from 30 minutes to two hours or more—the limit is posted); if you don't have the cardboard disk (located in the glove box of your rental car) to show what time you parked, you can use a piece of paper. The *parcometro,* the Italian version of metered parking in which you put coins into a machine for a stamped ticket that you leave on the dashboard, has been introduced in most large towns and cities.

Parking regulations are strictly enforced both in the cities and small towns. Fines run as high as €70 (more for taking a space designated for people with disabilities) and towing (or tire clamps) is possible in Florence. Car-rental companies may use your credit card to be reimbursed for any fines you incur during your rental period. In Tuscany and Umbria vandalism and theft of cars are rare. Nevertheless, **don't leave luggage or valuables in your car,** especially in cities and large towns where thieves target rental cars.

ROAD CONDITIONS

Driving on the back roads of Tuscany and Umbria isn't difficult as long as you're on the alert for bicycles, scooters, and passing cars. In addition, street and road signs are often missing or placed in awkward spots, so a good map and patience are essential. Be aware that some maps may not use the *SR* or *SP* (*stradale regionale* and *stradale provinciale*) highway designations, which took the place of the old *SS* designations in 2004. They may use the old *SS* designation or no numbering at all. Autostrade are well maintained, as are most interregional highways. The condition of provincial (county) roads varies, but road maintenance at this level is generally good in Italy. In many small hill towns the streets are winding and extremely narrow; consider parking at the edge of town and exploring on foot.

Most autostrade have two lanes in both directions; the left lane is used only for passing. Italians drive fast and are impatient with those who don't, so tailgating is the norm here; the only way to avoid it is to get out of the way.

ROAD MAPS

Michelin and Touring Club Italia, which has shops in major Italian cities, produce good road maps. The Michelin Web site is good for driving instructions and maps (⊕www.viamichelin. com). You can also get free street maps for most Tuscan and Umbrian towns at local information offices.

RULES OF THE ROAD

Driving is on the right. Regulations are largely as in the United States, except that the police have the power to levy on-the-spot fines. In most Italian towns the use of the horn is forbidden in certain, if not all, areas; a large sign, ZONA DI SILENZIO (silent zone), indicates where. Speed limits are 130 kph (80 mph) on autostrade and 100 kph (60 mph) on state and provincial roads, unless otherwise marked. Enforcement of these limits varies from region to region. Penalties, however, are stiff, including high fines and suspension of driving privileges. Penalties for driving after drinking are heavy, too, including license suspension and the additional possibility of six months' imprisonment. The relevant blood-alcohol level is 0.05.

Right turns on red lights are forbidden. Headlights are required to be on while driving on all roads (large or small) outside of municipalities. Seat belts are required for adults, and infant and children's car seats are compulsory for babies and toddlers.

▌ BY TRAIN

The fastest trains on the Ferrovie dello Stato (FS), the Italian State Railways, are the Eurostar trains, operating on several main lines, including Rome–Milan via Florence and Bologna. A new high-speed Eurostar called Alta Velocita runs between Rome and Naples and is also planned for Florence, Bologna, Venice, and Milan in the future. Seat reservations are mandatory on the Eurostar trains. Some Eurostar trains (the ETR 460 trains) have little aisle and luggage space (though there is a space near the door where you can put large bags). To avoid having to squeeze through narrow aisles, board only at your car (look for the number on the reservation ticket and match it to the number on the exterior of the car; it's usually on the door). The next-fastest trains are the Intercity (IC) trains, for which you pay a supplement and seat reservations may be required (which is always advisable). *Interregionale* trains usually make more stops and are a little slower. *Regionale* and *locale* trains are the slowest; many serve commuters.

There is refreshment service on all long-distance trains, with mobile carts and a cafeteria or dining car. Tap water on trains is not drinkable.

Traveling by night can be efficient and inexpensive (compared to the cost of a hotel room), but never leave your belong-ings unattended (even for a minute) and make sure the door of your compartment is locked.

Train service between Milan, Florence, Rome, and Naples is frequent throughout the day. For the most part, trains stick to the schedule, although delays may occur in the peak tourist season. Train strikes of various kinds are also frequent, so it's a good idea to make sure the train you want to take is in fact running.

The train from Rome to Florence takes 90 minutes; Rome to Perugia takes 2½ hours; Milan to Florence takes about three hours by train and then another two hours to Perugia.

CLASSES

Many Italian trains have first and second classes, but regional trains frequently don't have first class. On interregional trains the higher first-class fare gets you little more than a clean doily on the headrest of your seat, but on long-distance trains you get wider seats, more legroom, and better ventilation and lighting. At peak travel times, first-class train travel is worth the difference. One advantage of traveling first class is that the cars are almost always not crowded—or, at the very least, less crowded than the second-class compartments. A first-class ticket, in Italian, is *prima classe*; second is *seconda classe*. Remember always to **make seat reservations in advance,** for either class on Eurostar or Intercity (IC) trains.

CUTTING COSTS

If you're traveling only in Tuscany and Umbria, rail passes won't save you money. If Italy is your only destination in Europe, **consider purchasing a Eurail Italy Pass** (aka Trenitalia Pass or Italian Flexi Rail Card), which allows a limited number of travel days within one month. Four days of travel cost $278 (first class) or $223 (second class); additional days cost $30 (first class) or $25 (second class). If you are traveling with others, you should consider the discounted **Italian Flexi Rail**

Card Saver (aka Trenitalia Pass Saver), which allows a limited number of travel days within one month for groups of two to five people.

Four days of travel cost $238 (first class) or $190 (second class); additional days are $27 (first class) and $20 (second class).

Don't assume that a rail pass guarantees a seat on the trains you wish to ride; you need to reserve seats ahead even if you use a rail pass. There's a nominal fee (usually €5) for the reservation.

Information and Passes Rail Europe (☎914/682–5172 or 800/438–7245 ⊕www. raileurope.com). **RailPass** (☎877/724–5727 ⊕www.railpass.com).

FARES & SCHEDULES

You can buy train tickets for nearby destinations (within a 200-km range) at newsstands or tobacconists (usually only those inside the station) and at ticket machines in stations, as well as at the ticket windows at the station or at travel agencies in town. Tickets are good for two months after the date of issue, but right before departure you must **validate tickets in the yellow machines in the departure area.** Once stamped, tickets are valid for six hours on distances of less than 200 km (124 mi) or for 24 hours on longer distances. If you wish to stop along the way and your final destination is more than 200 km away, you can stamp the ticket a second time before it expires so as to extend its validity to a maximum of 48 hours from the time it was first stamped. If you forget to stamp your ticket in the machine, or you didn't make it to the station in time to buy the ticket, you must seek out a conductor and pay a €5.15 fine. Don't wait for the conductor to find out that you're without a valid ticket (unless the train is overcrowded and walking becomes impossible), as he might charge you a much heavier fine. However, you often can get out of paying the fine if you immediately write the time, date, and name of the departure station on the back of the ticket and sign it—essentially "validating" it and making it unusable for another trip.

PAYING

You can pay for your train tickets in cash or with any major credit card such as American Express, Diners Club, Master-Card, and Visa, except for the kilometric tickets purchased at a newsstand, which only accept cash.

RESERVATIONS

Trains can be very crowded; it is always a good idea to make a reservation. In summer it's fairly common to stand for a good part of the journey. On the fast, direct Eurostar trains reservations are mandatory. To avoid long lines at station windows, **buy tickets and make seat reservations up to two months in advance** at travel agencies in Italy displaying the FS emblem or from a travel agent or Web site (⊕www.railpass.com) before you leave home. Tickets can be purchased at the last minute, but seat reservations can be made at agencies (or the train station) up until about three hours before the train departs from its city of origin. For trains that require a reservation (all Eurostar and some Intercity), you may be able to get a seat assignment just before boarding the train; look for the conductor on the platform, but do this only as a last resort.

Train Information **Ferrovie dello Stato** (FS ☎147/888–088 in Italy ⊕www.ferrovie dellostato.it).**Trenitalia** (☎ 892021 in Italy (fee charged) ⊕www.trenitalia.comt).

ON THE GROUND

▮ COMMUNICATIONS

INTERNET

Getting online in Italian cities isn't difficult: public Internet stations and Internet cafés, some open 24 hours, are becoming more and more common. Prices differ from place to place, so spend some time to find the best deal. This isn't always readily apparent: a place might appear to have higher rates, but if it belongs to a chain, it might not charge you an initial flat fee again when you visit a branch in another city.

Wi-Fi hotspots are often within high-end hotels, major airports and train stations, Internet cafés, and shopping centers. Although there is no official map of Italian hotspots, you can check ⊕www.hotspots.com for locations in Tuscany and Umbria. Some hotels have in-room modem lines, but, as with phones, using the hotel's line is relatively expensive. Always check modem rates before plugging in.

You may need an adapter for your computer for the European-style plugs. If you are traveling with a laptop, carry a spare battery and an adapter. Never plug your computer into any socket before asking about surge protection. IBM sells a tiny modem tester that plugs into a telephone jack to check whether the line is safe to use.

Contacts **Cybercafes** (⊕www.cybercafes. com) lists over 4,000 Internet cafés worldwide.

PHONES

Telephone service in Tuscany and Umbria is efficient. Cell phones, however, are in wide use by Italians, resulting in a decrease in the number of public pay phones. Calling from a hotel land-line phone is almost always the most expensive option; hotels usually add huge surcharges to all calls, particularly international ones.

The country code for Italy is 39. Area codes for major cities are as follows: Florence, 055; Perugia, 075; Pisa, 050; Siena, 0577. For example, a call from New York City to Florence would be dialed as 011 + 39 + 055 + phone number.

When dialing an Italian number from abroad, do not drop the initial 0 from the local area code.

CALLING WITHIN ITALY

For all calls within Italy—local and long distance—you must dial the regional area code (*prefisso*), which begins with a 0, such as 055 for Florence. If you are calling from a public phone, you must deposit a coin or use a calling card to get a dial tone. Some of the newer public phones don't accept coins. Local calling cards are available at newsstands or tobacco shops. Rates on land-line phones vary during the day; it's less expensive to call within Italy during nonworking hours (before 9 AM and after 7 or 8 PM).

CALLING OUTSIDE ITALY

The country code for the United States is 1, so from most phones in Italy you will dial 001 + area code + phone number. To place international telephone calls and collect calls via English-speaking operator-assisted service, dial 170 (only available on land-line phones) or an international carrier's long-distance access code or use an international prepaid calling card.

You can also place a direct call to the United States using your U.S. phone calling-card number, through which you automatically reach a U.S. operator and thereby avoid all language difficulties.

Access Codes **AT&T USADirect** (☎800/172–444). **MCI Worldwide Access** (☎800/905–825). **Sprint Express** (☎800/172–405).

CALLING CARDS

Prepaid *carte telefoniche* (calling cards) for intra-country calls are prevalent throughout Italy and more convenient than coins. You buy the card (values vary) at post offices, tobacconists, most news stalls, and bars. Tear off the corner of the card and insert it in the slot on a public pay phone. When you dial, its value appears in the window. After you hang up, the card is returned so you can use it until its value runs out.

International phone cards are good value, allowing you to call Europe and the United States for less than 20 European cents a minute during peak hours. Follow the directions on the back of the card. These will include revealing the identification number on the card and calling an "800" number or other free number. If you wish to use this card at a public phone you may need a local calling card *(see above)* to activate the public phone. If you are using your hotel phone, the call should be charged as any other "800" number call.

MOBILE PHONES

If you have a multiband phone (some countries use different frequencies from what's used in the United States) and your service provider uses the world-standard GSM network (as do T-Mobile, Cingular, and Verizon), you can probably use your phone abroad. Roaming fees can be steep, however: 99¢ a minute is considered reasonable. And overseas you normally pay the toll charges for incoming calls. It's almost always cheaper to send a text message than to make a call, since text messages have a very low set fee (often less than 5¢).

If you just want to make local calls, consider buying a new SIM card (note that your provider may have to unlock your phone for you to use a different SIM card) and a prepaid service plan in the destination. You'll then have a local number and can make local calls at local rates. If your trip is extensive, you could also simply buy a new cell phone in your destination, as the initial cost will be offset over time.

■TIP➜ If you travel internationally frequently, save one of your old mobile phones or buy a cheap one on the Internet; ask your cell phone company to unlock it for you, and take it with you as a travel phone, buying a new SIM card with pay-as-you-go service in each destination.

The cost of cell phones is dropping and you can purchase a cell phone with a prepaid calling card (no monthly service plan) in Italy for less than €70. Inexpensive cell phones are dual band and will not allow you to call the United States, but using an international calling card and the cell phone solves that problem in a very inexpensive manner. Most medium to large towns in Tuscany and Umbria (Florence, Siena, Lucca, Pisa, and Perugia) have stores dedicated to selling cell phones. You will need to present your passport to purchase the SIM card that goes with the phone.

Rental cell phones are available in cities and large towns. Many Internet cafés offer them, but shop around for the best deal. Most rental contracts require a refundable deposit that covers the cost of the cell phone (€75–125) and then set up a monthly service plan that is automatically charged to your credit card. Frequently rental cell phones will be triple band and allow you to call the United States. Be sure to check the rate schedule before you rent a cell phone and commence calling to prevent a nasty surprise when you receive your credit-card bill two or three months later.

■TIP➜ Beware of cell-phone (and PDA) thieves. Keep your phone or PDA in a secure pocket or purse. Do not lay it on the bar when you stop for an espresso. Do not zip it into the outside pocket of your backpack in crowded cities. Do not leave it in your hotel room. If you are using a phone with a monthly service plan, notify your provider immediately if it is lost or stolen.

LOCAL DO'S & TABOOSLOCAL DO'S & TABOOS

CUSTOMS OF THE COUNTRY

Social behavior in Tuscany and Umbria tends to be more conservative and formal than in other parts of Italy.

GREETINGS

Upon meeting and leave-taking, both friends and strangers wish each other good day or good evening (*buon giorno, buona sera*); *ciao* isn't used between strangers. "Please" is *per favore*, "thank you" is *grazie*, and "you're welcome" is *prego*. When meeting, strangers will shake hands. Italians who are friends greet each other with a kiss, usually first on the left cheek, and then on the right.

SIGHTSEEING

Italy is full of churches, and many of them contain significant works of art. They are places of worship, therefore care should be taken to dress appropriately. Shorts, mini-skirts, tank tops, spaghetti straps, and sleeveless garments are taboo in most churches; short shorts are inappropriate anywhere. When touring churches—especially in the summer when it's hot and no sleeves are desirable—carry a sweater, large scarf, or a light shawl to wrap around your shoulders before entering the church, and always remember to take off your hat. Do not enter a church with food, and don't drink from your water bottle while inside. If a service is in progress, don't go inside. And if you have a cell phone, turn it off before entering.

OUT ON THE TOWN

Table manners are formal; rarely do Italians share food from their plates. Flowers, chocolates, or a bottle of wine are appropriate hostess gifts when invited to dinner at the home of an Italian.

Wiping your bowl clean with a small piece of bread is considered a sign of appreciation, not bad manners. Spaghetti should be eaten with a fork only, although a little help from a spoon won't horrify locals the way cutting spaghetti into little pieces might. Order your espresso (Italians don't usually drink cappuccino after breakfast time) after dessert, not with it. Don't ask for a doggy bag.

DOING BUSINESS

Showing up on time for business appointments is the norm and expected in Italy. There are more business lunches than business dinners, and even business lunches aren't common, as Italians view mealtimes as periods of pleasure and relaxation. Business cards are used throughout Italy, and business suits are the norm for both men and women.

LANGUAGE

One of the best ways to avoid being an Ugly American is to learn a little of the local language. You need not strive for fluency; even just mastering a few basic words and terms is bound to make chatting with the locals more rewarding.

In the main tourist cities, such as Florence, most hotels have English speakers at their reception desks, and you can always find someone who speaks at least a little English otherwise. Remember that the Italian language is pronounced exactly as it is written. You may run into a language barrier in the countryside, but a phrase book and the use of pantomime and expressive gestures will go a long way. Try to **master a few phrases for daily use** and familiarize yourself with the terms you'll need for deciphering signs, menus, and museum labels.

A phrase book and language-tape set can help get you started.

Fodor's Italian for Travelers (available at bookstores everywhere) is excellent.

Contacts **Cellular Abroad** (☎800/287–5072 ⊕www.cellularabroad.com) rents and sells GMS phones and sells SIM cards that work in many countries. **Mobal** (☎888/888–9162 ⊕www.mobalrental.com) rents mobiles and sells GSM phones (starting at $49) that will operate in 140 countries. Per-call rates vary throughout the world. **Planet Fone** (☎888/988–4777 ⊕www.planetfone.com) rents cell phones, but the per-minute rates are expensive.

▊ CUSTOMS & DUTIES

You're always allowed to bring goods of a certain value back home without having to pay any duty or import tax. But there's a limit on the amount of tobacco and liquor you can bring back duty-free, and some countries have separate limits for perfumes; for exact figures, check with your customs department. The values of so-called "duty-free" goods are included in these amounts. When you shop abroad, save all your receipts, as customs inspectors may ask to see them as well as the items you purchased. If the total value of your goods is more than the duty-free limit, you'll have to pay a tax (most often a flat percentage) on the value of everything beyond that limit.

Travelers from the United States should experience little difficulty clearing customs at any airports in Italy.

Of goods obtained anywhere outside the EU, the allowances are (1) 200 cigarettes or 100 cigarillos (under 3 grams) or 50 cigars or 250 grams of tobacco; (2) 2 liters of still table wine or 1 liter of spirits over 22% volume; and (3) 50 milliliters of perfume and 250 milliliters of toilet water.

Of goods obtained (duty and tax paid) within another EU country, the allowances are (1) 800 cigarettes or 400 cigarillos (under 3 grams) or 200 cigars or 1 kilogram of tobacco; (2) 90 liters of still table wine or 10 liters of spirits over 22%

volume or 20 liters of spirits under 22% volume or 110 liters of beer.

There is no quarantine period in Italy, so if you want to travel with Fido or Fifi, it's possible. Contact your nearest Italian consulate to find out what paperwork is needed for entry into Italy; generally, it is a certificate noting that the animal is healthy and up-to-date on its vaccinations. Keep in mind, however, that the United States has some stringent laws about reentry: pets must be free of all diseases, especially those communicable to humans, and they must be vaccinated against rabies at least 30 days before returning. This means that if you are in Italy for a short-term stay, you must find a veterinarian or have your pet vaccinated before departure. (This law does not apply to puppies less than three months old.) Pets should arrive at the point of entry with a statement, in English, attesting to this fact.

Information in Italy **Ministero delle Finanze, Direzione Centrale dei Servizi Doganali, Divisione I** (☎06/50242117 ⊕www.finanze.it). **Dogana Sezione Viaggiatori** (☎06/65954343 ⊕www.agenziadogane.it).

U.S. Information **U.S. Customs and Border Protection** (⊕www.cbp.gov).

▊ EATING OUT

The restaurants we list are the cream of the crop in each price category. Properties indicated by a ✕⊡ are lodging establishments whose restaurant warrants a special trip. Not too long ago, ristoranti tended to be more elegant and expensive than trattorie and osterie, which serve traditional, home-style fare in an atmosphere to match. But the distinction has blurred considerably, and an osteria in the center of town might be far fancier (and pricier) than a ristorante across the street. Although most restaurants in Tuscany and Umbria serve traditional local cuisine, you can find Asian and Middle Eastern alternatives in Florence, Perugia, and other cities. Menus are posted outside most restaurants (in English in tourist areas); if not, you might step inside and ask to take a look at the menu (but don't ask for a table unless you intend to stay).

Italians take their food as it is listed on the menu, seldom if ever making special requests such as "dressing on the side" or "hold the olive oil." If you have special dietary needs, however, make them known; they can usually be accommodated. Although mineral water makes its way to almost every table, you can order a carafe of tap water (*acqua di rubinetto* or *acqua semplice*) instead, but keep in mind that such water is frequently highly chlorinated.

The handiest and least expensive places for a quick snack between sights are probably bars, cafés, and pizza *al taglio* (by the slice) spots. Bars in Italy are primarily places to get a coffee and a bite to eat, rather than drinking establishments. Most have a selection of *panini* (sandwiches, often warmed up on the griddle) and *tramezzini* (sandwiches served on triangles of untoasted white bread). In larger cities, bars also serve prepared salads, fruit salads, cold pasta dishes, and yogurt around lunchtime. Most bars offer beer and a variety of alcohol, as well as wines by the glass. A café (*caffè* in Italian) is like a bar but usually with more tables. If you place your order at the counter, ask if you can sit down: some places charge extra for table service. In self-service bars and caffès, cleaning up your table before you leave is considered good manners. Note that in some places you have to pay before you place an order and then show your *scontrino* (receipt) when you move to the counter. Pizza al taglio shops are easy to negotiate. They sell pizza by weight: just point out which kind you want and how much. Very few pizza al taglio shops have seats.

MEALS & MEALTIMES

The Italian breakfast (*la colazione*) is typically a cappuccino and a sweet roll served at the local bar. For a larger breakfast, consider dining rooms of large hotels. For lunch Italians may eat a couple of small panini while standing at a local bar or self-serve caffè. A more substantial lunch (*il pranzo*) consists of one or two courses at a trattoria. Dinner (*la cena*) out is likely to be two or three courses at a restaurant or trattoria or pizza and beer at a pizzeria.

Menus separate dishes into *antipasti* (starters), *primi piatti* (first courses), *secondi piatti* (second courses), *contorni* (side dishes), and *dolci* (desserts). At ristoranti, trattorie, and osterie, you're generally expected to order at least a two-course meal: a *primo* and a *secondo*; an antipasto followed by either primo or secondo; or, perhaps, a secondo and a *dolce*. Italian cuisine is still largely regional, so ask about the local specialties.

In an *enoteca* (wine bar) or pizzeria, it's not inappropriate to order one dish. An enoteca menu is often limited to a selection of cheeses, cured meats, salads, and desserts; if there's a kitchen, you may also find soups, pasta, meat, and fish. Most pizzerias don't offer just pizza, but also a variety of antipasti, salads, and simple pasta dishes, as well as dolce. Pizza at a caffè is to be avoided—it's usually frozen and reheated in a microwave oven.

Breakfast is usually served 7–10:30, lunch 12:30–2, and dinner 7:30–9:30 or 10. Enoteche also are open in the morning and late afternoon for a snack at the counter. Most pizzerias open at 7:30 PM and close around midnight or 1 AM, or later in summer and on weekends. Most bars and caffès are open 7 AM–8 or 9 PM; a few stay open until midnight or so.

Unless otherwise noted, the restaurants listed in this guide are open daily for lunch and dinner.

PAYING

Major credit cards are widely accepted in Italian eating establishments, though cash is usually the preferred, and sometimes the only, means of payment—especially in small towns and rural areas. (More restaurants take Visa and MasterCard than American Express.) When you've finished your meal and are ready to go, **ask for the check** (*il conto*); unless it's well past closing time, no waiter will put a bill on your table until you've requested it.

Prices for goods and services in Italy include tax. The price of fish dishes is often given by weight (before cooking), so the price you see on the menu is for 100 grams of fish, not for the whole dish. (An average fish portion is about 350 grams.) Tuscan *bistecca fiorentina* is also often priced by weight (€4 for 100 grams or €40 for one kilogram [2.2 lbs]).

Most restaurants charge a separate "cover" charge per person, usually listed on the menu as *pane e coperto* (or just *coperto*); this charge is not for the service. It should be a modest charge (€1–€2.50 per person), except at the most expensive restaurants. Some restaurants instead charge for bread, which should be brought to you (and paid for) only if you order it. A charge for service (*servizio*) may be included either as part of the menu prices or the total bill; if it is, tipping is unnecessary. It is customary to leave a small tip (one to five euros) in appreciation of good service when the service charge is not included in the bill. Tips are always given in cash. Whenever in doubt, ask about the servizio and pane e coperto policies upon ordering to avoid unpleasant discussions about payment later.

When you leave a dining establishment, take your meal bill or receipt with you; although not a common experience, the Italian finance (tax) police can approach you within 100 yards of the establishment at which you've eaten and ask for a receipt. If you don't have one, they can fine you and will fine the business owner for not providing the receipt. The measure is intended to prevent tax evasion; it's not necessary to show receipts when leaving Italy.

For guidelines on tipping, see Tipping below.

RESERVATIONS & DRESS

Reservations are always a good idea in restaurants and trattorie, especially on weekends and holidays. We mention them only when they're essential or not accepted. Book as far ahead as you can, and reconfirm as soon as you arrive in town. (Large parties should always call ahead to check the reservations policy.)

Unless they're eating outdoors at a sea resort and perfectly tanned, Italian men never wear shorts or running shoes in a restaurant—no matter how humble—or in an enoteca. Shorts are acceptable in pizzerias and caffès. The same "rules" apply to women's casual shorts, running shoes, plastic sandals, and clogs.

We mention dress only when men are required to wear a jacket and tie.

WINES, BEER & SPIRITS

The grape has been cultivated in Italy since the time of the Etruscans, and Italians justifiably take pride in their local vintages. Though almost every region produces good-quality wine, Tuscany is one of the most renowned areas. Wine in Italy is considerably less expensive than almost anywhere else, so it's often affordable to order a bottle of wine at a restaurant rather than to stick with the house wine (which, nevertheless, is probably quite good). Many bars have their own *aperitivo della casa* (house aperitif); Italians are imaginative with their mixed drinks, so you may want to try one.

You may purchase beer, wine, and spirits in any bar, grocery store, or enoteca, any day of the week. Italian and German beers are readily available, but they can be more expensive than wine.

There's no minimum drinking age in Italy. Italian children begin drinking wine mixed with water at mealtimes when they are teens (or thereabouts). Italians are rarely seen drunk in public, and public drinking, except in a bar or eating establishment, isn't considered acceptable behavior. Bars usually close by 9 PM; hotel and restaurant bars stay open until midnight. Brew pubs and discos serve until about 2 AM.

▌ELECTRICITY

The electrical current in Italy is 220 volts, 50 cycles alternating current (AC); wall outlets take continental-type plugs, with two round prongs.

Consider making a small investment in a universal adapter, which has several types of plugs in one lightweight, compact unit. Most laptops and mobile phone chargers are dual voltage (i.e., they operate equally well on 110 and 220 volts), so require only an adapter. These days the same is true of small appliances such as hair dryers. Always check labels and manufacturer instructions to be sure. Don't use 110-volt outlets marked FOR SHAVERS ONLY for high-wattage appliances such as hair-dryers.

Contacts **Steve Kropla's Help for World Traveler's** (⊕www.kropla.com) has information on electrical and telephone plugs around the world. **Walkabout Travel Gear** (⊕www. walkabouttravelgear.com) has a good coverage of electricity under "adapters."

▌EMERGENCIES

No matter where you are in Italy, **dial 113 for all emergencies,** or find somebody (your concierge, a passerby) who will call for you, as not all 113 operators speak English; the Italian word to use to draw people's attention in an emergency is *aiuto* (help; pronounced "ah-YOU-toh"). *Pronto soccorso* means first aid and the emergency room of a hospital, and when said to an operator, it will get you an

ambulanza (ambulance). If you just need a doctor, you should ask for *un medico*; most hotels can refer you to a local doctor. Don't forget to ask the doctor for *una ricevuta* (an invoice) to show your insurance company in order to get a reimbursement. Other useful Italian words to use in an emergency are *al fuoco* (fire; pronounced "ahl fuh-WOE-co") and *al ladro* (follow the thief; pronounced "ahl LAH-droh").

Italy has a national police force (*carabinieri*) as well as local police (*polizia*). Both are armed and have the power to arrest and investigate crimes. Always report the loss of your passport to either the carabinieri or the police, as well as to your embassy. Local traffic officers are known as *vigili* (though their official name is *polizia municipale*)—they are responsible for, among other things, giving out parking tickets and clamping cars, so before you even consider parking the (illegal) Italian way, make sure you are at least able to spot their white (in summer) or black uniforms. Many are women. Should you find yourself involved in a minor car accident in town, you should contact the vigili. Many police stations have English-speaking staff to deal with travelers' problems. When reporting a crime, you'll be asked to fill out and sign a report form (*una denuncia*); keep a copy for your insurance company.

A country-wide toll-free number (112) is used to call the carabinieri in case of emergency.

United States Embassies **U.S. Consulate** (✉Via Lungarno Vespucci 38, Florence ☎055/266951). **U.S. Embassy** (✉Via Vittorio Veneto 121, Rome ☎06/46741 ⊕www.usembassy.it).

General Emergency Contacts **Carabinieri** (☎112). **Emergencies** (☎113).

HEALTH

The most common types of illnesses are caused by contaminated food and water. In Italy tap water is safe to drink, and eating out in Italy is perfectly safe. As in any part of the world, avoid fresh vegetables and fruits that you haven't washed or peeled yourself. If you have problems, mild cases of traveler's diarrhea may respond to Imodium (known generically as loperamide) or Pepto-Bismol. Be sure to drink plenty of fluids; if you can't keep fluids down, seek medical help immediately.

HOURS OF OPERATION

Business hours vary from region to region in Italy. In larger cities, such as Florence, Pisa, Lucca, Siena, and Perugia, stores and other businesses will generally be open 10–7. Many stores close 1–3:30 for a midday break, especially in small towns. More than half of the stores close on Sunday and on national holidays. Many businesses stay closed Monday morning but open in the afternoon. In August, many stores, restaurants, and other businesses shut down for two to four weeks for the traditional summer holiday.

HOLIDAYS
National holidays include New Year's Day (January 1); Epiphany (January 6); Easter Sunday and Monday (March 23-24 in 2008); Liberation Day (April 25); Labor Day or May Day (May 1); Assumption of Mary, also known as

Ferragosto (August 15); All Saints' Day (November 1); Immaculate Conception (December 8); Christmas Day and Boxing Day (December 25 and 26).

The feast days of patron saints are observed locally. Many businesses and shops may be closed in Florence on June 24 (St. John the Baptist).

MAIL

The Italian mail system is notoriously slow, but it is improving with some privatization. Allow from 7 to 15 days for mail to get to the United States. Receiving mail in Italy, especially packages, can take weeks.

Most post offices are open Monday–Saturday 9–12:30; central post offices are open weekdays 9–6:30, Saturday 9–12:30. On the last day of the month, post offices close at midday. You can buy stamps at tobacco shops as well as post offices.

Posta Prioritaria (for small letters and packages) is the name of the most commonly used postage. It supposedly guarantees delivery within Italy in three to five business days and abroad in five to six working days. The more expensive express delivery, *Postacelere* (for larger letters and packages), guarantees one-day delivery to most places in Italy and three-to five-day delivery abroad.

Mail sent as Posta Prioritaria to the United States costs €0.85 for up to 20 grams, €1.50 for 21–50 grams, and €1.85 for 51–100 grams. Mail sent as Postacelere to the United States costs €43–€50 for up to 500 grams.

Other package services to check are Quick Pack Europe, for delivery within Europe; and EMS Express Mail Service, a global three- to five-day service for letters and packages that can be less expensive than Postacelere.

Two-day mail is generally available during the week in all major cities and at popular resorts via UPS and Federal Express. Service is reliable; a Federal Express letter to the United States costs about €35. If your hotel can't assist you, try an Internet café, many of which also offer two-day mail services using major carriers.

SHIPPING PACKAGES

You can ship parcels via air or surface. Air takes about two weeks, and surface anywhere up to three months to most countries. If you have purchased antiques, ceramics, or other objects, ask if the vendor will do the shipping for you; in most cases, this is a possibility. If so, ask if the article will be insured against breakage. When shipping a package out of Italy, it is virtually impossible to find an overnight delivery option—the fastest delivery time is 48 to 72 hours.

▌ MONEY

As in most countries, prices vary from region to region and are a bit lower in the countryside than in cities. Umbria and the Marches offer good value for the money. Admission to the Galleria degli Uffizi is €9.50 (surcharges for reservations and special exhibits may increase the ticket price). A movie ticket is €7. A daily English-language newspaper is €2. A taxi ride (1 km [1 mi]) costs €9.

Prices throughout this guide are given for adults, in euros. Substantially reduced fees are sometimes available for children, students, and senior citizens from the EU; citizens of non-EU countries rarely get discounts, but be sure to inquire before you purchase your tickets because this situation is constantly changing.

■TIP➔ Banks never have every foreign currency on hand, and it may take as long as a week to order. If you're planning to exchange funds before leaving home, don't wait until the last minute.

ATMS & BANKS

Your own bank may charge a fee for using ATMs abroad or charge for the cost of conversion from euros to dollars. Nevertheless, you'll usually get a better rate of exchange at an ATM than you will at a currency-exchange office or even when changing money inside a bank with a teller. Extracting funds as you need them is also a safer option than carrying around a large amount of cash.

■TIP➔ PIN numbers with more than four digits are not recognized at ATMs in many countries. If yours has five or more, remember to change it before you leave. PIN numbers beginning with a 0 (zero) tend to be rejected in Italy.

Fairly common in banks in large and small towns, as well as in airports and train stations, ATMs are the easiest way to get euros in Italy. All major banks are members of Cirrus and/or Plus. You won't find an ATM (*bancomat* in Italian) in hotels or grocery stores, however. Before you leave home, **memorize your PIN in numbers,** not letters, because ATM keypads in Italy frequently don't show letters. Check with your bank to confirm that you have an international PIN (*codice segreto*), to find out your maximum daily withdrawal allowance, and to learn what the bank fee is for withdrawing money.

CREDIT CARDS

In Italy, Visa and MasterCard are preferred over American Express, but in tourist areas American Express is usually accepted. While increasingly common, credit cards aren't accepted at all establishments, and some places require a minimum expenditure. If you want to pay with a card in a small hotel, store, or restaurant, it's a good idea to make your intentions known early on. ■TIP➔ **Notify your credit-card companies of your travel plans before you leave home;** the recent fraud prevention programs frequently suspend a cardholder's credit when foreign activity is detected on the card.

Throughout this guide, the following abbreviations are used: **AE**, American Express; **DC**, Diners Club; **MC**, MasterCard; and **V**, Visa.

Record all your credit-card numbers—as well as the phone numbers to call if your cards are lost or stolen—in a safe place, so you're prepared should something go wrong. Both MasterCard and Visa have general numbers you can call (collect if you're abroad) if your card is lost, but you're better off calling the number of your issuing bank, since MasterCard and Visa usually just transfer you to your bank; your bank's number is usually printed on your card.

If you plan to use your credit card for cash advances, you'll need to apply for a PIN at least two weeks before your trip. Although it's usually cheaper (and safer) to use a credit card abroad for large purchases (so you can cancel payments or be reimbursed if there's a problem), note that some credit-card companies *and* the banks that issue them add substantial percentages to all foreign transactions, whether they're in a foreign currency or not. Check on these fees before leaving home, so there won't be any surprises when you get the bill.

■TIP➔ Before you charge something, ask the merchant whether or not he or she plans to do a dynamic currency conversion (DCC). In such a transaction the credit-card *processor* (shop, restaurant, or hotel, not Visa or MasterCard) converts the currency and charges you in dollars. In most cases you'll pay the merchant a 3% fee for this service in addition to any credit-card company and issuing-bank foreign-transaction surcharges.

Dynamic currency conversion programs are becoming increasingly widespread. Merchants who participate in them are supposed to ask whether you want to be charged in dollars or the local currency, but they don't always do so. And even if they do offer you a choice, they may

well avoid mentioning the additional surcharges. The good news is that you *do* have a choice. And if this practice really gets your goat, you can avoid it entirely thanks to American Express; with its cards, DCC simply isn't an option.

Reporting Lost Cards **American Express** (☎800/992–3404 in the U.S., 336/393–1111 collect from abroad ⊕www.american express.com). **Diners Club** (☎800/234–6377 in the U.S., 303/799–1504 collect from abroad ⊕www.dinersclub.com). **MasterCard** (☎800/622–7747 in the U.S., 636/722–7111 collect from abroad ⊕www.mastercard.com). **Visa** (☎800/847–2911 in the U.S., 410/581–9994 collect from abroad ⊕www.visa.com).

CURRENCY & EXCHANGE

The euro is the main unit of currency in Italy, as well as in 12 other European countries. Under the euro system, there are eight coins: 1, 2, 5, 10, 20, and 50 *centesimi* (cents, at 100 centesimi to the euro), and 1 and 2 euros. There are seven notes: 5, 10, 20, 50, 100, 200, and 500 euros.

At this writing, the exchange rate is about 68 European cents to US$1.

■TIP➔ Even if a currency-exchange booth has a sign promising no commission, rest assured that there's some kind of huge, hidden fee. (Oh…that's right. The sign didn't say no *fee*). And as for rates, you're almost always better off getting foreign currency at an ATM or exchanging money at a bank.

TRAVELER'S CHECKS & CARDS

Some consider this the currency of the cave man, and it's true that fewer establishments accept traveler's checks these days. Nevertheless, they're a cheap and secure way to carry extra money, particularly on trips to urban areas. Both Citibank (under the Visa brand) and American Express issue traveler's checks in the United States, but Amex is better known and more widely accepted; you can also avoid hefty surcharges by cashing Amex checks at Amex offices. Whatever you do, keep track of all the serial numbers in case the checks are lost or stolen.

Request checks in the local currency, the euro, to obtain the best exchange rate.

In Tuscany and Umbria, traveler's checks tend to be more trouble than they are worth. Most businesses and stores will not accept them and only Florence has an American Express agency—all other points for changing traveler's checks charge a commission, and American Express charges a commission for accepting competitors' checks. With the abundance of ATM (bancomat) machines, the best exchange rate and lower attendant costs are reached though use of your ATM card. Only if you don't use an ATM card at home do traveler's check have some utility in Tuscany and Umbria.

American Express now offers a stored-value card called a Travelers Cheque Card, which you can use wherever American Express credit cards are accepted, including ATMs. The card can carry a minimum of $300 and a maximum of $2,700, and it's a very safe way to carry your funds. Although you can get replacement funds in 24 hours if your card is lost or stolen, it doesn't really strike us as a very good deal. In addition to a high initial cost ($14.95 to set up the card, plus $5 each time you "reload"), you still have to pay a 2% fee for each purchase in a foreign currency (similar to that of any credit card). Further, each time you use the card in an ATM you pay a transaction fee of $2.50 on top of the 2% transaction fee for the conversion—add it all up and it can be considerably more than you would pay when simply using your own ATM card. Regular traveler's checks are just as secure and cost less.

Contacts American Express (☎888/412–6945 in the U.S., 801/945–9450 collect outside of the U.S. to add value and speak to customer service ⊕www.americanexpress.com).

▌RESTROOMS

Standards of cleanliness and comfort vary greatly in Tuscany and Umbria. The type of toilet might be small and low with no seat or even a porcelain hole in the floor with places for your feet. In cities, restaurants, hotel common areas, department stores, and McDonald's eateries tend to have the cleanest restrooms. Pubs and bars rank among the worst. Gas stations also have facilities; again, the cleanliness varies greatly. Carry tissues with you wherever you go, in case there's no paper.

Pay and attendant-supervised restrooms are available in large towns and cities. (You can get a map of the pay toilets in Florence at city tourist-information offices.) Expect to pay or tip 60 European cents. There are restrooms in most museums and all airports and train stations; in major train stations you'll also find well-kept pay toilets for 60 to 75 European cents. Churches, post offices, and public beaches don't have restrooms.

▌SAFETY

Don't wear an exterior money belt or a waist pack, both of which peg you as a tourist. If you carry a bag or camera, be absolutely sure it has straps; you should sling it across your body bandolier-style and adjust the height to hip level or higher. Always be astutely aware of pickpockets, especially when on city buses, when making your way through train corridors, and in busy piazzas.

Women traveling alone in Tuscany and Umbria encounter few special problems. Younger women have to put up with male attention, but it's rarely dangerous. Ignoring whistling and questions is a good way to get rid of unwanted attention; a firm *no, vai via* ("no, go away") usually works, too.

▐TIP➔ Distribute your cash, credit cards, IDs, and other valuables between a deep front pocket, an inside jacket or vest pocket, and a hidden money pouch. Don't reach for the money pouch once you're in public.

TAXES

A embarkation tax of €3.72 (between Italy and EU destinations) or €8.26 (international flights) will be included as part of your airline ticket cost.

When making a purchase, ask for a V.A.T. refund form and find out whether the merchant gives refunds—not all stores do, nor are they required to. Have the form stamped like any customs form by customs officials when you leave the country or, if you're visiting several European Union countries, when you leave the EU. After you're through passport control, take the form to a refund-service counter for an on-the-spot refund (which is usually the quickest and easiest option), or mail it to the address on the form (or the envelope with it) after you arrive home. You receive the total refund stated on the form, but the processing time can be long, especially if you request a credit-card adjustment.

Global Refund is a Europe-wide service with 225,000 affiliated stores and more than 700 refund counters at major airports and border crossings. Its refund form, called a Tax Free Check, is the most common across the European continent. The service issues refunds in the form of cash, check, or credit-card adjustment.

V.A.T. Refunds Global Refund (☎800/566–9828 ⊕www.globalrefund.com).

TIME

Italy is six hours ahead of New York (so when it's 1 PM in New York it's 7 PM in Florence). Like the rest of Europe, Italy uses the 24-hour (or "military") clock, which means that after 12 noon you continue counting forward: 13:00 is 1 PM, 23:30 is 11:30 PM.

TIPPING

The following guidelines apply in major cities, but Italians tip smaller amounts in smaller cities and towns. In restaurants in Tuscany and Umbria a service charge of 10% to 15% sometimes appears on your check. It's not necessary to tip in addition to this amount. If service is not included, leave a tip of €2 to not more than 10%. No one tips in bars in Florence.

Tip checkroom attendants 50 European cents per person and restroom attendants 50 European cents (more in expensive hotels and restaurants). Italians rarely tip taxi drivers, which is not to say that you shouldn't do it. A tip of 10%, depending on the length of the journey, is appreciated—but only if the driver is courteous and helps with your luggage. Railway and airport porters charge a fixed rate per bag. Tip an additional 5% if the porter is especially helpful. Give a barber €1–€1.50 and a hairdresser's assistant €1.50–€4 for a shampoo or cut, depending on the type of establishment.

On sightseeing tours, tip guides about €2 per person for a half-day group tour, more if they are very good. In museums and other sights where admission is free, a contribution (€1) is expected. Service-station attendants are tipped only for special services, for example, 50 European cents for checking your tires.

In hotels, give the portiere (concierge) about 10% of his bill for services, or €2.50–€5 if he has been generally helpful. For two people in a double room, leave the chambermaid about 75 European cents per day, or about €5 a week, in a moderately priced hotel; tip a minimum of €1 for valet or room service. Double amounts in an expensive hotel. In very expensive hotels, tip doormen €1 for calling a cab and €1 for carrying bags to the check-in desk, bellhops €2–€4 for carrying your bags to the room, and €2–€3 for room service.

INDEX